bon appétit
Desserts

bon appétit
Desserts

THE COOKBOOK FOR ALL THINGS
SWEET AND WONDERFUL

Barbara Fairchild

Photography by Con Poulos

**Andrews McMeel
Publishing, LLC**
Kansas City · Sydney · London

Bon Appétit Desserts text copyright © 2010 by Condé Nast Publications. Photographs © 2010 by Con Poulos. Illustrations © 2010 by Arthur Mount Illustration. All rights reserved. Printed in China. No part of this book may be used or reproduced in any manner whatsoever without written permission except in the case of reprints in the context of reviews. For information, write Andrews McMeel Publishing, LLC, an Andrews McMeel Universal company, 1130 Walnut Street, Kansas City, Missouri 64106.

10 11 12 13 14 SDB 10 9 8 7 6 5 4 3 2 1

ISBN: 978-0-7407-9352-3

Library of Congress Control Number: 2010924505

Photographs by Con Poulos
Food Styling by Susie Theodorou
Illustrations by Arthur Mount Illustration
Design by Jennifer Barry Design, Fairfax, California
Layout Production by Kristen Hall and Layla Bockhorst

www.andrewsmcmeel.com

www.bonappetit.com

ATTENTION: SCHOOLS AND BUSINESSES
Andrews McMeel books are available at quantity discounts with bulk purchase for educational, business, or sales promotional use. For information, please write to:
Special Sales Department
Andrews McMeel Publishing, LLC
1130 Walnut Street
Kansas City, Missouri 64106.

Classic Pumpkin Pie

contents

acknowledgments

What kind of people would take on the crazy challenge of creating three huge—and I do mean huge—cookbooks in the space of about five years?

Well, I guess that would be us.

But, really, the topic at hand is a natural. For more than fifty years, *Bon Appétit* has been creating the most luscious cakes, cheesecakes, pies, puddings, frozen desserts, candies, and cookies on the planet. Our commitment to dessert recipes is unparalleled in magazine history. The hard part was trimming the list down to "only" 650 recipes . . . or a few more (we couldn't help ourselves).

Of course, I turned to senior food editor Sarah Tenaglia and associate food editor Lena Birnbaum for the monumental task of selecting the recipes that would best represent the fantastic scope and delicious diversity of our acclaimed desserts. And that's just what they did—incorporating everything from a simple, classic vanilla ice cream to a showstopping three-tiered wedding cake. Then they and food department colleagues Janet McCracken and Selma Morrow evaluated every recipe to make sure each was up to date. They retested some (not many needed it) and even created a few brand-new ones just for this book. Then our longtime food editor Kristine Kidd evaluated the recipes and assigned each a "whisk rating" to let you know at a glance the difficulty level of those Old-Fashioned Brownies (one whisk) or the Profiteroles with Caramel Sauce (four whisks).

Because we also wanted this to be the definitive guide to dessert preparation, we included extensive recipe headnotes, tips, sidebars, and chapters on stocking your dessert pantry, buying the proper equipment, and mastering baking techniques. These were researched and written by an expert group of *Bon Appétit* staffers and contributors: Amy Albert, Nina Elder, Camille Hahn, Jeanne Thiel Kelley, Janet McCracken, and Rochelle Palermo. And on pages 636–37, you'll find the names of the dozens of men and women who made this book what it is by creating and testing recipes, copyediting and proofreading, and checking every fact. I'm grateful to all of them for their commitment to *Bon Appétit*'s legendary quality and exacting standards.

Executive editor Victoria von Biel saw from the beginning what this book could and should be—not just a compendium of delicious recipes, but the comprehensive desserts cookbook everyone would want to keep, and use repeatedly. Victoria—herself an enthusiastic and expert dessert maker who gets an eager assist in the kitchen from her two daughters—oversaw the book's creation and made sure that every aspect was considered from the point of view of the cook at home, whether that meant offering detailed instructions on beating egg whites or defining culinary terms we sometimes take for granted.

Needless to say, the logistics involved in putting together a book like this are daunting, and I'm beyond grateful to editorial business director Marcy MacDonald for handling with her usual aplomb the tasks of clearing rights to every recipe, obtaining permissions, shepherding the contract process, working with our colleagues at Andrews McMeel, and coordinating all the in-house business matters (which are endless and vital). Many thanks as well to Marcy's assistant, Zoë Alexander, and to my assistant, Marcia Hartmann Lewis, who did double duty: managing my insane schedule and working with Zoë to secure and give proper credit for each of the recipes in the book. Frederika Brookfield lent her considerable expertise to the publicity and public relations aspects.

Susan Champlin did an amazing job seeing this book through the entire process even as she was making a major change with a cross-country move from L.A. to New York. Susan still managed to balance all of the facets of the work, as well as the opinions of all the (very opinionated!) editors, production people, and others involved here, without losing her cool—or her moving van. She is an adept and skilled editor, and a gentle guiding force . . . and was also much better at deadlines on this project than I was. (That's why you hire people like Susan.)

I'm especially excited by the look of this book, which is just as beautiful, lush, and satisfying as you would expect a *Bon Appétit* desserts cookbook to be. Con Poulos was our gifted photographer, and captured not just the gorgeous finished desserts (though, of course, there are plenty of those), but also what inspires us as cooks: the excitement—and, yes, the fun—of the dessert-making process itself. Our talented design director, Matthew Lenning, lent his opinions and advice whenever I needed an expert sounding board, and I thank our photo editor Bailey Franklin—a man with a keen eye and much-appreciated natural calm—for his help during the photo-selection process. Arthur Mount's excellent illustrations clarify techniques throughout the book, and all of the elements are beautifully brought together in Jenny Barry's terrific, user-friendly design.

David Black, our agent extraordinaire, continues to impress me with the seeming ease of launching every project he helps create for us. We are lucky to have him, and his confidence in *Bon Appétit* helps me to focus and to think not just about the present project, but also into the future. He is a valued colleague and friend.

Working with the publishing team at Andrews McMeel has been a dream—starting with their enthusiastic reaction to our concept and continuing every step of the way through the creation of this beautiful book. I am in awe of Andrews McMeel president and publisher Kirsty Melville, who is a devoted foodie—talk about bonding with someone instantly—and a publishing maven who combines big-picture vision with amazing attention to detail (also, like Victoria, a busy mother of two and an enthusiastic home cook). Project editor Jean Lucas coordinated this massive project and kept us on track with seemingly endless patience, and I thank her.

I do have a few more personal notes. Si Newhouse, Chuck Townsend, John Bellando, and Tom Wallace continue to lead our parent company, Condé Nast, with diligence and care in the rapidly changing and sometimes confounding business of magazines, the Internet, and beyond. Paul Jowdy is our brilliant and talented leader on the business side as publisher of the magazine. His unwavering support and enthusiasm for what we do—and who we are—is appreciated beyond measure.

I owe eternal thanks to Paige Rense for reinventing *Bon Appétit* in 1975, and to Pat Brown for hiring me way back when (1978 to be exact) as an editorial assistant who apparently showed some promise. First Marilou Vaughn and then Bill Garry, in particular, helped me refine my skills, expanded my horizons, taught me to think and to challenge myself, and, basically, provided a career that became my life. During our almost twenty years together, Bill gave me great freedom to work with others inside and outside the magazine to help him shape it; I had many key roles and responsibilities even before I became editor-in-chief in 2000.

Finally, love and appreciation to my family: my mom, Ina Lieb (whose brownies, short-bread, and pumpkin pie are still the gold standard), sisters Cara and Devra, nephews, nieces, in-laws, and friends—blessedly, for I am very blessed—too numerous to mention here by name. But most of all to Paul Nagle, who continues to inspire and support me, always with love and care.

—Barbara Fairchild, editor-in-chief

When I was growing up, we had dessert every night.

It wasn't something that I really ever thought about, it just *was*. All of my schoolmates had dessert every night, too, not to mention a little something sweet at lunch every day. Of course, there was always a treat of some sort offered when my mom's friends came over for coffee and when she and Dad played bridge every week, and certainly something special when she hosted a dinner party. We always made cupcakes for school bake sales, and we had a big cookie-making night at holiday time to make gifts for the neighbors and our teachers, with plenty left over for us and anyone who might unexpectedly drop in.

But the weeknight selection was not to be ignored. The simpler desserts came up in rotation a lot: raisin-, nut-, and cinnamon-stuffed baked Rome apples; lime Jell-O studded with bananas; cut-up fresh fruit with a little sour cream on top. My mom was a good cook and baker—she still is—and so we also had wonderful apple pies in the fall; terrific brownies, chocolate chip cookies, and shortbread in the winter; and fresh fruit cobblers and shortcakes in the spring and summer. And at my grandfather's house in Maryland, my sisters and I took turns churning unforgettably good peach ice cream in a hand-cranked, salt-filled ice-cream maker.

Yes, I still have something after dinner every night, but times have changed and so have desserts. Many are lighter, certainly many are quick, and seasonality and local sourcing are more important than ever. Flavors that once would have seemed exotic—cardamom, pomegranate, lavender, chili-spiked chocolate—are exciting

Red Velvet Cake with Raspberries and Blueberries

Stained-Glass Lemon Cookies

additions to the modern dessert repertoire. During the week, I still keep it simple. I'll have fresh berries with a little Greek yogurt, a perfect Honeycrisp apple, or a buttery piece of shortbread. On weekends, I might make something grander for a dinner party (Red Wine and Pear Brioche, anyone?), or create a luscious new ice cream in my little electric churn. My philosophy is simple: A good dessert is all about that little hit of sweet that gives any dinner its official wrap-up and launches us into the rest of the evening.

It has been said that the soul of a baker is much different than the soul of a cook. Dessert making is more exacting and precise, and although there is a little room for improvising in some instances, generally it's best to stick to the recipe. That's where this book comes in. Each of the more than six hundred recipes here has been tested and retested by the experts in the *Bon Appétit* kitchens to guarantee sweet success every time. In addition to the recipes, you'll find notes that let you know what to expect from each recipe; extensive tips and sidebars offering do-ahead suggestions and test-kitchen secrets; step-by-step illustrations to guide you through preparation; and thorough chapters on stocking your pantry, buying the most useful equipment, and mastering the essential techniques of dessert making. We want this to be your ultimate dessert resource, guidebook, and helpmate in the kitchen, whether you're an enthusiastic beginner or a confident cook looking for some new ideas and tricks.

Bon Appétit Desserts has been a long time coming. After more than three decades of publishing recipes for cakes, cookies, pies, tarts, cheesecakes, ice creams, and so much more, we've been able to pack a lot of info and expertise into these pages. This gorgeous book truly is what we say on the cover: the cookbook for all things sweet and wonderful. Nothing provides the satisfaction, gets the attention, or creates memories like a great dessert. And there is little more in life that you can ask for than that.

—Barbara Fairchild, Los Angeles, California

Deep Dark Chocolate Cheesecake

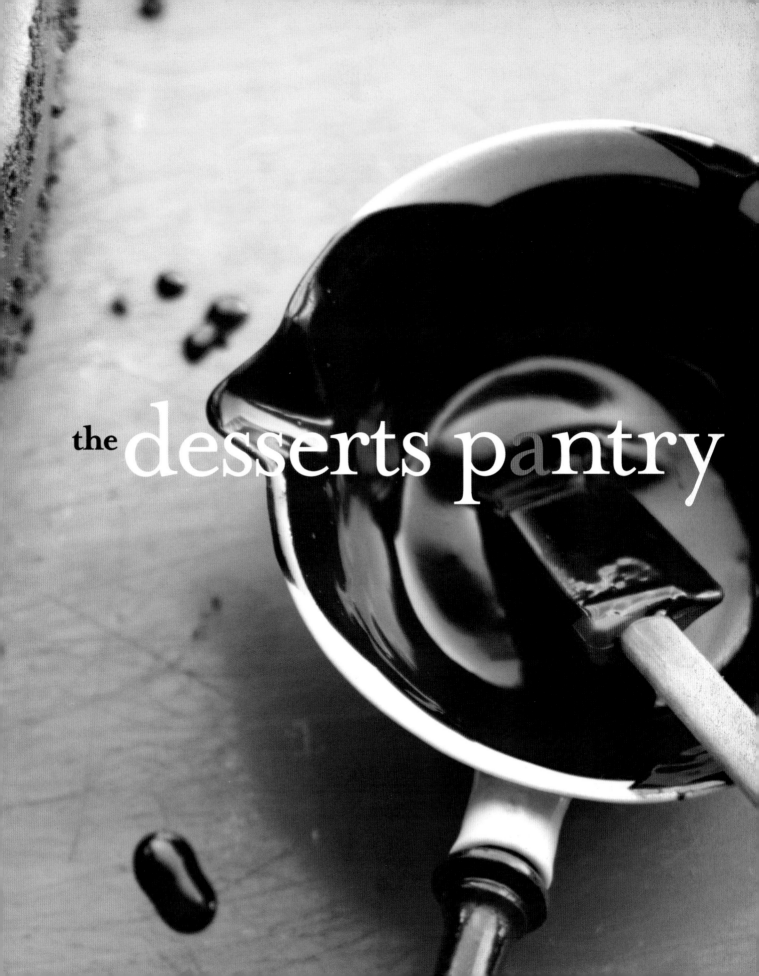

the desserts pantry

There are many wonderful things about making desserts,

not least that you get to eat them afterward. One of the other pluses is that you probably have most of the staples in your cupboard or refrigerator right now: flour, sugar, baking powder, eggs, butter, milk, vanilla extract, baking chocolate. From there, it's not a huge leap into the delicious world of cakes, pies, custards, ice creams, and cookies—not to mention Linzertortes, Pavlovas, baked Alaskas, tiered wedding cakes, and croquembouches. Following is a guide to the ingredients you'll be using most often as you bake and cook your way through the recipes in this book, from angel food cake to zabaglione.

Whisk Ratings

To help you determine at a glance which recipe fits your skill level, we've given every recipe in the book a "whisk rating," on a scale of one to four whisks. A complete Index of Whisk Ratings begins on page 638.

Very easy to make, with no special techniques required. Perfect for the novice.

A little more challenging. For the beginner with confidence.

Sophisticated, requiring more mastery of technique, such as caramelizing sugar. For the experienced cook.

A showstopping dessert with many steps and components. For the expert baker.

almond paste & marzipan

WHAT: Pliable sweet "doughs" made primarily of ground blanched almonds and sugar, with the addition of glucose or egg whites.

USES: Almond paste is usually used as an ingredient in desserts for flavor and texture. **Marzipan** is lighter, finer, and sweeter and is often tinted and sculpted into fruit, vegetable, or animal shapes. In the recipes here, it is usually rolled into sheets to cover cakes or to be cut into various shapes.

FIND: In tubes or cans at most supermarkets and at specialty foods stores.

STORE: Unopened in a dry, cool place for up to a year; once opened, store airtight in the refrigerator for up to three months.

baking powder & baking soda

WHAT: Key leavening agents for baked goods—in other words, they help cakes, cookies, and muffins rise and have an airy texture. **Baking soda** (bicarbonate of soda) has four times the leavening power of baking powder. It releases carbon dioxide gas when combined with an acidic ingredient (like buttermilk, molasses, sour cream, or yogurt) and causes dough and batter to rise. **Baking powder** is a mixture of baking soda, cornstarch, and one or more powdered acids, which release carbon dioxide gas first when moistened and a second time when heated, thus giving baking powder a double-acting leavening ability.

USES: When using baking soda or baking powder, whisk them with the other dry ingredients to distribute them evenly.

FIND: In the baking aisle. You can make your own baking powder by whisking 2 tablespoons of cream of tartar with 1 tablespoon of baking soda and 1½ table-spoons cornstarch three times to ensure that it is well blended.

STORE: In a cool, dry place for about six months. Store homemade baking powder airtight at room temperature for up to one month.

butter

WHAT: Butter is made by churning cream until it separates, forming a milky liquid and the solid butterfat. **Unsalted butter** is the preferred choice for baking since it allows you to control the amount of salt in recipes. **European butter** (also known in the U.S. as cultured butter) is made by churning fermented cream rather than regular cream; it has a higher percentage of milk fat and works well in desserts.

USES: Butter adds flavor and richness, makes baked goods tender and flaky, extends the shelf life of breads, and aids in browning. Well-chilled butter is crucial to the success of baked goods like biscuits, shortcakes, scones, and pie dough; however, when beating butter with sugar for cakes and most cookie doughs, the butter will "cream" better if it is at room temperature.

FIND: European butter, such as Plugrá (European-style butter) and Isigny Ste-Mère, can be found alongside regular butter in well-stocked supermarkets and at specialty foods stores.

STORE: Butter absorbs odors easily; store it airtight in the coldest part of the refrigerator and away from foods for one to two months (wrapped). Regular butter can be frozen for up to six months, European-style butter for up to four.

chocolate

WHAT: The purest form of chocolate is the cacao nib, formed after cacao beans are removed from their pods, fermented, dried, roasted, shelled, and cracked open. You can use nibs to add subtle chocolate flavor and a crunchy texture to baked goods, but most nibs are ground into a paste called chocolate liquor. Chocolate liquor is, basically, a combination of cocoa solids and cocoa butter; after further stages of refining, chocolate as we know it is formed.

USES: As a rule of thumb, use the best-quality chocolate you can find and afford. In fact, many of our recipes specify "high-quality chocolate" such as Lindt, Perugina, Valrhona, and Scharffen Berger, which reward you with incredible depth of flavor, sweetness, and smooth texture. Most labels on packages of chocolate now indicate the percentage of cacao—the higher the percentage of cacao, the less sugar and other ingredients.

- **Dark chocolate** includes unsweetened, bittersweet, and semisweet chocolates.
- **Unsweetened chocolate** (100 percent cacao) is pure chocolate with no other ingredients, including sugar; also referred to as baking chocolate.

- **Bittersweet and semisweet chocolates** contain sugar, vanilla, and lecithin, an emulsifier; sometimes you'll also see milk solids added to mellow the flavor. Bittersweet has a richer chocolate flavor and is less sweet since it has a higher percentage of cacao. In certain *Bon Appétit* recipes, to guarantee the best results, it's important to use a bittersweet or semisweet chocolate that doesn't have too high a percentage of cacao; in those cases, we specify that the chocolate should not exceed 61 percent cacao. In other recipes, the cacao percentage will not affect the outcome; those recipes will simply call for "bittersweet or semisweet chocolate."
- **Milk chocolate,** made with the addition of dry milk powder, has more sugar than bittersweet or semisweet chocolate.
- **White chocolate** is technically not chocolate because it doesn't contain chocolate liquor. It is a blend of cocoa butter, sugar, milk products, vanilla, and lecithin. For the best results when using white chocolate in a recipe, use the highest quality possible; make sure it contains cocoa butter, not vegetable oil. Lindt and Perugina are excellent brands.

FIND: In the baking aisle or the candy aisle. If your supermarket doesn't carry high-quality chocolate, check specialty foods stores or online (see Online and Mail-Order Sources on page 632).

STORE: Wrap tightly and store in a cool, dry place. Unopened, chocolate will keep for several months.

cocoa powder

WHAT: A powder made of the chocolate liquor extracted from cocoa beans.

USES: Natural cocoa (sometimes labeled simply "cocoa" or "nonalkalized cocoa") is slightly acidic and has a strong flavor and a slightly red color. Many baked goods rely on natural cocoa's acidity to help set the proteins in baked goods. **Dutch-process cocoa** has been treated with an alkali, which neutralizes its acidity, softens the harsh flavor, and dramatically darkens the color. But because it lacks acidity, it might not set the proteins properly in baked goods, resulting in cakes that collapse, for example. Use Dutch-process cocoa only in recipes that call for it; substituting Dutch-process for natural cocoa is not recommended.

FIND: In the baking aisle (natural cocoa) or the coffee and tea aisle.

STORE: In a tightly covered container in a cold, dark place for up to two years.

cookies

WHAT: Purchased cookies, such as graham crackers, chocolate or vanilla wafers, biscotti, shortbread, gingersnaps, or any other crisp cookie.

USES: Cookies are often used to make delicious, easy crumb crusts for pies, tarts, and cheesecakes. The cookies are ground into fine crumbs, then combined with butter or shortening and usually some sugar to form a moist, sandy texture that clumps together when squeezed, ensuring that the crumbs will stick to the sides of a pan.

FIND: In the cookie aisle or—depending on the cookie—in specialty foods stores or ethnic markets.

STORE: Unopened packages usually last a month or more.

cornstarch

WHAT: A white, silky powder made from dried and ground corn kernels.

USES: Lends a fine texture to cakes, cookies, and other pastries (it sometimes replaces part of the flour) and is used to thicken puddings, pastry creams, and cooked fruit fillings for pies and cobblers. Sauces thickened with cornstarch remain clear, whereas those thickened with flour turn opaque. To avoid lumps, mix cornstarch with a cold liquid, such as milk, then gradually whisk it into the hot liquid, or mix it with sugar, then add a cold liquid and stir while cooking. For cornstarch to thicken properly, it must come to a near boil.

FIND: In the baking aisle.

STORE: In a cool, dry place for up to a year.

corn syrup

WHAT: A derivative of cornstarch, corn syrup comes in light and dark varieties.

USES: It is often used in recipes for caramel, fudge, and frostings, as it inhibits sugar from crystallizing and creates a smooth texture. It also keeps ice cream creamy by preventing the formation of ice crystals. **Light corn syrup** is clear and thick and imparts a mild, sugar-like sweetness. **Dark corn syrup** contains caramel color and flavoring and adds a molasses-like sweetness. It can also be used as a topping for pancakes, waffles, and cornbread.

FIND: Light corn syrup can be found year-round in the baking aisle at the supermarket; dark corn syrup is available at many supermarkets and is especially easy to find at holiday time.

STORE: For up to six months in a cool, dry place.

cream cheese

WHAT: A soft, spreadable cheese made from cow's milk.

USES: Cream cheese is the basis for most cheesecakes and many frostings. When baking with cream cheese, we prefer Philadelphia brand, as it sets frostings and cheesecakes better than other brands. (Do not substitute whipped cream cheese or low fat or nonfat cream cheese.)

FIND: In the dairy case.

STORE: Once opened, cream cheese should be used within ten days. Unopened, it can be stored in the refrigerator for up to one month past the sell-by date.

cream of coconut, sweetened

WHAT: Cream of coconut is made from coconut milk that has been sweetened with sugar. (It is much sweeter than coconut milk, and these two items are not interchangeable.)

USES: Used mainly in desserts and mixed drinks.

FIND: It is available canned as Coco López or in a squeeze bottle as Coco Reál in the beverage and mixers section of most liquor stores and supermarkets.

STORE: Unopened, it will last for up to a year in a cool, dry place.

cream of tartar

WHAT: A fine white powder made from tartaric acid.

USES: It is beaten into egg whites when making meringue to help stabilize the egg foam and prevent it from weeping. It also serves as the acid in many baking powders. Because it inhibits the formation of sugar crystals, it is often used in candies and frosting to create a creamy texture.

FIND: In the spice section of the baking aisle.

STORE: In a cool, dry, dark cupboard for up to a year.

dairy products: buttermilk

WHAT: Originally, buttermilk was the liquid that remained after butter was churned. Today it's made in a similar way to yogurt and is known as "cultured buttermilk": Bacterial cultures are added to milk, and the mixture is heated at a low temperature. The bacteria cause the milk to ferment and thicken, resulting in buttermilk's creamy texture and slightly tart flavor. Despite its name, commercial buttermilk is low in fat, with only 0.5 percent to 2 percent butterfat.

USES: Buttermilk is used in many baked goods, such as cakes, scones, cornbread, and coffee cake, though it can also be used to make deliciously tangy ice cream, custard, and panna cotta.

FIND: In the dairy section of the supermarket.

STORE: In the refrigerator. Check the sell-by date on the package.

dairy products: cream

WHAT: Cream is formed naturally when milk separates into two layers—a thick, creamy top layer with a thin milky liquid below. The percentage of milk fat in the top layer determines what kind of cream it will be: **Heavy whipping cream,** which is what *Bon Appétit* dessert recipes call for, has 36 percent to 40 percent milk fat. For the thickest, richest whipped cream, use pasteurized (*not* ultra-pasteurized) heavy whipping cream. Note that organic whipping cream will take much longer to whip.

USES: Whipping cream lends an unmatched richness to desserts and a tenderness to many baked goods. Heavy whipping cream is the basis for rich custards, ice creams, ganache, and, of course, fluffy whipped cream. Whipping cream becomes thick and airy and doubles in size when whipped, and the process occurs more quickly when the cream, mixing bowl, and beaters are well chilled.

FIND: In the dairy section of the supermarket.

STORE: In the refrigerator. Check the sell-by date on the package.

dairy products: sour cream & crème fraîche

WHAT: **Sour cream** is similar to yogurt in that it is treated with a lactic acid culture to give it a tangy flavor and thick texture, but cream is used instead of milk. **Crème fraîche** is also made with a starter culture—the result is a sweet, tangy cream that's similar in consistency to sour cream.

USES: Sour cream, along with yogurt and buttermilk, is a key ingredient in baked goods, as its acidity not only helps tenderize cakes, quick breads, and pie crusts, but also helps set the proteins so that pie crusts don't slide down the sides of the pie dish. Crème fraîche is often used in place of sour cream or as a tangy alternative to whipped cream as a topping.

FIND: In the dairy section of the supermarket. Crème fraîche is available at some supermarkets and at specialty foods stores.

STORE: In the refrigerator. Check the sell-by date on the package.

dairy products: yogurt

WHAT: **Yogurt** is made by adding bacterial cultures to milk and cooking the mixture at a low temperature. The bacteria cause the milk to thicken, giving yogurt a creamy texture and slightly tart flavor. Most of the yogurt available in supermarkets is made from cow's milk, although sheep and goat's milk yogurts are also available. **Greek-style yogurt** is a type of strained yogurt, made by straining the yogurt through cheesecloth or a coffee filter to remove the excess liquid.

USES: Yogurt adds tanginess and moistness to cakes and quick breads. It is also a lighter alternative to sour cream and crème fraîche, which are made from cream.

FIND: In the dairy section of the supermarket. If you can't find Greek-style yogurt there, look for it at specialty foods stores (such as Trader Joe's and Whole Foods markets) and Greek markets.

STORE: In the refrigerator. Check the sell-by date on the package.

eggs

WHAT: Organic eggs are the preferred choice in baking, since the chickens are fed an organic diet and raised without antibiotics. The color of an eggshell—white, brown, green, or blue—makes no difference to the flavor or nutritional value of the egg (the shell color varies with the breed of hen).

USES: Most baking recipes call for large eggs, but always use the size that the recipe calls for to ensure the best results. For meringues, make sure the egg whites are at room temperature to ensure more volume. (You can use packaged egg whites if you prefer, but you may not achieve the same results; the *Bon Appétit* test kitchen uses only fresh egg whites.)

FIND: Most supermarkets now offer regular, free-range, and organic eggs; farmers' markets are also a good source for organic eggs.

STORE: In their carton in the coldest part of the refrigerator (usually the bottom shelf) for up to a month.

extracts

WHAT: Concentrated flavorings, such as vanilla, almond, and peppermint. Some are extracted from the oil of plants (such as mint and bitter almonds); others are made by distilling and pressing ingredients (such as vanilla beans).

USES: Always use pure extracts and avoid imitation extracts, which are inferior in quality and flavor. Extracts are useful in baking, as they can be added to batter, dough, sauce, ice cream, and custard without affecting the texture or consistency. Since their flavors are intense, they should be used sparingly. For the best results, add extracts to mixtures that are slightly cooled, since heat weakens the flavors. **Vanilla** extract is the most widely used extract, as it complements most other flavors (see page 14 for more on vanilla extract). **Almond** extract has a strong, sweet flavor that complements most pitted fruits, such as cherries, apricots, plums, and peaches. **Peppermint** extract pairs well with chocolate.

FIND: In the baking aisle.

STORE: Indefinitely in a cool, dark place.

flours

WHAT: Wheat flour is the essential ingredient of many desserts; hard and soft wheat are the two main types of wheat used to make it. The difference is the amount of protein in each. When flour is mixed with water to form dough, the proteins in the flour bond to create a gum-like substance called gluten. Gluten is stretchy and gives dough the elasticity to expand and trap the gas formed by leavening agents like yeast, baking powder, and baking soda. Hard wheat is high in protein and forms flour with stronger gluten; flour made from soft wheat has less protein.

USES: Getting the proper texture for various baked goods requires different types of flour:

- **All purpose flour** is a blend of hard and soft wheats; it is the most common flour used in home kitchens. It can be used for making most baked goods, including breads, cookies, pie crusts, and cakes (unless otherwise specified in the recipe). The recipes in this book call for unbleached all purpose flour, which has not been exposed to bleaching chemicals; instead the ground flour has turned from yellow to white naturally through exposure to oxygen.
- **Cake flour** is soft wheat flour and results in baked goods with a tender texture.
- **Pastry flour** is soft wheat flour with a bit more protein than cake flour; it's good for making pie doughs, muffins, biscuits, and pastries. Whole wheat pastry flour is also available.
- **Self-rising flour** is all purpose flour with baking powder and salt added. If you don't have self-rising flour on hand, you can add 1½ teaspoons of baking powder and ¼ teaspoon salt to 1 cup of all purpose flour to equal 1 cup of self-rising flour.
- **Bread flour** is unbleached flour made with hard wheat and is high in gluten. Because it results in a well-risen loaf, it is the best flour to use for making yeast breads.
- **Whole wheat flour** contains the grain's bran and germ and so has a higher fiber and oil content. White whole wheat flour is milled from white, rather than red, wheat. It has a milder flavor and lighter color than traditional whole wheat but the same fiber and nutrition.

FIND: Most flours can be found in the baking aisle; some specialty flours can be found online (see Online and Mail-Order Sources on page 632).

STORE: Airtight in a cool, dry place for up to six months. Whole wheat flour should be refrigerated (for up to six months) to keep the oils in the flour from turning rancid.

fruits, dried

WHAT: Fresh fruits that have been dehydrated, retaining only 15 percent to 25 percent of their original moisture; dried fruits have a more concentrated flavor than their fresh counterparts.

- **Dried tart cherries,** also known as dried sour cherries, have a wonderful sweet-tart flavor. **Dried Bing cherries** are sweeter and darker.
- **Dried apricots** are available sulphured and unsulphured. Sulphured dried apricots are more common. They are preserved with sulphur dioxide to extend the shelf life, lighten the color, and keep the dried fruit soft. Unsulphured and organic fruit is darker and sweeter.

- **Raisins** are dried grapes usually made from Thompson seedless or Muscat grapes. Thompson seedless grapes can be used to produce both dark and golden raisins. When the grapes are sun-dried for several weeks, the resulting raisins are darker and more shriveled. To produce golden raisins, the grapes are treated with sulphur dioxide, then dried with artificial heat; golden raisins are fatter and more moist. Raisins made from Muscat grapes are dark and very sweet.
- **Dried currants,** also called Zante currants, are actually not currants; they are tiny raisins made by drying Black Corinth seedless grapes (when fresh, these grapes are also known as Champagne grapes). Dried currants are not related to fresh currants.
- **Dried figs** come in two varieties—dried Calimyrna figs, with thick, beige skin, and dried black Mission figs, which have very dark skin. You can use these varieties interchangeably in *Bon Appétit* recipes, though the appearance will be different. The figs should be sweet and still relatively moist. Trim the tough tip of the stem, then chop them into a suitable size and add them to baked goods.
- **Dried coconut** is unsweetened shredded, shaved, or chipped coconut flesh. It is different from **sweetened flaked coconut,** which has been dried, flaked, rehydrated, and sweetened and tends to be moister; they are not interchangeable. Both types lend a mild, sweet, coconut flavor and texture to desserts and are often used as a garnish. When toasted, dried coconut becomes golden and crunchy with a slightly nuttier flavor.

USES: Dried fruits add flavor and sweetness as well as texture to pastries and baked goods. You can use dried fruits as is, or reconstitute them by soaking them in warm liquid—such as water, wine, fruit juice, or liqueur—until they are soft. (But reconstituted fruit is very different from fresh fruit, so don't try to substitute it for fresh.) Dried fruit can also be simmered in a fruit compote, where it softens considerably.

FIND: Most dried fruits are available in the dried fruit section or produce department of supermarkets and specialty foods stores. Unsulphured dried fruits, such as apricots, are available at natural foods stores and some supermarkets. Dried unsweetened shredded coconut is available at specialty foods stores, natural foods stores, and some supermarkets. Sweetened flaked coconut is available in the baking aisle at most supermarkets. See Online and Mail-Order Sources, page 632, for other places to find dried fruits.

STORE: Keep airtight at room temperature for several months or refrigerate in a tightly sealed bag for up to a year.

fruits, frozen

WHAT: Frozen fruit is a convenient alternative to fresh fruit since it is cleaned, peeled, pitted, cut up, and ready to use. The fruit is harvested at its peak and quickly frozen, so it is ripe, nutritious, and economical; most are available year-round (although frozen cranberries may be difficult to find in the summer).

USES: Frozen berries, cherries, and cranberries are especially good for baked goods (such as pies and cobblers), cooked sauces and compotes, and smoothies and shakes. For some recipes, the fruit does not need to be thawed before using.

FIND: In the frozen foods aisle. When purchasing frozen fruit, feel the bag to check that the pieces of fruit are separate; if they are clumped together in one large piece, this is a sign that the fruit may have been thawed due to improper handling and then refrozen. Most recipes call for unsweetened frozen fruit, but some frozen fruit is sweetened and packaged in syrup, so check the packaging carefully. To freeze your own fresh fruit, wash, trim, peel, seed or pit, and chop larger fruits, like bananas, mangoes, peaches, and strawberries (other berries and cranberries can be frozen as is), then arrange the fruit in a single layer on a baking sheet and freeze. Enclose frozen fruit in resealable plastic freezer bags and keep frozen.

STORE: In resealable plastic freezer bags in the freezer for up to six months. Unopened packages of purchased frozen fruit can be kept in the freezer for six months.

gelatin

WHAT: A thickener and stabilizer derived from animal bones, cartilage, tendons, and other connective tissue (therefore, not suitable for consumption by vegetarians).

USES: Thickens desserts such as panna cotta, gelatin, mousse, pudding, parfait, and marshmallows. It does not impart any color, flavor, or smell. It must be soaked in a cool liquid (usually water) to soften, then stirred over low heat until completely dissolved before it is blended with other ingredients. Once the dessert is chilled, the gelatin becomes firm like jelly, and depending on the amount used, it will set the dessert to the desired consistency, from thickening to firming completely. Some ingredients, such as fresh figs, ginger, guava, kiwi, mangoes, papaya, and pineapple, contain an enzyme that prevents gelatin from setting; however, once cooked, they can be used.

FIND: Gelatin is sold as unflavored, unsweetened tiny granules in small packets; it's available in the baking aisle of supermarkets. Agar, a thickener made from red algae, is a good vegetarian/vegan alternative that can be found in natural foods stores.

STORE: Gelatin keeps in an airtight container in a cool, dry place for up to a year. Dried agar can be stored for up to two years in an airtight container.

ginger

WHAT: Fresh ginger is a knobby root with bulbous offshoots and a spicy, sweet, pungent flavor. **Dried ground ginger** has a distinctive, strong flavor that is quite different than fresh ginger. **Crystallized ginger** is slightly chewy, candy-like pieces of ginger that have been cooked in sugar syrup and coated with sugar.

USES: Fresh ginger adds a clean and refreshing flavor to sorbets, ice creams, syrups, and sauces. Dried ground ginger is an essential ingredient in many desserts and baked goods, such as ginger cookies and gingerbread. Crystallized ginger adds spicy sweetness to cakes, scones, cookies, and ice cream. With its sparkly sugar coating, it also makes a pretty garnish.

FIND: Fresh ginger can be found in the produce section. It should be firm with smooth, tan, slightly shiny skin and a moist flesh with a fresh aroma. The skin needs to be peeled and, since fresh ginger has fibers that run down the length of the root, it should be thinly sliced crosswise or grated. Ground ginger is sold in the spice aisle. Crystallized ginger is available sliced, finely diced, and cubed at many supermarkets, natural foods stores, and Asian markets.

STORE: Fresh unpeeled ginger will keep at room temperature for up to three days, up to three weeks tightly wrapped and stored in the refrigerator, or frozen for up to six months. Dried ginger can be stored in a cool, dry place for up to six months. Crystallized ginger can be stored in an airtight container at room temperature for up to three months, in the refrigerator for up to six months, or in the freezer for up to a year.

honey

WHAT: There are hundreds of honeys available, ranging in taste and form from robustly flavored liquid honey to whipped honey. The flavor and color of honey depends on the type of flower from which the nectar is foraged. For instance, when bees forage for honey in a lavender patch or on the blossoms of orange trees, the honey can take on the subtle flavors of that flower.

USES: Honey is a natural sweetener that is used in many desserts and as a syrup for pastries, cornbread, and breakfast items such as pancakes and French toast. It lends its distinctive flavor to classic desserts and candies, such as baklava and nougat. Cakes and cookies made with honey stay moist longer than those made with sugar. And cookies made with honey are soft rather than crisp. Honey gives chocolate sauce a gooey, fudgy texture. **Clover honey,** the most widely used honey, imparts a traditional honey flavor, but **orange blossom honey** and **lavender honey** are two types of honey that are prized for their floral, perfumey flavors.

FIND: Clover and other honeys are available at the supermarket and at farmers' markets. Varietal honeys are often available in specialty foods stores, or online (see Online and Mail-Order Sources on page 632).

STORE: Airtight at room temperature for up to a year. If honey crystallizes, the jar can be heated in a pan of warm water for 10 to 20 minutes to dissolve the crystals.

jams & preserves

WHAT: Jams and preserves are fruits cooked with sugar and sometimes pectin; preserves feature larger pieces of fruit.

USES: Jams and preserves add a sweet, concentrated fruit flavor to a variety of desserts. They can be used as filling for Italian crostatas, French jam tarts, crepes, doughnuts, and layered cakes. They are often swirled in breakfast pastries and cakes and used in cookies such as thumbprints, pinwheels, sandwich cookies, and rugelach. Apricot jam has a light amber color and is often used as a glaze for fruit tarts.

FIND: In the peanut butter section of the supermarket.

STORE: Most jams and preserves will keep for up to a year in the refrigerator.

maple syrup

WHAT: Pure maple syrup is the boiled-down sap of maple trees; it takes 20 to 50 gallons of sap to make a single gallon of maple syrup. Maple syrup is classified according to the intensity of its amber color, going from light (AA) to dark (C), and its maple flavor, although the grade is not a reflection of quality. Generally, the darker the syrup, the more robust the flavor. Grade B is preferred for most of the recipes in this book because of its robust flavor.

USES: Maple syrup is a natural sweetener. Because it lends a mild maple flavor to baked goods and desserts, it can sometimes be used in place of other liquid sweeteners, such as honey and corn syrup.

FIND: Grade B maple syrup can be found at the supermarket or specialty foods stores. If you can't find Grade B, Grade A syrup can be used instead. Avoid syrups that are labeled "pancake syrup" but look like maple syrup—these less expensive imitators of maple syrup actually contain corn syrup and artificial flavors, but no maple syrup.

STORE: Once opened, maple syrup keeps in the refrigerator for up to a year.

mascarpone

WHAT: Although often referred to as cream cheese, Italian mascarpone is technically a very thick cream. It has an even richer, creamier flavor than heavy whipping cream and a thick, smooth, spreadable consistency. Its flavor is similar to cream cheese but has a sweeter, creamier taste compared to the tangy, salty flavor of cream cheese.

USES: Mascarpone's creamy qualities make it a blank slate for showcasing other flavors. Mascarpone is the essential ingredient in tiramisù and is often used in cheesecakes, frostings, and mousses. It can also be served in lieu of butter atop waffles, crepes, and French toast or spread onto toast and topped with jam.

FIND: In small plastic containers in the cheese or dairy section of most supermarkets, Italian markets, specialty foods stores, and natural foods stores.

STORE: In the refrigerator for up to a month.

molasses

WHAT: A sweet, thick, dark brown syrup with a distinctive roasted, tangy flavor that is characteristic of gingerbread. Molasses is the by-product of processing sugarcane or sugar beets into table sugar. There are three basic types of molasses available: **light,** which comes from the first boiling of the sugar syrup; **dark,** from the second; and **blackstrap** molasses, from the third boiling. Dark molasses is more robust and less sweet than light molasses, and blackstrap molasses is even darker and more bittersweet.

USES: We recommend unsulphured molasses because it is the purest. The recipes in this book specify whether to use light or dark molasses; blackstrap should never be used because its flavor is too bitter.

FIND: Near the maple syrups in the supermarket and at specialty foods stores.

STORE: Airtight in a cool, dry place for up to a year.

nuts

WHAT: Most nuts are fruits or seeds, although peanuts are technically legumes.

USES: Nuts add flavor, texture, and richness to baked goods and desserts. They are sold shelled or unshelled, raw or roasted, salted or unsalted, or seasoned. Some, such as almonds, are available slivered, sliced, chopped, and blanched. Most desserts and baking recipes call for shelled raw or toasted nuts that are unsalted.

FIND: Because nuts are high in fat, they can easily become rancid. It is best to buy them from sources that have a high turnover rate to ensure freshness—such as natural foods stores, farmers' markets, and online sources specializing in nuts. They're also available at supermarkets.

STORE: To help keep them fresh, store shelled nuts airtight in the refrigerator for up to six months, and in the freezer for up to a year.

peanut butter

WHAT: Natural peanut butter, also known as old-fashioned peanut butter, is made by blending roasted peanuts with some salt into a paste that is either creamy or crunchy. Many major-brand **regular peanut butters** contain sugar, molasses, and other additives. In recent years, these brands have replaced partially hydrogenated oils with palm oil; the palm oil prevents the natural oils found in peanut butter from separating from the peanut butter.

USES: The separation of oil and peanut butter is a common occurrence in natural peanut butter, so it must be stirred to blend before it is measured. At room temperature, natural peanut butter tends to be thinner than regular peanut butter, yet firmer when cold. Since natural and regular peanut butter are quite different in texture and flavor, it is important to use the style called for in the recipe.

FIND: In the supermarket.

STORE: After opening, store in the refrigerator for up to six months.

phyllo dough & puff pastry

WHAT: Although they both create decadent, flaky crusts for desserts, phyllo dough and puff pastry are quite different. **Phyllo dough** is paper-thin sheets of dough (made of flour, water, and oil); in many recipes, each layer is brushed with melted butter and then stacked to create a crust. **Puff pastry** is made by wrapping chilled butter in dough and repeatedly rolling and folding. For each, it is this layering of pastry dough with butter that makes them puff. When baked, the butter releases its moisture as steam, which is trapped by the dough, causing the layers of dough to separate and puff. Baked phyllo dough is crisper than puff pastry.

USES: Phyllo dough and puff pastry dough are two indispensable ingredients for making some of the most prized desserts and pastries, ranging from baklava and apple strudel to napoleons and elegant tarts.

FIND: Making these doughs from scratch is very labor-intensive and time-consuming, but, fortunately, they can easily be purchased. Both are widely available in the freezer section of supermarkets and specialty foods stores, near the frozen fruits and desserts. Look for frozen puff pastry that lists butter as a main ingredient. Phyllo dough can also be purchased fresh at Middle Eastern markets.

STORE: In the freezer for up to a year. Thaw frozen phyllo dough overnight in the refrigerator, puff pastry at room temperature for about 30 minutes.

salt

WHAT: Salt is a key ingredient in baked goods and desserts and comes in a variety of forms used in baking:

- **Table salt** is inexpensive common white salt; it's very fine grained and contains additives that help prevent it from clumping. Some bakers prefer this salt because its fine grains blend and dissolve easily in batters and dough. However, others avoid table salt because they feel it has a harsh, chemical flavor.
- **Kosher salt** is coarse-grained salt that is free of additives and has a smoother flavor than table salt. If a recipe calls for kosher salt, don't use table salt, as they are not interchangeable (table salt is far saltier).
- **Sea salt** has a fresh, smooth flavor and is available in fine and coarse grains. The fine grains are used like table salt, and the coarse grains are often used as a "finishing salt," sprinkled on food as a garnish just before serving. Some sea salts are rich in minerals, which gives them an off-white or gray color.
- **Fleur de sel** (meaning "flower of salt" in French) is a sea salt that is hand-harvested off the coast of France. Because only the very top layer of salt is collected in a labor-intensive process, it is more expensive than table salt and kosher salt. It has large, damp grains and is available at specialty foods stores and natural foods stores. It is used only as a finishing salt.

USES: A small amount of salt heightens and intensifies flavors; without it, breads, cakes, and cookies taste flat and can fall short of dazzling. When using salt in batters, whisk it with the other dry ingredients to ensure that it is evenly dispersed. When beating egg whites for meringues, add the salt toward the end, since salt can make egg foams unstable.

FIND: Table salt and kosher salt are available in the baking aisle at the supermarket. Sea salt and fleur de sel can be found in some supermarkets and at specialty foods stores.

STORE: Airtight in the cupboard indefinitely.

shortening

WHAT: Solid vegetable shortening is pure vegetable oil in a solid state. *Bon Appétit* recommends non-hydrogenated shortening, which is healthier because it contains no trans fats. Note that shortening is not the same thing as margarine, which usually contains water, whey, salt, and other ingredients. If a recipe calls for shortening, do not substitute margarine, as the added ingredients can alter the texture of the dessert.

Chocolate-Caramel Slice

spices

WHAT: Spices are aromatic seasonings derived from the bark, roots, seeds, buds, or berries of plants and trees. Allspice, cardamom, cinnamon, cloves, ginger, and nutmeg are among the most frequently used spices for desserts.

- **Allspice,** a brown berry, is available whole or ground. It's originally from tropical regions, including Jamaica, South America, and the West Indies, and tastes like a mixture of cinnamon, cloves, nutmeg, ginger, and black pepper.
- **Cardamom** is a small, pale green pod with small black seeds. It is sold as whole pods, seeds, and ground. Cardamom is native to India and frequently used in Southeast Asian cuisines, Middle Eastern cuisines, and Scandinavian breads and pastries. It has a warm, pungent aroma and flavor. The easiest way to remove the seeds from cardamom pods is to enclose the pods in a resealable plastic bag, then whack them a few times with a skillet, rolling pin, or meat mallet. Remove the husks from the bag, and keep whacking until the seeds are crushed as finely as you like.
- **Cinnamon,** the bark of an evergreen tree indigenous to India and Sri Lanka, is sold both in stick form and as a ground powder. However, much of the cinnamon on the market in the United States is actually cassia (also the bark of an evergreen tree), which has a stronger flavor than genuine cinnamon. Sticks of the two types appear quite different. True cinnamon quills consist of paper-thin layers of bark rolled together. Cassia sticks are a single layer of thick, stiff bark. If you prefer the flavor of true cinnamon (some people like cassia's more assertive character), look for jars labeled Ceylon cinnamon or plastic bags of Mexican cinnamon.
- **Cloves** are the dried, unopened flower buds of a tropical evergreen tree. They're sold whole or ground and have a very pungent flavor. A little goes a long way; using too much has a numbing effect and its flavor will overpower the dish.
- **Ginger** is the knobby root of a tropical plant. It is most frequently used fresh, dried and ground, and crystallized (see page 10 for more information).
- **Nutmeg** is an oval-shaped seed of a fruit native to East Indonesia. It is sold whole or ground, and has a warm, sweet flavor and aroma. Whole nutmeg can be grated with a Microplane grater or nutmeg grinder, and will have a much more intense flavor than purchased ground nutmeg.

USES: Ground spices are convenient to use, but their flavors deteriorate more quickly than whole spices. Toasting spices changes their flavor dramatically (consider how different a slice of bread tastes when toasted), so if a recipe calls for a spice to be toasted, don't skip that step—you'll be shortchanging the dish.

FIND: All of the spices listed here can be found in the spice aisle.

STORE: In tightly sealed canisters in a cool, dark cupboard; ground spices will keep for six months to a year; whole spices will keep about twice as long.

USES: Solid vegetable shortening is often used in combination with butter in crusts. Because it's more malleable than butter (which contains some milk solids), shortening makes the crust easier to work with and to roll out, preventing the dough from cracking and falling apart. It's helpful to novice pie makers for that reason. And because it's all fat, it helps make the crusts flaky. However shortening does not have any flavor, so it's best used in combination with butter. To measure solid vegetable shortening accurately, pack it firmly into a measuring cup and level it off with a knife. Rinsing the measuring cup with cold water first will make it easier to scrape the shortening from the cup with a rubber spatula.

FIND: Non-hydrogenated vegetable shortening is available at supermarkets, specialty markets, and natural foods stores. It's usually found in the aisle where vegetable oils and olive oils are sold; in some markets it's in the baking aisle.

STORE: Technically shortening does not need refrigeration after opening, but since it's usually used chilled for pie crusts, do keep it in the refrigerator. It will keep for at least a year, and will last even longer if stored in the freezer.

sugar

WHAT: Sugar is probably the first ingredient people think of when they think of desserts. It comes in a variety of forms, including the familiar granulated white sugar, powdered (or confectioners') sugar, raw sugar, and light and dark brown sugar.

USES: Sugar plays various roles, depending on the kind of sugar being used.

- **Granulated sugar** is highly refined from the juices of sugarcane or sugar beets. It is sold in cubes and in several different textures, from **superfine**—which dissolves easily, making it ideal for meringues and for sweetening drinks—to **coarse,** which is often colored and used as decoration.
- **Powdered sugar** (also known as confectioners' sugar) is white sugar that's been ground into a fine powder and mixed with a small amount of cornstarch to help absorb moisture and prevent caking. If powdered sugar is excessively clumpy, sift it before measuring. Because it dissolves easily, it's good for making icings, frostings, and whipped cream. It is frequently dusted over baked goods as a garnish.
- **Raw sugar** is a coarse-grained sugar with a light amber color, sparkly appearance, and sweet flavor with notes of caramel. **Turbinado sugar** and **demerara sugar** are varieties of raw sugar. Raw sugar is partially refined, but unlike granulated sugar, it retains a bit of molasses residue. Since raw sugar has large sparkly grains, it is often used as a finishing sugar—it is especially pretty sprinkled on scones and pie crusts before baking—and can be substituted for white or brown sugar when used as a garnish. However, it is not always interchangeable with white and brown sugar in recipes that call for a particular sugar.
- **Brown sugar** is white sugar mixed with molasses and comes in two main varieties: **golden brown sugar,** also called **light brown sugar,** and **dark brown sugar,** which has a stronger molasses flavor. When measuring brown sugar, always pack it firmly in the measuring cup, unless otherwise specified.

FIND: Granulated, powdered, and brown sugars are all sold in the baking aisle at the supermarket. Raw sugar is available in the baking section of many supermarkets and specialty foods stores.

STORE: In your cupboard or pantry. Brown sugar is a soft, moist sugar that hardens when exposed to air, so store it in an airtight container at room temperature. If it hardens, enclose it in an airtight container with a damp paper towel or wedge of apple on top and let it stand for a couple of days, or place it in a microwave-safe dish and cover with two damp paper towels, then microwave on high for about 30 seconds.

tapioca, quick-cooking

WHAT: A starchy thickener derived from the cassava plant.

USES: Thickens the fruit juices in cobblers, pies, crisps, and other desserts. Don't use regular tapioca pearls, which are much larger and won't soften and dissolve properly.

FIND: In the baking aisle.

STORE: Can be kept in a cool, dry place for two to three years.

vanilla

WHAT: Vanilla adds a sweet perfume and underlying flavor to desserts. It comes in three forms:

- **Vanilla beans** are actually long, thin, dried pods of a tropical orchid; Madagascar and Tahiti produce high-quality vanilla beans. Vanilla beans have an exotic flavor that is more complex than that of vanilla extract. The pods are usually split lengthwise with the point of a knife, exposing the fragrant tiny, black, sticky vanilla seeds (see page 38 for tips on doing this). Typically, the pods are then steeped in a hot liquid or the seeds are scraped out and added to the batters.
- **Vanilla extract** is the most commonly used type of vanilla. Vanilla beans are chopped and soaked in an alcohol-water solution, which is then aged for several months. Vanilla extract has a deep brown color, a slightly syrupy consistency, and a rich perfume. Always use pure vanilla extract, as imitation vanilla is inferior in quality and taste. One teaspoon of vanilla extract can be substituted for a 2-inch piece of vanilla bean (or a 1-inch piece of Tahitian vanilla bean). For the best results, add vanilla extract to mixtures that are slightly cooled; heat weakens vanilla extract's flavor.
- **Vanilla paste** is a concentrated form of vanilla extract and includes the pretty flecks of fresh vanilla bean seeds. If you have it on hand, you can use it as a substitute for vanilla beans; 1 tablespoon of vanilla paste is the equivalent of one whole vanilla bean.

USES: Vanilla is extremely versatile and can stand alone in puddings, custards, sauces, ice cream, cakes, and cookies, or be paired with other intense flavors such as chocolate, coffee, and spices.

FIND: Vanilla beans are available in the spice aisle of most supermarkets and at natural foods stores and specialty foods stores. Look for pods that are plump, pliable, and slightly moist. Vanilla extract is in the spice aisle at the supermarket. Vanilla paste is available at specialty foods stores and online.

STORE: Wrap vanilla beans in plastic and store in an airtight jar in the refrigerator for up to six months. Vanilla extract and vanilla paste keep indefinitely when stored airtight in a cool, dark place.

wine & spirits

WHAT: Wines, liqueurs, and spirits add sophisticated flavor and aroma to desserts. The following wines, liqueurs, and spirits are used most often in this book.

FORTIFIED WINES

Fortified wines are those that have had brandy or another spirit added to them, either during or after the fermentation process. When the spirit is added during fermentation, it stops the fermentation and leaves more sugar in the wine, resulting in a sweet and strong product.

- **Port** is a sweet, fortified wine. Available varieties include Porto, ruby Port, tawny Port, and vintage Port. Ruby is most frequently used in the recipes in this book; ruby Port has a darker red color and fruitier flavor than tawny Port.
- **Muscat** is a sweet wine made from Muscat grapes; it can range in color from white to deep, rich pink, but most of the versions called for in this book will be white (pale gold). Muscat wines are made in many countries and go by different names, including **Beaumes-de-Venise,** a type of fortified Muscat wine from the village of Beaumes-de-Venise, France; *moscato,* made in Italy; and **Essensia,** a brand of fortified sweet dessert wine made in California from perfumey Orange Muscat grapes.
- **Marsala** is an Italian fortified wine. It is commonly available as sweet or fine (dry), and is typically used in tiramisù and zabaglione.
- **Madeira** is a Portuguese fortified white wine with an amber color. It is similar to sherry and ranges from sweet to dry.
- **Sherry** is a fortified wine. It ranges from dry (fino or manzanilla) to sweet (oloroso; cream, a kind of oloroso sherry; amoroso; or amontillado, which has a nutty flavor).

LIQUEURS

Liqueurs are sweetened alcoholic beverages made by adding sugar to distilled alcohol and flavoring it with fruit, nuts, herbs, or spices.

- **Grand Marnier** is a Cognac-based liqueur with an orange flavor. Cointreau or other orange liqueurs can usually be substituted.
- **Amaretto** is a liqueur, originally from Italy, with an almond flavor.
- **Chambord** is a French liqueur with a black raspberry flavor and a deep ruby color.
- **Kahlúa** is a Mexican liqueur with a rich roasted coffee flavor and a dark brown color.
- **Frangelico** is a hazelnut-flavored liqueur with a pale golden color.

SPIRITS

- **Brandy** is distilled from either wine or another fermented fruit juice. Armagnac is the limousine of brandies. It has more flavor and a smoother texture than any other brandy. Cognac makes the best substitute.
- **Eau-de-vie** is a clear brandy or other spirit distilled from fermented wine or fruit juice. Kirsch (made from cherries), framboise (made from raspberries), and poire Williams (made from pears) are popular eaux-de-vies.
- **Rum** is distilled from fermented sugarcane. It is available clear (or light), and dark. Most recipes in this book that use rum call for dark rum.
- **Whiskey** is distilled from a mash of fermented grains such as corn, rye, and barley. Whisky from Scotland (spelled without an "e") is called Scotch and is made from a mash of barley. Bourbon is an American whiskey made mostly from a mash of corn. Irish whiskey is made from barley and other grains.

USES: Wines, liqueurs, and spirits can be paired with other ingredients of similar flavor—amaretto with almonds, for example, or Grand Marnier with fresh oranges. Or they may provide the focal point of flavor for a dessert.

FIND: All of these wines, liqueurs, and spirits can be found at liquor stores or in the liquor aisle of supermarkets and specialty foods stores.

STORE: In a cool, dry place. Unopened, liqueurs can last indefinitely. Once opened, fortified wines should be used within a few weeks (buy half-bottles if you don't think you'll be able to use a whole bottle that quickly). Liqueurs can last up to three years once opened; distilled spirits up to two years.

yeast, dry

WHAT: Dry yeast, also called active dry yeast, comes as dehydrated granules in small packets and jars. Dry yeast acts as the leavening (rising) agent in dough; when mixed with other ingredients, such as flour, water, and sugar, and allowed to sit in a warm place, yeast converts these ingredients into carbon dioxide and alcohol. The alcohol burns off while the carbon dioxide causes the dough to rise. Dry yeast is available as regular and quick-rising (also known as rapid-rise) yeast.

USES: To activate (or proof) yeast, combine it with a warm liquid (105°F to 115°F), as instructed in the recipe. Use an instant-read thermometer to check the temperature; never use a liquid that is too hot or too cold, as doing so can slow the yeast's growth or even kill it. If the mixture doesn't foam after 10 to 15 minutes, the yeast is not active, and you need to start again with a new package of yeast.

FIND: In the baking aisle.

STORE: In the refrigerator; use by the date indicated on the jar or packet.

equipment
the basics

Anyone can make desserts with equipment already on hand—

which probably includes measuring cups and spoons, a cake pan or two, baking dishes in a few sizes, a whisk, a spatula, maybe a food processor. All indispensable. But if you're serious about baking, and you plan to do it on anything like a regular basis, having a well-stocked kitchen will transform your life—making dessert preparation faster, more efficient, and simply more fun. Here's a guide to the essential elements of a dessert-maker's kitchen. (Note that you'll also find plenty of information throughout the book on other handy tools that will help with specific recipes.)

baking dishes & pans

Bon Appétit recipes are usually specific about the type of baking dish to use. It's wise to buy a variety of sizes and materials, including heavy-duty metal, tempered glass, earthenware, porcelain, and enameled cast iron.

A **heavy-duty metal baking pan** is preferable when high-temperature baking or broiling is involved, because metal can withstand higher heat than ceramic or glass.

For fruit crisps and cobblers, which contain acidic ingredients, **glass or ceramic baking dishes** are better than metal, which reacts with acidic ingredients—and they can go from freezer to microwave to oven with ease. Ceramic baking dishes have an added advantage: They're made in attractive colors and are pretty enough to serve from right at the table. The recipes in this book regularly call for 2-inch-deep baking dishes in these sizes: 8x8, 9x9, 11x7, and 13x9 inches.

baking sheets

Rimmed baking sheets, also known as **jelly-roll pans** or **sheet pans,** are usually about an inch deep. They're great for cookies and pastries; you'll want a few of them if you'll be baking multiple batches of cookies. They can also be used under fruit-filled items like cobblers, pies, tarts, and turnovers, which can bubble over during baking. Rimmed baking sheets are also great for organizing groups of prepped ingredients and ferrying them around the kitchen. Heavy-duty, commercial-weight aluminized sheets (available at well-stocked cookware and restaurant supply stores) are the best choice because they won't warp or buckle at high temperatures. Rimmed baking sheets come in quarter-sheet pan size (about 13x9 inches) and half-sheet pan size (about 18x13 or 17x12 inches). Note that pan dimensions may vary depending on the manufacturer.

Rimless baking sheets are helpful when it's necessary to slide free-form tarts and other delicate items directly from baking sheet to cooling rack; they're also good for baking cookies.

bowls

A set of nesting mixing bowls made of tempered glass, metal, or plastic is easy to store neatly. The various graduated sizes come in handy for mixing doughs and batters, tossing fruit salads, and organizing prepped ingredients.

cake pans

Heavy-duty **round metal cake pans** come in many diameters and depths. The recipes in this book regularly call for 8-, 9-, and 10-inch-diameter pans with 2-inch-high sides.

Rectangular or square metal cake pans are ideal for breakfast and snack-type cakes. Glass baking dishes can be used, but because cakes bake faster in glass pans than in metal ones (and because glass pans stay hot longer after being removed from the oven), you should reduce the oven temperature by 25 degrees and start checking for doneness a few minutes earlier than the recipe says. Avoid dark metal pans altogether—they tend to brown cakes too quickly.

Springform pans, which come in several diameters, are an excellent choice for creamy-textured cakes, like cheesecakes and mousse cakes. The high, removable sides provide a form for the cake and the latched sides make unmolding simple.

More specialized cakes—such as **Bundt** and **angel food**—require their own pans; a Bundt pan can also double as a **kugelhopf pan**.

cake turntable

For frosting and decorating cakes, a cake turntable offers excellent maneuverability (a lazy Susan would do the trick, too). It allows the cake to be rotated and also raises it several inches above the work surface so that all sides may be reached easily.

cherry pitter

To pit whole cherries quickly, try using a cherry pitter. In our test kitchen, we use the Oxo Good Grips cherry/olive pitter (about $13; oxo.com). It holds large cherries easily and has a splatter shield that protects you, your clothes, and your countertop from the staining juices. If you don't have a cherry pitter, use a chopstick: Push it into the fruit through the stem end, forcing the pit out the opposite end.

citrus juicers

Electric and manual citrus juicers are designed to squeeze juice from lemons, limes, oranges, and grapefruits. An **electric juicer** is an efficient way to extract the most juice quickly. Less expensive and also easy to use are **manual juicers**. A few different models are available. When just a few teaspoons of juice are needed, a **hand reamer** is an easy-to-use option. Press and twist this small fluted tool into the citrus half, working over a strainer to catch the seeds. With a **reamer set on a perforated base,** the perforated base catches the seeds and sits over a dish that catches the juice. A **scoop-shape juicer** works best for lemon and lime halves. This perforated, clamp-like squeezer resembles an oversize round garlic press and operates like one, too.

citrus zester

To get slender strands of peel from lemons, limes, grapefruit, and oranges, use a five-pronged zester, which removes the zest while leaving the bitter pith behind.

cookie & biscuit cutters

Cookie cutters in a variety of shapes and sizes will come in handy all year, and can be used for making cutouts to decorate the top crusts of pies, too. **Biscuit cutters,** which are deeper than cookie cutters, are sold in sets of three or four or more, all with different diameters. Fluted or straight edged, they are perfect for biscuits and shortcakes and can double as cookie cutters. Our recipes commonly call for 2- to 3-inch round cutters.

cooling rack

A cooling rack lets air circulate underneath cookies, cakes, and pies for rapid, even cooling.

cupcake pans

Cupcake pans, also known as muffin pans, are usually made of metal. They come in a variety of sizes, for baking standard-size, oversize, or mini muffins or cupcakes. *Bon Appétit* recipes usually call for standard (⅓-cup) cupcake pans, with cups that are 3 inches in diameter. For mini cupcakes, pans with 2-inch-diameter cups are the pan of choice.

custard cups, ramekins & soufflé dishes

Custard cups are handy for baking individual puddings and for organizing prepped ingredients, too. They're made in two basic styles: **Tempered-glass custard cups** are squat glass cups that are wider than they are tall. These have flared sides and come in sizes that range from 4 to 8 ounces in capacity. **Ceramic custard cups** have gently tapered, fluted sides. They're less squat than glass custard cups and range from 2 to 6 ounces in capacity.

Ramekins are squat dishes with flat bottoms and straight, fluted sides. Most are made of ceramic, though glass versions are also available. Ramekins come in a wide variety of sizes; the recipes in this book most often call for ½-, ¾-, ⅔-, and 1-cup ramekins. Stock a range: You'll use them for baking individual puddings, soufflés, and cheesecakes and for organizing prepped ingredients.

Soufflé dishes are bigger, straight-sided ceramic dishes that resemble oversize ramekins and hold a quart or more. Glass versions are also available. Soufflé dishes are pretty enough to sit on the table and double as serving dishes.

double boiler

A double boiler consists of two pans, one set on top of the other. It's useful for melting chocolate, making custard sauces, and other kitchen tasks that involve cooking above simmering water. If you don't have a double boiler, rig one up by placing a metal mixing bowl in a saucepan of simmering water, but not so low that the bottom touches the water. (The bottom of the bowl must sit close to but not touch the simmering water when cooking eggs for a custard. When melting chocolate, this is less of a concern.)

electric mixers

Because it's light, with a less powerful motor than a stand mixer, a **handheld electric mixer** is ideal for mixing or beating small amounts. And because it's portable, it's also useful for quick jobs like whipping cream for a dessert garnish or making zabaglione on the stovetop. Handheld mixers are much less expensive than stand mixers.

A **stand mixer** is a heavy-duty version of the handheld mixer that's capable of dealing with large and small quantities of dough or other mixtures, leaving your hands free for other tasks—it can mix and whip while you scoop, measure, and sift. And it comes with a variety of attachments that perform very different functions:

- The **wire whisk** incorporates the maximum amount of air into light mixtures—use it for whipping eggs and sugar for flourless chocolate cakes and angel food cakes, and for whipping cream.
- The **flat paddle beater** is best used for working with firmer mixtures, such as creaming butter and sugar for cake batter or mixing cookie dough. The BeaterBlade, a brand-name product, is a flat paddle beater with a flexible rubber edge that functions like a windshield wiper for the mixing bowl, almost eliminating the need to stop the machine to scrape down the sides of the bowl. It can be purchased separately from specialty cookware stores—or go to beaterblade.com for more outlets.
- You won't need to use the **dough hook** for the recipes in this book. Save it for mixing and kneading yeast dough for breads.

food processors

For quick chopping, pureeing, slicing, and grating, nothing beats a food processor. It comes with several attachments, including an S-shaped metal blade (which is probably the one you'll use most often when making desserts; it's perfect for making crumb crusts for cheesecakes, for example). A plastic dough blade, a shredding disk, and a slicing disk are other attachments.

Use a **large-capacity food processor,** which holds anywhere from 7 to 16 cups, to make purees and mix some doughs. Count on a **mini processor,** which holds around 2 cups, to pulverize small quantities of nuts or make flavored sugar.

graters

If you're in the market for a grater, choose a reputable brand, like Microplane. The problem with many graters is that the teeth on them aren't particularly efficient. Look for graters with super-sharp, razor-fine teeth: They're essential for grating citrus zest, fresh ginger, chocolate, and nutmeg. Graters come in several different styles.

Paddle-shaped graters with handles and **long, slender rasp graters** both come in coarse, ribbon, and extra-fine rasp styles that allow you to grate everything from whole nutmeg and fresh ginger to the outermost layer of citrus peel. (The long, thin grater makes grating citrus zest especially easy—its slender shape allows you to draw the grater back and forth over a piece of citrus fruit, as if bowing a cello.)

A **rotary grater,** crank operated and cylindrical with a small chamber, makes quick work of grating chocolate for sprinkling over a finished dessert.

A conventional **box grater** has four sides with different-size holes for grating, shredding, and slicing. Generally, this kind of grater is best used in savory cooking, but the side with large holes can be used for grating carrots for carrot cake, and the smaller holes are suitable for finely grating chocolate, ginger, and citrus zest. Use the holes with pronged perforations for hard, dry ingredients like nutmeg.

When grating or slicing large amounts, the grater and slicer disks on a food processor are the quickest way to get the job done.

ice-cream maker

See page 452 in the Frozen Desserts chapter.

kitchen scale

Used by professional bakers, a **kitchen scale** is helpful for measuring ingredients by weight rather than volume, which helps ensure consistent results in the commercial kitchen. Avid home bakers use kitchen scales, too, for measuring dry ingredients like flour, cornmeal, chocolate, nuts, and brown sugar. (For a list of weight-volume equivalencies, see page 634). Mechanical scales start at about $20, digital scales at about $50. Both can weigh items up to about 11 pounds, and should be able to measure in ¼-ounce increments.

knives

Designed to last, stay sharp, and feel comfortable in the hand, good knives make cooking a pleasure. Because you'll use them every day, it's worth the extra cost to go for top-quality knives. Most top-tier, long-lasting knives are forged from a single piece of high-carbon stain-resistant steel.

A 6- or 8-inch **chef's knife** is great for chopping nuts, fruit, and chocolate and for mincing fresh ginger.

A long, **serrated bread knife** is handy for halving cake layers, as well as for slicing Bundt cakes and pound cakes (a smaller serrated knife is good for cutting citrus and smaller cakes).

A **paring knife** serves well for peeling fruit, separating citrus pulp from pith, and mincing small quantities.

A long, thin-bladed **slicing knife** works well for cutting rich cheesecakes and flourless chocolate cakes.

Ceramic knives have a following among some cooks. With a blade made of hard, high-tech ceramic, these knives come in 3- to 6-inch sizes and are ultra-sharp—they can cut through an apple as if it were butter. Ceramic knives are also costly, prone to shattering if dropped on a hard surface, and require special equipment for both honing and sharpening.

To choose the knives that are right for you, visit a well-stocked kitchen supply store and try different models to figure out which design feels best in your hand.

loaf pans

Loaf pans come in metal, tempered glass, porcelain, and earthenware. Dimensions vary slightly depending on the manufacturer, but a full-size pan generally measures about 9x5 inches and is about 3 inches deep. Loaf pans are convenient for making quick breads, pound cakes, fruitcakes, and dessert terrines. At holiday time, **miniature loaf pans** are great for baking small, gift-size breads and cakes.

measuring cups

You'll need both dry and liquid measuring cups.

Dry measuring cups are sold in sets of ¼-, ⅓-, ½- and 1-cup capacities. Sets that also include ⅔-cup and ¾-cup measures are available.

Liquid measuring cups are essential because they provide extra space at the top so the liquid won't spill, and the pour spout makes it easy to add the liquid to a pot or mixing bowl. Look for ones that are made of heat-resistant glass with easy-to-read markings. You'll use 1-, 2-, and 4-cup measuring cups most often; an 8-cup measure is a bonus when making larger quantities—and it can double as another mixing bowl.

measuring spoons

A basic set of measuring spoons, usually made of metal or plastic, includes ¼-, ½-, and 1-teaspoon sizes, plus a 1-tablespoon size. Sets with ⅛-teaspoon and ½-tablespoon measures are also available. It's well worth buying more than one set of measuring spoons if you do a lot of baking so that you don't have to stop and clean spoons while making a cake or other dessert.

parchment paper

Ovenproof up to 420°F, parchment paper is often used to line baking sheets and cake pans. It's helpful for removing cakes from pans after baking. Plus, it eliminates the need for a spatula when transferring cookies, crostatas, and scones from a baking sheet to a cooling rack—simply slide the paper off the baking sheet and onto the rack.

pastry bags

Use a pastry bag, which can be fitted with a variety of tips, both plain and star shaped, for piping icing, cookie doughs, and meringues. Made of washable plastic-coated cloth, **traditional pastry bags** are reusable, while **disposable pastry bags,** suitable for one use only, are made of clear plastic. Available at specialty cookware stores and in the baking section of some supermarkets, disposable bags are sturdy and cheap, and a boon to bakers who like using multiple colors of frosting for decorating cookies and cupcakes.

No pastry bag? No problem. In the *Bon Appétit* test kitchen, we often use a heavy-duty **resealable plastic bag** with a corner snipped off.

pastry blender

Made for mixing pastry, biscuit, or scone dough by hand, a pastry blender is used to cut cold pieces of butter into dry ingredients instead of using your fingertips (the heat from your hands can melt the butter and result in a less flaky pastry). This simple hand tool consists of five or six closely spaced semicircular blades or wires on one end and a handle on the other. If you don't have a pastry blender, two table knives or a large fork would work, too, although it is not as convenient.

pastry brushes

Coating a pie crust with an egg glaze, brushing melted butter onto phyllo dough, buttering a Bundt pan, or brushing down the sides of a saucepan when making caramel—all of these jobs are most neatly done with a pastry brush. Brushes are available with natural or silicone bristles; both are effective for evenly applying egg washes and glazes. Silicone brushes are easier to clean, but some cooks prefer natural bristles when especially gentle brushing is required—such as when applying an egg wash to a yeast-raised dough that shouldn't be compressed or spreading fruit glaze on top of a carefully arranged fruit tart.

pie dishes

Pie dishes come in diameters ranging from 8 to 10 inches, in glass, metal, and ceramic. In the *Bon Appétit* test kitchen, recipes are tested with glass pie dishes, so you'll have the best results if you use the same. Avoid dark metal pans—they tend to brown what's inside too quickly.

pie weights

When blind baking (baking a tart or pie crust before filling it), metal or ceramic pie weights prevent the dough from buckling and shrinking during baking. Dried beans can also serve as pie weights—and the beans are reusable.

pot holders & oven mitts

Look for thick pads or gloves made of moisture-resistant fabric or silicone. To protect your forearms when reaching into the oven, choose extra-long gloves.

roasting pan

A large, heavy-duty roasting pan that measures about 16x13x3 inches can hold a water bath for baking cheesecakes, molten chocolate cakes, custards, and puddings, or an ice bath to use for cooling dessert sauces like hot fudge, custard, and butterscotch sauce. A roasting pan is deeper than a simple baking dish, and has sturdy handles that make moving a water-filled pan in and out of the oven much easier.

rolling pins

Rolling pins come in a few different shapes and are available at well-stocked cookware stores and restaurant supply stores.

A **straight rolling pin** is the simplest and most versatile. This wood dowel is about 20 inches long and 1¾ inches in diameter. Because you push the pin with your hands directly on the dowel, monitoring the texture and thickness of the dough as you roll is easy. Silicone-coated nonstick versions of a straight rolling pin are also available.

A **tapered rolling pin** is more slender than a straight pin. Thanks to its curved profile, a tapered pin permits rolling a round of dough with minimum effort. Silicone versions are available.

A **traditional rolling pin** with handles and ball bearings can be helpful for rolling out very stiff doughs because of its heft. Traditional pins come in wood, metal, and silicone-coated versions. However, these rolling pins with handles generally aren't as long as straight or tapered pins. Also, many bakers believe that using a rolling pin with handles on the sides puts distance between your hands and the dough, offering less opportunity to monitor the feel of the dough as you roll it out.

ruler

Keep an 18-inch ruler in the kitchen along with other hand tools. It's handy for measuring the diameter of rolled-out pie crusts and puff pastry, and for checking the measurements of cake, tart, and pie pans in case the dimensions are not visibly marked on the pan.

A **silicone pastry** or **baking mat** with markings for various diameters of pie crust makes easy work of rolling out pastry dough. Some pastry mats are also marked with a numbered grid, which helps ensure precision when rolling out square and rectangular pieces of dough. Pastry mats are available from specialty cookware stores and online.

saucepans

Saucepans come in small (1 to 1½ quarts), medium (2 to 3 quarts), and large (3 to 4 quarts). In the dessert kitchen, they're indispensable for making fruit compote, fudge sauce, and custard. When paired with a metal bowl, a saucepan makes a serviceable double boiler. A saucepan should feel heavy in your hand, with a snug lid and a handle that stays cool and is easy to grip. The best pans are made of a mix of materials. Effective heat-conducting metals like copper and aluminum are sandwiched between metals like anodized aluminum or stainless steel, which are hardy and don't react with acidic ingredients like fruit. A saucepan with a stainless interior has the added advantage of being shiny enough to make color change easily visible—especially important when making caramel syrup and other preparations in which color change is an indicator of doneness.

sifter

We don't use a sifter in the test kitchen. When dry goods need sifting, we use a strainer instead. In general, however, combining ingredients with a whisk aerates them sufficiently.

skillets

Skillets come in small (7 to 8 inches in diameter), medium (around 10 inches), and large (12 to 14 inches). Their shallow, sloping sides allow the most moisture to evaporate in the shortest amount of time. In the dessert kitchen, skillets come in handy for making small batches of preserves, for browning nuts, and for sautéing fresh fruit. A skillet should feel heavy in your hand, with a handle that stays cool and is easy to hold. Some large skillets have a loop handle on the opposite side from the long handle to ensure a good grip. The best skillets are made of a mix of materials. Effective heat-conducting metals like copper and aluminum are sandwiched between metals like anodized aluminum or stainless steel, which don't react with acidic ingredients. Nonstick skillets are handy for sautéing fruit, but their dark interior can make it hard to see color change. Cast-iron skillets are the best choice for dishes that go from stovetop to oven.

spatulas

Spatulas come in solid or slotted versions and a variety of heat-resistant materials, including silicone and metal. The pancake-flipper style is especially useful for transferring cookies from a baking sheet to a cooling rack.

Icing spatulas in flat and offset (bent at a 90-degree angle) styles offer ease of maneuverability for icing cakes and cupcakes. They come in 1- to 2-inch widths.

Silicone spatulas come in many shapes and sizes. They're great for stirring, folding, flipping crepes, and scraping doughs and batters off the bottom and sides of mixing bowls. In addition, silicone spatulas are flexible and easy to clean. Unlike the rubber variety, they're heat resistant up to 800°F and come in a wide range of colors. Buy several silicone spatulas in different thicknesses, shapes, and sizes. Silicone spatulas with a scooped head are effective for spooning batter. Those that are curved on one side and flat on the other, with thin sides, are especially effective for folding mousses and angel food cake batters, as well as for scraping mixtures from the sides of a mixing bowl. A silicone spatula with a long, thin head is effective for scraping the last bits of puree from the bottom of a blender or jar.

spice grinders

An **electric spice grinder** makes quick work of pulverizing seeds and whole spices. A **coffee grinder** works, too, but get a separate one for spices so that the flavor of your morning brew isn't affected. Using a **mortar and pestle** to grind spices has rustic appeal, though more time and muscle are required. Usually made of ceramic or marble, this time-honored two-piece grinder features a bowl-like mortar and a baton-like pestle.

springform pans

Springform pans have removable sides that seal shut with a spring-loaded latch. Making a cheesecake, mousse cake, or frozen dessert in a springform pan allows for especially easy removal of the pan sides at serving time. Springform pans come in several different sizes, but *Bon Appétit* recipes usually call for 9- or 10-inch-diameter pans.

strainers

Buy fine- and coarse-mesh strainers in a few different sizes. They're indispensable for straining fruit purees, custard sauces, and freshly squeezed citrus juice. A **coarse strainer** does double duty as a sifter for sifting dry ingredients together, as well as for removing lumps from sugar and cocoa. Use a **small strainer** to dust cookies and cakes with powdered sugar.

tart & tartlet pans

Tart pans range in size from just a few inches across (for tartlets) to 11 inches wide. They can be round, rectangular, or square. The pan's shallow depth and fluted edges give a professional pastry-shop look, and the removable bottom makes it easy to remove the tart from the pan.

testers

For testing the doneness of cakes, brownies, and scones, a thin bamboo skewer works well, as does a toothpick. You can also buy a cake tester, a thin steel skewer with a handle at one end.

thermometers, candy & instant-read

To check the doneness of caramels, syrups, candy mixtures, jams, and jellies, it's critical to use a **candy thermometer,** also called a **deep-fry thermometer.** Get one that clips onto the side of the pan so that your hands are free for cooking. A candy thermometer is different from an **instant-read thermometer,** which is used to read the temperature of custards and butter. Many instant-read thermometers aren't designed to withstand the high temperatures required for readings on sugar mixtures like dark caramel, which can get as hot as 380°F.

vegetable peeler

Choose a swivel-bladed peeler with a comfortable grip, which will offer the easiest maneuverability for removing the peel from fruits and for making chocolate curls.

whisks

A whisk's sturdy wires help blend ingredients and also beat air into whatever you're mixing. For combining dry ingredients and stirring sauces until smooth, use a **standard whisk,** which has a gently tapered profile. A **balloon whisk,** which is wider at the bottom than the top, is good for tasks that require aerating, such as whipping small amounts of cream by hand.

wooden spoons

Simple, heat resistant, and versatile, wooden spoons have countless uses. The spoons come with flat edges, angled edges, and, of course, curved bowls. They're sturdy enough for softening butter and stirring thick doughs, batters, compotes, and sauces. The simple, dowel-like handle is easy to hold. And the wooden surface is less slick than a metal spoon's, which makes it the tool of choice for stirring and softening thick ingredients, like buttery cookie doughs. Wooden spoons are inexpensive, so keep an assortment of sizes on hand.

techniques
the basics

Dessert preparation, like other kinds of cooking, comes with its own unique set of techniques, whether whipping cream to soft peaks or creating the perfect custard. Some techniques may require a little more practice than others, but all are well within the reach of every home cook. Here we offer step-by-step guidance to the most widely used dessert techniques—those that you'll use frequently throughout this book. In addition, you'll find more specific instructions (how to frost cakes, for example, or how to prepare perfect pie crusts) within each chapter.

how to follow a recipe

1. Read through the entire recipe before measuring or preparing a single ingredient. This may sound obvious, but many cooks dive right in, only to discover that they are missing ingredients, have not allowed enough time for preparation or chilling, or don't have the proper equipment on hand.
2. Pay special attention to the recipe headnote, which highlights useful information about the ingredients and techniques used in the recipe.
3. Ingredients are listed in the order that they are used in the recipe.
4. The French term *mise en place* means "setting in place"; in cooking, it refers to having all the ingredients prepped and ready to go—chocolate chopped, flour measured, strawberries hulled and sliced, etc. But, once again, read the recipe first before preparing the *mise en place*. You wouldn't want to peel and slice peaches for a cheesecake topping, for example, only to find that they are added to the recipe *after* the cake has chilled overnight.
5. Cooking times will vary depending on individual ovens, pan variations, and other elements. Always set the timer for a few minutes less than the recipe calls for, just to be on the safe side. Once you find that your baking times are in sync with the times stated in the recipes, or that they routinely run a minute or two slower or faster, set your timer accordingly.

NOTE: Baking is the most exacting form of cooking; even minor changes to a recipe can make a dramatic difference in the results. Therefore, we suggest that you *do not make substitutions* beyond what may be recommended in the recipe or headnote. Or, prepare the recipe at least once as written, then experiment with your own variations.

butter, browning

Brown butter, or *beurre noisette,* refers to butter that has been melted and cooked until golden brown. Browning—not burning—the butter over medium-low heat cooks the milk solids in the butter, thus intensifying the butter flavor. This is a classic French technique that adds a full, nutty, buttery flavor to foods. Here's how to do it.

1. Melt the butter in a heavy saucepan over medium-low heat.
2. Continue to cook, stirring occasionally, until the butter is browned to the desired color indicated in the recipe. The length of time will vary depending on the amount of butter. Remove from heat.

buttering & flouring a pan

Thoroughly buttering a baking pan and then coating it with a light layer of flour is the best way to ensure that your finished dessert releases from the pan completely.

1. Using a pastry brush or clean fingers, coat the inside surface of the baking pan thoroughly with softened butter, making sure to cover all surfaces and reaching into corners and grooves.
2. Sprinkle the pan with about 2 tablespoons of flour [1].
3. Tilt and tap the pan gently to coat all surfaces with flour [2].
4. Invert the pan and tap out any excess flour.

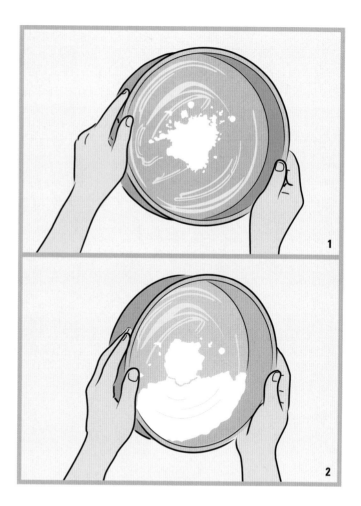

butter & sugar, creaming

Beating sugar and butter until fluffy is called "creaming." This step is important, as it incorporates air into the final product.

1. Make sure the butter is at room temperature and soft so that it creams properly with the sugar. If your butter is cold and firm, you can cut it into slices and microwave it on low for a few seconds (be sure not to melt the butter). The butter should be soft enough that you can easily press your finger into it and leave a distinct mark.
2. Beat butter and sugar in a large bowl until light and fluffy. This is easiest with an electric mixer, but can be done by hand with a wooden spoon.
3. The butter and sugar mixture should have the consistency of fluffy frosting and should be very pale in color.

caramel

Making caramel takes some practice. First make sure you have the right equipment, then follow the recipe directions precisely—and be very careful when working with hot caramel. If you're new to making caramel, keep in mind these tips:

1. Use a heavy-duty nonreactive pan with a secure handle and a shiny or light-colored interior. Heavy-duty pans ensure even heat. A secure grip helps keep the pan under control (getting burned by hot sugar is no fun). And a pan with a reflective (not dark) interior makes color changes easy to see.
2. Dissolve the sugar in the liquid according to the recipe directions. To make sure the sugar is totally dissolved, dip a spoon in, then rub a drop of the syrup between your thumb and finger (the syrup will still be cool enough to touch at this point). If you feel grainy bits, keep stirring over low heat. If not, continue with the recipe.
3. Brush down the sides of the pan with a wet pastry brush to dissolve any sugar crystals. Otherwise, the finished caramel may have a grainy texture.
4. As soon as the syrup in the pan turns golden, the difference between light, medium, and dark caramel occurs in a matter of seconds. What's in the pan is much too hot to taste safely and could burn you badly. Instead, rely on visual cues or a candy thermometer:

   Color: Light amber
   Temperature: 330°F to 340°F
   Flavor: Mild
   Color: Medium amber
   Temperature: 355°F to 360°F
   Flavor: Distinctively roasty
   Color: Dark amber
   Temperature: 375°F to 380°F
   Flavor: Intense, with an almost bitter edge

5. If you're adding cream (or other ingredients), stand back—the hot caramel syrup will bubble vigorously and could burn you.

chocolate, melting

1. Always chop chocolate to ensure even melting: Score lines in the chocolate with a large sharp knife; the pieces should be no larger than a half inch. Press a knife firmly with the heel of your hand along the score lines to chop.
2. Place the chopped chocolate in a metal bowl set over barely simmering water.
3. Stir the chocolate constantly; it can burn easily. A silicone spatula works well because the silicone will not impart any off flavors to the chocolate. Stir until the chocolate is smooth.
4. When melting chocolate with other ingredients, such as butter or cream, use a heavy saucepan over low heat and stir the mixture constantly.

chocolate curls

Chocolate curls lend a festive finish to all kinds of desserts, from simple cupcakes to sophisticated mousses. And they are incredibly easy to make.

1. Set a large chunk or bar of chocolate in a warm place to soften slightly (but not melt). Or gently warm chocolate in a microwave oven: Place the chocolate on a paper towel and heat it on the lowest setting at 5-second intervals until just warm.
2. Working over a sheet of waxed paper, firmly grasp the chocolate in one hand and, using a sharp vegetable peeler, shave curls from the chocolate onto the waxed paper. (If the chocolate breaks into small pieces, it is probably too cold.)
3. Use the waxed paper to transfer the chocolate curls: Lift the edges of the paper and carefully slide the chocolate curls and shavings onto the dessert or into an airtight plastic container. Store chocolate curls in a cool, dry place for up to a week.

chocolate leaves

Chocolate leaves are an elegant way to decorate cakes, mousses, and cheesecakes.

1. Select semirigid, waxy, nontoxic leaves. Camellia or citrus leaves, particularly lemon leaves, work well.
2. Line a large baking sheet with foil or waxed paper.
3. Using a small offset spatula or small brush, coat the back of a leaf with a thin, even layer of melted chocolate, about 1/16 inch thick, being careful not to let the chocolate drip over the edge of the leaf [1]. Transfer the leaf to the baking sheet.
4. Repeat the process, making as many leaves as desired.
5. Refrigerate or freeze the leaves until firm.
6. Grasp the stem end of the leaf with your fingertips or tweezers and carefully peel it away from the chocolate [2]. Store the leaves in the refrigerator in a single layer in a waxed paper–lined sealable plastic container. Handle the leaves as little as possible; the heat from your fingers will melt and mar the delicate chocolate.

cream, whipping

Beat chilled whipping cream (taken directly from the refrigerator) in a large bowl. To get the best texture and volume from whipped cream, be sure that the bowl and beaters are chilled as well.

If whipping by hand, use a large balloon whisk and whisk the cream until desired peaks form.

If using an electric mixer:

1. Begin whipping the cream at medium-high speed, then reduce the speed to low as soon as the cream begins to thicken.
2. Continue to whip the cream until desired peaks form.
3. Do not overbeat the cream; overwhipped cream will break and curdle— meaning that the dairy fat will separate from the liquid, forming small clumps of butter.
4. Sweeten and flavor whipped cream to your taste: Use honey, maple syrup, agave nectar, powdered sugar, or brown sugar in place of granulated sugar, if you like, and flavor with citrus zests, spices, liqueurs, and extracts.
5. When is cream whipped enough?
   - When serving whipped cream as a garnish, whip it just until it thickens and forms loose peaks when the beaters are lifted.
   - When using it as a frosting or in a mousse, whip the cream to medium peaks. (It will continue to thicken as it's used.)
   - For piping, whip the cream until firmer peaks form.

custard, crème anglaise, or ice-cream base

Here's how to make crème anglaise or a stirred custard for ice cream without curdling the eggs.

1. Bring the cream or milk mixture to a simmer in a heavy saucepan.
2. Whisk the egg yolk and sugar mixture in a large bowl until very well blended.
3. Gradually beat the hot milk or cream mixture into the egg-yolk mixture.
4. Return the custard mixture to the saucepan and stir with a wooden spoon or a silicone spatula over the heat level indicated in the recipe, just until thickened. Be very careful not to allow the custard to boil, as boiling will cause the eggs to curdle (which is basically scrambling).
5. It is fairly easy to judge with your eye whether the custard is properly cooked—it will thicken slightly and your finger will leave a path on the back of a spoon when drawn across it [1, above right]—but it is safest to use an instant-read thermometer. Cook the custard to 170°F to ensure proper thickening and to avoid curdling.
6. Once the custard reaches the proper temperature, immediately remove it from the heat and transfer to a large bowl.

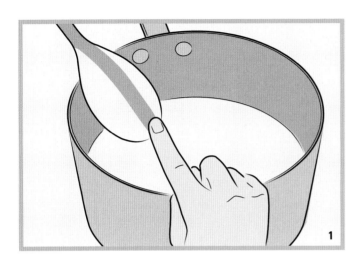

custard, zabaglione

Zabaglione (in Italian) or *sabayon* (in French) is a traditional custard preparation made by whisking egg yolks with sugar and liquid (usually wine) over a double boiler until light and fluffy. The beating is done over simmering water so that the egg yolks cook as they thicken into a light, foamy custard.

1. Select a metal bowl that fits above a medium-size saucepan so that the bulk of the bowl sits over the water (but does not touch the water) and does not come into direct contact with the heat from the sides of the saucepan.
2. Using a large wire whisk, beat vigorously and continuously until an instant-read thermometer reads 160°F.
3. Remove the bowl from over the water as soon as the zabaglione is cooked.

eggs, separating

1. Break the egg open by striking it against the edge of a bowl.
2. Carefully open the egg by pulling the top half of the shell from the bottom, making sure that the bottom half forms a cup that holds the egg yolk.
3. Let the egg white drain from the eggshell into the bowl. If necessary, pass the egg yolk carefully from one half of the eggshell to the other to remove all of the egg white.

egg whites, beating

Egg whites will increase eight times in volume as you beat them. To ensure that they don't lose volume, only beat the egg whites once all of your other ingredients are ready, your pan is prepared, and your oven is preheated.

1. Choose a large deep stainless steel, copper, or glass bowl. Do not use aluminum, as it will turn egg whites gray. Make sure the bowl is clean and dry.
2. Using the wire whip attachment of an electric mixer or a large balloon whisk, beat the egg whites without stopping until they form soft peaks [1] or firm peaks [2], according to the recipe instructions. Make sure not to overbeat them (egg whites can become dry and grainy).

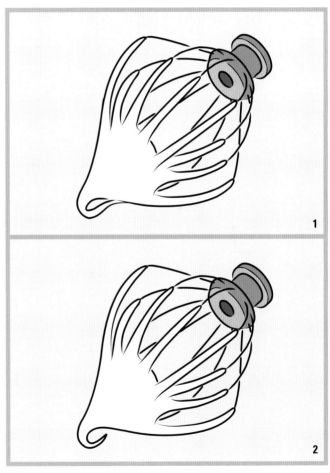

folding

Folding refers to the blending of two ingredients (usually including whipped cream or whipped egg whites) without stirring, so as not to deflate, or remove air from, the mixture.

1. Carefully draw a rubber spatula down [1] and across the ingredients in a large bowl toward the edge of the bowl, pulling the ingredients from the bottom and folding them over the top of the mixture [2].
2. Repeat the process just until the ingredients are thoroughly incorporated, being careful to work quickly but gently.

fruit, preparing

How to: dice a mango

1. Stand the mango on one end with a tapered side toward you. Slice off each long side, cutting as close to the pit as possible.
2. With the tip of a knife, cut a crosshatch pattern in the flesh of each section, cutting down to (but not through) the skin [1].
3. Press on the back of the skin on each section, turning it inside out so that the flesh pops up. Cut the cubes off the skin with a knife [2].
4. Slice any remaining flesh off the pit, then dice.

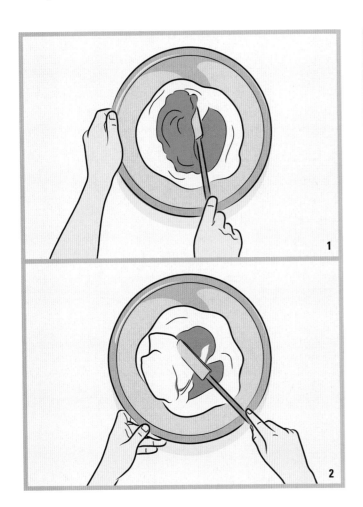

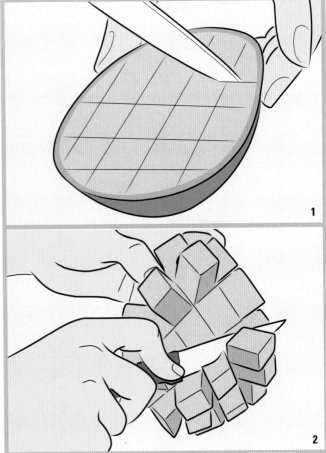

How to: grate citrus peel

1. Use a very sharp handheld grater. Hold the citrus firmly in one hand and draw the grater across the surface of the fruit to remove just the colored surface of the peel, not the white pith, which is bitter.

2. Continue turning the fruit and grating the peel until the peel is removed or you have the amount called for in the recipe.

How to: remove citrus peel (zest)

1. For long, thin strips of peel, remove the outer layer of the peel (not the white pith) with a vegetable peeler.

2. Trim the peel or thinly slice the peel according to the recipe instructions.

How to: segment citrus fruit

Citrus sections without any peel, pith, or membrane are called "supremes."

1. Use a thin knife to cut off the stem end of the fruit, just to the point of exposing the flesh. Cut off the opposite end [1].

2. Place the fruit, cut side down, on the work surface and cut away the peel and pith while following the contour of the flesh [2].

3. Place the citrus on its side and cut carefully between the membranes to release the segments [3].

How to: peel peaches

1. Bring a large saucepan of water to boil.

2. Using a small sharp knife, mark an X on the bottom of each peach.

3. Using a slotted spoon, gently lower the peaches into the boiling water and blanch (cook briefly) for 30 seconds.

4. Transfer the peaches to a strainer and rinse under cold water, or plunge into a bowl of ice water to cool.

5. Slip the skins off the peaches with your fingertips.

EVEN EASIER: Purchase a serrated peeler, which makes quick work of peeling fresh peaches and eliminates the need for blanching. Serrated peelers are available at many supermarkets and at kitchen supply stores.

How to: peel pineapple

1. Using a long serrated knife, cut off the leafy top end of the pineapple first, then cut off the base.

2. Stand the bottom of the pineapple on the cutting board. Starting at the top of the fruit, cut away the skin, following the contour of the fruit.

3. Using a small paring knife or the gouging end of a vegetable peeler, remove any remaining brown eyes from the flesh.

ice cream, softening

1. Let ice cream stand at room temperature for 10 to 15 minutes, until it is easy to scoop and serve.
2. Alternatively, place the ice-cream carton in the microwave and heat on low power at 10-second intervals until it is soft enough to scoop.

make your own ...

Baking powder: Whisk 2 tablespoons cream of tartar with 1 tablespoon baking soda and 1½ tablespoons cornstarch; make sure mixture is well blended.

Crème fraîche: Combine 1 cup heavy whipping cream and 2 tablespoons buttermilk in a glass container. Cover and let stand at room temperature until thickened, 8 to 24 hours. Stir well and chill until serving time.

Greek-style yogurt: Place regular yogurt in a cheesecloth-lined strainer set over a large bowl. Cover and chill overnight to drain (the yogurt will thicken).

Mascarpone cheese: Blend 8 ounces cream cheese with ¼ cup whipping cream and 2½ tablespoons sour cream.

Self-rising flour: Add 1½ teaspoons baking powder and ¼ teaspoon salt to 1 cup all purpose flour to equal 1 cup of self-rising flour.

measuring flour

It is critically important to measure flour properly when baking—even a tablespoon or so too many or too few can alter a recipe's results.

1. Today's supermarket flour is pre-sifted, so unless a recipe calls for flour to be sifted before measuring, it is not necessary to do so.
2. Use a large spoon to stir the flour in the bag or canister to loosen.
3. Dip the measuring cup into the flour, then use a knife to level the flour in the measuring cup, using a sweeping motion so as not to compress the flour.

measuring by weight

For greater precision, many experienced bakers prefer to measure their ingredients by weight rather than by volume. Here are the weight equivalencies for 1 cup of the most commonly used dry ingredients:

All purpose flour = 4½ ounces
Cake flour = 4 ounces
Whole wheat flour = 5 ounces
Granulated sugar = 7 ounces
Firmly packed brown sugar = 7½ ounces
Powdered sugar = 4 ounces
Cornmeal (regular) = 5½ ounces

measuring liquid ingredients

1. Use a glass measuring cup with the measurements marked on the side.
2. Set the cup on a flat counter or surface to fill.
3. Wait for the liquid to settle, then bend down and read the measurement at eye level for accuracy.

nuts, toasting

Toasting nuts brings out an incredible fragrance and flavor, so you should never skip this step in a recipe: What you might save in time you'll lose in the quality of the final product.

1. Preheat the oven to 350°F.
2. Arrange the nuts in a single layer on a large rimmed baking sheet.
3. Toast the nuts in the oven until slightly darker in color and fragrant. Always cool nuts completely before using them in recipes. Cooking times vary depending on the kind of nuts you're using:
Almonds, sliced: 7 to 10 minutes
Almonds, slivered: 7 to 10 minutes
Almonds, whole: 10 minutes
Hazelnuts*: 12 to 15 minutes
Pecans: 12 to 15 minutes
Pine nuts**
Walnuts: 10 to 15 minutes

* Some recipes call for removing the skin of (or "husking") hazelnuts. After toasting and cooling the hazelnuts slightly, transfer them to the center of a clean dishtowel spread out on a work surface. Gather the towel around the nuts and rub to remove skins (some bits of skin will remain, which is fine).

** Because of their high fat content, pine nuts burn very easily. It's best to toast them on the stovetop, where browning can be monitored. Stir pine nuts in a large heavy skillet over medium heat until they just begin to turn golden, about 3 minutes. Remove the nuts from the heat and continue stirring until they're almost cool, to avoid burning.

pastry dough textures

Bon Appétit pie crust and pastry dough recipes use visual descriptions to indicate what the dough should look like at various stages. When first combining the dry ingredients with the fat, the instructions generally say to mix the ingredients until "pea-size pieces" form [1] or until the mixture resembles "coarse meal" [2]. After adding liquid, instructions often say to combine "until moist clumps form" [3].

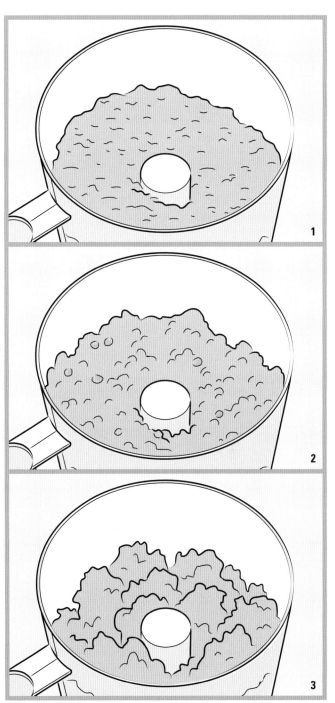

piping

Decorative piping gives desserts a beautiful bakery-window look—but it's easier than you'd think. If piping **whipped cream,** use a large pastry bag fitted with a medium or large star tip. For **frostings** and **buttercream,** use desired piping tip and a medium-size pastry bag. (See page 23 for more information on pastry bags.)

1. Insert the tip into the small end of the bag. Place the bag, tip side down, in a tumbler or a large measuring cup for support (this way, both of your hands are free to fill the bag). Fold the top of the bag over the rim of the tumbler like a cuff so that it stays clean while you fill it with cream or frosting.

2. Using a large silicone spatula, scoop the whipped cream or frosting into the bag [1]. After the bag is filled, uncuff it from over the tumbler, grab it by the top edge, and shake it gently to release any air pockets and settle the contents.

3. Twist the top of the bag just above the point where it's filled. Hold the twist firmly and squeeze to push out a bit of frosting.

4. Holding the twisted end of the bag closed with one hand, use the other hand to direct the piping tip while applying gentle pressure with the hand at the twisted end [2]. Practice on a clean plate before piping onto the dessert.

vanilla bean, seeding

1. Place the vanilla bean on a cutting board.

2. Using a small, sharp knife, slice the pod in half lengthwise, from the stem end to the opposite end [1].

3. Grasp one end of half of the pod and, using the same knife, scrape down the length of the split pod to remove the tiny, moist seeds [2].

4. Repeat with the remaining half of the vanilla bean.

Don't let those leftover vanilla beans go to waste. After you scrape out the seeds, turn the leftover pods into **vanilla sugar**—it's great in baked goods or stirred into your morning cup of coffee or tea.

1. First, dry the pods well, then chop them coarsely.

2. Blend 3 cups sugar with the pods in a food processor until the pods are finely ground.

3. Store the vanilla sugar in a covered container at room temperature for at least 2 days and up to a year.

4. Strain the vanilla sugar through a fine strainer before using.

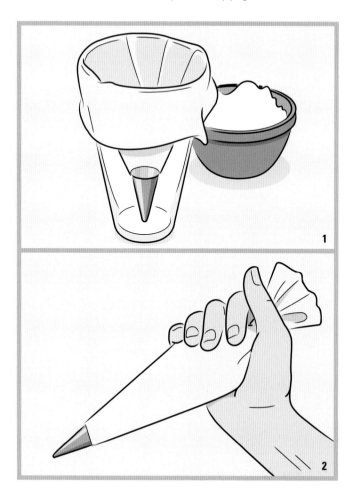

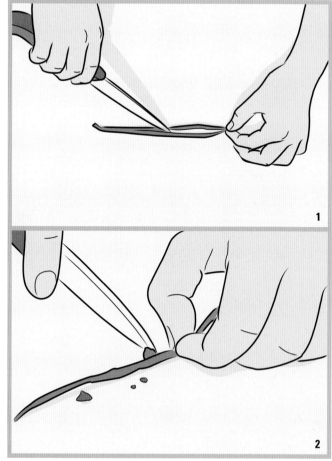

Chilled Lime-Coconut Pie with Macadamia-Coconut Crust

cakes

cakes

special-occasion cakes

Classic Pound Cake

Originally made with a pound each of eggs, flour, butter, and sugar, this cake has been an American and British staple for more than 200 years. Over time, cooks have tweaked the recipe by adjusting the original proportions; adding leavening, such as baking powder, and liquids, like sour cream or milk; and incorporating all kinds of flavorings, from vanilla to chocolate. Yet it remains a classically simple and delicious treat. **8 to 10 servings**

1¾   cups unbleached all purpose flour
½   teaspoon salt
1   cup (2 sticks) unsalted butter, room temperature
1½   cups sugar
3   large eggs
1¼   teaspoons vanilla extract
¼   cup whole milk

Preheat oven to 350°F. Butter and flour 9x5x3-inch metal loaf pan. Whisk flour and salt in medium bowl to blend. Using electric mixer, beat butter in large bowl until fluffy. Gradually add sugar, beating until blended well. Beat in eggs 1 at a time, occasionally scraping down sides of bowl. Beat in vanilla. Beat in half of flour mixture, then milk, then remaining flour mixture. Spread batter evenly in prepared pan.

Bake cake until golden and tester inserted into center comes out clean, about 1 hour 15 minutes. Cool cake in pan 10 minutes. Cut around pan sides to loosen cake. Turn cake out onto rack. Turn right side up and cool completely.

DO AHEAD: *Can be made 1 day ahead. Wrap in foil and store at room temperature.*

Deep Chocolate Pound Cake

Mixing boiling water into the cocoa powder is the key to creating a deep chocolate flavor: This melts the cocoa butter and disperses the cocoa through-out the batter. Adding mini chocolate chips that melt into the cake intensifies the flavor even more. Cut any leftover cake into cubes and layer it in glasses with sweetened whipped cream, fresh raspberries, and a touch of chocolate sauce for pretty individual trifles. **8 servings**

2¼   cups unbleached all purpose flour
1   teaspoon baking powder
¾   teaspoon coarse kosher salt
¼   teaspoon baking soda
½   cup sour cream
½   cup whole milk
¼   cup natural unsweetened cocoa powder
¼   cup honey
2   tablespoons boiling water
¾   cup sugar
½   cup (1 stick) unsalted butter, room temperature
2   large eggs
1   teaspoon vanilla extract
½   cup mini semisweet chocolate chips

Position rack in center of oven; preheat to 350°F. Butter and flour 9x5x3-inch metal loaf pan; tap out excess flour.

Whisk flour, baking powder, coarse salt, and baking soda in medium bowl. Whisk sour cream and milk in small bowl.

Sift cocoa into another small bowl. Whisk in honey and 2 tablespoons boiling water until smooth. Cool completely.

Using electric mixer, beat sugar and butter in another medium bowl until light and fluffy, about 3 minutes. Beat in eggs 1 at a time, occasionally scraping down sides of bowl. Beat in vanilla. Add cooled cocoa mixture; stir until smooth, occasionally scraping down bowl. Beat in flour mixture alternately with sour cream mixture in 2 additions each until just blended. Stir in chocolate chips.

Transfer batter to prepared pan; smooth top. Bake until tester inserted into center comes out clean, about 1 hour 8 minutes. Remove cake from pan and cool.

♕ Hot Fudge–Banana Pound Cake

Here, the banana split is re-created in pound cake form, served with chocolate sauce, vanilla ice cream, and banana slices. The cake needs to stand at room temperature overnight before serving. **10 servings**

Sauce

1½	**cups heavy whipping cream**
1½	**cups sugar**
6	**ounces unsweetened chocolate, chopped**
3	**tablespoons unsalted butter**
3	**tablespoons light corn syrup**
	Large pinch of salt
¾	**teaspoon vanilla extract**

Cake

2	**cups sifted unbleached all purpose flour (sifted, then measured)**
1	**teaspoon baking powder**
¾	**teaspoon salt**
½	**teaspoon baking soda**
1	**cup (about 2 large) mashed very ripe bananas**
1	**teaspoon fresh lemon juice**
¾	**cup (1½ sticks) unsalted butter, room temperature**
1¼	**cups sugar**
4	**large eggs, room temperature**
	Vanilla ice cream
	Fresh banana slices (optional)

SAUCE: Stir cream, sugar, chocolate, butter, corn syrup, and salt in heavy medium saucepan over low heat until chocolate melts. Increase heat to medium and bring to boil, stirring occasionally. Boil until reduced to 2¾ cups, stirring constantly, about 6 minutes. Cool; mix in vanilla. Set sauce aside.

CAKE: Position rack in center of oven and preheat to 350°F. Lightly butter 9x5x3-inch metal loaf pan. Line pan with waxed paper, leaving ½-inch overhang. Sift flour, baking powder, salt, and baking soda into medium bowl. Blend mashed banana and lemon juice in small bowl. Using electric mixer, beat butter and sugar in large bowl until fluffy. Add eggs 1 at a time, beating well after each addition. Using rubber spatula, mix in dry ingredients alternately with banana mixture, beginning and ending with dry ingredients.

Heat sauce until just slightly warm, stirring often. Spoon ⅓ of batter into prepared pan. Drizzle ⅓ cup sauce over and spread gently to within ½ inch of pan edge. Repeat with another layer of batter and sauce. Top with remaining batter. Run small sharp knife through cake in zigzag motion to swirl sauce slightly.

Bake cake until tester inserted into center comes out clean, about 1 hour 15 minutes. Cool in pan on rack 30 minutes. Turn cake out onto rack. Peel off paper and cool completely. Wrap cake in foil and store overnight at room temperature. Cover and chill remaining sauce.

DO AHEAD: *Can be made 2 days ahead. Let cake stand at room temperature.*

Rewarm sauce. Cut cake crosswise into ¾-inch-thick slices. Top each with scoop of ice cream. Spoon warm sauce over. Garnish with fresh banana slices, if desired, and serve.

Cornmeal Pound Cake with Rosemary Syrup, Poached Pears, and Candied Rosemary

Rosemary is typically used in savory dishes, but here it flavors a sweet syrup that plays off the pears, turning a humble pound cake into a sophisticated dessert. The rosemary syrup is also delicious in a cup of tea; candied rosemary makes a perfect decoration for a holiday Yule log. **8 servings**

Pears

3	cups water
2	cups sugar
1	cup dry or off-dry Riesling
3	fresh rosemary sprigs
1	vanilla bean, split lengthwise
¼	teaspoon whole black peppercorns
8	Forelle pears or other small pears, peeled, stems left intact

Pound Cake

1	cup unbleached all purpose flour
1	cup yellow cornmeal
1	cup (2 sticks) unsalted butter, room temperature
1⅓	cups sugar
¼	teaspoon salt
5	large eggs, beaten to blend in medium bowl
1	teaspoon vanilla extract

Syrup and Candied Rosemary

1	cup sugar
½	cup water
8	4-inch-long fresh rosemary sprigs
	Superfine sugar

PEARS: Combine 3 cups water, sugar, Riesling, rosemary, vanilla bean, and peppercorns in heavy large saucepan. Stir over medium heat until sugar dissolves. Add pears and bring syrup to boil, turning pears occasionally. Reduce heat to medium-low, cover, and simmer until pears are tender, about 20 minutes. Chill pears uncovered in syrup until cold, at least 3 hours.

DO AHEAD: *Can be made 2 days ahead. Cover and keep chilled.*

POUND CAKE: Preheat oven to 325°F. Butter and flour 9x5x3-inch metal loaf pan. Whisk flour and cornmeal in medium bowl to blend. Using electric mixer, beat butter in large bowl until light and fluffy. Gradually beat in sugar, then salt. Drizzle in beaten eggs by tablespoonfuls, beating constantly, then beat in vanilla. Add dry ingredients in 3 additions, beating just to blend after each addition. Transfer batter to prepared pan.

(continued page 48)

Cornmeal Pound Cake with Rosemary Syrup, Poached Pears, and Candied Rosemary *(continued)*

Bake cake until brown on top and tester inserted into center comes out clean, about 1 hour 15 minutes. Cool cake in pan 15 minutes. Turn cake out onto rack and cool completely.

DO AHEAD: *Can be made 1 day ahead. Wrap in foil and store at room temperature.*

SYRUP AND CANDIED ROSEMARY: Bring 1 cup sugar and ½ cup water to simmer in medium saucepan over medium-high heat, stirring until sugar dissolves. Add rosemary. Simmer until syrup reduces slightly, swirling pan occasionally, about 5 minutes. Using tongs, transfer rosemary sprigs to rack and drain. Cover and reserve rosemary syrup.

Pour superfine sugar into shallow bowl. Add drained rosemary sprigs to sugar, 1 at a time, turning to coat thickly. Place on paper towels. Dry at least 1 hour.

DO AHEAD: *Can be made 1 day ahead. Let sprigs and syrup stand at room temperature.*

Cut dark ends off cake. Cut eight ½- to ¾-inch-thick cake slices. Cut each slice diagonally in half. Arrange 2 halves on each plate. Drain pears. Stand 1 pear on each plate. Drizzle each dessert with reserved rosemary syrup and garnish with candied rosemary sprig. Serve, passing remaining rosemary syrup separately.

Kumquat-Cardamom Tea Bread

This recipe makes two tea breads—keep one and give the other as a gift. Since the pale orange–colored kumquat icing adorning the bread is so pretty, just place the bread in a clear cellophane bag, available at some kitchen-supply stores, then tie on a bow. A touch of instant iced tea powder adds an intriguingly subtle flavor, but it is optional. **Makes 2 loaves**

2   cups stemmed, quartered, seeded kumquats; plus 2 kumquats, sliced thinly
     Nonstick vegetable oil spray
3   cups unbleached all purpose flour
2   teaspoons instant iced tea powder (optional)
1½   teaspoons baking powder
1   teaspoon baking soda
½   teaspoon ground cardamom
2   teaspoons coarse kosher salt, divided
1¼   cups sugar
¾   cup plus 1 tablespoon corn oil
3   large eggs
2   teaspoons vanilla extract
1   8-ounce can crushed pineapple in juice
1   cup walnuts, toasted, chopped
¼   cup (½ stick) unsalted butter, room temperature
3   cups powdered sugar
1   tablespoon fresh lemon juice

Place quartered kumquats in processor; puree 3 minutes. Measure ⅓ cup puree for glaze; set aside.

Position rack in center of oven; preheat to 350°F. Spray two 8½x4½x2½-inch metal loaf pans with nonstick spray. Combine flour, tea powder (if using), baking powder, baking soda, cardamom, and 1½ teaspoons coarse salt in medium bowl; whisk to blend. Using electric mixer, blend 1¼ cups sugar and oil in large bowl. Beat in eggs 1 at a time, then vanilla, ⅔ cup kumquat puree, and pineapple with juice. Gradually add dry ingredients, beating just until blended. Fold in walnuts. Divide batter between prepared pans.

Bake cakes until tester inserted into center comes out clean, about 1 hour. Cool in pans on rack 5 minutes. Turn cakes out. Place cakes, top side up, on rack and cool.

Place reserved ⅓ cup kumquat puree in large bowl. Whisk in butter, powdered sugar, lemon juice, and remaining ½ teaspoon coarse salt. Spread glaze over cakes. Top with kumquat slices. Let stand until icing sets.

DO AHEAD: *Can be made 1 day ahead. Wrap in foil; store at room temperature.*

Cakes: Art and Science

The most basic ingredients in cakes—sugar, butter or vegetable oil, eggs, and flour—perform critical functions. Knowing their roles helps explain why precise measurements are so important in baking.

Sugar sweetens cakes, of course, but it also tenderizes them and helps keep them moist. Sugar also helps brown cake crusts.

Butter and vegetable oil moisten and tenderize cakes. Vegetable oil actually moistens cakes better than butter, but butter provides more flavor. When butter is creamed with sugar, it traps air bubbles that help leaven cakes.

Eggs provide the protein that holds cakes together. Egg whites help cakes rise and have a drying effect that prevents cakes from becoming too soggy. Egg yolks help emulsify large quantities of sugar, butter, and liquids, which produces very moist cakes.

Flour provides bulk and starch to hold the cake together.

🥄 Vanilla Chiffon Cake

When the chiffon cake was developed in the 1920s, it was an instant sensation. Using oil instead of butter and adding beaten egg whites result in an airy yet moist cake. Tropical fruits like mango, papaya, and pineapple would be a colorful and refreshing springtime garnish for this light cake, which is perfect for Passover. Serve it with the Rich Chocolate Sorbet (page 464). **8 servings**

1½   **cups sugar, divided**
½   **cup matzo cake meal**
½   **cup potato starch**
1½   **vanilla beans, chopped**
½   **teaspoon coarse kosher salt**
7   **large eggs, separated, room temperature**
2   **tablespoons vegetable oil**
2   **tablespoons brandy**

Preheat oven to 350°F. Blend ½ cup sugar, matzo cake meal, potato starch, vanilla beans, and coarse salt in processor until beans are finely chopped. Sift mixture into small bowl; discard beans in sieve.

Using electric mixer, beat egg whites in large bowl until medium-firm peaks form. Gradually add ¾ cup sugar, beating until stiff but not dry. Using same beaters, beat egg yolks and remaining ¼ cup sugar in another bowl until thick, about 5 minutes. Gradually beat in oil, then brandy. Beat in matzo mixture. Fold in egg white mixture in 3 additions.

Transfer batter to ungreased 10-inch-diameter angel food cake pan with removable bottom. Bake until tester inserted near center comes out clean, about 37 minutes. Immediately invert center tube of pan over neck of narrow bottle and cool cake completely.

DO AHEAD: *Can be made 1 day ahead. Cover cake in pan.*

Using sharp knife, cut around sides of pan and center tube to loosen cake. Holding center tube, lift cake from pan sides. Cut cake free from pan bottom. Turn cake out onto plate. Using serrated knife, cut cake into wedges.

{ Ingredient Tip: **Potato Starch**
Using potato starch is a great way to add tenderness to baked goods, and it's kosher for Passover. You'll find it in the kosher foods section and baking aisle of the supermarket, as well as at online baking sites. }

The Secret to Tender Cakes

The secret is in the flour and the mixing, both of which determine the amount of gluten in a cake. Too much gluten makes cakes tough. To ensure that your cake is tender:

USE THE RIGHT FLOUR. The more protein a flour has, the more gluten it can produce, so all purpose flour and cake flour are best. Cake flour has slightly less protein and creates an especially fine-textured cake. However, don't be tempted to use it in place of all purpose flour in a recipe. The two flours are not interchangeable; using cake flour when all purpose is called for can actually create a cake that's too tender and falls apart.

MIX BRIEFLY. Because mixing develops the gluten, don't overmix your batter once the flour is added. Mix just enough to incorporate the dry ingredients. This rule applies to cookie doughs, as well.

Angel Food Cake with Strawberry-Blueberry Sauce

Both the cake and the sauce can be prepared a day ahead. Let the cake stand at room temperature, and chill the sauce in a sealed container. It's important not to grease the cake pan when making an angel food cake, or the cake may not rise properly. **10 to 12 servings**

Sauce

2	12-ounce containers strawberries, hulled
1	12-ounce container blueberries
⅓	cup sugar
1	tablespoon fresh lemon juice
¼	cup amaretto

Cake

1¼	cups sifted cake flour (sifted, then measured)
2	teaspoons vanilla extract
2	teaspoons fresh lemon juice
½	teaspoon almond extract
14	large egg whites, room temperature
1½	teaspoons cream of tartar
½	teaspoon salt
1⅔	cups sugar
	Whole strawberries (optional)

SAUCE: Place half of strawberries in medium bowl. Crush with fork or potato masher. Slice remaining strawberries and add to bowl. Add half of blueberries to same bowl. Place remaining blueberries in medium saucepan and crush; add sugar and lemon juice. Stir over medium heat until sugar dissolves and juices become syrupy, about 4 minutes. Cool. Add to strawberry mixture. Stir in amaretto. Let stand 20 minutes.

DO AHEAD: *Can be made 8 hours ahead. Cover and refrigerate.*

CAKE: Position rack in center of oven and preheat to 300°F. Sift sifted flour into medium bowl. Combine vanilla, lemon juice, and almond extract in small bowl. Using electric mixer, beat egg whites in large bowl at medium speed until frothy. Add cream of tartar and salt and beat until soft peaks form. Add sugar ⅓ cup at a time and continue to beat until whites are stiff but not dry. Fold in vanilla mixture. Sift flour over in 4 batches, gently folding in each addition.

Spoon batter into ungreased 10-inch-diameter angel food cake pan with removable bottom. Bake until top of cake is golden brown and springy to touch, about 1 hour 10 minutes. Immediately invert center tube of cake pan over neck of narrow bottle and cool cake completely. Using sharp knife, cut around sides of pan and center tube to loosen cake. Holding center tube, lift cake from pan sides. Cut cake free from pan bottom. Turn cake out onto plate.

DO AHEAD: *Can be made 8 hours ahead. Cover and let stand at room temperature.*

Using serrated knife, cut cake into wedges. Place on plates. Spoon berry sauce over. Garnish each with whole strawberry, if desired, and serve.

Orange- and Vanilla-Scented Bundt Cake

Orange peel contains essential oils, which deliver the concentrated orange flavor and aroma in this fragrant cake. Blending the grated orange peel with the sugar first helps release the oils from the peel and turns the sugar a pretty pale orange color. **10 to 12 servings**

Cake

3	cups unbleached all purpose flour
¾	teaspoon salt
½	teaspoon baking soda
1⅔	cups sugar
1	tablespoon finely grated orange peel
1	vanilla bean, split lengthwise
¾	cup (1½ sticks) unsalted butter, room temperature
3	large eggs
⅔	cup fresh orange juice
⅔	cup buttermilk

Glaze

½	cup fresh orange juice
2	tablespoons sugar
2	tablespoons (¼ stick) unsalted butter

Icing

⅓	cup powdered sugar
2	teaspoons (about) fresh orange juice

CAKE: Position rack in center of oven and preheat to 350°F. Butter and flour 12- to 15-cup Bundt pan. Whisk flour, salt, and baking soda in medium bowl to blend. Using electric mixer, beat sugar and orange peel in large bowl at low speed to release essential oils from peel. Scrape seeds from vanilla bean into sugar mixture and beat to blend well. Add butter and beat until light. Add eggs 1 at a time, beating well after each addition. Mix in orange juice (mixture will look curdled). Stir in flour mixture, then buttermilk. Transfer batter to prepared pan; smooth top. Bake cake until tester inserted near center comes out clean, about 50 minutes.

GLAZE: Meanwhile, boil orange juice, sugar, and butter in heavy small saucepan over medium heat until reduced to ½ cup, swirling pan occasionally, about 5 minutes.

Brush 3 tablespoons glaze over cake. Cool cake in pan on rack 10 minutes. Using small sharp knife, cut around sides and center tube of pan to loosen cake. Turn cake out onto rack and brush with remaining glaze. Cool completely.

ICING: Place sugar in small bowl. Mix in orange juice, ½ teaspoonful at a time, until thick pourable consistency forms. Drizzle icing decoratively over cake. Let stand until icing sets.

DO AHEAD: *Can be made 1 day ahead. Cover with cake dome and store at cool room temperature.*

Bundt Pans

Bundt pans are fluted, ring-shaped cake pans that are available today in a seemingly endless variety of shapes and sizes. We call for a range of 12- to 15-cup capacity pans in our recipes in an effort to accommodate this variety. Because the width and depth of pans vary, it's a good idea to check for doneness about 10 minutes before the suggested baking time has elapsed.

Apple-Spice Cake with Brown Sugar Glaze

Grated apples and a caramel-like glaze keep this cake moist and delicious for a day or two after you make it. Serve it warm with a scoop of vanilla ice cream for a cake version of apple pie à la mode. **12 servings**

Cake

	Nonstick vegetable oil spray
3	cups unbleached all purpose flour
1	teaspoon baking soda
1	teaspoon ground cinnamon
¾	teaspoon salt
½	teaspoon ground nutmeg
¼	teaspoon ground cloves
¼	teaspoon ground allspice
1¾	pounds Granny Smith apples, peeled, cored, coarsely grated
1½	cups (3 sticks) unsalted butter, room temperature
1½	cups sugar
½	cup (packed) golden brown sugar
1	teaspoon finely grated lemon peel
3	large eggs
1	teaspoon vanilla extract
1	teaspoon fresh lemon juice

Glaze

½	cup (packed) golden brown sugar
¼	cup (½ stick) unsalted butter
¼	cup heavy whipping cream
½	teaspoon vanilla extract
½	teaspoon fresh lemon juice
¼	teaspoon salt

CAKE: Position rack in center of oven and preheat to 325°F. Spray 12- to 15-cup Bundt pan with nonstick spray. Sift flour, baking soda, cinnamon, salt, nutmeg, cloves, and allspice into medium bowl. Drain grated apples in strainer. Using hands or kitchen towel, squeeze out excess liquid from apples. Measure 2 cups grated apples.

Using electric mixer, beat butter, both sugars, and lemon peel in large bowl until fluffy. Beat in eggs 1 at a time. Mix in vanilla and lemon juice. Beat in flour mixture. Mix in grated apples. Transfer batter to prepared pan.

Bake cake until tester inserted near center comes out clean, about 1 hour. Cool in pan on rack 20 minutes.

GLAZE: While cake cools, prepare glaze. Stir sugar, butter, cream, vanilla, lemon juice, and salt in small nonstick skillet over medium-high heat until sugar dissolves and mixture comes to boil. Reduce heat to medium; whisk until glaze is smooth, about 1 minute. Remove from heat.

Invert cake onto rack set over baking sheet. Using small skewer, pierce holes all over top of warm cake. Pour hot glaze over top, allowing it to be absorbed before adding more. Cool cake 30 minutes. Serve warm or at room temperature.

Poured Glazes

A glaze coating gives a cake a beautiful, glossy finish. The easiest way to glaze a cake is to place it on a cardboard round that is slightly smaller than the cake, then place the cake on a rack over a rimmed baking sheet. Pour the glaze over the center of the cake, using an offset spatula to coax the glaze over the top and down the sides. Smooth the sides only as needed; the less the glaze is worked, the shinier it will remain. Allow the glaze to set (at room temperature or in the refrigerator, as indicated in the recipe), and then transfer the cake to a platter.

Maple-Walnut Pound Cake with Maple Glaze

While Grade A maple syrup is the most common variety, for this recipe it's worth seeking out Grade B, which packs much more robust flavor. Grade B is becoming easier to find at specialty foods stores and supermarkets.

12 servings

Cake

1¾	cups coarsely chopped walnuts, toasted
2¼	cups cake flour
1	teaspoon baking powder
½	teaspoon salt
1¼	cups (2½ sticks) unsalted butter, room temperature
1¼	cups sugar
5	large eggs
½	cup pure maple syrup
¾	teaspoon maple extract
½	teaspoon vanilla extract

Glaze

¼	cup (½ stick) unsalted butter
2	tablespoons pure maple syrup
2	tablespoons heavy whipping cream
10	tablespoons powdered sugar, sifted
⅛	teaspoon maple extract
12	walnut halves

CAKE: Preheat oven to 350°F. Butter and flour 12- to 15-cup Bundt pan. Finely grind walnuts in processor. Sift flour, baking powder, and salt into medium bowl. Using electric mixer, beat butter and sugar in large bowl until light and fluffy. Add eggs 1 at a time, beating well after each addition. Beat in maple syrup, maple extract, and vanilla (batter may look curdled). Mix in dry ingredients. Fold in ground walnuts.

Pour batter into prepared pan. Bake cake until top is golden and tester inserted near center comes out clean, about 1 hour. Transfer pan to rack; cool cake in pan 10 minutes. Using small knife, cut around sides and center tube of pan to loosen cake. Turn cake out onto rack and cool completely.

DO AHEAD: *Can be made 2 days ahead. Wrap cake tightly in foil and store at room temperature.*

GLAZE: Melt butter with maple syrup and cream in heavy small saucepan. Remove from heat. Add powdered sugar and maple extract; whisk until smooth. Cool glaze until slightly thickened, about 15 minutes. Drizzle glaze over cake. Arrange walnut halves decoratively on top of cake. Let cake stand until glaze sets, about 15 minutes.

Coconut Bundt Cake with Powdered Sugar Glaze

This pound cake gets its velvety texture from coconut milk. Look for it in the Asian foods section of the supermarket, or at Indian, Southeast Asian, or Latin markets. **12 to 16 servings**

3	cups cake flour
½	teaspoon salt
1	cup (2 sticks) unsalted butter, room temperature
2½	cups sugar
6	large eggs
2	teaspoons vanilla extract
½	teaspoon coconut extract
1¼	cups canned unsweetened coconut milk, divided
2	cups (packed) sweetened flaked coconut
1¾	cups powdered sugar
	Additional sweetened flaked coconut (optional)

Preheat oven to 350°F. Generously butter 12- to 15-cup Bundt pan; dust pan with flour. Stir flour and salt in medium bowl to blend. Beat butter in large bowl until fluffy. Gradually add 2½ cups sugar, beating until well blended. Beat in eggs 1 at a time, then both extracts. Beat in flour mixture in 4 additions alternately with 1 cup coconut milk in 3 additions. Fold in 2 cups flaked coconut. Transfer batter to prepared pan; smooth top.

Bake cake until top is golden brown and tester inserted near center comes out clean, about 1 hour 10 minutes. Cool cake in pan 5 minutes. Using small sharp knife, cut around sides and center tube of pan to loosen cake. Turn cake out onto rack; cool completely.

Whisk powdered sugar and remaining ¼ cup coconut milk in medium bowl to blend. Spoon glaze over cake. Top with additional coconut, if desired.

DO AHEAD: *Can be made 1 day ahead. Cover with cake dome and store at room temperature.*

Raspberry-Yogurt Cake

The yogurt helps make this moist cake especially tender. Coating the raspberries with flour keeps them suspended evenly in the cake. **10 to 12 servings**

3	cups unbleached all purpose flour, divided
1½	teaspoons baking powder
¼	teaspoon salt
1	cup (2 sticks) unsalted butter, room temperature
1¾	cups sugar
2	tablespoons fresh orange juice
1½	teaspoons almond extract, divided
1	teaspoon finely grated orange peel
3	large eggs, room temperature
1	cup plain low-fat yogurt
2½	cups raspberries (two 6-ounce containers)
1	cup powdered sugar
1	tablespoon (or more) water

Preheat oven to 350°F. Butter 12- to 15-cup Bundt pan. Whisk 2½ cups flour, baking powder, and salt in medium bowl.

Using electric mixer, beat butter and 1¾ cups sugar in large bowl until creamy. Beat in orange juice, 1 teaspoon almond extract, and orange peel. Beat in eggs 1 at a time. Mix in yogurt.

Add dry ingredients to batter and beat just until blended.

Toss remaining ½ cup flour and raspberries in large bowl. Fold berry mixture into batter. Spoon batter into prepared pan; smooth top.

Bake cake until tester inserted near center comes out clean, about 1 hour 10 minutes. Cool in pan on rack 30 minutes.

Invert cake onto plate and cool.

DO AHEAD: *Can be made 1 day ahead. Cover and let stand at room temperature.*

Whisk powdered sugar, 1 tablespoon water, and remaining ½ teaspoon almond extract in medium bowl. Add more water by ½ teaspoonfuls as needed for thick glaze. Drizzle over cake. Let stand until glaze sets.

Market Tip: **Raspberries**
The best raspberries are locally grown and sold at farmers' markets in open containers during mid- to late summer. Look for berries that have a bright, uniform color and avoid those that are dark and dull. Don't rinse raspberries, as this blunts their aroma—buy organic so that there's no concern about pesticides to wash away.

Almond Butter Crown

This yeast cake gets its name from the crown-like look, which is thanks to the Bundt pan it is baked in. It would be perfect for brunch or an afternoon tea. Almond paste is available in the baking aisle of most supermarkets and at specialty foods stores. **10 servings**

Dough

3	cups unbleached all purpose flour
1¼	cups (2½ sticks) chilled unsalted butter, cut into pieces
2	¼-ounce envelopes active dry yeast
¼	cup warm water (105°F to 115°F)
½	cup canned evaporated milk, room temperature
2	large eggs, room temperature
	Seeds from 6 cardamom pods, crushed
1	teaspoon salt
¼	cup sugar

Filling

½	cup (1 stick) unsalted butter, room temperature
½	cup sugar
½	cup almond paste
1	teaspoon almond extract
¼	cup sliced almonds
	Powdered sugar

DOUGH: Place flour in processor. Add butter and cut in, using on/off turns, until butter is size of kidney beans. Transfer to large bowl. Cover and refrigerate while dissolving yeast.

Sprinkle yeast and pinch of sugar over ¼ cup warm water in medium bowl; stir to dissolve. Let stand until foamy, about 5 minutes. Mix in milk, eggs, crushed cardamom seeds, salt, and ¼ cup sugar. Pour over flour-butter mixture and stir just until flour is moistened. Cover and refrigerate at least 5 hours.

DO AHEAD: *Can be made 1 day ahead. Keep refrigerated.*

Punch dough down. Dust hands with flour. Pat dough out on lightly floured surface to 20-inch square. Fold dough over into 3 equal sections as for business letter. Press edges lightly with rolling pin to seal. Turn dough so that 1 short side faces you. Roll dough out into 30x6½-inch rectangle. Starting at 1 short side, fold dough over into thirds, forming 10x6½-inch rectangle. Wrap dough in plastic. Refrigerate while preparing filling.

FILLING: Using electric mixer, beat butter, sugar, almond paste, and almond extract in medium bowl to blend.

Butter 12- to 15-cup Bundt pan. Sprinkle bottom with sliced almonds. Unwrap dough. Roll dough out on lightly floured work surface into 24x9-inch rectangle. Spread filling over. Starting at 1 long side, roll dough up jelly-roll style. Cut dough crosswise into 8 slices. Arrange dough slices, cut sides down, in prepared pan, spacing evenly apart. Let rise in warm draft-free area until almost doubled in volume, about 1½ hours.

Preheat oven to 375°F. Bake cake until top is dark golden brown, about 45 minutes. Turn out onto rack.

DO AHEAD: *Can be made 1 day ahead. Cool completely. Wrap tightly in foil. Let stand at room temperature. Before continuing, rewarm uncovered in 325°F oven about 10 minutes.*

Sift powdered sugar over. Serve warm.

Chocolate-Apricot Kugelhopf

This yeast-risen cake is surprisingly hands-off. It requires no kneading and gets set aside in a warm place to rise, doing lots of the work all by itself. If you don't have a kugelhopf pan (they are available at cookware stores), you can use a large Bundt pan. **12 servings**

Sponge

1½   cups apricot nectar
1½   cups sifted unbleached all purpose flour (sifted, then measured)
¼   cup sugar
¼   cup nonfat dry milk powder
1   ¼-ounce envelope quick-rising active dry yeast

Dough

½   cup (1 stick) unsalted butter, room temperature
1   cup sugar
2   large eggs
3   large egg yolks
3   tablespoons apricot brandy or apricot nectar
1¼   teaspoons salt
1   teaspoon vanilla extract
½   teaspoon ground ginger
1   ¼-ounce envelope quick-rising active dry yeast
2   tablespoons hot water (120°F to 125°F)
3   cups sifted unbleached all purpose flour (sifted, then measured)
12   ounces bittersweet or semisweet chocolate, coarsely chopped
6   ounces moist dried apricots, quartered
2   tablespoons (packed) golden brown sugar
1½   teaspoons ground cinnamon

     Powdered sugar
     Chocolate Swirl Whipped Cream (optional; see recipe)

SPONGE: Boil apricot nectar in heavy medium saucepan over high heat until reduced to 1 cup, about 5 minutes. Pour reduced nectar into large bowl. Cool to 120°F to 125°F. Whisk in flour, sugar, milk powder, and yeast. Cover tightly with plastic wrap and let rise in warm draft-free area until doubled in volume, about 30 minutes.

DOUGH: Generously butter 12-cup kugelhopf pan. Using electric mixer, beat butter and sugar in large bowl until fluffy. Beat in eggs and egg yolks 1 at a time. Beat in apricot brandy, salt, vanilla, and ginger. Combine yeast and 2 tablespoons hot water in small bowl and stir until yeast dissolves. Mix yeast mixture and sponge into butter mixture. Gradually mix in flour. Combine chocolate, dried apricots, brown sugar, and cinnamon in medium bowl. Mix into dough.

Spoon dough into prepared pan. Cover tightly with plastic wrap and kitchen towel. Let stand in warm draft-free area until dough rises just to top of pan, about 3 hours.

Position rack in center of oven and preheat to 350°F. Bake kugelhopf until deep brown and cracking on top and tester inserted near center comes out clean, about 48 minutes. Cool in pan on rack 20 minutes. Turn out onto rack and cool completely.

DO AHEAD: *Can be made 1 day ahead. Return to pan, cover tightly, and store at room temperature.*

Place kugelhopf on platter. Lightly sift powdered sugar over. Cut into wedges. Serve, passing Chocolate Swirl Whipped Cream separately, if desired.

Chocolate Swirl Whipped Cream

This luscious whipped cream is optional—but how could you resist? The apricot flavor complements the kugelhopf, and would add an unexpected, sophisticated touch to other chocolate cakes. **Makes 5 cups**

2   ounces bittersweet or semisweet chocolate (do not exceed 61% cacao), chopped
2   tablespoons plus 2 cups heavy whipping cream
2   tablespoons sugar
3   tablespoons apricot brandy or apricot nectar

Stir chocolate and 2 tablespoons cream in heavy small saucepan over low heat until chocolate melts and mixture is smooth. Cool. Beat remaining 2 cups cream and sugar in large bowl until soft peaks form. Add brandy and continue beating until stiff peaks form. Pour chocolate mixture over cream and fold together until whipped cream is lightly streaked with chocolate. Transfer to serving bowl.

DO AHEAD: *Can be made 8 hours ahead. Cover and refrigerate.*

Blueberry Coffee Cake

This cake tastes equally delicious whether made using fresh or frozen blueberries. **12 servings**

2⅓   cups unbleached all purpose flour, divided
¾   cup (1½ sticks) unsalted butter, room temperature, divided
1   cup sweetened flaked coconut
½   cup (packed) golden brown sugar
1   teaspoon ground cinnamon
2½   teaspoons baking powder
½   teaspoon salt
1   cup sugar
2   large eggs
1   cup milk
1   12-ounce package frozen blueberries, unthawed, or 2½ cups fresh blueberries

Combine ⅓ cup flour, ¼ cup butter, coconut, brown sugar, and cinnamon in medium bowl. Mix until moist and crumbly. Set topping aside.

Preheat oven to 375°F. Butter and flour 13x9x2-inch metal baking pan. Sift remaining 2 cups flour, baking powder, and salt into small bowl. Using electric mixer, beat remaining ½ cup butter in large bowl until fluffy. Gradually add sugar, beating until well blended. Beat in eggs 1 at a time. Mix dry ingredients into batter alternately with milk in 3 additions each. Fold in blueberries.

Transfer batter to prepared pan. Sprinkle topping evenly over batter. Bake cake until tester inserted into center comes out clean and topping is golden brown, about 40 minutes. Cool cake slightly. Serve warm or at room temperature.

Spiced Crumble Cake with Chocolate Frosting

The cake can be made a day ahead, and it keeps well after serving, too. The "crumble" refers to the cake's center: a layer of pecans, brown sugar, butter, and cocoa powder. **12 servings**

Crumble

1	cup pecans
⅓	cup (packed) golden brown sugar
2	tablespoons (¼ stick) chilled unsalted butter, diced
1	tablespoon natural unsweetened cocoa powder

Cake

2⅓	cups unbleached all purpose flour
1	tablespoon cornstarch
1	teaspoon baking soda
1	teaspoon ground cinnamon
¾	teaspoon salt
¼	teaspoon ground cloves
¼	teaspoon ground allspice
¾	cup sour cream
¼	cup whole milk
1	teaspoon vanilla extract
1	cup (2 sticks) unsalted butter, room temperature
1	cup sugar
¾	cup (packed) golden brown sugar
5	large eggs

Frosting

6	ounces bittersweet or semisweet chocolate (do not exceed 61% cacao), chopped
1	8-ounce package Philadelphia-brand cream cheese, room temperature
¼	cup (½ stick) unsalted butter, room temperature
1	teaspoon vanilla extract
2½	cups powdered sugar
2	tablespoons natural unsweetened cocoa powder

CRUMBLE: Blend pecans, sugar, butter, and cocoa in processor until nuts are finely chopped.

CAKE: Preheat oven to 350°F. Butter and flour 13x9x2-inch metal baking pan. Whisk flour, cornstarch, baking soda, cinnamon, salt, cloves, and allspice in medium bowl to blend. Whisk sour cream, milk, and vanilla in small bowl to blend.

Using electric mixer, beat butter in large bowl until fluffy. Gradually beat in both sugars. Beat in 3 eggs, 1 at a time. Beat in ½ cup dry ingredients. Beat in remaining 2 eggs, 1 at a time. Beat in remaining dry ingredients in 3 additions alternately with sour cream mixture in 2 additions.

Spread 3 cups batter in prepared pan. Sprinkle with crumble; press lightly into batter. Spread remaining batter over crumble to cover. Bake cake until tester inserted into center comes out clean, about 35 minutes. Cool cake in pan on rack.

FROSTING: Melt chocolate in top of double boiler over simmering water, stirring until just melted and smooth. Let stand just until cool but not set. Using electric mixer, beat cream cheese, butter, and vanilla in large bowl to blend. Beat in sugar in 3 additions, then cooled chocolate and cocoa.

Spread frosting over top of cake.

DO AHEAD: *Can be made 1 day ahead. Chill until frosting is set; cover and keep chilled. Let stand 1 hour at room temperature before serving.*

Sour Cream–Orange Coffee Cake with Chocolate-Pecan Streusel

Sour cream makes this coffee cake rich and moist, and a streusel in both the filling and the topping adds twice as much chocolate-pecan flavor.

12 servings

Streusel

1½	cups (packed) golden brown sugar
1	tablespoon ground cinnamon
6	tablespoons (¾ stick) chilled salted butter, diced
1½	cups coarsely chopped pecans
1	cup (6 ounces) semisweet chocolate chips

Cake

3	cups unbleached all purpose flour
1½	teaspoons baking soda
1½	teaspoons baking powder
1⅓	cups sugar
¾	cup (1½ sticks) salted butter, room temperature
3	large eggs
1½	teaspoons finely grated orange peel
1½	teaspoons vanilla extract
1½	cups sour cream
¼	cup fresh orange juice
	Powdered sugar

STREUSEL: Whisk sugar and cinnamon in medium bowl to blend. Add butter and rub in with fingertips until mixture holds together in small moist clumps. Mix in pecans and chocolate chips.

DO AHEAD: *Can be made 3 days ahead. Cover and refrigerate.*

CAKE: Preheat oven to 350°F. Butter and flour 13x9x2-inch metal baking pan. Sift flour, baking soda, and baking powder into medium bowl. Using electric mixer, beat sugar and butter in large bowl until blended and smooth. Beat in eggs 1 at a time, then orange peel and vanilla. Mix in flour mixture in 4 additions alternately with sour cream in 3 additions. Mix in orange juice. Spread half of batter in prepared pan. Sprinkle with half of streusel. Drop remaining batter over by heaping tablespoonfuls; carefully spread batter to make even layer. Sprinkle with remaining streusel.

Bake cake 30 minutes. Place sheet of foil loosely over pan to keep topping from browning too quickly. Continue baking until tester inserted into center of cake comes out clean, about 35 minutes longer. Remove foil. Cool cake in pan on rack 20 minutes. Sift powdered sugar over cake; serve warm or at room temperature.

DO AHEAD: *Can be made 2 days ahead. Cool completely. Store airtight at room temperature.*

Poppy Seed Coffee Cake with Cardamom Streusel

The streusel topping is delicious and adds a spicy, homey touch to this rustic cake. But if you're running short on time, go ahead and skip it—the cake is still delicious without it. **10 to 12 servings**

Streusel

6	tablespoons sugar
6	tablespoons unbleached all purpose flour
¼	cup (½ stick) unsalted butter, melted
¾	teaspoon ground cardamom
½	teaspoon ground cinnamon

Cake

2⅓	cups cake flour
1½	teaspoons baking powder
1	teaspoon baking soda
¾	teaspoon ground cardamom
¼	teaspoon salt
11	tablespoons unsalted butter, room temperature
1	cup plus 2 tablespoons sugar
2	large eggs
1	cup sour cream
¼	cup fresh orange juice
2	teaspoons finely grated orange peel
1	teaspoon vanilla extract
⅓	cup poppy seeds

STREUSEL: Mix sugar, flour, melted butter, cardamom, and cinnamon in small bowl until moist clumps form.

CAKE: Preheat oven to 350°F. Butter and flour 10-inch-diameter angel food cake pan with removable bottom. Sift cake flour, baking powder, baking soda, cardamom, and salt twice into medium bowl. Using electric mixer, beat butter and sugar in large bowl until well blended. Beat in eggs 1 at a time. Mix in sour cream, orange juice, orange peel, and vanilla. Beat in dry ingredients to blend. Mix in poppy seeds. Transfer batter to prepared pan (batter will fill less than half of pan).

Bake cake 25 minutes. Sprinkle streusel over top of cake. Continue to bake until tester inserted near center comes out clean, about 25 minutes longer. Cool cake completely in pan on rack.

Using sharp knife, cut around sides of pan and center tube to loosen cake. Holding center tube, lift cake from pan sides. Cut cake free from pan bottom. Placing hand gently atop cake for support, tilt cake just far enough over to release from center tube; remove tube. Place cake streusel side up on platter.

DO AHEAD: *Can be made 1 day ahead. Cover and let stand at room temperature.*

Testing for Doneness

The baking time indicated in a recipe provides the estimated time you can expect the cake to be done, but visual cues are your best bet for determining doneness. Here are three ways to determine if a cake is perfectly done.

1. Insert a toothpick, cake tester, or even a thin metal skewer (like the ones used to truss a turkey) into the center of the cake. It should come out clean or with just a few crumbs attached.

2. Gently press your finger onto the top of the cake. The cake should spring back without leaving an impression of your finger.

3. Check the sides of the cake. In most cases, the edges should just begin to pull away from the sides of the pan.

For a molten cake, the rules are different. A tester inserted into the center of the cake should come out with thick batter attached, and the tops and sides of the cake should be set, while the center should appear wobbly.

Raisin Streusel Cake

Made with matzo cake meal, potato starch, and nondairy creamer, this deliciously spiced coffee cake also satisfies the dietary requirements for Passover. **12 servings**

Streusel

¼   **cup (½ stick) unsalted margarine, room temperature**
⅔   **cup sugar**
4¼   **teaspoons ground cardamom**
2¼   **teaspoons ground cinnamon**
½   **cup matzo cake meal**

Cake

½   **cup matzo cake meal**
½   **cup potato starch**
½   **teaspoon salt**
½   **teaspoon ground ginger**
5   **large egg whites, room temperature**
1⅓   **cups sugar, divided**
5   **large egg yolks**
⅓   **cup liquid nondairy creamer**
¼   **cup (½ stick) unsalted margarine, melted, cooled**
2   **tablespoons finely grated lemon peel**
1½   **tablespoons fresh lemon juice**
⅔   **cup raisins**

STREUSEL: Position rack in center of oven and preheat to 350°F. Coat 9x9x2-inch metal baking pan generously with margarine. Mix margarine, sugar, cardamom, and cinnamon in medium bowl. Gradually add matzo cake meal and mix until crumbly. Spread half of streusel on baking sheet and bake until golden and crisp, about 10 minutes. Cool and break into bits.

CAKE: Combine matzo cake meal, potato starch, salt, and ginger in small bowl. Using electric mixer, beat egg whites in large bowl until soft peaks form. Gradually add 1 cup sugar and beat until stiff but not dry.

Using same beaters, beat egg yolks and remaining ⅓ cup sugar in another large bowl until mixture is thick and slowly dissolving ribbon forms when beaters are lifted. Beat in nondairy creamer, then margarine, lemon peel, and lemon juice at low speed. Add dry ingredients and stir until well blended. Fold in egg white mixture in 2 additions.

Pour half of batter into prepared pan. Sprinkle baked streusel over. Sprinkle with half of raisins. Spread remaining batter over. Sprinkle with unbaked streusel and remaining raisins. Bake until tester inserted into center of cake comes out dry, about 40 minutes.

Cool cake in pan on rack. Cover with foil and let stand 1 hour to soften topping.

DO AHEAD: *Can be made 2 days ahead. Keep covered and store at room temperature.*

Cut into squares and serve.

Cherry-Vanilla Tea Cake with Vanilla Sugar

A springform pan is ideal for this cake: The powdered sugar topping can be sifted over the hot cake while it's still in the pan—allowing some of the sugar to melt ever so slightly—then the sides can be slipped off without disturbing the topping. Tossing the cherries with the reserved flour mixture before they're added to the batter prevents them from sinking to the bottom. **10 servings**

1½	cups unbleached all purpose flour
1	teaspoon baking powder
½	teaspoon baking soda
¼	teaspoon salt
⅛	teaspoon ground nutmeg
½	cup (1 stick) unsalted butter, room temperature
1	cup plus 1 tablespoon sugar
2	large eggs, room temperature
2	teaspoons vanilla extract
⅔	cup sour cream
1	teaspoon finely grated lemon peel
1	cup canned pitted sweet cherries, halved, drained
½	vanilla bean, split lengthwise
2	tablespoons powdered sugar

Preheat oven to 350°F. Lightly butter and flour 10-inch-diameter springform pan with 2¾-inch-high sides. Sift flour, baking powder, baking soda, salt, and nutmeg into medium bowl. Using electric mixer, beat butter and 1 cup sugar in large bowl until well blended. Add eggs 1 at a time, beating well after each addition. Blend in vanilla extract. Transfer 2 tablespoons dry ingredients to small bowl. At low speed, beat half of remaining dry ingredients into butter mixture, then mix in sour cream and lemon peel. Beat in remaining half of dry ingredients. Mix cherries into reserved 2 tablespoons dry ingredients; fold cherries into batter.

Spoon batter into prepared pan; smooth top. Bake until tester inserted into center of cake comes out clean, about 30 minutes. Transfer cake to rack and cool 10 minutes.

Meanwhile, using small sharp knife, scrape seeds from vanilla bean into small bowl. Mix in remaining 1 tablespoon sugar, rubbing with fingertips to distribute seeds. Add powdered sugar and rub again.

Sift vanilla sugar over hot cake and cool. Cut around pan sides to loosen cake; remove pan sides.

DO AHEAD: *Can be made 1 day ahead. Cover; let stand at room temperature.*

Chocolate Chip Coffee Cake

With mini chocolate chips dotted throughout and a sweet and tangy drizzle on top, this moist coffee cake is great for either brunch or dessert. **12 servings**

Cake

	Nonstick vegetable oil spray
2	large egg whites (¼ cup)
⅓	cup (packed) golden brown sugar
	Pinch of salt
1½	cups coarsely chopped walnuts
1¼	cups mini semisweet chocolate chips, divided
2	cups cake flour
½	teaspoon salt
¼	teaspoon baking powder
¼	teaspoon baking soda
1	cup plus 2 tablespoons sugar
½	cup (1 stick) unsalted butter, room temperature
3	large eggs
¾	cup sour cream

Topping

¾	cup powdered sugar
2	tablespoons sour cream

CAKE: Position rack in center of oven and preheat to 350°F. Butter and flour 10-inch-diameter angel food cake pan with removable bottom, then spray with nonstick spray. Mix egg whites, brown sugar, and salt in medium bowl. Mix in walnuts and ¼ cup chocolate chips.

Whisk flour, salt, baking powder, and baking soda in another medium bowl. Using electric mixer, beat sugar and butter in large bowl to blend. Beat in eggs 1 at a time. Stir in flour mixture in 4 additions alternately with sour cream in 3 additions. Stir in remaining 1 cup chocolate chips.

Transfer batter to prepared pan; smooth top. Spoon walnut mixture evenly over. Bake cake until tester inserted near center comes out clean, about 1 hour 8 minutes. Cool cake in pan on rack 15 minutes. Using sharp knife, cut around sides of pan and center tube to loosen cake. Using oven mitt, grasp center tube and lift cake from sides of pan. Cool cake completely on rack. Cut cake free from pan bottom. Placing hand gently atop cake for support, tilt cake just far enough over to release from center tube; remove tube. Place cake, streusel side up, on platter (walnuts should be on top).

DO AHEAD: *Can be made 1 day ahead. Wrap in plastic.*

TOPPING: Mix sugar and sour cream in bowl; drizzle over cake.

Chocolate-Pecan Coffee Cake

This yeast-risen coffee cake needs to rise for an hour before being baked, so allow enough time before you plan to serve it. **12 servings**

Topping

1	8-ounce package Philadelphia-brand cream cheese, room temperature
¼	cup powdered sugar
1	large egg yolk
⅔	cup golden raisins

Cake

5	ounces bittersweet or semisweet chocolate, chopped
¾	cup (packed) golden brown sugar
1½	cups sifted unbleached all purpose flour (sifted, then measured)
½	cup natural unsweetened cocoa powder
¾	teaspoon salt
6	tablespoons (¾ stick) chilled unsalted butter, diced
⅓	cup warm water (105°F to 115°F)
1	teaspoon sugar
1	¼-ounce envelope active dry yeast
1	large egg, room temperature
6	tablespoons milk, room temperature

Pecans

1	large egg white
½	cup sugar
1	cup pecan halves

TOPPING: Using electric mixer, beat cream cheese, sugar, and egg yolk in small bowl to blend. Mix in raisins.

CAKE: Butter 9x9x2-inch metal baking pan. Finely grind chocolate and brown sugar in processor. Transfer to bowl. Blend flour, cocoa, and salt in processor 5 seconds. Add butter; using on/off turns, chop finely.

Combine ⅓ cup warm water, sugar, and yeast in large bowl. Stir to dissolve yeast. Let stand until foamy, about 8 minutes. Mix in egg, milk, chocolate mixture, and flour mixture. Spread batter in prepared pan. Drop topping over batter by tablespoonfuls and spread carefully to cover.

Pour boiling water in bottom of 8x8-inch pan to depth of 1½ inches. Place pan with dough over pan with water. Cover pan with dough tightly with plastic wrap, then kitchen towel. Let stand until dough has risen, about 1 hour.

Position rack in center of oven and preheat to 350°F.

PECANS: Meanwhile, beat egg white and sugar in medium bowl until thick. Add pecan halves and stir until well coated.

Arrange pecans, rounded side up, atop cake in irregular pattern (discard excess sugar mixture). Bake cake until tester inserted into center comes out with just a few crumbs attached, about 35 minutes. Cool cake in pan on rack. Serve warm or at room temperature.

Texas Sheet Cake

There's no clear consensus on why this cake is named for Texas, though it certainly is large like the Lone Star State (and Lady Bird Johnson is rumored to have created it). The chocolate glaze and crunchy pecan topping are easy decorations for the novice baker. And there are lots of ways to change up the topping, such as adding coarsely crushed toffee bars, chocolate-coated espresso beans, or toasted coconut; or add mini marshmallows and toasted walnuts for a rocky road rendition. **12 servings**

Cake

1²/₃   **cups unbleached all purpose flour**
²/₃   **cup natural unsweetened cocoa powder**
³/₄   **teaspoon baking soda**
³/₄   **teaspoon salt**
1½   **cups sugar**
³/₄   **cup (1½ sticks) unsalted butter, room temperature**
2   **large eggs**
1   **teaspoon vanilla extract**
1   **cup hot water**

Glaze

²/₃   **cup heavy whipping cream**
2   **tablespoons sugar**
6   **ounces bittersweet or semisweet chocolate (do not exceed 61% cacao), chopped**
2   **tablespoons (¼ stick) unsalted butter, cut into pieces**
1¼   **cups coarsely chopped pecans, toasted**

CAKE: Preheat oven to 350°F. Butter and flour 13x9x2-inch metal cake pan. Whisk flour, cocoa, baking soda, and salt in medium bowl to blend. Using electric mixer, beat sugar and butter in large bowl until light and fluffy. Add eggs 1 at a time, beating well after each addition. Mix in vanilla. Beat in half of dry ingredients, then 1 cup hot water, then remaining dry ingredients. Transfer batter to prepared pan; smooth top. Bake cake until tester inserted into center just comes out clean, about 25 minutes. Cool cake in pan on rack.

GLAZE: Bring cream and sugar to boil in heavy medium saucepan. Remove from heat and add chocolate and butter. Let stand 5 minutes; whisk until smooth. Drizzle half of glaze over cake; sprinkle with pecans. Drizzle with remaining glaze. Cool until glaze is set.

DO AHEAD: *Can be made 1 day ahead. Store airtight at room temperature.*

Cut cake into squares and serve.

The Right Icing

Certain frostings, icings, and glazes go particularly well with certain cakes. Here's how they match up.

LIGHT, SPONGY CAKES—like angel food and chiffon cakes—work best with thin, pourable icings made by dissolving powdered sugar with a liquid, such as milk, coffee, or citrus juice, or with fluffy whipped cream frostings that won't compete with the cake's airy crumb. Spongy cakes are able to soak up any excess moisture these creamy icings may exude. Powdered sugar icings and chocolate glazes also work well with Bundt cakes, since the decorative surface needs just a glossy finish.

RICH, MOIST LAYERED CAKES—like gingerbread, chocolate, and carrot cakes—work in harmony with buttercreams, whipped ganaches, and cream cheese frostings, which won't exude liquid and will help seal in the cake's moisture.

DENSE, FUDGY CAKES—like flourless chocolate cakes—are so rich that a simple sifting of powdered sugar is often the only embellishment needed. These cakes are even more extravagant when draped in ganache, covered in whipped cream, or served with a dessert sauce, such as crème anglaise.

Carrot Cake with Buttermilk Glaze and Cinnamon–Cream Cheese Frosting

There's nothing ordinary about this carrot cake. It's loaded with coconut, pineapple, and pecans, and includes both a glaze and a frosting. The glaze is hot when it's poured over the warm sheet cake, which gives this dessert a rich, moist texture. The frosting is truly the icing on the cake. Just be sure the glazed cake is completely cool before the frosting is spread over it, or the frosting will melt. **12 servings**

Cake

2	cups unbleached all purpose flour
2	teaspoons baking soda
2	teaspoons ground cinnamon
½	teaspoon salt
1½	cups sugar
3	large eggs
¾	cup buttermilk
¾	cup vegetable oil
1	teaspoon vanilla extract
2	cups coarsely grated peeled carrots
1½	cups sweetened flaked coconut
1	8-ounce can crushed pineapple in juice
1	cup coarsely chopped pecans

Glaze

1	cup sugar
½	cup buttermilk
½	cup (1 stick) unsalted butter, diced
1	tablespoon light corn syrup
1½	teaspoons baking soda
1	teaspoon vanilla extract

Frosting

1½	8-ounce packages Philadelphia-brand cream cheese, room temperature
½	cup (1 stick) unsalted butter, room temperature
1	1-pound box powdered sugar
2	tablespoons (packed) brown sugar
1½	teaspoons vanilla extract
1	teaspoon ground cinnamon

CAKE: Preheat oven to 350°F. Brush 13x9x2-inch metal baking pan with vegetable oil; dust with flour. Whisk flour, baking soda, cinnamon, and salt in medium bowl. Beat sugar, eggs, buttermilk, oil, and vanilla in large bowl until smooth. Beat in dry ingredients. Fold in carrots, coconut, pineapple with juice, and pecans. Transfer batter to prepared pan.

Bake cake 30 minutes. Tent loosely with foil. Continue to bake until tester inserted into center comes out clean, about 15 minutes longer. Remove from oven. Using bamboo skewer, poke deep holes all over cake.

GLAZE: Meanwhile, bring sugar, buttermilk, butter, corn syrup, and baking soda to boil in large saucepan, stirring until sugar dissolves. Boil until glaze is deep amber color, whisking often, 3 to 4 minutes (glaze will thin out when almost done). Remove from heat; mix in vanilla.

Spoon hot glaze evenly over warm cake. Cool cake completely in pan.

FROSTING: Beat cream cheese and butter in large bowl until fluffy. Add powdered sugar, brown sugar, vanilla, and cinnamon; beat until blended. Spread frosting over cooled cake in pan.

DO AHEAD: *Can be made 1 day ahead. Cover and chill.*

Parsnip Spice Cake with Ginger–Cream Cheese Frosting

Parsnips are closely related to carrots—they are similar in flavor but have creamy white flesh. Here, they give a new twist to carrot cake. Toasting the walnuts, or any other nuts, intensifies their rich nutty flavor; see page 36 for tips on toasting nuts. **12 to 16 servings**

1½   cups unbleached all purpose flour
1   cup sugar
1   tablespoon ground ginger
2   teaspoons baking powder
¼   teaspoons ground cinnamon
¾   teaspoon plus ⅛ teaspoon salt
¾   teaspoon ground nutmeg
¾   teaspoon ground allspice
¾   teaspoon ground cloves
3   large eggs
½   cup canola oil or other vegetable oil
½   cup whole milk
1½   teaspoons vanilla extract, divided
2   cups (packed) shredded peeled parsnips (about 3 large)
½   cup walnuts, toasted, chopped
4   ounces Philadelphia-brand cream cheese, room temperature
2   tablespoons (¼ stick) unsalted butter, room temperature
2   teaspoons grated peeled fresh ginger
3   cups (about 12 ounces) powdered sugar

Preheat oven to 350°F. Butter and flour 13x9x2-inch metal baking pan. Combine flour, 1 cup sugar, ground ginger, baking powder, cinnamon, ¾ teaspoon salt, nutmeg, allspice, and cloves in large bowl; whisk to combine. Whisk eggs, oil, milk, and 1 teaspoon vanilla in medium bowl to combine. Pour egg mixture over dry ingredients; stir until just combined. Stir in parsnips and walnuts. Transfer batter to prepared pan. Bake until tester inserted into center comes out clean, about 25 minutes. Cool cake completely in pan on rack.

Beat cream cheese and butter in large bowl until smooth. Beat in fresh ginger and remaining ⅛ teaspoon salt and ½ teaspoon vanilla. Gradually add powdered sugar and beat until frosting is smooth. Spread over cake.

DO AHEAD: *Can be made 1 day ahead. Cover and chill.*

Glazed Lime Cake

Here's a cake you can make any night of the week on a whim, since there are just seven staple ingredients used for both the cake and glaze—all of which you're likely to have on hand. If you don't have self-rising flour, use all purpose flour instead and add 1¾ teaspoons baking powder and ½ teaspoon salt. For a pretty garnish, grate some fresh lime peel over the cake just after it's been glazed and sprinkle with blackberries or raspberries. **9 servings**

¾   cup (1½ sticks) butter, room temperature
2½   cups powdered sugar, divided
2   large eggs, room temperature
¼   cup milk
1⅓   cups self-rising flour
4   large limes
6   tablespoons sugar

Preheat oven to 350°F. Butter and flour 8x8x2-inch metal baking pan. Using electric mixer, beat butter and 1½ cups powdered sugar in large bowl until well blended. Beat in eggs 1 at a time. Beat in milk, then flour. Transfer batter to prepared pan; smooth top. Bake cake until tester inserted into center comes out clean, about 33 minutes.

Meanwhile, finely grate enough lime peel to measure 1 tablespoon. Halve limes; squeeze enough juice to measure 6 tablespoons. Stir lime peel, lime juice, and 6 tablespoons sugar in small bowl until sugar dissolves. Set lime syrup aside.

Using skewer, poke holes all over cake. Spoon 2½ tablespoons lime syrup into another small bowl; reserve for glaze. Spoon all remaining lime syrup evenly over hot cake. Cool cake completely in pan on rack.

Whisk remaining 1 cup powdered sugar into reserved 2½ tablespoons lime syrup; drizzle glaze over cake. Let stand 1 hour. Cut cake into squares.

Double-Ginger Gingerbread with Orange-Ginger Sauce

The double hit of ginger comes from ground ginger and chopped crystallized ginger. **8 servings**

1½   cups unbleached all purpose flour
1   teaspoon baking soda
1   teaspoon ground ginger
1   teaspoon ground cinnamon
½   teaspoon salt
½   teaspoon freshly ground black pepper
½   cup (1 stick) unsalted butter, room temperature
½   cup (packed) dark brown sugar
2   large eggs
¼   cup robust-flavored (dark) molasses
⅔   cup buttermilk
¼   cup chopped crystallized ginger
½   cup chilled heavy whipping cream, whipped to soft peaks
     Orange-Ginger Sauce (see recipe)

Preheat oven to 325°F. Butter 8x8x2-inch metal baking pan; dust with flour. Sift flour, baking soda, ground ginger, cinnamon, salt, and pepper into small bowl. Using electric mixer, beat butter in large bowl until light and fluffy. Add sugar and beat until fluffy. Add eggs 1 at a time, beating well after each addition. Mix in molasses. Mix in half of dry ingredients, then buttermilk, then remaining dry ingredients. Fold in crystallized ginger.

Transfer batter to prepared pan. Bake cake until tester inserted into center comes out clean, about 45 minutes. Cool cake slightly in pan on rack.

DO AHEAD: *Can be made 6 hours ahead. Cool completely. Cover with foil and rewarm in 375°F oven 10 to 15 minutes.*

Cut warm cake into squares and place on plates. Top with whipped cream and Orange-Ginger Sauce and serve.

Orange-Ginger Sauce

This sauce would also be delicious over vanilla ice cream or spooned over thick Greek yogurt scattered with toasted almonds. **Makes about 1½ cups**

3   large oranges
1   cup (about) fresh orange juice
6   tablespoons sugar
1   cinnamon stick
3   tablespoons chopped crystallized ginger

Using small sharp knife, cut off peel and white pith from oranges. Working over small bowl, cut between membranes of oranges, releasing segments. Transfer segments to medium bowl. Pour accumulated orange juice into measuring cup. Add enough orange juice to measure 1 cup plus 2 tablespoons. Transfer juice to medium saucepan. Add sugar and cinnamon. Cook over low heat, stirring until sugar dissolves. Increase heat and simmer until juice mixture is syrupy and reduced to 6 tablespoons, about 12 minutes. Pour over oranges. Add ginger. Cool.

DO AHEAD: *Can be made 1 day ahead. Cover and refrigerate.*

Cranberry-Maple Pudding Cake

Pudding cakes form two wonderful layers all on their own as they bake—the pudding layer settles on the bottom, and a spongy cake forms on top. Serve this warm for breakfast or dessert. **6 to 8 servings**

2	cups fresh or frozen cranberries
1	cup pure maple syrup (Grade B or Grade A dark amber)
²/₃	cup heavy whipping cream
¾	teaspoon finely grated orange peel
	Pinch of salt plus ½ teaspoon salt
²/₃	cup unbleached all purpose flour
⅓	cup yellow cornmeal (preferably stone-ground)
1½	teaspoons baking powder
1	large egg
3	tablespoons sugar
½	cup whole milk
½	cup (1 stick) unsalted butter, melted
1	teaspoon vanilla extract
	Crème fraîche, softly whipped cream, or vanilla ice cream

Position rack in center of oven and preheat to 400°F. Combine cranberries, maple syrup, cream, orange peel, and pinch of salt in heavy medium saucepan. Bring to boil, stirring occasionally. Reduce heat and simmer 1 minute. Remove from heat.

Whisk flour, cornmeal, baking powder, and remaining ½ teaspoon salt in medium bowl. Whisk egg and sugar in another medium bowl. Whisk milk, melted butter, and vanilla into egg mixture. Add flour mixture to egg mixture; whisk to blend.

Pour warm cranberry mixture into 11x7x2-inch or 8x8x2-inch glass or ceramic baking dish. Pour batter over. Bake cake until golden and cranberry mixture bubbles at edges, about 28 minutes. Cool 15 minutes. Spoon warm cake with cranberry mixture onto plates. Serve cake topped with crème fraîche, whipped cream, or vanilla ice cream.

Apple-Cornmeal Upside-Down Cake

Yellow cornmeal gives this homey dessert great texture. Pippin apples can be used in place of Granny Smiths. When adding the batter to the cake pan, drop it by spoonfuls rather than pouring it over to help distribute it evenly and to avoid dislodging the apples. This cake isn't super-sweet, so serve it warm with vanilla or dulce de leche ice cream, if desired. **6 to 8 servings**

Nonstick vegetable oil spray
8   tablespoons (1 stick) unsalted butter, room temperature, divided
½   cup plus ⅔ cup sugar
3   7- to 8-ounce Granny Smith apples, peeled, cut into eighths, cored
1   cup unbleached all purpose flour
¼   cup yellow cornmeal
½   teaspoon baking soda
¼   teaspoon salt
1   large egg
½   cup buttermilk

Position rack in center of oven and preheat to 350°F. Generously spray 9-inch-diameter cake pan with 2-inch-high sides with nonstick spray. Melt 2 tablespoons butter in heavy large skillet over medium-high heat. Add ½ cup sugar and stir until sugar melts and turns golden brown, about 3 minutes. Add apples and sauté over medium heat until apples are just tender and coated with caramel, shaking pan occasionally, about 12 minutes. Immediately pour mixture into prepared pan; distribute apples and caramel evenly over bottom of pan.

Whisk flour, cornmeal, baking soda, and salt in medium bowl. Using electric mixer, beat remaining 6 tablespoons butter and ⅔ cup sugar in large bowl until fluffy. Beat in egg. Add half of flour mixture; stir in buttermilk. Add remaining flour mixture and mix well. Drop batter by spoonfuls evenly over apples and spread gently with offset spatula.

Bake until cake is golden brown and tester inserted into center comes out clean, about 40 minutes. Cool cake in pan on rack 5 minutes. Cut around pan sides to loosen cake. Place platter over pan. Using oven mitts or pot holders as aid, firmly grasp pan and platter together and turn over. Gently lift pan off cake. Serve warm.

Technique Tip: Flipping Out

Inverting an upside-down cake to get it out of the pan requires a leap of faith—and a firm grip. It's important, of course, to read the instructions in the recipe first. Then, just go for it: Using oven mitts or thick kitchen towels, make sure you've got the cake pan and the platter clasped tightly together [1]. Then flip the platter and cake quickly, let stand as directed, and carefully lift off the cake pan [2].

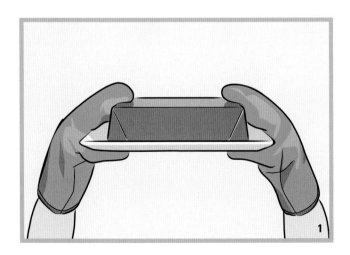

Caramel-Walnut Upside-Down Banana Cake

A new twist on pineapple upside-down cake: Walnuts replace the pineapple atop a super-moist banana cake, and a brown sugar caramel drips down the sides. **6 to 8 servings**

Topping

Nonstick vegetable oil spray

½   cup (1 stick) unsalted butter

1   cup (packed) golden brown sugar

3   tablespoons dark corn syrup

¾   cup walnut halves or pieces

Cake

1¾   cups cake flour

1   teaspoon baking powder

¾   teaspoon baking soda

½   teaspoon salt

½   cup (1 stick) unsalted butter, room temperature

½   cup sugar

½   cup (packed) golden brown sugar

2   large eggs

1   cup mashed very ripe bananas (2 to 3 large)

3   tablespoons sour cream

1   tablespoon dark rum

1   teaspoon vanilla extract

Whipped cream or vanilla ice cream

TOPPING: Spray 8-inch-diameter cake pan with 2-inch-high sides with nonstick spray. Bring butter, sugar, and corn syrup to boil in medium saucepan, stirring constantly until butter melts. Boil syrup 1 minute. Stir in nuts. Spread topping in prepared pan. Let topping cool completely.

CAKE: Preheat oven to 350°F. Sift flour, baking powder, baking soda, and salt into medium bowl. Using electric mixer, beat butter and both sugars in large bowl until blended. Beat in eggs 1 at a time, then mashed bananas, sour cream, rum, and vanilla. Beat in dry ingredients in 2 additions just until combined. Spoon batter into pan.

Bake cake until tester inserted into center comes out clean, about 55 minutes. Cool 15 minutes. Run small knife around pan sides to loosen cake. Place platter over pan. Using oven mitts or pot holders as aid, firmly grasp pan and platter together, then turn over. Let stand 5 minutes, then gently lift pan off cake. Cool at least 15 minutes for topping to set. Serve warm or at room temperature with whipped cream or vanilla ice cream.

Market Tip: Bananas

If you don't see any ripe bananas in the produce section, ask the produce manager if there are any in the back—sometimes they remove the ripe bananas to make room for the newest shipment.

Plum-Blueberry Upside-Down Cake

Upside-down cake, an old-fashioned favorite, is given a lustrous new look with plums and fresh blueberries. **8 servings**

Topping

½   **cup (1 stick) unsalted butter**
½   **cup (packed) dark brown sugar**
4   **plums, pitted, cut into ½-inch wedges**
1   **½-pint container blueberries**

Cake

1½   **cups unbleached all purpose flour**
2   **teaspoons baking powder**
¾   **teaspoon ground cinnamon**
¼   **teaspoon salt**
¼   **cup (½ stick) unsalted butter, room temperature**
1   **cup sugar**
2   **large eggs, room temperature**
1   **teaspoon vanilla extract**
½   **cup plus 1 tablespoon milk**

   Vanilla ice cream or whipped cream (optional)

TOPPING: Melt butter in heavy medium saucepan over low heat. Add sugar; whisk until well blended. Pour syrup into 9-inch-diameter cake pan with 2-inch-high sides, spreading to cover bottom evenly. Lightly press plums into syrup in circle around edge of pan. Spread berries in center.

DO AHEAD: *Can be made 3 hours ahead. Let stand at room temperature.*

CAKE: Position rack in center of oven and preheat to 350°F. Sift flour, baking powder, cinnamon, and salt into medium bowl. Beat butter in another medium bowl until smooth. Gradually add sugar to butter and beat until well combined. Add eggs 1 at a time, beating well after each addition. Beat in vanilla. Stir dry ingredients and milk alternately into butter mixture, beginning and ending with dry ingredients. Spoon batter over topping in pan.

Bake cake until top is golden and firm and tester inserted into center comes out clean, about 55 minutes. Let stand 10 minutes. Run small sharp knife around pan sides to loosen cake. Place platter over pan. Using oven mitts or pot holders as aid, firmly grasp pan and platter together, then turn over. Let stand 3 minutes, then gently lift pan off cake. Serve warm or at room temperature with ice cream or whipped cream, if desired.

Pineapple Upside-Down Pumpkin Gingerbread

Upside-down cake gets warmed up for autumn with the addition of pumpkin, molasses, and a mix of spices. To peel the pineapple, use a large serrated knife to cut through the tough skin with ease. Using round cookie cutters of different sizes to cut the pineapple pieces is a clever twist that adds a modern look.

10 servings

Topping

Nonstick vegetable oil spray

²⁄₃	cup (packed) golden brown sugar
½	cup (1 stick) unsalted butter
2	tablespoons frozen pineapple juice concentrate, thawed
1	teaspoon mild-flavored (light) molasses
1	ripe pineapple, peeled

Cake

2	cups unbleached all purpose flour
2	teaspoons baking soda
2	teaspoons baking powder
1¼	teaspoons ground cinnamon
¾	teaspoon ground ginger
½	teaspoon salt
½	cup (1 stick) unsalted butter, room temperature
1	cup sugar
2	large eggs
½	cup mild-flavored (light) molasses
½	cup canned pure pumpkin
½	cup boiling water

Whipped cream

{ Market Tip: **Pineapple**
When selecting a pineapple, look for one that feels heavy for its size—a good sign that it will be juicy—and has a fragrant smell, a hint that it will be flavorful. Then tug at one of the inner leaves; it will release easily if the pineapple is ripe. }

TOPPING: Preheat oven to 350°F. Spray 9x9x2-inch metal baking pan with nonstick spray. Combine sugar, butter, pineapple juice concentrate, and molasses in heavy small saucepan. Bring to boil over medium heat, whisking until sugar dissolves and syrup is smooth; boil 1 minute. Pour evenly into prepared pan.

Cut off one ⅓-inch-thick round from pineapple; cut out core. Place round in syrup in pan. Stand pineapple on end. Cut lengthwise into ⅓-inch-thick slices. Using 3 round cutters of different sizes, cut out rounds from pineapple slices, avoiding core. Arrange rounds close together in single layer in free-form design in syrup.

CAKE: Whisk flour, baking soda, baking powder, cinnamon, ginger, and salt in medium bowl. Beat butter in large bowl until fluffy. Add sugar and beat to blend. Beat in eggs 1 at a time. Beat in molasses, then pumpkin. Beat in dry ingredients just until blended, occasionally scraping down sides of bowl. Beat in ½ cup boiling water. Pour batter evenly into pan.

Bake cake until tester inserted into center comes out clean, about 50 minutes. Cool cake in pan 45 minutes. Place platter over pan. Using oven mitts or pot holders as aid, firmly grasp pan and platter together and turn over. Let stand 5 minutes, then gently lift pan off cake. Serve cake warm or at room temperature with whipped cream.

Upside-Down Spiced Peach Cake with Honey-Sweetened Whipped Cream

A touch of honey in the brown sugar mixture, fresh peaches instead of canned pineapple, and a bit of yogurt in place of some of the butter update the classic cake. When removed from the heat, the honey mixture will begin to harden quickly, so be ready to pour it into the cake pan immediately. As the cake bakes, the honey mixture melts into the peaches and into the bottom of the cake, creating a luscious topping. **6 servings**

6   tablespoons (¾ stick) unsalted butter, room temperature, divided
¼   cup honey
¼   cup (packed) golden brown sugar
1¼   cups unbleached all purpose flour
1½   teaspoons ground cardamom
½   teaspoon ground cinnamon
¼   teaspoon baking soda
¼   teaspoon salt
¾   cup sugar
1   large egg
½   cup plain whole-milk yogurt
3   small or 2 medium ripe peaches (about 1 pound total), pitted, thinly sliced
      Honey-Sweetened Whipped Cream (see recipe)

Position rack in center of oven and preheat to 350°F. Generously butter 9-inch-diameter cake pan with 2-inch-high sides. Melt 2 tablespoons butter in heavy small saucepan over medium-high heat. Stir in honey and brown sugar. Boil until mixture darkens slightly, stirring often, about 2 minutes. Immediately pour honey mixture into prepared pan to coat bottom completely. Let stand while preparing batter.

Whisk flour, cardamom, cinnamon, baking soda, and salt in medium bowl to blend. Using electric mixer, beat sugar and remaining 4 tablespoons butter in large bowl until fluffy. Beat in egg. Mix in half of flour mixture, then all of yogurt. Add remaining flour mixture and mix just until blended.

Arrange sliced peaches decoratively over honey mixture (it will be firm), covering completely. Drop batter by spoonfuls evenly over peaches and gently spread batter over peaches to cover completely. Bake until cake begins to pull away from sides of pan and tester inserted into center comes out clean, about 40 minutes. Cool cake in pan on rack 5 minutes. Run small knife around pan sides to loosen cake. Place platter over pan. Using oven mitts or pot holders as aid, firmly grasp pan and platter together, then turn over. Gently lift off pan. Serve warm or at room temperature with Honey-Sweetened Whipped Cream.

Honey-Sweetened Whipped Cream

Using honey to sweeten the cream adds a subtle nuance; a bit of yogurt creates a perfect balance of sweet, creamy, and tangy flavors. **Makes about 1¾ cups**

¾   cup chilled heavy whipping cream
3   tablespoons honey
¼   cup plain whole-milk yogurt

Using electric mixer, beat cream and honey in large bowl until soft peaks form. Fold in yogurt.

DO AHEAD: *Can be made 8 hours ahead. Cover and refrigerate.*

Brown Sugar–Almond Cake with Caramel Frosting

Buttermilk helps make this cake tender, and brown sugar gives it a roasty, old-fashioned sweetness. **12 servings**

Cake

2	cups cake flour
¾	teaspoon baking powder
¾	teaspoon baking soda
¼	teaspoon salt
1	15-ounce can pear halves in light syrup, well drained
¾	cup blanched slivered almonds
¾	cup buttermilk
¾	cup sugar
½	cup (packed) golden brown sugar
½	cup (1 stick) unsalted butter, room temperature
2	large eggs
1	teaspoon vanilla extract
¾	teaspoon almond extract

Frosting

¾	cup (packed) dark brown sugar
½	cup heavy whipping cream
1	tablespoon light corn syrup
½	cup (1 stick) unsalted butter, room temperature
1	cup powdered sugar, sifted
1	teaspoon vanilla extract

Toasted sliced almonds
Additional powdered sugar

CAKE: Preheat oven to 350°F. Butter 9x9x2-inch metal baking pan. Line pan with waxed paper; butter paper. Sift flour, baking powder, baking soda, and salt into large bowl.

Place pears and nuts in processor; blend to thick puree. Add buttermilk, both sugars, butter, eggs, and both extracts. Process until well blended (mixture may look curdled). Add to dry ingredients; stir to blend. Transfer to prepared pan.

Bake cake until tester inserted into center comes out clean, about 30 minutes. Cool cake in pan on rack 10 minutes. Run small sharp knife around pan sides to loosen cake. Turn cake out onto rack; peel off paper. Cool cake completely.

FROSTING: Combine brown sugar, cream, and corn syrup in heavy medium saucepan. Stir over medium heat until mixture comes to boil. Boil 2 minutes, swirling pan occasionally. Pour mixture into medium bowl. Chill until cold and beginning to thicken, stirring occasionally, about 1 hour.

Using electric mixer, beat butter and powdered sugar in medium bowl until smooth. Gradually beat in cold brown sugar mixture, then vanilla.

Place cake on platter. Spread frosting over cake. Sprinkle nuts on top of cake.

DO AHEAD: *Can be made 1 day ahead. Chill until cold, then cover.*

Sprinkle additional powdered sugar over cake.

Walnut-Orange Cake

Instead of the vegetable oil or butter usually found in cakes, olive oil is used here, lending a mild aroma and flavor that complement the walnuts and orange. Regular olive oil works best, as its mild taste won't compete with the other flavors. Nutty but delicate, this cake would be delicious with just a dollop of lightly sweetened whipped cream. Serve it for breakfast, brunch, or tea, or after dinner. **8 to 10 servings**

	Nonstick olive oil spray
1½	cups chopped walnuts
1	cup unbleached all purpose flour
1	tablespoon baking powder
4	large eggs
1½	cups sugar
½	cup fresh orange juice
1	tablespoon finely grated orange peel
½	cup olive oil
	Powdered sugar

Preheat oven to 350°F. Spray 9-inch-diameter springform pan with nonstick olive oil spray. Place parchment paper round in bottom of pan; spray parchment.

Grind walnuts in processor until finely ground but not powdery. Combine ground walnuts, flour, and baking powder in medium bowl.

Using electric mixer, beat eggs in large bowl until frothy, about 2 minutes. Gradually add sugar, beating until light, thick, and pale yellow, about 4 minutes. Gradually add walnut-flour mixture, then orange juice, orange peel, and olive oil, beating just until blended. Transfer batter to prepared pan. Place pan on rimmed baking sheet and bake cake until tester inserted into center comes out clean, about 1 hour. Cool cake completely in pan on rack.

Run knife around pan sides to loosen cake. Release pan sides. Carefully invert cake onto platter and remove parchment. Sift powdered sugar over cake.

Cinnamon-Sugar Plum Cake

Fresh, ripe, seasonal fruit is essential in desserts that feature it—such as this one. So make this cake when summer plums are at their peak. Other summer fruits that would be delicious in this recipe: pitted fresh cherries or sliced peaches and nectarines. During fall and winter, use sliced cored unpeeled pears. **6 to 8 servings**

1¼	cups unbleached all purpose flour
1	teaspoon baking powder
¼	teaspoon salt
½	cup (1 stick) unsalted butter, room temperature
¾	cup plus 1½ tablespoons sugar
2	large eggs
1	tablespoon fresh lemon juice
1	teaspoon finely grated lemon peel
5	large plums (about 1¼ pounds), pitted, cut into ½-inch wedges
¼	teaspoon ground cinnamon

Preheat oven to 350°F. Butter 9-inch-diameter springform pan. Whisk flour, baking powder, and salt in small bowl to blend. Using electric mixer, beat butter in large bowl until fluffy. Beat in ¾ cup sugar. Add eggs 1 at a time, then lemon juice and lemon peel, beating until blended after each addition. Beat in flour mixture. Spread batter in prepared pan.

Press plum wedges halfway into batter in concentric circles, spacing slightly apart. Mix remaining 1½ tablespoons sugar and cinnamon in small bowl; sprinkle over plums.

Bake cake until browned on top and tester inserted into center comes out clean, about 50 minutes. Cut around cake; release pan sides. Serve cake warm or at room temperature.

Raspberry Cake with Marsala, Crème Fraîche, and Raspberries

This tender raspberry cake has the texture of a fresh cake doughnut, so it would be great for brunch. Very lightly sweetened whipped cream could be substituted for the crème fraîche. **10 servings**

1½	**cups unbleached all purpose flour**
1	**teaspoon baking powder**
1	**teaspoon salt**
¼	**teaspoon baking soda**
¼	**teaspoon ground nutmeg**
½	**cup Marsala**
¼	**cup fresh orange juice**
14	**tablespoons (1¾ sticks) unsalted butter, room temperature, divided**
1	**cup plus 4 tablespoons sugar, divided**
2	**large eggs**
1	**teaspoon vanilla extract**
1	**teaspoon finely grated lemon peel**
4	**cups fresh raspberries, divided**
2	**cups crème fraîche or sour cream**

Position rack in center of oven and preheat to 400°F. Butter 10-inch-diameter springform pan with 2¾-inch-high sides. Whisk flour, baking powder, salt, baking soda, and nutmeg in medium bowl to blend. Combine Marsala and orange juice in small bowl. Beat 12 tablespoons butter and 1 cup sugar in large bowl until well blended. Beat in eggs, vanilla, and lemon peel. Beat in flour mixture in 3 additions alternately with Marsala mixture in 2 additions. Transfer batter to prepared pan. Sprinkle with 1½ cups raspberries; reserve remaining berries for serving.

Bake cake until top is gently set, about 20 minutes. Reduce oven temperature to 375°F. Dot top of cake with remaining 2 tablespoons butter and sprinkle with 2 tablespoons sugar. Continue baking until tester inserted into center of cake comes out clean, about 15 minutes. Cool cake in pan on rack. Release pan sides; transfer cake to platter. Cool to room temperature.

Mix crème fraîche and remaining 2 tablespoons sugar in small bowl.

DO AHEAD: *Cake and crème fraîche mixture can be made 8 hours ahead. Let cake stand at room temperature. Cover and chill crème fraîche mixture.*

Cut cake into wedges. Top each with dollop of crème fraîche and fresh raspberries and serve.

♝ Tarte au Sucre

Similar to a rustic coffee cake, this Belgian classic is a light and fluffy yeast-risen treat with a custardy brown sugar topping. Often served with fresh berries as dessert, the tart is also lovely for brunch or as an afternoon snack with coffee or tea. **10 to 12 servings**

1½   cups unbleached all purpose flour
¼   cup sugar
2   teaspoons active dry yeast
1   teaspoon finely grated lemon peel
½   teaspoon salt
6   tablespoons (¾ stick) chilled unsalted butter, cut into
        ½-inch cubes
¼   cup whole milk
3   large egg yolks
2   large eggs
⅔   cup heavy whipping cream
⅔   cup (packed) dark brown sugar, divided

Butter and flour 9-inch-diameter springform pan with 2¾-inch-high sides. Mix flour, ¼ cup sugar, yeast, lemon peel, and salt in processor. Add butter; using on/off turns, blend until mixture resembles coarse meal. Add milk and egg yolks; using on/off turns, blend until soft dough forms. Using wet fingertips, press dough over bottom and 1 inch up sides of prepared pan. Cover tightly with plastic and let rise in warm draft-free area until light and puffy (dough will not double in volume), about 2 hours.

Preheat oven to 400°F. Whisk whole eggs and cream in small bowl to blend. Sprinkle ⅓ cup brown sugar over bottom of tart. Pour cream mixture over. Sprinkle with remaining ⅓ cup brown sugar. Bake until dough puffs and browns and filling browns in spots, about 25 minutes. Transfer to rack. Cut around pan sides to loosen tart. Release pan sides. Cool 30 minutes. Serve warm or at room temperature.

♝ Chocolate Decadence

Although the pan is buttered and floured to prevent sticking, the cake itself is flourless. The decadence comes from a generous dose of bittersweet chocolate and butter, accented with Grand Marnier, Cognac, and espresso powder. **12 servings**

1   pound bittersweet or semisweet chocolate (do not exceed
        61% cacao), chopped
10   tablespoons (1¼ sticks) unsalted butter
2   tablespoons Grand Marnier or other orange liqueur
1   tablespoon Cognac or brandy
1   tablespoon instant espresso powder or coffee powder
6   large eggs
¾   cup sugar
     Lightly sweetened whipped cream
     Fresh raspberries

Preheat oven to 350°F. Butter and flour 9-inch-diameter springform pan with 2¾-inch-high sides. Stir chocolate and butter in heavy large saucepan over low heat until melted and smooth. Remove from heat. Whisk in Grand Marnier, Cognac, and espresso powder. Cool to lukewarm.

Using electric mixer, beat eggs and sugar in large bowl until tripled in volume, about 5 minutes. Fold ¼ of beaten egg mixture into cooled chocolate mixture to lighten, then fold chocolate mixture into remaining egg mixture. Transfer batter to prepared pan.

Bake cake until tester inserted into center comes out with moist crumbs still attached, about 45 minutes. Cool cake in pan on rack (cake will sink as it cools). Run knife around pan sides to loosen cake. Release pan sides.

DO AHEAD: *Can be made 1 day ahead. Cover and let stand at room temperature.*

Cut cake into wedges. Serve with whipped cream and berries.

Technique Tip: **Whip It Up**
Since there's no leavening agent in this cake other than eggs to make it rise, a good whipping of the eggs and sugar is key. Use room-temperature eggs and a hand-held mixer or stand mixer at medium speed to create a fluffy foam that will literally triple in volume. The chocolate mixture should be just lukewarm when the foam is added or the heat will deflate the foam. Bake the cake immediately, while the foam is at its highest volume.

Chocolate-Pistachio Torte with Warm Chocolate Ganache

Characteristic of tortes, this is a decadent flourless cake loaded with nuts. Pistachio paste lends a wonderful flavor but is not readily available and is fairly expensive. Fortunately, this recipe demonstrates how simple it is to make your own, and by making the paste yourself, you control its purity and freshness. There will be a bit of pistachio paste left over—stir it into your next batch of brownies. **12 servings**

Pistachio Paste

12	ounces unsalted natural pistachios
2	tablespoons sugar
2	large egg whites

Torte

12	ounces bittersweet or semisweet chocolate (do not exceed 61% cacao), chopped
½	cup (1 stick) unsalted butter, room temperature
6	large eggs, separated, room temperature
¼	teaspoon salt
2	tablespoons sugar
2	tablespoons (packed) golden brown sugar

Ganache

2	cups heavy whipping cream
15	ounces bittersweet or semisweet chocolate (do not exceed 61% cacao), chopped
	Chopped pistachios

PISTACHIO PASTE: Finely grind nuts and sugar in processor. Add egg whites and blend well.

DO AHEAD: *Can be made 3 days ahead. Transfer pistachio paste to small bowl, cover, and refrigerate.*

TORTE: Preheat oven to 350°F. Butter 8-inch-diameter springform pan with 2¾-inch-high sides. Line pan bottom with parchment paper; butter paper. Place chocolate in medium metal bowl. Set bowl over saucepan of simmering water and stir until chocolate is melted and smooth. Remove bowl from over water. Cool chocolate to lukewarm.

Measure ⅓ cup pistachio paste and transfer to small bowl (cover and reserve for another use). Place remaining pistachio paste in large bowl; add butter. Using electric mixer, beat until blended. Beat in egg yolks, then melted chocolate. Using clean dry beaters, beat egg whites with salt in another large bowl until soft peaks form. Gradually add 2 tablespoons sugar, beating until firm peaks form. Sift brown sugar over and fold in. Using flexible rubber spatula, fold egg white mixture into chocolate mixture in 4 additions; transfer batter to prepared pan.

Bake torte until center is slightly puffed and tester inserted into center of torte comes out with some batter still attached, about 1 hour. Cool torte completely in pan on rack.

DO AHEAD: *Can be made 1 day ahead. Cover and let stand at room temperature.*

GANACHE: Bring cream to simmer in small saucepan. Remove from heat; add chocolate and whisk until melted and smooth.

DO AHEAD: *Can be made 1 day ahead. Chill. Rewarm before using.*

Cut torte into wedges; place on plates. Pour warm ganache over. Sprinkle with chopped pistachios and serve.

Chocolate Gâteau with Lemon, Raisins, Almonds, and Muscat Custard Sauce

This recipe uses Muscat de Beaumes de Venise, a sweet white French wine that imparts a floral aroma to the raisins and custard sauce. If you can't find this particular wine, a sweet Muscat from Italy or California is fine as a substitute. **6 to 8 servings**

Cake

1	cup sweet Muscat wine (such as Muscat de Beaumes de Venise)
1	cup raisins
1	cup sliced almonds, toasted, divided
8	ounces bittersweet or semisweet chocolate (do not exceed 61% cacao), chopped
1	cup (2 sticks) unsalted butter
5	large eggs
1	cup sugar
2	teaspoons finely grated lemon peel
⅓	cup unbleached all purpose flour
½	teaspoon salt

Sauce

1½	cups heavy whipping cream
5	large egg yolks
¼	cup sugar
	Powdered sugar

CAKE: Bring wine and raisins to boil in heavy medium saucepan. Remove from heat; cover and let stand at least 30 minutes.

Preheat oven to 325°F. Butter 9-inch-diameter springform pan with 2¾-inch-high sides. Line bottom of pan with parchment paper. Generously butter parchment paper. Sprinkle half of almonds evenly over bottom of pan. Melt chocolate and butter in heavy medium saucepan over low heat, stirring until smooth. Cool slightly. Whisk eggs, sugar, and lemon peel in large bowl until well blended. Stir in chocolate mixture, then flour and salt. Using slotted spoon, strain raisins, reserving wine mixture; mix raisins into batter. Stir remaining almonds into batter. Carefully pour batter into prepared pan.

Bake cake until set on top and tester inserted into center comes out with a few moist crumbs attached, about 50 minutes. Cool completely in pan on rack. Release pan sides and invert cake onto platter. Remove pan bottom and parchment.

SAUCE: Simmer reserved wine over medium heat until reduced to ¼ cup, about 5 minutes. Bring cream to simmer in heavy medium saucepan. Meanwhile, whisk egg yolks and sugar in medium bowl until well blended. Gradually stir in hot cream; return mixture to saucepan. Stir constantly over medium-low heat until mixture thickens enough to coat back of spoon, about 4 minutes (do not boil). Immediately add reduced wine. Strain sauce into large bowl. Chill uncovered until cold, stirring occasionally, about 3 hours.

DO AHEAD: *Cake and sauce can be made 1 day ahead. Cover and keep sauce refrigerated. Wrap cake with plastic and keep at cool room temperature.*

Sift powdered sugar over cake. Cut into wedges and serve with sauce.

Semisweet Chocolate Layer Cake with Vanilla Cream Filling

This impressive cake has rich chocolate flavor, deep brown color, and a moist, tender crumb, all layered with a whipped cream filling and cloaked in a luxurious chocolate glaze. You can also make this cake using bittersweet chocolate; just be sure it has a cacao content no higher than 61 percent. If eight-inch cake pans are not available in the baking aisle at your supermarket, look for them at cookware stores. **10 servings**

Cake

½	cup natural unsweetened cocoa powder
2	ounces semisweet or bittersweet chocolate (do not exceed 61% cacao), chopped
½	cup boiling water
½	cup buttermilk
1⅓	cups cake flour
1	teaspoon baking soda
½	teaspoon salt
1⅓	cups (packed) golden brown sugar
½	cup (1 stick) unsalted butter, room temperature
2	large eggs
1	teaspoon vanilla extract

Cream Filling

3	tablespoons cold water
1¾	teaspoons unflavored gelatin
2¼	cups chilled heavy whipping cream, divided
½	cup powdered sugar
1	teaspoon vanilla extract

Ganache

1¼	cups heavy whipping cream
⅓	cup light corn syrup
16	ounces semisweet or bittersweet chocolate (do not exceed 61% cacao), chopped
1	teaspoon vanilla extract
	Unsweetened cocoa powder or powdered sugar

Ganache Two Ways

Ganache is a mixture of melted chocolate and warm heavy cream. Its simplicity and versatility (not to mention its decadent richness and flavor) make it a delicious essential in the pastry kitchen. With cakes, there are two ways to use ganache.

WARM: Dip the tops of cupcakes into it; spread it over cakey brownies to create a silky smooth, no-fuss glaze; or pour it over a torte to create an elegant, glossy finish. When the ganache cools, it sets into a fudgy coating. If you plan to use the ganache as a glaze, make sure to stir the cream and chocolate just until blended—overstirring can diminish the ganache's glossy appearance.

COOL: Whip the ganache until it becomes airy and fluffy; it's an ideal filling and frosting for layered cakes.

CAKE: Position rack in center of oven and preheat oven to 350°F. Butter three 8-inch-diameter cake pans with 2-inch-high sides. Line pan bottoms with parchment paper; butter parchment. Combine cocoa powder and semisweet chocolate in medium bowl. Pour ½ cup boiling water over cocoa powder and chocolate and whisk until smooth. Whisk in buttermilk. Set chocolate mixture aside.

Whisk flour, baking soda, and salt in another medium bowl to blend. Using electric mixer, beat brown sugar and butter in large bowl until well blended (mixture will not be smooth). Add eggs and vanilla and beat until light and creamy. Beat in dry ingredients and chocolate mixture. Transfer batter to prepared pans, dividing equally. Bake cakes until tester inserted into center comes out clean, about 15 minutes. Cool cakes in pans on racks 15 minutes. Cut around pan sides to loosen cakes. Turn cakes out onto racks; peel off parchment. Cool completely.

(continued next page)

Semisweet Chocolate Layer Cake with Vanilla Cream Filling (continued)

CREAM FILLING: Place 3 tablespoons cold water in small bowl. Sprinkle gelatin over. Let stand until gelatin softens, about 10 minutes. Bring ½ cup cream just to simmer in heavy small saucepan. Add hot cream to softened gelatin; stir until gelatin dissolves. Place in refrigerator just until cool but not set, stirring frequently, 5 to 8 minutes. Using electric mixer, beat remaining 1¾ cups cream, sugar, and vanilla in medium bowl until peaks form. Gradually add gelatin mixture, beating until medium-firm peaks form.

Place 1 cake layer on 8-inch cardboard round or tart pan bottom. Spread half of filling over. Top with second cake layer. Spread remaining filling over. Top with third cake layer. Using icing spatula, remove any excess filling that may have oozed out between cake layers. Chill on cardboard round until filling sets, about 2 hours.

GANACHE: Meanwhile, bring cream and corn syrup to simmer in heavy small saucepan. Remove from heat. Add chocolate; whisk until smooth. Stir in vanilla. Cool until thick enough to spread, about 2 hours.

Place cake, still on cardboard, on rack set in center of baking sheet. Spread ¼ of ganache over top and sides of cake. Chill cake 15 minutes. Spread ¼ of remaining ganache over top and sides of cake again. Chill cake 1 hour. Rewarm remaining ganache in small saucepan over low heat just until lukewarm and pourable, stirring constantly. Pour ganache over cold cake, spreading as needed to cover top and sides. Chill until ganache is set, about 2 hours.

DO AHEAD: *Can be made 1 day ahead. Keep chilled. Let stand at room temperature 2 hours before continuing.*

Cut out paper heart shapes of differing sizes and lay flat atop cake. Sift cocoa powder or powdered sugar over. Carefully lift hearts from cake, revealing design, and serve.

Slicing a Cake into Layers

Cutting a cake into horizontal layers might seem like a daunting task, but really it just requires a little precision and the right tools.

1. Choose a long, thin, serrated knife.

2. If dividing a cake into more than two layers, stand a ruler next to the cake and use toothpicks around the side of the cake to mark off even layers. Otherwise, start halfway down.

3. With the blade parallel to the work surface, cut 1 inch into the side of the cake with a back-and-forth sawing motion. Then turn the cake a bit and cut 1 inch into that portion. Repeat, stopping every few inches to check that you're maintaining a level cut. Score all the way around the cake.

4. Using the scored line as a guide and keeping the knife level, cut toward the center until the cake layer is divided in two [1].

5. If a layer isn't even, shave it slightly to make it level. Slice the remaining layers, if required.

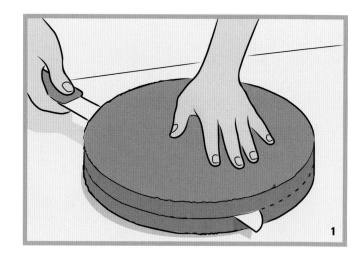

Black Bottom Devil's Food Cake

With its cheesecake topping, this deep, dark cake is a riff on black-bottom cupcakes—chocolate cupcakes with a cheesecake-style filling. The cake can be prepared a day ahead and chilled. It will taste best if it sits at room temperature for a couple of hours before serving. **12 to 16 servings**

Cake

2	cups (packed) dark brown sugar
1¾	cups unbleached all purpose flour
¾	cup natural unsweetened cocoa powder, sifted
2	teaspoons baking soda
1	teaspoon baking powder
¼	teaspoon ground cinnamon
¼	teaspoon salt
1	cup buttermilk
1	cup strong coffee, room temperature
½	cup vegetable oil
2	large eggs

Cheesecake Topping

4	ounces Philadelphia-brand cream cheese, room temperature
2	tablespoons sugar
1	large egg
1	tablespoon unbleached all purpose flour
½	cup mini semisweet chocolate chips

Icing

1¼	cups canned evaporated milk
2	12-ounce packages semisweet chocolate chips
10	ounces Philadelphia-brand cream cheese, room temperature

CAKE: Preheat oven to 350°F. Lightly butter two 9-inch-diameter cake pans with 1½-inch-high sides. Line pan bottoms with parchment paper. Whisk sugar, flour, cocoa, baking soda, baking powder, cinnamon, and salt in large bowl to blend. Add buttermilk, coffee, oil, and eggs and whisk until smooth. Divide batter between prepared pans.

CHEESECAKE TOPPING: Beat cream cheese and sugar in medium bowl to blend. Beat in egg, then flour. Spoon topping over batter in 1 pan (topping will not cover batter completely). Sprinkle chocolate chips over topping.

Place cakes in oven. Bake plain cake until tester inserted into center comes out clean, about 30 minutes. Bake topping-covered cake until center springs back when lightly touched, about 35 minutes. Cool cakes completely in pans on racks, then freeze cakes 3 hours.

ICING: Bring evaporated milk to boil in heavy medium saucepan over high heat. Reduce heat to low. Add chocolate chips and stir until melted and smooth. Cool completely.

Using electric mixer, beat cream cheese in large bowl until fluffy. Gradually beat in chocolate mixture.

Cut around pan sides to loosen cakes. Turn cakes out onto work surface. Peel off parchment. Using serrated knife, cut each cake horizontally in half. Set 1 plain cake layer on platter. Spread ⅔ cup icing over. Top with second plain cake layer. Spread ⅔ cup icing over. Top with third plain cake layer. Spread ⅔ cup icing over. Top with cake layer with cheesecake topping. Spread top and sides of cake with 1⅔ cups icing. Spoon remaining icing into pastry bag fitted with star tip. Pipe icing in rosettes atop cake. Refrigerate until cake is slightly chilled and icing sets, at least 30 minutes.

DO AHEAD: *Can be made 1 day ahead. Cover with cake dome and keep refrigerated. Let cake stand at room temperature 2 hours before serving.*

Devil's Food Cake with Chocolate-Orange Buttercream Frosting

The subtle hint of lavender is a nice accent in this cake. Dried lavender blossoms are available in the spice section of some supermarkets, at natural foods stores, and at some specialty foods stores and farmers' markets, but the blossoms can be omitted, if you prefer. **12 servings**

Cake

4	ounces bittersweet or semisweet chocolate (do not exceed 61% cacao), chopped
1½	cups unbleached all purpose flour
½	cup natural unsweetened cocoa powder
1	teaspoon baking powder
½	teaspoon coarse kosher salt
¼	teaspoon baking soda
½	cup whole milk
½	cup plain whole-milk yogurt
1½	cups (packed) golden brown sugar
¾	cup (1½ sticks) unsalted butter, room temperature
2	teaspoons dried lavender blossoms, finely ground in spice mill (optional)
4	large eggs

Buttercream Frosting

8	ounces bittersweet or semisweet chocolate (do not exceed 61% cacao), chopped
½	cup natural unsweetened cocoa powder
7	tablespoons (or more) water
4	cups powdered sugar, divided
1½	cups (3 sticks) unsalted butter, room temperature
1	tablespoon finely grated orange peel
2	teaspoons vanilla extract
½	teaspoon coarse kosher salt
1	tablespoon Grand Marnier or other orange liqueur
	Chocolate curls

CAKE: Position rack in center of oven and preheat to 325°F. Butter and flour two 9-inch-diameter cake pans with 1½-inch-high sides. Line pan bottoms with parchment paper. Stir chocolate in medium metal bowl set over saucepan of simmering water until melted and smooth. Remove bowl from over water. Cool to barely lukewarm.

Sift flour, cocoa, baking powder, coarse salt, and baking soda into medium bowl. Whisk milk and yogurt in small bowl to blend. Using electric mixer, beat sugar, butter, and lavender (if using) in large bowl until smooth. Beat in eggs 1 at a time. Beat in melted chocolate. Beat in dry ingredients alternately with milk mixture in 3 additions each. Divide batter between prepared pans.

Bake cakes until tester inserted into center comes out clean, about 30 minutes. Cool cakes in pans on racks 15 minutes. Cut around pan sides to loosen cakes. Turn cakes out onto racks; remove parchment and cool completely.

BUTTERCREAM FROSTING: Stir chocolate in medium metal bowl set over saucepan of simmering water until melted and smooth. Remove bowl from over water. Cool until barely lukewarm but still pourable. Combine cocoa and 7 tablespoons water in heavy small saucepan. Stir over medium-low heat until smooth and thick but still pourable, adding more water by teaspoonfuls if necessary to thin. Cool.

Beat ⅓ cup powdered sugar, butter, and orange peel in large bowl to blend. Add melted chocolate, vanilla, and coarse salt; beat until smooth. Beat in cocoa mixture. Gradually add remaining 3⅔ cups powdered sugar and beat until frosting is smooth. Mix in Grand Marnier.

Place 1 cake layer on platter. Spread 1½ cups frosting over. Top with second cake layer. Spread remaining frosting over top and sides of cake, swirling decoratively. Mound chocolate curls in center of cake.

DO AHEAD: *Can be made 1 day ahead. Cover with cake dome and refrigerate. Let cake stand at room temperature 2 hours before serving.*

Chocolate Stout Cake

Stout (a kind of dark beer) has creamy chocolate and coffee notes that lend a mildly sweet flavor to this three-layer cake. Be sure the stout and butter mixture is simmering when the cocoa is added. Whisking the cocoa powder into this simmering mixture actually creates an even more intense chocolate flavor. **12 servings**

Cake

2	cups stout (such as Guinness)
2	cups (4 sticks) unsalted butter, diced
1½	cups unsweetened cocoa powder (preferably Dutch-process)
4	cups unbleached all purpose flour
4	cups sugar
1	tablespoon baking soda
1½	teaspoons salt
4	large eggs
1⅓	cups sour cream

Icing

2	cups heavy whipping cream
1	pound bittersweet or semisweet chocolate (do not exceed 61% cacao), chopped

CAKE: Preheat oven to 350°F. Butter three 8-inch-diameter cake pans with 2-inch-high sides. Line pan bottoms with parchment paper; butter paper. Bring stout and butter to simmer in heavy large saucepan over medium heat, whisking to melt butter. Add cocoa and whisk until mixture is smooth. Cool to lukewarm.

Whisk flour, sugar, baking soda, and salt in large bowl to blend. Using electric mixer, beat eggs and sour cream in another large bowl to blend. Add stout-chocolate mixture to egg mixture and beat just to combine. Add flour mixture and beat 10 to 15 seconds at low speed. Using rubber spatula, gently fold batter until completely combined. Divide batter among prepared pans.

Bake cakes until tester inserted into center comes out clean, about 35 minutes. Cool cakes in pans on racks 10 minutes. Cut around pan sides to loosen cakes. Turn cakes out onto rack, peel off parchment, and cool completely.

ICING: Bring cream to simmer in heavy medium saucepan. Remove from heat. Add chocolate and whisk until melted and smooth. Refrigerate until icing thickens to spreadable consistency, stirring frequently, about 2 hours.

Place 1 cake layer on plate. Spread ⅔ cup icing over. Top with second cake layer. Spread ⅔ cup icing over. Top with third cake layer. Spread remaining icing over top and sides of cake.

Step by Step to Picture-Perfect Frosting

A cake is truly more than the sum of its delicious parts—but a beautiful frosting is key to making a fantastic first impression. Here are some ways to create professional-looking frosted cakes.

1 **PREP:** If the cooled cake layers are domed, use a serrated knife to carefully trim the tops and make them level. Set one cake layer on a cardboard round that is slightly smaller in diameter than the cake so that it's concealed, or set the cake layer on a flat cake plate. A dab of frosting on the cardboard or plate helps anchor the cake.

2 **FILL AND LAYER:** Spread the filling over the cake layer, keeping it half an inch from the edge of the cake [1]; then top with the second cake layer (this allows some wiggle room for the filling to ooze) [2]. It's best to place the bottom layer cut side up and the top layer cut side down; the cut surfaces absorb some of the filling, while the

smooth, flat surface forms a nice shape for the finished cake. Sometimes the top layer slides around, which makes frosting the cake difficult. To solve this, cover the layered cake with plastic and chill it until the filling becomes firm and the top layer is securely set in place.

3 **ADD THE CRUMB COAT:** Spread a thin layer of frosting over the entire cake [3], then chill the cake until the frosting is cold. Don't worry if the cake doesn't look attractive; the crumb coating is simply used to glue any loose cake crumbs to the cake's surface to make it easier to apply the final coating of frosting. (Not all recipes call for this step.)

4 **FROST:** Finally, spread the remaining frosting decoratively over the sides and top of the cake [4]. Setting the cake on a cake turntable or lazy Susan and using a long offset spatula will help you create a perfectly smooth finish.

1

3

2

4

Cappuccino-Chocolate Layer Cake

For more roasted-coffee flavor, instant espresso powder could substitute for the instant coffee powder in both the cake and the frosting. **12 servings**

Coffee Syrup

6	tablespoons water
3	tablespoons sugar
1	tablespoon instant coffee powder

Cake

4	ounces unsweetened chocolate, chopped
2	cups unbleached all purpose flour
1½	teaspoons baking powder
1	teaspoon ground cinnamon
¼	teaspoon salt
1½	cups whole milk
2	teaspoons instant coffee powder
2	cups sugar
½	cup (1 stick) unsalted butter, room temperature
2	large eggs
2	teaspoons vanilla extract
	Fudge Frosting (see recipe)

COFFEE SYRUP: Combine all ingredients in small saucepan. Stir over low heat until sugar and coffee powder dissolve. Let cool.

DO AHEAD: *Can be made 2 days ahead. Cover and chill.*

CAKE: Position rack in center of oven and preheat to 350°F. Butter two 9-inch-diameter cake pans with 2-inch-high sides. Line pan bottoms with waxed paper; butter paper. Dust pans with flour. Stir chocolate in top of double boiler set over simmering water until melted and smooth. Remove from over water.

Sift flour, baking powder, cinnamon, and salt into medium bowl. Stir milk and coffee powder in another medium bowl until coffee dissolves. Using electric mixer, beat sugar and butter in large bowl until well blended. Beat in eggs 1 at a time. Mix in melted chocolate and vanilla. Beat in dry ingredients alternately with milk mixture in 3 additions each. Divide batter between pans.

Bake cakes until tester inserted into center comes out clean, about 35 minutes. Cool cakes in pans on racks 10 minutes. Cut around pan sides to loosen cakes. Turn cakes out onto racks. Peel off paper and cool completely.

Cut each cake horizontally in half. Using bottom of tart pan as aid, transfer 1 cake layer, cut side up, to platter. Brush cake layer with 2 tablespoons coffee syrup. Spread ¾ cup Fudge Frosting over. Repeat layering 2 times, using 1 cake layer, 2 tablespoons syrup, and ¾ cup frosting each time. Top with fourth cake layer, cut side down. Spread remaining frosting over top and sides of cake.

DO AHEAD: *Can be made 1 day ahead. Cover and let stand at room temperature.*

Fudge Frosting

Allow enough time, one to two hours, to chill the frosting so that it's firm enough to spread. **Makes about 4 cups**

¾	cup (1½ sticks) unsalted butter
¾	cup sugar
¾	cup half and half
4	teaspoons instant coffee powder
6	ounces unsweetened chocolate, chopped
4	ounces bittersweet or semisweet chocolate (do not exceed 61% cacao), chopped
1	teaspoon vanilla extract
2½	cups powdered sugar
4	teaspoons ground cinnamon

Combine butter, ¾ cup sugar, half and half, and coffee powder in large saucepan. Stir over medium heat until sugar and coffee powder dissolve and mixture comes to simmer. Remove from heat. Add both chocolates; whisk until melted and smooth. Whisk in vanilla. Transfer chocolate mixture to large bowl. Sift in powdered sugar and cinnamon; whisk to blend. Chill just until firm enough to spread, stirring occasionally, about 1½ hours.

DO AHEAD: *Can be made 1 day ahead. Press plastic wrap onto surface of frosting and keep chilled. Let stand at room temperature until soft enough to spread before using.*

♥♥♥♥ Chocolate Cake with Fleur de Sel–Caramel Filling

This grand four-layer chocolate cake is filled with both chocolate ganache and salted caramel and is worthy of the most celebratory occasion. Fleur de sel, a type of sea salt, is available at some supermarkets, specialty foods stores, and natural foods stores. It is smooth and pure, without any chemical after-taste. For tips on piping the ganache, see page 38. **12 servings**

Caramel Filling

1	cup sugar
¼	cup water
2	tablespoons light corn syrup
½	cup heavy whipping cream
¼	cup (½ stick) unsalted butter, diced
¼	cup crème fraîche or sour cream
½	teaspoon fresh lemon juice
	Large pinch of fine fleur de sel plus additional for assembling

Ganache Filling and Frosting

1½	pounds bittersweet or semisweet chocolate (do not exceed 61% cacao), chopped
3	cups heavy whipping cream

Cake

2	cups sugar
1¾	cups unbleached all purpose flour
¾	cup natural unsweetened cocoa powder
1½	teaspoons baking powder
1½	teaspoons baking soda
1	teaspoon salt
1	cup whole milk
2	large eggs
½	cup (1 stick) unsalted butter, melted, cooled
1	cup hot water
1	tablespoon instant espresso powder or instant coffee powder

1¼	cups almonds, toasted, coarsely chopped, divided

CARAMEL FILLING: Stir sugar, ¼ cup water, and corn syrup in deep medium saucepan over low heat until sugar dissolves. Increase heat to medium; cover pan and cook 4 minutes. Uncover; increase heat to high. Boil without stirring until syrup is deep amber color, occasionally brushing down pan sides with wet pastry brush and swirling pan, about 6 minutes. Remove from heat. Add cream (mixture will bubble vigorously). Whisk in butter, then crème fraîche, lemon juice, and pinch of fleur de sel. Cool caramel completely.

DO AHEAD: *Can be made 3 days ahead. Cover and chill. Bring to room temperature before using.*

GANACHE FILLING AND FROSTING: Place chocolate in large bowl. Bring cream to simmer in medium saucepan. Pour cream over chocolate; let soften 1 minute. Whisk until chocolate is melted and smooth. Cool, then cover and chill overnight.

DO AHEAD: *Can be made 3 days ahead. Keep chilled. Bring to room temperature before using.*

CAKE: Position rack in center of oven and preheat to 350°F. Butter two 9-inch-diameter cake pans with 2-inch-high sides. Line pan bottoms with parchment paper; butter paper and dust pan with flour.

Sift sugar, flour, cocoa, baking powder, baking soda, and salt into large bowl. Add milk, eggs, and melted butter. Using electric mixer, beat at low speed until blended. Increase speed and beat 2 minutes. Stir 1 cup hot water and espresso powder in small bowl to dissolve. Add to batter; beat until blended (batter will be thin). Divide batter between pans (about 3 cups each).

Bake cakes until tester inserted into center comes out clean, about 32 minutes. Cool cakes in pans on racks 10 minutes. Cut around pan sides to loosen cakes; turn out onto racks. Peel off parchment and cool completely.

Using long serrated knife, cut each cake horizontally in half. Place 1 layer on platter; spread ½ cup room-temperature ganache over. Spoon ¾ cup ganache into pastry bag fitted with ¼-inch plain round tip. Pipe ring of ganache around edge of layer. Spread ¼ cup room-temperature caramel filling evenly inside ring. Sprinkle caramel with large pinch of fleur de sel, then 1 tablespoon almonds. Top with second cake layer, ganache, ganache ring, caramel filling, fleur de sel, and almonds. Repeat with third cake layer. Top with fourth cake layer, cut side down. Spread remaining ganache over top and sides of assembled cake. Press remaining almonds onto sides.

DO AHEAD: *Can be made 2 days ahead. Cover with cake dome and chill. Let cake stand at room temperature 1 hour before serving.*

Chocolate Cake with Caramel-Coconut-Almond Filling

This is a delicious version of the classic German chocolate cake. For tips on creating perfect caramel, see page 31. **12 servings**

Cake

4	ounces unsweetened chocolate, chopped
1	cup water
1	tablespoon instant espresso powder or coffee powder
2¼	cups (packed) dark brown sugar
1	cup (2 sticks) unsalted butter, room temperature
3	large eggs
1	teaspoon vanilla extract
2	cups cake flour
2	teaspoons baking soda
1	teaspoon baking powder
½	teaspoon salt
1	cup sour cream

Filling

1	cup sugar
¼	cup water
1	cup heavy whipping cream
1	cup sweetened flaked coconut, toasted
1	cup thinly sliced almonds, toasted

Frosting

½	cup (1 stick) unsalted butter
3	ounces unsweetened chocolate, chopped
½	teaspoon vanilla extract
2	cups powdered sugar, sifted, divided
½	cup sour cream, divided
2	cups sliced almonds, toasted

CAKE: Preheat oven to 350°F. Butter three 9-inch-diameter cake pans with 1½-inch-high sides. Line pan bottoms with waxed paper; butter paper. Combine chocolate, 1 cup water, and espresso powder in heavy small saucepan. Stir over low heat until chocolate melts and mixture is smooth. Remove from heat. Cool completely, stirring occasionally.

Using electric mixer, beat sugar and butter in large bowl until light and fluffy. Beat in eggs 1 at a time. Beat in chocolate mixture and vanilla. Sift flour, baking soda, baking powder, and salt into medium bowl. Beat dry ingredients into butter mixture alternately with sour cream in 3 additions each, beginning with dry ingredients. Divide batter among prepared pans.

Bake cakes until tester inserted into center comes out clean, about 30 minutes. Cool cakes in pans on racks 10 minutes. Cut around pan sides to loosen cakes. Turn cakes out onto racks. Remove waxed paper; cool completely.

FILLING: Combine sugar and ¼ cup water in heavy medium saucepan. Stir over low heat until sugar dissolves. Increase heat to high and boil without stirring until syrup turns deep amber, occasionally brushing down sides of pan with wet pastry brush and swirling pan, about 10 minutes. Remove from heat. Add cream (mixture will bubble vigorously). Place pan over medium-low heat and stir until any caramel bits melt, about 5 minutes. Remove from heat; stir in coconut and almonds. Cool filling until thick enough to spread, stirring occasionally, about 45 minutes.

FROSTING: Stir butter and chocolate in heavy small saucepan over low heat until melted and smooth. Transfer to large bowl. Whisk in vanilla, then 1 cup powdered sugar and ¼ cup sour cream. Whisk in remaining 1 cup powdered sugar and ¼ cup sour cream.

Place 1 cake layer on platter. Spread half of filling evenly over, leaving ½-inch plain border. Top with second cake layer. Spread remaining filling over, leaving ½-inch plain border. Top with remaining cake layer. Spread frosting over top and sides of cake. Press almonds onto sides of cake. Using small spatula, swirl frosting decoratively over top of cake.

DO AHEAD: *Can be made 1 day ahead. Cover with cake dome; store at room temperature.*

Black Pearl Layer Cake

This Asian-influenced creation is named after a popular chocolate truffle by Vosges Haut-Chocolat. The unexpected combination of wasabi and black sesame seeds that infuses the truffle also flavors this inspired cake. You'll find wasabi powder and black sesame seeds in the Asian foods section of some supermarkets, at specialty foods stores, and at Asian and Indian markets.

10 to 12 servings

Black Pearl Ganache

6	ounces bittersweet or semisweet chocolate (do not exceed 61% cacao), chopped
¾	cup heavy whipping cream
1	teaspoon ground ginger
½	teaspoon wasabi powder
2	tablespoons black sesame seeds
1	tablespoon corn syrup
2	tablespoons (¼ stick) unsalted butter, room temperature

Ginger Syrup

1	cup water
½	cup sugar
⅓	cup matchstick-size strips peeled fresh ginger
1	vanilla bean, split lengthwise

Cake

2	cups boiling water
1	cup natural unsweetened cocoa powder
2¾	cups unbleached all purpose flour
2	teaspoons baking soda
½	teaspoon baking powder
½	teaspoon salt
2¼	cups sugar
1	cup (2 sticks) unsalted butter, room temperature
4	large eggs
1	tablespoon vanilla extract

Whipped Cream Frosting

2	cups chilled heavy whipping cream
6	tablespoons powdered sugar
½	teaspoon vanilla extract
½	teaspoon ground ginger
	Additional black sesame seeds

BLACK PEARL GANACHE: Place chocolate in medium bowl. Bring cream, ginger, and wasabi to boil in small saucepan. Pour hot cream mixture over chocolate; cover with plastic wrap and let stand 5 minutes. Whisk cream and chocolate until smooth. Mix sesame seeds and corn syrup in small bowl to coat; stir into chocolate mixture. Let cool to lukewarm. Whisk in butter. Cover and let stand at room temperature overnight to set.

GINGER SYRUP: Place 1 cup water, sugar, and ginger in small saucepan. Scrape in seeds from vanilla bean; add bean. Bring to simmer over medium heat, stirring until sugar dissolves. Simmer 2 minutes; remove from heat. Let stand at room temperature 1 hour for flavors to blend. Strain syrup into small bowl. Chop ginger; place in another small bowl.

DO AHEAD: *Can be made 1 day ahead. Cover ginger and syrup and chill.*

CAKE: Preheat oven to 350°F. Butter and flour three 8-inch-diameter cake pans with 2-inch-high sides. Line pan bottoms with parchment paper.

Whisk 2 cups boiling water, cocoa, and reserved chopped ginger in medium heatproof bowl to blend. Whisk flour, baking soda, baking powder, and salt in large bowl to blend. Using electric mixer, beat sugar and butter in another large bowl until fluffy, about 1 minute. Beat in eggs 1 at a time, then vanilla. Beat in flour mixture in 4 additions alternately with cocoa mixture in 3 additions. Divide batter among prepared pans; smooth tops.

Bake cakes until tester inserted into center comes out clean, about 30 minutes. Cool in pans 5 minutes. Turn cakes out onto racks; cool completely.

DO AHEAD: *Can be made 1 day ahead. Cover with plastic wrap and store at room temperature.*

WHIPPED CREAM FROSTING: Using electric mixer, beat cream in large bowl until soft peaks form. Add sugar, vanilla, and ginger. Beat until stiff peaks form.

Using long serrated knife, trim rounded tops off cakes to create flat surface. Place 1 cake layer, cut side up, on plate. Brush top with ⅓ cup ginger syrup. Spread half of ganache over. Top with second layer, cut side up. Brush with ⅓ cup syrup; spread remaining ganache over. Top with third cake layer. Brush with remaining syrup. Spread whipped cream frosting over top and sides of cake. Sprinkle black sesame seeds over. Refrigerate until ganache is set, about 4 hours. Let stand at room temperature 30 minutes before serving.

DO AHEAD: *Can be made 1 day ahead. Keep refrigerated.*

Chocolate–Peanut Butter Cake with Cream Cheese and Butterfinger Frosting

The truffle-like filling for this decadent cake needs to chill overnight to thicken, so make it one day before you assemble the cake. Old-fashioned natural peanut butter is key to this recipe, so don't use anything else. Since the old-fashioned variety tends to separate, be sure to stir it until well blended before using.
12 servings

Filling

2¼	cups heavy whipping cream
½	cup (packed) golden brown sugar
12	ounces bittersweet or semisweet chocolate (do not exceed 61% cacao), chopped
½	cup old-fashioned (natural) chunky peanut butter

Cake

2½	cups unbleached all purpose flour
1	teaspoon baking powder
1	teaspoon baking soda
½	teaspoon salt
10	tablespoons (1¼ sticks) unsalted butter, room temperature
½	cup old-fashioned (natural) chunky peanut butter
1	pound golden brown sugar
4	large eggs
1	teaspoon vanilla extract
1	cup buttermilk

Frosting

12	ounces Philadelphia-brand cream cheese, room temperature
2	cups powdered sugar, divided
6	tablespoons (¾ stick) unsalted butter, room temperature
1	teaspoon vanilla extract
¾	cup chilled heavy whipping cream
	Butterfinger candy bars, coarsely chopped
	Glazed peanuts

FILLING: Bring cream and sugar to simmer in medium saucepan, whisking to dissolve sugar. Remove from heat. Add chocolate; let stand 1 minute. Whisk until melted and smooth. Whisk in peanut butter. Chill uncovered overnight.

CAKE: Preheat oven to 350°F. Butter three 9-inch-diameter cake pans with 1½-inch-high sides. Line pan bottoms with parchment paper. Sift flour, baking powder, baking soda, and salt into medium bowl. Using electric mixer, beat butter and peanut butter in large bowl until blended. Beat in sugar. Beat in eggs 1 at a time, then vanilla. At low speed, beat in flour mixture in 4 additions alternately with buttermilk in 3 additions. Divide batter among prepared pans; smooth tops.

Bake cakes until tester inserted into center comes out clean, about 25 minutes. Cool cakes in pans on racks 5 minutes. Cut around pan sides to loosen cakes. Turn cakes out onto racks; peel off parchment. Cool cakes completely.

FROSTING: Using electric mixer, beat cream cheese, 1¼ cups sugar, butter, and vanilla in large bowl to blend. Whisk cream and remaining ¾ cup sugar in medium bowl until medium-firm peaks form. Fold cream mixture into cream cheese mixture in 3 additions; chill frosting until firm but spreadable, about 1 hour.

Place 1 cake layer, bottom side up, on 9-inch-diameter tart pan bottom. Spread half of filling over. Place second cake layer, bottom side up, on work surface; spread remaining filling over and place, filling side up, atop first layer. Top with remaining cake layer, bottom side up. Spread frosting over top and sides of cake.

DO AHEAD: *Can be made 1 day ahead. Cover with cake dome; chill. Let stand at room temperature 2 hours before continuing.*

Press candy and peanuts onto top of cake.

More to Try

You can use the cake filling to make truffles by rolling the chilled mixture into balls and coating them with finely chopped roasted peanuts or unsweetened cocoa powder.

Coconut-Chocolate Marjolaine

Multiple layers of soft coconut meringue and a dark chocolate and rum ganache give a tropical spin to the classic French gâteau. At 90°F, the melted ganache is the perfect consistency for coating the marjolaine, so use an instant-read thermometer to gauge it just right. Two types of unsweetened coconut are used here: finely shredded coconut for the meringue layers and shaved coconut, sometimes called coconut chips, for the garnish. Both are available at some supermarkets and at many natural foods stores. **8 servings**

Ganache
4	ounces bittersweet or semisweet chocolate (do not exceed 61% cacao), chopped
1	cup heavy whipping cream
1	tablespoon dark rum

Meringue
1½	cups unsweetened shredded coconut (about 4½ ounces)
⅔	cup sugar, divided
2	tablespoons unbleached all purpose flour
¼	teaspoon salt
6	large egg whites, room temperature
½	teaspoon cream of tartar

Glaze
12	ounces bittersweet or semisweet chocolate (do not exceed 61% cacao), chopped
1	cup heavy whipping cream
2	tablespoons dark rum
1	cup coconut shavings, lightly toasted

GANACHE: Place chocolate in medium metal bowl. Bring cream to simmer in small saucepan. Pour cream over chocolate; whisk until chocolate is melted and smooth. Whisk in rum. Cover and chill at least 6 hours.

DO AHEAD: *Can be made 2 days ahead. Keep chilled.*

MERINGUE: Position rack in center of oven and preheat to 325°F. Line 17x11x1-inch rimmed baking sheet with parchment paper. Mix shredded coconut, ⅓ cup sugar, flour, and salt in medium bowl. Using electric mixer, beat egg whites and cream of tartar in large bowl until soft peaks form. Gradually add remaining ⅓ cup sugar; beat until stiff but not dry. Fold coconut mixture into meringue just until incorporated. Spread meringue evenly over parchment on prepared sheet, covering completely. Bake until light golden and just springy to touch, about 20 minutes (meringue will be soft). Cool completely on baking sheet.

DO AHEAD: *Can be made 1 day ahead. Cover tightly with foil; store at room temperature.*

GLAZE: Place chocolate in medium metal bowl. Bring cream to simmer in small saucepan. Pour cream over chocolate; whisk until chocolate is melted and smooth. Whisk in rum. Let glaze stand at room temperature until thickened and spreadable, about 1 hour.

Place sheet of waxed paper on work surface. Cut around edges of meringue to loosen. Invert meringue onto waxed paper. Peel off parchment. Cut meringue crosswise in half, then cut lengthwise in thirds, forming six 8½x3⅔-inch rectangles. Cut piece of cardboard into 8½x3⅔-inch rectangle; cover cardboard with foil. Place 1 meringue rectangle on cardboard.

Using electric mixer, beat ganache just until lighter in color and firm enough to spread. Using offset spatula, spread 3 generous tablespoons ganache evenly over meringue. Top with second meringue rectangle; press to adhere. Spread 3 tablespoons ganache over. Repeat procedure with 3 more meringue rectangles and remaining ganache. Top with remaining meringue rectangle. Chill cake until ganache is firm, about 1 hour.

Place cake on rack set over rimmed baking sheet. Spread top and sides of cake with some of glaze. Chill 30 minutes.

Place bowl with remaining glaze in skillet of barely simmering water and rewarm just until instant-read thermometer inserted into glaze registers 90°F. Pour glaze over top of cake, allowing glaze to drip down sides, spreading evenly over sides. Using spatula, scoop up excess glaze on sheet; spread over sides of cake to cover. Press toasted coconut shavings onto glaze over bottom 1 inch of cake. Transfer cake to platter. Chill until glaze is set, at least 1 hour.

DO AHEAD: *Can be made 1 day ahead. Cover and keep chilled. Let cake stand at room temperature 30 minutes before serving.*

Using serrated knife, cut cake crosswise into slices and serve.

Pecan Praline Cake

This luscious southern-style cake features flavors reminiscent of Louisiana pralines (brown sugar–pecan confections). **12 servings**

Cake

2½	**cups cake flour**
1½	**teaspoons baking powder**
½	**teaspoon salt**
2	**cups sugar**
1	**cup (2 sticks) unsalted butter, room temperature**
4	**large eggs**
2	**teaspoons vanilla extract**
1	**cup whole milk**
1½	**cups chopped pecans**

Syrup

3	**tablespoons water**
3	**tablespoons sugar**
1	**tablespoon bourbon**

Vanilla Cream Cheese Frosting (see recipe)
Pecan Praline Topping (see recipe)

CAKE: Position rack in center of oven and preheat to 350°F. Butter two 9-inch-diameter cake pans with 2-inch-high sides. Line pan bottoms with waxed paper; butter paper. Whisk flour, baking powder, and salt in medium bowl to blend. Using electric mixer, beat sugar and butter in large bowl until fluffy. Beat in eggs 1 at a time, then vanilla. Beat in dry ingredients in 3 additions alternately with milk in 2 additions. Stir in pecans. Divide batter between prepared pans.

Bake cakes until tester inserted into center comes out clean and cakes begin to pull away from pan sides, about 35 minutes. Cool cakes in pans on racks 10 minutes. Cut around pan sides to loosen cakes. Turn cakes out onto racks; peel off waxed paper. Cool cakes completely.

DO AHEAD: *Can be made 1 day ahead. Wrap in foil and store at room temperature.*

SYRUP: Stir 3 tablespoons water and sugar in small saucepan over medium heat until sugar dissolves and mixture comes to simmer. Remove from heat. Stir in bourbon. Cool.

Place 1 cake layer, flat side up, on platter. Brush some of syrup over. Spread 1 cup Vanilla Cream Cheese Frosting over. Top with second cake layer, flat side up. Brush top and sides of cake with remaining syrup. Spread remaining frosting over top and sides of cake. Arrange Pecan Praline Topping all over top of cake, mounding slightly in center.

DO AHEAD: *Can be made 1 day ahead. Cover with cake dome and refrigerate. Let stand at room temperature 1 hour before serving.*

Vanilla Cream Cheese Frosting

Using slightly softened, room-temperature butter ensures easier mixing and a smoother frosting. **Makes about 3¼ cups**

12	**ounces Philadelphia-brand cream cheese, room temperature**
½	**cup (1 stick) unsalted butter, room temperature**
2	**teaspoons vanilla extract**
4	**cups powdered sugar**

Using electric mixer, beat cream cheese, butter, and vanilla in large bowl until smooth. Beat in sugar 1 cup at a time, scraping down bowl occasionally.

Pecan Praline Topping

These crunchy brown-sugar pecans are also delicious on their own. **Makes about 1½ cups**

1	large egg white, room temperature
1	tablespoon water
½	cup (packed) golden brown sugar
1½	cups pecan halves

Preheat oven to 300°F. Butter rimmed baking sheet. Using fork, beat egg white and 1 tablespoon water in medium bowl until foamy. Add sugar and stir until sugar dissolves. Add pecan halves and toss to coat. Spread pecan mixture on prepared baking sheet (some egg white mixture will flow out onto baking sheet). Bake until nuts are deep brown and crisp, stirring occasionally, about 25 minutes. Remove from oven; stir to loosen nuts from baking sheet. Cool nuts completely on sheet.

DO AHEAD: *Can be made 3 days ahead. Store airtight at room temperature.*

Can This Cake Be Saved?

Even professional pastry chefs run into sticky situations when making cakes. Here are some tricks to fix the peskiest problems.

DRY CAKES

- Split the cake layers in half horizontally, then brush them with simple syrup (equal parts sugar and water, heated and stirred until the sugar dissolves). If cupcakes come out too dry or a sheet cake is dry, poke holes in the top, then brush with the simple syrup. Once the syrup is absorbed, assemble and fill the cake layers and apply the frosting. Keep the cakes under a cake dome to ensure they don't dry out any further.
- Serve slices of cake with a vanilla custard sauce (crème anglaise), caramel sauce, chocolate sauce, or ice cream.
- Cut the cake into cubes and layer it in parfait glasses with whipped cream, lemon curd, raspberry sauce, and fresh berries.

FALLEN OR LUMPY CAKES

- Use a serrated knife to even out the surface of the cake.
- Make extra frosting and use it to create a smooth surface.
- If the cake is completely beyond hope, cut it into squares and use them to make sundaes or parfaits.

IMPERFECTLY FROSTED CAKES

- Use chopped toasted nuts, sweetened flaked coconut, coarsely crushed cookies, or cake crumbs to coat the sides of the cake and mask frosting flaws. Select the coatings that pair best with the flavors of your cake.
- Make a chocolate band (see the Chocolate Panna Cotta Layer Cake on page 122–23) to wrap around the cake and hide any imperfections.
- If the top of the frosted cake looks sparse, cover it with whipped cream and top it with assorted fresh berries just before serving.

♟♟♟ Raspberry–Whipped Cream Truffle Cake

The framboise in the filling has a beautiful raspberry aroma and a nice kick, but the cake also tastes fine without it. You'll find framboise at liquor stores and some specialty foods stores. **12 servings**

Glaze

1	cup heavy whipping cream
¼	cup (½ stick) unsalted butter, diced
2	tablespoons sugar
12	ounces bittersweet or semisweet chocolate (do not exceed 61% cacao), chopped
1	teaspoon vanilla extract

Cake

2	ounces unsweetened chocolate, chopped
2	cups cake flour
⅔	cup natural unsweetened cocoa powder
1	teaspoon baking soda
½	teaspoon salt
2	cups sugar
½	cup (1 stick) unsalted butter, room temperature
3	large eggs
1½	teaspoons vanilla extract
1¼	cups buttermilk

Filling

1¾	cups plus 2 tablespoons chilled heavy whipping cream
3	tablespoons powdered sugar
2	teaspoons framboise (clear raspberry brandy; optional)
¾	teaspoon vanilla extract
2	cups fresh raspberries or frozen unsweetened raspberries, thawed, drained

Additional fresh raspberries (optional)

GLAZE: Combine cream, butter, and sugar in heavy large saucepan. Stir over medium heat until butter melts, sugar dissolves, and mixture comes to simmer. Remove from heat. Add chocolate and vanilla. Stir until chocolate melts and glaze is smooth. Let stand until thick enough to spread, stirring occasionally, about 1 hour.

DO AHEAD: *Can be made 1 week ahead. Cover and refrigerate. Before using, whisk over low heat just until spreadable.*

CAKE: Preheat oven to 350°F. Butter two 9-inch-diameter cake pans with 2-inch-high sides. Line pan bottoms with waxed paper; butter paper. Stir chocolate in top of double boiler set over simmering water until melted. Remove from over water.

Sift flour, cocoa, baking soda, and salt into medium bowl. Using electric mixer, beat sugar and butter in large bowl until well blended. Beat in eggs 1 at a time, occasionally scraping down sides of bowl. Beat in melted chocolate and vanilla. Beat in dry ingredients alternately with buttermilk in 3 additions each. Divide batter between prepared pans.

Bake cakes until tester inserted into center comes out clean, about 35 minutes. Cool cakes in pans on racks 10 minutes. Cut around pan sides to loosen cakes. Turn cakes out onto racks; peel off waxed paper. Cool cakes completely.

DO AHEAD: *Can be made 1 day ahead. Wrap and store at room temperature.*

FILLING: Using electric mixer, beat cream, powdered sugar, framboise (if using), and vanilla in large bowl until firm peaks form. Transfer 1½ cups whipped cream mixture to small bowl and chill. Fold raspberries into remaining whipped cream mixture for filling.

Using long serrated knife, cut each cake layer horizontally in half. Using large tart pan bottom as aid, transfer 1 layer to platter. Slide waxed paper strips under edges of cake. Spread ⅔ cup chocolate glaze over cake. Spread half of raspberry whipped cream over. Place second cake layer on work surface. Spread ⅔ cup glaze, then remaining raspberry cream over. Place atop first layer, using tart pan bottom as aid. Top with third cake layer, cut side down, pressing lightly to adhere (reserve fourth layer for another use). Smooth filling at edges of cake. Spread thin layer of glaze over sides of cake. Chill until glaze sets, about 10 minutes.

Spread remaining glaze over sides of cake. Spread or pipe reserved 1½ cups whipped cream mixture over top of cake. Garnish with additional berries, if desired. Gently pull waxed paper strips from under cake. Cover cake with cake dome; chill at least 1 hour and up to 8 hours.

Sour Cream Layer Cake with Pecan Brittle

With additions like sour cream and grated chocolate, a brown sugar frosting, and a simple crunchy pecan brittle, a box of cake mix is transformed into some-thing special. During the brittle-making process, the syrup will begin to harden immediately once it's removed from the heat, so be sure to have the baking sheet prepared and a metal offset spatula or knife at the ready to spread the syrup. **10 to 12 servings**

Pecan Brittle

	Nonstick vegetable oil spray
¾	cup sugar
¼	cup water
⅛	teaspoon cream of tartar
¾	cup pecan halves, toasted, coarsely chopped

Cake

	Nonstick vegetable oil spray
1	18.25-ounce box yellow cake mix
4	large eggs
1	cup sour cream
⅓	cup vegetable oil
½	teaspoon vanilla extract
½	teaspoon almond extract
2	ounces bittersweet or semisweet chocolate, coarsely grated

Frosting

½	cup (packed) dark brown sugar
3	tablespoons water
¼	cup heavy whipping cream
6	cups (about) powdered sugar, divided
1	cup (2 sticks) unsalted butter, room temperature

PECAN BRITTLE: Spray rimmed baking sheet with nonstick spray. Combine sugar, ¼ cup water, and cream of tartar in heavy small saucepan. Stir over medium-low heat until sugar dissolves. Increase heat and boil without stirring until syrup is deep amber color, occasionally brushing down sides of pan with wet pastry brush and swirling pan, about 9 minutes. Add pecans and swirl to blend. Pour out onto prepared baking sheet; spread evenly. Cool brittle completely. Cut 3 large pieces of brittle (each about 1½ inches). Cut remaining brittle into ⅓-inch pieces.

DO AHEAD: *Can be made 1 week ahead. Store airtight at room temperature.*

CAKE: Preheat oven to 350°F. Spray two 9-inch-diameter cake pans with 1½-inch-high sides with nonstick spray. Line pan bottoms with waxed paper. Combine cake mix, eggs, sour cream, oil, vanilla, and almond extract in large bowl. Using electric mixer, beat mixture until well blended, about 3 minutes; fold in grated chocolate. Divide batter between prepared pans.

Bake cakes until brown on top and tester inserted into center comes out clean, about 30 minutes. Cool cakes in pans on racks 10 minutes. Cut around pan sides to loosen cakes. Turn cakes out onto racks. Peel off paper and cool completely.

FROSTING: Combine brown sugar and 3 tablespoons water in heavy small saucepan. Stir over medium-low heat until sugar dissolves. Increase heat; boil until slightly thickened, about 3 minutes. Remove from heat; cool 5 minutes. Whisk in cream. Using electric mixer, beat 3 cups powdered sugar and butter in large bowl until well blended. Beat in brown sugar mixture. Beat in enough remaining powdered sugar, ½ cup at a time, to form frosting that is thick enough to spread.

Place 1 cake layer, flat side up, on platter. Spread 1 cup frosting over. Sprinkle with ½ cup small brittle pieces; press into frosting. Top with second cake layer, flat side down. Spread remaining frosting over top and sides of cake. Stand large brittle pieces in center of cake. Arrange smaller brittle pieces in 1-inch-wide border around top edge of cake.

DO AHEAD: *Can be made 1 day ahead. Cover with cake dome and refrigerate. Let stand at room temperature 1 hour before serving.*

Tres Leches Cake

Tres leches ("three milks") cake, popular in Mexico, gets its name from the evaporated milk, sweetened condensed milk, and heavy cream that soak the cake. Temperature is the key to soaking this cake perfectly: The cake should be completely cooled, but the milk syrup must be lukewarm when it's drizzled and smoothed over each layer. The warmth of the syrup allows it to penetrate the cake thoroughly. **8 servings**

Cake

1½	cups cake flour
1½	teaspoons baking powder
½	teaspoon salt
1	cup sugar
½	cup (1 stick) unsalted butter, room temperature
2	large eggs
1	teaspoon vanilla extract
¾	cup canned evaporated milk

Caramel Milk Syrup

½	cup sugar
2	tablespoons water
½	cup heavy whipping cream
½	cup canned sweetened condensed milk
¼	cup canned evaporated milk

Frosting and Filling

1¾	cups chilled heavy whipping cream
1½	teaspoons vanilla extract
3	1-pint containers strawberries, hulled, divided
1	½-pint container blackberries

CAKE: Preheat oven to 350°F. Butter 9-inch-diameter cake pan with 2-inch-high sides. Line pan bottom with parchment paper. Butter and flour parchment. Whisk flour, baking powder, and salt in medium bowl to blend. Using electric mixer, beat sugar and butter in large bowl until light and fluffy. Beat in eggs 1 at a time, then vanilla. Beat in dry ingredients alternately with evaporated milk in 3 additions each. Transfer batter to prepared pan; smooth top.

Bake cake until golden and tester inserted into center comes out clean, about 38 minutes. Cool in pan on rack 10 minutes. Cut around pan sides to loosen cake. Cool cake in pan on rack 15 minutes longer. Turn cake out onto rack; remove parchment and cool completely.

CARAMEL MILK SYRUP: Stir sugar and 2 tablespoons water in heavy small saucepan over medium heat until sugar dissolves, occasionally brushing down sides of pan with wet pastry brush. Increase heat and boil without stirring until syrup is deep amber color, occasionally brushing down sides of pan with wet pastry brush and swirling pan, about 12 minutes. Remove pan from heat. Immediately whisk in cream (mixture will bubble vigorously). Whisk in sweetened condensed milk and evaporated milk. Cool to lukewarm.

DO AHEAD: *Cake and caramel milk syrup can be made 1 day ahead. Wrap cake airtight in plastic wrap and store at room temperature. Cover and refrigerate milk syrup, then reheat to lukewarm before using.*

Using long serrated knife, cut cake horizontally in half. Place 1 cake layer, cut side up, on cake plate. Drizzle ⅔ cup lukewarm caramel milk syrup over. Using small offset spatula, spread syrup to cover completely. Let stand 5 minutes.

FROSTING AND FILLING: Whisk cream and vanilla in large bowl until medium peaks form. Spread 1 cup whipped cream mixture over syrup on cake layer. Top with second cake layer, cut side up. Drizzle remaining milk syrup over second layer, spreading with spatula to cover completely. Let stand 5 minutes. Spread remaining whipped cream over top and sides of cake. Decorate top of cake with half of strawberries and all blackberries.

DO AHEAD: *Can be made 4 hours ahead. Cover with cake dome and refrigerate. Let stand at room temperature 30 minutes before serving.*

Slice remaining strawberries. Cut cake into wedges; spoon sliced strawberries alongside each wedge and serve.

Banana Layer Cake with Caramel Cream and Sea Salt–Roasted Pecans

The caramel sauce for the filling is made with brown sugar instead of white sugar, so it has a golden caramel color right off the bat, but it won't have rich, deep caramel flavor until it is cooked to the right temperature. Use a candy thermometer or deep-fry thermometer to ensure that it reaches 218°F. **10 to 12 servings**

Cake

2½	cups unbleached all purpose flour
1	tablespoon baking powder
½	teaspoon (generous) fine sea salt
2½	cups sugar, divided
¾	cup (1½ sticks) unsalted butter, room temperature
6	large eggs
1	cup plus 2 tablespoons buttermilk
2	small ripe bananas, peeled, cut into ¼-inch cubes (about 1½ cups)

Banana-Caramel Cream

1½	cups (packed) golden brown sugar
1	small ripe banana, peeled, cut into 1-inch pieces
3	tablespoons unsalted butter, room temperature
3¾	cups chilled heavy whipping cream, divided
4½	teaspoons fresh lime juice, divided
4½	teaspoons dark rum, divided

Sea Salt–Roasted Pecans (see recipe)

CAKE: Preheat oven to 350°F. Butter and flour two 9-inch-diameter cake pans with 1½-inch-high sides. Sift flour, baking powder, and sea salt into medium bowl. Beat 1 cup sugar and butter in large bowl until well blended. Add 2 eggs; beat until blended. Beat dry ingredients into butter mixture in 4 additions alternately with buttermilk in 3 additions. Beat remaining 4 eggs and remaining 1½ cups sugar in medium bowl until mixture is thick and pale in color, about 4 minutes. Fold egg mixture into batter. Fold in bananas. Divide batter between prepared pans (about 3½ cups for each).

Bake cakes until tester inserted into center comes out clean, about 35 minutes. Cool cakes in pans on racks 15 minutes. Cut around pan sides to loosen cakes. Turn cakes out onto racks; cool completely.

DO AHEAD: *Can be made 1 day ahead. Wrap in foil; store at room temperature.*

BANANA-CARAMEL CREAM: Combine sugar, banana, and butter in processor; blend until smooth. Add 1½ cups cream; process to blend. Transfer to heavy medium saucepan. Whisk over medium heat until sugar dissolves and mixture comes to boil. Attach candy thermometer to side of pan; cook without stirring or swirling pan until thermometer registers 218°F, about 10 minutes. Pour caramel into medium bowl. Cool to room temperature, whisking occasionally.

Whisk remaining 2¼ cups cream in large bowl until cream mounds softly. Gradually fold in cooled caramel mixture. Chill until caramel cream is firm enough to spread, about 3 hours.

Cut each cake horizontally into 2 layers. Place 1 layer, cut side up, on platter. Drizzle 1½ teaspoons lime juice and 1½ teaspoons rum over. Spread 1¼ cups caramel cream over. Top with second cake layer. Drizzle 1½ teaspoons lime juice and 1½ teaspoons rum over. Spread 1½ cups caramel cream over. Repeat with third cake layer, lime juice, rum, and caramel cream. Top with fourth cake layer, cut side down; spread remaining caramel cream over top. Scatter Sea Salt–Roasted Pecans over top of cake.

DO AHEAD: *Can be made 1 day ahead. Cover with cake dome and refrigerate.*

Sea Salt–Roasted Pecans

A simple recipe with endless uses—these pecans would be delicious tossed into salads, crumbled atop grilled fish, or sprinkled over hot fudge sundaes. The melted butter adds wonderful flavor and helps the sea salt cling to the nuts; be sure to use unsalted butter to keep the salty flavor in perfect balance. **Makes 2 cups**

2	cups pecan halves
3	tablespoons unsalted butter, melted
1¼	teaspoons fine sea salt

Preheat oven to 325°F. Toss pecans and melted butter in medium bowl to coat. Add sea salt and toss. Spread pecans in single layer on rimmed baking sheet. Bake pecans until fragrant and slightly darkened in color, stirring occasionally, about 15 minutes. Cool pecans on sheet.

DO AHEAD: *Can be made 2 days ahead. Store airtight at room temperature. Before using, rewarm in 350°F oven 5 minutes, then cool.*

Triple-Ginger Layer Cake

Crystallized ginger in the moist cake, the frosting, and the garnish lends lively flavor that's enhanced with ground ginger and cinnamon. Crystallized ginger is sometimes labeled candied ginger. It can be found in the spice aisle or Asian foods section of most supermarkets, or in the bulk section of natural foods stores. It should be tender and chewy with a fresh coating of sugar. **8 to 10 servings**

Cake

	Nonstick vegetable oil spray
3	cups cake flour, sifted
1	cup finely chopped crystallized ginger (about 6 ounces)
2	teaspoons ground ginger
1	teaspoon ground cinnamon
1	teaspoon baking soda
¼	teaspoon salt
¾	cup (1½ sticks) unsalted butter, room temperature
¾	cup (packed) golden brown sugar
2	large eggs
1	cup plus 2 tablespoons buttermilk

Frosting

2	8-ounce packages Philadelphia-brand cream cheese, room temperature
½	cup (1 stick) unsalted butter, room temperature
¾	cup (packed) golden brown sugar
⅔	cup powdered sugar
½	teaspoon ground cinnamon
¼	teaspoon ground ginger
¼	teaspoon vanilla extract
½	cup finely chopped crystallized ginger (about 3 ounces), divided

{ Technique Tip: **Cover Up**
Don't have a cake dome? Invert a bowl or pot large enough to cover the cake without touching it. }

CAKE: Preheat oven to 350°F. Spray two 8-inch-diameter cake pans with 2-inch-high sides with nonstick spray. Line pan bottoms with parchment paper. Whisk flour, crystallized ginger, ground ginger, cinnamon, baking soda, and salt in medium bowl to blend, separating ginger pieces. Using electric mixer, beat butter and sugar in large bowl until light and fluffy. Beat in eggs 1 at a time. Beat in dry ingredients alternately with buttermilk in 3 additions each, occasionally scraping down sides of bowl. Divide batter between prepared pans.

Bake cakes until tester inserted into center comes out clean, about 30 minutes. Cool cakes in pans on racks 10 minutes. Cut around pan sides to loosen cakes. Turn cakes out onto racks, peel off parchment, and cool completely.

FROSTING: Using electric mixer, beat cream cheese and butter in large bowl until fluffy. Add brown sugar, powdered sugar, cinnamon, ground ginger, and vanilla; beat until well blended. Mix in ¼ cup crystallized ginger.

Place 1 cake layer on platter. Spread 1 cup frosting over. Top with second cake layer. Spread remaining frosting over top and sides of cake. Sprinkle remaining ¼ cup crystallized ginger decoratively atop cake.

DO AHEAD: *Can be made 1 day ahead. Cover with cake dome and refrigerate. Let stand at room temperature 2 hours before serving.*

Ginger-Lime Coconut Cake with Marshmallow Frosting

A ginger-scented lime curd fills this buttermilk cake. For this recipe, be sure to sift the flour before measuring it. Since this cake is four layers tall, you'll need 3 or 4 bamboo skewers to help hold the layers in place as you frost the cake.

10 to 12 servings

Ginger-Lime Curd

3	large eggs
3	large egg yolks
½	cup sugar
½	cup fresh lime juice
¼	cup finely grated lime peel (from about 12 limes)
1	tablespoon grated peeled fresh ginger
	Pinch of salt
6	tablespoons (¾ stick) unsalted butter, cut into pieces, room temperature

Cake

5	cups sifted cake flour (sifted, then measured)
1	teaspoon baking soda
1	teaspoon salt
1½	cups (3 sticks) unsalted butter, room temperature
3	cups sugar
8	large eggs
2	cups buttermilk, room temperature

Frosting

1½	cups sugar
2	large egg whites
⅓	cup water
2	teaspoons light corn syrup
¼	teaspoon cream of tartar
1	teaspoon vanilla extract
1	7-ounce package sweetened flaked coconut

GINGER-LIME CURD: Whisk eggs, egg yolks, sugar, lime juice, lime peel, ginger, and salt in large metal bowl to blend. Place bowl over saucepan of barely simmering water and whisk constantly until curd thickens, about 8 minutes. Remove bowl from over water; whisk butter into hot curd. Strain curd through fine strainer set over bowl; discard solids in strainer. Press plastic wrap directly onto surface of curd; chill overnight.

DO AHEAD: *Can be made 2 days ahead. Keep refrigerated.*

CAKE: Position 1 rack in top third and 1 rack in bottom third of oven and preheat to 350°F. Butter four 9-inch-diameter cake pans with 1½-inch-high sides. Line pan bottoms with parchment paper. Butter parchment; dust with flour. Sift flour, baking soda, and salt into large bowl. Using electric mixer, beat butter in another large bowl until smooth. Gradually add sugar and beat until well blended, about 5 minutes. Beat in eggs 1 at a time, scraping down sides of bowl often. Beat in flour mixture in 3 additions alternately with buttermilk in 2 additions. Divide batter among prepared pans.

Place 2 cake pans on upper rack of oven and 2 pans on lower rack. Bake cakes until golden and tester inserted into center comes out clean, reversing pans after 15 minutes, about 30 minutes total. Cool cakes in pans on racks 10 minutes. Turn cakes out onto racks; peel off parchment. Cool cakes completely.

Place 3 cake layers on work surface. Spread ⅓ of ginger-lime curd (about ½ cup) over each, leaving ½-inch plain border at edge. Let cake layers stand 10 minutes. Stack cake layers, curd side up, on platter. Top with fourth cake layer. Insert 3 or 4 bamboo skewers from top to bottom into cake to hold stacked layers in place while preparing frosting.

FROSTING: Whisk sugar, egg whites, ⅓ cup water, corn syrup, and cream of tartar in large metal bowl to blend. Set bowl over saucepan of barely simmering water. Using handheld electric mixer, beat at medium speed until mixture resembles soft marshmallow fluff, about 4 minutes. Increase mixer speed to high and beat until mixture is very thick, about 3 minutes longer. Remove bowl from over water. Add vanilla and continue beating until marshmallow frosting is completely cool, about 5 minutes.

Spread marshmallow frosting thinly over top and sides of cake. Remove bamboo skewers. Press flaked coconut into marshmallow frosting on top and sides of cake.

DO AHEAD: *Can be made 1 day ahead. Cover with cake dome and refrigerate. Let stand at room temperature 2 hours before serving.*

Gingerbread Layer Cake with Candied Kumquats

Cola in gingerbread cake? Absolutely—the warm caramel flavors in cola actually complement the molasses and brown sugar in this triple-layer cake. Use a cola made the good old-fashioned way, with cane sugar instead of high-fructose corn syrup. You'll have some candied kumquats left over; they're delicious served with vanilla ice cream or creamy Greek-style yogurt.

12 servings

Cake

1	cup cola
1½	teaspoons baking soda
1	cup mild-flavored (light) molasses
2	cups unbleached all purpose flour
2	tablespoons ground ginger
1½	teaspoons baking powder
1¼	teaspoons ground cinnamon
¾	teaspoon ground cloves
½	teaspoon ground nutmeg
½	teaspoon salt
1	cup (packed) dark brown sugar
¾	cup vegetable oil
3	large eggs

Candied Kumquats

1	cup water
¾	cup honey
¼	cup sugar
15	whole cloves
2	cinnamon sticks, broken in half
1	vanilla bean, split lengthwise
22	ounces kumquats, cut into ¼-inch-thick rounds, seeded

Frosting

1⅓	cups (packed) dark brown sugar
½	cup plus 1 tablespoon whipping cream
2	8-ounce packages Philadelphia-brand cream cheese, room temperature
¾	cup (1½ sticks) unsalted butter, room temperature
1	tablespoon vanilla extract
1	cup pecans, toasted, chopped
⅓	cup chopped crystallized ginger

CAKE: Preheat oven to 350°F. Butter and flour 3 nonstick 9-inch-diameter cake pans with 1½-inch-high sides. Bring cola to boil in heavy medium saucepan. Remove from heat; whisk in baking soda, then molasses. Transfer to large bowl; cool to room temperature. Whisk flour, ginger, baking powder, cinnamon, cloves, nutmeg, and salt in medium bowl to blend. Whisk sugar, oil, and eggs into molasses mixture. Whisk in flour mixture. Divide batter among prepared pans (about 1⅔ cups batter for each).

Bake cakes until tester inserted into center comes out clean, about 18 minutes. Cool cakes in pans on racks 15 minutes. Turn cakes out onto racks; cool completely.

CANDIED KUMQUATS: Bring 1 cup water, honey, sugar, cloves, and cinnamon to boil in heavy large skillet, stirring to dissolve sugar. Scrape in seeds from vanilla bean; add bean. Add kumquats; reduce heat to medium and simmer until almost tender, stirring often, about 6 minutes. Using slotted spoon, transfer kumquats to plate. Boil syrup until reduced to ⅔ cup, stirring often, about 8 minutes. Strain syrup and cool.

FROSTING: Stir sugar and cream in heavy small saucepan over medium heat until sugar dissolves; cool caramel completely. Transfer ¼ cup caramel to small bowl and reserve. Using electric mixer, beat cream cheese, butter, and vanilla in large bowl until smooth. Beat remaining caramel into frosting until well blended.

Chop enough candied kumquats to measure ⅓ cup; mix in small bowl with 1 tablespoon kumquat syrup. Place 1 cake layer on platter; spread ¾ cup frosting over. Dot with half of chopped kumquat mixture. Drizzle with half of reserved caramel. Top with second cake layer; spread ¾ cup frosting over. Dot with remaining chopped kumquat mixture. Drizzle with remaining reserved caramel. Top with third cake layer; spread remaining frosting over top and sides of cake. Arrange enough sliced kumquats in single layer atop cake just to cover. Mix pecans and ginger in small bowl. Press nut mixture halfway up sides of cake. Chill 1 hour.

DO AHEAD: *Cake can be made 1 day ahead. Cover with cake dome and chill overnight. Cover remaining kumquat syrup; let stand at room temperature.*

Drizzle some kumquat syrup over kumquats atop cake. Serve cake cold or at room temperature.

Apple Cake with Maple-Walnut Cream Cheese Frosting

If you can't find Pippin apples, choose another variety that's good for cooking. Golden Delicious, Winesap, Pink Lady, Granny Smith, and Jonagold are good options. **8 to 10 servings**

Cake

1	pound Pippin apples (about 2 medium), peeled, cored, diced
¼	cup water
2½	cups plus 1 tablespoon unbleached all purpose flour
2	teaspoons baking soda
1½	teaspoons ground cinnamon
½	teaspoon salt
¼	teaspoon ground nutmeg
¼	teaspoon ground cloves
1	cup dried currants
1	cup walnuts, toasted, chopped
2	cups sugar
1	cup (2 sticks) unsalted butter, room temperature
1	tablespoon brandy
1½	teaspoons vanilla extract
4	large eggs

Frosting

1	cup (2 sticks) unsalted butter, room temperature
1	cup (packed) dark brown sugar
2	8-ounce packages Philadelphia-brand cream cheese, room temperature
½	cup pure maple syrup
¼	teaspoon maple flavoring
2	cups walnuts, toasted, chopped

CAKE: Preheat oven to 350°F. Butter and flour three 9-inch-diameter cake pans with 1½-inch-high sides. Combine apples and ¼ cup water in small saucepan. Cover; simmer over medium-low heat until apples are tender, about 20 minutes. Place in processor; puree until smooth. Cool puree.

Sift 2½ cups flour, baking soda, cinnamon, salt, nutmeg, and cloves into medium bowl. Toss currants with remaining 1 tablespoon flour in small bowl to coat; mix in walnuts.

Using electric mixer, beat sugar, butter, brandy, and vanilla in large bowl until blended. Beat in eggs 1 at a time. Beat in half of flour mixture, then 1¼ cups apple puree (reserve any remaining puree for another use). Beat in remaining flour mixture. Stir in currants and walnuts. Divide batter among prepared pans.

Bake cakes until tester inserted into center comes out clean, about 20 minutes. Cut around pan sides to loosen cakes; turn cakes out onto racks and cool.

FROSTING: Using electric mixer, beat butter and sugar in large bowl until blended. Beat in cream cheese, then maple syrup and maple flavoring. Chill frosting until beginning to set, about 20 minutes.

Place 1 cake layer on platter. Spread ¾ cup frosting over. Top with second layer; spread ¾ cup frosting over. Top with third layer. Spread 1 cup frosting in thin layer over top and sides of cake. Chill 15 minutes. Spread remaining frosting all over cake. Press walnuts halfway up sides of cake. Chill until frosting is set, at least 30 minutes.

DO AHEAD: *Can be made 1 day ahead. Cover with cake dome; keep chilled. Let stand at room temperature 1 hour before serving.*

Pumpkin Spice Layer Cake with Caramel–Cream Cheese Frosting

This nice autumnal cake features a festive garnish of candied orange peel, which is available seasonally at most supermarkets and year-round at specialty foods stores and from chefshop.com. Look for a peel that's made with high-quality ingredients and no artificial colors, flavors, or preservatives.

12 servings

Cake

3	cups unbleached all purpose flour
2	teaspoons baking soda
2	teaspoons baking powder
1	teaspoon ground cinnamon
½	teaspoon ground ginger
¼	teaspoon ground cloves
¼	teaspoon freshly grated nutmeg
¼	teaspoon ground allspice
¼	teaspoon ground cardamom
1	15-ounce can pure pumpkin
1½	cups sugar
1¼	cups vegetable oil
4	large eggs
2	teaspoons finely grated orange peel

Frosting

1	1-pound box powdered sugar, divided
½	cup plus 1 tablespoon heavy whipping cream
1	teaspoon vanilla extract
¼	teaspoon salt
1	8-ounce package Philadelphia-brand cream cheese, room temperature
¼	cup (½ stick) unsalted butter, room temperature

Candied orange peel

Technique Tip: Let It Melt

When making the caramel for the frosting, do not stir the powdered sugar until it has melted completely, or else the sugar will crystallize and seize. Keep a watchful eye on it, shaking and tilting the pan, if necessary, to allow the sugar to melt evenly.

CAKE: Preheat oven to 350°F. Butter and flour two 9-inch-diameter cake pans with 1½-inch-high sides. Whisk flour, baking soda, baking powder, cinnamon, ginger, cloves, nutmeg, allspice, and cardamom in large bowl to blend. Using electric mixer, beat pumpkin, sugar, and oil in another large bowl until blended. Beat in eggs 1 at a time, then orange peel. Add flour mixture; beat at low speed just to blend. Divide batter between prepared pans.

Bake cakes until tester inserted into center comes out clean, about 33 minutes. Cool cakes in pans on racks 10 minutes. Cut around pan sides to loosen cakes. Invert cakes onto racks and cool completely.

FROSTING: Sprinkle ½ cup sugar over bottom of small nonstick skillet. Cook without stirring over medium heat until sugar melts, swirling pan occasionally. Continue cooking until sugar turns deep amber color, stirring occasionally, about 2 minutes. Add ½ cup cream, vanilla, and salt (mixture will bubble vigorously). Stir until any caramel bits dissolve. Stir in remaining 1 tablespoon cream. Strain into small bowl. Cool caramel to room temperature.

Sift remaining sugar into medium bowl. Using electric mixer, beat cream cheese and butter in large bowl. Gradually beat in sugar. Beat in cooled caramel. Cover and chill frosting until firm enough to spread, about 2 hours.

Using long serrated knife, trim rounded tops from cakes. Place 1 cake layer, cut side up, on cake plate. Spread ¾ cup frosting over. Place second cake layer, cut side down, atop frosting. Spread remaining frosting smoothly over top and sides of cake.

DO AHEAD: *Can be made 2 days ahead. Cover with cake dome or large bowl and chill. Let stand at room temperature 2 hours before serving.*

Sprinkle candied orange peel over top of cake. Cut into wedges and serve.

Cranberry-Glazed Orange Layer Cake

Be sure to use clean, dry beaters and a clean, dry mixing bowl to beat the egg whites. Even a trace of oil can keep them from expanding properly. The glaze for this lovely autumn cake should be made a day ahead. **12 servings**

3	cups sifted cake flour (sifted, then measured)
2½	teaspoons baking powder
¼	teaspoon salt
1	cup (2 sticks) unsalted butter, room temperature
3½	cups sifted powdered sugar (sifted, then measured)
6	large eggs, separated, room temperature
2	teaspoons finely grated orange peel
1½	teaspoons vanilla extract
1½	teaspoons orange extract
1	cup whole milk
¼	cup plain whole-milk yogurt
	Creamy Brown Sugar Frosting (see recipe)
	Cranberry Glaze (see recipe)

Preheat oven to 350°F. Butter and flour two 9-inch-diameter cake pans with 2-inch-high sides. Sift flour, baking powder, and salt into medium bowl. Using electric mixer, beat butter in large bowl until fluffy. Gradually beat in sugar, occasionally scraping down sides of bowl. Beat in egg yolks 1 at a time, then orange peel, vanilla, and orange extract. Whisk milk and yogurt in small bowl to blend. Beat dry ingredients into butter mixture in 3 additions alternately with milk mixture in 2 additions.

Using clean dry beaters, beat egg whites in another large bowl until stiff but not dry. Fold whites into batter in 2 additions. Divide batter between prepared pans. Smooth tops.

Bake cakes until tester inserted into center comes out clean, about 35 minutes. Cool cakes in pans on racks 15 minutes. Cut around pan sides to loosen cakes. Turn cakes out onto racks and cool completely.

DO AHEAD: *Can be made 1 day ahead. Wrap cakes in plastic and store at room temperature.*

Place 1 cake layer, flat side up, on platter. Spread ¾ cup Creamy Brown Sugar Frosting over. Spread 1 cup Cranberry Glaze over frosting, leaving ½-inch border around edge. Top with second cake layer, flat side down; press lightly to adhere. Spread 2 cups frosting over sides of cake. Spoon remaining frosting into pastry bag fitted with medium-size star tip. Pipe decorative border around top edge of cake. Refrigerate until frosting is firm, about 1 hour. Spread remaining glaze over top center of cake. Chill until glaze is set.

DO AHEAD: *Can be made 1 day ahead. Cover with cake dome and refrigerate.*

Creamy Brown Sugar Frosting

Adding the powdered sugar in several stages helps prevent it from flying out of the mixing bowl. **Makes about 3½ cups**

12	ounces Philadelphia-brand cream cheese, room temperature
¾	cup (1½ sticks) unsalted butter, room temperature
¾	cup (packed) golden brown sugar
2¼	cups powdered sugar
1½	tablespoons frozen orange juice concentrate, thawed
1½	teaspoons vanilla extract

Using electric mixer, beat cream cheese and butter in large bowl until fluffy. Beat in brown sugar. Beat in powdered sugar scant ½ cup at a time. Beat in orange juice concentrate and vanilla. Chill frosting until firm enough to spread, about 30 minutes.

Cranberry Glaze

Make the glaze a day ahead so the flavors can meld and the texture can firm up. **Makes about 2⅓ cups**

1	12-ounce package fresh or frozen cranberries
1	cup sugar
1	cup water
1½	teaspoons finely grated orange peel

Combine cranberries and sugar in processor. Using on/off turns, coarsely chop cranberries. Transfer mixture to heavy medium saucepan. Add 1 cup water and orange peel and bring to boil, stirring occasionally. Reduce heat; simmer until mixture is reduced to 2⅓ cups, stirring occasionally, about 10 minutes. Cool to room temperature. Cover; chill at least 1 day or up to 2 days (mixture will thicken).

Coffee, Hazelnut, and Raspberry Torte

If you're planning a special dinner party, save yourself some stress by making this dessert a day ahead. (But be sure to make the raspberry filling a day before baking the cake, as it needs to chill overnight.) Any leftover filling would be delicious on pancakes, waffles, yogurt, or even whole wheat toast.

8 to 10 servings

Filling

1	cup frozen raspberries, thawed, drained
1	cup raspberry jam

Frosting

2½	cups chilled heavy whipping cream, divided
10	ounces high-quality white chocolate (such as Lindt or Perugina), chopped
3	tablespoons plus 1 teaspoon instant coffee crystals

Cake

1	cup hazelnuts, toasted, husked
1	cup sifted unbleached all purpose flour (sifted, then measured)
1¼	cups sugar, divided
1	teaspoon instant coffee crystals
¼	teaspoon salt
6	large eggs, separated, room temperature
¼	cup water
1	teaspoon vanilla extract
	Fresh raspberries (optional)

FILLING: Press raspberries through fine sieve into small bowl. Press jam through same sieve into raspberry puree; discard seeds. Stir to blend well. Cover and chill overnight.

DO AHEAD: *Can be made 3 days ahead. Keep chilled.*

FROSTING: Combine ¾ cup cream, white chocolate, and coffee crystals in heavy medium saucepan. Stir over low heat just until chocolate melts, coffee dissolves, and mixture is smooth. Remove from heat. Let stand until cool and thick, whisking occasionally, about 1½ hours.

Using electric mixer, beat remaining 1¾ cups cream in large bowl until firm peaks form. Fold large spoonful of whipped cream into chocolate mixture to lighten. Fold chocolate mixture into whipped cream in 4 additions. Cover and refrigerate frosting until very firm, about 6 hours.

DO AHEAD: *Can be made 1 day ahead. Keep chilled.*

CAKE: Preheat oven to 350°F. Line three 9-inch-diameter cake pans with 1½-inch-high sides with parchment paper. Butter and flour parchment. Combine nuts, flour, ¼ cup sugar, coffee crystals, and salt in processor. Blend until nuts are finely ground.

Using electric mixer, beat egg yolks and ½ cup sugar in large bowl until very thick, about 5 minutes. Beat in ¼ cup water and vanilla. Stir in flour mixture. Using clean dry beaters, beat egg whites in large bowl until soft peaks form. Gradually add remaining ½ cup sugar, beating until stiff but not dry. Fold whites into yolk mixture in 3 additions. Transfer batter to prepared pans.

Bake cakes until tester inserted into center comes out clean, about 18 minutes. Cool cakes in pans on racks. Cut around pan sides to loosen cakes. Turn cakes out onto racks; peel off parchment.

Place 1 cake layer on platter and second cake layer on piece of foil. Spread ⅓ cup filling over each; let stand 20 minutes to set up. Spread 1 cup frosting over filling on each. Lift cake layer off foil; place atop cake layer on platter. Top with third cake layer. Spread remaining frosting over top and sides of torte.

DO AHEAD: *Can be made 1 day ahead. Cover with cake dome and refrigerate.*

Garnish torte with fresh berries, if desired. Cut into wedges and serve.

Hazelnut Crunch Cake with Honeyed Kumquats

Tender cake, creamy filling, crunchy nuts, and tart-sweet kumquats add up to one glamorous dessert. For the pretty flower-like garnish, kumquats are quartered with the stem ends left intact, then cooked in a honey and wine syrup. To get the look, bend back the petals of the kumquats at varying angles and arrange them over the cake in a random fashion. These kumquat flowers also look beautiful on cheesecakes, carrot cakes, and chocolate cakes. **10 servings**

Nut Crunch

1	cup sugar
¼	cup water
2	cups unhusked hazelnuts, toasted

Kumquats

55	kumquats (about 21 ounces)
1½	cups Chardonnay
¾	cup sugar
¾	cup honey
10	whole star anise or whole cloves
1	vanilla bean, split lengthwise

Cake

1	cup unhusked hazelnuts, toasted
2	cups unbleached all purpose flour
1	tablespoon baking powder
1½	teaspoons Chinese five-spice powder
¾	teaspoon salt
¾	cup (1½ sticks) unsalted butter, room temperature
1½	cups sugar
3	large egg yolks
1	tablespoon vanilla extract
1	teaspoon almond extract
1¼	cups whole milk
5	large egg whites, room temperature

Frosting

1½	8-ounce containers mascarpone cheese
1½	cups chilled heavy whipping cream
3	tablespoons sugar
4	teaspoons Cognac or brandy
1	tablespoon vanilla extract

NUT CRUNCH: Line baking sheet with foil. Stir sugar and ¼ cup water in heavy medium saucepan over medium-low heat until sugar dissolves. Increase heat; boil without stirring until syrup turns deep amber, occasionally brushing down sides of pan with wet pastry brush and swirling pan. Mix in nuts. Pour onto foil; cool completely. Coarsely chop nut crunch. Set aside.

KUMQUATS: Starting at rounded end, cut cross into each kumquat to within ¼ inch of stem end. Bring wine, sugar, honey, and star anise to boil in heavy large saucepan, stirring until sugar dissolves. Scrape in seeds from vanilla bean; add bean. Add kumquats; simmer until almost tender, about 8 minutes. Using slotted spoon, transfer kumquats to plate; cool. Seed and finely chop enough kumquats to measure ⅔ cup (reserve remaining kumquats). Gently boil kumquat syrup until reduced to 1¼ cups, about 12 minutes. Strain syrup and cool.

CAKE: Preheat oven to 350°F. Line 15½x10½x1-inch or 17x11x¾-inch baking sheet with foil; butter and flour foil. Finely grind nuts with flour in processor; transfer to medium bowl. Whisk in baking powder, five-spice powder, and salt. Using electric mixer, beat butter and sugar in large bowl until well blended. Beat in egg yolks and both extracts. Beat in flour mixture alternately with milk in several additions, just until combined. Using clean dry beaters, beat egg whites in another large bowl until stiff but not dry. Fold ⅓ of whites into batter to lighten, then fold in remaining whites. Spread batter evenly in prepared sheet.

Bake cake until tester inserted into center comes out clean, about 28 minutes for 15½x10½-inch cake or 20 minutes for 17x11-inch cake. Cool cake in pan on rack 20 minutes. Run knife around cake to loosen. Turn cake out onto foil-lined rack; cool completely. Peel foil off cake. Cut hazelnut cake crosswise into 3 equal pieces.

FROSTING: Combine all ingredients in large bowl; beat to soft peaks (do not overbeat or mixture will curdle).

Place 1 cake piece on platter; spread ¾ cup frosting over. Sprinkle with ⅓ cup chopped kumquats and ⅓ cup nut crunch, then drizzle with 2 tablespoons kumquat syrup. Top with second cake piece; spread ¾ cup frosting over. Sprinkle with ⅓ cup chopped kumquats and ⅓ cup nut crunch, then drizzle with 2 tablespoons kumquat syrup. Top with third cake piece; spread remaining frosting over top and sides of cake. Drain reserved kumquats; remove seeds and any attached pulp. Top cake with kumquats, arranging like flowers.

DO AHEAD: *Can be made 1 day ahead. Cover and chill cake. Store remaining nut crunch and kumquat syrup separately at room temperature.*

Press remaining nut crunch around sides of cake. Drizzle 2 tablespoons syrup over cake and serve.

Ingredient Tips: **Kumquats, Star Anise, and Chinese Five-Spice Powder**

Kumquats will start to appear at the market in late fall and are available until June. Look for those that are on the small side to make the decorative flowers used here. The star anise (brown, star-shaped seedpods) and Chinese five-spice powder (a spice blend that usually contains star anise, cinnamon, cloves, fennel seeds, and Szechuan peppercorns) are available in the spice section of some supermarkets and at specialty foods stores and Asian markets.

♥♥♥♥ Apricot-Pistachio Torte with Honey Buttercream

This is a classic French torte featuring layers of rich genoise (a sponge cake enriched with melted butter) made with pistachios in place of some of the flour. The torte is completed with a jammy apricot filling and honey buttercream. The cake can be prepared up to eight hours ahead. Any leftover apricot filling makes a wonderful breakfast spread for toast or English muffins. **10 servings**

Filling

1	cup water
⅓	cup sugar
¼	cup orange blossom honey
1⅓	cups (packed) moist dried apricots

Cake

1	cup unbleached all purpose flour
¾	cup roasted unsalted natural pistachios
	Pinch of salt
5	large eggs
2	large egg yolks
¾	cup plus 2 tablespoons sugar
1	teaspoon vanilla extract
3	tablespoons unsalted butter, melted and cooled to barely lukewarm
	Powdered sugar

Buttercream

½	cup sugar
¼	cup plus 2 tablespoons orange blossom honey
⅓	cup water
6	large egg yolks
½	teaspoon vanilla extract
1	cup plus 2 tablespoons (2¼ sticks) unsalted butter, room temperature, cut into 18 pieces
¾	cup roasted unsalted natural pistachios, chopped
	Glazed Apricots (see recipe)

FILLING: Stir 1 cup water, sugar, and honey in heavy medium saucepan over medium heat until sugar dissolves. Increase heat and bring to boil. Add apricots; reduce heat, cover, and simmer 5 minutes. Uncover and simmer 3 minutes to thicken syrup slightly. Puree in processor. Transfer to bowl and cool.

DO AHEAD: *Can be made 4 days ahead. Cover and chill. Bring to room temperature before using.*

CAKE: Position rack in center of oven and preheat to 350°F. Butter 15½x10½x1-inch baking sheet. Line bottom with parchment or waxed paper. Dust sheet with flour; tap out excess. Finely grind flour, pistachios, and salt in processor.

Combine eggs, egg yolks, sugar, and vanilla in large bowl. Set bowl over saucepan of simmering water (do not let bowl touch water); whisk just until warm, about 3 minutes. Remove from over water. Using electric mixer, beat until mixture triples in volume and thick ribbon falls when beaters are lifted. Gently fold in flour-nut mixture in 2 batches. Pour 1 cup batter into small bowl; fold in melted butter. Gently but thoroughly fold butter mixture into remaining cake batter. Transfer batter to prepared sheet; smooth top. Bake cake until top is golden brown and tester inserted in center comes out clean, about 20 minutes. Cool in pan on rack.

Lightly dust 15½x10½-inch piece of parchment or waxed paper with powdered sugar. Run small sharp knife around pan sides to loosen cake. Turn cake out onto sugared parchment. Peel off top parchment. Cut cake crosswise into three 10x5-inch rectangles.

BUTTERCREAM: Stir sugar, honey, and ⅓ cup water in heavy medium saucepan over low heat until sugar dissolves. Brush sides of pan with cold water. Increase heat and boil without stirring until syrup registers 238°F on candy thermometer, tilting pan if necessary to submerge thermometer, about 10 minutes.

Meanwhile, using electric mixer, beat egg yolks with vanilla in large bowl until tripled in volume.

Gradually beat hot syrup into yolks. Continue beating until mixture is cool, about 10 minutes. Gradually add butter and beat until smooth. (If buttercream looks broken or curdled, place bowl with buttercream over medium heat on stove burner and whisk 5 to 10 seconds to warm mixture slightly. Then remove from heat and beat mixture again at medium speed. Repeat warming and beating as many times as needed until buttercream is smooth.)

Spoon ¾ cup buttercream into pastry bag fitted with small star tip (No. 1). Place 1 cake layer on plate; spread ⅓ cup apricot filling over. Spread ½ cup buttercream over filling. Top with second cake layer; spread with ⅓ cup apricot filling. Spread ½ cup buttercream over filling. Top with third cake layer; spread with ⅓ cup filling (reserve remaining filling for another use). Spread top and sides of cake with remaining buttercream. Press chopped nuts onto sides of cake.

Halve Glazed Apricots and arrange decoratively down center of cake. Pipe buttercream in pastry bag decoratively around apricots or base of cake.

DO AHEAD: *Can be made 8 hours ahead. Cover and let stand at cool room temperature.*

{ Technique Tip: **Genoise**

There are a number of pastry tricks at play in this cake, and one of the most important involves the genoise. Melted butter is folded into a light and airy batter to make genoise, but if the butter is not evenly dispersed it sinks to the bottom of the cake as it bakes, creating an undesirable texture throughout. To avoid this, a portion of the batter is first stirred into the melted butter, then the lightened butter-batter mixture can be more evenly incorporated into the remaining batter. Be careful not to overfold the batter, as that can cause it to deflate, resulting in a dense and heavy cake. }

 ## Glazed Apricots

Dried apricots become plump and shiny in honey-sugar syrup. They make a beautiful cake garnish and a delicious after-dinner treat. Using orange blossom honey gives them a floral scent, but clover honey would work, too. For a different flavor and aroma, try lavender honey instead. **Makes 20**

½   **cup water**
½   **cup orange blossom honey**
½   **cup sugar**
20   **jumbo moist dried apricots**

Stir ½ cup water, honey, and sugar in heavy large saucepan over medium heat until sugar dissolves. Add apricots; cook until apricots are tender and syrup is reduced and thinly coats spoon, stirring frequently, about 20 minutes. Cool apricots in syrup at least 2 hours.

DO AHEAD: *Can be made 1 day ahead. Cover and let stand at room temperature.*

Remove apricots from syrup (apricots will be sticky). Drain on paper towels to remove any excess syrup.

Lemon and Pistachio Praline Meringue Torte

This cake, made of layered pistachio praline meringues and lemon buttercream, has a winning creamy-crispy contrast. It's assembled and refrigerated a day ahead of serving so that the flavors meld. **12 servings**

Praline
¾	cup sugar
3	tablespoons water
1	cup unsalted natural pistachios

Meringues
5	large egg whites, room temperature
½	teaspoon cream of tartar
½	cup sugar
½	teaspoon almond extract
1	cup powdered sugar

Lemon Buttercream
4	ounces high-quality white chocolate (such as Lindt or Perugina), chopped
4	large egg whites, room temperature
¼	teaspoon cream of tartar
2	tablespoons plus ⅔ cup sugar
3	tablespoons water
1	tablespoon light corn syrup
1	cup (2 sticks) unsalted butter, room temperature
2	tablespoons fresh lemon juice
1	tablespoon plus 2 teaspoons finely grated lemon peel
1	teaspoon vanilla extract

PRALINE: Oil large baking sheet. Stir sugar and 3 tablespoons water in heavy small saucepan over medium-low heat until sugar dissolves. Increase heat and boil without stirring until syrup is deep amber color, occasionally brushing down sides of pan with wet pastry brush and swirling pan. Stir in pistachios. Immediately pour mixture onto prepared sheet. Cool praline completely.

Finely chop praline. Grind ½ cup praline to powder in processor.

MERINGUES: Position 1 rack in center and 1 rack in top third of oven; preheat to 225°F. Line 2 large baking sheets with parchment paper. Using 8-inch-diameter cake pan bottom as guide, trace 2 circles on 1 parchment sheet and 1 circle on second sheet. Turn over parchment on baking sheets, marked side down. Using electric mixer, beat egg whites and cream of tartar in large bowl until soft peaks form. Gradually add ½ cup sugar; beat until egg whites are stiff but not dry. Beat in almond extract. Stir powdered sugar and praline powder in bowl to blend. Fold into meringue in 2 additions.

Divide meringue among traced circles. Using spatula, spread mixture to edges. Bake until crisp and pale golden, reversing baking sheets after 45 minutes, about 1 hour 45 minutes. Cool meringues completely.

LEMON BUTTERCREAM: Stir white chocolate in top of double boiler set over simmering water until melted and smooth. Remove from over water. Let stand until just cool but not set.

Using electric mixer, beat egg whites and cream of tartar in large bowl until soft peaks form. Gradually beat in 2 tablespoons sugar.

Meanwhile, combine remaining ⅔ cup sugar, 3 tablespoons water, and corn syrup in heavy small saucepan. Stir over medium-low heat until sugar dissolves. Increase heat and boil without stirring until candy thermometer registers 238°F, about 5 minutes.

Immediately pour hot syrup in thin steady stream into beaten egg whites, beating until mixture is completely cool, about 4 minutes. Beat in butter 2 tablespoons at a time. Beat in white chocolate, lemon juice, lemon peel, and vanilla. Chill just until thickened to spreadable consistency, stirring occasionally, about 45 minutes. (If buttercream looks broken or curdled, place bowl with buttercream over medium heat on stove burner and whisk 5 to 10 seconds to warm mixture slightly, then remove from heat and beat mixture again at medium speed. Repeat warming and beating as many times as needed until buttercream is smooth.)

Place 1 meringue layer on platter. Spread scant 1 cup buttercream evenly over. Top with another meringue layer. Spread scant 1 cup buttercream evenly over. Top with remaining meringue. Spread remaining buttercream evenly over top and sides of torte. Press chopped praline onto sides and in 1-inch border along top edge of torte. Refrigerate until buttercream sets, then cover and chill overnight. Let torte stand uncovered at room temperature 30 minutes before serving.

♫♫♫ Maple Crunch Layer Cake

The "crunch" comes from the candy—much like peanut brittle, but made with maple syrup and walnuts—that goes between the layers and on the sides and top edge of the cake. Have all of your ingredients and equipment ready before you begin making the candy, as the action happens quickly. You'll need a candy thermometer to ensure that the syrup reaches 300°F so that it will harden to the right consistency when cooled. **14 servings**

Candy

	Vegetable oil
1	cup pure maple syrup
½	cup sugar
2	teaspoons apple cider vinegar
2	teaspoons baking soda
1	cup coarsely chopped walnuts

Cake

	Nonstick vegetable oil spray
2½	cups unbleached all purpose flour
2	teaspoons baking powder
1	teaspoon baking soda
½	teaspoon salt
¼	teaspoon ground cinnamon
½	cup (1 stick) unsalted butter, room temperature
½	cup (packed) golden brown sugar
1	cup pure maple syrup
2	large eggs
2	teaspoons vanilla extract
½	cup buttermilk

Buttercream

½	cup pure maple syrup
4	large egg whites, room temperature
2	cups (4 sticks) unsalted butter, cut into ½-inch-thick slices, room temperature

{
Ingredient Tip: **Secret Weapons**
Why baking soda and vinegar? Baking soda makes the caramel-like maple syrup foam up, giving the candy that crisp and porous brittle texture. The vinegar eliminates any trace of an unpleasant soapy flavor that baking soda can sometimes leave behind.
}

CANDY: Line rimmed baking sheet with foil; brush foil with oil. Stir maple syrup, sugar, and vinegar in heavy medium saucepan until sugar is moistened. Attach candy thermometer to side of pan. Without stirring, bring mixture to boil over medium-high heat and boil until thermometer registers 300°F, occasionally brushing down pan sides with wet pastry brush and swirling pan, about 7 minutes. Remove pan from heat; mix in baking soda, then nuts (mixture will bubble vigorously).

Immediately pour maple mixture onto prepared baking sheet and spread to even ½-inch thickness (candy begins to firm quickly). Let stand until candy cools and hardens, at least 30 minutes.

DO AHEAD: *Can be made 1 day ahead. Cover baking sheet tightly with plastic wrap and store candy at room temperature.*

CAKE: Preheat oven to 350°F. Spray two 8-inch-diameter cake pans with 2-inch-high sides with nonstick spray. Line pan bottoms with parchment paper; spray parchment. Whisk flour, baking powder, baking soda, salt, and cinnamon in medium bowl to blend.

Using electric mixer, beat butter in large bowl until fluffy. Beat in sugar. Gradually beat in maple syrup (batter may look curdled). Beat in eggs 1 at a time, then vanilla. Beat in dry ingredients in 3 additions alternately with buttermilk in 2 additions. Divide batter between prepared pans.

Bake cakes until tester inserted into center comes out clean, about 30 minutes. Cool cakes in pans on racks 5 minutes. Cut around pan sides to loosen cakes. Turn cakes out onto racks, peel off parchment paper, and cool completely.

DO AHEAD: *Can be made 1 day ahead. Wrap tightly; store at room temperature.*

(continued next page)

Maple Crunch Layer Cake (continued)

BUTTERCREAM: Bring maple syrup to boil in small saucepan.

Meanwhile, using electric mixer, beat egg whites in large bowl until stiff peaks form. Without letting hot maple syrup touch beaters, pour ¼ cup syrup down side of bowl into egg whites and beat to blend. Gradually beat in remaining hot maple syrup, avoiding beaters. Continue to beat until whites are stiff and cool, about 15 minutes. Beat in butter, 1 slice at a time. Beat until smooth. (If buttercream looks broken or curdled, place bowl with buttercream over medium heat on stovetop burner and whisk 5 to 10 seconds to warm mixture slightly, then remove from heat and beat mixture again at medium speed. Repeat warming and beating as many times as needed until buttercream is smooth.)

Chop enough maple candy into ¼-inch pieces to measure 1 cup; wrap remaining maple candy tightly in plastic. Place 1 cake layer on platter. Spread 1 cup buttercream over. Sprinkle 1 cup maple candy pieces over and press lightly to adhere. Top with second cake layer. Spread remaining buttercream smoothly over top and sides of cake.

DO AHEAD: *Can be made 1 day ahead. Cover with cake dome; chill. Bring to room temperature before continuing.*

Chop enough of remaining maple candy into ¼-inch pieces to measure 2 cups. Mince enough maple candy to measure 2 tablespoons. Press ¼-inch pieces of maple candy onto sides of cake. Sprinkle minced maple candy around top edge of cake. Serve cake within 2 hours.

 Marzipan-Topped Strawberry Layer Cake

Also called fraisier *(French for "strawberry plant") and usually made with almonds, this delicate pistachio cake is layered with fresh whole strawberries and a fluffy white chocolate buttercream, then topped with green-tinted marzipan. Scrolling the name of the cake on top is a French custom, but feel free to write whatever message you like. Cake decorating stores and cookware stores carry the little leaf-shape cookie cutters that are used to make the strawberry leaves on this cake. If you can't find them, use a small sharp knife to cut out the leaves by hand. Or, if you have a strawberry plant, use fresh leaves instead.* **10 servings**

Cake
2   **large eggs, room temperature**
⅓   **cup plus 2 tablespoons sugar**
½   **cup ground unsalted natural pistachios**
½   **cup unbleached all purpose flour**
¼   **teaspoon baking powder**
4   **large egg whites, room temperature**

Buttercream
6   **large egg yolks**
⅓   **cup sugar**
2   **tablespoons unbleached all purpose flour**
1½ **cups half and half**
8   **ounces high-quality white chocolate (such as Lindt or Perugina), chopped**
2   **teaspoons vanilla extract**
1   **cup (2 sticks) unsalted butter, room temperature**
5   **tablespoons fraise eau-de-vie or framboise (clear strawberry or raspberry brandies) or other brandy, divided**

Assembly
6   **tablespoons strawberry jam**
3   **1-pint containers strawberries, hulled**
7   **ounces marzipan**
     Green food coloring
     Powdered sugar
2   **ounces high-quality white chocolate (such as Lindt or Perugina), chopped**
4   **strawberries, cut in half through stem end**

CAKE: Position rack in center of oven and preheat to 350°F. Butter 9-inch square metal pan with 2-inch-high sides. Line bottom with parchment paper. Butter and flour parchment.

Using electric mixer, beat eggs and ⅓ cup sugar at high speed in large bowl until slowly dissolving ribbon forms when beaters are lifted, about 4 minutes. Mix nuts, flour, and baking powder in medium bowl. Fold nut mixture into egg mixture. Using clean dry beaters, beat egg whites in another medium bowl until soft peaks form. Gradually add remaining 2 tablespoons sugar and beat until stiff peaks form. Fold egg white mixture into batter in 2 additions. Transfer batter to prepared pan. Bake cake until tester inserted in center comes out clean, about 18 minutes. Cool cake in pan on rack 5 minutes. Using small sharp knife, cut around sides of pan to loosen cake. Turn cake out onto rack. Peel off parchment; cool cake completely.

BUTTERCREAM: Whisk egg yolks, sugar, and flour in medium bowl until well blended. Bring half and half to simmer in heavy medium saucepan. Slowly pour hot half and half into egg mixture, whisking constantly. Return egg mixture to same saucepan and cook until mixture is very thick and boils, whisking constantly. Transfer mixture to medium bowl. Add white chocolate and vanilla; stir until chocolate melts and mixture is smooth. Press plastic wrap directly onto surface of pastry cream to prevent skin from forming; cool.

DO AHEAD: *Can be made 1 day ahead. Chill. Bring to room temperature before continuing.*

Using electric mixer, beat butter and 1 tablespoon brandy in large bowl until fluffy. Add pastry cream ¼ cup at a time, beating after each addition until mixture is just blended.

> ## Technique Tip: **One-of-a-Kind Buttercream**
> The buttercream in this recipe is unlike any other in this book. White chocolate and vanilla are mixed into pastry cream, then beaten into butter, which creates a wonderful, mousse-like texture. Be sure to add the pastry cream to the butter a ¼ cup at a time so that it blends in properly and does not separate.

ASSEMBLY: Melt jam in heavy small saucepan over medium heat. Stir remaining 4 tablespoons brandy into jam. Cut cake horizontally into 2 even layers. Place 1 layer on 8-inch cardboard square. Brush half of jam over cake. Spread 1 cup buttercream over jam. Cover buttercream layer completely with whole strawberries, stem ends down. Set aside ½ cup buttercream. Spoon remaining buttercream over berries, spreading buttercream between and around berries. Spread remaining jam over second cake layer. Place cake, jam side down, atop buttercream, pressing gently to adhere. Chill cake until buttercream is firm.

DO AHEAD: *Can be made 1 day ahead. Cover cake and remaining buttercream separately and chill. Bring buttercream to room temperature before continuing.*

Knead marzipan and 2 drops green food coloring in large bowl until color is evenly distributed. Dust work surface with powdered sugar. Roll out marzipan on sugar to 12-inch-diameter circle, sprinkling with powdered sugar as needed to prevent sticking. Spread reserved ½ cup buttercream over top of cake. Using rolling pin as aid, drape marzipan over top of cake; press gently to adhere. Trim marzipan even with top of cake; reserve trimmings. Brush excess powdered sugar off marzipan. Using long sharp knife, cut ⅓ inch off each side of dessert to expose strawberries. Using small cutter, cut marzipan trimmings into leaf shapes.

Stir 2 ounces white chocolate in top of double boiler until melted and smooth. Transfer chocolate to small parchment cone. Cut off tip to form small opening. Pipe the word "fraisier" atop marzipan layer. Garnish with strawberry halves and marzipan leaves. Chill.

DO AHEAD: *Can be made 4 hours ahead. Keep chilled.*

Red Velvet Cake with Raspberries and Blueberries

The stunning contrast of red cake and fluffy white cream cheese frosting has made this a southern tradition for festive occasions. Mixing a touch of cocoa powder with the buttermilk and vinegar creates a reddish brown color, but it's the red food coloring that earns this cake its name. For an even deeper red color, add an extra tablespoon of food coloring. **12 servings**

Cake

2¼	cups sifted cake flour (sifted, then measured)
2	tablespoons natural unsweetened cocoa powder
1	teaspoon baking powder
1	teaspoon baking soda
½	teaspoon salt
1	cup buttermilk
1	tablespoon red food coloring
1	teaspoon distilled white vinegar
1	teaspoon vanilla extract
1½	cups sugar
½	cup (1 stick) unsalted butter, room temperature
2	large eggs

Frosting

2	8-ounce packages Philadelphia-brand cream cheese, room temperature
½	cup (1 stick) unsalted butter, room temperature
1	tablespoon vanilla extract
2½	cups powdered sugar
3	½-pint containers raspberries
3	½-pint containers blueberries

CAKE: Preheat oven to 350°F. Butter and flour two 9-inch-diameter cake pans with 1½-inch-high sides. Sift flour, cocoa, baking powder, baking soda, and salt into medium bowl. Whisk buttermilk, food coloring, vinegar, and vanilla in small bowl to blend. Using electric mixer, beat sugar and butter in large bowl until well blended. Beat in eggs 1 at a time. Beat in dry ingredients in 4 additions alternately with buttermilk mixture in 3 additions. Divide batter between prepared pans.

Bake cakes until tester inserted into center comes out clean, about 27 minutes. Cool in pans on racks 10 minutes. Cut around pan sides to loosen cakes. Turn cakes out onto racks; cool completely.

FROSTING: Using electric mixer, beat cream cheese and butter in large bowl until smooth. Beat in vanilla. Add sugar and beat until smooth.

Place 1 cake layer, flat side up, on platter. Spread 1 cup frosting over. Arrange 1 container raspberries and ½ container blueberries atop frosting, pressing lightly to adhere. Top with second cake layer, flat side down. Spread remaining frosting over top and sides of cake. Arrange remaining berries decoratively over top of cake.

DO AHEAD: *Can be made 1 day ahead. Cover with cake dome and refrigerate. Let stand at room temperature 1 hour before serving.*

⫿⫿⫿⫿ Chocolate Panna Cotta Layer Cake

Panna cotta, a very rich and creamy custard, makes a luxurious filling for this double-decker chocolate cake. The easy-to-make chocolate band wraps this cake up with style for a stunning, bakery-worthy look. Begin making this a day ahead, as the assembled layers need to chill overnight. **12 servings**

Cake

	Nonstick vegetable oil spray
4	ounces bittersweet or semisweet chocolate (do not exceed 61% cacao), chopped
3	tablespoons natural unsweetened cocoa powder
½	cup strong hot coffee
½	cup hot water
1	cup plus 1 tablespoon unbleached all purpose flour
1	teaspoon baking powder
½	teaspoon baking soda
⅛	teaspoon salt
½	cup sugar
½	cup (packed) golden brown sugar
⅓	cup vegetable oil
3	large eggs
½	cup sour cream

Panna Cotta

½	cup water
5	teaspoons unflavored gelatin
7½	ounces bittersweet or semisweet chocolate (do not exceed 61% cacao), chopped
5	ounces high-quality milk chocolate (such as Lindt or Perugina), chopped
2½	cups heavy whipping cream
2½	cups whole milk
½	cup plus 2 tablespoons sugar
1¼	teaspoons vanilla extract
1¼	vanilla beans, split lengthwise

Chocolate Band

2	16x3-inch strips waxed paper
5	ounces semisweet or bittersweet chocolate, finely chopped

CAKE: Preheat oven to 350°F. Spray two 10-inch-diameter springform pans with 2½-inch-high sides with nonstick spray. Place chocolate and cocoa in medium bowl. Pour hot coffee and ½ cup hot water over; whisk until melted and smooth. Whisk flour, baking powder, baking soda, and salt in another medium bowl to blend. Using electric mixer, beat both sugars and oil in large bowl 1 minute (mixture will be crumbly). Beat in eggs 1 at a time. Beat in sour cream. Beat in half of dry ingredients, then chocolate mixture. Beat in remaining dry ingredients at low speed (batter will be thin). Divide batter between pans (layers will be shallow).

Bake cakes until tester inserted into center comes out clean, about 20 minutes. Cool in pans on rack.

PANNA COTTA: Place ½ cup water in small bowl. Sprinkle gelatin over; let stand until softened, about 10 minutes. Place both chocolates in large metal bowl. Combine cream, milk, sugar, and vanilla extract in large saucepan. Scrape in seeds from vanilla beans; add beans. Bring to boil, stirring until sugar dissolves; remove from heat. Add gelatin mixture to hot cream mixture; whisk to dissolve. Discard vanilla bean. Pour cream mixture over chocolates in large metal bowl; whisk until melted and smooth. Place bowl over larger bowl of ice water. Stir often until panna cotta mixture thickens like pudding, draining off water and adding more ice to larger bowl as needed, about 30 minutes. Remove smaller bowl from over ice water.

Pour half of panna cotta mixture over cake in 1 pan (mixture may drip down sides of cake). Freeze until firm, about 45 minutes. Keep remaining panna cotta mixture at room temperature.

Remove pan sides from second cake. Using large metal spatula, carefully slide cake onto panna cotta in first cake pan. Pour remaining panna cotta mixture over, filling pan completely. Cover tightly with foil and chill overnight.

DO AHEAD: *Can be frozen for 2 weeks. Defrost overnight in refrigerator before continuing.*

CHOCOLATE BAND: Line large baking sheet with foil. Place another large sheet of foil on work surface; top with waxed paper strips, spaced apart. Stir chocolate in medium bowl set over pan of simmering water until melted and smooth. Pour half of melted chocolate down center of each waxed paper strip. Using small offset spatula, spread chocolate to cover strips evenly and completely (some chocolate may extend beyond edges of paper strips). Using fingertips, lift chocolate-coated strips and place on foil-lined sheet. Refrigerate until chocolate just begins to set but is still completely flexible, about 2 minutes.

Cut around pan sides to release assembled cake; remove pan sides. Using fingertips, lift 1 chocolate strip from foil. Wrap band around cake, chocolate side in, lining up 1 long edge with bottom of cake (band will be higher than cake and only go about halfway around). Repeat with second band, pressing band onto uncovered side of cake and arranging so ends meet. If bands overlap, trim any excess paper and chocolate. Using fingertips, press top edge of band in toward cake, forming slight ruffle. Chill until chocolate sets, at least 5 minutes. Gently peel off waxed paper. Chill cake.

DO AHEAD: *Can be made 1 day ahead. Cover with cake dome and keep chilled.*

Shopping Tip: **The Best Chocolate**

If ever there was a time to splurge on the finest-quality chocolate, it would be for this cake and its panna cotta filling. Panna cotta is smooth and creamy, and superior chocolate gives it a silky texture that lesser-quality chocolates just can't provide. If brands like Lindt or Perugina are not in the baking aisle at your supermarket, check the candy aisle.

Winter-Spiced Molten Chocolate Cakes with Rum-Ginger Ice Cream

These cakes can be completely assembled the day before, then quickly baked before serving. Even though it goes against all the traditional rules of baking cakes, be sure to remove these from the oven while the centers are still soft and gooey—or "molten." Once the tops of the cakes are broken with a spoon, the soft centers become the sauce. **Makes 8**

Ice Cream
1	pint vanilla ice cream, softened
2	tablespoons chopped crystallized ginger
1	tablespoon dark rum

Cakes
14	ounces bittersweet or semisweet chocolate (do not exceed 61% cacao), chopped
1¼	cups (2½ sticks) unsalted butter
2	teaspoons ground coriander
2	teaspoons ground cardamom
1	teaspoon ground cinnamon
½	teaspoon ground cloves
½	teaspoon freshly ground white pepper
6	large eggs
6	large egg yolks
2	teaspoons vanilla extract
3	cups powdered sugar
1	cup unbleached all purpose flour

Additional powdered sugar
Crystallized ginger strips

ICE CREAM: Place softened ice cream in medium bowl. Using plastic spatula, fold ginger and rum into ice cream. Transfer to airtight container. Freeze ice cream mixture until firm, about 4 hours.

DO AHEAD: *Can be made 1 day ahead. Keep frozen.*

CAKES: Generously butter eight ¾-cup soufflé dishes. Stir chocolate, butter, coriander, cardamom, cinnamon, cloves, and white pepper in heavy medium saucepan over low heat until melted and smooth. Cool slightly. Whisk eggs, egg yolks, and vanilla in large bowl to blend. Whisk in powdered sugar, then chocolate mixture, then flour. Transfer batter to prepared dishes, filling to top.

DO AHEAD: *Can be made 1 day ahead. Cover and refrigerate.*

Preheat oven to 425°F. Bake cakes until batter has risen above sides of dish, top edges are dark brown, and center is still soft and runny, about 15 minutes (or about 18 minutes for refrigerated batter). Run small knife around cakes to loosen. Allow cakes to stand in dishes 5 minutes. Place small plate atop 1 dish with cake. Using oven mitts or pot holders, hold plate and dish firmly together and invert, allowing cake to settle onto plate. Repeat with remaining cakes. Sift additional powdered sugar over cakes. Top with crystallized ginger strips. Serve cakes with rum-ginger ice cream.

♥♥ Chocolate-Mint Pudding Cakes

To avoid overbaking the pudding in the middle of these cakes, start checking early for doneness—unlike most other traditional cakes, the tester should come out with wet batter attached. You can make your own superfine sugar by pulverizing granulated sugar in a food processor until it is finely ground; but this recipe can also be made with regular sugar. **Makes 6**

6   ounces bittersweet or semisweet chocolate (do not exceed
          61% cacao), chopped
½   cup (1 stick) unsalted butter, cut into 4 pieces
3   large eggs
3   large egg yolks
⅓   cup superfine sugar or regular sugar
¼   cup unbleached all purpose flour
1¼   teaspoons peppermint extract
¼   teaspoon salt
        Powdered sugar
        Peppermint stick ice cream or mint chocolate chip ice cream
        Fresh mint leaves

Preheat oven to 375°F. Lightly butter six ¾-cup ramekins or custard cups. Stir chocolate and butter in heavy small saucepan over low heat until melted and smooth. Remove from heat and cool slightly.

Using electric mixer, beat eggs, egg yolks, and sugar in large bowl until slightly thickened, about 5 minutes. Add flour and beat until blended. Add chocolate mixture, peppermint extract, and salt; beat just until incorporated. Divide chocolate mixture among prepared ramekins. Place ramekins on baking sheet.

DO AHEAD: *Can be made 1 hour ahead. Let stand at room temperature.*

Bake cakes until edges are set but center looks shiny and still moves slightly when ramekins are gently shaken and tester inserted into center comes out with wet batter attached, about 11 minutes. Run small knife around each cake to loosen.

Place small plate atop 1 ramekin with pudding cake. Using oven mitts or pot holders, hold plate and ramekin firmly together and invert, allowing cake to settle onto plate. Repeat with remaining cakes. Sift powdered sugar over cakes. Place scoop of ice cream alongside. Garnish with mint leaves and serve.

Warm Lemon Pudding Cakes with Marbled Raspberry Cream

These little lemon cakes hide a sweet surprise: a soft, pudding-like center. They're best served warm with the cool contrast of the swirled raspberry whipped cream, but they can also be made ahead and served at room temperature. **Makes 6**

¾   cup plus 4 tablespoons sugar, divided
6   tablespoons (¾ stick) unsalted butter, room temperature
1   tablespoon finely grated lemon peel
3   large eggs, separated, room temperature
⅓   cup unbleached all purpose flour
⅓   cup fresh lemon juice
1½   cups whole milk
     Powdered sugar
     Marbled Raspberry Cream (see recipe)

Preheat oven to 350°F. Butter six ¾-cup soufflé dishes or custard cups. Place dishes in 13x9x2-inch metal baking pan. Using electric mixer, beat ¾ cup plus 2 tablespoons sugar, butter, and lemon peel in medium bowl until well blended. Add egg yolks 1 at a time, beating well after each addition. Beat in flour, then lemon juice. Gradually whisk in milk (mixture will be thin and may look curdled).

Using clean dry beaters, beat egg whites in large bowl until soft peaks form. Add remaining 2 tablespoons sugar and beat until stiff but not dry. Fold whites into yolk mixture in 3 additions (mixture will be runny). Divide batter among prepared soufflé dishes. Add enough hot water to pan to come halfway up sides of dishes.

Bake pudding cakes until puffed and firm to touch, about 25 minutes. Transfer dishes to plates. Sprinkle with powdered sugar and serve warm, or let stand up to 8 hours and serve at room temperature. Top with dollops of Marbled Raspberry Cream.

Marbled Raspberry Cream

A bright pink raspberry puree is swirled into sweetened whipped cream. It would be beautiful as a topping for flourless chocolate cake, or even waffles. **Makes about 1⅔ cups**

1   cup frozen raspberries, thawed
4   tablespoons sugar, divided
¾   cup chilled heavy whipping cream

Puree raspberries and 2 tablespoons sugar in processor. Strain puree into small bowl; discard seeds. Whisk cream and remaining 2 tablespoons sugar in medium bowl until peaks form. Drizzle raspberry puree over cream. Using knife, swirl raspberry puree into cream just until marbled in appearance.

DO AHEAD: *Can be made 4 hours ahead. Cover and chill.*

Hot-Milk Cakes with Strawberries and Cream

Hot-milk cake is a nice old-fashioned dessert, but its simplicity gives it a modern appeal. The moist, delicate cake gets its name from the hot milk that is added to the batter just before baking. In this recipe, the individual cakes are split, then topped with fresh strawberries and lightly sweetened whipped cream, like shortcakes. **Makes 6**

	Nonstick vegetable oil spray
2	large eggs
⅔	cup plus ½ cup sugar
¾	teaspoon vanilla extract, divided
1	cup plus 2 tablespoons self-rising flour
⅔	cup whole milk
5	tablespoons unsalted butter
1	1-pound container strawberries, hulled, thinly sliced lengthwise
½	cup chilled heavy whipping cream
1	tablespoon powdered sugar

Preheat oven to 425°F. Spray six ¾-cup custard cups with nonstick spray. Place cups on rimmed baking sheet. Using electric mixer, beat eggs in medium bowl at high speed until thick, about 3 minutes. Gradually add ⅔ cup sugar, beating until thick and pale yellow, about 1 minute longer. Beat in ½ teaspoon vanilla. Add flour and beat 30 seconds. Bring milk and butter just to boil in small saucepan, stirring until butter melts. Beat hot milk mixture into batter. Continue to beat 30 seconds. Divide batter among prepared cups.

Bake cakes until firm to touch and pale golden, and tops form rounded peak in center, about 16 minutes. Cool in cups at least 20 minutes. Serve warm or at room temperature.

DO AHEAD: *Can be made 8 hours ahead. Cool completely in cups, then cover and let stand at room temperature.*

Toss strawberries and remaining ½ cup sugar in medium bowl to coat; let stand 20 minutes for juices to form. Using electric mixer, beat cream, powdered sugar, and remaining ¼ teaspoon vanilla in another medium bowl until peaks form.

Remove cakes from cups and transfer to bowls. Cut off rounded top of each cake. Spoon some of berries and juices over. Cover berries with tops of cakes. Spoon whipped cream over, garnish with remaining berries and juices, and serve.

Devil's Food Cupcakes with Chocolate Frosting

Moist and chocolaty with a tender, airy crumb, these cupcakes live up to their seductive good looks. A fudgy frosting makes them even harder to resist. For a slightly sweeter frosting, use up to ½ cup of powdered sugar. **Makes 16**

Cupcakes

½	cup natural unsweetened cocoa powder
2	ounces high-quality milk chocolate (such as Lindt or Perugina), chopped
½	cup boiling water
½	cup buttermilk
1	cup cake flour
¾	teaspoon baking soda
½	teaspoon salt
⅔	cup (packed) dark brown sugar
½	cup canola oil
½	cup sugar
2	large eggs
1	teaspoon vanilla extract

Frosting

4	ounces bittersweet or semisweet chocolate (do not exceed 61% cacao), chopped
2	ounces high-quality milk chocolate (such as Lindt or Perugina), chopped
2	tablespoons heavy whipping cream
2	tablespoons (¼ stick) unsalted butter
½	cup sour cream
1	teaspoon vanilla extract
¼	cup powdered sugar

CUPCAKES: Preheat oven to 350°F. Line 16 standard (⅓-cup) muffin cups with paper liners. Combine cocoa powder and chocolate in medium bowl. Pour ½ cup boiling water over; whisk until smooth. Whisk in buttermilk.

Whisk flour, baking soda, and salt in another medium bowl to blend. Using electric mixer, beat brown sugar, oil, ½ cup sugar, eggs, and vanilla in large bowl until light and creamy, about 2 minutes. Beat in flour mixture, alternating with chocolate mixture in 2 additions. Divide batter among paper liners.

Bake until tester inserted into center comes out with some crumbs attached, about 18 minutes. Cool in pans on cooling rack 10 minutes. Transfer cupcakes to rack and cool completely.

FROSTING: Stir both chocolates, cream, and butter in medium bowl over saucepan of simmering water until melted and smooth. Remove from over water. Whisk in sour cream and vanilla, then powdered sugar. Let stand until thick enough to spread, about 10 minutes.

DO AHEAD: *Can be made 3 days ahead. Store frosted cupcakes airtight at room temperature.*

Vanilla Cupcakes with Vanilla Frosting

These cupcakes are a delicious blank canvas: Enjoy them as the classic cupcakes they are, or dress them up with anything from fresh raspberries to edible flowers (see Icing on the Cupcake, page 133, for more ideas). **Makes 12**

Cupcakes

1⅓	**cups cake flour**
1	**teaspoon baking powder**
½	**teaspoon salt**
⅓	**cup whole milk**
3	**large egg whites, room temperature**
2	**tablespoons sour cream**
1	**teaspoon vanilla extract**
½	**cup (1 stick) unsalted butter, room temperature**
1	**cup sugar**

Frosting

3	**cups powdered sugar**
½	**cup (1 stick) unsalted butter, room temperature**
6	**tablespoons (about) heavy whipping cream**
1½	**teaspoons vanilla extract**

CUPCAKES: Preheat oven to 350°F. Line 12 standard (⅓-cup) muffin cups with paper liners. Whisk flour, baking powder, and salt in medium bowl. Whisk milk, egg whites, sour cream, and vanilla in another medium bowl until sour cream is completely incorporated. Using hand-held electric mixer, beat butter and sugar in large bowl until very light and fluffy, about 8 minutes. Add flour mixture to butter mixture in 2 additions alternately with milk mixture in 2 additions, beating on low speed until blended between additions. Divide batter equally among paper liners (about ⅓ cup each). Bake cupcakes until tester inserted into center comes out clean, 18 to 20 minutes. Cool in pans on rack 5 minutes. Transfer cupcakes to rack to cool completely.

FROSTING: Beat powdered sugar, butter, 2 tablespoons cream, and vanilla in large bowl until blended. Continue beating, adding 1 tablespoon cream at a time, until mixture is light and fluffy, about 3 minutes. Using butter knife, spread frosting on cupcakes or, if desired, refrigerate frosting just until thick enough to pipe, then spoon frosting into pastry bag and pipe decoratively atop cupcakes.

DO AHEAD: *Can be made and frosted 1 day ahead. Cover and let stand at room temperature.*

Banana–Chocolate Chunk Cupcakes with Cream Cheese Frosting

These moist banana cupcakes with walnuts and chocolate chunks are a great bring-along for a potluck brunch. If you like, the frosting can be tinted with a couple of drops of food coloring for special occasions. **Makes 12**

Cupcakes

2½	cups unbleached all purpose flour
1	teaspoon baking soda
½	teaspoon baking powder
¼	teaspoon salt
¾	cup sugar
¾	cup (packed) dark brown sugar
½	cup (1 stick) unsalted butter, room temperature
1	teaspoon vanilla extract
2	large eggs
2	cups mashed ripe bananas (about 4 large)
½	cup sour cream
¼	cup buttermilk
8	ounces high-quality milk chocolate (such as Lindt or Perugina), cut into small pieces
1	cup coarsely chopped walnuts, lightly toasted

Frosting

1	cup (2 sticks) unsalted butter, room temperature
1	8-ounce package Philadelphia-brand cream cheese, room temperature
1	cup powdered sugar, sifted
1	teaspoon vanilla extract

CUPCAKES: Position rack in center of oven and preheat to 350°F. Line 12 standard (⅓-cup) muffin cups with paper liners. Sift flour, baking soda, baking powder, and salt into medium bowl. Using electric mixer, beat both sugars, butter, and vanilla in large bowl until light and fluffy. Beat in eggs 1 at a time. Beat in bananas (mixture may look broken). Beat in sour cream. Reduce speed to very low. Beat in half of dry ingredients, then buttermilk, then remaining dry ingredients. Stir in chocolate and walnuts. Divide batter among paper liners.

Bake cupcakes until tester inserted into center comes out clean, about 30 minutes. Transfer to racks and cool.

FROSTING: Using electric mixer, beat butter and cream cheese in large bowl until smooth and fluffy. Reduce speed to low and beat in sugar and vanilla. Increase speed to high and beat until fluffy. Spread frosting thickly over cupcakes.

DO AHEAD: *Can be made 1 day ahead. Cover and refrigerate. Bring to room temperature before serving.*

{ Ingredient Tip: **Storing Ripe Bananas**
After you've ripened them at room temperature, bananas can be stored in the fridge. The peel will turn brown, but that's okay. Just be sure to use the bananas within a couple of days. }

Lemon-Raspberry Cupcakes

These gorgeous lemon cupcakes are filled with dollops of raspberry jam. Half of the cupcakes have a pale yellow lemon glaze; the rest are topped with a pink raspberry-lemon glaze. They're also delicious warm from the oven and simply dusted with powdered sugar. **Makes 12**

¾   cup (1½ sticks) unsalted butter, room temperature
3   cups powdered sugar, divided
4½   teaspoons finely grated lemon peel, divided
2   large eggs
1¼   cups self-rising flour
¼   cup buttermilk
4   tablespoons fresh lemon juice, divided
12   teaspoons plus 1 tablespoon seedless raspberry jam
       Fresh raspberries

Preheat oven to 350°F. Line 12 standard (⅓-cup) muffin cups with paper liners. Using electric mixer, beat butter, 1½ cups sugar, and 3 teaspoons lemon peel in large bowl until fluffy and pale yellow. Beat in eggs 1 at a time. Beat in half of flour. Beat in buttermilk and 2 tablespoons lemon juice, then remaining flour.

Drop 1 rounded tablespoonful batter into each paper liner. Drop 1 teaspoon raspberry jam onto center of batter. Cover jam with remaining batter.

Bake cupcakes until tester inserted halfway into center comes out clean, about 23 minutes. Cool cupcakes in pan on rack.

Meanwhile, whisk remaining 1½ cups sugar, 2 tablespoons lemon juice, and 1½ teaspoons lemon peel in small bowl to blend for icing. Spoon half of icing over 6 cupcakes. Whisk 1 tablespoon raspberry jam into remaining icing. Spoon over remaining cupcakes. Let stand until icing sets, about 30 minutes. Garnish with raspberries.

Icing on the Cupcake

Decorating cupcakes is the perfect chance to be truly creative and have fun. It's also a great way to get kids involved in baking.

WRAP IT UP: There are a number of pretty, whimsical, and even elegant foil and paper cupcake liners and wraparounds now available. Try baking supply stores for the biggest selection (see Online and Mail-Order Sources, page 632, for details).

FROST WITH FLAIR: There are two ways to frost a cupcake. You can spread the frosting on with a knife or offset spatula, or you can pipe it on using a piping bag (see Techniques—The Basics, page 27) or a resealable plastic bag with the corner snipped off. Pipe dots all over the surface of the cupcake for a pretty effect, or draw lines from the edge of the cupcake to the center, all the way around the circumference. Place a candied violet or other decoration in the center.

Create tinted frostings by dividing plain vanilla frosting among as many bowls as you want and adding drops of different food colorings to each. If using the piping method, use a different disposable pastry bag for each color.

TOP IT OFF: There's no end to the decorative elements that can go on top of a frosted cupcake. Try chocolate or colored sprinkles, colored sugar crystals, candied confetti, small or cut-up candies, candied or edible flowers, crystallized ginger, chocolate curls, candied orange peel, and whole berries (never use cut fruit; the juices will make the frosting run). For inspiration, play off the occasion, the time of year, or just the flavor of the cupcake when choosing your decorations. A dried banana chip would be clever atop a banana cupcake, for example, and appropriate holiday colors are always a good bet. If your supermarket doesn't carry a variety of decorations, try a specialty baking store.

TOPPING TIPS: Dip plain frosted cupcakes in sprinkles or colored sugar crystals (for a completely covered look), or sprinkle them by hand over the tops of the cupcakes (for a lighter look). Create geometric designs using colored candies. On chocolate frosting, use decorations in colors that will stand out against a dark background, such as candied flowers or fresh rose petals, pansies, or edible flowers (purple works especially well on chocolate). Gold leaf and glittery sprinkles in metallic colors are also stunning.

Dip a spoon into melted chocolate (use white chocolate for chocolate frosting) and create zigzag patterns directly atop the cupcakes. Or drizzle the chocolate in thick, heavy irregular lines over a piece of foil; sprinkle with crystallized ginger, chopped nuts, or crushed toffee bits, if desired. Chill until the chocolate is set, then peel pieces off the foil and stand them on edge in the frosting.

Coconut Cupcakes

Cream of coconut gives these cupcakes a delicate coconut flavor. Don't confuse it with coconut milk—cream of coconut is sweetened with sugar and is available in the liquor or mixers section of most supermarkets. Coconut milk is unsweetened and commonly used in savory Asian soups and curries. **Makes 30**

Cupcakes

2¾	cups unbleached all purpose flour
1	teaspoon baking powder
¾	teaspoon salt
½	teaspoon baking soda
1⅔	cups sugar
1	cup (2 sticks) unsalted butter, room temperature
1	teaspoon vanilla extract
4	large eggs
1	cup buttermilk
⅔	cup canned sweetened cream of coconut (such as Coco Reál or Coco López)

Frosting

6	ounces Philadelphia-brand cream cheese, room temperature
¾	cup (1½ sticks) unsalted butter, room temperature
3	cups powdered sugar
½	cup canned sweetened cream of coconut (such as Coco Reál or Coco López)
1	7-ounce package sweetened flaked coconut

CUPCAKES: Position rack in center of oven and preheat to 350°F. Line 30 standard (⅓-cup) muffin cups with paper liners. Whisk flour, baking powder, salt, and baking soda in medium bowl to blend. Using electric mixer, beat sugar, butter, and vanilla in large bowl until light and fluffy. Beat in eggs 1 at a time. Beat in half of dry ingredients, then buttermilk, then remaining dry ingredients. Beat in cream of coconut. Fill each paper liner ⅔ full with batter.

Bake cupcakes until tester inserted into center comes out clean, about 18 minutes. Let cool in pans on racks 10 minutes, then transfer cupcakes to racks and cool completely.

FROSTING: Using electric mixer, beat cream cheese and butter in large bowl until light and fluffy. Gradually beat in sugar. Beat in cream of coconut. If frosting is too soft to spread, cover and refrigerate until firm enough to spread. Using offset spatula, spread frosting over cupcakes. Place coconut in large shallow bowl. Holding each cupcake over bowl, sprinkle coconut over frosting.

DO AHEAD: *Can be made 1 day ahead. Arrange cupcakes in roasting pan. Cover pan with foil and let stand at cool room temperature.*

Key Lime Cupcakes

Neon green food coloring gives these cupcakes a vibrant chartreuse color and a fun retro feel, but it can be omitted if desired. The lime peel is what really enhances the fresh lime flavor in the cupcakes. **Makes 12**

Cupcakes

1	cup unbleached all purpose flour
¾	cup self-rising flour
½	cup (1 stick) unsalted butter, room temperature
1¼	cups sugar
2	large eggs
2½	tablespoons fresh lime juice
1	tablespoon finely grated lime peel
¼	teaspoon neon green food coloring (optional)
¾	cup buttermilk

Frosting

1½	cups powdered sugar
1	8-ounce package Philadelphia-brand cream cheese, room temperature
½	cup (1 stick) unsalted butter, room temperature
1	tablespoon finely grated lime peel
½	teaspoon vanilla extract

CUPCAKES: Preheat oven to 350°F. Line 12 standard (⅓-cup) muffin cups with paper liners. Whisk both flours in medium bowl to blend. Using electric mixer, beat butter in large bowl until smooth. Add sugar; beat to blend. Beat in eggs 1 at a time, then lime juice, lime peel, and food coloring, if using. (Batter may look curdled.) Beat in flour mixture in 3 additions alternately with buttermilk in 2 additions. Spoon scant ⅓ cup batter into each liner.

Bake cupcakes until tester inserted into center comes out clean, 20 to 25 minutes. Cool 10 minutes in pan. Remove cupcakes from pan; cool completely.

FROSTING: Using electric mixer, beat all ingredients in medium bowl until smooth. Spread over cupcakes.

Market Tip: **Food Coloring**

Food coloring comes in a rainbow of shades these days, so check the color name on the container to be sure it's the shade you want. You'll find food coloring in the baking aisle of supermarkets and a wider variety of high-quality food colorings at craft stores like Michael's and cookware stores like Sur La Table.

🥄 Pumpkin Cupcakes

These moist, spicy cupcakes are decorated with kid-friendly candy to resemble mini pumpkins. But they're packed with lots of good-for-you ingredients like pumpkin puree, walnuts, and dried cranberries, so unfrosted, they're delicious for breakfast or with brunch. **Makes 12**

Cupcakes

1	cup unbleached all purpose flour
¾	cup sugar
1	teaspoon baking soda
1	teaspoon ground cinnamon
½	teaspoon ground ginger
½	teaspoon salt
⅛	teaspoon ground cloves
1	large egg
½	cup canned pure pumpkin
⅓	cup canola oil or other vegetable oil
¼	cup buttermilk
⅓	cup chopped walnuts
⅓	cup dried cranberries

Frosting

4	ounces Philadelphia-brand cream cheese, room temperature
¼	cup (½ stick) unsalted butter, room temperature
2	cups powdered sugar
1	teaspoon vanilla extract
	Orange gel food coloring
	Sour green apple straws
	Sour green apple candy tape

CUPCAKES: Preheat oven to 350°F. Line 12 standard (⅓-cup) muffin cups with paper liners. Whisk flour, sugar, baking soda, cinnamon, ginger, salt, and cloves in medium bowl to blend.

Whisk egg in large bowl to blend; whisk in pumpkin, oil, and buttermilk. Stir in flour mixture until just blended. Stir in walnuts and cranberries. Spoon batter into paper liners. Bake cupcakes until golden brown and tester inserted into center comes out clean, about 20 minutes. Cool in pan on rack 5 minutes. Transfer cupcakes to rack and cool completely.

FROSTING: Using electric mixer, beat cream cheese and butter in large bowl until light. Beat in sugar and vanilla. Mix in orange food coloring by drops to reach desired shade. If frosting is very soft, cover and refrigerate until firm enough to hold shape.

Frost cupcakes, mounding slightly in center. Cut 1-inch-long pieces of apple straws and stick 1 piece in top of each cupcake to resemble stem. Using leaf-shaped cutters, cut out leaves from candy tape. Drape leaves atop cupcakes.

DO AHEAD: *Can be made 1 day ahead. Cover with cake dome and store at cool room temperature.*

White Chocolate Cupcakes with Candied Kumquats

The candied kumquats add a tang that contrasts nicely with the sweet white chocolate and creamy coconut milk. Coconut milk is available at many supermarkets and at Indian, Southeast Asian, and Latin markets. Shake the can well before opening it. **Makes 18**

Cupcakes

8	ounces high-quality white chocolate (such as Lindt or Perugina), chopped
1¾	cups unbleached all purpose flour
1	teaspoon baking powder
½	teaspoon coarse kosher salt
1	cup sugar
¾	cup (1½ sticks) unsalted butter, room temperature
1	tablespoon vanilla extract
½	cup canned unsweetened coconut milk
3	large egg whites, room temperature

Frosting

4½	ounces high-quality white chocolate (such as Lindt or Perugina), chopped
6	ounces Philadelphia-brand cream cheese, room temperature
6	tablespoons (¾ stick) unsalted butter, room temperature
¼	cup powdered sugar
½	teaspoon vanilla extract
¼	teaspoon coarse kosher salt
	Candied Kumquats (see recipe)

CUPCAKES: Preheat oven to 325°F. Line 18 standard (⅓-cup) muffin cups with paper liners. Place white chocolate in medium metal bowl set over saucepan of barely simmering water. Stir until melted and smooth. Remove bowl from over water; cool to lukewarm.

Whisk flour, baking powder, and coarse salt in medium bowl to blend. Using electric mixer, beat sugar, butter, and vanilla in large bowl until blended. Stir white chocolate into sugar mixture. Beat in flour mixture in 3 additions alternately with coconut milk in 2 additions. Using clean dry beaters, beat egg whites in medium bowl until soft peaks form. Gently fold whites into batter in 3 additions. Divide batter among paper liners (about ¼ cup each).

Bake cupcakes until tester inserted into center comes out clean, about 25 minutes. Cool completely in pans on rack.

DO AHEAD: *Can be made 1 day ahead. Store in airtight container at room temperature.*

FROSTING: Stir white chocolate in medium metal bowl set over saucepan of barely simmering water until melted and smooth. Cool slightly. Using electric mixer, beat cream cheese, butter, sugar, vanilla, and coarse salt in another medium bowl until fluffy. Gradually beat in melted white chocolate. Cool until thickened to spreadable consistency.

Spread frosting over cupcakes. Drain Candied Kumquats; arrange kumquats decoratively atop cupcakes.

DO AHEAD: *Can be assembled 2 hours ahead. Let stand at room temperature.*

Candied Kumquats

Cooking the kumquat slices in simple syrup gently mellows the tart citrus flavor. These candied kumquats would be a great addition to many other desserts—in trifles, atop cheesecakes and custards, and between layers of a gingerbread cake. And try stirring the kumquat syrup into cocktails. **Makes about ⅔ cup**

½	cup water
½	cup sugar
20	kumquats, sliced into rounds, seeded

Stir ½ cup water and sugar in small saucepan over medium heat until sugar dissolves. Increase heat and bring syrup to boil. Add kumquats and return to boil. Reduce heat to medium and simmer until fruit is tender and syrup thickens slightly, about 20 minutes. Transfer to bowl; cool to room temperature.

DO AHEAD: *Can be made 1 week ahead. Cover and chill.*

ⅢⅢⅢ Chocolate Fudge Torte

A velvety frosting and tender cake make this Passover dessert rich and decadent enough for any special occasion. The use of nondairy creamer and pareve margarine makes it lactose-free, and Passover-friendly matzo cake meal and potato starch are used in place of flour. (When Passover food restrictions are not a concern, the recipe is great using heavy cream and butter.) Potato starch, made from cooked, dried, and ground potatoes, is a gluten-free thickener. Look for it in the kosher or baking aisle of your supermarket. Freezing the cake just until it becomes firm makes removing it from the pan and assembling it easier.

8 to 10 servings

Frosting

10	ounces bittersweet or semisweet chocolate (do not exceed 61% cacao), chopped
¾	cup sugar
¾	cup (1½ sticks) unsalted pareve margarine, diced
3	large eggs, beaten to blend
½	cup liquid nondairy creamer
	Pinch of coarse salt

Cake

1½	cups sugar, divided
1	cup natural unsweetened cocoa powder
6	tablespoons matzo cake meal
2	tablespoons potato starch
5	large eggs, separated, room temperature
¼	teaspoon salt
¼	cup vegetable oil
¼	cup liquid nondairy creamer
	Chocolate shavings (optional)
	Fresh mint leaves (optional)

FROSTING: Combine all ingredients in heavy large saucepan. Whisk over medium heat until chocolate melts and mixture is smooth and just begins to bubble, about 8 minutes. Chill until just thick enough to spread, stirring occasionally, about 1½ hours.

CAKE: Preheat oven to 350°F. Line 15½x10½x1-inch baking sheet with foil, leaving overhang. Grease foil. Sift ½ cup sugar, cocoa, cake meal, and potato starch into medium bowl.

Combine egg whites and salt in large bowl. Using handheld electric mixer, beat egg whites until soft peaks form. Gradually add ½ cup sugar; beat until stiff but not dry. Using same beaters, beat egg yolks and remaining ½ cup sugar in another large bowl until thick, about 2 minutes. Gradually beat in oil, then nondairy creamer. Add dry ingredients; beat just until blended. Fold egg white mixture into egg yolk mixture in 3 additions.

Spread batter on prepared sheet. Bake until tester inserted into center comes out dry and cake feels firm to touch, about 20 minutes. Cool cake in pan on rack. Freeze cake just until firm, about 30 minutes.

Using foil as aid, lift cake onto work surface. Cut cake crosswise into 3 rectangles, each about 10x5 inches. Slide large spatula under 1 cake rectangle; transfer to platter. Spread ⅔ cup frosting over. Top with second layer. Spread ⅔ cup frosting over. Top with third layer. Spread very thin layer of frosting over top and sides of cake to coat thinly and anchor crumbs. Chill cake 15 minutes to set thin coat of frosting. Spread remaining frosting decoratively over cake. Chill until cold, about 4 hours.

DO AHEAD: *Can be made 3 days ahead. Cover loosely with foil; keep chilled.*

Cover top of cake with chocolate shavings and garnish with mint, if desired. Cut crosswise into slices and serve.

Chocolate, Walnut, and Prune Fudge Torte

Prunes add moisture to this rich torte, which can be made up to three days before you plan to serve it. Slice it thinly: It's very rich, and a little goes a long way. To serve this dessert during Passover, make it with margarine for a meat meal or with butter for a dairy meal. Note that the cake needs to chill overnight after it's baked. **16 servings**

Cake

	Natural unsweetened cocoa powder
1½	cups diced pitted prunes (about 8 ounces)
1	cup prune juice
1	cup (2 sticks) unsalted margarine or unsalted butter
8	ounces bittersweet or semisweet chocolate (do not exceed 61% cacao), chopped
¾	cup natural unsweetened cocoa powder
1	cup coarsely chopped toasted walnuts
8	large eggs, room temperature
2	large egg yolks
1¾	cups sugar
	Pinch of salt

Glaze

1	cup prune juice
¼	cup (½ stick) unsalted margarine or unsalted butter
10	ounces bittersweet or semisweet chocolate (do not exceed 61% cacao), chopped
24	walnut halves

> ### Technique Tip: Slicing the Torte
> For thin, cleanly sliced portions of this dense chocolate torte, use a thin sharp knife dipped in very hot water. Wipe the knife dry with a thick dish towel, and dip it back into the hot water before each slice.

CAKE: Position rack in center of oven and preheat to 350°F. Brush 9-inch-diameter springform pan with 2¾-inch-high sides with margarine. Dust pan with cocoa; tap out excess. Wrap outside of pan with triple layer of heavy-duty foil. Combine prunes and prune juice in small bowl. Let stand 15 minutes.

Melt margarine in heavy medium saucepan over low heat. Add chocolate and whisk until melted and smooth. Remove from heat. Add ¾ cup cocoa and whisk until smooth. Mix in walnuts, then prune mixture. Cool to lukewarm.

Using electric mixer, beat eggs, egg yolks, sugar, and salt in large bowl at medium speed until well blended and just beginning to foam, about 1 minute. Fold in chocolate mixture. Transfer batter to prepared springform pan. Set springform pan in roasting pan. Pour enough hot water into roasting pan to come halfway up sides of springform pan.

Set roasting pan in oven and bake torte until top looks dry and crusty and tester inserted into center comes out with some moist crumbs attached, about 1 hour 5 minutes. Cool torte in pan on rack 30 minutes. Place in refrigerator uncovered and chill overnight.

GLAZE: Bring prune juice and margarine to boil in heavy medium saucepan over medium heat. Remove from heat. Add chocolate and whisk until smooth. Cool glaze until thick but still pourable, stirring occasionally, about 45 minutes.

Line plate with foil. Dip walnuts halfway into glaze. Arrange on foil and refrigerate until chocolate is set.

Meanwhile, cut around pan sides to loosen torte. Remove pan sides. Set torte on rack. Pour glaze over and spread to coat completely. Arrange walnuts, chocolate half at outer edge, around top of cake. Refrigerate until glaze is completely set, at least 3 hours.

DO AHEAD: *Can be made 3 days ahead. Cover loosely with foil or cake dome and keep refrigerated.*

Cut torte into wedges and serve.

Raspberry Ganache Marjolaine

Marjolaine is a classic French gâteau with a rectangular shape and multiple layers of nutty meringue and buttercream. This rendition features layers of raspberry ganache and hazelnut meringue. The absence of flour and the use of ground nuts, egg whites, and chocolate makes this a sophisticated gluten-free cake and Passover-friendly dessert (as long as you use "kosher for Passover" vanilla and almond extracts). Because it does use dairy ingredients, serve the marjolaine at a meatless Passover meal. **8 servings**

Ganache

2¼	**cups heavy whipping cream**
21	**ounces bittersweet or semisweet chocolate (do not exceed 61% cacao), chopped**
½	**cup raspberry preserves**
2	**tablespoons (¼ stick) unsalted butter, room temperature**
2	**tablespoons kosher Concord grape wine**

Meringue

2	**cups hazelnuts, toasted, husked, divided**
½	**cup plus 6 tablespoons sugar**
1	**tablespoon potato starch**
4	**large egg whites, room temperature**
½	**teaspoon fresh lemon juice**
½	**teaspoon vanilla extract**
¼	**teaspoon almond extract**
¼	**teaspoon salt**
1	**½-pint container raspberries**

> ## Technique Tip: **Meringue Layers**
> You won't need a special pan to make this stylish cake, just two baking sheets and parchment paper. Use a ruler and a pencil to trace perfect rectangles on the parchment as templates for the meringue layers, then turn the paper upside down so the pencil markings don't come in contact with the meringue. Add a dab of meringue under the corners of the paper to glue it in place on the baking sheet. Spread the meringue inside the traced rectangles.

GANACHE: Bring cream to boil in heavy medium saucepan. Remove from heat. Add chocolate and stir until melted and smooth. Stir in preserves, butter, and wine. Cover and chill overnight.

DO AHEAD: *Can be made 2 days ahead. Keep chilled.*

MERINGUE: Preheat oven to 275°F. Trace five 10×4-inch rectangles on 2 sheets of parchment paper. Invert parchment onto 2 baking sheets. Coarsely grind 1 cup hazelnuts in processor. Combine with ½ cup sugar and potato starch in medium bowl.

Using electric mixer fitted with clean dry beaters, beat egg whites in large bowl until foamy. Add lemon juice, both extracts, and salt; continue beating until soft peaks form. Gradually add remaining 6 tablespoons sugar and beat until egg whites are stiff and glossy. Gently fold in hazelnut-sugar mixture.

Place 1 cup meringue on parchment in center of 1 rectangle. Spread with small spatula to fill in rectangle. Repeat with remaining meringue and parchment. Bake until meringues are golden brown and just dry to touch, about 25 minutes. Cool on baking sheets. Carefully peel off paper (meringues will deflate slightly).

Place 1 meringue rectangle on 10×4-inch cardboard rectangle. Spread ½ cup ganache over meringue. Repeat layering with 3 more meringue rectangles and 1½ cups ganache. Top with remaining meringue rectangle. Spread top and sides of marjolaine with ¾ cup ganache. Chill marjolaine until firm, about 1 hour.

Rewarm remaining ganache in heavy medium saucepan over very low heat just until melted, stirring constantly. Cool to room temperature, about 20 minutes. Place marjolaine on wire rack set over baking sheet. Spread some ganache over sides of marjolaine. Pour remaining ganache over top; smooth with spatula if necessary. Let stand at room temperature until glaze is set, about 30 minutes.

Chop remaining 1 cup hazelnuts. Gently press hazelnuts onto sides of marjolaine. Decorate top with raspberries. Chill marjolaine 1 hour.

DO AHEAD: *Can be made 3 hours ahead. Keep chilled.*

Halloween Candy Cake

Peanut lovers will fall hard for this creation: roasted peanuts in the cake and topping, creamy peanut butter and peanut butter cups in the filling, and peanut butter candies on top. And with the fall colors of the candy topping, this would be a fun Halloween treat. The cake layers can be assembled a day ahead, but the whipped cream frosting will begin to weep if made too far in advance, so frost and decorate the cake a couple of hours before serving it. **12 servings**

Cake

1	**cup unsalted roasted peanuts**
¾	**cup unbleached all purpose flour**
6	**large eggs**
2	**large egg yolks**
1	**cup (packed) golden brown sugar**
1	**teaspoon vanilla extract**

Filling

½	**cup creamy peanut butter (do not use old-fashioned style or freshly ground)**
½	**cup (1 stick) unsalted butter, room temperature**
5	**tablespoons powdered sugar**
½	**cup heavy whipping cream**
5	**1.8-ounce packages Reese's Peanut Butter Cups, finely chopped**

Topping

1½	**cups chilled heavy whipping cream**
3	**tablespoons (packed) golden brown sugar**
1½	**teaspoons vanilla extract**
½	**cup unsalted roasted peanuts, coarsely chopped**
3	**2.1-ounce Butterfinger candy bars, cut into ¾-inch wedges**
⅓	**cup Reese's Pieces**

Technique Tip: Chopping Nuts

A food processor can chop nuts into uniform pieces in seconds. But just as quickly, it can turn the nuts to peanut butter. Use the pulse button to control how much the nuts are chopped, and stop the machine long enough to give the bowl a scrape and ensure all the nuts get equal chop time. Nuts start to release oil as they break down, so adding a little flour absorbs some of the oil and prevents the finely ground nuts from clumping and becoming paste.

CAKE: Preheat oven to 375°F. Butter and flour two 9-inch-diameter cake pans with 2-inch-high sides. Grind nuts and flour in processor until fine. Using electric mixer, beat eggs, egg yolks, sugar, and vanilla in large bowl until mixture whitens and triples in volume, about 4 minutes. Fold in nut mixture. Divide batter between prepared pans; smooth tops. Bake cakes until toothpick inserted in center comes out clean, about 20 minutes. Cool cakes in pans on rack.

FILLING: Blend peanut butter, butter, and sugar in processor until smooth. With machine running, add cream through feed tube and blend until mixture is light and fluffy.

Run small sharp knife around cake pan sides to loosen. Invert cakes onto work surface. Using serrated knife, cut each cake into 2 layers. Place 1 cake layer on platter, cut side up. Spread with ⅓ of filling and sprinkle with ⅓ of chopped peanut butter cups. Top with second cake layer, cut side down. Continue layering with remaining filling, peanut butter cups, and cake, ending with cake, cut side down.

DO AHEAD: *Can be made 1 day ahead. Cover and chill.*

TOPPING: Using electric mixer, beat cream, sugar, and vanilla in large bowl until almost stiff. Transfer ½ cup to small bowl and reserve for garnish.

Spread remaining whipped cream over top and sides of cake. Press nuts around base of cake, forming 1½-inch-high border. Cover top of cake with Butterfinger candy bars, leaving ½-inch border. Spoon reserved whipped cream into pastry bag fitted with medium star tip; pipe stars around top edge. Garnish with Reese's Pieces.

DO AHEAD: *Can be made 2 hours ahead. Chill. Let stand 1 hour at room temperature before serving.*

Chocolate Heart Layer Cake with Chocolate-Cinnamon Mousse

A chocolate-cinnamon mousse filling and chocolate glaze spiced with the flavors of chai tea give this cake a surprising, exotic twist. Begin preparing the cinnamon cream a day ahead since it needs to chill overnight. Cherry jam and kirsch moisten and flavor the cake layers. **4 servings**

Cake

4	tablespoons (½ stick) unsalted butter, melted, divided
⅓	cup unbleached all purpose flour
⅓	cup natural unsweetened cocoa powder
¼	teaspoon salt
4	large eggs
¾	cup sugar

Mousse Base

1	cup heavy whipping cream
4	cinnamon sticks, broken in half

Mousse and Cake Assembly

⅔	cup cherry jam
2	tablespoons kirsch (clear cherry brandy)
4	ounces bittersweet or semisweet chocolate (do not exceed 61% cacao), finely chopped

Glaze

½	cup heavy whipping cream
¼	cup water
2	tablespoons light corn syrup
1	teaspoon chai-spiced tea leaves or Lapsang Souchong black tea leaves (from 1 tea bag)
5	ounces bittersweet or semisweet chocolate (do not exceed 61% cacao), chopped

CAKE: Preheat oven to 400°F. Place 8x2-inch heart-shaped cake ring on sheet of foil. Wrap foil around sides of ring, folding, pressing, and crimping firmly to adhere (to prevent batter from leaking out). Brush foil and inside of ring with 1 tablespoon melted butter; dust with flour. Place on baking sheet.

Sift flour, cocoa, and salt into medium bowl. Combine eggs and sugar in large metal bowl. Set bowl over saucepan of simmering water (do not allow bowl to touch water). Whisk until sugar dissolves, about 2 minutes. Remove from over water. Using electric mixer, beat mixture until thick and billowy and heavy ribbon falls when beaters are lifted, about 5 minutes. Sift half of flour mixture over; fold in gently. Repeat with remaining flour mixture. Transfer ¼ cup batter to small bowl; fold in remaining 3 tablespoons melted butter. Gently fold butter mixture into batter; do not overmix or batter will deflate. Pour batter into ring.

Bake cake until tester inserted into center comes out clean, about 20 minutes. Transfer cake with foil to rack; cool completely.

DO AHEAD: *Can be made 1 day ahead. Cover and store at room temperature.*

MOUSSE BASE: Bring cream and cinnamon just to simmer in heavy medium saucepan. Remove from heat; let steep 1 hour at room temperature. Cover and chill cinnamon cream overnight.

MOUSSE AND CAKE ASSEMBLY: Stir jam and kirsch in small bowl to blend. Cut around sides of cake; lift off ring. Using metal spatula, loosen cake from foil. Using serrated knife, cut cake horizontally in half. Using tart pan bottom, transfer top cake layer to work surface; turn cut side up. Spread jam mixture on cut side of both cake layers.

Strain cinnamon cream into large bowl; beat until soft peaks form. Stir finely chopped chocolate in heavy small saucepan over low heat until smooth. Quickly fold warm chocolate into whipped cream (chocolate must be warm to blend smoothly). Immediately drop mousse by dollops over bottom cake layer; spread to within ¾ inch of edge. Gently press second cake layer, jam side down, atop mousse. Smooth sides of cake with offset spatula. Chill assembled cake on rack while preparing glaze.

GLAZE: Bring cream, ¼ cup water, corn syrup, and tea to boil in small saucepan, stirring constantly. Remove from heat; steep 5 minutes. Strain into another small saucepan; return to boil. Remove from heat. Add chopped chocolate; whisk until smooth. Cool glaze until thickened but still pourable, about 30 minutes. Place rack with cake over baking sheet. Slowly pour glaze over cake to cover, using spatula if necessary to spread evenly. Chill until glaze is firm, at least 2 hours.

DO AHEAD: *Can be made 1 day ahead. Keep chilled.*

Place cake on platter and serve.

Tiered Almond Cake with Mixed Berries and White Chocolate–Cream Cheese Frosting

This pretty, two-tiered cake is flavored with almond, filled with assorted berries, and frosted with a rich mixture of white chocolate and cream cheese. It's perfect for a bridal shower, a small intimate wedding, a sweet 16 party, or any other special occasion. To make sure the frosting sets properly, use a high-quality white chocolate, such as Lindt or Perugina. The piped whipped cream dots are very easy to create, but you can omit them if you prefer. You'll need dowels to separate the tiers; they are available at cake supply stores and most hardware stores. The cake can be prepared up to two days ahead. **25 servings**

Cake

2¼	cups blanched slivered almonds
2	cups cake flour
1	tablespoon baking powder
1	cup plus 2 tablespoons (2¼ sticks) unsalted butter, room temperature
1½	cups sugar
21	ounces almond paste, cut into small pieces
12	large eggs, room temperature
1	tablespoon vanilla extract

Filling

2	cups frozen blueberries, thawed
2	cups frozen boysenberries or blackberries, thawed
2	cups fresh raspberries
⅔	cup sugar

Frosting

15	ounces high-quality white chocolate (such as Lindt or Perugina), chopped
2¼	cups (4½ sticks) unsalted butter, room temperature
2½	pounds Philadelphia-brand cream cheese, room temperature
3	tablespoons vanilla extract
1¼	teaspoons almond extract
6½	cups powdered sugar
1	cup sour cream

Assembly

1	11-inch-diameter cardboard round
1	7-inch-diameter cardboard round
2	yards lavender or pink ribbon (about 1 inch wide)
4	6-inch-long, ¼-inch-diameter wood dowels
	Assorted fresh flowers

CAKE: Preheat oven to 325°F. Butter and flour one 8-inch-diameter cake pan with 2-inch-high sides and one 12-inch-diameter cake pan with 2-inch-high sides. Finely grind almonds in processor. Sift flour and baking powder into small bowl. Set aside.

Using electric mixer, cream butter with sugar in large bowl until blended. Beat in almond paste a few pieces at a time. Beat until mixture resembles smooth paste. Add eggs 1 at a time, beating well after each addition. Add vanilla and beat until batter increases slightly in volume, about 5 minutes. Mix in ground almonds, then flour mixture.

Divide batter between prepared pans. Bake until tester inserted in center of cakes comes out clean, about 55 minutes for 8-inch cake and about 1 hour 5 minutes for 12-inch cake. Cool cakes in pans on rack 10 minutes. Run small sharp knife around cake pan sides to loosen. Turn cakes out onto racks and cool completely.

DO AHEAD: *Can be made 1 day ahead. Wrap tightly in plastic and store at room temperature.*

FILLING: Combine all berries in heavy large saucepan. Sprinkle with sugar. Let stand 45 minutes, stirring occasionally. Bring berry mixture to boil. Reduce heat and simmer until mixture is reduced to 2 cups, stirring occasionally, about 20 minutes. Transfer to bowl. Cover and chill until well chilled.

DO AHEAD: *Can be made 1 day ahead. Keep chilled.*

FROSTING: Melt chocolate in top of double boiler over barely simmering water, stirring until smooth. Cool chocolate until just slightly warm.

Using electric mixer, beat butter in large bowl until light. Gradually add cream cheese, beating until just combined. Beat in both extracts. Add sugar and beat just until smooth. Add melted chocolate and beat until just combined. Stir in sour cream. If necessary, chill frosting until spreadable.

(continued next page)

Tiered Almond Cake with Mixed Berries and White Chocolate–Cream Cheese Frosting *(continued)*

ASSEMBLY: Using serrated knife, cut each cake horizontally into 3 layers. Place bottom 12-inch cake layer on 11-inch-diameter cardboard round. Spread with ⅔ cup berry filling, leaving ½-inch border uncovered. Carefully spread 2 cups frosting over entire layer. Top with middle 12-inch cake layer. Spread with ⅔ cup berry filling, leaving ½-inch border uncovered. Carefully spread 2 cups frosting over entire layer. Top with top 12-inch cake layer, cut side down. Spread 3 cups frosting over top and sides of cake.

Place bottom 8-inch cake layer on 7-inch-diameter cardboard round. Spread with ¼ cup berry filling, leaving ¼-inch border uncovered. Carefully spread ¾ cup frosting over entire layer. Top with middle 8-inch cake layer. Spread with ¼ cup berry filling, leaving ¼-inch border uncovered. Carefully spread ¾ cup frosting over entire layer. Top with top 8-inch cake layer, cut side down. Spread 2 cups frosting over top and sides of cake.

Cut one 40-inch long piece of ribbon and wrap around base of 12-inch cake. Press gently onto sides to adhere. Cut one 27-inch-long piece of ribbon and wrap around base of 8-inch cake. Press gently onto sides to adhere. Chill both cakes until frosting sets, about 3 hours.

Place 12-inch cake on platter. Press dowel into center of cake. Mark dowel ⅛ inch above top of cake. Remove and cut with serrated knife at marked point. Cut remaining dowels to same length. Carefully press dowels into bottom cake tier 3½ to 4 inches in from cake edges, spacing evenly. Gently place 8-inch cake on cardboard atop bottom cake tier, centering carefully, with cake resting on dowels.

Spoon remaining frosting into pastry bag fitted with small round tip. Pipe dots of frosting on top edge of both cakes. Chill until frosting sets, about 1 hour.

DO AHEAD: *Can be made 2 days ahead. Cover loosely with plastic wrap and keep chilled.*

Arrange flowers atop cake.

DO AHEAD: *Can be made 4 hours ahead.*

Serve cake cold or at room temperature. Remove top tier; cut into slices. Remove dowels from bottom cake. Starting 3 inches in from edge of bottom cake and cutting through from top to bottom, cut 6-inch-diameter circle in center of cake. Cut outer portion of cake into slices, then cut inner portion into slices.

Making Tiered Cakes

When making tiered cakes for special occasions, a few non-food items are essential to stack the cakes beautifully. Most items can be found at cake supply stores, some craft stores, and online (see Online and Mail-Order Sources, page 632).

- Use cardboard cake circles to support each layered cake (usually you'll want to use circles that are slightly smaller than the diameter of the cakes, so they're not visible).
- Dowels, either wooden or plastic, provide a firm foundation for the top tiers. Wooden dowels can also be found at most hardware stores.
- A 1-inch-wide ribbon looks pretty when wrapped around the base of a cake—it hides any imperfections along the bottom edge and gives the cake a polished look. (Remove the ribbon just before serving the cake.)
- Cake boxes and nonslip shelf liners keep the cake tiers safe while they're being transported. A piece of shelf liner under the cake box prevents the box from sliding around in the car.
- Select a cake base on which the finished cake will be displayed. These range in style to suit different cakes.

Tiramisù Wedding Cake with Mixed Berries

This cake has all the flavors of tiramisù, the popular Italian dessert. The cake layers are brushed with espresso syrup, covered with a luscious Marsala–cream cheese frosting, and sprinkled with ground chocolate. Assemble and frost the cakes one day ahead. Tier the cakes and add the finishing frosting touches up to eight hours ahead and keep refrigerated. The cake can stand at cool room temperature throughout the ceremony and reception (up to six hours). **50 servings**

Cake

7½	cups unbleached all purpose flour
3	tablespoons baking powder
2	teaspoons salt
2¾	cups (5½ sticks) unsalted butter, room temperature
5⅔	cups sugar
2½	tablespoons vanilla extract
2	teaspoons almond extract
3¾	cups whole milk (do not use low-fat or nonfat)
18	large egg whites (about 2⅓ cups), room temperature

Syrup

2	cups Kahlúa or other coffee-flavored liqueur
1½	cups water
½	cup plus 1 tablespoon instant espresso powder or instant coffee powder

Frosting

14	8-ounce packages Philadelphia-brand cream cheese, room temperature
7	cups powdered sugar
2⅓	cups chilled heavy whipping cream
7	tablespoons sweet Marsala
3½	tablespoons vanilla extract

Assembly

12	ounces bittersweet or semisweet chocolate, chopped
1	6-inch-diameter cardboard cake round
1	9-inch-diameter cardboard cake round
1	12-inch-diameter cardboard cake round
1	11-inch-diameter revolving cake stand (optional)
9	12-inch-long, ¼-inch-diameter wood dowels
4½	cups assorted whole berries (such as raspberries, blueberries, blackberries, and strawberries)
	Fresh mint sprigs

Topping

12	cups mixed berries (such as raspberries, blueberries, blackberries, and hulled, quartered strawberries)
6	tablespoons sugar

(continued next page)

> ## Presentation Tip: **Transporting the Cake**
> If the cake is being transported to another location, bring each chilled layer inserted with dowels to the site, along with the remaining frosting in a pastry bag and a large metal spatula. Assemble the cake tiers, do the final piping of frosting, and garnish with berries on the table where the cake will be served. Never leave a cake in a warm area or in direct sunlight, as the frosting will melt.

Tiramisù Wedding Cake
with Mixed Berries *(continued)*

CAKE: Position 1 rack in top third and 1 rack in bottom third of oven and preheat to 350°F. Butter one 12-inch-diameter cake pan with 3-inch-high sides, one 9-inch-diameter cake pan with 3-inch-high sides, and one 6-inch-diameter cake pan with 3-inch-high sides. Line pan bottoms with parchment paper. Sift flour, baking powder, and salt into medium bowl. Using electric mixer, beat butter in 12-quart bowl at medium-high speed until light. Gradually add sugar and beat until well blended. Beat in both extracts. At medium-low speed, beat in flour mixture alternately with milk in 3 additions each, beating just until combined (batter will be thick).

Using electric mixer fitted with clean dry beaters, beat egg whites in another large bowl until stiff but not dry. Fold ⅓ of whites into batter to lighten. Fold in remaining whites. Spoon batter into prepared pans, making sure that depth of batter is the same in each pan; smooth tops. Bake until tops are deep golden brown and tester inserted into centers comes out clean, about 55 minutes for 6-inch cake, about 1 hour 5 minutes for 9-inch cake, and about 1 hour 20 minutes for 12-inch cake. Cool cakes in pans on racks 20 minutes. Run knife around pan sides to loosen cakes. Turn out cakes onto racks and peel off parchment. Cool cakes completely.

SYRUP: Mix all ingredients in heavy large saucepan. Boil over medium-high heat until mixture is reduced to 2⅔ cups, stirring occasionally, about 10 minutes. Cool syrup completely.

FROSTING: Using electric mixer, beat cream cheese in large bowl until light. Gradually add sugar and beat until fluffy. Add cream, Marsala, and vanilla; beat until well blended. Cover and let stand at room temperature up to 1 hour.

ASSEMBLY: Finely grind chocolate in processor (do not overprocess or chocolate will soften and clump together). Using serrated knife, cut each cake horizontally into 3 equal layers. Spread dab of frosting on 6-inch-diameter cardboard round; top with bottom layer of 6-inch cake, cut side up. Brush cake with 2 tablespoons syrup, then spread ½ cup frosting over and sprinkle with 2 tablespoons ground chocolate. Top with middle layer of 6-inch cake. Brush with 2 tablespoons syrup, then spread ½ cup frosting over and sprinkle with 2 tablespoons ground chocolate. Brush 2 tablespoons syrup over cut side of top layer of 6-inch cake. Using hands, turn cake layer over and place cut side down atop frosted cake layers. Cover and chill cake.

Spread dab of frosting on 9-inch-diameter cardboard round; top with bottom layer of 9-inch cake, cut side up. Brush with ¼ cup syrup, then spread 1 cup frosting over and sprinkle with ¼ cup ground chocolate. Top with middle layer of 9-inch cake. Brush with ¼ cup syrup [1], then spread 1 cup frosting over and sprinkle with ¼ cup ground chocolate. Brush ¼ cup syrup over cut side of top layer of 9-inch cake. Slide large tart pan bottom or springform cake pan bottom under cake layer. Using pan bottom as aid, lift cake layer and turn cut side down atop frosted cake layers. Cover and chill cake.

Spread dab of frosting on 12-inch-diameter cardboard round; top with bottom layer of 12-inch cake, cut side up. Brush with ½ cup syrup, then spread 2 cups frosting over and sprinkle with ½ cup ground chocolate. Top with middle layer of 12-inch cake. Brush with ½ cup syrup, then spread 2 cups frosting over and sprinkle with ½ cup ground chocolate. Brush ½ cup syrup over cut side of top layer of 12-inch cake. Slide large tart pan bottom or cake pan bottom under

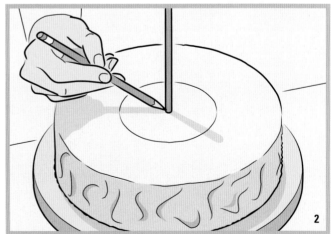

cake. Using pan bottom as aid, lift cake layer and turn cut side down atop frosted cake layers. Cover and chill all cakes until firm, about 4 hours. Cover remaining frosting and let stand at room temperature.

Place 12-inch cake on cardboard round atop large flat platter. Place platter on cake stand if using. Using icing spatula, spread 4 cups frosting over top and sides of cake; smooth top. Swirl frosting decoratively on sides of cake. Press 1 dowel into center of 12-inch cake. Mark dowel ¼ inch above top of cake [2]. Remove dowel and cut with serrated knife at marked point. Cut 4 more dowels to same length. Press 4 cut dowels into 12-inch cake, inserting 4 inches in from cake edges and spacing evenly. Press 1 dowel into center of cake. Chill cake on platter.

Place 9-inch cake on cardboard round atop large flat plate or tart pan bottom. Place plate on cake stand. Using icing spatula, spread 3 cups frosting over top and sides of cake; smooth top. Swirl frosting decoratively on sides of cake. Press 1 dowel into center of 9-inch cake. Mark dowel ¼ inch above top of cake. Remove dowel and cut at marked point. Cut remaining 3 dowels to same length. Press 4 cut dowels into 9-inch cake, inserting 3 inches in from cake edges and spacing evenly. Chill 9-inch cake on plate.

Place 6-inch cake on cardboard round atop large flat plate or tart pan bottom. Place plate on cake stand. Using icing spatula, spread 2 cups frosting over top and sides of cake; smooth top. Swirl frosting decoratively on sides of cake. Chill all cakes until frosting sets, about 2 hours.

DO AHEAD: *Can be made 1 day ahead. Cover cakes and remaining frosting separately with plastic wrap; keep refrigerated. Bring frosting to room temperature before continuing.*

Using metal spatula as aid, gently place 9-inch cake on cardboard round atop 12-inch cake, centering carefully on dowels. Gently place 6-inch cake on cardboard round atop dowels in 9-inch cake.

Spoon remaining frosting into pastry bag fitted with medium star tip. Pipe decorative border around base of 12-inch cake and around top edge of each tier. Arrange berries decoratively inside piped borders atop each tier.

DO AHEAD: *Can be made 8 hours ahead. Keep chilled.*

Let cake stand at room temperature at least 3 hours and up to 6 hours before serving. Garnish with mint.

TOPPING: Toss berries with sugar in large bowl. Let stand at least 30 minutes and up to 2 hours at room temperature.

Remove top and middle cake tiers. Remove dowels from middle cake. Cut top and middle cakes into slices; transfer to plates. Remove dowels from bottom cake. Starting 3 inches in from edge of bottom cake and cutting through from top to bottom, cut 6-inch-diameter circle in center of cake. Cut outer portion of cake into slices [3], then cut inner portion into slices. Spoon berries around cake slices and serve.

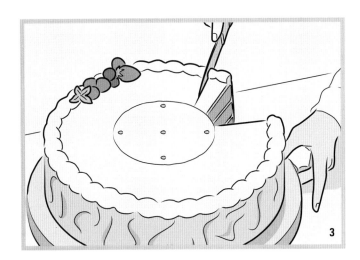

White Chocolate and Lemon Wedding Cake

Clear instructions, simple techniques, and plenty of do-aheads make this impressive wedding cake foolproof. The result is a take on a classic American silver cake (which is made with egg whites) filled with lemon mousse and lemon curd (which uses the egg yolks). The tiers are frosted with a delicate icing made of white chocolate and cream cheese. A delicious bonus: An elegant, colorful compote made with fresh berries accompanies each slice. **50 servings**

Lemon Curd

Make the curd in two separate batches. It's used as a filling between the cake layers and as a component in the mousse. **Makes about 10½ cups**

6   cups sugar, divided
9   teaspoons cornstarch, divided
3   cups fresh lemon juice, divided
36 large egg yolks, divided
3   cups (6 sticks) unsalted butter, cut into 24 pieces, divided

Whisk 3 cups sugar and 4½ teaspoons cornstarch in heavy medium saucepan to blend. Gradually whisk in 1½ cups lemon juice, then 18 egg yolks. Add 1½ cups butter. Cook over medium heat until curd thickens and boils, whisking constantly, about 18 minutes. Transfer curd to medium bowl. Press plastic wrap directly onto surface of curd. Make second batch of curd, using same amount of each ingredient. Chill at least 1 day.

DO AHEAD: *Can be made 7 days ahead. Keep chilled.*

Frosting

Make the frosting in two separate batches at least one day ahead. One batch is for the 12-inch cake; the second batch is for the other two cakes. Cream replaces butter in this variation of standard cream cheese frosting, so it's spreadable straight from the fridge. For the best results, use heavy whipping cream. **Makes about 16 cups**

16 ounces high-quality white chocolate (such as Lindt or Perugina), chopped, divided
6   8-ounce packages Philadelphia-brand cream cheese, room temperature, divided
5   cups (packed) powdered sugar (about 1¼ pounds), divided
4   cups chilled heavy whipping cream, divided

Place 8 ounces chocolate in top of double boiler set over barely simmering water. Stir until chocolate is melted, smooth, and just warm (do not overheat); remove from over water. Using electric mixer, beat 3 packages cream cheese in large bowl until fluffy. Beat in 1¼ cups sugar, then warm chocolate. Beat 2 cups cream and 1¼ cups sugar in medium bowl until medium-firm peaks form. Fold into cream cheese mixture in 3 additions. Cover; chill. Make second batch of frosting, using same amount of each ingredient. Chill frosting at least 1 day.

DO AHEAD: *Can be made 4 days ahead. Keep chilled.*

Lemon–White Chocolate Mousse
Makes about 7 cups

4	cups lemon curd (see left)
14	ounces high-quality white chocolate (such as Lindt or Perugina), chopped
1⅓	cups chilled heavy whipping cream

Place lemon curd in large bowl and chill. Place white chocolate in top of double boiler set over barely simmering water. Stir until chocolate is melted, smooth, and just warm (do not overheat); remove from over water. Using electric mixer, beat cream in another large bowl until medium-firm peaks form; add warm chocolate and fold together. Fold mixture into lemon curd in 3 additions. Cover bowl and chill mousse until cold and set, at least 1 day.

DO AHEAD: *Can be made 4 days ahead. Keep chilled.*

Orange Buttermilk Cake
Use half of these ingredients to make the 12-inch cake and half to make both the 9- and 6-inch cakes.

11	cups sifted cake flour (sifted, then measured), divided
11	teaspoons baking powder, divided
2½	teaspoons salt, divided
3	cups buttermilk, divided
6	tablespoons thawed frozen orange juice concentrate, divided
5	tablespoons vanilla extract, divided
1½	cups (3 sticks) unsalted butter, room temperature, divided
6½	cups sugar, divided
1½	cups vegetable oil, divided
2½	cups egg whites (about 20 large), room temperature, divided
½	teaspoon cream of tartar, divided

Position rack just below center of oven and preheat to 350°F. Butter and flour 12-inch-diameter cake pan with 3-inch-high sides and removable bottom. Butter and flour 9-inch-diameter cake pan with 3-inch-high sides and removable bottom. Butter and flour 6-inch-diameter cake pan with 3-inch-high sides and removable bottom. Sift 5½ cups sifted flour, 5½ teaspoons baking powder, and 1¼ teaspoons salt into large bowl 3 times. Mix 1½ cups buttermilk, 3 tablespoons orange juice concentrate, and 2½ tablespoons vanilla in small bowl.

Using electric mixer, beat ¾ cup (1½ sticks) butter in large bowl until smooth and fluffy. Gradually beat in 1¼ cups sugar, then ¾ cup oil. Beat in 1 more cup sugar. Beat in flour mixture in 4 additions alternately with buttermilk mixture in 3 additions, scraping down sides of bowl often. Using clean dry beaters, beat 1¼ cups (about 10) egg whites and ¼ teaspoon cream of tartar in another large bowl until soft peaks form. Gradually add 1 cup sugar, beating until egg whites fall from beaters in thick, puffy (not stiff) ribbon, about 4 minutes. Fold egg white mixture into batter in 4 additions. Transfer batter to prepared 12-inch pan.

Bake cake until brown and tester inserted into center comes out clean, about 1 hour 25 minutes. Cool cake in pan on rack 30 minutes. Cut around cake to loosen; remove pan sides. Maintain oven temperature.

Make second batch of cake batter following same technique as for first cake and using same amount of each ingredient. Transfer 8½ cups batter to prepared 9-inch pan; transfer 4 cups batter to prepared 6-inch pan. Bake cakes until brown and tester inserted into centers comes out clean, about 1 hour 10 minutes for 6-inch cake, and about 1 hour 18 minutes for 9-inch cake. Cool cakes in pans on racks 30 minutes. Cut around cakes to loosen. Remove pan sides. Let cakes stand until cooled completely.

DO AHEAD: *Can be made 1 day before filling and frosting the cakes. Return cakes to pans. Cover with foil and store at room temperature.*

(continued next page)

White Chocolate and
Lemon Wedding Cake *(continued)*

Assembling Cakes
To make filling and frosting the cakes easier, use the removable bottoms of tart pans or buy cardboard rounds from a cake or candy supply store.

2	**11-inch-diameter tart-pan bottoms or cardboard rounds**
1	**8-inch-diameter tart-pan bottom or cardboard round (cut from 9-inch round)**
1	**5-inch-diameter tart-pan bottom or cardboard round (cut from 6-inch round)**
14	**12-inch-long, ¼-inch-diameter wood dowels**

Push 12-inch cake up to release from pan. Using large serrated knife, cut off enough of top crust to make cake 2½ inches high. Cut cake horizontally into 3 layers, each about ¾ inch thick. Using tart-pan bottom or 11-inch-diameter cardboard round, transfer top layer of cake to work surface and cover; transfer middle layer of cake to work surface and cover. Cut bottom layer of cake from pan bottom and place on tart-pan bottom or cardboard round. Spread generous 1¾ cups mousse over. Drop 1¾ cups curd over by table-spoonfuls and spread to cover mousse in even layer. Chill until mousse and curd are firm, about 1 hour. Using tart-pan bottom, place middle layer of cake atop bottom layer. Spread with same amounts of mousse and curd. Using tart-pan bottom, place top layer of cake atop middle layer and press lightly. Chill assembled cake.

Push 9-inch cake up to release from pan. Cut off enough of top crust to make cake 2½ inches high. Cut cake horizontally into 3 layers, each about ¾ inch thick. Using tart-pan bottom or cardboard round, transfer top layer of cake to work surface and cover; repeat with middle layer of cake. Cut bottom layer of cake from pan bottom and place on 8-inch-diameter tart-pan bottom or cardboard round. Spread 1¼ cups mousse over. Drop generous ⅔ cup curd over by tablespoonfuls and spread to cover mousse in even layer. Chill until mousse and curd are firm, about 1 hour. Using tart-pan bottom, place middle layer of cake atop bottom layer. Spread with same amount of mousse and curd. Using tart-pan bottom, place top layer of cake atop middle layer and press lightly. Chill assembled cake.

Push 6-inch cake up to release from pan. Cut off enough of top crust to make cake 2½ inches high. Cut cake horizontally into 3 layers, each about ¾ inch thick. Transfer top layer of cake to work surface and cover; repeat with middle layer of cake. Cut bottom layer of cake from pan bottom and place on 5-inch-diameter tart-pan bottom or cardboard round. Spread generous ½ cup mousse over. Drop 6 tablespoons curd over by tablespoonfuls and spread to cover mousse in even layer. Chill until mousse and curd are firm, about 1 hour. Using large spatula, place middle layer of cake atop bottom layer. Spread with same amount of mousse and curd. Using large spatula, place top layer of cake atop middle layer and press lightly. Chill assembled cake.

Spread 2¼ cups frosting thinly over top and sides of 12-inch assembled cake. Spread 1½ cups frosting thinly over top and sides of 9-inch assembled cake. Spread ¾ cup frosting thinly over top and sides of 6-inch assembled cake. Chill cakes 1 hour.

Spread 5 cups frosting over 12-inch cake. Spread 3⅔ cups frosting over 9-inch cake. Spread 2 cups frosting over 6-inch cake. Chill 6-inch cake.

Place 12-inch cake on platter. Press 1 dowel into center and through to bottom of cake. Mark dowel 1¼ inches above level of frosting. Remove dowel and cut with serrated knife at marked point. Cut 7 more dowels to same length. Press 1 dowel into center of cake. Press remaining 7 dowels into cake, spacing apart equally, 3 to 3¼ inches from center dowel. Chill cake with dowels.

Press 1 dowel into center of 9-inch cake. Mark dowel 1¼ inches above level of frosting. Remove dowel and cut with serrated knife at marked point. Cut 5 more dowels to same length. Press 1 dowel into center of cake. Press remaining 5 dowels into cake, spacing apart equally, 2 inches from center. Chill cake with dowels in place.

DO AHEAD: *Can be made 2 days ahead. After frosting is firm, cover cakes with cake domes or loosely with foil; keep chilled.*

Assembly and Decoration

Mix of large and tiny white roses and freesias (about 5 dozen)

Place 9-inch cake atop dowels in 12-inch cake. Place 6-inch cake atop dowels in 9-inch cake. Place large roses between bottom and middle tiers, fitting in tiny roses and freesias to fill space. Fill space between middle and top tiers with mix of flowers.

Berry Compote
Makes about 16 cups

8	1-pint containers strawberries, hulled, halved
2	½-pint containers blackberries
2	½-pint containers raspberries
2	½-pint containers blueberries
1	cup sugar

Combine all berries and sugar in large bowl; toss to coat. Cover; chill until juices form, at least 1 hour and up to 6 hours.

SERVING: Place top and middle cake tiers on work surface. Remove flowers and dowels from cakes. Cut top cake into 8 slices. Cut middle cake into 16 slices. Insert knife straight down into 12-inch cake 3 inches from edge. Continue to cut around cake 3 inches from edge, making 6-inch-diameter circle in center. Cut outer ring into 18 slices. Cut 6-inch center into 8 slices. Place cake slices on plates; spoon compote alongside each.

Tiered Cake Timeline

Don't wait until the last minute to make multi-tiered cakes—it's not like baking a simple batch of cupcakes. But a bit of timing and planning makes baking multiple cakes completely manageable. Since each cake recipe includes suitable do-aheads, abide by their guidelines to ensure the best results. When in doubt, this breakdown can help you map out each step.

- 7 days before the event, have all your ingredients and equipment on hand.

- 5 days ahead, clear enough room in the refrigerator to store the filling, frostings, and cakes.

- 4 days before the event, make the frosting and fillings.

- 3 days ahead, bake the cakes and store them properly to maintain freshness.

- 2 days ahead, fill and frost the cakes, and insert dowels into the bottom tiers.

- 1 day ahead, buy fresh flowers (if using). Stand the flowers in water and refrigerate.

- 4 hours before the event, transport the cakes and assemble them upon arrival. Bring extra frosting and tools, such as offset spatulas and piping bags.

♥♥♥♥ Triple-Chocolate Celebration Cake

Any time one dessert features three forms of chocolate—chocolate cake, chocolate ganache, and chocolate mousse—there's going to be a celebration. Serve this stunning dessert at a bridal shower, a graduation, on Father's Day, or for any other summertime occasion when berries are full of flavor. Begin making the cake one day ahead; you'll need a 9-inch tart pan bottom or cardboard round when you assemble the cake. Enjoy the extra mousse and cake later with fresh berries. **20 servings**

Cake

2¾	**cups cake flour**
1	**cup natural unsweetened cocoa powder**
2	**teaspoons baking soda**
¾	**teaspoon salt**
½	**teaspoon baking powder**
2¾	**cups sugar**
4	**large eggs**
2	**large egg yolks**
1	**cup vegetable oil**
1	**cup sour cream**
1	**tablespoon vanilla extract**
¾	**cup mini semisweet chocolate chips**

Ganache

3	**cups heavy whipping cream**
1½	**pounds bittersweet or semisweet chocolate (do not exceed 61% cacao), chopped**

Mousse

4⅓	**cups chilled heavy whipping cream, divided**
½	**cup light corn syrup**
1¼	**pounds bittersweet or semisweet chocolate (do not exceed 61% cacao), chopped**

Assembly and Serving

⅔	**cup seedless raspberry jam**
1	**15¾x11¾-inch transfer sheet with gold-thread design**
¾	**pound bittersweet or semisweet chocolate, chopped**
3	**½-pint containers raspberries**
½	**pound cherries**
1	**1-pint container small strawberries**
1	**½-pint container blueberries**
1	**½-pint container blackberries**

Decorating Made Easy

Pliable plastic sheets called transfers are coated with a mixture of cocoa butter and food coloring and etched with repetitive designs. The ones used here create an exquisite gold-thread pattern on the band of chocolate that's wrapped around the cake. The sheets are see-through, so be sure the pattern side is facing up (you can tell by touching the raised surface with your fingertips). They're easy to use, too; the melted chocolate is simply spread over the sheets, and once the chocolate becomes firm, the plastic sheets are peeled away, leaving an edible design on the chocolate's surface. You can purchase transfer sheets at some cake and candy supply stores or by mail from Beryl's Cake Decorating & Pastry Supplies (beryls.com or 800-488-2749).

CAKE: Position rack in center of oven and preheat to 350°F. Butter and flour two 10-inch-diameter cake pans with 2-inch-high sides; line each with round of parchment paper or waxed paper. Combine flour, cocoa, baking soda, salt, and baking powder in medium bowl; whisk to blend well. Using electric mixer, beat sugar, eggs, and egg yolks in large bowl until very thick and heavy ribbon falls when beaters are lifted, about 6 minutes. Add oil, sour cream, and vanilla, then flour mixture all at once to egg mixture. Beat at low speed until just blended, about 1 minute. Scrape down sides of bowl. Beat at high speed until well blended, about 3 minutes. Fold in chocolate chips; divide batter between prepared pans (about 3¾ cups batter in each).

Bake cakes until tester inserted into center comes out clean, about 40 minutes. Cool cakes completely in pans on racks. Cover and let cakes stand at room temperature overnight.

GANACHE: Bring cream to simmer in heavy large saucepan over medium-high heat. Remove from heat. Add chocolate and whisk until chocolate is melted and mixture is smooth. Transfer ganache to glass bowl. Let stand until thick enough to spread, about 4 hours.

DO AHEAD: *Can be made 1 day ahead. Cover; chill.*

MOUSSE: Using electric mixer, beat 3⅓ cups cream in large bowl until peaks form; chill. Combine remaining 1 cup cream and corn syrup in heavy medium saucepan and bring to simmer. Remove from heat. Add chocolate and whisk until melted, smooth, and still warm to touch. Pour warm chocolate mixture directly onto whipped cream and fold in gently. Chill until mousse is set, at least 8 hours.

DO AHEAD: *Can be made 1 day ahead. Cover and keep chilled.*

ASSEMBLY AND SERVING: Cut around pan sides; turn out cakes. Peel off parchment. Cut each cake horizontally in half. Place 1 cake layer, cut side up, on 9-inch-diameter tart pan bottom or cardboard round. Place another cake layer, cut side up, on clean baking sheet. Spread each with ⅓ cup raspberry jam. Chill until jam sets, about 15 minutes.

If ganache is chilled, microwave on defrost setting in 15-second intervals until just soft enough to spread, stirring occasionally. Drop 1 cup ganache by rounded teaspoonfuls over each jam layer. Using offset spatula, gently spread ganache to cover jam. Drop 3 cups mousse by heaping spoonfuls onto each ganache layer; gently spread to cover. Chill cake layers 30 minutes. Using large metal spatula, place cake layer from baking sheet, mousse side up, atop cake layer on tart pan bottom. Place third cake layer, cut side down, atop cake (reserve remaining cake layer for another use). Spread 1 cup mousse over top of assembled cake. Using long offset spatula, spread sides of assembled cake with enough ganache (about 1½ cups) to fill gaps and make smooth surface. Transfer cake on tart pan bottom to platter.

Turn 1 large baking sheet upside down on work surface. Arrange two 20-inch-long pieces of foil on work surface. Cut two 15¾x4½-inch-strips from transfer sheet. Lay 1 transfer sheet strip, rough-textured design facing up, onto each sheet of foil.

Place chocolate in medium metal bowl; set bowl over saucepan of simmering water (do not allow bowl to touch water). Stir until chocolate is smooth and very warm to touch (about 115°F). Remove bowl from over water.

Pour thick ribbon of melted chocolate (about ⅔ cup) onto 1 transfer sheet strip. Using long offset spatula, spread chocolate evenly over transfer strip, covering completely (chocolate will run over sides of strip) [1]. Using tip of knife, lift edge of chocolate-coated strip. Slide hands between transfer strip and foil; lift entire transfer strip and place it, chocolate side up, on inverted baking sheet [2]. Chill until chocolate on strip is set and loses gloss but is still flexible (do not let chocolate become too firm), about 1½ minutes. Using fingertips, lift chocolate-coated strip and attach, chocolate side in, to side of cake [3]. Press strip to seal chocolate to side of cake (strip will stand about 1 inch above top edge of cake). Coat remaining transfer strip with chocolate and transfer to inverted baking sheet; chill until set but still flexible. Arrange 1 end of second strip against (but not overlapping) 1 end of first strip. Press second strip to seal chocolate to side of cake (both strips will just encircle cake). Chill cake until chocolate strips are firm, about 30 minutes. Carefully peel transfer paper off chocolate strips [4]. Chill cake at least 3 hours and up to 1 day.

Mound fruit atop cake. Chill until ready to serve.

DO AHEAD: *Cake can be assembled up to 8 hours ahead. Keep chilled.*

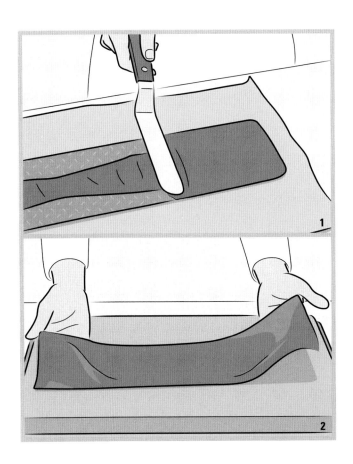

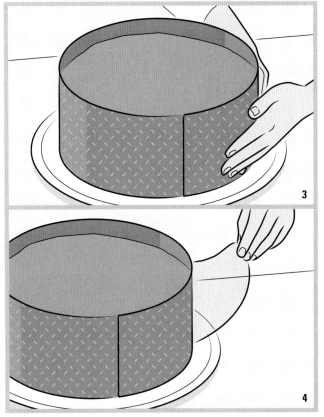

Spiced Chocolate Torte Wrapped in Chocolate Ribbons

Adorned with a ribbon and a big bow, this cake looks like a delicious present. Adding corn syrup to the melted chocolates creates a pliable mixture known as modeling chocolate. Using a pasta machine makes it easy to roll out sheets of chocolate to cut into ribbons, but the cake would look stunning with just the glaze and fresh flowers. **12 to 14 servings**

Cake

1½	cups (3 sticks) butter, room temperature
2	cups sugar
8	eggs, separated, room temperature
10	ounces bittersweet or semisweet chocolate (do not exceed 61% cacao), melted, lukewarm
1½	cups finely chopped pecans
2	teaspoons vanilla
1	teaspoon ground cinnamon
1	teaspoon ground cloves
1	teaspoon freshly grated nutmeg
1⅓	cups unbleached all purpose flour, sifted (measured, then sifted)
	Pinch of salt
	Pinch of cream of tartar

Buttercream

¾	cup sugar
½	cup light corn syrup
4	jumbo egg yolks
1½	cups (3 sticks) butter, cut into small pieces, room temperature
6	ounces bittersweet or semisweet chocolate (do not exceed 61% cacao), melted and cooled (but still pourable)
¼	cup dark rum

Glaze

12	ounces bittersweet or semisweet chocolate (do not exceed 61% cacao), chopped
¾	cup (1½ sticks) unsalted butter, cut into 12 pieces
2	tablespoons honey
¾	teaspoon instant espresso powder or instant coffee powder

Chocolate Ribbons

7	ounces high-quality white chocolate (such as Lindt or Perugina), chopped
½	cup light corn syrup, divided
7	ounces bittersweet or semisweet chocolate (do not exceed 61% cacao), broken into pieces

CAKE: Position rack in center of oven and preheat to 350°F. Butter and flour three 9-inch-diameter cake pans with 1½-inch-high sides. Line bottom of each with waxed paper; butter and flour paper.

Using electric mixer, cream butter in large bowl. Gradually beat in sugar until smooth. Beat in egg yolks 1 at a time. Blend in melted chocolate. Slowly mix in pecans, vanilla, and spices. Gently fold in flour in 4 batches (batter will be very thick and dense).

Using electric mixer fitted with clean dry beaters, beat egg whites with salt and cream of tartar in another large bowl until medium peaks form. Gently fold ¼ of whites into batter to lighten, then fold in remaining whites. Divide batter among prepared pans, spreading evenly. Bake until toothpick inserted into center of cake comes out clean, 35 to 40 minutes. Run knife around sides of each cake. Let stand 10 minutes. Invert cakes onto racks. Cool to room temperature.

DO AHEAD: *Can be made 2 weeks ahead. Wrap tightly and freeze.*

BUTTERCREAM: Stir sugar and corn syrup in heavy medium saucepan over medium heat until sugar dissolves. Increase heat and boil 1 minute. Meanwhile, using electric mixer, beat egg yolks in medium bowl until pale and thick.

Gradually beat in hot sugar syrup; continue beating until mixture is completely cool, about 5 minutes. Beat in butter 1 piece at a time, incorporating each piece completely before adding next. Blend in melted chocolate, then rum. (If buttercream looks broken or curdled, place bowl with buttercream over medium heat on stove burner and whisk 5 to 10 seconds to warm mixture slightly, then remove from heat and beat mixture again on medium speed. Repeat warming and beating as many times as needed until buttercream is smooth.)

Reserve ½ cup buttercream. Set 1 cake layer flat side up on rack; spread with half of remaining buttercream. Top with second cake layer; spread with remaining buttercream. Top with third cake layer; use reserved ½ cup buttercream to fill in seam where cake layers meet. Freeze cake until buttercream is firm, about 2 hours.

GLAZE: Stir all ingredients in top of double boiler over gently simmering water until mixture is melted and smooth. Remove from over water. Stir until glaze is thickened, about 5 minutes (do not allow to set).

Pour ¾ of glaze over top of cake. Carefully and quickly tilt cake back and forth so glaze coats sides; smooth sides with spatula, adding some of remaining glaze where necessary. Chill cake until glaze is set.

CHOCOLATE RIBBONS: Melt white chocolate in top of double boiler over gently simmering water; stir until smooth. Stir in ¼ cup corn syrup. Pour onto baking sheet. Chill until firm, 30 to 40 minutes. Transfer white chocolate to work surface and knead several minutes. Shape white chocolate dough into ball. Wrap in plastic. Let stand at room temperature 1 hour.

Repeat with bittersweet chocolate and remaining ¼ cup corn syrup.

Cut white chocolate dough into 4 pieces. Flatten 1 piece into rectangle. Turn pasta machine to widest setting. Run chocolate through 3 times, folding into thirds before each run. Adjust machine to next narrower setting. Run chocolate through machine without folding. If chocolate is more than ¹⁄₁₆ inch thick, run through next narrower setting. Lay chocolate piece on rimless baking sheet. Repeat flattening, folding, and rolling with remaining chocolate pieces. Repeat process with bittersweet chocolate dough.

Cut four 8x1-inch strips from rolled white chocolate dough and four 8x½-inch strips from rolled bittersweet chocolate dough. Center bittersweet chocolate strips atop white chocolate strips to form 4 ribbons. Run 1 ribbon from base of cake to center. Arrange remaining 3 ribbons equidistant from each other in same fashion, so ribbons meet in center [1].

Cut ten 6½x1-inch strips from rolled white chocolate dough and ten 6½x½-inch strips from rolled bittersweet chocolate dough. Center bittersweet chocolate strips atop white chocolate strips to form 10 ribbons. Cut ends off 2 ribbons on diagonal. Starting at center, drape ribbons over top and sides of cake to form trailers. To form loops for bows, fold remaining 8 ribbons in half, layered side out. Cut ends into V shapes [2]. Arrange ribbon halves with V shapes at center of cake to form bow [3].

Cut one 3x1-inch strip of white chocolate and one 3x½-inch strip of bittersweet chocolate. Center bittersweet chocolate strip atop white chocolate strip. Fold in ends and pinch to resemble knot; place in center of bow. Transfer cake to platter.

DO AHEAD: *Can be made 1 day ahead. Chill. Bring cake to room temperature before serving.*

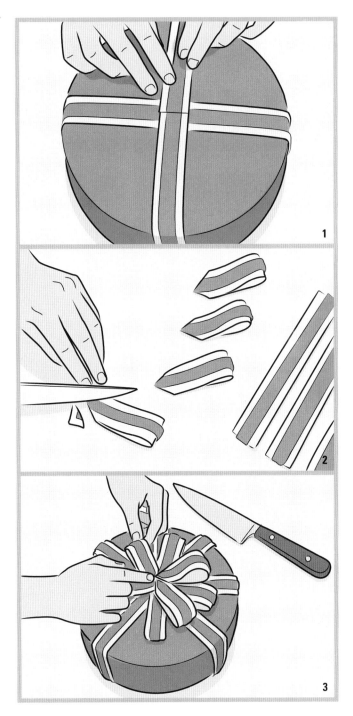

🥄🥄🥄🥄 The Ultimate Valentine Cake

Heart shaped and decorated with a big white-and-dark-chocolate heart and fresh berries, this cake makes a showstopping centerpiece for Valentine's Day or any other romantic occasion, such as an anniversary or engagement cele-bration. When the cake is assembled, the chocolate heart will look like a candy-box lid propped open at an angle. To serve, remove the chocolate heart and break it into pieces to nibble along with the cake. For an all-occasion cake, use a round 8x2-inch springform pan and form the chocolate into a disk. **12 servings**

Chocolate Heart

3   ounces high-quality white chocolate (such as Lindt or Perugina), chopped

3   ounces bittersweet or semisweet chocolate, chopped

Cake

9   ounces high-quality white chocolate (such as Lindt or Perugina), chopped

5   large eggs, separated, room temperature

½   cup plus 1 tablespoon sugar

1   tablespoon framboise or Chambord (black raspberry liqueur)

1   teaspoon vanilla extract

6   tablespoons (¾ stick) unsalted butter, melted, warm

¾   cup cake flour

Icing

12   ounces bittersweet or semisweet chocolate (do not exceed 61% cacao), chopped

1¼   cups (2½ sticks) unsalted butter

3   tablespoons light corn syrup

3   tablespoons framboise or Chambord (black raspberry liqueur)

Assembly

1   1-pint container strawberries, hulled, halved

1   ½-pint container raspberries

1   1-pint container strawberries with stems, halved through stem end (stems left intact)

Compote

2   1-pint containers strawberries, hulled, sliced

3   tablespoons sugar

2   tablespoons framboise or Chambord (black raspberry liqueur)

2   ½-pint containers raspberries

Shopping Tip: **Finding Specialty Items**

Two specialty items help make this cake spectacular: an 8x2-inch bottomless heart-shaped cake ring and framboise liqueur. Cake rings are available at many cookware and candy stores and from online cake decorating suppliers. Framboise, a raspberry liqueur, is available at some liquor stores and specialty foods stores.

CHOCOLATE HEART: Cut piece of waxed paper into heart shape about 4 inches larger than 8x2-inch heart-shaped cake ring. Place on baking sheet. Lightly oil inside of heart ring with vegetable oil. Butter outside of ring. Place heart ring atop waxed paper on baking sheet. Press paper up onto outsides of buttered ring to adhere (to prevent chocolate from leaking out).

Place white chocolate in medium metal bowl. Set bowl over saucepan of simmering water; stir until smooth. Remove from over water. Place bitter-sweet chocolate in another medium metal bowl. Set bowl over saucepan of simmering water; stir until smooth. Remove from over water.

Drop white chocolate by spoonfuls into heart ring, spacing apart and allowing some to touch inner edge of ring. Drop bittersweet chocolate by spoonfuls into spaces. Move heart ring gently from side to side to distribute chocolate evenly and fill in heart completely. Swirl mixtures together using tip of knife. Holding cake ring to baking sheet with hands, tap sheet firmly on counter to flatten chocolate. Chill until firm, about 1 hour.

Run small sharp knife around outside of ring to loosen chocolate. Remove pan. Chill chocolate heart until ready to use.

DO AHEAD: *Can be made 1 week ahead. Cover chocolate heart with plastic wrap and keep chilled.*

CAKE: Preheat oven to 350°F. Butter and flour 8x2-inch heart-shaped cake ring. Cut piece of heavy-duty foil into heart shape 4 inches larger than heart-shaped cake ring. Butter and flour foil. Place on heavy large baking sheet. Center heart ring on foil. Wrap foil around outsides of ring, folding, pressing, and crimping firmly to adhere (to prevent batter from leaking out).

Place white chocolate in medium metal bowl. Set bowl over saucepan of simmering water; stir until smooth. Remove from over water. Using electric mixer, beat egg yolks and ½ cup sugar in large bowl until pale yellow and slowly dissolving ribbon forms when beaters are lifted, about 3 minutes. Beat in framboise and vanilla, then melted butter. Add melted white chocolate and beat until mixture is just combined.

Using electric mixer fitted with clean dry beaters, beat egg whites in large bowl to soft peaks. Gradually add remaining 1 tablespoon sugar and beat until just stiff. Mix flour into chocolate mixture (batter will be very thick). Stir in ¼ of whites to lighten. Gradually fold in remaining whites. Pour batter into prepared ring. Bake 45 minutes. Cover top with foil and continue to bake until tip of small knife inserted into center of cake comes out clean, about 20 minutes (cake will be well browned). Cool in ring on rack.

ICING: Melt chocolate, butter, and corn syrup in heavy medium saucepan over low heat, stirring until smooth. Stir in framboise. Cool icing until firm enough to spread, about 2 hours.

Run small sharp knife around sides of cake; lift off ring. Using metal spatula, loosen cake from foil. Using serrated knife, cut cake horizontally in half. Place bottom cake layer on platter, cut side up. Spread ⅔ cup icing over. Cover with top cake layer, cut side down. Spread all but ½ cup icing over top and sides of cake. Chill cake until icing is set, about 1 hour.

DO AHEAD: *Can be made 1 day ahead. Cover and chill cake and remaining icing separately. Rewarm icing over very low heat until just spreadable.*

ASSEMBLY: Mound some hulled strawberries and raspberries on right half of heart cake. Position chocolate heart atop berries at angle, moving berries around so that left edge of heart rests on left edge of cake (chocolate heart will be angled so that berries are visible at opposite side). Tuck half of strawberries with stems, stems facing out, between cake and chocolate heart. Spread remaining ½ cup icing over side of cake where heart is attached, smoothing with spatula to create box-like appearance. Reserve remaining strawberries and raspberries for garnish. Chill cake until icing is set, about 1 hour.

DO AHEAD: *Can be assembled 12 hours ahead. Keep chilled.*

COMPOTE: Toss strawberries with sugar and framboise in large bowl. Chill at least 1 hour or up to 6 hours. Add raspberries and toss gently.

Arrange reserved berries on platter around cake. Serve cake, spooning compote over each piece.

Gingerbread Roulade with Caramel and Glacéed Fruits

This recipe has all the makings of a perfect holiday dessert: a spiral of brandy–whipped cream filling in gingerbread cake that is coated with a spiced brown sugar frosting and drizzled with caramel. It is particularly stunning when accompanied by a glistening array of glacéed fruits. **10 to 12 servings**

Cake

6	large eggs, separated, room temperature
¾	cup plus 2 tablespoons sugar
2	tablespoons (¼ stick) unsalted butter, melted
1	tablespoon mild-flavored (light) molasses
1	teaspoon vanilla extract
¾	cup unbleached all purpose flour
1	teaspoon baking powder
1½	teaspoons ground ginger
1½	teaspoons ground allspice
¼	teaspoon salt
¾	teaspoon cream of tartar
	Powdered sugar
¼	cup brandy

Filling

¾	cup chilled heavy whipping cream
¼	cup chilled sour cream
¼	cup powdered sugar
1	tablespoon brandy

Frosting

¾	cup (packed) golden brown sugar
½	cup heavy whipping cream
¾	cup (1½ sticks) unsalted butter, room temperature
3	cups powdered sugar
¾	teaspoon ground ginger
¾	teaspoon ground allspice

Caramel

½	cup sugar
3	tablespoons water
½	tablespoon light corn syrup
	Glacéed Fruits (optional; see recipe)

(continued next page)

Gingerbread Roulade with Caramel and Glacéed Fruits (continued)

CAKE: Preheat oven to 350°F. Butter 15½x10½x1-inch baking sheet. Line with waxed paper; butter and flour paper.

Using electric mixer, beat egg yolks and ¾ cup sugar in large bowl until mixture falls in heavy ribbon when beaters are lifted, about 5 minutes. Beat in melted butter, molasses, and vanilla. Sift flour, baking powder, spices, and salt over yolk mixture; fold in gently. Using clean dry beaters, beat egg whites and cream of tartar in another large bowl until soft peaks form. Gradually add remaining 2 tablespoons sugar, beating until stiff but not dry. Fold egg white mixture into egg yolk mixture in 3 additions. Spread batter evenly in prepared sheet.

Bake cake until tester inserted into center comes out clean, about 15 minutes. Cut around sides of baking sheet to loosen cake. Lay kitchen towel on work surface; dust with powdered sugar. Turn cake out onto towel; peel off paper. Brush cake with brandy. Starting at 1 long side, roll warm cake and towel jelly-roll style. Cool cake in towel.

FILLING: Beat all ingredients in medium bowl until stiff peaks form. Unroll cake; spread with filling. Reroll cake only (not towel); place seam side down on long platter and chill.

FROSTING: Stir brown sugar and cream in heavy small saucepan over medium-low heat until sugar dissolves and mixture simmers. Place in freezer until cold, about 15 minutes. Beat butter, powdered sugar, and spices in medium bowl until fluffy. Beat in cold brown sugar mixture. Spread frosting all over cake. Chill until set, at least 2 hours.

DO AHEAD: *Can be made 2 days ahead. Cover; chill.*

CARAMEL: Stir sugar, 3 tablespoons water, and corn syrup in heavy small saucepan over low heat until sugar dissolves, occasionally brushing down pan sides with wet pastry brush. Increase heat and boil without stirring until syrup is deep amber color, swirling pan occasionally, about 5 minutes. Using teaspoon and working quickly, drizzle caramel over cake.

DO AHEAD: *Can be made 6 hours ahead. Chill.*

Serve cake with Glacéed Fruits, if desired.

 ## Glacéed Fruits

A caramel coating gives fresh and dried fruits a glossy, jewel-like look. Using a candy thermometer, be sure the caramel reaches 340°F before dipping the fruit so that it hardens to the right texture when cooled. The fruits can be made up to 6 hours ahead—but no more than that, or the caramel will begin to soften and melt. **Makes 24 to 36**

24	to 36 pieces assorted fresh and dried fruits (such as fresh cranberries, whole strawberries, orange segments with membranes intact, kumquats, dried apricot halves, and small grape clusters)
24	to 36 wooden skewers
4½	cups sugar
1	cup water
⅓	cup light corn syrup
4	thin rounds peeled fresh ginger

Line large baking sheet with foil. Wipe fruits clean. Insert 1 skewer halfway into each fruit (excluding grape clusters).

Combine sugar and 1 cup water in heavy medium 4-inch-deep saucepan. Stir over medium-low heat until sugar dissolves. Add corn syrup and ginger. Increase heat and bring to boil, occasionally brushing down sides of pan with wet pastry brush. Attach candy thermometer to saucepan. Boil without stirring until syrup is golden amber color and candy thermometer registers 340°F, swirling pan occasionally, about 20 minutes. Remove pan from heat.

Holding skewer and working quickly, carefully dip 1 fruit into hot caramel, coating completely. If necessary, carefully tilt pan to submerge fruits in caramel. Hold fruit over pan, allowing some of excess caramel to drip off. Place fruit, still on skewer, on prepared sheet. Repeat dipping with remaining fruits and caramel. Hook stem end of each grape cluster in tines of fork; dip into caramel to coat. Place on prepared sheet.

DO AHEAD: *Can be made ahead. Let stand at room temperature up to 6 hours.*

White Chocolate, Almond, and Apricot Roulade

A roulade is a soft, soufflé-like cake that's spread with jam, buttercream, or another filling, then rolled up jelly-roll style. The frosting needs to firm up in the fridge before beating, so it's best to prepare it a day ahead of making the cake. If you have any apricot puree left over, it would be delicious on toast the next morning. **12 servings**

Puree

1	6-ounce package dried apricots
1	cup apricot nectar
½	cup sugar

Frosting

1¼	cups heavy whipping cream
2	ounces high-quality white chocolate (such as Lindt or Perugina), chopped
½	teaspoon vanilla extract

Cake

1⅓	cups sliced almonds, toasted
10	tablespoons sugar, divided
2	ounces high-quality white chocolate (such as Lindt or Perugina), chopped
½	cup sifted cake flour (sifted, then measured)
½	teaspoon salt
¼	teaspoon baking powder
⅛	teaspoon ground ginger
4	large eggs, separated, room temperature
1	tablespoon milk
¼	teaspoon almond extract
2	tablespoons powdered sugar, divided

Garnish

1⅓	cups sliced almonds, toasted
½	cup chilled heavy whipping cream
1	tablespoon sugar

PUREE: Stir all ingredients in heavy medium saucepan over medium heat until sugar dissolves and mixture comes to simmer. Cover and simmer until apricots soften, about 5 minutes. Cool to lukewarm. Puree in processor (mixture will have some tiny pieces of apricot). Transfer to medium bowl; cover and refrigerate.

DO AHEAD: *Can be made 4 days ahead. Keep refrigerated.*

FROSTING: Combine cream and white chocolate in heavy medium saucepan. Stir over medium-low heat until chocolate melts and mixture is smooth. Mix in vanilla. Transfer to bowl and chill overnight, stirring occasionally.

Using electric mixer, beat cream mixture until stiff peaks form. Fold in 1 cup apricot puree. Cover and chill at least 1 hour.

DO AHEAD: *Can be made 1 day ahead. Keep refrigerated.*

CAKE: Position rack in center of oven and preheat to 350°F. Butter 15x10x1-inch baking sheet. Line sheet with waxed paper; butter and flour paper. Finely grind almonds in processor. Transfer ½ cup ground almonds to small bowl and reserve. Add 2 tablespoons sugar and white chocolate to remaining almonds in processor and grind finely. Combine flour, salt, baking powder, and ginger in another small bowl. Using electric mixer, beat egg whites in large bowl until soft peaks form. Gradually add 6 tablespoons sugar and beat until stiff but not dry.

Using same beaters, beat egg yolks and remaining 2 tablespoons sugar in another large bowl until slowly dissolving ribbon forms when beaters are lifted, about 5 minutes. Mix in milk and almond extract. Fold in almond–white chocolate mixture; fold in flour mixture. Fold in egg white mixture in 2 additions. Spread batter in prepared pan. Bake until tester inserted into center comes out clean, about 17 minutes.

Sift 1 tablespoon powdered sugar over hot cake. Cut around edges of cake to loosen. Turn pan over onto kitchen towel. Lift off pan. Peel off paper. Sift remaining 1 tablespoon powdered sugar over hot cake. Fold 2 to 3 inches of towel over 1 long edge of cake and gently roll up cake in towel. Cool cake completely, about 1 hour.

Unroll cake. Spread ½ cup apricot puree over. Sprinkle with reserved ½ cup ground almonds. Spread 1¼ cups frosting over. Starting at 1 long side and using towel as aid, roll up cake. Transfer to platter. Spread remaining frosting over entire outside of cake.

GARNISH: Press sliced almonds along sides but not top of cake. Whip cream and sugar in medium bowl to stiff peaks. Transfer to pastry bag fitted with small star tip. Pipe row of rosettes atop cake just above almonds. Refrigerate cake at least 1 hour.

DO AHEAD: *Can be made 6 hours ahead. Keep refrigerated.*

Black Forest Boule-de-Neige

The components of Germany's famous Black Forest torte—chocolate and cherries—combine in this moist, fudgy cake. It's baked in a metal bowl and covered with whipped cream, so it resembles a snowball, or boule-de-neige *in French. Begin making this dessert at least one day ahead, as the cake needs to stand overnight. Candied violet petals are available at some supermarkets and at specialty foods stores and some cookware shops; they can also be ordered from cheftools.com.* **14 servings**

Cake

	Nonstick vegetable oil spray
⅓	cup cherry preserves
2	tablespoons kirsch (clear cherry brandy)
1½	cups dried tart cherries (about 8 ounces)
1	pound bittersweet or semisweet chocolate (do not exceed 61% cacao), chopped
1	cup (2 sticks) unsalted butter, cut into 16 pieces
1¼	cups sugar
1	teaspoon vanilla extract
6	large eggs
⅓	cup unbleached all purpose flour

Whipped Cream

2	cups chilled heavy whipping cream
¼	cup powdered sugar
4	teaspoons kirsch (clear cherry brandy)
¼	teaspoon almond extract
16	candied violet petals

CAKE: Position rack in lowest third of oven and preheat to 350°F. Line 10-cup metal bowl with foil, extending 3 inches over sides. Spray foil with nonstick spray. Stir preserves with kirsch in medium skillet over medium heat until preserves melt. Add dried cherries; bring to boil. Cover; remove from heat. Let cool.

Melt chocolate with butter in heavy large saucepan over medium-low heat, stirring until smooth. Remove from heat. Whisk in sugar and vanilla, then whisk in eggs 1 at a time. Mix in flour, then cherry mixture. Transfer batter to prepared bowl.

Bake cake in bowl 30 minutes. Fold foil overhang over edges of cake to prevent overbrowning. Continue to bake cake until top is cracked and dry and tester inserted into center comes out with some moist batter attached, about 55 minutes longer. Cool cake completely in bowl on rack (cake may fall in center). Press edge of cake firmly to level with center of cake. Cover and let stand at room temperature overnight.

WHIPPED CREAM: Using electric mixer, beat cream, sugar, kirsch, and almond extract in large bowl until cream holds peaks.

Invert cake onto platter. Peel off foil. Spoon whipped cream into large pastry bag fitted with medium star tip. Pipe whipped cream stars over cake, covering completely. Pipe additional stars over top flat center of cake to form dome.

DO AHEAD: *Can be made 1 day ahead. Cover with cake dome and chill.*

Decorate with candied violet petals.

Cranberry-Chocolate Soufflé Cake

Don't be alarmed when this cake falls in the center as it cools—it's the nature of soufflés and flourless chocolate cakes like this one. Whipped chocolate cream cleverly covers the top of the cake, hiding the sunken center and adding a luxurious touch. The cranberries need to stand in syrup overnight, so begin making this a day ahead. **10 servings**

Poached Cranberries

2½	cups sugar
1	cup water
3	cups fresh cranberries
1	tablespoon finely grated orange peel
¼	teaspoon cinnamon
⅛	teaspoon ground allspice

Cake

4	ounces unsweetened chocolate, chopped
6	ounces bittersweet or semisweet chocolate (do not exceed 61% cacao), chopped
10	tablespoons (1¼ sticks) unsalted butter
7	extra-large eggs, separated, room temperature
1	cup plus 1 tablespoon sugar, divided
⅓	cup Grand Marnier or other orange liqueur

Topping

3	ounces bittersweet or semisweet chocolate (do not exceed 61% cacao), chopped
1	cup chilled heavy whipping cream
1	tablespoon Grand Marnier or other orange liqueur

Ingredient Tip: **Room-Temperature Eggs**

This recipe calls for room-temperature eggs. Although it's easier to separate eggs when they're cold, you'll get more volume from egg whites when they're at room temperature. To take the chill off the eggs, place them in a bowl of very warm water for 5 minutes. Drain and wipe dry before separating the yolks from the whites. Egg whites will form firm peaks rather quickly when whipped, but when sugar is added, the peaks take longer to form. So, to speed along the process, gradually add the sugar when the egg whites have formed very soft peaks.

POACHED CRANBERRIES: Bring sugar and 1 cup water to boil in heavy medium saucepan, stirring until sugar dissolves. Add cranberries, orange peel, cinnamon, and allspice. Simmer until cranberries pop, about 2 minutes. Remove from heat. Let stand in syrup overnight. Drain cranberries before using.

CAKE: Preheat oven to 350°F. Butter and sugar 9-inch-diameter springform pan with 2½-inch-high sides. Melt both chocolates and butter in top of double boiler set over simmering water, stirring until smooth. Remove from over water. Combine egg yolks with ¾ cup plus 1 tablespoon sugar in large bowl. Using electric mixer, beat until thick and pale, about 3 minutes. Gradually beat in Grand Marnier on low speed. Add chocolate mixture and stir just until incorporated. Using electric mixer fitted with clean dry beaters, beat egg whites in another large bowl until soft peaks form. Gradually add remaining ¼ cup sugar; continue beating until mixture is stiff but not dry. Gently fold into chocolate mixture.

Pour batter into prepared pan. Bake cake until top forms crust but inside is still moist, about 45 minutes. Cool completely in pan on rack (cake may fall while cooling).

DO AHEAD: *Cake can be made up to 6 hours ahead. Keep at room temperature.*

TOPPING: Melt chocolate in top of double boiler over simmering water, stirring until smooth. Remove from over water and cool until just warm to touch. Using electric mixer, beat cream in large bowl until soft peaks form. Add melted chocolate to cream and fold together. Fold in Grand Marnier.

Place cake on platter; remove pan sides. Spread top of cake with 1½ cups chocolate cream, leaving ½-inch border around edge of cake. Top with poached cranberries. Spoon remaining cream into pastry bag fitted with large star tip. Pipe cream decoratively around top edge of cake.

DO AHEAD: *Can be made 3 hours ahead. Chill. Let cake stand about 1 hour at room temperature before serving.*

Chocolate, Orange, and Macadamia Bûche de Noël

The bûche de Noël, or yule log, was created in France during the late 19th century by pastry chefs who were inspired by the wood logs that burned on hearths throughout Christmas Eve. A bûche de Noël is basically a jelly roll—a rolled sponge cake with a spiral of buttercream—frosted and decorated with meringue mushrooms to resemble a real tree stump. Sometimes a dusting of powdered sugar is added to resemble fallen snow. Any rolled cake can be decorated to create a bûche de Noël. This one has a chocolate sponge cake, an orange buttercream filling, chocolate frosting, and, of course, all the trimmings. It would look beautiful garnished with the candied rosemary on pages 46–48. **8 servings**

Cake

4	large eggs, room temperature
1	large egg yolk
¼	cup sugar
	Pinch of salt
⅓	cup unbleached all purpose flour
⅓	cup natural unsweetened cocoa powder
1½	teaspoons finely grated orange peel

Buttercreams

1½	cups plus 1½ tablespoons sugar
1½	cups water
5	large egg yolks, room temperature
6	tablespoons Cointreau or other orange liqueur
2¼	cups (4½ sticks) unsalted butter, room temperature
4½	tablespoons frozen orange juice concentrate, thawed
4½	ounces unsweetened chocolate, melted and cooled
⅔	cup macadamia nuts, toasted, coarsely chopped
	Meringue Mushrooms (see recipe)

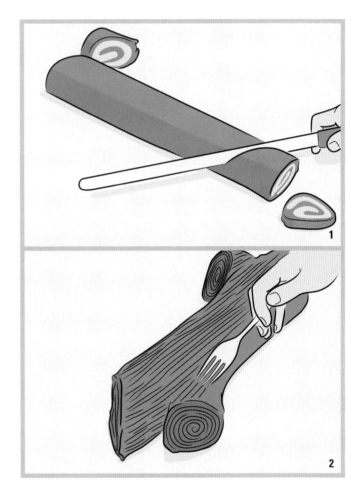

CAKE: Preheat oven to 400°F. Line 17½x11x1-inch baking sheet with parchment paper. Using electric mixer, beat eggs, egg yolk, sugar, and salt in large bowl at medium speed until stiff peaks form. Sift in flour and cocoa. Add orange peel; gently fold together. Spread batter evenly in prepared sheet. Bake until cake is springy to touch and just begins to pull from sides of pan, about 7 minutes. Using small sharp knife, cut around cake edges to loosen. Transfer cake and parchment to work surface and let cool.

Recipe Tip: Buttercream Styles

There are three primary styles of buttercream: French, Italian, and simple. This cake recipe uses French buttercream, which is made by beating hot syrup into egg yolks and finishing with butter. Italian buttercream is made by beating butter into Italian meringue. Simple buttercream is made by beating powdered sugar and butter together. Save the egg whites to use in the Meringue Mushrooms.

BUTTERCREAMS: Bring sugar and 1½ cups water to boil in heavy medium saucepan, stirring until sugar dissolves. Continue boiling without stirring until candy thermometer registers 240°F (soft-ball stage), occasionally brushing down sides of pan with wet pastry brush.

Meanwhile, using electric mixer, beat egg yolks in medium bowl until thickened. Add Cointreau. Gradually beat in hot syrup. Continue beating until bottom of bowl cools to room temperature, about 5 minutes. Add butter, 3 tablespoons at a time, beating at medium speed after each addition until smooth. Mix in orange juice concentrate. Transfer 3¼ cups buttercream to small bowl. Mix melted chocolate into remaining buttercream. (If buttercream looks broken or curdled, place bowl with buttercream over medium heat on stove burner and whisk 5 to 10 seconds to warm mixture slightly. Then remove from heat and beat mixture again at medium speed. Repeat warming and beating as many times as needed until buttercream is smooth.)

Invert cake onto sheet of plastic wrap. Carefully remove parchment. Spread orange buttercream over cake, leaving 1-inch border on long side. Sprinkle with macadamias. Using plastic wrap as aid, roll up cake jelly-roll style, starting at long side and rolling toward side with uncovered border.

Trim to make ends of roll even. Cut 2 inches off each end of roll at 45-degree angle [1]. Using plastic as aid, transfer roll to platter, seam side down. Spread some chocolate buttercream on cut ends of 2-inch pieces. With buttercream touching cake, place 1 piece atop cake off center; place second piece on 1 long side of cake to resemble tree stump. Transfer 1 cup chocolate buttercream to pastry bag fitted with ¼-inch plain tip. Spread remaining chocolate buttercream over cake. Pipe buttercream in spirals over ends of bûche and stumps, starting at center of each. Run fork tines through buttercream to create bark pattern [2].

DO AHEAD: *Can be made 1 day ahead. Chill. Let stand at room temperature 2 hours before serving.*

Garnish with Meringue Mushrooms just before serving.

Meringue Mushrooms

These little meringue cookies make the perfect embellishment to any bûche de Noël. Here, powdered sugar and egg white form the glue that sticks the meringue caps and stems together, but melted dark chocolate could also be used. Don't worry if your caps and stems aren't uniform; they'll only look more natural. A tap of sifted cocoa powder just before serving creates mushroom freckles. **Makes about 15**

¼   **cup egg whites (about 2 large), room temperature**
     Pinch of salt
2   **tablespoons sugar**
2   **tablespoons powdered sugar**
1   **tablespoon powdered sugar mixed with ¼ teaspoon egg white (paste)**
     Natural unsweetened cocoa powder

Preheat oven to 150°F. Line baking sheet with parchment. Using electric mixer, beat egg whites and salt in medium bowl 1 minute to blend. Combine sugar and 2 tablespoons powdered sugar in small bowl. Add to egg whites in 3 additions, beating 20 seconds after each. Continue beating until meringue is stiff and glossy. Transfer mixture to pastry bag fitted with ½-inch plain tip. Pipe about fifteen ½- to 1-inch domed rounds on prepared sheet for mushroom caps. Smooth top of each with damp finger. Pipe about fifteen ½- to 1-inch peaked mounds on prepared sheets for stems. Bake until meringues are dry and beginning to color, about 1 hour 45 minutes. Let cool completely.

Using small knife, cut small hole in bottom of each mushroom cap. Dip peaked end of stem in sugar paste and push into hole in mushroom cap. Repeat with remaining stems and caps.

DO AHEAD: *Can be made 1 day ahead. Store in airtight container at room temperature.*

Dust mushrooms with cocoa before serving.

Storage Tip: Meringues

The long baking time dries out the meringue so that the cookies become crunchy; the low temperature is what keeps them white. Any dampness or humidity will soften the meringues. Keep them crunchy by storing them in an airtight container, such as a cookie tin.

♟ Chocolate Fruitcake

Natural foods stores and Middle Eastern markets are both good places to find the dried fruits called for in this recipe. **16 servings**

Cake

1½	cups diced stemmed dried Calimyrna figs
1	cup diced pitted prunes
1	cup diced dried peaches
1	cup diced pitted dates
¼	cup spiced rum or dark rum
¼	cup fresh orange juice
3	tablespoons minced orange peel (orange part only)
3	cups sifted unbleached all purpose flour (sifted, then measured)
¾	cup natural unsweetened cocoa powder
1½	teaspoons baking powder
1½	teaspoons baking soda
¾	teaspoon ground cinnamon
¾	teaspoon salt
2	cups (packed) dark brown sugar
3	ounces bittersweet or semisweet chocolate (do not exceed 61% cacao), coarsely chopped
½	cup (1 stick) unsalted butter, room temperature
4	large eggs
1	cup purchased mincemeat with brandy and rum
2½	cups large walnut pieces, toasted

Glazes

3	tablespoons light corn syrup
2	tablespoons spiced rum or dark rum
3	ounces bittersweet or semisweet chocolate (do not exceed 61% cacao), chopped
3	tablespoons unsalted butter
	Orange peel strips

CAKE: Position rack in center of oven and preheat to 325°F. Generously butter 12- to 15-cup Bundt pan. Dust pan with cocoa; tap out excess. Combine figs, prunes, dried peaches, dates, rum, orange juice, and orange peel in large bowl. Let stand 30 minutes, stirring occasionally. Sift flour, cocoa, baking powder, baking soda, cinnamon, and salt into medium bowl. Finely grind sugar and chocolate in processor.

Using electric mixer, beat butter in another large bowl until fluffy. Beat in sugar-chocolate mixture in 3 additions (mixture will be grainy). Beat in eggs 1 at a time. Using rubber spatula, mix in ⅓ of dry ingredients. Mix in half of mincemeat. Mix in half of remaining dry ingredients, then remaining mincemeat. Add remaining dry ingredients and walnuts to dried fruit mixture, tossing to coat evenly. Add to batter and blend well. Spoon batter into prepared pan.

Bake cake until tester inserted near center comes out with just a few crumbs attached, covering cake loosely with foil if browning too quickly, about 1½ hours. Cool cake in pan on rack 20 minutes. Turn pan over onto rack. Let stand 3 minutes; gently lift off pan. Cool cake completely.

GLAZES: Stir corn syrup and rum in small bowl to blend. Place cake on plate. Brush all of rum glaze over cake. Double-wrap in foil and store at room temperature at least 2 days.

DO AHEAD: *Can be made up to 3 months ahead. Store in refrigerator. Bring to room temperature before continuing.*

Stir chocolate and butter in heavy small saucepan over low heat until melted and smooth. Cool 15 minutes. Drizzle chocolate glaze decoratively over top of cake. Garnish with strips of orange peel and serve.

Gingerbread Christmas Pudding with Orange Hard Sauce

English Christmas "pudding" is really a dense, moist spiced cake that's steamed on the stove rather than baked in the oven. Pudding molds are available at cookware stores. Some molds come with a lid that can be used in place of the foil covering. **8 to 10 servings**

Hard Sauce

1½   cups powdered sugar
½   cup (1 stick) unsalted butter, room temperature
2   tablespoons brandy
1   teaspoon finely grated orange peel

Pudding

     Nonstick vegetable oil spray
1¼   cups unbleached all purpose flour
1   tablespoon ground ginger
2   teaspoons ground cinnamon
1   teaspoon baking powder
½   teaspoon salt
½   teaspoon baking soda
¼   teaspoon ground cloves
¾   cup sugar
6   tablespoons (¾ stick) unsalted butter, room temperature
3   large eggs
½   cup orange marmalade
¼   cup mild-flavored (light) molasses
1   teaspoon finely grated orange peel

{ ## Technique Tip: **Two Coats**
Coating the pudding mold with both nonstick cooking spray and butter might seem excessive, but they both serve a purpose: The spray helps ensure that the pudding will unmold easily, and while the butter helps in this effort, it also adds extra richness and flavor. }

HARD SAUCE: Combine all ingredients in small bowl; stir to blend well.

DO AHEAD: *Can be made 4 days ahead. Cover and refrigerate. Bring to room temperature before serving.*

PUDDING: Coat inside and center tube of 6- to 8-cup pudding mold or Bundt pan with nonstick spray, then coat generously with butter. Sift flour, ginger, cinnamon, baking powder, salt, baking soda, and cloves into medium bowl. Using electric mixer, beat sugar and butter in large bowl until well blended. Beat in eggs 1 at a time, then marmalade, molasses, and orange peel. Beat in flour mixture. Transfer batter to prepared mold. Cover mold tightly with buttered foil, buttered side down.

Place steamer rack in large pot. Place pudding mold on rack. Fill pot with enough water to come halfway up sides of mold. Bring water to boil. Reduce heat to medium. Cover pot and steam pudding until tester inserted near center comes out clean, adding more boiling water as needed to maintain water level, about 1 hour 15 minutes. Using oven mitts as aid, remove mold from pot. Uncover and let stand 10 minutes. Cut around top center and sides of pudding to loosen. Turn pudding out onto rack and cool 20 minutes.

DO AHEAD: *Can be made 1 day ahead. Cool completely. Return pudding to mold; cover and chill. Resteam, covered, 45 minutes to heat through, then turn out of mold.*

Transfer pudding to platter. Cut pudding into wedges; serve with sauce.

Steamed Cranberry-Marmalade Pudding with Grand Marnier Hard Sauce Rosettes

This traditional English dessert—in which the pudding is really a moist, rich cake—gets its texture from being baked in a covered container surrounded by a water bath. The traditional mold used to make steamed pudding looks like a Bundt pan with a lid. If you don't have one, just use a loaf pan covered tightly with foil. **8 servings**

Pudding

1	cup unbleached all purpose flour
1	teaspoon baking powder
½	teaspoon ground ginger
½	teaspoon ground nutmeg
¼	teaspoon salt
½	cup (1 stick) unsalted butter, room temperature
¾	cup sugar
2	large eggs
¼	cup Sherry
½	cup orange marmalade
2	cups coarsely chopped fresh or frozen cranberries

Candied Cranberries

¾	cup sugar, divided
½	cup water
½	cup fresh cranberries

Grand Marnier Hard Sauce Rosettes (see recipe)

PUDDING: Preheat oven to 350°F. Butter and flour 1-quart pudding mold or loaf pan. Sift flour, baking powder, ginger, nutmeg, and salt into medium bowl. Using electric mixer, beat butter in large bowl until light and fluffy. Beat in sugar. Beat in eggs 1 at a time. Beat in half of dry ingredients, then Sherry, then remaining dry ingredients. Fold in marmalade. Gently fold in chopped cranberries.

Spoon batter into prepared mold; smooth top. Top pudding mold with cover or cover tightly with large sheet of buttered foil, buttered side down. Place pudding in Dutch oven or large baking pan. Pour enough hot water into pan to come halfway up sides of mold. Bake until small knife inserted near center of pudding comes out clean, about 2½ hours. Remove from water. Cool 10 minutes.

Cut around edge of pan to loosen pudding. Turn out onto plate.

DO AHEAD: *Can be made 4 days ahead. Cool completely. Wrap tightly in plastic; chill. Reheat before serving: Remove plastic; wrap pudding in foil. Reheat in 350°F oven until heated through, about 45 minutes.*

CANDIED CRANBERRIES: Line small baking sheet with waxed paper. Bring ½ cup sugar and ½ cup water to boil in heavy medium saucepan, stirring until sugar dissolves. Attach candy thermometer to side of pan. Continue boiling until thermometer registers 238°F, about 6 minutes. Remove from heat; stir in cranberries. Let stand until cranberries are tender but still retain shape, about 3 minutes. Using slotted spoon, carefully transfer cranberries to prepared baking sheet. Let stand until almost dry, about 20 minutes.

Place remaining ¼ cup sugar in shallow bowl. Add cranberries and toss until completely coated.

DO AHEAD: *Can be made 6 hours ahead. Cover and let stand at room temperature.*

Serve steamed pudding warm with candied cranberries and Grand Marnier Hard Sauce Rosettes.

Grand Marnier Hard Sauce Rosettes

Hard sauce—a rich blend of butter, sugar, and flavoring—is often made with brandy or rum, but here takes an orange flavor from Grand Marnier. Piping the hard sauce into rosettes is fun and adds a playful touch, but if you don't feel like doing that, just put the sauce in a serving bowl and pass it at the table.

Makes 8

½   cup (1 stick) unsalted butter, room temperature
1½   cups powdered sugar
2   tablespoons Grand Marnier or other orange liqueur

Line small baking sheet with waxed paper. Using electric mixer, beat butter in medium bowl until light and fluffy. Beat in sugar, then liqueur. Transfer to pastry bag fitted with large star tip. Pipe 8 large rosettes onto prepared baking sheet. Chill until set, about 1 hour.

DO AHEAD: *Can be made 3 days ahead. Cover and keep chilled.*

Wine with Cake

Cake is synonymous with celebration, and a glass of wine alongside adds to the special-occasion feeling. But serving dry wine with sweet cake makes both things taste awful: The sugar in the dessert wrecks the flavors in the wine and makes it taste bitter. (If you've ever been served dry [brut] Champagne with birthday cake, you've experienced this.) Both still wine and sparkling wine can taste great with cake. A good rule of thumb: Make sure that what's in the glass is as sweet if not sweeter than what's on the plate. But the best dessert wines shouldn't overwhelm with their sugar level: They should have enough acidity to balance their sweetness. Typically, dessert wines can have flavors of peach, apricot, citrus, nuts, and toffee, among others. Here are a few to look for:

MOSCATO D'ASTI, a gently fizzy Italian wine, which also has a low alcohol content

VOUVRAY MOUSSEUX, a bubbly Chenin Blanc from France's Loire Valley

LATE-HARVEST RIESLING grown from sweet Riesling grapes; especially good ones come from Germany, France, and Australia.

SWEET CHAMPAGNE from France, of course. Look for extra-dry or the sweeter demi-sec.

SAUTERNES, from the Bordeaux region of France, arguably the greatest dessert wine in the world. It's some of the most expensive, too, especially if aged.

cheesecakes

cheesecakes

New York–Style Cheesecake

Made popular in New York City in the 1920s by Jewish delicatessens, this cake is identified by its graham cracker crust and smooth cream cheese filling. Baking the cake in a water bath allows the rich filling to cook at an even, steady heat, giving the cheesecake its signature creamy quality. For a slightly fluffier and drier version (which may crack as it cools), bake the cake directly on the oven rack at 300°F until the center is softly set, about 1 hour 20 minutes. **12 servings**

Crust
9	whole graham crackers, broken into pieces
5	tablespoons chilled unsalted butter, cut into ½-inch cubes
3	tablespoons sugar

Filling
5	8-ounce packages Philadelphia-brand cream cheese, room temperature
1½	cups sugar
4	large eggs
1	large egg yolk
1	tablespoon fresh lemon juice
1½	teaspoons vanilla extract
	Pinch of salt
1	tablespoon unbleached all purpose flour

CRUST: Preheat oven to 325°F. Grind graham crackers to coarse crumbs in processor. Add butter and sugar. Process until blended and crumb mixture begins to stick together. Press crumb mixture onto bottom (not sides) of 9-inch-diameter springform pan with 2¾-inch-high sides. Bake crust until golden and firm to touch, about 25 minutes. Cool crust in pan on rack. Wrap outside of pan with 3 layers of heavy-duty foil. Maintain oven temperature.

FILLING: Using electric mixer, beat cream cheese in large bowl until fluffy. Gradually add sugar, beating until blended. Beat in eggs and egg yolk 1 at a time just until blended, occasionally scraping down sides of bowl. Beat in lemon juice, vanilla, and salt. Sift flour over; beat on low speed until blended. Scrape filling over crust in pan.

Place cake pan in large roasting pan. Add enough hot water to roasting pan to come halfway up sides of cake pan; place in oven. Bake cheesecake in water bath until center is softly set, about 1 hour 15 minutes. Remove from oven. Let stand in water bath 5 minutes. Place cheesecake in pan on rack. Cut around pan sides to loosen cake. Cool completely at room temperature. Cover and chill overnight.

DO AHEAD: *Can be made 2 days ahead. Keep chilled.*

Cut around pan sides again; remove pan sides. Cut cheesecake into wedges.

Technique Tip: Give It Time
When making cheesecake, plan ahead. Many of the recipes in this chapter require that the cheesecake chill overnight to firm up properly—this results in the best texture and easiest slicing.

Crumb Crusts

Virtually every cheesecake in this chapter (unless it's a crustless cheesecake) features a crumb crust made from graham crackers, gingersnaps or another kind of cookie, or nuts. In many ways, these are the simplest crusts to make, as they don't involve preparing or rolling out dough. But there are still a few handy tricks to know.

1. To grind cookies, wafers, and graham crackers into crumbs, try one of two methods:

BY MACHINE Put broken-up cookies or crackers in a food processor. Use on/off turns to pulse until the crumbs are evenly ground to the desired coarseness.

UNPLUGGED Enclose broken-up cookies or crackers in a heavy-duty resealable plastic bag. Pass a rolling pin over them until they're evenly crushed to the desired coarseness.

2. Blending the butter, crumbs, or ground nuts with other crust ingredients in a food processor will give you the quickest and most uniform results (although some simple crust recipes call for the ingredients to be blended in a bowl, so check the instructions).

3. To press crumb crusts evenly into a pan, wrap your fingertips in plastic wrap to prevent sticking and press firmly. Make sure to create a crust of even thickness.

♕ Red-Berry Cheesecake

This cheesecake is the perfect dessert for showcasing summer's best berries. It's worth scouring the farmers' market for the ripest, most fragrant raspberries and strawberries you can get your hands on. **12 servings**

1	tablespoon unsalted butter, room temperature
⅔	cup coarsely ground graham cracker crumbs
3	8-ounce packages Philadelphia-brand cream cheese, room temperature
1¼	cups sugar, divided
1½	teaspoons vanilla extract, divided
4	large egg whites, room temperature
2	cups sour cream
2	½-pint containers raspberries
1	1-pint container strawberries

Preheat oven to 350°F. Spread 1 tablespoon butter evenly over bottom of 9-inch-diameter springform pan with 2¾-inch-high sides. Sprinkle with graham cracker crumbs. Using electric mixer, beat cream cheese in large bowl until smooth. Add 1 cup sugar and 1 teaspoon vanilla and beat until well blended. Using clean dry beaters, beat egg whites in another large bowl until stiff but not dry. Gently fold beaten whites into cheese mixture in 3 additions. Pour batter into prepared pan.

Bake cheesecake until filling is puffed and cracks begin to form around edges, about 35 minutes. Remove from oven. Combine sour cream, remaining ¼ cup sugar, and remaining ½ teaspoon vanilla in small bowl; stir until blended. Spoon sour cream mixture over filling. Using spatula, spread sour cream mixture evenly over hot cheesecake, covering completely.

Bake cake 5 minutes longer. Transfer cake to rack. Cool completely. Cover and chill overnight.

Cut around pan sides to loosen cake; remove pan sides. Garnish cake with some berries. Cut into wedges and serve with remaining berries.

♕ Lemon Cheesecake with Gingersnap Crust

Simple yet surprising—fresh lemon juice and freshly grated lemon peel transform the classic cheesecake, and leaves from a lemon tree are a simple, perfect garnish. To grind gingersnap cookies, break them into large pieces and whirl them in a food processor until evenly ground. **16 servings**

2	cups ground gingersnap cookies
6	tablespoons (¾ stick) unsalted butter, melted
5	8-ounce packages Philadelphia-brand cream cheese, room temperature
2	cups sugar
¼	teaspoon salt
7	large eggs
3	cups sour cream
2	tablespoons finely grated lemon peel
2	tablespoons fresh lemon juice
	Lemon leaves (optional)

Preheat oven to 350°F. Stir cookie crumbs and melted butter in medium bowl until evenly moistened. Press crumb mixture onto bottom (not sides) of 9-inch-diameter springform pan with 3-inch-high sides. Bake crust until deep golden, about 12 minutes. Cool completely. Reduce oven temperature to 325°F. Wrap outside of pan with 3 layers of heavy-duty aluminum foil.

Using electric mixer, beat cream cheese in large bowl until smooth and fluffy. Gradually beat in sugar, then salt. Beat in eggs 1 at a time. Beat in sour cream, lemon peel, and lemon juice. Pour filling into crust. Place wrapped cake pan in large roasting pan. Pour enough hot water into roasting pan to come halfway up sides of cake pan.

Bake cake until filling is slightly puffed and moves only slightly when pan is shaken gently, about 1 hour 25 minutes. Remove cake pan from water bath; remove foil. Cool cake in pan on rack 2 hours. Chill uncovered until cold; cover and keep chilled at least 1 day and up to 2 days.

Cut around pan sides to loosen cake; remove pan sides. Place cake on platter. Garnish with lemon leaves, if desired.

Orange Blossom Cheesecake with Raspberry-Pomegranate Sauce

Orange-flower water and pomegranate juice lend Moroccan style to the New York cheesecake. The rich filling is citrusy and floral, and the tart, red pomegranate sauce offers a deliciously tangy contrast. Orange-flower water is an aromatic flavoring extract that is sold at some supermarkets and at liquor stores and Middle Eastern markets. **12 servings**

Crust

1¾	cups graham cracker crumbs (from about 12 whole graham crackers)
1¼	cups walnuts
6	tablespoons sugar
½	teaspoon salt
¼	teaspoon ground cloves
½	cup (1 stick) unsalted butter, melted

Filling

5	8-ounce packages Philadelphia-brand cream cheese, room temperature
1⅔	cups sugar
3	tablespoons unbleached all purpose flour
2	tablespoons finely grated orange peel
2	teaspoons orange-flower water
5	large eggs
2	large egg yolks

Sauce

4	cups chilled fresh pomegranate juice
2	12-ounce bags frozen raspberries (unthawed)
¼	cup sugar
½	cup honey

CRUST: Wrap 3 layers of heavy-duty aluminum foil around outside of 9-inch-diameter springform pan with 2¾-inch-high sides. Butter pan. Blend graham cracker crumbs, walnuts, sugar, salt, and cloves in processor until nuts are ground. Add melted butter. Using on/off turns, blend until moist crumbs form. Press crumb mixture onto bottom and 2 inches up sides of pan.

FILLING: Preheat oven to 500°F. Using electric mixer, blend cream cheese, sugar, flour, orange peel, and orange-flower water in large bowl. Beat in eggs and egg yolks 1 at a time. Pour filling into crust.

Bake cheesecake until slightly puffed and beginning to brown in spots, about 12 minutes. Reduce oven temperature to 200°F and continue baking until cake is gently set in center (edges may crack), about 1 hour. Transfer cake to rack and cool 5 minutes. Cut around pan sides to loosen cake. Cool completely. Cover and chill overnight.

DO AHEAD: *Can be made 2 days ahead; keep chilled.*

SAUCE: Bring juice to boil in heavy large saucepan. Reduce heat; simmer until reduced to 1 cup, about 35 minutes. Mix in raspberries and sugar. Simmer until reduced to 3 cups, stirring frequently, about 20 minutes. Mix in honey and return to simmer. Cool sauce slightly. Cover; chill until cold.

DO AHEAD: *Can be made 1 day ahead; keep chilled.*

Cut around pan sides again; remove pan sides. Cut cheesecake into wedges and transfer to plates. Spoon sauce over cheesecake and serve.

Glazed Plum Cheesecake

Glistening concentric circles of red-skinned plum wedges—which have been bathed in a syrup of orange juice, red currant jelly, brown sugar, and ginger— create a stunning presentation for a dinner-party dessert. Plum varieties that will look especially beautiful atop this cheesecake include Satsuma, Red Beauty, and Grand Rosa. **10 to 12 servings**

Crust

11	whole graham crackers, coarsely broken
¼	cup (packed) golden brown sugar
¼	teaspoon ground cinnamon
	Pinch of salt
5	tablespoons unsalted butter, melted

Filling

3	8-ounce packages Philadelphia-brand cream cheese, room temperature
1	cup sugar
4	large eggs
1	cup sour cream
1	tablespoon finely grated lemon peel
2	teaspoons vanilla extract

Plums

¾	cup orange juice
½	cup red currant jelly
¼	cup (packed) golden brown sugar
3	¼-inch-thick slices peeled fresh ginger
6	large ripe red-skinned plums, halved, pitted, cut into ½-inch-thick wedges

CRUST: Preheat oven to 350°F. Lightly butter 9-inch-diameter springform pan with 2¾-inch-high sides. Combine graham crackers, brown sugar, cinnamon, and salt in processor. Process until fine crumbs form. Mix in melted butter. Transfer crumb mixture to prepared pan; press over bottom (not sides) of pan. Bake crust until set and golden, about 10 minutes. Cool on rack while preparing filling. Reduce oven temperature to 300°F.

FILLING: Using electric mixer, beat cream cheese in large bowl until smooth. Beat in sugar. Beat in eggs 1 at a time, then mix in sour cream, lemon peel, and vanilla. Pour filling over crust.

Bake cake until sides puff slightly and center is just set, about 1 hour 15 minutes. Turn oven off. Leave cake in oven with door slightly open 30 minutes.

Transfer cake to rack. Cut around pan sides to loosen cake. Cool cake completely in pan on rack, about 3 hours (cake may crack slightly as it cools). Cover and chill cake overnight.

PLUMS: Whisk orange juice, jelly, brown sugar, and ginger in heavy large skillet over medium-high heat until jelly dissolves. Add plums. Bring mixture to boil. Reduce heat to medium-low. Cover and simmer gently until plums are just tender but still hold shape, about 3 minutes. Using slotted spoon, transfer plums to large plate and cool. Boil cooking liquid in skillet until thickened to syrup consistency, stirring occasionally, about 7 minutes. Discard ginger.

DO AHEAD: *Plums and syrup can be made 4 hours ahead. Cover separately and chill.*

Cut around pan sides again; remove pan sides. Arrange plum wedges in concentric circles atop cheesecake, covering completely. Brush some syrup over plums. Cut cake into wedges. Serve with remaining syrup.

Peach Cheesecake with Gingersnap Crust

The gingersnap crust here has a little more spice than the familiar graham cracker crust and provides a delicious complement to the sweet peach compote, which is "hidden" between two layers of cream cheese filling. If you're headed to a potluck dinner or celebration feast, this cheesecake travels well. Glaze the cake in its springform pan, chill it, and transport it in the same pan. Come serving time, release the pan sides, then top the cake with fresh peach slices.

12 servings

Crust

25	gingersnap cookies (about 6 ounces), coarsely broken
¼	cup (½ stick) unsalted butter, melted

Filling

4	small peaches (about 1¼ pounds), peeled, pitted, sliced ¼ inch thick
2	tablespoons plus 1¼ cups sugar
½	teaspoon fresh lemon juice
4	8-ounce packages Philadelphia-brand cream cheese, room temperature
4	large eggs
½	cup sour cream
1½	teaspoons vanilla extract

Glaze

½	cup peach preserves
1½	teaspoons fresh lemon juice
½	large peach, peeled, pitted, very thinly sliced

Technique Tip: Room Temperature
Removing the cream cheese from the fridge and letting it come to room temperature for 30 minutes will make the filling much easier to mix.

CRUST: Preheat oven to 350°F. Grind gingersnaps in processor to coarse crumbs. Add melted butter and blend until evenly moistened. Press crumb mixture onto bottom and 1 inch up sides of 9-inch-diameter springform pan with 2¾-inch-high sides. Bake crust until beginning to brown, about 8 minutes. Cool in pan on rack. Reduce oven temperature to 325°F.

FILLING: Combine peaches, 2 tablespoons sugar, and lemon juice in heavy large saucepan. Cover and cook over medium-high heat until sugar dissolves and peaches are juicy, stirring occasionally, about 5 minutes. Uncover and cook until peaches are tender and juices thicken, about 5 minutes. Cool compote.

Using electric mixer, beat cream cheese in large bowl until fluffy. Gradually add remaining 1¼ cups sugar and beat until smooth. Beat in eggs 1 at a time. Mix in sour cream and vanilla. Spoon half of cheese mixture (about 3 cups) into crust. Spoon peach compote over by tablespoonfuls, spacing apart. Top with remaining cheese mixture.

Place large piece of foil on oven rack. Place pan with cheesecake on foil. Bake cake until puffed, set in center, and beginning to brown, about 1 hour. Place hot cake on rack; cool 5 minutes. Cut around pan sides to loosen cake; chill uncovered overnight.

DO AHEAD: *Can be made 2 days ahead. Cover; keep chilled.*

GLAZE: Combine preserves and lemon juice in heavy small saucepan. Stir over medium heat until glaze comes to simmer. Strain into small bowl. Cut around pan sides again; remove pan sides. Place cheesecake on platter. Spread glaze over top of cake to within ¼ inch of edge. Chill until glaze sets, at least 30 minutes and up to 8 hours. Arrange peach slices in center of cake and serve.

Cranberry Swirl Cheesecake with Cranberry-Raspberry Compote

The red swirls that run through this creamy cheesecake look impressive,
but all it takes to create them is a butter knife and a few twists of the wrist.

12 servings

Puree

2	cups fresh or thawed frozen cranberries
⅔	cup sugar
⅔	cup fresh orange juice
2	tablespoons finely grated orange peel
½	teaspoon ground cinnamon
¼	teaspoon ground nutmeg
4	teaspoons vanilla extract

Crust

	Nonstick vegetable oil spray
2¾	cups finely ground butter biscuit cookies or butter cookies
2	tablespoons sugar
1	teaspoon ground cinnamon
½	cup (1 stick) unsalted butter, melted

Filling

4	8-ounce packages Philadelphia-brand cream cheese, room temperature
1	cup sugar
4	large eggs
1	cup sour cream
½	cup heavy whipping cream
1	tablespoon vanilla extract

Cranberry-Raspberry Compote (see recipe)

PUREE: Combine all ingredients except vanilla in heavy large saucepan. Bring to boil over medium-high heat, stirring until sugar dissolves. Reduce heat to medium and cook until mixture thickens, stirring occasionally, about 5 minutes. Cool slightly. Transfer to processor. Add vanilla; puree until smooth. Strain into medium bowl; discard solids. Cover with plastic and chill at least 6 hours.

CRUST: Spray 10-inch-diameter springform pan with 2¾-inch-high sides with nonstick spray. Wrap outside of pan with 3 layers of heavy-duty foil. Blend cookies, sugar, and cinnamon in processor. Add melted butter; blend until moist clumps form. Press crumb mixture onto bottom and up sides of pan. Chill crust while preparing filling.

FILLING: Position rack in center of oven and preheat to 350°F. Using electric mixer, beat cream cheese in large bowl until fluffy. Beat in sugar. Beat in eggs 1 at a time. Mix in sour cream, whipping cream, and vanilla.

Spread ⅓ of filling over prepared crust. Dollop ⅓ of cranberry puree atop filling. Repeat layering of filling and puree 2 more times. Using butter knife, make a few zigzag cuts through batter to swirl puree and create marbled design [1].

Place cake pan in large roasting pan. Pour enough hot water into roasting pan to come halfway up sides of cake pan. Place in oven and bake cheesecake until puffed around edges, about 1 hour 15 minutes. Turn off oven. Let cake stand in oven 1 hour, leaving oven door slightly ajar.

Transfer cake to rack. Cut around pan sides to loosen cake. Cool completely.

Remove foil from pan sides. Cover cake and chill overnight.

DO AHEAD: *Can be made 2 days ahead. Keep chilled.*

Remove pan sides. Serve cake with Cranberry-Raspberry Compote.

(continued next page)

Cranberry Swirl Cheesecake with Cranberry-Raspberry Compote *(continued)*

Cranberry-Raspberry Compote

In addition to being a beautiful crowning touch for the cheesecake, this compote is great over vanilla-flavored frozen yogurt or thick and creamy plain Greek yogurt. **Makes about 2 cups**

1	12-ounce package frozen raspberries, thawed
1	cup fresh or frozen cranberries
¾	cup (packed) golden brown sugar
1	tablespoon fresh lemon juice
2	teaspoons finely grated lemon peel
½	teaspoon ground cinnamon
¼	teaspoon ground nutmeg
1	tablespoon vanilla extract

Combine all ingredients except vanilla in heavy medium saucepan. Simmer over medium heat until cranberries burst and mixture thickens, stirring occasionally, about 10 minutes. Remove from heat. Cool slightly. Stir in vanilla. Cool to room temperature. Cover and chill until cold, at least 6 hours.

DO AHEAD: *Can be made 2 days ahead. Keep chilled.*

Key Lime Cheesecake with Tropical Dried-Fruit Chutney

Key limes are round, golf-ball-size limes from Florida that are usually more fragrant and juicy than common Persian limes, with skin that is thinner and more yellow. They're the star players in Key lime pie, and this cheesecake is a denser, richer version of that Florida classic. Key limes are increasingly available in the produce section of supermarkets and at specialty foods stores. The peak season is late spring and summer. If you can't find them, you can use the juice and peel of regular limes. **12 servings**

Crust

⅔	cup unbleached all purpose flour
⅔	cup sweetened flaked coconut
⅓	cup sugar
¼	cup (½ stick) unsalted butter, melted

Filling

3	8-ounce packages Philadelphia-brand cream cheese, room temperature
½	cup sour cream
1	cup sugar
5	large eggs
3	tablespoons fresh Key lime juice
2	teaspoons finely grated Key lime peel
¾	teaspoon vanilla extract
	Tropical Dried-Fruit Chutney (see recipe)

CRUST: Preheat oven to 350°F. Stir flour, coconut, and sugar in medium bowl to blend. Drizzle melted butter over and stir until mixture sticks together. Press mixture firmly onto bottom (not sides) of 9-inch-diameter springform pan with 2¾-inch-high sides. Bake crust until golden brown, about 25 minutes. Cool crust. Wrap outside of pan with 3 layers of heavy-duty foil.

FILLING: Using electric mixer, beat cream cheese in large bowl until smooth. Beat in sour cream, then sugar. Beat in eggs 1 at a time, occasionally scraping down sides of bowl. Beat in lime juice, lime peel, and vanilla. Pour batter over crust. Place wrapped cheesecake in large roasting pan. Pour enough hot water into roasting pan to come halfway up sides of cake pan. Cover cake pan (not roasting pan) loosely with foil.

Bake 1 hour. Uncover and continue to bake until cake is just set in center when pan is gently shaken, about 20 minutes longer. Remove cake from water, remove foil, and place directly into refrigerator; chill uncovered overnight.

Cut around pan sides to loosen cake. Remove pan sides. Slice cake; serve with Tropical Dried-Fruit Chutney.

Tropical Dried-Fruit Chutney

Cooking dried fruits in Sherry and adding pineapple juice off the heat adds luscious moistness to the fruit; adding chopped mint and cilantro lends a sweet-savory touch. Dried mango, papaya, and pineapple are available at natural foods stores and specialty markets. Star anise, a star-shaped, slightly licorice-flavored seedpod, is available in the spice section of some supermarkets and at specialty food stores and Asian markets. **Makes about 3 cups**

1   **vanilla bean, split lengthwise**
1   **cup imported dry Sherry**
2   **cinnamon sticks**
2   **whole star anise**
1   **cup ½-inch dice dried mango**
1   **cup ½-inch dice dried papaya**
½   **cup ½-inch dice dried pineapple**
½   **cup raisins**
    Pineapple juice
3   **tablespoons chopped fresh mint**
3   **tablespoons chopped fresh cilantro**

Scrape seeds from vanilla bean into heavy medium saucepan. Add bean, Sherry, cinnamon sticks, and star anise. Bring to simmer over medium heat. Add all dried fruits; return to simmer, stirring occasionally. Simmer until Sherry is almost evaporated, stirring occasionally, about 15 minutes. Remove from heat. Mix in enough pineapple juice by tablespoonfuls to moisten chutney. Transfer to bowl, cover, and chill until cold, at least 3 hours.

DO AHEAD: *Chutney can be made 1 day ahead. Keep chilled.*

Remove vanilla bean, cinnamon sticks, and star anise from chutney. Mix in mint and cilantro and serve.

Vanilla Bean Cheesecake with Guava Topping and Mango-Lime Salad

The Tropics get dressed up: An intensely vanilla-flavored cheesecake—prepared with two vanilla beans—is covered with a guava gelatin topping and accompanied by a refreshing salad of mango and lime (with a splash of rum to up the Caribbean influence). Because the cheesecake needs to chill after baking and again after the guava topping is added, begin preparing this two days ahead. **8 to 10 servings**

Crust
  Nonstick vegetable oil spray
1¼ cups graham cracker crumbs
2   tablespoons sugar
¼   cup (½ stick) unsalted butter, melted

Filling
3   8-ounce packages Philadelphia-brand cream cheese, room temperature
1   cup sugar
2   vanilla beans, split lengthwise
4   large eggs
¾   cup sour cream

Topping
2   tablespoons plus ½ cup water
1   ¼-ounce envelope unflavored gelatin
½   cup sugar
2   cups guava nectar or guava juice

  Mango-Lime Salad (see recipe)
  Sweetened flaked coconut, toasted

CRUST: Preheat oven to 350°F. Spray 8-inch-diameter springform pan with 2¾-inch-high sides with nonstick spray. Mix graham cracker crumbs and sugar in processor. Add melted butter; process until crumbs are evenly moistened. Press crumb mixture onto bottom (not sides) of prepared pan. Bake until crust is set and deep golden, about 12 minutes. Cool crust while making filling. Maintain oven temperature.

FILLING: Using electric mixer, beat cream cheese in large bowl until smooth. Add sugar, then scrape in seeds from vanilla beans (reserve beans for another use); beat until smooth. Add eggs 1 at a time, blending well after each addition. Beat in sour cream. Pour filling over crust.

Bake cake until puffed, golden on top, set around edges, and center moves just slightly when pan is gently shaken, about 1 hour (top may crack). Cool 30 minutes. Chill uncovered overnight. Using back of spoon, smooth any cracks on top of cake.

TOPPING: Pour 2 tablespoons water into small bowl. Sprinkle gelatin over; let stand until gelatin softens, about 15 minutes. Bring sugar and remaining ½ cup water to boil in medium saucepan, stirring until sugar dissolves. Boil until reduced to ½ cup, about 3 minutes. Add guava nectar to sugar syrup; stir over medium-low heat just until mixture is hot. Add gelatin mixture and stir just until gelatin dissolves. Place in freezer until topping begins to thicken slightly but is still pourable, stirring occasionally, about 20 minutes. Spoon guava topping over cheesecake, spreading to edges. Chill until topping sets, at least 8 hours and up to 1 day.

Cut around pan sides to loosen cake. Remove pan sides. Cut cake into wedges and transfer to plates. Spoon Mango-Lime Salad alongside. Sprinkle with toasted coconut.

Mango-Lime Salad

This would also make a nice salad for brunch—especially topped with toasted coconut; the recipe is easy to double or triple. To choose a flavorful mango, smell the stem end. You should get a whiff of pine and peaches. The mango is ripe if it gives slightly when pressed gently. For tips on dicing a mango, see page 34. **Makes about 2⅔ cups**

3   firm but ripe mangoes, peeled, pitted, cut into ¼-inch cubes
4½ tablespoons sugar
3   tablespoons fresh lime juice
1½ tablespoons dark rum
1   tablespoon finely grated lime peel

Mix all ingredients in small bowl. Let stand at room temperature 30 minutes, tossing occasionally. Serve chilled or at room temperature.

Deep Dark Chocolate Cheesecake

For this rich, dense dessert, you'll want to use a delicious, top-tier bittersweet chocolate (with a 70% cacao content) like Scharffen Berger; if it's not available, try Valrhona, Callebaut, or Lindt. **12 servings**

Crust

24	chocolate wafer cookies (from one 9-ounce package)
1	tablespoon sugar
¼	cup (½ stick) unsalted butter, melted

Filling

1	9.7-ounce bar Scharffen Berger bittersweet chocolate (70% cacao), chopped
4	8-ounce packages Philadelphia-brand cream cheese, room temperature
1¼	cups plus 2 tablespoons sugar
¼	cup natural unsweetened cocoa powder (preferably Scharffen Berger)
4	large eggs

Topping

¾	cup heavy whipping cream
6	ounces Scharffen Berger bittersweet chocolate (70% cacao), chopped
1	tablespoon sugar
	Bittersweet chocolate curls

CRUST: Preheat oven to 350°F. Butter 9-inch-diameter springform pan with 2¾-inch-high sides. Blend cookies and sugar in processor until cookies are finely ground. Add melted butter and process until well blended. Press crumb mixture evenly onto bottom (not sides) of prepared pan. Bake just until crust is set, about 8 minutes. Cool while preparing filling. Maintain oven temperature.

FILLING: Stir chopped chocolate in metal bowl set over saucepan of simmering water until melted and smooth. Remove bowl from over water; cool chocolate until lukewarm but still pourable. Blend cream cheese, sugar, and cocoa powder in processor until smooth, occasionally scraping down sides of bowl. Blend in eggs 1 at a time. Mix in lukewarm chocolate. Pour filling over crust; smooth top.

Bake cheesecake until center is just set and top looks dry, about 1 hour. Cool 5 minutes. Cut around sides of pan to loosen cake. Place warm cake in pan in refrigerator and chill uncovered overnight.

TOPPING: Stir cream, chopped chocolate, and sugar in heavy medium saucepan over low heat until chocolate melts and topping is smooth. Cool slightly. Pour over center of cheesecake and spread to within ½ inch of edge, covering any cracks. Chill until topping is set, about 1 hour.

DO AHEAD: *Can be made 3 days ahead. Cover with foil and keep chilled.*

Cut around pan sides again; remove pan sides. Transfer cheesecake to platter. Top with chocolate curls. Let stand 2 hours at room temperature before serving.

♨ Cappuccino Cheesecake

With espresso and chocolate flavors combined in the filling, this cheesecake is dessert and after-dinner coffee in one. Using semisweet chocolate chips will make this recipe go faster, but if you have a favorite semisweet or bittersweet chocolate, go ahead and use it—just be sure to chop it into chip-size pieces. **12 servings**

8	whole graham crackers, crushed
5	tablespoons unsalted butter, melted
1½	cups sugar, divided
1½	cup heavy whipping cream
4	teaspoons instant espresso powder or coffee powder
1½	teaspoons vanilla extract
4	8-ounce packages Philadelphia-brand cream cheese, room temperature
4	large eggs
2	tablespoons unbleached all purpose flour
1	cup semisweet chocolate chips
	Chocolate curls (optional)

Preheat oven to 350°F. Mix graham crackers, melted butter, and ¼ cup sugar in medium bowl to blend. Press crumb mixture onto bottom (not sides) of 9-inch-diameter springform pan with 2¾-inch-high sides. Bake crust 10 minutes. Cool crust in pan on rack. Maintain oven temperature.

Combine cream, espresso powder, and vanilla in small bowl. Stir until espresso powder dissolves. Using electric mixer, beat cream cheese in large bowl until smooth. Gradually beat in remaining 1¼ cups sugar, then eggs 1 at a time. Beat in flour, then espresso mixture. Stir in chocolate chips. Pour batter over crust.

Bake cake until edges are puffed and beginning to crack and center is just set, about 1 hour 5 minutes. Cool in pan on rack 30 minutes. Chill cake uncovered until cold, about 6 hours. Cover; keep chilled at least 1 day and up to 2 days. Cut around pan sides to loosen cake. Remove pan sides. Top cheesecake with chocolate curls, if desired.

♨♨♨ Almond Joy Cheesecake

Here's a delicious ode to the chocolate, coconut, and almond candy bars— coconut and almonds are even added to the crust. **10 to 12 servings**

Crust

1½	cups graham cracker crumbs
1½	cups sweetened flaked coconut, toasted
½	cup sliced almonds, toasted
¼	cup sugar
½	cup (1 stick) unsalted butter, melted

Filling

4	8-ounce packages Philadelphia-brand cream cheese, room temperature
1	cup sugar
4	large eggs
1	cup sweetened flaked coconut, toasted
1	tablespoon coconut extract
1	cup sliced almonds, toasted

Glaze

1	cup semisweet chocolate chips
¾	cup heavy whipping cream
1½	teaspoons vanilla extract

CRUST: Preheat oven to 350°F. Wrap outside of 9-inch-diameter springform pan with 2¾-inch-high sides with foil. Finely grind cracker crumbs, coconut, almonds, and sugar in processor. Add melted butter; process until moist crumbs form. Press crumb mixture onto bottom and 1 inch up sides of pan. Bake crust until set and beginning to brown, about 12 minutes. Cool. Reduce oven temperature to 325°F.

FILLING: Using electric mixer, beat cream cheese and sugar in large bowl until smooth. Add eggs 1 at a time, beating just until blended after each addition. Fold in flaked coconut and coconut extract, then almonds. Pour batter over crust in pan.

Bake cake until puffed and no longer jiggling in center when pan is gently shaken, about 1 hour 15 minutes. Cool cake completely in pan on rack.

GLAZE: Combine chocolate chips, cream, and vanilla in small saucepan. Stir over medium-low heat until smooth. Cool until glaze begins to thicken but is still pourable, about 30 minutes. Pour glaze over cooled cake; spread evenly. Chill cake overnight.

Cut around pan sides to loosen cake. Remove pan sides and serve cake.

Black Forest Cheesecake

This is a cheesecake riff on Black Forest cake, the chocolate-and-cherry dessert named for Germany's Black Forest. Sour cherry syrup is available at specialty foods stores and from online retailers such as amazon.com.

12 to 14 servings

Cherry Topping

1   pound frozen dark sweet cherries, thawed

¼   cup kirsch (clear cherry brandy)

¼   cup (about) Morello cherry syrup or sour cherry syrup

Crust

8½   ounces chocolate wafer cookies (from one 9-ounce package)

6   tablespoons (¾ stick) chilled unsalted butter, cut into
       ½-inch cubes

Filling

1½   cups chilled heavy whipping cream

12   ounces bittersweet or semisweet chocolate (do not exceed
       61% cacao), coarsely chopped

2   8-ounce packages Philadelphia-brand cream cheese,
       room temperature

¾   cup sugar

4   large eggs, room temperature

1   teaspoon vanilla extract

Kirsch Whipped Cream

1   cup chilled heavy whipping cream

2   tablespoons sugar

1   tablespoon kirsch (clear cherry brandy)

     Chocolate curls (optional)

CHERRY TOPPING: Combine cherries and kirsch in medium bowl. Steep 6 hours, stirring occasionally.

Place cherries with juices in strainer set over medium bowl. Let drain 2 hours, shaking occasionally.

Pour cherry juices from bowl into 1-cup measuring cup; add enough cherry syrup to measure 1 cup. Pour 6 tablespoons juice mixture into heavy medium skillet (reserve remaining liquid for filling). Halve cherries and add to skillet. Boil until syrup is thickened and mixture resembles preserves, stirring occasionally, about 6 minutes.

DO AHEAD: *Can be made 2 days ahead. Cover and chill.*

CRUST: Generously butter 9-inch-diameter springform pan with 2¾-inch-high sides. Using on/off turns, finely crush cookies in processor. Add butter; using on/off turns, blend until mixture begins to stick together. Press crumb mixture onto bottom and 2 inches up sides of pan. Chill crust at least 30 minutes and up to 1 day.

FILLING: Preheat oven to 325°F. Stir cream and chocolate in heavy medium saucepan over low heat until chocolate melts. Cool 10 minutes.

Using electric mixer, beat cream cheese and sugar in large bowl until smooth. Beat in eggs 1 at a time. Beat in chocolate mixture, then remaining cherry juice mixture and vanilla. Pour filling into crust.

Bake cheesecake until outer 2 inches of cake are firm but center still moves slightly, about 1 hour 15 minutes (top may crack). Cool completely in pan on rack. Top cake pan with paper towels and cover tightly with foil. Chill 1 to 2 days.

Remove foil and paper towels. Cut around pan sides to loosen cake; remove pan sides. Spread cherry topping over cake.

KIRSCH WHIPPED CREAM: Whisk cream, sugar, and kirsch in large bowl until peaks form. Spoon into center of cake. Top with chocolate curls, if desired.

DO AHEAD: *Can be made 2 hours ahead; chill.*

Let stand at room temperature 15 minutes before serving.

S'mores Cheesecake with Summer Berries

The ingredients for s'mores, that classic American cookout dessert, translate wonderfully into this chocolate cheesecake with a graham cracker crust and marshmallow topping. Serving juicy, in-season berries alongside is the crowning summery touch. **8 to 10 servings**

Crust
9   whole graham crackers, finely ground in processor
3   tablespoons sugar
6   tablespoons (¾ stick) unsalted butter, melted

Filling
9   ounces high-quality milk chocolate (such as Lindt or Perugina), chopped
2   8-ounce packages Philadelphia-brand cream cheese, room temperature
¾   cup sugar
⅛   teaspoon salt
¾   cup heavy whipping cream
3   large eggs

Topping
1   cup sugar
2   large egg whites, room temperature
3   tablespoons water
1   teaspoon cream of tartar
⅛   teaspoon salt
12   large marshmallows, cut into quarters with wet kitchen scissors
½   teaspoon vanilla extract

1   1-pint container raspberries
1   1-pint container blueberries

CRUST: Position rack in center of oven and preheat to 350°F. Mix crumbs and sugar in medium bowl. Add melted butter; stir until crumbs are evenly moistened. Press crumb mixture onto bottom (not sides) of 9-inch-diameter springform pan with 2¾-inch-high sides. Bake crust until set, about 12 minutes. Remove from oven and cool. Reduce oven temperature to 325°F.

FILLING: Stir chocolate in medium metal bowl set over saucepan of barely simmering water until melted and smooth. Remove from over water and cool to lukewarm, stirring occasionally.

Combine cream cheese, sugar, and salt in processor; blend until smooth, occasionally scraping down sides of bowl. With motor running, add whipping cream through feed tube and process just until blended. With motor running, add melted chocolate, then add eggs 1 at a time, blending and scraping down sides of bowl after each addition until batter is smooth. Pour batter over crust in pan.

Bake cake until outer edge is slightly puffed and cake is barely set in center (center will look shiny and move slightly when pan is gently shaken), about 55 minutes. Transfer cake to rack. Cut around pan sides to loosen cake. Chill uncovered until cold, at least 8 hours and up to 1 day.

DO AHEAD: *Can be made 2 days ahead. Cover and keep chilled.*

TOPPING: Whisk sugar, egg whites, 3 tablespoons water, cream of tartar, and salt in large metal bowl to blend. Set bowl over saucepan of simmering water and whisk constantly until sugar dissolves and mixture thickens and is hot to touch, about 3 minutes. Remove bowl from over water and stir in marshmallows (keep water simmering in saucepan). Let stand until marshmallows soften, about 3 minutes. Set bowl with mixture over simmering water again. Using handheld electric mixer, beat until stiff shiny peaks form, about 4 minutes. Beat in vanilla. Scrape topping onto cheesecake. Using offset metal spatula, spread topping to edges of cake, swirling decoratively. Let stand until set, about 15 minutes. Using kitchen torch, lightly brown topping in spots. (Or preheat broiler; place cake at least 4 inches from heat source and broil just until topping is lightly browned in spots, watching closely to avoid burning, about 2 minutes.) Chill cake uncovered until cold.

DO AHEAD: *Can be made 1 day ahead. Cover with cake dome and keep chilled.*

Cut around pan sides again; remove pan sides. Place cake on platter.

Mix raspberries and blueberries in medium bowl. Cut cake into wedges. Serve berries alongside.

⫲ Double-Decker Raspberry and White Chocolate Cheesecake

The raspberry flavor lends a nice summertime feeling to this dessert, but since the recipe calls for frozen raspberries, it can be made year-round. Leftover raspberry puree is delicious in club soda with a squeeze of lime. **12 servings**

1	**9-ounce package chocolate wafer cookies, coarsely broken**
6	**tablespoons (¾ stick) unsalted butter, melted**
1	**12-ounce package frozen raspberries, thawed, juices reserved**
6	**ounces high-quality white chocolate (such as Lindt or Perugina), finely chopped**
4	**8-ounce packages Philadelphia-brand cream cheese, room temperature**
1⅓	**cups sugar**
2	**tablespoons unbleached all purpose flour**
4	**large eggs**
2	**tablespoons heavy whipping cream**
2	**teaspoons vanilla extract**
½	**teaspoon almond extract**
	White chocolate curls (optional)

Preheat oven to 325°F. Butter 9-inch-diameter springform pan with 2¾-inch-high sides. Wrap outside of pan with 3 layers of heavy-duty foil. Place cookies in processor and blend until coarse crumbs form. Add melted butter and process until evenly moistened. Press crumb mixture firmly onto bottom and halfway up sides of prepared pan. Bake crust 8 minutes; cool in pan on rack. Maintain oven temperature.

Press raspberries with juices through fine strainer into small bowl; discard seeds in strainer. Measure ½ cup puree to use for filling (reserve remaining puree for another use). Stir white chocolate in small metal bowl set over saucepan of barely simmering water until just melted and smooth.

Using electric mixer, beat cream cheese and sugar in large bowl until smooth and fluffy. Beat in flour, then beat in eggs 1 at a time. Beat in whipping cream and vanilla. Transfer 2¼ cups batter to medium bowl; stir in melted white chocolate. Stir reserved ½ cup raspberry puree and almond extract into remaining batter in large bowl.

Pour raspberry batter into prepared crust. Place cake pan in large roasting pan. Pour enough hot water into roasting pan to come 1 inch up sides of cake pan.

Bake cake until raspberry filling is softly set in center and beginning to puff at edges, about 50 minutes. Remove roasting pan from oven; let raspberry layer cool 5 minutes to firm slightly.

Starting at edge of pan, spoon white chocolate batter in concentric circles onto raspberry layer. Smooth top. Bake cake until white chocolate filling is set in center, about 30 minutes. Remove cake pan from water bath and remove foil from pan sides. Chill hot cake uncovered until cold, at least 4 hours.

DO AHEAD: *Can be made 2 days ahead; cover and keep chilled.*

Cut around pan sides to loosen cheesecake; remove pan sides. Garnish cheesecake with white chocolate curls, if desired.

Pumpkin Cheesecake with Marshmallow–Sour Cream Topping and Gingersnap Crust

Just because it has pumpkin in the filling and marshmallows on the top, don't relegate this amazing cheesecake to just one month out of the year—friends and family will give thanks any time you make it. The sour cream in the topping provides excellent balance to the sweet marshmallows. **12 servings**

Crust

	Nonstick vegetable oil spray
2	cups gingersnap cookie crumbs
1	cup pecans
¼	cup (packed) golden brown sugar
2	tablespoons chopped crystallized ginger
¼	cup (½ stick) unsalted butter, melted

Filling

4	8-ounce packages Philadelphia-brand cream cheese, room temperature
2	cups sugar
1	15-ounce can pure pumpkin
5	large eggs
3	tablespoons unbleached all purpose flour
1	teaspoon ground cinnamon
½	teaspoon ground ginger
¼	teaspoon freshly grated nutmeg
¼	teaspoon ground allspice
¼	teaspoon salt
2	tablespoons vanilla extract

Topping

2	cups mini marshmallows or large marshmallows cut into ½-inch cubes
¼	cup whole milk
1	teaspoon vanilla extract
⅛	teaspoon salt
1	cup sour cream

CRUST: Preheat oven to 350°F. Spray 9-inch-diameter springform pan with 2¾-inch-high sides with nonstick spray. Blend cookie crumbs, pecans, brown sugar, and ginger in processor until nuts are finely ground. Add melted butter; using on/off turns, process until crumbs stick together. Press crumb mixture onto bottom and 2 inches up sides of prepared pan. Bake crust until set and lightly browned, about 10 minutes. Cool completely.

FILLING: Preheat oven to 350°F. Using electric mixer, beat cream cheese and sugar in large bowl until light and fluffy, about 2 minutes. Beat in pumpkin. Add eggs 1 at a time, beating on low speed to blend after each addition and occasionally scraping down sides of bowl. Add flour, spices, and salt; beat just to blend. Beat in vanilla. Transfer filling to cooled crust.

Bake cake until edges begin to crack and filling is just set in center (filling will move only slightly in center when pan is gently shaken), about 1 hour 20 minutes. Cool 1 hour. Cut around pan sides to loosen cake; chill uncovered in cake pan overnight.

TOPPING: Stir marshmallows and milk in large saucepan over low heat until marshmallows are melted. Remove from heat; stir in vanilla and salt. Cool marshmallow mixture to room temperature, stirring occasionally. Fold sour cream into marshmallow mixture. Pour topping over cheesecake and spread evenly, leaving ½ inch plain border around edges. Chill to set topping, at least 1 hour.

DO AHEAD: *Can be made 1 day ahead. Keep chilled.*

Cut around pan sides again. Remove pan sides. Cut cheesecake into wedges and serve.

{ **Technique Tip: A Clean Slice**
For neat cheesecake slices, dip a thin-bladed knife into a large glass of very hot water before cutting (the cheesecake filling won't stick to the hot blade). Dip the blade and wipe it clean after cutting each slice. }

Crème Fraîche Cheesecake with Honey-Rum-Roasted Pineapple

Crème fraîche brings extra tanginess to this tropical-flavored cheesecake, while dark rum gives it a decidedly grown-up kick. **12 servings**

Crust
1 cup graham cracker crumbs
¼ cup (½ stick) unsalted butter, melted
1 tablespoon sugar

Filling
3 8-ounce packages Philadelphia-brand cream cheese, room temperature
1 cup sugar
1 vanilla bean, split lengthwise
2 large eggs
¾ cup crème fraîche or sour cream

Topping
1 pineapple, peeled, cut into ½-inch-thick rounds, cored
1 cup water
¼ cup honey
2 tablespoons sugar
2 tablespoons dark rum

CRUST: Preheat oven to 350°F. Blend all ingredients in bowl until crumbs stick together. Press crumb mixture onto bottom (not sides) of 9-inch-diameter springform pan with 2¾-inch sides. Bake crust until golden, about 12 minutes. Transfer to rack; cool. Wrap outside of pan with 3 layers of heavy-duty foil. Reduce oven temperature to 325°F.

FILLING: Using electric mixer, beat cream cheese in large bowl until fluffy. Gradually beat in sugar. Scrape in seeds from vanilla bean (reserve bean for another use) and blend 1 minute. Beat in eggs 1 at a time. Mix in crème fraîche. Pour filling over crust. Place pan in roasting pan. Add enough hot water to roasting pan to come 1 inch up sides of cake pan.

Bake cake until top is dry-looking and slightly puffed, about 1 hour. Turn off oven. Let cake cool in closed oven 1 hour. Remove from water bath; remove foil. Chill uncovered until cold, at least 6 hours.

DO AHEAD: *Can be made 1 day ahead. Cover and keep chilled.*

TOPPING: Preheat oven to 400°F. Place pineapple rings on large foil-lined rimmed baking sheet. Bring 1 cup water, honey, sugar, and rum to boil in small saucepan, stirring until sugar dissolves. Boil 3 minutes, stirring occasionally. Spoon syrup over pineapple. Roast pineapple 12 minutes. Turn rings over; roast until tender and syrup thickens, turning rings every 5 minutes, about 20 minutes longer. Cool pineapple on sheet. Cut into ⅓-inch cubes; transfer pineapple and syrup to bowl.

DO AHEAD: *Can be made 1 day ahead. Chill.*

Drain pineapple, reserving syrup. Cover top of cheesecake with some pineapple; stir remainder back into syrup. Serve cake, passing pineapple in syrup separately.

Mascarpone Cheesecake with Balsamic Strawberries

Cheesecake gets an irresistible Italian accent with mascarpone (Italian cream cheese), biscotti, and balsamic vinegar. The vinegar is used along with sugar to macerate the strawberries, which gives them a tang that contrasts wonderfully with the rich, creamy cheesecake. You can find all three of these ingredients at Italian markets, of course, but many supermarkets carry them as well. **8 to 10 servings**

1½   **cups ground crumbs from purchased almond biscotti**
         (about 6 ounces)
6   **tablespoons (¾ stick) unsalted butter, melted**
4   **8-ounce packages Philadelphia-brand cream cheese,**
         room temperature
8   **ounces mascarpone cheese**
1¾   **cups plus 2 tablespoons sugar, divided**
2   **large eggs**
3   **cups quartered hulled strawberries (about 18 ounces)**
¼   **cup balsamic vinegar**

Tightly wrap outside of 9-inch-diameter springform pan with 2¾-inch-high sides with 3 layers of heavy-duty foil. Mix biscotti crumbs and melted butter in bowl until evenly moistened. Press crumb mixture evenly onto bottom (not sides) of prepared pan. Chill crust 30 minutes.

Preheat oven to 350°F. Using electric mixer, beat cream cheese, mascarpone, and 1¼ cups sugar in large bowl until smooth. Add eggs 1 at a time; beat just until blended after each addition. Spread cheese mixture evenly over crust in pan. Place cake pan in large roasting pan. Pour enough hot water into roasting pan to come halfway up sides of cake pan.

Bake until cheesecake is golden and center of cake moves only slightly when pan is shaken, about 1 hour 10 minutes. Transfer cake to rack; cool 1 hour. Remove foil from pan sides. Chill cake uncovered overnight.

DO AHEAD: *Cake can be made 2 days ahead. Cover and keep chilled. Remove from refrigerator 30 minutes before serving.*

Mix strawberries, remaining ½ cup plus 2 tablespoons sugar, and vinegar in large bowl. Let stand at room temperature until juices form, tossing occasionally, about 30 minutes.

Cut cake into wedges. Spoon strawberries with juices alongside.

Cream Cheese vs. Mascarpone

Cream cheese is a soft unripened cheese made of cow's milk and cream (by law, it has to contain 33% milk fat)—and it's far and away the most widely used ingredient in cheesecake. When cream cheese is called for in *Bon Appétit* recipes, the Test Kitchen specifies "Philadelphia-brand." This is a result of side-by-side testings with several other brands, in which we found that the cheesecakes made with Philadelphia cream cheese set up far better than those made with other brands, which didn't have the desired firmness after chilling.

Mascarpone, sometimes called Italian cream cheese, is different from American cream cheese. Both are rich, but while cream cheese is dense, with a pronounced tanginess, mascarpone is mellower and more buttery and lends a lighter texture to the finished cheesecake. Mascarpone is fairly widely available in supermarkets these days, but if you can't find it at yours, look for it in specialty foods stores or in Italian markets.

Mascarpone Cheesecake with Candied Pecans and Dulce de Leche

Dulce de leche—the Latin version of caramel sauce that is made with condensed milk—creates a rich layer atop the mascarpone cheesecake. If you don't have time to make your own, you'll find dulce de leche sold in jars with other ice-cream toppings at many supermarkets and at Latin markets. **14 servings**

8	ounces purchased shortbread cookies
1/3	cup pecans
2	tablespoons (1/4 stick) unsalted butter, melted
12	ounces Philadelphia-brand cream cheese, room temperature
2	8-ounce containers mascarpone cheese, room temperature
1 1/2	tablespoons all purpose flour
1 1/4	cups sugar
1	teaspoon vanilla extract
1/2	teaspoon fresh lemon juice
4	large eggs, room temperature
	Candied Pecans (see recipe)
	Dulce de Leche (see recipe)

Preheat oven to 350°F. Wrap outside of 9-inch-diameter springform pan with 2¾-inch-high sides with 3 layers of heavy-duty foil. Finely grind shortbread cookies and pecans in processor. Add melted butter and process until crumbs are moistened. Press crumb mixture onto bottom (not sides) of prepared pan. Bake crust until golden, about 15 minutes. Cool crust completely in pan on rack. Reduce oven temperature to 325°F.

Using electric mixer, beat cream cheese in large bowl until smooth. Add mascarpone and flour; beat until smooth, occasionally scraping down sides of bowl with rubber spatula. Gradually add sugar and beat until smooth. Beat in vanilla and lemon juice. Add eggs 1 at a time, beating just until blended after each addition.

Pour filling over crust in pan. Place cake pan in large roasting pan. Pour enough hot water into roasting pan to come halfway up sides of cake pan.

Bake cheesecake until top is golden and cake is almost set (center 2 inches will move only slightly when pan is gently shaken), about 1 hour 15 minutes. Cool cake on rack 1 hour. Remove foil from pan sides. Chill cake uncovered overnight.

DO AHEAD: *Can be made 2 days ahead. Cover and keep chilled.*

Arrange Candied Pecans decoratively atop cake. Cut cake into wedges. Serve with Dulce de Leche.

Candied Pecans

These would also be good served on their own after dinner with coffee— or tossed in a salad. **Makes about 1 cup**

	Nonstick vegetable oil spray
1/2	cup sugar
2	tablespoons water
	Pinch of cream of tartar
3/4	cup pecan halves

Line rimmed baking sheet with foil; spray foil with nonstick spray. Combine sugar, 2 tablespoons water, and cream of tartar in heavy small saucepan. Stir over medium-low heat until sugar dissolves. Increase heat and boil without stirring until syrup is deep amber color, occasionally brushing down sides of pan with wet pastry brush and swirling pan, about 7 minutes. Remove from heat. Immediately stir in pecans. Quickly pour mixture out onto prepared baking sheet. Using 2 forks and working quickly, separate pecans. Cool completely. Break candied pecans apart, leaving each pecan half intact with some crisp caramel attached.

DO AHEAD: *Can be made 1 week ahead. Store airtight at room temperature.*

Dulce de Leche

Dulce de leche is also delicious on ice cream, or you can even spread it on whole wheat toast. **Makes about 1 1/3 cups**

1	cup heavy whipping cream
1	cup (packed) dark brown sugar
1/2	cup sweetened condensed milk

Combine cream and sugar in heavy medium saucepan. Stir over medium heat until sugar dissolves. Boil until mixture is reduced to 1 cup, stirring occasionally, about 5 minutes. Stir in sweetened condensed milk.

DO AHEAD: *Can be made 1 day ahead. Cover and chill. Rewarm over medium-low heat just until warm and pourable.*

Mascarpone Cheesecake with Quince Compote

This cheesecake, which requires baking only the crust, has a silky texture that may remind you of panna cotta, the Italian custard dessert. The cake is made with mascarpone (Italian cream cheese), heavy cream, and gelatin instead of regular cream cheese and eggs. This would be a delicious addition to a Thanksgiving feast. **12 servings**

1⅓   cups pecans, toasted
½   cup walnuts, toasted
½   cup (packed) golden brown sugar
½   cup (1 stick) unsalted butter, melted
3½   cups heavy whipping cream, divided
¼   cup water
3½   teaspoons unflavored gelatin (from 2 envelopes)
3½   cups plus 2 tablespoons mascarpone cheese (measured from
        four 8-ounce containers)
1¼   cups powdered sugar, sifted
        Quince Compote (see recipe)

Preheat oven to 375°F. Coarsely grind all nuts and brown sugar in processor. Add melted butter and blend well. Press nut mixture onto bottom (not sides) of 9-inch-diameter springform pan with 2¾-inch-high sides. Bake until crust is set, about 12 minutes. Cool crust completely.

Pour 3 cups cream into medium bowl. Pour ¼ cup water into medium heatproof bowl; sprinkle gelatin over. Let stand until gelatin softens, about 15 minutes. Place bowl with gelatin in small skillet of barely simmering water; stir until gelatin dissolves, about 2 minutes. Remove bowl from water. Pour remaining ½ cup cream into gelatin. Pour gelatin mixture into cream in bowl; whisk gently until well blended.

Using electric mixer, beat mascarpone and powdered sugar in large bowl until smooth. Add cream-gelatin mixture and beat just until blended. Pour filling over cooled crust. Cover and chill overnight.

DO AHEAD: *Can be made 2 days ahead. Keep chilled.*

Cut around pan sides to loosen cheesecake. Remove pan sides. Place cake on platter. Cut cake into wedges and serve with Quince Compote.

Ingredient Tip: Quince

An ancient apple-like fruit used extensively in Asia and the Mediterranean, the quince is extremely hard, so is always cooked in recipe preparations. It's used in preserves because of its high pectin content, and also in savory dishes like stews.

Quince Compote

Quinces are golden yellow fruits that look a bit like pears, but are rounder and harder. Cooking transforms them from astringent to mellow. Look for them at the market in the fall. **Makes about 3 cups**

4   pounds quinces, peeled, quartered, cored, cut into ½-inch cubes
2   cups water
2   cups sugar
2   cups dry white wine
1   vanilla bean, split lengthwise

Bring quinces, water, sugar, and wine to boil in heavy large saucepan, stirring until sugar dissolves. Scrape in seeds from vanilla bean; add bean. Reduce heat, cover, and simmer until fruit is soft, stirring occasionally, about 40 minutes. Using slotted spoon, transfer fruit to bowl. Boil juices uncovered until reduced to 3 cups, about 30 minutes. Pour syrup over fruit. Cover and chill overnight. Remove vanilla bean before serving.

Almond Cheesecake with Sour Cream and Blackberries

This cake gets intense almond flavor from almond paste, almond extract, and ground almonds—and that flavor pairs beautifully with the blackberry and sour cream topping. Almond paste can be found in the baking section of most supermarkets and at specialty foods stores and some online retailers. **8 to 10 servings**

Crust

1	**7-ounce tube almond paste**
6	**whole graham crackers, coarsely broken**
½	**cup whole almonds, toasted, cooled**
¼	**cup (½ stick) chilled unsalted butter, cut into ½-inch cubes**

Filling

½	**cup sugar**
2	**8-ounce packages Philadelphia-brand cream cheese, cut into 1-inch pieces, room temperature**
3	**large eggs**
½	**cup heavy whipping cream**
¼	**teaspoon almond extract**

Topping

1	**cup sour cream**
3	**tablespoons plus ½ cup sugar, divided**
1	**pound frozen blackberries, thawed, drained, juices reserved**
1½	**teaspoons unflavored gelatin**

CRUST: Preheat oven to 350°F. Set aside ½ cup (packed) almond paste for filling. Combine remaining almond paste, graham crackers, and almonds in processor and grind finely. Add butter; process until moist crumbs form. Press crumb mixture over bottom and 2 inches up sides of 9-inch-diameter springform pan with 2¾-inch-high sides. Bake until crust darkens in color, about 10 minutes. Cool crust. Maintain oven temperature.

FILLING: Wipe out processor. Blend sugar and reserved ½ cup almond paste in processor until mixture resembles fine meal, about 1 minute. Add half of cream cheese and process until smooth, about 1 minute. Add remaining cream cheese and process until smooth. Add eggs, cream, and almond extract and blend until just combined, occasionally scraping down sides of bowl. Pour filling into crust.

Bake cake until just set in center and beginning to crack at edges, about 40 minutes. Cool 10 minutes. Maintain oven temperature.

TOPPING: Mix sour cream and 1 tablespoon sugar in small bowl; spoon over hot cake. Bake 3 minutes. Chill cake uncovered until cold, about 1½ hours.

Mix remaining 2 tablespoons plus ½ cup sugar and reserved berry juices in heavy small saucepan. Sprinkle gelatin over. Let stand until gelatin softens, about 15 minutes. Stir mixture over low heat until sugar and gelatin dissolve (do not boil). Pour into medium bowl; mix in berries. Chill berry topping until cold and beginning to set, stirring occasionally, about 1½ hours.

Spoon berry topping over chilled cake. Chill uncovered until berry topping is fully set, at least 3 hours and up to 1 day.

Hazelnut Praline Cheesecake

Using cake flour for the crust is important: It is lower in protein than all purpose flour and results in a more tender crust. The praline gives nutty flavor and crunchy contrast to the rich cheesecake filling. Wrapping a triple layer of foil around the cake pan provides a seal that guards against leaking when the cake is in the water bath. **12 servings**

1¼   **cups cake flour**
½   **cup plus 2 tablespoons (1¼ sticks) chilled unsalted butter,
     cut into ½-inch cubes**
¼   **cup (packed) golden brown sugar
     Hazelnut Praline (see recipe)**
4   **8-ounce packages Philadelphia-brand cream cheese,
     room temperature**
1   **cup sugar**
2   **tablespoons unbleached all purpose flour**
2   **tablespoons heavy whipping cream**
1   **teaspoon vanilla extract**
4   **large eggs**

Position rack in center of oven and preheat to 350°F. Butter 9-inch-diameter springform pan with 2¾-inch-high sides. Blend cake flour, butter, and brown sugar in processor until moist clumps form. Press crust mixture onto bottom (not sides) of prepared pan. Bake until crust is golden, about 25 minutes. Cool. Wrap outside of pan with 3 layers of heavy-duty foil.

Reserve ½ cup Hazelnut Praline for garnish. Grind remaining praline to powder in processor. Using electric mixer, beat cream cheese and 1 cup sugar in large bowl until smooth. Beat in all purpose flour, then cream and vanilla. Beat in eggs 1 at a time. Fold in praline powder. Pour filling over crust.

Place cake pan in roasting pan. Pour enough hot water into roasting pan to come halfway up sides of cake pan. Bake cake until center is just set, about 1 hour 20 minutes.

Transfer cake to rack. Cut around pan sides to loosen cake. Cool completely. Remove foil from pan sides. Chill cake uncovered overnight.

DO AHEAD: *Can be made 3 days ahead. Cover and keep chilled.*

Cut around pan sides again. Remove pan sides. Transfer cake to platter. Mound reserved ½ cup coarsely crushed Hazelnut Praline in center of cake and serve.

Hazelnut Praline

This distinctive praline uses hazelnuts instead of the traditional almonds or pecans. Husked hazelnuts are often available at specialty foods stores, but it's easy enough to toast and husk them yourself—see the guidelines on page 36.
Makes about 10 ounces

     Vegetable oil
¾   **cup sugar**
¼   **cup water**
1   **cup hazelnuts, toasted, husked**

Lightly oil baking sheet. Combine sugar and ¼ cup water in heavy medium saucepan. Stir over low heat until sugar dissolves. Increase heat and boil without stirring until syrup is deep amber color, occasionally brushing down sides of pan with wet pastry brush and swirling pan, about 8 minutes. Add hazelnuts and stir until well coated, about 1 minute. Carefully pour hot praline onto prepared baking sheet. Cool until praline hardens. Break praline into pieces. Transfer to resealable plastic bag. Using rolling pin or mallet, coarsely crush praline.

DO AHEAD: *Can be made 1 month ahead. Wrap airtight and freeze.*

Pistachio Brittle Cheesecake

Stained-glass-like shards of amber-colored pistachio brittle stand on edge atop the cheesecake, creating a truly gorgeous dessert. The cake should be refrigerated overnight, but wait until you're ready to serve it before arranging the pieces of brittle on top. **10 to 12 servings**

Crust

1	5½-ounce package shortbread cookies
½	cup unsalted natural pistachios
¼	cup sugar
¼	cup (½ stick) chilled unsalted butter, diced

Filling and Topping

3	8-ounce packages Philadelphia-brand cream cheese, room temperature
1¼	cups sugar
1	teaspoon ground cardamom
4	large eggs, room temperature
2¼	cups sour cream, divided
½	cup pear nectar
2	tablespoons unbleached all purpose flour
2	teaspoons vanilla extract
5	ounces high-quality white chocolate (such as Lindt or Perugina), finely chopped

Pistachio Brittle (see recipe)

CRUST: Preheat oven to 350°F. Blend shortbread, nuts, and sugar in processor until nuts are finely ground. Add butter; process until moist clumps form. Press crust mixture onto bottom (not sides) of 9-inch-diameter springform pan with 2¾-inch-high sides. Wrap outside of pan with 3 layers of heavy-duty aluminum foil. Bake crust until golden, about 15 minutes. Cool crust. Maintain oven temperature.

FILLING AND TOPPING: Beat cream cheese, sugar, and cardamom in large bowl until smooth. Beat in eggs 1 at a time. Add 1 cup sour cream, pear nectar, flour, and vanilla; beat until blended. Pour filling over crust.

Bake cheesecake until puffed at edges and softly set in center, about 1 hour 5 minutes. Transfer cake to rack; cool 10 minutes.

Meanwhile, stir white chocolate in medium metal bowl set over saucepan of barely simmering water until melted and smooth. Cool chocolate to luke-warm; whisk in remaining 1¼ cups sour cream.

Spread topping over warm cake. Chill cake uncovered overnight. Cut around pan sides to loosen cake; remove pan sides. Place cake on platter. Stand Pistachio Brittle pieces on edge in topping on cheesecake.

Pistachio Brittle

In addition to being an impressive cheesecake topping, this brittle makes a delicious gift; break it into shards and wrap in iridescent cellophane. **Makes 12 to 16 pieces**

	Nonstick vegetable oil spray
1	cup sugar
¼	cup water
¼	cup unsalted natural pistachios

Spray baking sheet with nonstick spray. Stir sugar and ¼ cup water in heavy small saucepan over medium-low heat until sugar dissolves. Increase heat and boil without stirring until syrup is deep amber color, occasionally brushing down sides of pan with wet pastry brush and swirling pan, about 12 minutes. Stir nuts into caramel and immediately pour onto prepared baking sheet. Working quickly and carefully (caramel is very hot and hardens fast), press tip of small knife into edge of caramel and stretch gently. Continue stretching at several points around edge of caramel to form very thin sheet, approximately 12 by 10 inches. Cool brittle completely.

Break brittle into irregular pieces.

DO AHEAD: *Can be made 3 days ahead. Store airtight at room temperature.*

Peanut Butter–Brownie Cheesecake

This recipe combines two homey favorites: A peanut butter–cream cheese filling is baked in a brownie crust. For the best texture, don't use old-fashioned or freshly ground peanut butter; you'll get better results with a creamy variety.
12 servings

Crust

3	ounces unsweetened chocolate, chopped
¼	cup (½ stick) unsalted butter, diced
½	cup sifted unbleached all purpose flour (sifted, then measured)
⅛	teaspoon salt
⅛	teaspoon baking powder
2	large eggs
1	cup (packed) golden brown sugar
1½	teaspoons vanilla extract
½	ounce bittersweet or semisweet chocolate, finely chopped

Filling

12	ounces Philadelphia-brand cream cheese, room temperature
1	cup (packed) golden brown sugar
3	large eggs
½	cup sour cream
1⅓	cups creamy peanut butter

Topping

¾	cup sour cream
2	teaspoons sugar
½	cup creamy peanut butter

CRUST: Position rack in center of oven and preheat to 350°F. Butter 9-inch-diameter springform pan with 2¾-inch-high sides. Dust pan lightly with flour; tap out excess.

Stir unsweetened chocolate and butter in heavy small saucepan over low heat until melted and smooth. Cool. Whisk flour, salt, and baking powder in small bowl to blend. Using electric mixer, beat eggs and brown sugar in medium bowl until very thick, about 4 minutes. Scrape down sides of bowl. Beat in melted chocolate mixture, vanilla, and chopped bittersweet chocolate. Add flour mixture and beat until just blended.

Spread 1 cup brownie batter over bottom of prepared pan. Bake until firm, about 17 minutes. Cool bottom crust in pan in freezer 15 minutes. Maintain oven temperature.

FILLING: Blend cream cheese and brown sugar in processor until smooth. Add eggs and sour cream; using on/off turns, process until mixture is smooth, occasionally scraping down sides of bowl. Using on/off turns, blend in peanut butter. Using small knife, spread remaining brownie batter evenly around sides of pan, sealing batter to bottom crust. Pour in filling (filling will not be as high as brownie batter).

Bake until center of cheesecake is gently set and brownie sides have fallen to form 1-inch-wide ring around filling, about 30 minutes.

TOPPING: Whisk sour cream and sugar in small bowl to blend. Spread evenly atop hot cheesecake to within ¾ inch of edge. Bake cheesecake 1 minute longer.

Set cake on rack. Cut around top edge of pan sides to loosen cake. Cool cake completely. Place peanut butter in pastry bag fitted with small (No.1) star tip. Pipe tiny rosettes of peanut butter around edge of sour cream. Chill cake until rosettes are firm, about 30 minutes. Cover pan tightly with foil and chill cake overnight.

Cut around pan sides to loosen cake. Remove pan sides. Transfer cheesecake to platter. Cut into wedges and serve.

Baklava Cheesecake

Inspired by the flaky, honey-sweetened Middle Eastern dessert pastry, this cheesecake forgoes the usual cookie- or cracker-crumb crust and is instead sandwiched between fine layers of phyllo pastry. To clarify butter, simmer it over low heat for a few minutes, then let it cool 5 minutes. Skim off the foamy top, then spoon the clear (clarified) butter into a small bowl. Discard the milk solids in the bottom of the pan. **16 servings**

Filling
4	8-ounce packages Philadelphia-brand cream cheese, room temperature
1	cup clover honey
¼	cup fresh lemon juice
2	teaspoons vanilla extract
6	large eggs

Pastry
½	cup (1 stick) unsalted butter, clarified
1	pound fresh phyllo pastry sheets or thawed frozen phyllo (each sheet about 17x11 inches)

Topping
½	cup walnuts
½	cup blanched almonds
1	tablespoon plus ½ cup sugar
1	teaspoon ground cinnamon
½	cup (1 stick) unsalted butter, clarified
¼	cup water
1	tablespoon fresh lemon juice
1	1½-inch piece cinnamon stick
1	tablespoon Cognac or other brandy

FILLING: Position rack in lower third of oven and preheat to 350°F. Using electric mixer, beat cream cheese in large bowl until light and fluffy. Gradually beat in honey, then lemon juice and vanilla. Beat in eggs 1 at a time.

PASTRY: Brush 10-inch-diameter springform pan with 2¾-inch-high sides with clarified butter. Arrange 1 phyllo pastry sheet with long edge parallel to edge of work surface (cover remaining sheets with dampened towel to prevent drying). Brush left half of pastry with clarified butter; fold right half over. Brush top of pastry with butter; place in prepared pan, buttered side up, leaving 5-inch overhang at 1 side. Cover with another dampened towel. Butter and fold second pastry sheet in same way and arrange in pan, overlapping first sheet by 3 inches. Repeat with 4 more sheets, covering entire pan. (Wrap remaining phyllo pastry sheets airtight and chill to make topping later.)

Whisk filling to reblend; pour into crust. Fold pastry overhang over filling, pressing gently to make flat surface. Bake until pastry is light brown and filling is firm to touch, about 50 minutes. Cut around pan sides to loosen cake; remove pan sides. Using toothpick, poke several holes in top of cake to allow steam to escape. Cool cake completely on rack. Chill uncovered 1 day, then cover and keep chilled 1 more day to mellow flavors.

TOPPING: Preheat oven to 350°F. Cover rimmed baking sheet with 2 sheets of parchment paper. Coarsely grind all nuts, 1 tablespoon sugar, and cinnamon in processor. Stack 10 reserved phyllo pastry sheets on work surface. Set rim of 10-inch-diameter springform pan atop pastry stack. Using sharp knife, cut around inside rim of pan through entire pastry stack, making 10 pastry rounds. Cover rounds with damp towel. Set pan rim on prepared baking sheet. Brush parchment and inside of pan rim with clarified butter. Place 1 pastry round inside pan rim on baking sheet and brush with butter. Repeat with 4 more pastry rounds. Spread nut mixture evenly over pastry. Top with remaining 5 pastry rounds, brushing each with butter. Using ruler as guide, cut pastry into 16 wedges with sharp knife. Sprinkle lightly with several drops of water. Bake pastry until crisp and golden, about 30 minutes.

Meanwhile, stir remaining ½ cup sugar, ¼ cup water, and lemon juice in heavy small saucepan over low heat until sugar dissolves. Add cinnamon stick; increase heat to medium and boil until mixture reduces to syrup, about 4 minutes. Remove from heat. When bubbles subside, stir in Cognac.

Flatten the pastry that is atop cake. Remove pan rim from topping. Set topping on cake, using large spatula. Recut wedges in topping. Replace pan rim on assembled cake. Immediately pour hot syrup all over topping. Cool 1 hour. Chill cake 1 to 6 hours. Let cake stand at room temperature for 20 minutes before serving.

⫴ Upside-Down Honey Cheesecakes

These crustless, upside-down cheesecakes have a built-in sauce: When the ramekins are inverted, a gooey honeyed topping is revealed. Since these are individual cheesecakes, you'll need twelve ¾-cup ramekins or custard cups to bake them in. **Makes 12**

1	cup sugar
⅓	cup honey
¼	cup (½ stick) unsalted butter
⅓	cup water
3	8-ounce packages Philadelphia-brand cream cheese, room temperature
⅔	cup (packed) golden brown sugar
1	cup sour cream
2	teaspoons fresh lemon juice
2	teaspoons vanilla extract
4	large eggs
	Assorted fresh berries

Preheat oven to 300°F. Butter twelve ¾-cup ramekins or custard cups. Place 1 cup sugar, honey, and butter in heavy medium saucepan. Stir over medium heat until butter melts and mixture is blended. Increase heat to medium-high and bring to boil. Whisk until mixture darkens slightly and candy thermometer registers 300°F, about 5 minutes. Remove from heat. Add ⅓ cup water (mixture will bubble vigorously); whisk to blend. Divide topping among ramekins (about 2 tablespoonfuls for each). Divide ramekins between two 13x9x2-inch metal baking pans and chill while preparing filling.

Using on/off turns, blend cream cheese and brown sugar in processor, occasionally scraping down sides of bowl. Add sour cream, lemon juice, and vanilla; process until smooth. Add eggs 1 at a time, processing just to blend between each addition. Divide filling equally among ramekins. Add enough hot water to baking pans to come halfway up sides of ramekins.

Bake cheesecakes until set, about 35 minutes. Remove from pans and chill uncovered until firm, about 1 hour.

DO AHEAD: *Can be made 2 days ahead. Cover and keep chilled.*

Cut around sides of ramekins. Invert cheesecakes onto plates, spooning any remaining topping in ramekins over. Garnish with berries.

⫴ Individual Cheesecakes with Mixed Berry Sauce

Sometimes smaller is better—when it means everyone gets his or her own dessert. Custard cups, ramekins, or even ovenproof ceramic teacups are good vessels for these little cheesecakes. Just make sure they hold 10 ounces (1¼ cups). **Makes 6**

Crust and Cake

2	cups ground vanilla wafer cookies or shortbread cookies (about 10 ounces)
¼	cup (½ stick) unsalted butter, melted
3	8-ounce packages Philadelphia-brand cream cheese, room temperature
¾	cup sugar
½	teaspoon vanilla extract
2	large eggs
2	large egg yolks

Berry Sauce

¼	cup (½ stick) unsalted butter
¼	cup sugar
2	½-pint containers raspberries
2	½-pint containers blueberries
6	tablespoons black raspberry liqueur (such as Chambord) or black currant liqueur (such as crème de cassis)

CRUST AND CAKE: Preheat oven to 325°F. Butter six 1¼-cup custard cups. Stir ground cookies with melted butter in medium bowl until crumbs are evenly moistened. Press 3 tablespoons crumb mixture evenly onto bottom of each custard cup; reserve remaining crumb mixture.

Using electric mixer, beat cream cheese, sugar, and vanilla in large bowl until fluffy, occasionally scraping down sides of bowl. Add eggs and egg yolks 1 at a time, blending well after each addition. Divide filling equally among prepared cups. Sprinkle reserved crumb mixture evenly atop filling. Place custard cups in large roasting pan. Add enough hot water to roasting pan to reach halfway up sides of cups.

Bake cheesecakes until set in center, about 45 minutes. Remove cakes from water bath. Cool completely. Cover cakes with plastic wrap and chill until cold, about 2 hours.

DO AHEAD: *Can be made 1 day ahead. Keep chilled.*

BERRY SAUCE: Melt butter in medium skillet over high heat. Mix in sugar. Add raspberries and blueberries; toss until sugar dissolves and berries are heated through, about 3 minutes. Remove skillet from heat; stir in liqueur.

Cut around cup sides to loosen cheesecakes. Turn cakes out onto plates. Pour warm berry sauce around cakes and serve.

Fixing the Cracks

Cheesecakes often crack a bit on the top, and the most likely culprit is overbaking. To prevent cracks, start checking doneness 5 to 10 minutes before the indicated cooking time. When the center two to three inches of the cheesecake are still slightly jiggly (give the cake pan a gentle nudge to check), remove the cake from the oven. The residual heat will set the very center.

But if a cheesecake cracks despite your best efforts, there are a few quick fixes.

Cool the cheesecake completely, then cover the crack by mixing 1 cup of sour cream with 1 tablespoon of sugar. Spread the sour cream mixture over the cheesecake, filling the crack, then bake the cheesecake at 350°F for 5 minutes just to set the topping. Refrigerate until cold. A few pretty strawberries can hide any remaining cracks.

Or mix up a streusel (for instance, a streusel topping from one of the crisp or crumble recipes in the Fruit Desserts chapter), scatter it over a cookie sheet, and bake it. Just before serving, sprinkle the streusel strategically over the cheesecake.

Coeur à la Crème

This classic heart-shaped dessert is basically a no-bake, crustless cheesecake. For an extra treat, use small wild strawberries (fraises des bois) *if available. They're sometimes available at farmers' markets in spring and early summer.*
Makes 4

4	10x10-inch squares cheesecloth
1	8-ounce package Philadelphia-brand cream cheese, room temperature
1	cup crème fraîche or sour cream
6	tablespoons powdered sugar, divided
1	teaspoon fresh lemon juice
½	teaspoon vanilla extract
	Pinch of salt
1	pound small strawberries, hulled, quartered (about 1⅔ cups)

Rinse cheesecloth under water; squeeze until just damp. Line each of four 3- to 4-inch coeur à la crème molds with 1 square of cheesecloth. Using electric mixer, beat cream cheese, crème fraîche, 4 tablespoons powdered sugar, lemon juice, vanilla, and salt in large bowl until smooth, about 4 minutes. Divide mixture among molds. Fold cheesecloth over mixture. Place molds on rimmed baking sheet; cover with plastic wrap. Chill at least 4 hours and up to 1 day.

Toss strawberries and remaining 2 tablespoons powdered sugar in medium bowl to coat; let stand 30 minutes. Unwrap molds; invert onto plates and peel off cheesecloth. Spoon strawberries around each and serve.

Equipment Tip: **Make Your Own Molds**
Coeur à la crème molds, perforated and heart shaped, are available online at fantes.com. You can also rig up makeshift molds by cutting the sides of four 12-ounce paper cups to 3 inches high. With a toothpick, poke 12 holes in the bottom of each cup. Line with cheesecloth; fill as directed. You'll get a drum-shaped "coeur."

♯♯ Cream Cheese Pie Topped with Peaches and Blackberries

The no-bake filling makes this pie perfect for the hot summer months. If possible, top the pie with fresh peaches and blackberries from your local farmers' market. **8 servings**

Crust
½ cup (1 stick) unsalted butter, melted
½ teaspoon almond extract
2½ cups shortbread cookie crumbs (about 10 ounces)

Filling and Topping
1 8-ounce package Philadelphia-brand cream cheese, room temperature
¾ cup powdered sugar
½ cup heavy whipping cream
1 teaspoon vanilla extract
½ teaspoon almond extract
3 large peaches, peeled, halved, pitted, sliced
2 ½-pint containers blackberries
¼ cup peach jam, melted

CRUST: Preheat oven to 325°F. Butter 10-inch-diameter glass pie dish. Blend melted butter and almond extract in medium bowl. Add crumbs and stir until evenly moistened. Press crumb mixture over bottom and up sides of prepared dish. Bake crust until just golden, about 8 minutes. Cool crust completely.

FILLING AND TOPPING: Blend cream cheese in processor until smooth. Add sugar, cream, vanilla extract, and almond extract and blend until very smooth, occasionally scraping down sides of bowl. Spread filling in prepared crust. Chill until filling is firm, about 2 hours.

DO AHEAD: *Can be made 1 day ahead. Cover and keep chilled.*

Arrange peach slices around edge of pie. Arrange blackberries in center. Brush warm jam lightly over fruit to glaze. Chill pie up to 3 hours before serving.

♯♯♯ Vanilla Cheesecake Tartlets with Vanilla-Vodka Berries

These tartlets have intense vanilla flavor and a sophisticated edge thanks to vodka in the filling and the berry topping. **Makes 8**

Crusts
2½ cups graham cracker crumbs
½ cup (packed) dark brown sugar
½ cup (1 stick) unsalted butter, melted

Filling
8 teaspoons vodka
4½ teaspoons vanilla extract, divided
½ teaspoon unflavored gelatin
2 8-ounce packages Philadelphia-brand cream cheese, room temperature
⅔ cup sugar
2 vanilla beans, split lengthwise
6 tablespoons heavy whipping cream

Topping
3 cups mixed berries (such as raspberries, blueberries, and halved strawberries)
¼ cup sugar
4 teaspoons vodka
2 teaspoons vanilla extract

CRUSTS: Preheat oven to 350°F. Mix graham cracker crumbs, brown sugar, and melted butter in large bowl until evenly moistened. Divide mixture among eight 4½x¾-inch tartlet pans with removable bottoms. Press crumb mixture over bottoms and up sides of pans. Bake until crusts are light brown, about 12 minutes. Cool crusts completely in pans on racks.

FILLING: Mix vodka and 4 teaspoons vanilla extract in small saucepan; sprinkle gelatin over. Let stand until gelatin softens, about 15 minutes. Stir over very low heat just until gelatin dissolves. Cool to barely lukewarm.

Using electric mixer, beat cream cheese, sugar, and remaining ½ teaspoon vanilla extract in large bowl until blended. Scrape in seeds from vanilla beans and beat to blend. Beat in cream, then gelatin mixture. Divide filling among crusts. Press bottoms of pans up, releasing tartlets. Arrange tartlets on rimmed baking sheet. Chill until filling sets, at least 3 hours and up to 1 day.

TOPPING: Gently stir berries, sugar, vodka, and vanilla extract in bowl. Let stand 15 minutes. Spoon berry mixture atop tartlets.

No-Bake Berry Cheesecake with Graham Cracker Crust

Though the crust bakes briefly, the fresh blueberry filling doesn't require any baking at all, making this an ideal summertime dessert. Chilling the cheesecake overnight will enhance the blueberry flavor. **10 servings**

Crust

9	whole graham crackers
½	cup old-fashioned oats
3	tablespoons (packed) golden brown sugar
⅛	teaspoon salt
5	tablespoons unsalted butter, melted
1	teaspoon vanilla extract

Filling

¼	cup water
1	tablespoon unflavored gelatin (from 2 envelopes)
1½	8-ounce packages Philadelphia-brand cream cheese, room temperature
1	cup heavy whipping cream
1	cup sugar
1	tablespoon fresh lemon juice
3	cups blueberries

Topping

1	cup chilled heavy whipping cream
1	tablespoon sugar
4	½-pint containers blueberries
⅔	cup blueberry jam

CRUST: Preheat oven to 350°F. Blend graham crackers, oats, brown sugar, and salt in processor until graham crackers are finely ground. Add melted butter and vanilla; process until moist crumbs form. Press crumb mixture onto bottom and 1 inch up sides of 9-inch-diameter springform pan with 2¾-inch-high sides. Bake crust until deep golden brown, about 12 minutes. Cool.

FILLING: Pour ¼ cup water into small saucepan; sprinkle gelatin over. Let stand until gelatin softens, about 15 minutes. Stir over very low heat just until gelatin dissolves. Blend cream cheese, cream, sugar, and lemon juice in processor until smooth, occasionally scraping down sides of bowl. Add berries; puree until smooth (some blueberry bits will remain). With machine running, add warm gelatin mixture through feed tube and blend well. Pour filling into crust. Cover; chill overnight.

DO AHEAD: *Can be made 2 days ahead. Keep chilled.*

Cut around pan sides to loosen cake; remove pan sides. Transfer cake to platter.

TOPPING: Using electric mixer, beat cream and sugar in medium bowl until peaks form. Spread cream mixture thickly over top of cheesecake. Place berries in bowl. Heat jam in small saucepan over low heat until just melted. Pour jam over berries; toss to coat. Mound coated berries on cream, leaving 1-inch plain border. Chill cake at least 1 hour and up to 1 day.

pies, tarts & pastries

pies, tarts & pastries

Cranberry-Lime Tart

Classic Double-Crust Apple Pie

Tart and sweet apples combine in this all-American pie. See Crust 101 (page 212) for tips on preparing, rolling, and crimping the crust. **8 servings**

Crust

2½	cups unbleached all purpose flour
½	teaspoon salt
10	tablespoons (1¼ sticks) chilled unsalted butter, cut into ½-inch cubes
½	cup chilled solid non-hydrogenated vegetable shortening, cut into ½-inch pieces
3	tablespoons (or more) ice water

Filling

	Nonstick vegetable oil spray
1¾	pounds sweet apples, such as Spartan or Golden Delicious, peeled, cored, thinly sliced (about 5½ cups)
1¾	pounds tart apples, such as Granny Smith or Pippin, peeled, cored, thinly sliced (about 5½ cups)
¾	cup plus 1 tablespoon sugar
1	teaspoon fresh lemon juice
½	teaspoon plus large pinch of ground cinnamon
½	teaspoon vanilla extract
1	tablespoon unbleached all purpose flour
3	tablespoons unsalted butter, diced
1	tablespoon whole milk

CRUST: Whisk flour and salt in large bowl to blend. Add butter and shortening and rub in with fingertips until very coarse meal forms. Sprinkle 3 tablespoons ice water over; toss until moist clumps form, adding more ice water by teaspoonfuls if mixture is dry. Gather dough into ball; divide in half. Flatten each half into disk. Wrap in plastic; chill at least 1 hour.

DO AHEAD: *Can be made 1 day ahead. Keep refrigerated. Soften slightly at room temperature before using.*

FILLING: Preheat oven to 400°F. Spray 9-inch-diameter deep-dish glass pie dish with nonstick spray. Stir all apples, ¾ cup sugar, lemon juice, ½ teaspoon cinnamon, and vanilla in large bowl to blend. Let stand until juices form, tossing occasionally, about 15 minutes. Mix in flour.

Roll out 1 dough disk on lightly floured surface to 12-inch round. Place dough in prepared pie dish. Spoon in filling; dot with butter. Roll out second dough disk to 13-inch round. Using small bottle cap, cut out ten ½-inch-diameter circles from

Technique Tip: Easy on the Dough

There are two ways to transfer rolled-out pie crust dough from the work surface to the pie dish (see below): Roll the dough gently onto the rolling pin, then unroll it in the dish [1]; or fold the dough carefully into quarters, and unfold it in the pie dish [2].

dough for decoration; discard circles. Drape dough over filling. Seal top and bottom crust edges together; trim to ½-inch overhang. Fold overhang under; crimp decoratively. Brush pie with milk. Stir remaining 1 tablespoon sugar and large pinch of cinnamon in small bowl; sprinkle over pie.

Transfer pie to baking sheet; place in oven. Immediately reduce temperature to 375°F. Bake pie until crust is golden brown, apples are tender, and filling is bubbling thickly, covering edge with foil if browning too quickly, about 2 hours. Cool 30 minutes. Serve warm or at room temperature.

DO AHEAD: *Can be made 1 day ahead. Cover loosely; store at room temperature.*

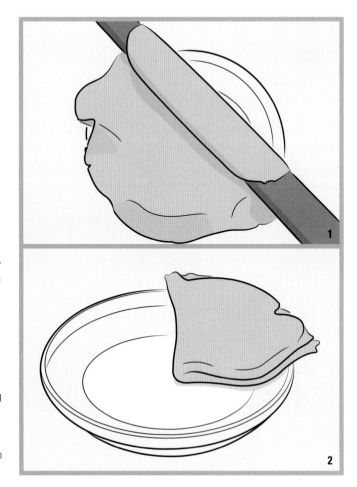

Apple and Blackberry Pie

Tart green apples and blackberries are a delicious combination. The crust has a texture more like that of a biscuit than a typical pie crust. **8 servings**

Crust

2	**cups self-rising flour**
9	**tablespoons sugar**
¾	**cup (1½ sticks) chilled unsalted butter, cut into ½-inch cubes**
1	**large egg, beaten to blend**
1	**tablespoon (or more) ice water**

Filling

2	**pounds tart green apples (such as Granny Smith), peeled, quartered, cored, cut into ¼-inch-thick slices**
1½	**cups frozen blackberries, unthawed**
⅓	**cup plus 2 teaspoons sugar**
2	**tablespoons unbleached all purpose flour**

Milk
Sweetened whipped cream

CRUST: Combine flour and sugar in medium bowl. Add butter and rub in with fingertips until mixture resembles coarse crumbs. Mix in beaten egg. Mix in 1 tablespoon ice water, adding more ice water by teaspoonfuls as needed until moist clumps form. Gather dough into ball; divide in half. Flatten each half into disk. Wrap separately in plastic and chill at least 30 minutes.

DO AHEAD: *Can be made 1 day ahead. Keep chilled. Let soften slightly at room temperature before rolling out.*

FILLING: Preheat oven to 375°F. Mix apples, blackberries, ⅓ cup sugar, and flour in large bowl.

Roll out 1 dough disk on floured surface to 12-inch round. Transfer to 9-inch-diameter glass pie dish.

Spoon filling into crust. Roll out second dough disk on floured surface to 12-inch round; place atop filling. Fold top crust edge under bottom edge and pinch to seal. Crimp edges decoratively. Brush crust with milk. Sprinkle with remaining 2 teaspoons sugar. Cut several slits in top crust to allow steam to escape.

Bake pie until crust is golden brown and fruit is tender, covering crust edges with foil collar if browning too quickly, about 55 minutes. Cool pie on rack 30 minutes. Serve warm with sweetened whipped cream.

Equipment Check

What you need to make perfect pies and tarts.

PIE DISHES: In the *Bon Appétit* test kitchen, we use glass pie dishes. Ceramic pie dishes (such as from Emile Henry) also work well. Most recipes call for a 9- or 10-inch-diameter pan that's about 1½ inches deep. If you like to make deep-dish pies, also consider buying a deep-dish pie dish, which is usually about 2 inches deep.

ROLLING PIN: You'll need one to roll out pastry crust, but the style you use is up to you. Some cooks believe that the tapered wooden French-style rolling pin (with no handles) gives you a better feel for the dough. Others prefer a heavy marble rolling pin because it keeps cool, which is helpful when you're working with a sticky dough. Still others swear by a straight rolling pin with a nonstick silicone-lined barrel or a classic wooden pin with handles.

TART PANS: Tart pans are usually made of metal with fluted sides and a removable bottom. The most common shapes are round, square, and rectangular. Most of the recipes in this book call for 9-, 10-, or 11-inch-diameter tart pans. If you like making tartlets, buy a collection of 4½-inch mini pans.

ROLLING MATS: You can buy silicone mats, made just for rolling out dough. The nonstick surface makes the dough easy to roll and has circles (9-inch, 10-inch, 13-inch) drawn right on the mat, which help you create perfectly round, perfectly sized crusts. These mats are also handy for rolling out dough for pizza, scones, and biscuits.

Technique Tip: **Keep It Clean**

Place fruit pies on a baking sheet lined with foil or a Silpat baking mat before putting them in the oven. This will help avoid a sticky, baked-on mess on the bottom of your oven should the fruit filling bubble up and over.

Cinnamon-Apple Pie with Raisins and Crumb Topping

Raisins and brown sugar enhance the apples in this homey pie. Because they're firm and tart, Pippin apples would make an excellent alternative to the Granny Smiths in the filling. Don't skip the teaspoon of vinegar in the pie dough—it helps to make the crust tender. **8 servings**

Crust

1½	cups unbleached all purpose flour
1	tablespoon sugar
½	teaspoon salt
⅛	teaspoon baking powder
½	cup (1 stick) chilled unsalted butter, cut into ½-inch cubes
¼	cup (or more) ice water
1	teaspoon apple cider vinegar

Filling

1	cup (packed) golden brown sugar
3	tablespoons unbleached all purpose flour
2	teaspoons finely grated lemon peel
1¼	teaspoons ground cinnamon
2¾	pounds Granny Smith apples (about 6 medium), peeled, halved, cored, cut into ⅛-inch-thick slices (about 8 cups)
1	cup raisins
2	teaspoons vanilla extract

Crumb Topping

1	cup unbleached all purpose flour
½	cup (packed) golden brown sugar
1	teaspoon ground cinnamon
⅛	teaspoon salt
½	cup (1 stick) chilled unsalted butter, cut into ½-inch cubes

Lightly sweetened whipped cream or vanilla ice cream

CRUST: Blend flour, sugar, salt, and baking powder in processor. Add butter; using on/off turns, cut in until mixture resembles coarse meal. Mix ¼ cup ice water and vinegar in small bowl; add to processor. Using on/off turns, blend until moist clumps form, adding more ice water by teaspoonfuls if mixture is dry. Gather dough into ball; flatten into disk. Wrap in plastic and chill at least 1 hour.

DO AHEAD: *Can be made 1 day ahead. Keep chilled. Let soften slightly at room temperature before rolling out.*

Roll out dough disk on floured surface to 13-inch round. Transfer to 9-inch-diameter deep-dish glass pie dish. Fold edges under and crimp, forming crust sides ¼ inch above rim of pie dish. Freeze crust 20 minutes.

FILLING: Position rack in center of oven and preheat to 375°F. Mix brown sugar, flour, lemon peel, and cinnamon in large bowl. Add apple slices, raisins, and vanilla; toss until well coated. Transfer filling to unbaked crust, mounding slightly in center. Bake pie until apples begin to soften, about 40 minutes.

CRUMB TOPPING: Meanwhile, whisk flour, sugar, cinnamon, and salt in small bowl. Add butter and rub in with fingertips until mixture begins to clump together.

Sprinkle topping evenly over hot pie. Continue to bake pie until apples are tender and topping is browned and crisp, tenting pie with sheet of foil if browning too quickly, about 50 minutes. Cool pie on rack at least 2 hours.

DO AHEAD: *Can be made 8 hours ahead. Let stand at room temperature.*

Cut pie into wedges and serve warm or at room temperature with whipped cream or vanilla ice cream.

Crust 101

A tender, flaky pie crust is a thing of beauty—and it is within the reach of every home cook. Just remember that baking is a science, so it's important to measure carefully and follow the recipe exactly. Follow these tips from the *Bon Appétit* test kitchen and you'll be a pie-crust pro in no time.

1 **STAY COOL:** Chilled or—even better—frozen fat (butter, shortening, and/or lard) will create a dough that's easy to work with and will produce a flaky, tender crust; room-temperature fat won't. Using ice water is an important part of the process because the chilled water helps keep the fat cold.

2 **LESS IS MORE:** For a perfectly tender crust, you want short, weak strands of gluten (a protein that's in flour). The more you work the dough, the longer those strands of gluten become, and that can make the dough tough. The bottom line? Mix the dough just until it comes together, then stop.

3 **CHILL THE DOUGH:** Don't rush it. After you've made your dough, wrap it in plastic wrap, flatten it into a disk, and chill it for at least the minimum time recommended in the recipe. This will give the gluten a chance to relax, which will make the dough easier to roll out. It's also not a bad idea to put the rolled-out crust (once it's in the pan) in the freezer while you prepare the pie filling; that will keep the crust from shrinking while it bakes and will also ensure the fat stays cold.

4 **ROLL THE DOUGH:** Give it space. Before you even get the dough out of the fridge, make sure you have a large, clean space for rolling. Lightly flour your work surface to prevent the dough from sticking—and flour your rolling pin, too. Roll out the dough gently, rotating the dough occasionally to create an even circle [1,2]. If the dough begins to stick, sprinkle the work surface and/or the rolling pin with a little more flour. Make sure that the dough round is two to four inches larger in circumference than your pie plate. The extra dough will allow you to create a decorative edge on your pie. To transfer the dough to the pie pan, wrap the dough loosely around the rolling pin, then carefully unroll it into the pan. Ease the dough into the edges of the pan [3], being careful not to stretch the dough to the corners (which will cause the crust to shrink as it bakes). Lightly press the dough onto the bottom and up the sides of the pan.

5 **A DIFFERENT WAY TO ROLL:** Temperamental dough? Brand new to baking? Consider rolling out the dough between two large sheets of parchment paper. Lightly flour one sheet of parchment. Unwrap the chilled dough disk, set it in the center of the parchment, then pound it with the rolling pin until it's about six inches in diameter. Lightly dust the dough with flour and lay the second piece of parchment on top. Starting at the center and rolling out to the edges, roll the dough using even pressure. To keep the thickness of the dough uniform, turn the parchment 90 degrees and flip the parchment and dough over after every few rolls. When you have a dough round that's two to four inches larger than your pan, remove the top sheet of parchment. Pick up the remaining parchment and dough and quickly flip the round into the pie pan. Center the dough in the pan and tear off the parchment in strips (peeling it off in one piece may tear the tender dough).

6 **CRIMP THE EDGE:** Finish your pie crust with a pretty design around the edge. Fold the extra dough under to make it even with the rim of the pan. For a classic crimp, pinch the crust with your thumb and index finger on one side and your other index finger on the other side [4]. For an easier crust, press the crust with the back of a spoon, the tines of a fork, or a chopstick.

7 EXTRA CREDIT: The ultimate show-off crust? The beautiful, interwoven strips of dough known as lattice. For a classic lattice top, cut strips from the dough round (the quantity and width of the strips will be specified in the recipe). Evenly space half of the strips atop the filling. To weave the dough, fold every other strip in half over itself. Place a new strip of dough perpendicular to the folded strips [5]. Return the folded strips to the edge of the pie, laying them over the perpendicular strip. Repeat the process, alternating the remaining strips of dough as you go.

8 CHEAT SHEET: If you want all of the glory of a lattice crust with a fraction of the work, do a quick and easy overlay technique. Arrange half of the dough strips across your filled pie. Top with the remaining strips perpendicular or diagonal to the first.

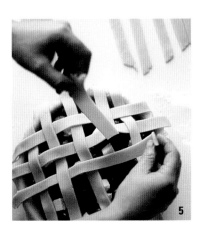

♥♥♥ Golden Raisin and Apple Lattice Pie

Golden Delicious apples become tender yet still retain their shape and pleasant firmness after baking. The apple slices are baked in the oven prior to filling the crust for the pie. To keep the lattice strips intact, roll and cut the dough on a piece of floured parchment paper, then gently slide the strips from the parchment onto the pie to assemble the lattice crust. **8 servings**

Crust

1½   cups unbleached all purpose flour
½   cup cake flour
1   tablespoon plus 1½ teaspoons sugar
¾   teaspoon salt
9   tablespoons (1 stick plus 1 tablespoon) chilled unsalted butter, cut into ½-inch cubes
3   tablespoons chilled non-hydrogenated solid vegetable shortening, cut into ½-inch pieces
6   tablespoons (or more) ice water

Filling

3¼   pounds Golden Delicious apples, peeled, quartered, cored, each quarter cut crosswise into ¼-inch-thick slices
3   tablespoons plus 2 teaspoons sugar
3   tablespoons unsalted butter, melted, divided
2   teaspoons fresh lemon juice
1   cup golden raisins
2   tablespoons (packed) dark brown sugar

1   large egg yolk beaten to blend with 1 tablespoon heavy whipping cream

CRUST: Blend both flours, sugar, and salt in processor. Add butter and shortening; using on/off turns, cut in until mixture resembles coarse meal. Add 6 tablespoons ice water and process just until moist clumps form, adding more ice water by teaspoonfuls if dough is dry. Gather dough into ball; divide into 2 pieces, 1 slightly larger than the other. Flatten larger piece into disk and smaller piece into rectangle; wrap separately in plastic and chill at least 1 hour.

DO AHEAD: *Can be made 1 day ahead. Keep chilled. Let soften slightly at room temperature before rolling out.*

FILLING: Position rack in bottom third of oven and preheat to 375°F. Spread apple slices on large rimmed baking sheet. Sprinkle 3 tablespoons sugar over apples, then drizzle with 2 tablespoons melted butter and lemon juice; toss to coat. Bake just until apples begin to soften, stirring once, about 15 minutes. Cool apples completely on baking sheet. Maintain oven temperature.

Transfer apples and any accumulated juices to large bowl. Mix in raisins and brown sugar.

Butter 9-inch-diameter glass pie dish. Roll out dough disk on floured surface to 12-inch round. Transfer to prepared pie dish. Spoon apple filling into crust. Drizzle remaining 1 tablespoon melted butter over. Roll out dough rectangle on floured surface to 11x7-inch rectangle. Cut lengthwise into twelve ½-inch-wide strips. Place 6 strips 1 inch apart atop apple filling. Place remaining 6 strips diagonally atop first 6 strips, forming diamond lattice pattern. Trim strips even with bottom crust. Fold dough overhang in, pressing onto edge of pie dish. Using fork, press dough edge decoratively to seal.

Brush dough strips with egg glaze. Sprinkle strips with remaining 2 teaspoons sugar. Bake pie 15 minutes. Reduce oven temperature to 350°F. Continue to bake pie until crust is golden and apples are tender, covering crust edges with foil collar if browning too quickly, about 1 hour 15 minutes longer. Cool pie on rack at least 2 hours. Serve slightly warm or at room temperature.

DO AHEAD: *Can be made 1 day ahead. Cool completely, then cover and store at room temperature.*

Pear-Cardamom Pie with Almond Crust

The foolproof cookie-like crust is perfect for the pie-making novice. Consider serving this dessert with a scoop of vanilla ice cream or a dollop of lightly sweetened whipped cream. **8 servings**

Crust

2¾	cups unbleached all purpose flour
1	7-ounce package marzipan or almond paste, coarsely crumbled
¾	teaspoon salt
½	cup (1 stick) chilled unsalted butter, cut into ½-inch cubes
5	tablespoons chilled non-hydrogenated solid vegetable shortening, cut into ½-inch pieces
3	tablespoons (or more) pear nectar
½	teaspoon almond extract

Filling

⅓	cup (packed) dark brown sugar
1	vanilla bean, coarsely chopped
3	tablespoons cornstarch
¼	teaspoon ground cardamom
3	pounds firm but ripe Bartlett pears, peeled, halved, cored, cut into ½- to ¾-inch-thick wedges
2	tablespoons pear nectar
1	egg, beaten to blend
1	tablespoon sugar

CRUST: Blend flour, marzipan, and salt in processor until marzipan is finely ground. Add butter and shortening; using on/off turns, cut in until mixture resembles coarse meal. Mix 3 tablespoons pear nectar and almond extract in small bowl; add mixture to processor. Using on/off turns, blend mixture, gradually adding more pear nectar by teaspoonfuls as needed until moist clumps form. Gather dough into ball; divide in half. Flatten each half into disk. Wrap separately in plastic and chill at least 2 hours.

DO AHEAD: *Can be made 1 day ahead. Keep chilled. Let soften slightly at room temperature before rolling out.*

FILLING: Grind brown sugar and chopped vanilla bean in processor 1 minute. Add cornstarch and cardamom and process until vanilla bean is very finely ground. Transfer mixture to large bowl. Add pears and pear nectar; toss to coat.

Position rack in bottom third of oven and preheat to 400°F. Roll out 1 dough disk between sheets of floured parchment paper to 13-inch round. Peel off top sheet of parchment. Invert dough into 9-inch-diameter glass pie dish. Peel off second sheet of parchment and press dough into dish. Trim dough overhang to ½ inch. Transfer pear filling to crust. Roll out second dough disk between sheets of floured parchment to 13-inch round. Peel off top sheet of parchment and invert dough onto filling. Peel off second sheet of parchment. Trim dough overhang to ½ inch. Press top and bottom crust edges together to seal. Fold edge under and crimp decoratively.

Gather dough scraps and reroll between sheets of floured parchment. Using leaf-shaped cookie cutter, cut out cookies. Arrange atop pie. Brush top of crust (not edge) with egg glaze. Sprinkle with sugar. Cut several slits in top crust to allow steam to escape during baking.

Bake pie 15 minutes. Cover crust edge with foil collar to prevent over-browning. Continue baking until crust is golden brown and pears are almost tender when pierced with skewer, about 40 minutes. Cool pie on rack at least 1½ hours. Serve slightly warm or at room temperature.

Pear and Fig Pie with Hazelnut Crust

With its pairing of fresh pears and dried figs, this is a wonderful autumn dessert. Hazelnuts add crunch and rich flavor to the crust. **8 servings**

Crust

½   **cup hazelnuts, toasted, husked, cooled**
4½   **teaspoons sugar**
½   **teaspoon salt**
2½   **cups unbleached all purpose flour**
¾   **cup (1½ sticks) chilled unsalted butter, cut into ¼-inch cubes**
4   **tablespoons (or more) ice water**

Filling

1   **cup dried black Mission figs, stemmed, quartered**
½   **cup sugar**
2   **tablespoons unbleached all purpose flour**
1   **tablespoon fresh lemon juice**
1   **teaspoon finely grated lemon peel**
2¼   **pounds pears, peeled, quartered, cored, thinly sliced**

CRUST: Finely grind nuts, sugar, and salt in processor. Blend in flour. Add butter; using on/off turns, cut in until butter is reduced to rice-size pieces. Blend in 4 tablespoons ice water, adding more ice water by teaspoonfuls until dough comes together in moist clumps. Gather dough into ball; divide in half. Flatten each half into disk. Wrap separately in plastic and chill at least 45 minutes.

DO AHEAD: *Can be made 1 day ahead. Keep chilled. Let soften slightly at room temperature before rolling out.*

FILLING: Preheat oven to 400°F. Combine figs, sugar, flour, lemon juice, and lemon peel in large bowl. Add pears and toss to blend.

Roll out 1 dough disk on lightly floured surface to 12-inch round. Transfer to 9-inch-diameter glass pie dish. Fill crust with pear mixture. Roll out second dough disk on lightly floured surface to 12-inch round; place atop filling. Trim overhang of top and bottom crusts to ½ inch; press together and fold under. Crimp edge decoratively. Cut several slits in top crust to allow steam to escape during baking.

Bake pie 20 minutes. Reduce oven temperature to 350°F. Continue to bake until juices bubble thickly through slits and crust is golden, about 50 minutes longer. Cool pie on rack 45 minutes. Serve warm or at room temperature.

Pie Troubleshooting

Soggy crusts? Overflowing filling? Holes in the dough? We have the solution—or the prevention—for common pie problems.

PROBLEM: Holes and tears in the dough.
SOLUTION: When transferring the dough to the pie pan, rips, tears, and holes sometimes appear. To fix this, just use any leftover dough pieces to patch the problem areas. Press the dough patch to adhere it to the crust. If needed, brush over the patch with a little beaten egg white.

PROBLEM: Soggy bottom crust.
SOLUTION: Pies with soft, wet fillings can sometimes become soggy on the bottom. To avoid this, partially bake the crust before adding the filling: Line the crust with foil and add dried beans or commercial pie weights, then bake it until it's just light brown.

PROBLEM: Unevenly baked crust.
SOLUTION: First, press the dough gently into the bottom of the pie pan. A crust that touches the pan in all spots has a better chance of browning evenly. Before you preheat the oven, move the rack to the bottom third of the oven. Baking the pie lower in the oven will help the crust brown. And last but not least, we recommend baking your pies in a glass pie pan, which allows you to check the bottom of the crust during baking.

PROBLEM: Overflowing filling.
SOLUTION: As some pies bake, the filling bubbles up—and over. To prevent the mess in your oven, place pies on a rimmed baking sheet. Using a baking sheet also makes it easy to remove the pie from the oven.

PROBLEM: Burned crust edges.
SOLUTION: Because they aren't protected by filling, the thin edges of the crust have a tendency to brown more quickly than the rest of the crust. Keep a close eye on the pie as it bakes. When the crust edge turns light golden, cover it with a pie-crust shield (a thin metal or silicone ring that fits over the pie), or make your own with a long strip of aluminum foil. The edge of the crust will continue to brown after you cover it, so it's important not to wait too long.

Rhubarb Lattice Pie with Cardamom and Orange

Rhubarb comes into season early in spring when there's little else at the farmers' market to cook with. It is delicious in pies, cobblers, and crisps, and it is particularly pretty bubbling out from beneath a lattice crust. Look for rhubarb with deep-red stalks, as they make the best-looking pie. If you're running short on time, skip the lattice and top with a second crust.

8 servings

Crust

2	cups unbleached all purpose flour
2	tablespoons sugar
¾	teaspoon salt
¾	cup (1½ sticks) chilled unsalted butter, cut into ½-inch cubes, then frozen 15 minutes
6	tablespoons (or more) ice water

Filling

10	cups 1-inch pieces trimmed fresh rhubarb (about 2½ pounds)
⅔	cup plus 2 teaspoons sugar
¼	cup orange juice
2½	teaspoons finely grated orange peel
½	teaspoon ground cardamom
¼	cup strawberry preserves
1	tablespoon heavy whipping cream
	Vanilla ice cream

CRUST: Blend flour, sugar, and salt in processor 5 seconds. Add butter; using on/off turns, blend until mixture resembles coarse meal. Add 6 tablespoons ice water. Using on/off turns, blend until moist clumps form, adding more ice water by teaspoonfuls if dough is dry. Gather dough into ball; divide into 2 pieces, 1 slightly larger than the other. Flatten each into disk. Wrap separately in plastic and chill at least 1 hour.

DO AHEAD: *Can be made 1 day ahead. Keep chilled. Let soften slightly at room temperature before rolling out.*

FILLING: Combine rhubarb, ⅔ cup sugar, orange juice, orange peel, and cardamom in large deep skillet. Toss over medium-high heat until liquid starts to bubble. Reduce heat to medium. Cover and simmer until rhubarb is almost tender, occasionally stirring very gently to keep rhubarb intact, about 8 minutes. Using slotted spoon, transfer rhubarb to colander set over bowl. Drain well. Add syrup from bowl to skillet. Boil until juices in skillet are thick and reduced to ⅔ cup, adding any additional drained syrup from bowl, about 7 minutes. Mix in preserves. Cool mixture in skillet 15 minutes. Very gently fold in rhubarb (do not overmix or rhubarb will fall apart).

Preheat oven to 375°F. Roll out larger dough disk on lightly floured surface to 12-inch round. Transfer to 9-inch-diameter glass pie dish. Roll out smaller dough disk on lightly floured surface to 11-inch round; cut into ½-inch-wide strips. Spoon filling into crust. Arrange 6 dough strips atop filling, spacing evenly. Place 5 dough strips at right angle atop first 6 strips, forming lattice. Seal strip ends to crust edge. Stir cream and remaining 2 teaspoons sugar in small bowl to blend. Brush over lattice, but not crust edge.

Bake pie until filling bubbles thickly and crust is golden, covering edge with foil collar if browning too quickly, about 55 minutes. Cool pie completely on rack. Cut into wedges and serve with ice cream.

Classic Sour-Cherry Pie with Lattice Crust

You've never had a cherry pie this good. It's got an incredible sour-cherry filling, a light and flaky crust, and vanilla ice cream to top it all off. Sour-cherry season is short—in the United States it runs from mid-June to early July—and fresh ones are not widely available. If you can't find fresh sour cherries, you can sometimes buy them frozen (thaw and drain them before measuring), or you can substitute sweet cherries and extra lemon juice. Frozen sour cherries can be ordered online from Friske Orchards in Michigan (apples-cherries.com). To create a woven lattice crust for this pie, see Crust 101 on page 213 for instructions. For a more rustic look, trim the excess crust instead of forming a crimped edge. **8 servings**

Crust

2½	**cups unbleached all purpose flour**
1	**tablespoon sugar**
¾	**teaspoon salt**
1	**cup (2 sticks) chilled unsalted butter, cut into ½-inch cubes**
5	**tablespoons (or more) ice water**

Filling

1	**cup plus 1 tablespoon sugar**
3	**tablespoons cornstarch**
¼	**teaspoon salt**
5	**cups whole pitted sour cherries or dark sweet cherries (from about 2 pounds whole unpitted cherries)**
1	**teaspoon fresh lemon juice (if using sour cherries) or 3 tablespoons fresh lemon juice (if using dark sweet cherries)**
½	**teaspoon vanilla extract**
2	**tablespoons (¼ stick) unsalted butter, cut into ½-inch cubes**

Milk
Vanilla ice cream

CRUST: Whisk flour, sugar, and salt in large bowl to blend. Add butter and rub in with fingertips until small pea-size clumps form. Add 5 tablespoons ice water; mix lightly with fork until dough holds together when small pieces are pressed between fingertips, adding more ice water by teaspoonfuls if dough is dry. Gather dough into ball; divide in half. Flatten each half into disk. Wrap separately in plastic and chill at least 30 minutes.

DO AHEAD: *Can be made 2 days ahead. Keep chilled. Let soften slightly at room temperature before rolling out.*

FILLING: Position rack in bottom third of oven and preheat to 425°F. Whisk 1 cup sugar, cornstarch, and salt in medium bowl to blend. Stir in cherries, lemon juice, and vanilla; set aside.

Roll out 1 dough disk on floured surface to 12-inch round. Transfer to 9-inch-diameter glass pie dish. Trim dough overhang to ½ inch. Roll out second dough disk on floured surface to 12-inch round. Using large knife or pastry wheel with fluted edge, cut ten ¾-inch-wide strips from dough round. Transfer filling to dough-lined dish, mounding slightly in center. Dot with butter. Arrange 5 dough strips atop filling, spacing evenly. Place remaining 5 dough strips at right angle atop first 5 strips, forming lattice. Trim dough strip overhang to ½ inch. Fold bottom crust over ends of dough strips; crimp edges to seal. Brush lattice crust (not edges) with milk. Sprinkle lattice with remaining 1 tablespoon sugar.

Place pie on rimmed baking sheet and bake 15 minutes. Reduce oven temperature to 375°F. Continue to bake until filling is bubbling and crust is golden brown, covering edges with foil collar if browning too quickly, about 1 hour longer. Transfer pie to rack and cool completely. Serve with vanilla ice cream.

Cherry Crumble Pie

A simple crumble topping of oats, almonds, and brown sugar gives this pie a rustic touch. **8 servings**

Crust

1½	cups unbleached all purpose flour
1	tablespoon sugar
¼	teaspoon salt
6	tablespoons (¾ stick) chilled unsalted butter, cut into ½-inch cubes
2	tablespoons chilled non-hydrogenated solid vegetable shortening, cut into ½-inch pieces
2	tablespoons (or more) ice water
1	large egg yolk

Topping

1	cup plus 2 tablespoons old-fashioned oats
¾	cup unbleached all purpose flour
¾	cup (packed) golden brown sugar
½	cup sliced almonds
¾	teaspoon ground cinnamon
¼	teaspoon salt
½	cup (1 stick) chilled unsalted butter, cut into ½-inch cubes

Filling

6	cups fresh cherries, pitted, or 2 pounds frozen pitted sweet cherries, thawed, juices reserved
1	cup sugar
2½	tablespoons quick-cooking tapioca
1	tablespoon kirsch (clear cherry brandy) or brandy
	Pinch of salt

CRUST: Blend flour, sugar, and salt in processor 5 seconds. Add butter and shortening; using on/off turns, cut in until mixture resembles coarse meal. Beat 2 tablespoons ice water and egg yolk in small bowl to blend; add to processor. Using on/off turns, blend until moist clumps form, adding more ice water by teaspoonfuls if dough is dry. Gather dough into ball; flatten into disk. Wrap in plastic and chill at least 30 minutes.

DO AHEAD: *Can be made 1 day ahead. Keep chilled. Let soften slightly at room temperature before rolling out.*

TOPPING: Blend oats, flour, sugar, almonds, cinnamon, and salt in medium bowl. Add butter. Rub in with fingertips, pressing mixture together until moist clumps form. Chill at least 30 minutes.

DO AHEAD: *Can be made 1 day ahead. Keep chilled.*

FILLING: Mix cherries with any juices, sugar, tapioca, kirsch, and salt in large bowl. Let stand until tapioca looks translucent, stirring occasionally, about 1 hour.

Preheat oven to 425°F. Roll out dough disk on lightly floured surface to 13- to 14-inch round. Transfer to 9-inch-diameter deep-dish glass pie dish. Trim dough overhang to ¾ inch. Fold edge under and crimp decoratively. Spoon filling into crust. Sprinkle with topping.

Bake pie 30 minutes. Reduce oven temperature to 400°F. Continue to bake until filling is bubbling thickly and topping is brown and crisp, covering edges with foil collar if browning too quickly, about 25 minutes longer. Cool pie on rack at least 30 minutes. Serve warm or at room temperature.

Spiced Peach Pie with Buttermilk Crust

The ultimate summer dessert: a peach filling spiked with cinnamon and cardamom between two layers of tender, flaky, slightly tangy buttermilk crust.

8 servings

Crust

2½	cups unbleached all purpose flour
5	teaspoons sugar
½	teaspoon salt
6	tablespoons (¾ stick) chilled unsalted butter, cut into ½-inch cubes
¼	cup frozen lard or non-hydrogenated solid vegetable shortening, cut into ½-inch pieces
¾	cup (or more) chilled buttermilk

Filling

¾	cup plus 1 tablespoon sugar
¼	cup unbleached all purpose flour
1½	teaspoons fresh lemon juice
½	teaspoon ground cinnamon
¼	teaspoon ground cardamom
3¾	to 4 pounds ripe peaches
2	tablespoons (¼ stick) unsalted butter, cut into ½-inch cubes
1	egg, beaten to blend

CRUST: Blend flour, sugar, and salt in processor. Add butter and lard; using on/off turns, cut in until fat is reduced to pea-size pieces, about 25 turns. Using on/off turns, blend in ¾ cup buttermilk until dough just comes together in moist clumps, adding more buttermilk by tablespoonfuls if dough is dry. Gather dough into ball; divide into 2 pieces, 1 slightly larger than the other. Flatten each into disk. Wrap separately in plastic and chill at least 1 hour.

DO AHEAD: *Can be made 1 day ahead. Keep chilled. Let soften slightly at room temperature before rolling out.*

FILLING: Mix ¾ cup sugar, flour, lemon juice, cinnamon, and cardamom in large bowl. Bring large pot of water to boil. Add peaches to boiling water for 30 seconds. Using slotted spoon, transfer peaches to bowl of cold water; cool. Peel, halve, and pit peaches. Slice peaches into bowl with sugar mixture; toss to coat. Let filling stand until juices form, stirring often, about 20 minutes.

Place 1 rack in center and 1 rack at lowest position in oven and preheat to 400°F. Roll out larger dough disk on floured surface to 12- to 13-inch round. Transfer to 9-inch-diameter glass pie dish. Trim overhang to ¾ inch. Mound filling in crust; dot with butter. Roll out smaller dough disk on floured surface to 12-inch round. Gently roll up dough onto rolling pin and unroll, draping over filling. Pinch together overhang of bottom crust and edge of top crust. Fold edge under and crimp decoratively. Cut several slits in top crust to allow steam to escape during baking. Brush crust with beaten egg; sprinkle with remaining 1 tablespoon sugar.

Place pie on center rack in oven. Place baking sheet on lowest oven rack to catch any drippings. Bake pie until crust is golden brown and juices bubble thickly through slits, covering very loosely with foil if crust browns too quickly, about 1 hour 10 minutes. Cool pie on rack at least 1 hour. Serve warm or at room temperature.

Peach Pie with Pecan Crumb Topping

This is summer's perfect pie, with a not-too-sweet filling, a tender flaky crust, and a crunchy nut topping. The peaches can be peeled by either using a very sharp serrated peeler, available online and at cookware stores, or plunging the peaches into boiling water for 30 seconds before cooling and slipping the skins off. **8 servings**

Crust

1¼	cups unbleached all purpose flour
1	teaspoon sugar
½	teaspoon salt
¼	cup (½ stick) chilled unsalted butter, cut into ½-inch cubes
¼	cup non-hydrogenated solid vegetable shortening or lard, frozen, cut into ½-inch pieces
3	tablespoons (or more) ice water

Filling

6	large ripe peaches (about 2½ pounds total), peeled, pitted, cut into ¾-inch-thick slices
½	cup sugar
2	tablespoons quick-cooking tapioca
½	teaspoon ground cinnamon

Topping

½	cup unbleached all purpose flour
⅓	cup (packed) golden brown sugar
½	teaspoon salt
6	tablespoons (¾ stick) chilled unsalted butter, cut into ½-inch cubes
1	cup pecan pieces
¾	cup old-fashioned oats

CRUST: Blend flour, sugar, and salt in processor. Add butter and shortening; using on/off turns, cut in until mixture resembles coarse meal. Transfer mixture to medium bowl. Using fork, stir in 3 tablespoons ice water, adding more ice water by teaspoonfuls if dough is dry, and pressing dough together with fingertips until moist clumps form. Gather dough into ball; flatten into disk. Wrap in plastic and chill at least 30 minutes.

DO AHEAD: *Can be made 1 day ahead. Keep chilled. Let soften slightly at room temperature before rolling out.*

FILLING: Toss peach slices, sugar, tapioca, and cinnamon in large bowl to coat. Let stand 15 minutes, tossing occasionally.

TOPPING: Meanwhile, blend flour, brown sugar, and salt in processor. Add butter; using on/off turns, process until mixture resembles fine moist clumps. Add pecans and oats. Using on/off turns, blend until nuts are chopped.

Position rack in bottom third of oven and preheat to 400°F. Roll out dough disk on lightly floured surface to 12-inch round. Transfer to 9-inch-diameter glass pie dish. If necessary, trim overhang to ¾ inch. Fold overhang under and crimp edge decoratively. Spoon filling into crust. Sprinkle pecan topping evenly over peaches. Bake pie 30 minutes. Reduce oven temperature to 350°F. Continue to bake until topping is brown, juices bubble thickly, and peaches are tender when pierced with small sharp knife, about 1 hour longer. Cool pie on rack 1 hour. Serve warm or at room temperature.

Peach and Blackberry Pie

There is just enough flour in the fruit filling to thicken the juices slightly. If you prefer a thicker pie filling, go ahead and add another tablespoon of flour to the fruit. Nectarines make good substitutes for the peaches, with the added benefit that they don't need to be peeled. **8 servings**

1½   **pounds ripe peaches (about 6 small)**
3   **cups fresh blackberries**
⅔   **cup plus 1 tablespoon sugar**
3   **tablespoons unbleached all purpose flour**
2   **Best-Ever Pie Crust dough disks (see recipe)**
   Heavy whipping cream
   Vanilla ice cream

Bring large saucepan of water to boil. Drop peaches into water; cook 30 seconds. Remove with slotted spoon. Rinse peaches under cold water to cool. Slip skins off peaches, then halve, pit, and slice (yielding 3¾ to 4 cups).

Position rack in bottom third of oven and preheat to 400°F. Mix peaches, blackberries, ⅔ cup sugar, and flour in large bowl; toss to blend.

Roll out 1 dough disk on lightly floured surface to 12-inch round. Transfer to 9-inch-diameter glass pie dish. Trim dough overhang to ½ inch. Spoon peach filling into crust. Roll out second dough disk on lightly floured surface to 12-inch round; drape over filling. Trim dough overhang to 1½ inches. Fold edges of top and bottom crusts under, pressing to seal. Crimp edges decoratively. Brush pie with cream and sprinkle with remaining 1 tablespoon sugar. Cut one 2-inch X in center of top crust to allow steam to escape during baking. Bake until crust is golden brown, peaches are tender when pierced with small sharp knife, and juices bubble thickly through X in crust, about 1 hour 10 minutes. Cool pie on rack at least 1 hour.

DO AHEAD: *Can be made 8 hours ahead. Let stand at room temperature.*

Serve warm or at room temperature with vanilla ice cream.

Best-Ever Pie Crust

Use this pie crust for any single-crust, double-crust, or lattice-top pie. Butter gives the crust a wonderful flavor; shortening makes it tender. **Makes 2 dough disks (enough for 1 double-crust pie or 1 lattice-top pie)**

2½   **cups unbleached all purpose flour**
1½   **teaspoons sugar**
1   **teaspoon salt**
½   **cup (1 stick) chilled unsalted butter, cut into ½-inch cubes**
½   **cup non-hydrogenated solid vegetable shortening or lard, frozen, cut into ½-inch pieces**
5   **tablespoons (or more) ice water**

Blend flour, sugar, and salt in processor. Add butter and shortening; using on/off turns, cut in until mixture resembles coarse meal. Transfer mixture to large bowl. Mix in 5 tablespoons ice water, adding more ice water by teaspoonfuls, if needed, until moist clumps form. Gather dough into ball; divide in half. Flatten each half into disk. Wrap separately in plastic and chill at least 20 minutes.

DO AHEAD: *Can be made ahead and chilled up to 1 day or frozen up to 1 month. If frozen, thaw overnight in refrigerator.*

Let soften slightly at room temperature before rolling out.

Old-Fashioned Blueberry-Maple Pie

This is blueberry pie the way it's meant to be: pure, simple, and utterly delicious. Be sure to place a baking sheet in the bottom of the oven before putting the pie in to bake. The sheet will catch any juices that bubble out of the crust. **8 servings**

Crust

2¼   cups unbleached all purpose flour
3   tablespoons sugar
1½   teaspoons baking powder
¾   teaspoon salt
6   tablespoons chilled non-hydrogenated solid vegetable
        shortening, cut into ½-inch pieces
3   tablespoons chilled unsalted butter, cut into ½-inch cubes
6   tablespoons (or more) ice water

Filling

4   cups fresh blueberries
1   cup pure maple syrup
¼   cup unbleached all purpose flour
¼   cup quick-cooking tapioca
4   teaspoons fresh lemon juice

CRUST: Blend flour, sugar, baking powder, and salt in processor. Add shortening and butter; using on/off turns, cut in until mixture resembles coarse meal. Mix in 6 tablespoons ice water, adding more ice water by teaspoonfuls, if needed, until moist clumps form. Gather dough together; divide into 2 pieces, 1 slightly larger than the other. Flatten each into disk. Wrap disks separately in plastic and chill 1 hour.

DO AHEAD: *Can be made 1 day ahead. Keep chilled. Let soften slightly at room temperature before rolling out.*

FILLING: Place baking sheet in bottom of oven and position rack in center; preheat to 375°F. Combine blueberries, maple syrup, flour, tapioca, and lemon juice in medium bowl; toss to blend. Let stand 15 minutes.

Roll out larger dough disk on floured surface to 12-inch round. Transfer to 9-inch-diameter glass pie dish. Pour filling into crust. Roll out smaller dough disk on floured surface to 12-inch round; arrange over filling. Press top and bottom crusts together at edge of dish to seal. Trim dough overhang to ¾ inch; fold under and crimp edge decoratively. Using small sharp knife, cut several slits in top crust to allow steam to escape during baking.

Bake pie until juices bubble thickly and crust is golden, about 1 hour. Cool pie completely on rack. Serve at room temperature.

Lattice-Topped Blueberry Pie

In this pie, the blueberries are cooked separately to ensure that the filling has the perfect consistency. **8 servings**

32   ounces frozen wild blueberries or regular blueberries (unthawed)
        or 7 cups fresh wild blueberries or regular blueberries
1   cup sugar
¼   cup cornstarch
2   tablespoons fresh lemon juice
1   teaspoon finely grated lemon peel
2   Best-Ever Pie Crust dough disks (see recipe on page 224)
        Heavy whipping cream
        Vanilla ice cream

Combine blueberries, sugar, cornstarch, lemon juice, and lemon peel in heavy large saucepan. Cook over medium heat until mixture thickens and bubbles, stirring occasionally, about 15 minutes. Continue to cook 1 minute longer, stirring constantly. Cool until warm.

DO AHEAD: *Can be made 3 days ahead. Cover and refrigerate.*

Position rack in bottom third of oven and preheat to 400°F. Roll out 1 dough disk on lightly floured surface to 12-inch round. Transfer to 9-inch-diameter glass pie dish. Trim dough overhang to 1 inch. Spoon filling into crust. Roll out remaining dough disk to 13x10-inch rectangle; cut into ¾-inch-wide strips. Arrange half of dough strips atop filling, spacing evenly. Arrange remaining dough strips at right angle atop first strips, weaving if desired, to form lattice. Brush crust edge with cream and press strips to adhere. Trim dough strips even with overhang on lower crust. Fold edge of crust up over strips, pressing gently to seal. Crimp edges decoratively. Brush lattice and edges lightly with cream.

Place pie on baking sheet. Bake until crust is golden, about 1 hour. Cool pie on rack at least 1 hour.

DO AHEAD: *Can be made 8 hours ahead. Let stand at room temperature.*

Serve pie warm or at room temperature with vanilla ice cream.

Wild Blueberry Pie with Almond Crumble Topping

Wild blueberries are small and flavorful. They can be found fresh at farmers' markets and frozen at supermarkets and specialty foods stores. If you can't find wild blueberries, regular fresh or frozen blueberries make a fine substitute. The little bit of marzipan or almond paste in the topping amps up the flavor of the berries. **8 servings**

1	**Best-Ever Pie Crust dough disk (see recipe on page 224)**
¾	**cup plus 2 tablespoons (or more) sugar**
¼	**cup cornstarch**
7	**cups fresh wild blueberries or regular blueberries (about 32 ounces) or 32 ounces frozen wild blueberries or regular blueberries (unthawed)**
2	**tablespoons fresh lemon juice**
⅔	**cup unbleached all purpose flour**
4	**ounces marzipan or almond paste, broken into ⅓-inch pieces (about ¾ cup loosely packed)**
¼	**cup (½ stick) chilled unsalted butter, cut into ½-inch cubes**
½	**teaspoon salt**
	Whipped cream or ice cream

Roll out pie dough disk on floured surface to 12-inch round. Transfer to 9-inch-diameter glass pie dish. Turn crust edges under and crimp decoratively, forming crust edge ¼ inch above sides of pie dish. Refrigerate while preparing filling and topping.

Whisk ¾ cup plus 2 tablespoons sugar and cornstarch in heavy large saucepan to blend. Stir in blueberries and lemon juice. Cook over medium heat until mixture bubbles and thickens, frequently stirring gently, about 13 minutes. Chill filling until cool, about 1 hour. If more sweetness is desired, stir in sugar by tablespoonfuls.

Combine flour, marzipan, butter, and salt in processor; blend until mixture begins to clump together. Transfer topping to small bowl; chill 30 minutes.

Position rack in bottom third of oven and preheat to 400°F. Spread blueberry filling evenly in unbaked crust. Sprinkle topping evenly over. Place pie on rimmed baking sheet and bake until crust and topping are golden and filling bubbles thickly, about 50 minutes. Transfer pie to rack and cool completely.

DO AHEAD: *Can be made 8 hours ahead. Let stand at room temperature.*

Serve at room temperature with whipped cream or ice cream.

Blueberry–Sour Cream Pie

A bit of almond extract gives the blueberry filling a subtle flavor. The crunchy pecan streusel provides a nice contrast to the custardy filling. **8 servings**

Crust

1¼	**cups unbleached all purpose flour**
½	**cup (1 stick) chilled unsalted butter, cut into ½-inch cubes**
2	**tablespoons sugar**
	Pinch of salt
3	**tablespoons (or more) ice water**

Filling

1	**cup sour cream**
¾	**cup sugar**
2½	**tablespoons unbleached all purpose flour**
1	**egg, beaten to blend**
¾	**teaspoon almond extract**
¼	**teaspoon salt**
2½	**cups fresh blueberries**

Topping

6	**tablespoons unbleached all purpose flour**
¼	**cup (½ stick) chilled unsalted butter, cut into ½-inch cubes**
⅓	**cup chopped pecans**
2	**tablespoons sugar**

CRUST: Blend flour, butter, sugar, and salt in processor until coarse meal forms. Using on/off turns, add 3 tablespoons ice water and blend until moist clumps form, adding more ice water by teaspoonfuls if dough is dry. Gather dough into ball; flatten into disk. Wrap in plastic and chill until firm, at least 30 minutes.

DO AHEAD: *Can be made 1 day ahead. Keep chilled. Let soften slightly at room temperature before rolling out.*

Preheat oven to 400°F. Roll out dough disk on floured surface to 13-inch round. Transfer to 9-inch-diameter glass pie dish. Trim dough overhang to ½ inch. Fold edge under and crimp decoratively. Freeze 10 minutes. Line crust with foil; fill with dried beans or pie weights. Bake until sides are set, about 15 minutes. Remove foil and beans.

FILLING: Whisk sour cream, sugar, flour, egg, almond extract, and salt in medium bowl. Mix in blueberries. Spoon filling into warm crust. Bake pie until filling is just set, about 25 minutes.

TOPPING: Using fingertips, mix flour and butter in medium bowl until small clumps form. Mix in pecans and sugar. Sprinkle topping over pie. Bake until topping is lightly browned, about 12 minutes. Cool pie completely on rack. Serve at room temperature.

♈♈♈ Blueberry Pie with Cornmeal Crust and Lemon Curd

Rolling the pie dough between two sheets of floured parchment paper gives maximum maneuverability. By handling the parchment (not the dough), it's easy to flip the dough frequently, which helps with rolling an even round. The top crust is sprinkled with raw sugar, creating a sparkling effect. **8 servings**

Crust

2½	cups unbleached all purpose flour
¼	cup cornmeal (preferably stone-ground, medium grind)
3	tablespoons sugar
¾	teaspoon salt
14	tablespoons (1¾ sticks) chilled unsalted butter, cut into ½-inch cubes
¼	cup non-hydrogenated solid vegetable shortening, frozen, cut into ½-inch pieces
4	tablespoons (or more) ice water

Filling

5	cups fresh blueberries (about 27 ounces)
¾	cup sugar
¼	cup cornstarch
1	tablespoon fresh lemon juice
1	tablespoon water
	Milk
1½	tablespoons raw sugar
	Lemon Curd (see recipe)

CRUST: Blend flour, cornmeal, sugar, and salt in processor. Add butter and shortening; using on/off turns, blend until mixture resembles coarse meal. Add 4 tablespoons ice water; blend just until moist clumps begin to form, adding more ice water by teaspoonfuls if dough is dry. Gather dough into ball; divide in half. Flatten each half into disk. Wrap separately in plastic and chill at least 1 hour.

DO AHEAD: *Can be made 1 day ahead. Keep chilled. Soften dough 10 minutes at room temperature before rolling out.*

FILLING: Combine blueberries, sugar, cornstarch, lemon juice, and 1 tablespoon water in large bowl; toss to blend. Let stand at room temperature until juices begin to form, about 30 minutes.

Preheat oven to 400°F. Place rimmed baking sheet in bottom of oven. Roll out 1 dough disk between 2 sheets of generously floured parchment paper to 12-inch round. Peel off top parchment sheet; invert dough into 9-inch-diameter glass pie dish. Carefully peel off second parchment sheet. Gently press dough into pie dish, pressing any cracks together as needed to seal and leaving dough overhang. Spoon filling into crust.

Roll out second dough disk between 2 sheets of generously floured parchment paper to 12-inch round. Peel off top parchment sheet. Carefully invert dough evenly atop filling. Peel off second parchment sheet. Trim overhang of both crusts to 1 inch. Fold overhang under and press to seal. Crimp edges decoratively. Cut five 2-inch-long slits in top crust of pie to allow steam to escape during baking. Lightly brush top crust (not edges) with milk. Sprinkle with raw sugar.

Bake pie 15 minutes. Reduce oven temperature to 350°F and continue baking until crust is golden brown and filling is bubbling thickly through slits in crust, about 1 hour 15 minutes. Cool pie completely on rack. Cut into wedges and serve with Lemon Curd.

 **Lemon Curd**

This thick, sweet-tart topping is also superb on scones or whole wheat toast.

Makes about 2 cups

1	cup plus 2 tablespoons sugar
½	cup fresh lemon juice
4	large eggs
1	large egg, separated
1	tablespoon finely grated lemon peel
10	tablespoons (1¼ sticks) chilled unsalted butter, cut into ½-inch cubes
	Pinch of salt

Combine 1 cup sugar, lemon juice, 4 eggs, egg yolk, and lemon peel in heavy medium saucepan and whisk to blend. Add butter and salt. Whisk constantly over medium heat until mixture thickens and coats back of spoon thickly (do not boil), about 12 minutes. Pour mixture through strainer into medium bowl. Place bowl in larger bowl filled with ice water and whisk occasionally until lemon curd is cooled completely, about 15 minutes.

Whisk egg white and remaining 2 tablespoons sugar in small metal bowl to blend. Set bowl over small saucepan of barely simmering water and whisk constantly until sugar dissolves and mixture is just warm to touch, about 1 minute (do not overheat or mixture will curdle). Immediately remove bowl from over water. Using electric mixer, beat egg white mixture until thick and glossy (texture will resemble marshmallow creme; volume of beaten egg white will be very small). Gently fold egg white mixture into cooled lemon curd.

DO AHEAD: *Can be made 1 day ahead. Cover and chill.*

Mixed Berry Pie with Pecan-Orange Lattice Crust

This is a wonderful pie to make in the fall, when fresh cranberries are just starting to appear at the market; combined with frozen raspberries and blueberries, they create a pie that's delightfully sweet and tart. A little grated orange peel adds fresh flavor to the pie crust. **8 servings**

Crust

½   cup pecans, toasted
2¼ cups unbleached all purpose flour
½   cup sugar
1   tablespoon finely grated orange peel
¾   teaspoon salt
¾   cup (1½ sticks) chilled unsalted butter, cut into ½-inch cubes
4   tablespoons (or more) ice water

Filling

1⅓ cups plus 1 tablespoon sugar
¼   cup orange marmalade
¼   cup cornstarch
1   tablespoon finely grated orange peel
¼   teaspoon ground allspice
1¾ cups frozen raspberries, thawed, drained
1½ cups frozen blueberries, thawed, drained
1¼ cups fresh or thawed frozen cranberries
1   egg, beaten to blend

CRUST: Finely grind pecans in processor. Add flour, sugar, orange peel, and salt and process until well blended. Add butter; using on/off turns, cut in until mixture resembles coarse meal. Using on/off turns, blend in 4 tablespoons ice water, adding more ice water by teaspoonfuls, if needed, until moist clumps form. Gather dough together; divide into 2 pieces, 1 slightly larger than the other. Flatten each into disk. Wrap separately in plastic and chill 1 hour.

DO AHEAD: *Can be made 1 day ahead. Keep chilled. Let soften slightly at room temperature before rolling out.*

FILLING: Position rack in bottom third of oven and preheat to 375°F. Combine 1⅓ cups sugar, orange marmalade, cornstarch, orange peel, and allspice in large bowl. Add all berries and toss gently.

Roll out larger dough disk on floured surface to 13-inch round. Transfer round to 9-inch-diameter glass pie dish. Trim overhang to 1½ inches.

Roll out smaller dough disk on floured surface to 12-inch round; cut into fourteen ½-inch-wide strips.

Mound filling in crust. Arrange 7 dough strips atop filling, spacing evenly. Place remaining 7 dough strips at right angle atop first 7 strips, forming lattice. Trim ends of dough strips even with overhang of bottom crust. Fold strip ends and overhang under, pressing to seal and forming high-standing rim. Brush lattice (not crust edge) with egg and sprinkle with remaining 1 tablespoon sugar.

Line baking sheet with foil; place in bottom of oven under rack to catch any drippings. Place pie on oven rack and bake until crust is golden brown and filling bubbles thickly, covering crust edge with foil collar if browning too quickly, about 1 hour 15 minutes. Transfer pie to rack and cool at least 1 hour. Serve slightly warm or at room temperature.

Pumpkin-Butterscotch Pie

Brown sugar, butter, salt, and Scotch whisky are quickly simmered into a tasty butterscotch, then pumpkin, cream, eggs, and spices round out the filling in this new take on the Thanksgiving classic. Spiking whipped cream with a little whisky to serve alongside brings out the "spirit" in the pie. **8 servings**

Crust

1¼	cups unbleached all purpose flour
½	teaspoon sugar
¼	teaspoon salt
10	tablespoons (1¼ sticks) chilled unsalted butter, cut into ½-inch cubes
3	tablespoons (or more) ice water

Filling

¾	cup (packed) golden brown sugar, divided
2	tablespoons (¼ stick) unsalted butter
¼	teaspoon salt
¼	cup Scotch
1¼	cups heavy whipping cream
1	cup canned pure pumpkin
3	large eggs
1	teaspoon ground cinnamon
½	teaspoon ground ginger
¼	teaspoon ground cloves
¼	teaspoon ground allspice

Whipped Cream

1	cup chilled heavy whipping cream
1	tablespoon sugar
1	tablespoon Scotch

CRUST: Mix flour, sugar, and salt in processor. Add butter; using on/off turns, process until very coarse meal forms. Add 3 tablespoons ice water; using on/off turns, process until moist clumps form, adding more ice water by teaspoonfuls if dough is dry. Gather dough into ball; flatten into disk. Wrap and chill 1 hour.

Roll out dough disk on floured surface to 12- to 13-inch round. Transfer to 9-inch-diameter glass pie dish. Fold edges under and crimp decoratively. Chill crust at least 1 hour.

DO AHEAD: *Can be made 1 day ahead. Cover and keep chilled.*

Preheat oven to 350°F. Line crust with foil; fill with dried beans or pie weights. Bake 20 minutes. Remove foil and beans. Bake crust until just beginning to turn golden brown, piercing with fork if bubbles form, about 15 minutes longer. Cool crust completely on rack.

FILLING: Combine ½ cup brown sugar, butter, and salt in medium saucepan; bring to boil over medium heat, stirring to dissolve sugar. Boil until deep brown, about 5 minutes. Remove from heat. Add Scotch, then cream (mixture will bubble vigorously) and whisk until smooth. Return to medium heat and stir until most caramel bits dissolve. Strain butterscotch mixture into small bowl. Cool to room temperature, stirring occasionally.

Whisk remaining ¼ cup brown sugar and pumpkin in large bowl. Whisk in eggs, then cinnamon, ginger, cloves, and allspice. Add reserved butterscotch mixture; whisk to blend.

DO AHEAD: *Can be made 1 day ahead. Cover and chill. Rewhisk before using.*

Preheat oven to 350°F. Pour filling into crust. Bake pie until filling is just set, about 50 minutes. Cool to room temperature, about 3 hours.

DO AHEAD: *Can be made 8 hours ahead. Store at room temperature.*

WHIPPED CREAM: Using electric mixer, beat cream, sugar, and Scotch in medium bowl until peaks form.

DO AHEAD: *Can be made 4 hours ahead. Cover and chill. Rewhisk if necessary before serving.*

Cut pie into wedges. Serve with dollops of whipped cream.

Classic Pumpkin Pie

A bit of sour cream gives the filling of this special pie a subtle tang and a little extra richness. If you'd like to decorate the pie with pastry leaves, prepare and roll out a second pie-crust dough disk; sprinkle the leaf-shaped cutouts with sugar before baking. Serve the pie with whipped cream, if desired. **8 servings**

Flaky Pie Crust dough disk (see recipe)
- ¾   **cup sugar**
- 2   **tablespoons (packed) dark brown sugar**
- 1   **tablespoon cornstarch**
- 2   **teaspoons ground cinnamon**
- ¾   **teaspoon ground ginger**
- ¼   **teaspoon (generous) salt**
- 1   **15-ounce can pure pumpkin**
- ¾   **cup chilled heavy whipping cream**
- 3   **large eggs, beaten to blend**
- ½   **cup sour cream**
- ¼   **cup apricot preserves**

Roll out dough disk on lightly floured surface to 13-inch round. Transfer to 9-inch-diameter glass pie dish. Trim dough overhang to ½ inch. Fold overhang under and shape edge to form high-standing rim. Make cut in crust edge at ½-inch intervals. Bend alternate edge pieces inward. Freeze crust 15 minutes. Preheat oven to 375°F. Line crust with foil and beans or pie weights. Place crust on large rimmed baking sheet. Bake crust until sides are set and dry, about 15 minutes. Remove foil and beans. Continue to bake crust until cooked through and pale golden, piercing with fork if crust bubbles, 13 to 15 minutes longer. Cool crust on sheet 30 minutes. Reduce oven temperature to 325°F.

Whisk both sugars, cornstarch, cinnamon, ginger, and salt in medium bowl until no lumps remain. Whisk in pumpkin, whipping cream, eggs, and sour cream. Gently spread apricot preserves evenly over inside of crust to coat. Pour filling into crust.

Bake pie on sheet until filling puffs at edges and center is almost set, 1 hour to 1 hour 5 minutes. Cool pie completely on rack. Cover and chill until cold.

DO AHEAD: *Can be made 1 day ahead. Keep chilled.*

> ## This Pie in History
> The Pilgrims didn't have pumpkin pie at their first Thanksgiving feast. The dessert reportedly made its debut at the second Thanksgiving, in 1623.

Flaky Pie Crust

All purpose flour and cake flour combine to make a tender crust, while the mixture of butter and shortening lends flavor and a flaky texture. If you don't own a food processor, simply use your fingertips or a pastry blender to combine the butter and shortening with the dry ingredients until the mixture resembles coarse meal. **Makes 1 dough disk (enough for one 9-inch or 10-inch crust)**

- 1   **cup unbleached all purpose flour**
- ⅓   **cup cake flour**
- 1   **tablespoon sugar**
- ¼   **teaspoon salt**
- 6   **tablespoons (¾ stick) chilled unsalted butter, cut into ½-inch cubes**
- 2   **tablespoons chilled non-hydrogenated solid vegetable shortening, cut into ½-inch pieces**
- 3   **tablespoons (or more) ice water**

Mix both flours, sugar, and salt in processor. Add butter and shortening; using on/off turns, process until mixture resembles very coarse meal. Add 3 tablespoons ice water and process until large moist clumps form, adding more ice water by teaspoonfuls if dough is dry. Gather dough into ball; flatten into disk. Wrap in plastic and chill until cold and firm, at least 1 hour.

DO AHEAD: *Can be made 1 day ahead. Let soften slightly at room temperature before rolling out.*

Pumpkin Chiffon Pie with Pecan–Graham Cracker Crust and Ginger Whipped Cream

A chiffon pie is any pie with an airy, fluffy filling. This velvety-textured pumpkin pie has a crunchy nutty crust, delicate spicing, a hint of bourbon, and zingy crystallized ginger that decorates the whipped cream topping. Try it as an alternative to a traditional pumpkin pie for Thanksgiving. **8 servings**

Crust

1	cup graham cracker crumbs
¾	cup finely chopped pecans
¼	cup (packed) golden brown sugar
⅛	teaspoon salt
5	tablespoons unsalted butter, melted

Filling

1	¼-ounce envelope unflavored gelatin
2	tablespoons bourbon
1¼	cups canned pure pumpkin
¾	cup whole milk
⅔	cup (packed) golden brown sugar
4	large egg yolks
1	teaspoon ground cinnamon
1	teaspoon ground ginger
¼	teaspoon ground cloves
¼	teaspoon salt

Ginger Whipped Cream

1½	cups chilled heavy whipping cream, divided
2	tablespoons powdered sugar
½	teaspoon vanilla extract
1½	tablespoons chopped crystallized ginger

CRUST: Preheat oven to 350°F. Butter 9-inch-diameter glass pie dish. Stir graham cracker crumbs, pecans, brown sugar, and salt in medium bowl to blend. Add butter and mix until crumbs are moistened. Press crumb mixture onto bottom and up sides of prepared dish. Bake crust until golden brown, about 10 minutes. Cool, then chill crust until cold.

FILLING: Sprinkle gelatin over bourbon in small bowl; set aside until gelatin softens, about 10 minutes. Meanwhile, whisk pumpkin, milk, brown sugar, egg yolks, cinnamon, ginger, cloves, and salt in heavy medium saucepan to blend. Stir over medium-low heat until mixture thickens slightly and instant-read thermometer inserted into mixture registers 160°F, about 8 minutes. Remove from heat and pour into large metal bowl. Immediately add softened gelatin mixture and stir until gelatin dissolves. Set bowl with pumpkin mixture over large bowl of ice water and stir until mixture is cold to touch but not set, about 5 minutes.

Beat ¾ cup cream in medium bowl until soft peaks form. Fold whipped cream into pumpkin mixture. Pour filling into chilled crust. Chill pie until filling is set, at least 3 hours.

DO AHEAD: *Can be made 1 day ahead. Cover loosely with foil and keep chilled.*

GINGER WHIPPED CREAM: Using electric mixer, beat remaining ¾ cup cream, powdered sugar, and vanilla in medium bowl until medium-firm peaks form. Transfer whipped cream to pastry bag fitted with large star tip. Pipe whipped cream rosettes around edge of pie. Alternately, spread whipped cream decoratively over pie. Sprinkle crystallized ginger over whipped cream.

DO AHEAD: *Can be made 6 hours ahead. Chill uncovered.*

Sweet Potato Cream Pie

Cooking the sweet potatoes in the microwave helps this pie come together quickly, a fact you'll appreciate when you're rushing to make all those desserts for the Thanksgiving feast. **10 to 12 servings**

Flaky Pie Crust dough disk (see recipe on page 233)
2   **large red-skinned sweet potatoes (yams; about 1¾ pounds total)**
¾   **cup (packed) dark brown sugar**
5   **large egg yolks**
2   **tablespoons fresh lemon juice**
1   **teaspoon vanilla extract**
1   **teaspoon ground cinnamon**
¼   **teaspoon salt**
¼   **teaspoon ground nutmeg**
1   **cup heavy whipping cream**
    Sweetened whipped cream

Position rack in bottom third of oven and preheat to 375°F. Butter 10-inch-diameter glass pie dish. Roll out dough disk on floured surface to 13-inch round. Transfer to prepared pie dish. Trim dough overhang to ½ inch if necessary. Fold overhang under, forming edge, and crimp decoratively. Freeze 15 minutes.

Line crust with foil; fill with dried beans or pie weights. Bake until edge of crust is pale golden, about 25 minutes. Remove foil and beans. Continue to bake until bottom of crust is pale golden, about 5 minutes. Cool crust on rack. Reduce oven temperature to 325°F.

Meanwhile, pierce sweet potatoes in several places with fork or toothpick. Cook in microwave on high until tender, turning once, about 10 minutes. Cut potatoes open; cool. Scrape flesh into medium bowl; discard skins. Mash potatoes. Measure enough potatoes to equal 2 cups (reserve remainder for another use).

Combine 2 cups mashed sweet potatoes, brown sugar, egg yolks, lemon juice, vanilla, cinnamon, salt, and nutmeg in processor; puree until smooth. Transfer to bowl; mix in whipping cream. Pour into crust.

Bake pie until filling is set in center and top is no longer shiny, about 50 minutes. Transfer to rack and cool completely.

DO AHEAD: *Can be made 1 day ahead. Chill uncovered until cold, then cover and keep chilled.*

Serve pie cold with whipped cream.

🥄 Toasted-Pecan Pie

Some of the pecans for this pie are toasted to an aromatic brown before being finely ground and stirred into the otherwise traditional pecan-pie filling. The results are rich and delicious. Avoid an oily mess by making sure that the nuts are cooled completely before grinding them. **10 servings**

Crust

1⅓	cups unbleached all purpose flour
½	teaspoon salt
½	cup (1 stick) chilled unsalted butter, cut into ½-inch cubes
4	tablespoons (or more) ice water

Filling

3	cups pecans, divided
6	large eggs
2	cups sugar
2	cups dark corn syrup
¼	cup (½ stick) unsalted butter, melted
1	tablespoon vanilla extract
¼	teaspoon salt
	Lightly sweetened whipped cream

CRUST: Blend flour and salt in processor 10 seconds. Add butter; using on/off turns, cut in until mixture resembles coarse meal. Add 4 tablespoons ice water and blend just until moist clumps form, adding more ice water by teaspoonfuls if mixture is dry. Gather dough into ball; flatten into disk. Wrap in plastic and chill 1 hour.

DO AHEAD: *Can be made 1 day ahead. Keep chilled. Let soften slightly at room temperature before rolling out.*

FILLING: Preheat oven to 350°F. Coarsely chop 2 cups pecans and reserve. Spread remaining 1 cup pecans on rimmed baking sheet. Toast in oven until nuts are aromatic and darker in color, about 12 minutes. Cool nuts completely, then grind finely in processor. Maintain oven temperature.

Roll out dough disk on lightly floured surface to 13-inch round (crust will be thin). Transfer to 10-inch-diameter glass pie dish. Fold dough overhang under, forming high-standing rim; crimp edges decoratively. Freeze crust 20 minutes.

Whisk eggs in large bowl until frothy. Add sugar, corn syrup, melted butter, vanilla, salt, and ground toasted pecans; whisk until blended. Mix in chopped pecans. Pour filling into crust.

Bake pie until crust is golden and filling is puffed and set (center may still move slightly when dish is shaken), about 1 hour 10 minutes. Transfer to rack and cool at least 3 hours.

DO AHEAD: *Can be made 8 hours ahead. Let stand at room temperature.*

Serve slightly warm or at room temperature with whipped cream.

Chocolate-Almond Pie

The rich, gooey filling of this sweet treat is reminiscent of a pecan pie. For an intense chocolate flavor, choose bittersweet chocolate; for a milder taste, go for semisweet. **8 servings**

4   ounces bittersweet or semisweet chocolate, chopped
3   tablespoons unsalted butter
1¼   cups dark corn syrup
¾   cup sugar
4   large eggs
2   teaspoons vanilla extract
¾   teaspoon almond extract
     Pinch of salt
3   cups sliced almonds, toasted
1   Cinnamon Pastry Crust (see recipe), chilled

Position rack in center of oven and preheat to 350°F. Stir chocolate and butter in large metal bowl set over saucepan of simmering water until melted and smooth. Remove bowl from over water. Mix in corn syrup and sugar. Whisk in eggs, vanilla extract, almond extract, and salt. Stir in toasted almonds.

Pour filling into prepared crust. Bake pie until filling is set around edges but moves slightly in center when pie is gently shaken and crust is golden brown, tenting with foil if crust browns too quickly, about 1 hour. Transfer pie to rack and cool slightly.

Serve warm or at room temperature.

 ## Cinnamon Pastry Crust

Toasted nuts and a bit of cinnamon make this the perfect crust for fall pies.
Makes one 9-inch crust

1½   cups unbleached all purpose flour
⅓   cup walnuts or slivered almonds, toasted
2   tablespoons sugar
1   teaspoon ground cinnamon
½   teaspoon salt
½   cup (1 stick) chilled unsalted butter, cut into ½-inch cubes
2   tablespoons chilled non-hydrogenated solid vegetable shortening, cut into ½-inch pieces
2   tablespoons (or more) ice water

Blend flour, nuts, sugar, cinnamon, and salt in processor until nuts are coarsely ground. Add butter and shortening; using on/off turns, process until coarse meal forms. Add 2 tablespoons ice water; using on/off turns, blend until small moist clumps form, adding more ice water by teaspoonfuls if dough is dry. Gather dough into ball; flatten into disk. Wrap in plastic and chill until cold, at least 30 minutes.

DO AHEAD: *Can be made 1 day ahead. Keep chilled. Let soften slightly at room temperature before rolling out.*

Roll out dough disk on floured surface to 12-inch round. Transfer to 9-inch-diameter glass pie dish. Press dough into dish. Fold dough overhang under and crimp edges decoratively. Cover and chill until cold, about 30 minutes.

DO AHEAD: *Can be made 1 day ahead. Keep chilled.*

California Walnut Pie with Orange and Cinnamon

This pie is aptly named, as virtually all walnuts in the United States (and two-thirds of those in the world) come from California. The texture is similar to that of a pecan pie, but this dessert is perfumed with another famous California crop, the orange. **8 servings**

1   **Flaky Pie Crust dough disk (see recipe on page 233)**
3   **large eggs**
1   **cup light corn syrup**
½   **cup sugar**
½   **cup (1 stick) unsalted butter, melted**
1   **teaspoon finely grated orange peel**
1   **teaspoon ground cinnamon**
1   **teaspoon vanilla extract**
1½   **cups coarsely chopped walnuts**

Position rack in bottom third of oven and preheat to 400°F. Roll out dough disk on floured surface to 12-inch round. Transfer to 9-inch-diameter glass pie dish. Fold crust edge under; crimp decoratively. Refrigerate 15 minutes.

Whisk eggs in medium bowl until well blended. Add corn syrup, sugar, melted butter, orange peel, cinnamon, and vanilla; whisk until smooth. Stir in walnuts. Pour walnut filling into chilled crust.

Bake 10 minutes. Reduce oven temperature to 350°F. Continue baking pie until puffed and set in center when dish is gently shaken, about 40 minutes longer. Cool pie completely on rack.

DO AHEAD: *Can be made 1 day ahead. Cover and store at room temperature.*

Maple-Hazelnut Pie

Hazelnuts and maple combine in a northern version of the southern favorite. Use dark Grade B maple syrup for the most intense maple flavor. **8 servings**

1   **Flaky Pie Crust dough disk (see recipe on page 233)**
¾   **cup pure maple syrup (preferably Grade B)**
½   **cup (packed) golden brown sugar**
½   **cup light corn syrup**
¼   **teaspoon salt**
2   **tablespoons bourbon**
¼   **cup (½ stick) unsalted butter, cut into ½-inch cubes**
1   **large egg white, lightly beaten to loosen**
1   **cup hazelnuts, husked, coarsely chopped**
3   **large eggs**
1   **teaspoon vanilla extract**

Position rack in center of oven and preheat to 375°F. Roll out dough disk on floured surface to 12-inch round. Transfer to 9-inch-diameter glass pie dish. Fold crust edge under; crimp decoratively. Refrigerate 20 minutes.

Line crust with foil; fill with dried beans or pie weights. Bake crust until sides are set, about 15 minutes. Remove foil and beans. Continue to bake until set, pressing gently with back of spoon if crust bubbles, 10 to 12 minutes. Transfer crust to rack and cool completely. Reduce oven temperature to 350°F.

Meanwhile, bring maple syrup, brown sugar, corn syrup, and salt to boil in medium saucepan over medium heat, stirring until sugar dissolves. Continue boiling 1 minute, reducing heat as needed to prevent mixture from boiling over. Remove pan from heat. Add bourbon, then butter; whisk until butter melts. Let mixture cool to lukewarm, whisking occasionally, about 20 minutes.

Brush crust with egg white to coat. Scatter hazelnuts over. Whisk eggs and vanilla in medium bowl until blended. Whisk cooled maple mixture into egg mixture. Pour filling over hazelnuts in crust.

Bake pie until filling is set and slightly puffed, covering crust edges with foil collar if browning too quickly, about 50 minutes. Cool pie completely on rack.

DO AHEAD: *Can be made 1 day ahead. Cover and store at room temperature.*

North Carolina Peanut Pie

Sorghum syrup is derived from a cereal-grass crop that grows in the South. Golden syrup comes from sugar cane, but unlike molasses, it is light in color and flavor. Salted North Carolina peanuts (sold as Golden Gourmet Peanuts) and sorghum syrup are available online at southernthings.com. Golden syrup can be found in some supermarkets or at specialty foods stores where maple syrup and other syrups are sold. **8 servings**

Crust

1½	cups unbleached all purpose flour
1	teaspoon sugar
½	teaspoon salt
½	cup (1 stick) chilled unsalted butter, cut into ½-inch cubes
4	tablespoons (or more) ice water

Filling

⅓	cup (packed) dark brown sugar
2	tablespoons unbleached all purpose flour
½	teaspoon coarse kosher salt
¼	teaspoon ground cinnamon
¼	teaspoon cayenne pepper
3	large eggs
½	cup golden syrup (such as Lyle's Golden Syrup)
½	cup sorghum syrup, or ½ cup golden syrup (such as Lyle's Golden Syrup) mixed with 1 teaspoon apple cider vinegar
¼	cup (½ stick) unsalted butter, melted, cooled slightly
1	teaspoon vanilla extract
1½	cups coarsely chopped salted North Carolina peanuts or coarsely chopped salted cocktail peanuts
	Vanilla ice cream

CRUST: Blend flour, sugar, and salt in processor. Add butter; using on/off turns, cut in until mixture resembles coarse meal. Add 4 tablespoons ice water; using on/off turns, blend just until moist clumps form, adding more ice water by teaspoonfuls if dough is dry. Gather dough into ball; flatten into disk. Wrap in plastic and chill at least 1 hour.

Preheat oven to 375°F. Roll out dough disk on lightly floured surface to 12-inch round. Transfer to 9-inch-diameter glass pie dish. Fold dough edges under and crimp decoratively. Freeze crust 15 minutes.

Line crust with foil; fill with dried beans or pie weights. Bake until crust is set, about 20 minutes. Remove foil and beans. Continue to bake until edges begin to color, piercing with fork if crust bubbles, about 13 minutes. Cool crust on rack while making filling. Maintain oven temperature.

FILLING: Whisk brown sugar, flour, coarse salt, cinnamon, and cayenne in medium bowl. Whisk eggs in another medium bowl to blend. Add golden syrup, sorghum syrup, melted butter, and vanilla to eggs and whisk to blend. Add brown sugar mixture and whisk until smooth. Mix in peanuts. Pour filling into cooled crust.

Bake pie 15 minutes. Reduce oven temperature to 350°F. Continue to bake until crust is golden and filling is set (center of filling may move slightly when dish is gently shaken), covering crust edges with foil if browning too quickly, about 40 minutes. Cool pie completely on rack.

DO AHEAD: *Can be made 1 day ahead. Cover loosely; store at room temperature.*

Cut pie into wedges. Serve with vanilla ice cream.

🥄 Classic Lemon Meringue Pie

Fresh lemon juice and lemon peel add a nice pucker to the filling. A sweet cloud of meringue balances the tartness. When beating egg whites for the meringue, be sure to use a perfectly clean metal or glass mixing bowl. Using a copper bowl will result in an especially fluffy texture. Using nonstick aluminum foil (available at supermarkets) makes it easy to blind bake the crust; or simply spray regular foil with nonstick spray. **8 servings**

Crust
1¼	cups unbleached all purpose flour
1	tablespoon sugar
½	teaspoon finely grated lemon peel
½	cup (1 stick) chilled unsalted butter, cut into ½-inch cubes
2	tablespoons (or more) ice water

Filling
1	cup sugar
4	teaspoons cornstarch
⅔	cup fresh lemon juice
4	large egg yolks
1	tablespoon finely grated lemon peel

Meringue
3	large egg whites, room temperature
	Pinch of salt
½	cup sugar

Technique Tip: Chill and Bake
If you have time, chill the pie crust dough before baking as long as one day or overnight. This allows the glutens in the flour to rest, reducing the amount the crust will shrink when baked.

CRUST: Blend flour, sugar, and lemon peel in processor. Add butter and process until mixture resembles coarse meal. Transfer mixture to medium bowl. Drizzle 2 tablespoons ice water over and stir with fork until moist clumps form, adding more ice water by teaspoonfuls if mixture is dry. Gather dough into ball; flatten into disk. Wrap in plastic and chill at least 20 minutes.

DO AHEAD: *Can be made 1 day ahead. Keep chilled. Let soften slightly at room temperature before rolling out.*

Roll out dough disk on lightly floured surface to 12-inch round. Gently roll up dough onto rolling pin and unroll into 9-inch-diameter glass pie dish. Press into dish. Fold dough overhang under, even with edge of pie dish. Crimp dough edges decoratively. Freeze crust until firm, about 15 minutes.

Preheat oven to 400°F. Line frozen crust with nonstick aluminum foil. Fill foil with dried beans or pie weights. Bake until crust is set, about 15 minutes. Remove foil and beans. Continue baking crust until golden, about 10 minutes longer. Remove crust from oven. Reduce oven temperature to 350°F. Let crust cool on rack while preparing filling.

FILLING: Whisk sugar and cornstarch in heavy medium saucepan to blend. Gradually whisk in lemon juice. Whisk in egg yolks 1 at a time. Stir in lemon peel. Whisk constantly over medium heat until mixture thickens and boils, about 10 minutes. Spoon warm filling into crust; smooth top.

MERINGUE: Using electric mixer fitted with whisk attachment, beat egg whites and salt in large bowl until very soft peaks form. Gradually beat in sugar; continue beating until mixture is stiff and glossy. Using silicone spatula, spread meringue over warm filling, covering to crust edges and creating peaks and swirls. Bake until meringue is pale golden, about 15 minutes. Cool pie completely on rack and serve.

Lemon Macaroon Pie

The tang of the lemon juice and lemon peel balances the richness of the coconut in this bright, sunny pie. **8 servings**

Crust

1	cup unbleached all purpose flour
⅓	cup cake flour
1	tablespoon sugar
½	teaspoon salt
6	tablespoons (¾ stick) chilled unsalted butter, cut into 4 pieces
2	tablespoons chilled non-hydrogenated solid vegetable shortening, cut into ½-inch pieces
3	tablespoons (or more) ice water

Filling

3	large eggs
2	large egg yolks
¼	teaspoon salt
1¼	cups sugar
1¼	cups sweetened flaked coconut
¼	cup chilled heavy whipping cream
¼	cup fresh lemon juice
2	tablespoons (¼ stick) unsalted butter, melted
2	teaspoons finely grated lemon peel
1½	teaspoons vanilla extract
½	teaspoon almond extract

Topping

¾	cup heavy whipping cream
2	teaspoons powdered sugar
¾	teaspoon vanilla extract
8	thin lemon slices

CRUST: Blend both flours, sugar, and salt in processor. Add butter and shortening; using on/off turns, cut in until mixture resembles coarse meal. Add 3 tablespoons ice water and process until moist clumps form, adding more ice water by teaspoonfuls if dough is dry. Gather dough into ball; flatten into disk. Wrap in plastic and chill at least 1 hour.

DO AHEAD: *Can be made 2 days ahead. Keep chilled. Let soften slightly at room temperature before rolling out.*

Position rack in bottom third of oven and preheat oven to 350°F. Butter 9-inch-diameter glass pie dish. Roll out dough disk on lightly floured surface to 12-inch round. Transfer to prepared dish. Trim dough overhang to ½ inch; fold under and crimp edge decoratively. Freeze crust 15 minutes.

Line crust with foil; fill with dried beans or pie weights. Bake until crust is set and edge is pale golden, about 20 minutes. Remove foil and beans. Cool crust completely on rack. Maintain oven temperature.

FILLING: Using electric mixer, beat eggs, egg yolks, and salt in large bowl to blend. Add sugar and beat until mixture is thick and fluffy, about 1 minute. Beat in coconut, whipping cream, lemon juice, melted butter, lemon peel, and vanilla and almond extracts. Pour filling into crust.

Bake until filling is golden and set, about 40 minutes. Cool pie completely on rack, then chill until cold, about 3 hours.

DO AHEAD: *Can be made 1 day ahead. Cover and keep chilled.*

TOPPING: Beat cream, powdered sugar, and vanilla in large bowl until stiff peaks form. Fill pastry bag fitted with large star tip with whipped cream mixture and pipe around border of pie. Garnish with lemon slices and serve.

🍴 Coconut Cream Pie

This luscious version of the classic pie features a rich pastry cream filling and a triple dose of coconut flavor: in the filling, in the whipped cream topping, and in the toasted coconut flakes sprinkled atop the pie. The pie filling needs to chill overnight, so begin making this one day ahead. **8 servings**

Crust

1½	**cups unbleached all purpose flour**
1	**tablespoon sugar**
½	**teaspoon salt**
6	**tablespoons (¾ stick) chilled unsalted butter, cut into ½-inch cubes**
3	**tablespoons chilled solid non-hydrogenated vegetable shortening, cut into ½-inch pieces**
4	**tablespoons (or more) ice water**

Filling

½	**cup sugar**
2	**large eggs**
1	**large egg yolk**
3	**tablespoons unbleached all purpose flour**
1½	**cups whole milk**
1½	**cups sweetened flaked coconut**
1	**teaspoon vanilla extract**
⅛	**teaspoon coconut extract**

Topping

⅔	**cup sweetened flaked coconut**
1¼	**cups chilled heavy whipping cream**
2	**tablespoons sugar**
⅛	**teaspoon coconut extract**

CRUST: Blend flour, sugar, and salt in processor. Add butter and shortening; using on/off turns, cut in until mixture resembles coarse meal. Drizzle 4 tablespoons ice water over mixture. Using on/off turns, process just until moist clumps form, adding more ice water by teaspoonfuls if dough is dry. Gather dough into ball; flatten into disk. Wrap in plastic. Chill 1 hour.

Roll out dough between 2 sheets of plastic wrap to 13-inch round. Transfer dough to 9-inch-diameter glass pie dish. Fold overhang under. Crimp edges decoratively. Pierce bottom of crust all over with fork. Freeze crust 15 minutes.

DO AHEAD: *Can be made 1 day ahead. Keep frozen.*

Preheat oven to 375°F. Line crust with aluminum foil. Fill with pie weights or dried beans. Bake 20 minutes. Remove weights and foil. Bake until golden and set, about 10 minutes. Cool.

DO AHEAD: *Crust can be made 1 day ahead. Wrap with foil or plastic wrap. Let stand at room temperature.*

FILLING: Whisk sugar, eggs, egg yolk, and flour in medium bowl. Bring milk and coconut to simmer in medium saucepan over medium heat. Gradually add hot milk mixture to egg mixture, whisking constantly. Return to same saucepan; cook until pastry cream thickens and boils, stirring constantly, about 4 minutes. Remove from heat. Mix in vanilla and coconut extracts. Transfer pastry cream to medium bowl. Press plastic wrap directly onto surface to prevent skin from forming. Chill until cold, at least 2 hours and up to 1 day. Transfer filling to crust. Cover; chill overnight.

TOPPING: Meanwhile toast coconut in heavy small skillet over medium heat until light golden, stirring often, about 3 minutes. Cool completely.

Using electric mixer, beat cream, sugar, and coconut extract in medium bowl until peaks form. Spread whipped cream all over top of filling. Sprinkle evenly with toasted coconut. Serve cold.

DO AHEAD: *Can be made 4 hours ahead. Cover and refrigerate.*

Bittersweet Chocolate Pudding Pie with Crème Fraîche Topping

Bittersweet chocolate and crème fraîche, now available at most supermarkets and at specialty foods stores, update the diner-style chocolate pudding pie. When making the filling, be sure to whisk the milk into the sugar mixture gradually to avoid clumps. **8 servings**

Crust

- 1 **cup chocolate wafer cookie crumbs (about half of 9-ounce package; about 23 cookies, finely ground in processor)**
- 2 **tablespoons sugar**
- 5 **tablespoons unsalted butter, melted**
- 2 **ounces bittersweet or semisweet chocolate (do not exceed 61% cacao), chopped**

Filling

- 1/3 **cup sugar**
- 1/3 **cup unsweetened cocoa powder (preferably Dutch-process)**
- 2 **tablespoons cornstarch**
- 1/8 **teaspoon salt**
- 1¾ **cups whole milk, divided**
- 1/4 **cup heavy whipping cream**
- 4 **ounces bittersweet or semisweet chocolate (do not exceed 61% cacao), chopped**
- 1 **tablespoon dark rum**
- 1 **teaspoon vanilla extract**

Topping

- 1 **cup chilled crème fraîche**
- 1 **cup chilled heavy whipping cream**
- 1/4 **cup sugar**
- 1 **teaspoon vanilla extract**
  Bittersweet chocolate shavings or curls (optional)

CRUST: Position rack in center of oven and preheat to 350°F. Blend cookie crumbs and sugar in processor. Add melted butter; process until crumbs are evenly moistened. Press crumb mixture onto bottom and up sides (not rim) of 9-inch-diameter glass pie dish. Bake until crust begins to set and no longer looks moist, pressing gently with back of fork if crust puffs, about 12 minutes. Remove crust from oven. Sprinkle chopped chocolate over bottom of crust. Let stand until chocolate softens, 1 to 2 minutes. Using offset spatula or small silicone spatula, gently spread chocolate over bottom and up sides of crust to cover. Chill crust until chocolate sets, about 30 minutes.

FILLING: Whisk sugar, cocoa, cornstarch, and salt to blend in heavy medium saucepan. Gradually add 1/3 cup milk, whisking until smooth paste forms. Whisk in remaining milk, then cream. Using flat-bottom wooden spoon or heatproof spatula, stir mixture constantly over medium heat, scraping bottom and sides of pan until pudding thickens and begins to bubble at edges, about 5 minutes. Add chocolate; stir until mixture is smooth. Remove from heat; stir in rum and vanilla. Pour hot pudding into crust and spread evenly. Cool 1 hour at room temperature. Cover with plastic wrap; chill overnight.

DO AHEAD: *Can be made 2 days ahead. Keep chilled.*

TOPPING: Using electric mixer, beat crème fraîche, whipping cream, sugar, and vanilla in medium bowl just until stiff peaks form and mixture is thick enough to spread (do not overbeat or mixture may curdle). Spread topping decoratively over top of pie, swirling to create peaks, if desired.

DO AHEAD: *Can be made 6 hours ahead. Cover with cake dome and chill.*

Sprinkle chocolate shavings decoratively atop pie, if desired.

Caramel-Pecan Black Bottom Pie

Triple threat: This decadent dessert features a crust filled with chocolate custard, vanilla-brandy custard, and a delicious caramel that's flecked with toasted pecans. **8 servings**

Crust

1⅓	cups sifted unbleached all purpose flour (sifted, then measured)
3	tablespoons sugar
¼	teaspoon salt
7	tablespoons chilled unsalted butter, cut into ½-inch cubes
2	tablespoons ice water
1	large egg yolk
½	teaspoon vanilla extract

Filling

2	tablespoons brandy
½	teaspoon vanilla extract
1	teaspoon unflavored gelatin
5	ounces bittersweet or semisweet chocolate, chopped
½	cup sugar
3	tablespoons cornstarch
¼	teaspoon salt
2	cups half and half
4	large egg yolks

Topping

⅔	cup sugar
⅓	cup water
½	cup plus 1 tablespoon heavy whipping cream
¼	cup (½ stick) unsalted butter
1	cup pecans, toasted, chopped

CRUST: Combine flour, sugar, and salt in processor. Add butter; using on/off turns, blend until mixture resembles coarse meal. Whisk 2 tablespoons ice water, egg yolk, and vanilla in small bowl to blend. Add egg mixture to processor and blend until large moist clumps form. Gather dough into ball; flatten into disk. Wrap in plastic and chill at least 30 minutes.

DO AHEAD: *Can be made 1 day ahead. Keep chilled. Let soften slightly at room temperature before rolling out.*

Position rack in center of oven and preheat to 350°F. Lightly butter 9-inch-diameter glass pie dish. Roll out dough disk on floured surface to 13-inch round. Transfer to prepared pie dish. Fold dough edges under and crimp to form high-standing fluted edge. Freeze crust until firm, about 15 minutes. Line crust with foil; fill with dried beans or pie weights. Bake until sides of crust are set, about 20 minutes. Remove foil and beans. Pierce bottom of crust in several places with fork and continue to bake until crust is golden brown, about 20 minutes. Cool on rack.

FILLING: Combine brandy and vanilla in small bowl. Sprinkle gelatin over and let stand 10 minutes. Place chocolate in medium bowl. Mix sugar, cornstarch, and salt in heavy medium saucepan. Gradually whisk half and half and egg yolks into sugar mixture. Whisk constantly over medium-high heat until custard is thick and smooth and begins to boil, about 3 minutes. Quickly add 1¼ cups custard to chocolate. Stir until chocolate is melted and mixture is smooth. Add brandy mixture to remaining hot custard; stir until gelatin dissolves. Spread chocolate filling evenly in crust. Spread brandy filling over. Refrigerate uncovered until pie is completely cool.

TOPPING: Heat sugar and ⅓ cup water in heavy small saucepan over low heat, stirring until sugar dissolves. Increase heat and boil without stirring until mixture is deep amber color, occasionally brushing down sides of pan with wet pastry brush and swirling pan, about 11 minutes. Remove from heat and add cream (mixture will bubble vigorously). Add butter and stir until smooth. Stir over low heat until color deepens and caramel thickens slightly, about 3 minutes. Mix in pecans. Transfer topping to small bowl. Chill until cool but not set, stirring occasionally, about 30 minutes.

Spoon topping over brandy layer. Chill pie until topping is set, about 2 hours.

DO AHEAD: *Can be made 1 day ahead. Cover and keep chilled.*

Banoffee Pie

Originally created in England, this delicious dessert gets its name from the combination of banana (the filling is topped with sliced fresh bananas) and toffee (the filling has a toffee flavor). **8 servings**

Crust

- **¾ cup unbleached all purpose flour**
- **6 tablespoons (¾ stick) chilled unsalted butter, cut into ½-inch cubes**
- **2 tablespoons sugar**
- **¼ teaspoon salt**
- **½ cup dry-roasted macadamia nuts**
- **1 large egg yolk**
- **1 teaspoon vanilla extract**

Filling

- **2 14-ounce cans sweetened condensed milk**
- **½ cup heavy whipping cream**
- **1 tablespoon dark rum**
- **1 tablespoon vanilla extract**
- **4 bananas, peeled, sliced**

Topping

- **3 tablespoons instant coffee crystals**
- **1 tablespoon water**
- **2 cups chilled heavy whipping cream**
- **½ cup sugar**

CRUST: Combine flour, butter, sugar, and salt in processor. Using on/off turns, blend until mixture resembles coarse meal. Add nuts; using on/off turns, process until nuts are finely chopped. Add egg yolk and vanilla; process until moist clumps form. Press dough onto bottom and up sides of 9-inch-diameter glass pie dish. Freeze 30 minutes.

Preheat oven to 350°F. Bake crust until golden and cooked through, 25 to 30 minutes. Cool on rack.

FILLING: Simmer sweetened condensed milk in heavy medium saucepan over medium heat until very thick and color of peanut butter, stirring frequently, about 25 minutes. Remove from heat. Stir in whipping cream, rum, and vanilla (mixture will be sticky and candy-like). Transfer warm filling to crust, spreading evenly. Cool completely.

DO AHEAD: *Can be made 1 day ahead. Cover loosely and chill.*

Top pie with sliced bananas, covering filling completely.

TOPPING: Stir instant coffee and 1 tablespoon water in small bowl until coffee dissolves. Combine coffee mixture, whipping cream, and sugar in large bowl; beat until peaks form. Spoon coffee whipped cream into pastry bag fitted with large star tip. Pipe whipped cream rosettes decoratively atop pie, covering completely.

DO AHEAD: *Can be made 2 hours ahead. Chill uncovered.*

Peanut Butter and White Chocolate Cream Pie

Here's a killer combination: layers of peanut butter crumble, white chocolate custard, and fresh bananas. The pie needs to chill for at least three hours, so be sure to plan accordingly. **8 servings**

1	**Flaky Pie Crust dough disk (see recipe on page 233)**
1	**cup sifted powdered sugar (sifted, then measured)**
¾	**cup smooth old-fashioned peanut butter**
2½	**teaspoons vanilla extract, divided**
2	**tablespoons Grape-Nuts cereal**
2½	**cups whole milk, divided**
4	**large egg yolks**
¾	**cup sugar**
¼	**cup unbleached all purpose flour**
¼	**cup cornstarch**
6	**ounces high-quality white chocolate (such as Lindt or Perugina), chopped**
2	**ripe bananas, peeled, sliced**
1½	**cups chilled heavy whipping cream, beaten to firm peaks**

Position rack in center of oven and preheat to 375°F. Roll out dough disk on floured surface to 12-inch round. Transfer to 9-inch-diameter glass pie dish. Fold crust edge under; crimp decoratively. Refrigerate 20 minutes.

Line crust with foil; fill with dried beans or pie weights. Bake crust until sides are set, about 15 minutes. Remove foil and beans. Continue to bake until set, pressing gently with back of spoon if crust bubbles, 10 to 12 minutes. Transfer crust to rack and cool completely.

Using fork, mix powdered sugar, peanut butter, and 1 teaspoon vanilla extract in medium bowl until mixture resembles coarse dry crumbs. Place cereal in small bowl. Mix ½ cup peanut butter mixture into cereal; set aside.

Whisk ¼ cup milk, egg yolks, sugar, flour, and cornstarch in another medium bowl to blend. Pour remaining 2¼ cups milk into heavy medium saucepan; bring to simmer. Gradually whisk hot milk into yolk mixture. Return mixture to saucepan. Whisk constantly over medium heat until custard boils and thickens, about 2 minutes. Remove from heat. Add white chocolate and remaining 1½ teaspoons vanilla; whisk until chocolate melts. Cool completely.

Sprinkle ½ cup plain (no cereal) peanut butter mixture over bottom of pie shell. Spoon half of custard filling over. Top with bananas, then remaining plain peanut butter mixture. Spoon remaining custard filling over, mounding in center. Chill pie until cold, about 3 hours.

DO AHEAD: *Can be made 6 hours ahead. Keep chilled.*

Top pie with whipped cream and sprinkle with peanut butter–cereal mixture.

Nectarine–White Chocolate Cream Pie

This no-bake treat is similar in style to a banana cream pie; enjoy it in the summer, when nectarines are ripe—and when you don't want to turn on the oven. To make sure the filling isn't too loose, chill the finished pie at least two hours before serving. **8 servings**

Crust

	Nonstick vegetable oil spray
7	whole graham crackers (about 4 ounces)
½	cup whole almonds
4	ounces high-quality white chocolate (such as Lindt or Perugina), chopped
3	tablespoons unsalted butter, cut into 6 pieces
¼	teaspoon salt

Filling

2⅓	cups whole milk
½	vanilla bean, split in half lengthwise
¼	cup cornstarch
¼	cup sugar
3	large egg yolks
	Pinch of salt
5	ounces high-quality white chocolate (such as Lindt or Perugina), chopped
1	tablespoon amaretto or other almond liqueur
2	ripe nectarines or peaches, pitted, sliced

Topping

1	cup chilled heavy whipping cream
2	tablespoons sugar
	White chocolate shavings or curls (optional)
	Nectarine or peach slices (optional)

CRUST: Spray 9-inch-diameter glass pie dish with nonstick spray. Finely grind graham crackers and almonds in processor. Combine white chocolate, butter, and salt in heavy small saucepan. Stir constantly over low heat until melted and smooth. Pour chocolate mixture over crumbs in processor and blend in using on/off turns. Press crumb mixture evenly over bottom and up sides of pie dish. Chill until cold and set.

FILLING: Bring milk and vanilla bean to simmer in heavy medium saucepan over medium heat; remove from heat. Whisk cornstarch, sugar, egg yolks, and salt in large bowl to blend. Gradually whisk in hot milk mixture; return to saucepan and whisk over medium-high heat until pudding thickens and boils, 3 to 4 minutes. Remove from heat. Add white chocolate and amaretto; whisk until chocolate is melted and pudding is smooth. Chill filling uncovered until cold, then cover and keep chilled.

DO AHEAD: *Crust and filling can be made 1 day ahead. Cover separately and keep chilled.*

Stir pudding until smooth; remove vanilla bean. Spoon half of pudding into crust. Arrange nectarines over pudding, then top nectarines with remaining pudding. Refrigerate until pie is set, about 2 hours.

TOPPING: Using electric mixer, beat cream and sugar in large bowl until soft peaks form. Spread whipped cream decoratively over pie. Garnish pie with chocolate shavings and nectarine slices, if desired, and serve.

Coffee-Coconut Tart

This cream pie is baked in a tart shell and every element of it is packed with flavor. The crust is amped up with coffee and flaked coconut, the coffee pudding filling gets a tropical hit from cream of coconut, and the topping is a coconut-scented whipped cream decorated with toasted coconut. Sweetened cream of coconut is found in the liquor or mixers section of most supermarkets.

8 servings

Crust
¾	cup unbleached all purpose flour
½	cup sweetened flaked coconut, toasted, cooled
7	tablespoons chilled unsalted butter, cut into ½-inch cubes
⅓	cup powdered sugar
1	teaspoon instant coffee crystals
¼	teaspoon salt

Filling
¼	cup sugar
6¼	teaspoons instant coffee crystals
2	tablespoons cornstarch
½	cup plus 2 tablespoons heavy whipping cream
6	tablespoons sweetened cream of coconut (such as Coco Reál or Coco López)
4	large egg yolks
½	teaspoon vanilla extract

Topping
¾	cup chilled heavy whipping cream
¼	cup sweetened cream of coconut (such as Coco Reál or Coco López)
2	tablespoons powdered sugar
	Sweetened flaked coconut, toasted

Technique Tip: Give It a Whirl
Sweetened coconut milk sometimes separates in the can. To get the creamy consistency you want for this recipe, mix the cream of coconut in the blender before measuring it.

CRUST: Preheat oven to 350°F. Combine flour, coconut, butter, powdered sugar, coffee crystals, and salt in processor. Process until moist clumps form, about 1 minute. Press dough onto bottom and up sides of 9-inch-diameter tart pan with removable bottom. Freeze crust until firm, about 10 minutes.

Place crust on baking sheet. Pierce all over with fork. Bake crust until golden brown, about 25 minutes. Cool.

FILLING: Whisk sugar, coffee crystals, and cornstarch in heavy medium saucepan until no cornstarch lumps remain. Gradually whisk in whipping cream, then cream of coconut (coffee crystals will not dissolve completely). Mix in egg yolks. Whisk over medium heat until mixture thickens and boils, about 8 minutes. Remove from heat. Cool in pan, whisking occasionally. Whisk in vanilla. Spread filling in crust. Chill uncovered until cold, about 2 hours.

DO AHEAD: *Can be made 1 day ahead. Cover and keep chilled.*

TOPPING: Beat whipping cream, cream of coconut, and powdered sugar in medium bowl until firm peaks form. Spoon into pastry bag fitted with medium star tip. Pipe whipped cream mixture decoratively over filling. Sprinkle with toasted flaked coconut.

DO AHEAD: *Can be made 2 hours ahead. Chill uncovered.*

Cut into wedges. Serve cold.

Chilled Lime-Coconut Pie with Macadamia-Coconut Crust

The combination of lime, coconut, and macadamia nuts gives this pie a tropical flavor. You can find sweetened cream of coconut in the liquor or mixers section of most supermarkets. **8 to 10 servings**

Crust

35	vanilla wafer cookies (about 5 ounces)
1/3	cup dry-roasted macadamia nuts
1/3	cup sweetened flaked coconut
1/4	cup (1/2 stick) unsalted butter, melted

Filling

1	15-ounce can sweetened cream of coconut (such as Coco Reál or Coco López)
2/3	cup plain low-fat yogurt
1/2	cup fresh lime juice
2	teaspoons finely grated lime peel
3	tablespoons cold water
2	teaspoons unflavored gelatin

Topping

3/4	cup chilled heavy whipping cream
2	tablespoons powdered sugar
1	lime, thinly sliced into rounds
	Additional powdered sugar (optional)

CRUST: Finely grind cookies and nuts in processor. Transfer to medium bowl. Mix in coconut. Add melted butter and stir until blended. Press crumb mixture onto bottom and up sides of 9-inch-diameter metal or glass pie dish. Freeze 30 minutes.

DO AHEAD: *Can be made 1 week ahead. Cover and keep frozen.*

Preheat oven to 350°F. Bake crust until golden, about 20 minutes. Cool completely.

FILLING: Whisk cream of coconut, yogurt, lime juice, and lime peel to blend in 4-cup measuring cup or large bowl.

Pour 3 tablespoons cold water into small metal bowl. Sprinkle gelatin over. Let stand until gelatin softens, about 10 minutes. Set bowl in small skillet of barely simmering water; whisk until gelatin dissolves, about 1 minute. Whisk into coconut mixture and pour into crust (filling will reach top of crust). Chill pie until filling is set, about 4 hours.

DO AHEAD: *Can be made 1 day ahead. Cover and keep chilled.*

TOPPING: Beat cream and 2 tablespoons powdered sugar in medium bowl until stiff peaks form. Transfer to pastry bag fitted with large star tip. Pipe whipped cream around edge of pie. Dip lime rounds into additional powdered sugar, if desired, and arrange around top edge or in center of pie.

Apricot and Cherry Crostata

Folding the crust around the filling gives this tart a beautifully rustic look. Serve with scoops of ice cream or frozen yogurt, or with a little slightly sweetened whipped cream. **6 servings**

Crust

1	**cup unbleached all purpose flour**
⅛	**teaspoon sugar**
	Pinch of salt
6	**tablespoons (¾ stick) chilled unsalted butter, cut into ½-inch cubes**
2	**tablespoons (or more) ice water**

Filling

2	**tablespoons unbleached all purpose flour**
2	**teaspoons plus 4½ tablespoons sugar, divided**
8	**large apricots, halved, pitted**
1	**cup pitted fresh cherries (about 6 ounces) or frozen, thawed**
2	**tablespoons (¼ stick) unsalted butter, melted, cooled**
	Vanilla ice cream or frozen yogurt

CRUST: Stir flour, sugar, and salt in bowl to blend. Add butter; rub in with fingertips until coarse meal forms. Add 2 tablespoons ice water and stir until moist clumps form, adding more ice water by teaspoonfuls if dough is dry. Gather dough into ball; flatten into disk. Wrap in plastic and chill 1 hour.

DO AHEAD: *Can be made 1 day ahead. Keep chilled. Let stand at room temperature 20 minutes to soften slightly before rolling out.*

Preheat oven to 400°F. Line baking sheet with parchment paper. Roll out dough disk on floured surface to 11-inch round. Transfer to prepared baking sheet.

FILLING: Mix flour and 2 teaspoons sugar in bowl. Sprinkle over crust, leaving 1½-inch plain border. Place apricots cut side down on crust, placing close together and leaving 1½-inch plain border at outer edge. Scatter cherries over apricots [1]. Top with 4 tablespoons sugar. Fold pastry edges up around apricots, pressing against apricots to form scalloped border [2]. Brush crust with butter; sprinkle with remaining ½ tablespoon sugar.

Bake until crust is golden and fruit is tender (some juices from fruit will leak onto parchment), about 1 hour. Remove from oven. Using pastry brush, brush tart with juices on parchment. Gently slide parchment with tart onto rack. Carefully run long knife under tart to loosen (crust is fragile). Cool on parchment until lukewarm. Slide 9-inch-diameter tart pan bottom under tart; use as aid to transfer tart to platter. Serve with ice cream or frozen yogurt.

Apricot and Raspberry Croustade with Sour Cream Crust and Topping

Sour cream enriches the pastry while also giving it elasticity. Scattering additional fresh raspberries over the top of the baked croustade makes for a stunning presentation. **8 servings**

Crust

1½	cups unbleached all purpose flour
⅓	cup powdered sugar
½	teaspoon salt
½	cup (1 stick) chilled unsalted butter, cut into ½-inch cubes
¼	cup chilled sour cream

Filling

1	pound ripe apricots (6 to 8), halved, pitted
⅓	cup apricot preserves
1	rounded teaspoon unbleached all purpose flour
8	ounces raspberries
	Whole milk
1	tablespoon sugar

Topping

1	cup sour cream
2	tablespoons sugar

CRUST: Blend flour, powdered sugar, and salt in processor. Add butter; using on/off turns, process until mixture resembles coarse meal. Add sour cream; using on/off turns, blend until moist clumps form. Gather dough into ball; flatten into disk. Wrap in plastic and chill 30 minutes.

DO AHEAD: *Can be made 1 day ahead. Keep chilled. Let stand at room temperature 20 minutes to soften slightly before rolling out.*

Preheat oven to 400°F. Roll out dough disk between 2 sheets of lightly floured parchment paper, lifting parchment and replacing it occasionally if paper wrinkles, forming 13-inch round. Remove top sheet of parchment. Slide bottom sheet of parchment with dough onto heavy rimless cookie sheet.

FILLING: Gently stir apricots, preserves, and flour in large bowl until apricots are lightly coated. Carefully fold in raspberries. Spoon filling onto center of dough. Arrange apricots, alternating cut side up and cut side down, leaving 1½- to 2-inch plain border at outer edge. Using parchment as aid, fold pastry edges up around filling, pressing gently to seal. Brush crust lightly with milk and sprinkle with sugar. Bake until crust is golden brown, fruit is tender, and juices bubble thickly in center (some juices from fruit will leak onto parchment paper), about 55 minutes. Cool until warm.

TOPPING: Stir sour cream and sugar in small bowl to blend. Carefully run long knife under tart to loosen (crust is fragile). Using tart pan bottom of 9-inch-diameter tart pan as aid, carefully transfer tart to platter. Serve with sweetened sour cream.

Apple-Cranberry Croustade

This version of the French free-form tart combines the flavors of fall. Raw sugar, also called turbinado or demerara sugar, has large golden granules that make for an attractive, sparkling-sweet crust. Dried cherries or raisins can be substituted for the dried cranberries in the topping. Serve with scoops of vanilla ice cream. **8 servings**

Crust

1½	cups unbleached all purpose flour
⅓	cup powdered sugar
½	teaspoon salt
½	cup (1 stick) chilled unsalted butter, cut into ½-inch cubes
¼	cup chilled sour cream

Filling

3	tablespoons unsalted butter
8	small Granny Smith apples (about 3 pounds), peeled, cored, each cut into 12 wedges
⅓	cup sugar
1	teaspoon ground cardamom
1	teaspoon ground cinnamon
½	cup dried cranberries
	Whole milk
2	tablespoons raw sugar

> ### Recipe Tip: Croustade, Crostata
> The French call this free-form tart a croustade, the Italians a crostata, but it's generally the same delicious dessert. A sheet or round of pastry is filled with fruit and/or nuts, with an inch or two of the crust edges folded up over the filling, creating a rustic, homey look.

CRUST: Combine flour, powdered sugar, and salt in food processor. Add butter; using on/off turns, process until mixture resembles coarse meal. Add sour cream; using on/off turns, process until moist clumps form. Gather dough into ball; flatten into disk. Wrap in plastic and chill 30 minutes.

DO AHEAD: *Can be made 1 day ahead. Keep chilled. Let stand at room temperature 20 minutes to soften slightly before rolling out.*

FILLING: Melt butter in heavy large skillet over medium-high heat. Add apples and sprinkle with ⅓ cup sugar. Cook until apples are tender and golden brown, about 12 minutes. Sprinkle with cardamom and cinnamon; mix in cranberries. Set aside to cool.

DO AHEAD: *Can be made up to 1 day ahead. Cover and chill.*

Preheat oven to 400°F. Roll out dough disk between 2 sheets of lightly floured parchment paper, lifting parchment and replacing it occasionally if paper wrinkles, to form 13-inch round. Remove top sheet of parchment. Slide bottom sheet of parchment with dough onto heavy rimless cookie sheet. Spoon filling onto center of dough, spreading toward edges and leaving 1½- to 2-inch plain border. Using parchment as aid, fold border over filling. Brush crust border with milk. Sprinkle crust border and apples with raw sugar.

Bake until crust begins to brown, about 15 minutes. Reduce heat to 375°F. Continue baking until crust is golden brown and filling is heated through, about 20 minutes longer. Cool until warm. Run thin knife under tart to loosen from parchment paper. Slide 10-inch-diameter bottom of tart pan with removable sides under tart and use as aid to transfer tart to plate.

Pear and Medjool Date Croustade

"King of Dates" and "Diamond of Dates" are just two of the nicknames for the Medjool date. Both are fitting for this large, rich, moist date that was once reserved for Moroccan royalty. Here, the dates are paired with pears and spices in a rustic, comforting dessert with an exotic flare. Raw sugar is available at most supermarkets and at natural foods stores. **8 servings**

Crust

1⅓	cups unbleached all purpose flour
½	cup powdered sugar
⅓	cup cornmeal
¾	teaspoon salt
10	tablespoons (1¼ sticks) chilled unsalted butter, cut into ½-inch cubes
1	chilled large egg, beaten to blend, divided

Filling

2	pounds (about 3 large) ripe Anjou pears, peeled, cored, each cut into 8 wedges
3	tablespoons sugar
1	tablespoon unbleached all purpose flour
½	teaspoon ground cardamom
½	teaspoon ground cinnamon
⅛	teaspoon ground cloves
7	large Medjool dates, pitted, torn into ¼- to ½-inch-wide strips
1½	teaspoons raw sugar

CRUST: Blend flour, powdered sugar, cornmeal, and salt in processor. Add butter; using on/off turns, process until mixture resembles coarse meal. Add all but 2 tablespoons egg (reserved for glaze); using on/off turns, process until moist clumps form. Gather dough into ball; flatten into disk. Wrap in plastic and chill 30 minutes.

DO AHEAD: *Can be made 1 day ahead. Keep chilled. Let stand at room temperature 20 minutes to soften slightly before rolling out.*

FILLING: Preheat oven to 375°F. Toss pear wedges with sugar, flour, cardamom, cinnamon, and cloves in large bowl. Roll out dough disk between 2 sheets of lightly floured parchment paper, lifting parchment and replacing it occasionally if paper wrinkles, to form 13- to 14-inch round. Slide crust with parchment onto rimless baking sheet; remove top layer of parchment. Arrange ⅔ of pear mixture over crust, leaving about 2-inch plain border. Arrange date strips amongst pears. Top with remaining pear slices. Using parchment as aid, fold edges of crust up over pear mixture, creating border. Brush crust edge with some of remaining egg and sprinkle crust with raw sugar.

Bake until crust is golden brown and filling bubbles thickly in center, about 1 hour. Cool until warm. Using 10-inch-diameter bottom of tart pan as aid, slide croustade onto serving platter.

Honey-Roasted Peach Croustade with Almonds and Honey-Sweetened Greek Yogurt

This rustic tart is rich with flavor: The peaches are roasted prior to topping the crust, and the almonds are chopped and rolled into the surface of the dough so that they become toasted to their fragrant and colorful best while baking. Thick, honey-sweetened Greek-style yogurt is a great alternative to vanilla ice cream. Greek-style yogurt can be found at some supermarkets and at Trader Joe's and other specialty foods stores. If unavailable, use regular plain yogurt. The topping will be thinner, but just as tasty. **8 servings**

Peaches

1½	pounds small ripe yellow peaches (about 6), unpeeled, quartered, pitted
2	tablespoons honey
2	tablespoons (packed) golden brown sugar

Crust

⅔	cup slivered almonds
1	cup unbleached all purpose flour
¼	cup sugar
½	teaspoon salt
7	tablespoons chilled unsalted butter, cut into ½-inch cubes
1	large egg yolk
2	tablespoons honey

Honey Yogurt

1½	cups plain Greek-style yogurt
3	tablespoons honey

PEACHES: Preheat oven to 400°F. Line heavy large baking sheet with foil. Arrange peaches, skin side down, on foil. Drizzle with honey and sprinkle with brown sugar. Roast peaches until just tender and beginning to brown, about 20 minutes. Using offset spatula, turn peaches and continue roasting until fruit is very tender and honey begins to turn dark brown on edges of pan, about 12 minutes longer. Cool peaches on foil-lined sheet.

CRUST: Using on/off turns, coarsely chop almonds in processor. Transfer nuts to bowl (do not wash processor). Blend flour, sugar, and salt in processor. Add butter; using on/off turns, process until mixture resembles coarse meal. Drop egg yolk through feed tube; using on/off turns, blend just until moist clumps form. Gather dough into ball; flatten into disk. Wrap in plastic and freeze 30 minutes.

DO AHEAD: *Can be made 1 day ahead. Keep chilled. Let stand at room temperature 20 minutes to soften slightly before rolling out.*

Position rack in top third of oven and preheat to 375°F. Roll out dough disk between 2 floured sheets of parchment paper to 10-inch round, sprinkling with additional flour as necessary. Remove top sheet of parchment. Sprinkle dough evenly with ½ cup chopped almonds. Replace parchment atop crust and roll to 11-inch round, embedding nuts into dough. Invert crust and parchment onto heavy baking sheet, nut side down. Remove top sheet of parchment. Arrange peaches over center of crust in concentric circles, alternating skin side up and skin side down and leaving 1½- to 2-inch plain border. Using parchment as aid, fold outer edge of crust over edges of peaches. Drizzle peaches with honey. Sprinkle with remaining chopped almonds.

Bake until crust is golden brown, about 30 minutes. Cool 20 minutes. Slide metal spatula under croustade to loosen from parchment. Using tart pan bottom from 11-inch-diameter tart pan as aid, carefully transfer croustade to platter.

HONEY YOGURT: Mix yogurt and honey in small bowl to blend.

Cut croustade into wedges and serve warm, passing honey yogurt separately.

Dark Chocolate and Pine Nut Crostata

Although a crostata is generally a rustic free-form tart, here the Italian moniker is used to suggest the dessert's thin crispness. Honey enhances the deep chocolate filling of this rich candy-bar-like tart. Look for 70% cacao chocolate at specialty foods stores, where it is sometimes called extra-bitter chocolate.

8 servings

Crust

1²/₃	cups unbleached all purpose flour
1	cup powdered sugar
½	teaspoon salt
6	tablespoons (¾ stick) unsalted butter, cut into ½-inch cubes, room temperature
2	large egg yolks
1	large egg

Filling

10	ounces bittersweet chocolate (70% cacao), chopped
2	cups heavy whipping cream
¼	cup honey
¼	cup pine nuts, toasted
	Lightly sweetened whipped cream

CRUST: Blend flour, powdered sugar, and salt in processor. Add butter, egg yolks, and whole egg. Using on/off turns, blend until moist clumps form. Gather dough into ball; flatten into disk. Wrap in plastic and chill 1 hour.

DO AHEAD: *Can be made 1 day ahead. Keep chilled. Let stand at room temperature 20 minutes to soften slightly before rolling out.*

Roll out dough disk on lightly floured surface to 14-inch round. Transfer to 10-inch-diameter tart pan with removable bottom. Press onto bottom and up sides of pan. Cut off all but ½-inch dough overhang. Fold overhang in, pressing to form double-thick sides extending ¼ inch above rim. Chill crust 30 minutes.

Preheat oven to 375°F. Bake crust 5 minutes. Using back of fork, press crust up sides of pan if slipping. Bake until golden, pressing up sides and piercing with fork if crust bubbles, about 25 minutes longer. Cool crust completely.

FILLING: Place chocolate in medium bowl. Bring cream to simmer in saucepan. Pour cream over chocolate; whisk until smooth. Whisk in honey. Pour filling into crust. Chill until set, at least 2 hours and up to 1 day.

Sprinkle tart with pine nuts. Serve with lightly sweetened whipped cream.

 # Tarte Tatin

This classic dessert was created by the Tatin sisters of France's Loire Valley. Legend has it that in trying to repair a baking error, they ended up with the renowned upside-down tart. A tarte Tatin is sometimes made with puff pastry; this version has a rich buttery crust that's easy to make. Red Delicious apples are a good choice here, because they hold their shape when cooked for long periods of time. **8 servings**

Crust

1½	cups unbleached all purpose flour
¼	cup sugar
1	teaspoon ground cinnamon
¾	teaspoon salt
10	tablespoons (1¼ sticks) chilled unsalted butter, cut into ½-inch cubes
2	large chilled egg yolks

Filling

¼	cup (½ stick) unsalted butter
¾	cup sugar
10	small Red Delicious apples (about 3½ pounds), peeled, halved, cored

Cinnamon Whipped Cream

1	cup chilled heavy whipping cream
2	tablespoons sugar
¼	teaspoon ground cinnamon

CRUST: Blend flour, sugar, cinnamon, and salt in processor. Add butter; using on/off turns, cut in until mixture resembles coarse meal. Add egg yolks and blend until moist clumps form. Gather into ball; flatten into disk. Wrap in plastic and chill 30 minutes.

DO AHEAD: *Can be made 1 day ahead. Keep chilled. Let stand at room temperature 20 minutes to soften slightly before rolling out.*

FILLING: Melt butter in heavy 9½-inch-diameter ovenproof skillet (preferably cast-iron) over medium heat. Add sugar; stir until melted and mixture is smooth and golden brown, about 5 minutes. Remove skillet from heat. Arrange half of apple halves, rounded side down, over caramel. Top with remaining apples, rounded side up, covering apples on bottom and filling pan completely. Cover and cook over medium-low heat until apples on bottom are almost tender, about 25 minutes. Uncover skillet. Increase heat to medium and simmer until apples are very tender and syrup is thick and deep amber color and thinly coats bottom of pan, shaking skillet gently to prevent sticking and to distribute syrup evenly, about 20 minutes longer. Remove from heat.

Preheat oven to 400°F. Roll out dough disk between 2 sheets of parchment paper to 9½-inch round. Remove top sheet of parchment. Using bottom sheet of parchment as aid, invert dough round onto hot apples; remove parchment and pierce dough several times with knife to allow steam to escape. Bake tart until crust is golden brown, about 20 minutes. Remove from heat. Cool 5 minutes.

CINNAMON WHIPPED CREAM: Using electric mixer, beat cream, sugar, and cinnamon in large bowl until very thick and soft peaks form.

Place flat platter atop tart and pan. Using oven mitts as aid, grasp platter and pan together and quickly turn over, releasing tart onto platter. Carefully remove pan. Replace any apples that may have become dislodged. Serve tart warm or at room temperature with cinnamon whipped cream.

♥♥♥ Apple and Pomegranate Tarte Tatin

The classic French upside-down apple tart gets an exotic touch from allspice and pomegranate syrup that's made from reduced pomegranate juice. A portion of the syrup is added to the caramelizing apples, while the rest is served alongside with vanilla ice cream. Any leftover syrup would be delicious served with Greek yogurt. **8 servings**

Crust
1   **cup unbleached all purpose flour**
2   **tablespoons sugar**
¼   **teaspoon salt**
6   **tablespoons (¾ stick) chilled unsalted butter, cut into ½-inch cubes**
¼   **cup crème fraîche or sour cream**

Filling
3   **cups pomegranate juice**
¼   **cup (½ stick) unsalted butter, room temperature**
¾   **cup sugar**
7   **medium Golden Delicious apples (about 3¼ pounds), peeled, quartered, cored**
⅛   **teaspoon ground allspice**
       Large pinch of coarse kosher salt

       Vanilla ice cream

CRUST: Blend flour, sugar, and salt in processor. Add butter; using on/off turns, blend until coarse meal forms. Add crème fraîche; using on/off turns, blend until moist clumps form. Gather dough into ball; flatten into disk. Wrap in plastic and chill 1 hour. Roll out dough disk on lightly floured surface to 11-inch round. Slide onto rimless baking sheet. Cover and chill.

FILLING: Boil pomegranate juice in heavy large saucepan until reduced to scant 1 cup syrup, about 15 minutes.

DO AHEAD: *Pomegranate syrup and crust can be made 1 day ahead. Cover syrup and chill. Keep crust chilled.*

Position rack in center of oven and preheat to 400°F. Spread room-temperature butter evenly over bottom and up sides of heavy 10-inch-diameter ovenproof skillet. Sprinkle sugar evenly over butter. Cook over medium heat without stirring until mixture bubbles all over, about 3 minutes. Remove from heat. Stand apple quarters on 1 end around edge of skillet, leaning 1 cut side against pan side and fitting snugly. Stand as many apples in center as will fit. Sprinkle apples with allspice and coarse salt.

Cook apples over medium-high heat until thick, deep-amber syrup bubbles up, shaking skillet gently to prevent sticking and to distribute syrup evenly, adding any remaining apples as space permits (apples will shrink as they cook), about 20 minutes. Pour ¼ cup pomegranate syrup over (mixture will bubble). Cook until juices thicken, 4 to 5 minutes (syrup will be deep amber). Remove from heat.

Using spatula, press apples gently toward center, then down to compact. Slide crust over apples. Tuck crust down around apples at edge of skillet. Cut 4 slits in top for steam to escape.

Bake tart until crust is brown and juices at edge are thick and dark scarlet in color, 25 to 30 minutes. Remove skillet from oven; let stand 1 minute.

Place large plate over skillet. Using oven mitts and holding plate and skillet firmly together, quickly invert tart onto plate. Carefully lift off skillet. Return any apples to tart that may be stuck in skillet. Let cool at least 15 minutes. Serve tarte Tatin warm or at room temperature with vanilla ice cream and drizzles of remaining pomegranate syrup.

♟♟♟ Plum Tarte Tatin

This version of the classic features plums instead of apples—think of it as a tarte Tatin for the summer. The recipe includes orange-flavored crème fraîche, but the dessert would be equally delicious served with vanilla ice cream or whipped cream. **6 servings**

1	**cup crème fraîche**
1	**teaspoon finely grated orange peel**
1	**sheet frozen puff pastry (half of 17.3-ounce package), thawed**
2¼	**pounds sweet firm red plums (such as Burgundies or Satsumas), halved, pitted**
2	**tablespoons plus ⅔ cup sugar**
1	**tablespoon fresh lemon juice**
1½	**teaspoons finely grated lemon peel**
⅛	**teaspoon ground nutmeg**
½	**vanilla bean, split lengthwise**
6	**tablespoons (¾ stick) unsalted butter**

Whisk crème fraîche and orange peel in small bowl. Cover; chill. Roll out pastry on lightly floured surface to 10-inch square; trim corners to create circle. Place on plate.

DO AHEAD: *Crème fraîche and crust can be made 1 day ahead. Cover separately and chill.*

Place plums, 2 tablespoons sugar, lemon juice, lemon peel, and nutmeg in large bowl. Scrape in seeds from vanilla bean (reserve bean for another use). Toss to coat. Let stand 30 minutes, tossing occasionally.

Melt butter in heavy 9-inch-diameter ovenproof skillet over medium heat. Sprinkle remaining ⅔ cup sugar evenly over melted butter. Tightly arrange plums, cut side up, in concentric circles in skillet (plums will appear slightly uneven but will soften while cooking, creating even layer). Drizzle accumulated juices from bowl over top. Cook over medium heat, shaking skillet gently to prevent sticking and to distribute syrup evenly. Continue cooking until syrup turns deep red, pressing plums slightly to form compact layer, about 35 minutes. Remove skillet from heat; cool 10 minutes.

Preheat oven to 400°F. Slide crust atop plums in skillet. Tuck crust edges down around plums at edge of skillet. Cut several slits in crust to allow steam to escape. Bake until golden brown, about 30 minutes. Cool tart completely in skillet.

Rewarm in skillet set over high heat to loosen, about 3 minutes. Place large platter over skillet. Using oven mitts, hold skillet and platter together and quickly invert, allowing tart to settle onto platter. Slowly lift off skillet. Let stand at least 30 minutes and up to 4 hours at room temperature. Serve with orange crème fraîche.

Spiced Apple Turnovers

A sweet treat that's like an apple pie, only portable. Cutting slits in each turnover before baking allows steam to escape. Be certain that the edges of the dough are sealed completely so that the filling doesn't escape out the sides. **Makes 6**

Pastry

1½	cups unbleached all purpose flour
1	teaspoon sugar
¼	teaspoon salt
½	cup (1 stick) chilled unsalted butter, cut into ½-inch cubes
4	tablespoons (or more) ice water

Filling

1½	pounds Golden Delicious apples, peeled, cored, cut into ½-inch pieces
⅓	cup sugar
2	tablespoons (packed) dried currants
1	teaspoon brandy
½	teaspoon ground cinnamon
½	teaspoon vanilla extract
¼	teaspoon finely grated lemon peel
¼	teaspoon finely grated orange peel
¼	teaspoon ground nutmeg
⅛	teaspoon ground cloves
6	teaspoons plus 2 tablespoons unsalted butter
	Additional sugar

PASTRY: Whisk flour, sugar, and salt in large bowl. Add butter and rub in with fingertips until mixture resembles coarse meal. Add 4 tablespoons ice water; using fork, stir until small moist clumps form, adding more ice water by teaspoonfuls if dough is dry. Transfer dough to floured surface; divide into 6 equal pieces. Form each piece into ball; flatten each into disk. Wrap separately in plastic and chill 1 hour.

DO AHEAD: *Can be made 1 day ahead. Keep chilled. Let stand at room temperature 10 minutes to soften slightly before rolling out.*

Line 2 heavy large baking sheets with parchment paper. Roll out each dough disk on floured work surface to 8-inch round. Transfer rounds to prepared baking sheets. Cover and refrigerate 30 minutes.

FILLING: Mix apples, sugar, currants, brandy, cinnamon, vanilla, lemon peel, orange peel, nutmeg, and cloves in large bowl. Cover and let stand 30 minutes to blend flavors.

Preheat oven to 400°F. Spoon ½ cup apple mixture onto bottom half of 1 pastry round, leaving ¾-inch plain border around edges. Dot filling with 1 teaspoon butter. Lightly brush edges with water. Fold top half of dough over filling to enclose completely. Gently press edges together to seal. Lightly brush edge with more water and fold edge inward. Using fork, gently press edge to seal. Repeat with remaining pastry rounds, filling, and butter.

Melt remaining 2 tablespoons butter in small saucepan. Using small sharp knife, cut 3 slits in top of each turnover to allow steam to escape. Brush butter over turnovers and sprinkle with additional sugar.

Bake turnovers until golden brown, about 30 minutes. Cool slightly. Transfer to plates and serve warm.

Chaussons aux Pommes (French Apple Turnovers)

To make this French version of the apple turnover, look for all-butter frozen puff pastry, available in the freezer section of specialty foods stores and at Trader Joe's markets. **Makes 8**

¾   **pound Granny Smith apples**
¾   **pound Golden Delicious apples**
¼   **cup water**
3   **tablespoons sugar**
¾   **teaspoon fresh lemon juice**
1   **14- to 16-ounce package all-butter frozen puff pastry**
      (1 or 2 sheets, depending on brand), thawed
1   **large egg, beaten to blend**
      Superfine sugar (optional)

Peel, core, and cut apples into 1-inch cubes (about 4 cups). Place apples in medium saucepan; add ¼ cup water, sugar, and lemon juice. Bring to boil, stirring occasionally until sugar dissolves. Cover; reduce heat to medium-low and simmer until apples are very tender, stirring frequently, about 12 minutes. Remove from heat. Gently mash apples with fork or potato masher until mixture is very soft but still chunky. Cool completely.

DO AHEAD: *Can be made 2 days ahead. Cover and chill.*

Position 1 rack in top third and 1 rack in bottom third of oven and preheat to 400°F. Line 2 baking sheets with parchment paper.

If using 14-ounce package (1 sheet) of pastry, roll out on lightly floured surface to 15-inch square. If using 16-ounce package (2 sheets), stack sheets together and roll out on lightly floured surface to 15-inch square. Cut pastry into nine 5-inch squares.

Place 1 generous tablespoon filling in center of each of 8 squares (reserve remaining square for another use). Lightly brush edges of 1 pastry with beaten egg. Fold half of pastry square over filling, forming triangle. Press and pinch pastry edges with fingertips to seal tightly. Lightly brush pastry with beaten egg. Sprinkle lightly with superfine sugar, if desired. Repeat with remaining pastry squares. Using thin, sharp knife, make 3 small slits on top of each triangle to allow steam to escape. Place triangles on prepared baking sheets. Refrigerate until firm, about 15 minutes.

Bake turnovers until beginning to color, about 15 minutes. Reverse baking sheets from top to bottom. Reduce oven temperature to 350°F; continue baking until turnovers are firm and golden, 10 to 15 minutes longer. Cool at least 15 minutes before serving. Serve warm or at room temperature.

Pear and Amaretti Turnovers

These clever "turnovers" are actually pear-shaped pastries—each with an almond-sliver stem—filled with ripe, brandy-soaked pear slices and crushed almond-flavored amaretti cookies. The cookies are available at some supermarkets and at Italian markets. Serve the turnovers with grapes, apples, and figs alongside. **Makes 6**

2   ripe Bartlett pears (about 7 ounces each), peeled, halved
       lengthwise, cored, cut into ⅛- to ¼-inch-thick slices
2   tablespoons sugar
2   tablespoons brandy
1   17.3-ounce package frozen puff pastry (2 sheets), thawed
6   tablespoons crushed amaretti cookies (Italian macaroons; from
       about 10 cookies)
6   blanched almond slivers
1   large egg, beaten to blend

Combine pears, sugar, and brandy in large bowl. Toss to coat.

Draw one 4x4-inch pear shape and one 4½x4½-inch pear shape on parchment paper. Using scissors, cut out shapes.

Line baking sheet with parchment paper. Roll out 1 pastry sheet on lightly floured surface to 12-inch square. Using 4x4-inch parchment template, cut out 6 pear shapes from pastry. Transfer pear-shaped pastries to baking sheet, spacing evenly.

Sprinkle half of crushed cookies over pastries, leaving ½-inch plain border. Arrange pear slices over crushed cookies. Sprinkle remaining cookies over pears.

Roll out second pastry sheet on lightly floured surface to 14½-inch square. Using 4½x4½-inch parchment template, cut out 6 pear shapes from pastry. Brush plain edges of crusts on baking sheet with water. Arrange larger pear-shaped pastries atop pears [1], pressing pastry edges together to adhere. Press edges with fork to seal [2]. Using skewer, poke small hole in top of each turnover to allow steam to escape. Press 1 almond sliver in tip of each turnover to represent stem. Cover and refrigerate 20 minutes.

Preheat oven to 375°F. Brush turnovers with egg. Bake until golden brown, about 30 minutes. Transfer to rack and cool.

DO AHEAD: *Can be made 8 hours ahead. Store in airtight container at room temperature.*

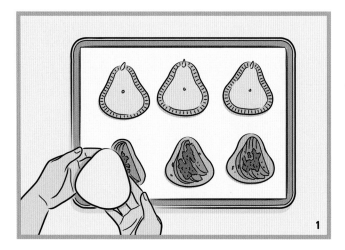

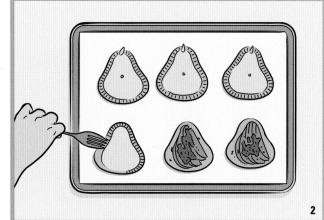

Sweet-and-Sour Cherry Turnovers with Goat Cheese Cream

Fresh sour cherries are not only more fragile than sweet ones, but they also have a very short season, which means they can be hard to find. Frozen sour cherries can be found online at apples-cherries.com. If you can't locate them, just double the amount of sweet cherries and increase the lemon juice to 1½ tablespoons. Raw sugar, also called turbinado or demerara sugar, is available at most supermarkets and at natural foods stores. **Makes 6**

Filling

1½	cups pitted fresh dark sweet cherries or frozen dark sweet cherries, thawed
1½	cups pitted fresh sour cherries or frozen sour cherries, thawed
¼	cup sugar
2	teaspoons cornstarch
1	teaspoon fresh lemon juice
½	teaspoon vanilla extract

Goat Cheese Cream

1½	cups chilled heavy whipping cream
3	ounces soft fresh goat cheese, crumbled
¼	cup powdered sugar
1	2-inch piece vanilla bean, split lengthwise

Turnovers

1	17.3-ounce package frozen puff pastry (2 sheets), thawed
1	large egg, beaten to blend
2	tablespoons raw sugar

FILLING: Combine sweet cherries and sour cherries with sugar, cornstarch, lemon juice, and vanilla in medium saucepan; toss to coat. Let cherry mixture stand 30 minutes at room temperature. Stir gently over medium-high heat until mixture boils and thickens slightly, about 2 minutes. Cool cherry filling completely.

DO AHEAD: *Can be made 1 day ahead. Cover and chill.*

GOAT CHEESE CREAM: Combine heavy cream, goat cheese, and powdered sugar in medium bowl. Scrape in seeds from vanilla bean (reserve bean for another use). Using electric mixer, beat until mixture is smooth and peaks form (do not overbeat or mixture may curdle).

DO AHEAD: *Can be made 6 hours ahead. Cover and chill. Rewhisk just until thick and smooth before using.*

TURNOVERS: Position rack in center of oven and preheat to 375°F. Roll out 1 puff pastry sheet on lightly floured work surface to 11½-inch square. Cut into 4 equal squares. Repeat with second puff pastry sheet.

Arrange 6 pastry squares like diamonds on work surface, spacing apart (reserve remaining 2 squares puff pastry for another use). Place ⅙ of cherry filling in center of lower half of each pastry diamond. Brush edges of pastry with beaten egg. Fold top half of pastry over filling on lower half, forming triangle. Press firmly on pastry edges to adhere, then fold edges over, enclosing filling completely and creating double edges; press with fork to seal.

Place turnovers on large rimmed baking sheet, spacing 2 to 3 inches apart. Using tines of fork, pierce top crust of each turnover in 3 places to allow steam to escape during baking. Brush tops and edges of turnovers with beaten egg; sprinkle with raw sugar.

Bake turnovers until crust is golden and filling is bubbling thickly through steam holes in crust, about 35 minutes. Cool slightly. Serve turnovers warm or at room temperature with goat cheese cream.

Golden Delicious Apple Tart

For this pretty tart, a custardy filling is topped with sautéed apple slices. Golden Delicious apples are a good choice for baking because they retain their shape when cooked. Since this crust gets pressed into the pan instead of being rolled out, it's wonderful for the beginning baker. **8 servings**

Crust

1¼   **cups unbleached all purpose flour**
¼   **cup sugar**
½   **teaspoon salt**
10   **tablespoons (1¼ sticks) chilled unsalted butter, cut into ½-inch cubes**
1   **large egg yolk**
1   **tablespoon (or more) ice water**

Filling

2   **large egg yolks**
6   **tablespoons sugar, divided**
1   **tablespoon cornstarch**
⅓   **cup heavy whipping cream**
⅓   **cup frozen apple juice concentrate, thawed**
3   **tablespoons unsalted butter**
3   **large Golden Delicious apples, peeled, cored, each cut into 16 slices**

CRUST: Whisk flour, sugar, and salt in medium bowl. Add butter; using fingertips, rub in until mixture resembles coarse meal. Whisk egg yolk and 1 tablespoon ice water in small bowl. Add to flour mixture and mix just until moist clumps form, adding more ice water by teaspoonfuls if dough is dry. Gather dough into ball; flatten into disk. Cover with plastic wrap and chill 1 hour.

Break dough into small pieces and scatter over bottom of 9-inch-diameter tart pan with removable bottom. Using fingertips, press dough onto bottom and up sides of pan in even layer. Trim excess dough and reserve. Freeze crust until firm, about 25 minutes.

Preheat oven to 400°F. Line crust with foil; fill with dried beans or pie weights. Bake until sides are set, about 15 minutes. Remove foil and beans. Continue to bake until crust is light golden, piercing bottom with fork if crust bubbles and patching with reserved dough if crust cracks, about 10 minutes longer. Cool crust completely on rack.

FILLING: Whisk egg yolks, 2 tablespoons sugar, and cornstarch in medium bowl to blend. Bring whipping cream and apple juice concentrate to simmer in heavy medium saucepan. Whisk into yolk mixture. Return mixture to saucepan. Whisk over medium heat until mixture boils and thickens, about 2 minutes. Transfer to bowl and cool.

DO AHEAD: *Can be prepared 1 day ahead. Cover crust and store at room temperature; refrigerate filling.*

Preheat oven to 375°F. Melt butter in heavy large skillet over medium heat. Add apples and sauté until tender and light golden, about 10 minutes. Add 3 tablespoons sugar; toss until sugar dissolves and apples are glazed, about 3 minutes. Cool until just warm to touch, about 15 minutes.

Spread cream filling over bottom of crust. Arrange apples in concentric circles atop filling. Bake tart 15 minutes. Sprinkle with remaining 1 tablespoon sugar; bake until filling is set and apples are glazed, about 10 minutes longer. Serve tart slightly warm or at room temperature.

Warm Cinnamon-Apple Tart with Currants

This simple French-style fruit tart is a lifesaver when you need a quick but sophisticated dessert. **4 servings**

2	**tablespoons sugar**
¾	**teaspoon ground cinnamon, divided**
1	**sheet frozen puff pastry (half of 16-ounce package all-butter puff pastry or half of 17.3-ounce package regular puff pastry), thawed**
1	**large egg, beaten to blend**
8	**tablespoons apricot preserves, divided**
1	**Golden Delicious apple (6 ounces), peeled, cored, very thinly sliced**
2	**tablespoons fresh lemon juice**
1½	**tablespoons unsalted butter**
	Dried currants
	Vanilla ice cream

Ingredient Tip: **All-Butter Pastry**

If possible, use all-butter frozen puff pastry, which tastes better than regular frozen puff pastry and doesn't have any of those bad-for-you trans fats. Look for all-butter frozen puff pastry at some supermarkets, specialty foods stores, and restaurant supply stores.

Position rack in center of oven and preheat to 400°F. Mix sugar and ½ teaspoon cinnamon in small bowl. Unfold thawed puff pastry on lightly floured baking sheet. Brush some of egg over 1-inch border of pastry on all sides. Fold 1-inch border over to form raised edge on all sides; press edge to adhere. Using sharp knife, make ½-inch-long cuts all around pastry edge, spacing ½ inch apart. Pierce center of pastry (not edge) all over with fork. Spread 2 tablespoons apricot preserves over center of pastry. Arrange apple slices atop apricot preserves in 3 rows, overlapping apples and fitting tightly together. Brush pastry edge with some of egg. Sprinkle cinnamon-sugar mixture over apples and pastry edge.

Bake tart until apples are tender and pastry is brown, about 30 minutes. Transfer tart to rack.

Meanwhile, mix remaining ¼ teaspoon cinnamon, remaining 6 tablespoons apricot preserves, lemon juice, and butter in small saucepan. Stir apricot sauce over medium heat until melted and hot.

Lightly dab some of apricot sauce over apples. Sprinkle with dried currants. Cut warm tart into 4 squares. Top each square with scoop of vanilla ice cream. Drizzle remaining apricot sauce over ice cream and serve.

Apple Frangipane Tart

Frangipane is a sweet almond mixture that is used as a filling or topping for pastries and cakes. Here, the almond mixture is combined with thinly sliced Golden Delicious apples for a luscious fall treat. Look for almond paste in specialty foods stores and in the baking aisle of most supermarkets.

6 to 8 servings

Crust

1	cup unbleached all purpose flour
1	tablespoon sugar
¼	teaspoon salt
6	tablespoons (¾ stick) chilled unsalted butter, cut into ½-inch cubes
3	tablespoons (or more) ice water

Filling

¼	cup (½ stick) unsalted butter, room temperature
4	ounces almond paste, crumbled
1	large egg
⅓	cup unbleached all purpose flour
2	medium Golden Delicious apples, peeled, quartered, cored, cut into ⅛-inch-thick slices
½	tablespoon sugar
1	tablespoon melted unsalted butter
1	tablespoon warm honey

Ingredient Tip: Almond Paste
Leftover almond paste should be wrapped tightly in plastic and stored in the refrigerator. If it becomes hard, heat the almond paste in the microwave for two or three seconds until soft and pliable.

CRUST: Blend flour, sugar, and salt in processor. Add butter; using on/off turns, cut in until coarse crumbs form. Add 3 tablespoons ice water. Process until small moist clumps form, adding more ice water by teaspoonfuls if dough is dry. Gather dough into ball; flatten into disk. Wrap dough in plastic and chill until cold, about 1 hour.

Roll out dough disk between 2 sheets of plastic wrap to 11-inch round. Remove top sheet of plastic. Using bottom sheet of plastic as aid, invert dough into 9-inch-diameter tart pan with removable bottom. Using plastic wrap, press dough onto bottom and up sides of pan. Remove plastic. Fold dough overhang in; press to form high-standing, double-thick sides. Pierce dough all over with fork. Freeze 30 minutes.

DO AHEAD: *Can be prepared 1 day ahead. Cover and keep frozen.*

Preheat oven to 400°F. Bake crust until golden, about 25 minutes. Cool on rack. Maintain oven temperature.

FILLING: Combine butter and almond paste in processor and blend until smooth. Add egg and process until well blended. Add flour and process just until blended. Spread filling evenly over bottom of crust. Toss apples with sugar in large bowl. Arrange apples in concentric circles atop filling. Brush apples with melted butter.

Place tart on baking sheet. Bake until apples are tender and light golden, about 40 minutes. Transfer tart to rack; cool 15 minutes. Brush apples with honey. Serve warm or at room temperature.

♥♥♥ Red Wine and Pear Brioche Tart

Brioche is an egg-and-butter-enriched light yeast bread. Here, it's used as a wonderful cakey crust for wine-poached pears. The brioche rises for about two hours, allowing plenty of time to poach the pears. If you prefer, poach the pears and reduce the syrup up to one day ahead and keep them covered at cool room temperature. **6 to 8 servings**

Brioche Crust

1½	**cups unbleached all purpose flour**
3	**tablespoons sugar**
2	**teaspoons active dry yeast**
¾	**teaspoon salt**
6	**tablespoons (¾ stick) chilled unsalted butter, cut into ½-inch cubes**
2	**large eggs**
2	**tablespoons whole milk**

Filling and Sauce

1¾	**cups dry red wine**
¾	**cup plus 2 tablespoons sugar**
1¼	**pounds firm but ripe Bosc pears (about 3 medium), peeled, quartered, cored, each quarter cut into 3 wedges**
1	**teaspoon cornstarch**
1	**teaspoon water**
	Crème fraîche or sour cream

BRIOCHE CRUST: Butter 9-inch-diameter springform pan with 2¾-inch-high sides. Blend flour, sugar, yeast, and salt in processor. Add butter; using on/off turns, blend until butter is reduced to pea-size pieces. Add eggs and milk. Using on/off turns, blend until sticky dough forms. Using buttered fingertips, press dough onto bottom of prepared springform pan. Cover with plastic. Let dough rise in warm draft-free area until light and puffy (dough will not double in volume), about 2 hours.

FILLING AND SAUCE: Meanwhile, stir wine and ¾ cup sugar in medium saucepan over medium-high heat until sugar dissolves and mixture boils. Add pears. Reduce heat to medium-low and simmer until pears are tender, about 8 minutes. Cool mixture 30 minutes.

Using slotted spoon, transfer pears to plate. Boil wine syrup in pan until reduced to 1 cup, about 4 minutes. Mix cornstarch and 1 teaspoon water in small bowl; stir into wine syrup. Cook until syrup thickens and boils, whisking occasionally, about 1 minute longer. Set sauce aside.

Position rack in top third of oven; preheat to 400°F. Starting at edge and leaving ½-inch plain border, arrange pear slices close together in concentric circles atop dough. Sprinkle pears and dough edge with remaining 2 tablespoons sugar.

Bake tart until edge is brown, pears are tender, and crust is cooked through, about 30 minutes. Transfer to rack; remove pan sides. Cool at least 15 minutes. Cut tart into wedges; place on plates. Drizzle with sauce. Spoon dollops of crème fraîche alongside and serve.

Classic Fruit Tart

This is a French patisserie-style tart with pâte sucrée ("sweet pastry"), vanilla pastry cream, and a glazed fruit topping. Instead of kiwi, you can use any combination of stone fruit (think sliced peaches, plums, and apricots) and berries. For a casual look, simply toss the fruit in a bowl with the glaze, mound atop the pastry cream, and serve. **8 servings**

Crust

	Nonstick vegetable oil spray
1	**cup unbleached all purpose flour**
¼	**cup sugar**
1	**teaspoon finely grated lemon peel**
½	**teaspoon salt**
½	**cup (1 stick) chilled unsalted butter, cut into ½-inch cubes**
2	**large egg yolks, chilled**

Filling

1	**cup whole milk**
½	**vanilla bean, split lengthwise**
¼	**cup sugar**
3	**large egg yolks**
1½	**tablespoons cornstarch**

Topping

1½	**6-ounce containers raspberries**
2	**kiwis, peeled, thinly sliced**
⅓	**cup apricot preserves**
2	**tablespoons water**

CRUST: Preheat oven to 400°F. Spray bottom of 9-inch-diameter tart pan with removable bottom with nonstick spray. Combine flour, sugar, lemon peel, and salt in processor. Add butter; using on/off turns, cut in until mixture resembles coarse meal. Add egg yolks; using on/off turns, process until moist clumps form. Press dough evenly over bottom and up sides of prepared tart pan. Freeze until firm, about 30 minutes. Bake crust until golden, about 18 minutes. Cool crust completely.

FILLING: Bring milk and vanilla bean just to simmer in heavy medium saucepan over medium-high heat. Meanwhile, beat sugar, egg yolks, and cornstarch in medium bowl to blend. Gradually whisk in hot milk mixture. Return mixture to saucepan and whisk over medium heat until mixture thickens and boils gently, about 1 minute. Transfer to small bowl. Press plastic wrap directly onto surface of pastry cream and chill completely.

DO AHEAD: *Can be made 2 days ahead. Keep chilled.*

Remove vanilla bean from filling; rewhisk until smooth. Spread filling into crust.

TOPPING: Arrange raspberries and kiwi decoratively over filling. Simmer apricot preserves and 2 tablespoons water in small saucepan over medium-high heat until mixture boils thickly, about 1 minute. Strain into small bowl. Brush apricot glaze generously over fruit. Chill tart to set, at least 30 minutes.

♯ Strawberry–Lemon Curd Tart

The crust of this pretty tart resembles shortbread; make the tart in spring, when strawberries are at their peak. Slicing off the stem ends of the strawberries will give them a flat base to stand on in the rich lemon curd.

10 servings

Curd

2	large eggs
½	cup sugar
3	tablespoons fresh lemon juice
¼	cup (½ stick) unsalted butter, cut into 4 pieces
1½	teaspoons finely grated lemon peel

Crust

1½	cups unbleached all purpose flour
3	tablespoons sugar
¼	teaspoon salt
½	cup (1 stick) chilled unsalted butter, cut into ½-inch cubes
2	tablespoons (or more) chilled heavy whipping cream
1	large egg yolk

Topping

1½	quarts strawberries, stem ends cut flat
½	cup strawberry jam

CURD: Whisk eggs, sugar, and lemon juice in heavy small saucepan to blend. Add butter and lemon peel. Stir over medium heat until butter melts and curd thickens to pudding consistency, about 8 minutes. Transfer to small bowl. Press plastic wrap directly onto surface of curd and chill at least 2 hours.

CRUST: Blend flour, sugar, and salt in processor. Add butter; using on/off turns, blend until mixture resembles coarse meal. Add 2 tablespoons cream and egg yolk. Blend until moist clumps form, adding more cream by teaspoonfuls if dough is dry. Gather dough into ball; flatten into disk. Wrap and chill 1 hour.

DO AHEAD: *Curd and dough can be made 2 days ahead. Keep chilled. Let dough soften slightly at room temperature before rolling out.*

Roll out dough disk on lightly floured surface to 13-inch round. Transfer to 9-inch-diameter tart pan with removable bottom. Press dough onto bottom and up sides of pan. Trim dough overhang to ½ inch; fold in and press firmly, forming double-thick sides. Pierce crust all over with fork; refrigerate 1 hour.

Preheat oven to 400°F. Bake crust until golden, pressing with back of fork if crust bubbles, about 20 minutes. Cool crust completely on rack.

TOPPING: Spread curd in crust. Stand berries in curd, cut side down. Stir jam in small saucepan over medium heat until melted; strain into small bowl. Brush jam over berries. Chill tart until glaze sets, at least 1 hour and up to 6 hours.

Remove pan sides from tart. Transfer to plate and serve.

Lemon Cream Tart

A splash of wine and the addition of cream mellow the tartness of the fresh lemons. Be sure that the lemon, egg yolk, and sugar mixture just boils when initially preparing the filling. Serve the tart with Raspberry-Apricot Compote with Champagne and Lemon Verbena (page 437). **8 servings**

Crust

1	cup unbleached all purpose flour
¼	cup sugar
1	teaspoon finely grated lemon peel
½	teaspoon salt
½	cup (1 stick) chilled unsalted butter, cut into ½-inch cubes
2	large egg yolks

Filling

½	cup sugar
2	large eggs
2	large egg yolks
1	tablespoon (packed) finely grated lemon peel
⅓	cup fresh lemon juice
2	tablespoons dry white wine (such as Sauvignon Blanc)
¾	cup heavy whipping cream

CRUST: Butter bottom (not sides) of 9-inch-diameter tart pan with removable bottom. Blend flour, sugar, lemon peel, and salt in processor. Add butter and blend until coarse meal forms. Add egg yolks and blend until moist clumps form. Gather dough into ball. Press onto bottom and up sides of prepared pan. Freeze crust until firm, about 15 minutes.

DO AHEAD: *Can be made 1 day ahead. Cover and keep frozen.*

Preheat oven to 400°F. Bake crust 5 minutes. Press up sides of crust with back of fork if sliding down. Continue to bake crust until golden, pressing up sides as needed, about 18 minutes longer. Cool completely. Maintain oven temperature.

FILLING: Whisk sugar, eggs, egg yolks, and lemon peel in heavy medium saucepan. Whisk in lemon juice and wine. Cook over medium heat until custard thickens and just begins to bubble, whisking constantly, about 5 minutes. Transfer to medium bowl. Cool to just warm, stirring occasionally, about 15 minutes. Gradually whisk in cream. Pour filling into crust.

Bake tart until filling is set in center and begins to puff at edges, about 20 minutes. Cool tart in pan on rack. Chill at least 2 hours.

DO AHEAD: *Can be made 6 hours ahead. Keep chilled.*

Lemon and Honey Tart with Walnut Crust and Honeyed Figs

The combination of lemon, honey, walnuts, and fresh figs gives this dessert a Provençal flavor. If fresh figs aren't available, use sliced plums instead.

6 servings

Crust

1⅓	cups unbleached all purpose flour
⅓	cup walnuts
2	tablespoons sugar
¼	teaspoon salt
½	cup (1 stick) chilled unsalted butter, cut into ½-inch cubes
1	large egg yolk
1½	tablespoons (or more) ice water

Filling

¾	cup buttermilk
⅓	cup fresh lemon juice
2	large eggs
2	tablespoons unbleached all purpose flour
½	teaspoon finely grated lemon peel
½	cup honey

Topping

6	fresh figs, cut crosswise (or pitted plums, cut lengthwise) into ¼-inch-thick slices
1	tablespoon honey
¼	cup walnuts, toasted, chopped

CRUST: Mix flour, walnuts, sugar, and salt in processor. Add butter; using on/off turns, cut in until mixture resembles coarse meal. Whisk egg yolk and 1½ tablespoons ice water in small bowl to blend; add to dry ingredients and process just until moist clumps form, adding more ice water by teaspoonfuls if mixture is dry. Gather dough into ball; flatten into disk. Wrap in plastic and chill at least 1 hour.

DO AHEAD: *Can be made 1 day ahead. Keep chilled. Let soften slightly at room temperature before rolling out.*

Butter and flour 9-inch-diameter tart pan with removable bottom. Roll out dough disk on floured surface to ⅛-inch-thick round. Transfer to tart pan. Press crust onto bottom and up sides of pan. Trim edges; reserve trimmings. Freeze crust 30 minutes.

Preheat oven to 350°F. Line crust with foil; fill with dried beans or pie weights. Bake until crust is set, about 12 minutes. Remove foil and beans. Continue to bake until crust is golden, about 25 minutes longer. Repair any cracks in crust with reserved dough. Cool crust. Maintain oven temperature.

FILLING: Whisk buttermilk, lemon juice, eggs, flour, and lemon peel in bowl. Add honey and stir until dissolved. Pour into crust. Bake until filling is set, about 30 minutes. Cool tart in pan on rack. Chill until cold.

DO AHEAD: *Can be made 8 hours ahead. Keep chilled.*

TOPPING: Arrange figs atop tart. Drizzle with honey and sprinkle with walnuts.

{ Market Tip: **Figs**
Keep in mind that fresh figs don't ripen off the tree, so only buy figs that feel ripe. They should be soft and have a fragrant scent. Nicks or tears in the skin won't affect the fruit. Ripe, fresh figs are very fragile, so take care when transporting them. Once home, put the figs in the fridge, where they'll keep for a couple of days. }

Blood Orange Tart with Orange Caramel Sauce

Blood oranges are increasingly available at some supermarkets, specialty foods stores, and farmers' markets from December through June. If you can't find blood oranges, navel oranges are fine substitutes. **10 to 12 servings**

Orange Curd

1½	cups sugar
⅓	cup fresh blood orange juice
⅓	cup fresh lemon juice
6	large eggs
2	large egg yolks
1	tablespoon finely grated blood orange peel
½	cup (1 stick) unsalted butter, cut into 8 pieces

Crust

1½	cups unbleached all purpose flour
2	tablespoons sugar
¼	teaspoon salt
½	cup (1 stick) chilled unsalted butter, cut into ½-inch cubes
2	tablespoons heavy whipping cream
1	large egg yolk

8	blood oranges
	Orange Caramel Sauce (see recipe)

ORANGE CURD: Whisk sugar, orange juice, lemon juice, eggs, egg yolks, and orange peel in medium metal bowl to blend. Add butter; set bowl over saucepan of simmering water and whisk constantly until curd thickens and instant-read thermometer inserted into curd registers 175°F, about 12 minutes (do not boil). Remove bowl from over water. Press plastic wrap directly onto surface of curd; chill overnight.

DO AHEAD: *Can be made 3 days ahead. Keep chilled.*

CRUST: Blend flour, sugar, and salt in processor. Add butter; using on/off turns, cut in until mixture resembles coarse meal. Add cream and egg yolk and process until moist clumps form. Gather dough into ball; flatten into disk. Cover with plastic wrap and chill 1 hour.

DO AHEAD: *Can be made 1 day ahead. Keep chilled. Let stand at room temperature 20 minutes to soften slightly before rolling out.*

Roll out dough disk on lightly floured surface to 13-inch round. Transfer to 10-inch-diameter tart pan with removable bottom. Press crust onto bottom and up sides of pan. Fold dough overhang in and press onto pan, forming double-thick sides. Pierce crust all over with fork; freeze 30 minutes.

Preheat oven to 375°F. Bake crust until cooked through, about 30 minutes. Cool crust completely in pan on rack. Spread curd evenly in cooled crust.

DO AHEAD: *Can be made 1 day ahead. Cover and chill.*

Cut peel and white pith from oranges. Working over medium bowl and using small sharp knife, cut between membranes to release orange segments. Transfer segments to paper towels and pat dry. Arrange orange segments in concentric circles atop orange curd. Chill tart up to 1 hour.

Remove pan sides from tart. Cut tart into wedges. Drizzle lightly with Orange Caramel Sauce and serve.

Orange Caramel Sauce

This complex sauce has orange notes on deep caramel. When making the caramel, be sure to use a heavy-bottomed stainless steel or copper saucepan for even browning and good visibility. The sauce is equally delicious when made with navel oranges or Valencia oranges. **Makes about ⅔ cup**

⅔	cup sugar
¼	cup water
½	cup fresh blood orange juice
½	teaspoon finely grated blood orange peel

Combine sugar and ¼ cup water in heavy small saucepan. Stir over medium-low heat until sugar dissolves. Increase heat and boil without stirring until syrup is deep amber color, occasionally brushing down pan sides with wet pastry brush and swirling pan, about 8 minutes. Carefully add orange juice and orange peel (mixture will bubble vigorously). Stir over low heat until smooth and any caramel bits dissolve. Cool completely.

DO AHEAD: *Can be prepared 1 day ahead. Cover and let stand at room temperature.*

Apricot Tart with Honey and Almonds

The apricot halves peeking out of the custard filling give this tart a whimsical polka-dot look. For a smooth custard, the cornstarch should be fully incorporated into the yolk and sugar mixture. **12 servings**

²⁄₃	cup whole milk
1	2-inch piece vanilla bean, split lengthwise
2	large egg yolks
3	tablespoons sugar
1	tablespoon cornstarch
	Pastry Crust dough disk (see recipe)
½	cup slivered almonds
⅓	cup powdered sugar
¼	cup (½ stick) unsalted butter, room temperature
1	large egg
1	teaspoon almond extract
	Pinch of salt
3	15.25-ounce cans unpeeled apricot halves in heavy syrup, well drained
3	tablespoons honey

Pour milk into small saucepan. Scrape in seeds from vanilla bean; add bean. Bring to simmer. Remove from heat. Whisk egg yolks, sugar, and cornstarch in bowl to blend. Gradually whisk milk mixture into yolk mixture. Return mixture to pan. Whisk over medium heat until custard thickens and boils, about 2 minutes. Discard vanilla bean. Transfer custard to bowl. Place plastic wrap directly onto surface of custard; cover and refrigerate until cold, about 4 hours.

DO AHEAD: *Can be made 2 days ahead. Cover and keep chilled.*

Roll out pastry crust dough disk on floured surface to 14-inch round. Transfer to 11-inch-diameter tart pan with removable bottom. Press crust onto bottom and up sides of pan. Trim dough overhang to ½ inch; fold in and press, forming double-thick sides. Freeze crust until firm, about 30 minutes.

Preheat oven to 400°F. Bake crust until light golden, about 20 minutes. Cool. Maintain oven temperature.

Finely grind almonds and powdered sugar in processor. Add cooled custard; blend using on/off turns. Blend in butter, then whole egg, almond extract, and salt. Pour into crust; smooth top. Arrange apricot halves, round side up, atop filling.

Bake tart until filling is set and golden, about 45 minutes. Remove from oven. Drizzle honey over and return to oven for 3 minutes. Cool tart completely in pan. Remove pan sides from tart. Transfer to plate.

Pastry Crust (Pâte Sucrée)

This rich, sweet dough is great for tarts. It results in a crust that's halfway between a traditional pie crust and a cookie. **Makes 1 dough disk (enough for one 11-inch tart crust)**

2	cups unbleached all purpose flour
⅓	cup sugar
1	teaspoon salt
½	teaspoon finely grated orange peel
1	cup (2 sticks) chilled unsalted butter, cut into ½-inch cubes
3	large egg yolks, beaten to blend

Mix flour, sugar, salt, and orange peel in large bowl. Add butter; rub in with fingertips until mixture resembles coarse meal. Add egg yolks; mix with fork until dough begins to clump together. Shape dough into ball; flatten into disk. Wrap in plastic and chill 30 minutes.

DO AHEAD: *Can be made 2 days ahead. Keep chilled. Let soften slightly at room temperature before rolling out.*

Strawberry and White Chocolate Mousse Tart

The pastry shell of this elegant dessert is "blind baked"—meaning it's fully baked before being filled (in this case, with lush white chocolate mousse). Begin preparing the tart one day before you plan to serve it to allow the mousse to set. **8 servings**

Crust

1¼   cups unbleached all purpose flour
¼   cup sugar
¼   teaspoon salt
½   cup (1 stick) chilled unsalted butter, cut into ½-inch cubes
1   large egg yolk
1   tablespoon (or more) ice water

Mousse

6   ounces high-quality white chocolate (such as Lindt or Perugina), chopped
1¼   cups chilled heavy whipping cream, divided
½   teaspoon vanilla extract
2   large egg whites, room temperature
⅛   teaspoon cream of tartar

⅓   cup seedless strawberry jam
1   tablespoon fresh lemon juice
1   16-ounce container strawberries, hulled, thinly sliced lengthwise

CRUST: Blend flour, sugar, and salt in processor. Add butter; using on/off turns, cut in until mixture resembles coarse meal. Whisk egg yolk and 1 tablespoon ice water in small bowl to blend. Add to processor and blend until moist clumps form, adding more ice water by teaspoonfuls if dough is dry. Gather dough into ball; flatten into disk. Wrap in plastic and chill 1 hour.

DO AHEAD: *Can be made 1 day ahead. Keep chilled. Let stand at room temperature 20 minutes to soften slightly before rolling out.*

Roll out dough disk on floured surface to 13-inch round. Transfer to 9-inch-diameter tart pan with removable bottom. Trim dough overhang to ½ inch; fold in and press onto pan, forming double-thick sides. Pierce crust all over with fork. Freeze crust 30 minutes.

Preheat oven to 375°F. Line crust with foil; fill with dried beans or pie weights. Bake until crust sides are light brown, about 25 minutes. Remove foil and beans. Continue to bake until crust is cooked through and golden brown, about 20 minutes longer. Cool crust completely in pan on rack.

MOUSSE: Combine white chocolate and ¼ cup whipping cream in large metal bowl. Set bowl over saucepan of simmering water and stir until chocolate is melted and smooth. Remove bowl from over water; cool chocolate mixture until lukewarm, about 15 minutes.

Beat remaining 1 cup chilled whipping cream and vanilla in large bowl until peaks form. Using clean dry beaters, beat egg whites with cream of tartar in medium bowl until stiff but not dry. Fold whites into chocolate mixture, then fold in whipped cream. Transfer mixture to cooled crust; smooth top. Cover with plastic wrap and chill overnight.

Combine jam and lemon juice in small saucepan; bring to simmer, stirring over medium heat until jam melts. Remove from heat. Arrange sliced strawberries in concentric circles atop tart. Brush berries with melted jam mixture. Chill tart up to 2 hours. Remove pan sides from tart. Transfer tart to platter.

⑂⑂⑂ Cherry Lattice Tart

This thin, cookie-like tart with a lattice crust is inspired by a feast-day dessert from the Mediterranean island of Malta. The recipe calls for cherry preserves and dried cherries in the filling, but apricot preserves and dried apricots would be great, too. **8 to 10 servings**

Crust

2	cups unbleached all purpose flour
½	cup sugar
1	teaspoon salt
1	cup (2 sticks) chilled unsalted butter, cut into ½-inch cubes
1	large egg

Filling

1	cup cherry preserves
½	cup chopped dried Bing cherries or other dried sweet cherries (about 2½ ounces)
½	teaspoon finely grated lemon peel
¼	teaspoon almond extract
¼	cup unsalted natural pistachios, chopped

Glaze

1	large egg
2	tablespoons whole milk
2	tablespoons sugar

CRUST: Blend flour, sugar, and salt in processor. Add butter; using on/off turns, cut in until mixture resembles coarse meal. Add egg and process just until moist clumps form. Gather dough into ball; divide in half. Flatten each half into disk. Wrap in plastic and chill until firm enough to roll, about 1 hour.

DO AHEAD: *Can be prepared 1 day ahead. Keep chilled. Let stand at room temperature 20 minutes to soften slightly before rolling out.*

FILLING: Mix preserves, chopped cherries, lemon peel, and almond extract in medium bowl.

Position rack in bottom third of oven and preheat to 325°F. Roll out 1 dough disk on lightly floured surface to 11-inch round. Transfer to 9-inch-diameter tart pan with removable bottom. Press dough onto bottom and up sides of pan; trim overhang even with top of pan sides. Spread filling in crust; sprinkle with pistachios. Roll out second dough disk on lightly floured surface to 11-inch round; cut into ¾-inch-wide strips. Arrange several strips, spaced ¾ inch apart, over filling. Top with more strips at slight angle, forming lattice. Press strip ends to edge of pan, trimming overhang.

GLAZE: Beat egg and milk to blend in small bowl for glaze. Brush some of glaze over lattice crust; sprinkle with sugar.

Bake tart until crust is golden brown and cherry filling is bubbling thickly, about 1 hour 5 minutes. Cool tart completely in pan on rack.

DO AHEAD: *Can be prepared 1 day ahead. Cover and store at room temperature.*

 # Cherry Linzertorte

Although the fillings may vary, the Linzertorte always has a tender nut crust (usually made with hazelnuts or almonds). This recipe makes enough dough for the torte and for a few extra cookies. To make cookies, roll out the dough to ¼-inch thickness. Cut out decorative shapes and bake at 350°F on a parchment-lined baking sheet until golden, about 10 minutes. **8 to 10 servings**

1¼	**cups hazelnuts, toasted, husked, cooled**
2⅓	**cups unbleached all purpose flour, divided**
¾	**cup sugar**
2	**teaspoons ground cinnamon**
½	**teaspoon baking powder**
½	**teaspoon salt**
¼	**teaspoon ground nutmeg**
1	**cup (2 sticks) chilled unsalted butter, cut into ½-inch cubes**
3	**large egg yolks**
1	**tablespoon vanilla extract**
1½	**cups cherry preserves (preferably imported; about 18 ounces)**
	Powdered sugar (optional)

Preheat oven to 350°F. Butter 9-inch-diameter tart pan with removable bottom. Combine nuts and ⅓ cup flour in processor; finely chop nuts. Transfer mixture to large bowl. Add remaining 2 cups flour, sugar, cinnamon, baking powder, salt, and nutmeg to bowl; whisk to blend. Add butter. Using electric mixer at low speed, blend ingredients until coarse meal forms (this will take several minutes). Add egg yolks and vanilla. Beat until moist clumps form.

Gather dough into ball; press 1½ cups (packed) dough over bottom and up sides of prepared pan. Spread preserves on dough. Roll remaining dough out on sheet of parchment paper to 13x10-inch rectangle. Freeze rectangle 5 minutes to firm. Cut twelve ½-inch-wide lengthwise strips from rectangle. Arrange 6 strips across torte, spacing evenly. Arrange 6 more strips across torte in opposite direction, forming lattice. Seal ends of strips to dough edge; trim excess. Reserve all dough scraps to make cookies, if desired.

Bake torte until crust is golden brown and preserves are bubbling thickly, about 40 minutes. Cool torte completely on rack.

DO AHEAD: *Can be made 2 days ahead. Cover with foil; store at room temperature.*

Push bottom of pan up to free torte from pan. Sift powdered sugar over edge of torte, if desired, and serve.

Sour Cream Tart with Santa Rosa Plum Compote

This tart combines a nutty short crust with a vanilla bean–infused, sour cream–lightened pastry cream. It then gets topped with a lovely plum compote. Alternatively, you could top the tart with fresh raspberries or sliced strawberries.
8 servings

Crust

¾	**cup unbleached all purpose flour**
¾	**cup assorted nuts (such as walnuts, almonds, and hazelnuts), toasted, cooled**
¼	**cup sugar**
¾	**teaspoon salt**
6	**tablespoons (¾ stick) chilled unsalted butter, cut into ½-inch cubes**
1	**large egg yolk**

Filling

2	**teaspoons water**
¼	**teaspoon unflavored gelatin**
3	**large egg yolks**
¼	**cup sugar**
1½	**tablespoons cornstarch**
1	**cup whole milk**
½	**vanilla bean, split lengthwise**
½	**cup sour cream**
	Santa Rosa Plum Compote (see recipe)

CRUST: Butter bottom of 9-inch-diameter tart pan with removable bottom. Finely grind flour, nuts, sugar, and salt in processor. Add butter; using on/off turns, blend until coarse meal forms. Add egg yolk; blend until moist clumps form. Press dough over bottom and up sides of pan. Pierce crust all over with fork. Freeze until firm, about 30 minutes.

Preheat oven to 400°F. Bake crust until golden, 15 to 20 minutes. Cool completely.

FILLING: Place 2 teaspoons water in very small cup. Sprinkle gelatin over. Let stand until gelatin softens, about 10 minutes.

Whisk egg yolks, sugar, and cornstarch in medium bowl to blend. Pour milk into medium saucepan. Scrape in seeds from vanilla bean; add bean. Bring milk to simmer. Gradually whisk hot milk mixture into yolk mixture; return to saucepan. Stir over medium-high heat until custard thickens and boils, about 2 minutes. Remove from heat. Scrape in gelatin mixture and stir to dissolve. Let stand 5 minutes.

Transfer custard to medium metal bowl. Discard vanilla bean. Set bowl over another bowl filled with ice and water; stir until custard is cool but not set, about 15 minutes. Fold in sour cream. Spread filling evenly in crust. Chill tart until filling sets, at least 2 hours and up to 6 hours.

Cut tart into wedges. Spoon Santa Rosa Plum Compote over and serve.

Santa Rosa Plum Compote

Santa Rosa plums are large fruits with purplish crimson skin and red-blushed yellow flesh. When stewed into a compote, they become intensely colored and flavored. The pits are left in while cooking, which also adds to the flavor. The compote is great when paired with the tart, but it's also delicious served over vanilla ice cream. **8 servings**

2	**pounds red plums (preferably Santa Rosa), quartered**
1⅓	**cups (about) sugar, divided**
2	**cinnamon sticks**
1	**vanilla bean, split lengthwise**

Combine plums, 1 cup sugar, and cinnamon sticks in large saucepan. Scrape in seeds from vanilla bean; add bean. Stir over low heat until plums are very tender and compote thickens, stirring often and adding ⅓ cup sugar if desired, about 45 minutes. Remove from heat. Cool completely. Transfer compote to bowl, discarding plum pits, vanilla bean, and cinnamon sticks.

DO AHEAD: *Can be made 2 days ahead. Cover and chill.*

🥄 Cheesecake Tart with Tropical Fruits

Mango, papaya, kiwi, and passion fruit top this cheesecake-filled tart. Guava jelly, which is found at many supermarkets and at specialty foods stores and Latin markets, adds a lovely glaze and tropical perfume to the fruit. Passion fruit may not be available at your market year-round, but the tart is still wonderful without it. **8 to 10 servings**

Crust

1½	cups unbleached all purpose flour
2	tablespoons sugar
⅛	teaspoon salt
10	tablespoons (1¼ sticks) chilled unsalted butter, cut into ½-inch cubes
2	tablespoons (or more) ice water
1	large egg yolk
¼	cup guava jelly or crab apple jelly

Filling

2	8-ounce packages Philadelphia-brand cream cheese, room temperature
⅔	cup sugar
1	large egg
¼	teaspoon vanilla extract
½	cup sour cream

Topping

¼	cup guava jelly or crab apple jelly
3	small red-fleshed papayas or regular papayas, halved, peeled, seeded, cut lengthwise into ¼-inch-thick slices
2	kiwis, peeled, cut into ¼-inch-thick rounds
1	large ripe mango, peeled, pitted, diced
2	passion fruits, halved (optional)

CRUST: Combine flour, sugar, and salt in processor. Add butter; using on/off turns, cut in until mixture resembles coarse meal. Whisk 2 tablespoons ice water and egg yolk in small bowl; add to processor and blend just until soft moist clumps form, adding more ice water by teaspoonfuls if dough is dry. Gather dough into ball; flatten into disk. Wrap in plastic and chill at least 1 hour.

DO AHEAD: *Can be made 1 day ahead. Keep chilled. Let soften slightly at room temperature before rolling out.*

Roll out dough disk on lightly floured surface to 13- to 14-inch round. Transfer to 11-inch-diameter tart pan with removable bottom. Press in dough overhang, forming double-thick sides. Pierce crust all over with fork. Freeze crust 30 minutes.

Preheat oven to 375°F. Bake crust until golden brown, pressing with back of fork if crust bubbles or slips, about 30 minutes. Transfer tart pan with crust to rack. Spread jelly over bottom of crust and cool completely. Reduce oven temperature to 350°F.

FILLING: Using electric mixer, beat cream cheese in large bowl until smooth. Add sugar and beat until light and fluffy. Beat in egg, then vanilla. Add sour cream and beat just to blend. Pour filling into tart crust.

Bake until filling is slightly puffed and center moves slightly when pan is gently shaken, about 35 minutes. Transfer tart to rack and cool completely in pan. Chill tart until cold, at least 4 hours.

DO AHEAD: *Can be made 1 day ahead. Cover and keep chilled.*

TOPPING: Melt jelly in heavy small saucepan over low heat. Brush over top of tart. Overlap papaya slices atop tart in circle. Arrange kiwis in overlapping slices in center. Sprinkle diced mango around edge. Spoon pulp of passion fruits into center of tart, if desired.

DO AHEAD: *Can be made 3 hours ahead. Cover and chill. Serve chilled.*

♀♀♀ Passion Fruit Tart with Crisp Meringue Top

Passion fruit has an exotic citrus flavor that makes for a luscious curd. While fresh passion fruit is abundant in New Zealand and Australia, it is still considered a specialty fruit in many parts of the States. This curd uses frozen passion fruit juice concentrate from the freezer aisle, which is always convenient. Before setting the meringue atop the passion fruit curd, don't forget to give it a light coating of melted white chocolate. Not only does the chocolate balance the tart flavor of the curd, it also forms a protective barrier over the meringue, preventing it from becoming soggy. **10 to 12 servings**

Crust

⅓	cup sugar
5	tablespoons unsalted butter, room temperature
¼	teaspoon salt
3	teaspoons (or more) heavy whipping cream
1	large egg yolk
1	cup unbleached all purpose flour

Passion Fruit Curd

1	cup frozen passion fruit juice concentrate, thawed
8	large egg yolks
2	large eggs
⅓	cup sugar
½	cup (1 stick) unsalted butter, diced

Meringue

3	large egg whites, room temperature
⅔	cup sugar
1½	ounces high-quality white chocolate (such as Lindt or Perugina), chopped
	White chocolate curls

CRUST: Using electric mixer, beat sugar, butter, and salt in medium bowl until blended. Beat in 3 teaspoons cream and egg yolk. Add flour and beat until moist clumps form, adding more cream by teaspoonfuls if dough is dry. Gather dough into ball; flatten into disk. Wrap in plastic and chill at least 1 hour.

DO AHEAD: *Can be made 1 day ahead. Keep chilled. Let soften slightly at room temperature before rolling out.*

PASSION FRUIT CURD: Whisk passion fruit juice concentrate, egg yolks, eggs, and sugar in heavy large saucepan. Add butter and whisk over medium-low heat until butter melts. Stir until filling thickens and leaves path on back of spoon when finger is drawn across, about 11 minutes (do not boil). Transfer to medium bowl. Press plastic wrap directly onto surface of curd. Chill until firm, at least 6 hours.

DO AHEAD: *Can be made 1 day ahead. Keep chilled.*

MERINGUE: Preheat oven to 275°F. Using plate or cake pan as aid, draw 9-inch-diameter circle on sheet of parchment paper. Turn parchment over and place on baking sheet (circle will show through). Using electric mixer, beat egg whites in medium bowl until soft peaks form. Gradually add sugar, beating until meringue is stiff and shiny. Spoon meringue into pastry bag fitted with ⅜-inch plain round tip. Starting in center, pipe tight spiral of meringue to fill circle. Bake meringue until pale golden and puffed but still slightly soft to touch, about 45 minutes. Cool on baking sheet.

Roll out dough disk on floured surface to 12-inch round. Transfer to 9-inch-diameter tart pan with removable bottom. Trim dough overhang to ¼ inch; fold in and press, forming double-thick sides. Pierce crust all over with fork. Chill 30 minutes.

Preheat oven to 350°F. Bake crust 5 minutes. Press up sides of crust with back of fork. Continue to bake crust until golden, pressing occasionally with back of fork to keep shape, about 15 to 20 minutes longer. Cool completely.

Spread curd in crust; chill tart. Place 1½ ounces white chocolate in microwave-safe cup. Microwave at low setting in 10-second intervals until softened; stir until smooth. Spread chocolate over bottom of meringue. Chill meringue, chocolate side up, until chocolate sets, about 30 minutes. Place meringue, chocolate side down, atop tart. Mound chocolate curls atop meringue.

DO AHEAD: *Can be made 8 hours ahead. Chill uncovered.*

Release tart from pan; place on platter and serve.

Technique Tip: **Microwaving Chocolate**

Chocolate is often melted in a bowl set over a saucepan of simmering water, but melting it in the microwave provides a quick and convenient alternative. Whether you're melting white chocolate or dark chocolate in the microwave, remember these key tips: Use a microwave-safe bowl or measuring cup (such as Pyrex), use a low-power setting so that the chocolate melts gently, use 10-second intervals so the chocolate doesn't overheat and burn, and stir the chocolate (even if it doesn't look melted) between each interval to ensure it melts evenly.

Cranberry-Lime Tart

Lime curd and tart cranberries are balanced by a layer of sweet white chocolate cream and a rich buttery crust. The vibrant red topping and green-speckled curd make this dessert perfect for the holidays. Begin preparing the tart at least two days ahead so that the lime curd can chill overnight before it's used and the assembled tart can chill overnight before it's served. If you like, the cranberries can be lightly flavored with Chinese five-spice powder, which is a blend of star anise, cinnamon, cloves, fennel seeds, and Szechuan peppercorns; it's available in the spice section of most supermarkets. **14 to 16 servings**

Curd

½	cup fresh lime juice
½	teaspoon cornstarch
¾	cup sugar
6	large egg yolks
½	cup (1 stick) unsalted butter, cut into 8 pieces
2½	teaspoons finely grated lime peel

Crust

1¼	cups unbleached all purpose flour
½	cup powdered sugar
⅓	cup whole almonds, toasted, cooled
½	teaspoon salt
¾	cup (1½ sticks) chilled unsalted butter, cut into ½-inch cubes
1	teaspoon vanilla extract

Topping

¼	cup water
1½	teaspoons cornstarch
⅔	cup sugar
3	tablespoons honey
1½	teaspoons Chinese five-spice powder (optional)
1	12-ounce bag (3 cups) fresh or partially thawed frozen cranberries

Cream

5	ounces high-quality white chocolate (such as Lindt or Perugina), chopped
½	cup plus 2 tablespoons sour cream
½	teaspoon vanilla extract
	White chocolate curls
8	thin lime twists

Technique Tip: Lime Twists
Sugared lime twists make a pretty garnish for this tart. To make them, remove the lime peel in 2-inch lengths using a lemon stripper or the large V-shaped cutter on a citrus zester. Twist the strips to form coils, dip them into ice water, and lightly roll them in sugar to coat.

CURD: Whisk lime juice and cornstarch in heavy medium saucepan. Whisk in sugar and egg yolks, then add butter. Whisk constantly over medium heat until mixture simmers and thickens, about 8 minutes. Strain into small bowl. Mix in lime peel. Cover; chill overnight.

CRUST: Finely grind flour, sugar, almonds, and salt in processor. Add butter and vanilla; using on/off turns, cut in until mixture just forms soft moist clumps. Gather dough into ball; flatten into disk. Wrap in plastic. Chill 1 hour. Press dough onto bottom and up sides of 11-inch-diameter tart pan with removable bottom. Using thumb, press dough up sides to extend ⅛ inch above rim of pan. Freeze crust 30 minutes.

Preheat oven to 350°F. Bake crust until golden brown, pressing with back of spoon if crust bubbles, about 25 minutes. Transfer to rack and cool completely.

TOPPING: Whisk ¼ cup water and cornstarch in heavy large saucepan to blend. Add sugar, honey, and five-spice powder, if desired. Stir over medium-high heat until mixture comes to boil. Add cranberries; cook until mixture boils and berries just begin to pop but still maintain shape, occasionally stirring gently, about 5 minutes. Cool completely (mixture will thicken).

CREAM: Stir chocolate in top of double boiler over simmering water until melted and smooth. Remove from over water; whisk in sour cream and vanilla. Cool completely.

Spread chocolate cream into crust; freeze 15 minutes. Spoon lime curd over; spread evenly. Spoon cranberry topping by tablespoonfuls over, then spread carefully to cover completely. Cover and chill overnight.

DO AHEAD: *Can be made 2 days ahead. Keep chilled.*

Remove pan sides; transfer tart to platter. Sprinkle chocolate curls around edge of tart. Garnish with lime twists.

Speculaas Tart with Almond Filling

Dutch speculaas *cookies are similar in flavor to gingerbread cookies. This tart combines the spiced* speculaas *dough with another treat—almond tart filling. During the holidays, use a 2-inch gingerbread man cookie cutter to form the cookies for the top of the tart. At other times of the year, any 2-inch cutter, such as a heart or a star, can be used instead.* **12 to 16 servings**

Dough

2¾	cups unbleached all purpose flour
2	teaspoons ground cinnamon
1	teaspoon ground ginger
½	teaspoon salt
½	teaspoon baking powder
¼	teaspoon ground nutmeg
1	cup (2 sticks) unsalted butter, room temperature
1	cup (packed) dark brown sugar
1	large egg

Filling

1½	cups blanched slivered almonds
¾	cup sugar
¼	cup (½ stick) unsalted butter, room temperature
1	large egg
2	teaspoons finely grated lemon peel
2	teaspoons fresh lemon juice
1	teaspoon vanilla extract
¾	teaspoon almond extract

Powdered sugar
Apricot preserves

DOUGH: Sift flour, cinnamon, ginger, salt, baking powder, and nutmeg into medium bowl. Using electric mixer, beat butter and sugar in large bowl until blended. Beat in egg. Add flour mixture and beat until moist clumps form. Gather dough into ball; divide into 2 pieces, 1 slightly larger than the other. Flatten dough into disks; wrap separately and chill at least 2 hours.

DO AHEAD: *Can be made 2 days ahead. Keep chilled. Let soften slightly at room temperature before rolling out.*

FILLING: Blend almonds, sugar, butter, egg, lemon peel, lemon juice, and both extracts in processor until nuts are finely chopped. Transfer to small bowl. Cover; chill at least 2 hours and up to 2 days.

Preheat oven to 325°F. Butter 9-inch-diameter springform pan with 2¾-inch-high sides. Roll out larger dough disk on lightly floured surface to 13-inch round. Transfer to prepared pan and press gently over bottom and up sides, pressing to seal any tears. Spread filling in dough. Trim dough on sides to ½ inch above level of filling. Fold dough in over filling.

Roll out second dough disk on lightly floured surface to 12- to 13-inch round. Using bottom of cake pan as aid, cut out 9-inch-diameter round of dough. Slide dough round onto plate and freeze 5 minutes to firm. Reserve dough scraps for cookies. Place chilled dough round on tart; press to adhere and seal edges.

Bake tart until crust is brown, about 50 minutes. Remove sides of springform pan; cool tart completely on pan bottom. Maintain oven temperature.

Line 2 baking sheets with parchment paper. Roll out dough scraps on lightly floured work surface to scant ¼-inch thickness. Using 2-inch gingerbread man cookie cutter, cut out cookies. Transfer cutouts to prepared baking sheets. Repeat, using all of dough.

Bake cookies until golden, about 8 minutes. Cool cookies on sheets.

DO AHEAD: *Tart and cookies can be made ahead. Cover separately and store at room temperature 1 day or chill up to 3 days.*

Sift powdered sugar over top of tart. Place small dab of apricot preserves on back of 1 cookie; place at top edge of tart. Repeat with more cookies, forming border around tart. Transfer tart to platter. Let stand at room temperature at least 1 hour.

Hazelnut Macaroon and Strawberry Tart

This dessert is kosher for Passover (with kosher almond extract), but don't think of it as only a holiday treat. The nutty, cookie-like crust is the perfect foil for the strawberry filling. **12 servings**

Filling

2	12-ounce containers strawberries, hulled, diced
¾	cup sugar
3	tablespoons Passover brandy
1	tablespoon fresh lemon juice
	Pinch of ground cloves

Crust and Berries

	Matzo cake meal
2	cups hazelnuts, toasted, husked
1	cup sugar
⅛	teaspoon salt
	Pinch of ground cloves
1	large egg
¼	teaspoon almond extract
3	1-pint containers strawberries, hulled, thinly sliced

FILLING: Combine all ingredients in heavy large skillet. Stir over high heat until sugar dissolves and mixture comes to boil. Boil until very thick, stirring frequently, about 13 minutes. Cool in pan.

DO AHEAD: *Can be made 2 days ahead. Transfer to bowl, cover, and chill.*

CRUST AND BERRIES: Position rack in center of oven and preheat to 350°F. Line 11-inch-diameter tart pan with removable bottom with heavy-duty foil, pressing firmly into scalloped sides of pan and overlapping sides. Grease foil and dust with cake meal. Finely grind nuts, sugar, salt, and cloves in processor. Add egg and almond extract; process until mixture just holds together. Reserve ½ cup dough for another use. Using moistened fingertips, press remaining dough onto bottom and up sides of prepared pan. Bake until crust is golden and crinkled and feels dry, about 13 minutes. Cool crust completely in pan on rack. Remove tart pan sides. Carefully peel foil off crust. Return crust to pan.

DO AHEAD: *Can be made 1 day ahead. Wrap pan with tart tightly and store at room temperature.*

Spread filling over crust. Starting at edge, cover tart with berry slices in overlapping concentric circles, with first circle leaning against crust edge.

DO AHEAD: *Can be made 3 hours ahead. Chill.*

Remove tart from pan. Cut into wedges and serve.

More to Try

Turn the leftover dough from this recipe into soft, chewy macaroon cookies. Here's how: Preheat the oven to 350°F. Line a baking sheet with parchment paper. Form teaspoonfuls of dough into balls, place on prepared sheet, and, using wet fingertips, flatten to ½ inch thick. Bake the cookies until they begin to color, 10 to 12 minutes.

Almond Tart with Honey and Orange

This rich dessert is like almond candy in a crust. Because the crust requires no chilling or baking prior to being filled, the entire tart can be made from start to finish in a little more than an hour. If you like, you can serve it with softly whipped, honey-sweetened cream. **8 to 10 servings**

Crust

1¾	cups unbleached all purpose flour
⅓	cup powdered sugar
1	teaspoon (scant) salt
10	tablespoons (1¼ sticks) chilled unsalted butter, cut into ½-inch cubes
1	teaspoon finely grated orange peel
2	tablespoons (or more) ice water

Filling

1	cup heavy whipping cream
½	cup sugar
¼	cup (packed) golden brown sugar
¼	cup honey
2¼	cups sliced almonds, toasted

CRUST: Blend flour, powdered sugar, and salt in food processor. Add butter and orange peel. Using on/off turns, process until mixture resembles coarse meal. Add 2 tablespoons ice water and process until moist clumps form, adding more ice water by teaspoonfuls if mixture is dry. Gather dough into ball. Break into small pieces and scatter over bottom of 10- to 10½-inch-diameter tart pan with removable bottom. Using fingertips, press dough evenly onto bottom and up sides of pan. Freeze crust 25 minutes.

FILLING: Meanwhile, preheat oven to 350°F. Combine cream, both sugars, and honey in heavy medium saucepan. Bring to boil over medium-high heat, stirring until sugar dissolves. Continue to boil until mixture darkens and thickens slightly, about 4 minutes. Remove from heat. Stir in almonds. Spoon filling evenly into crust.

Bake tart until filling is deep golden brown and bubbles thickly and crust is golden, about 38 minutes. Transfer tart to rack and cool completely in pan. Carefully remove pan sides from tart. Place tart on platter.

DO AHEAD: *Can be made 2 days ahead. Cover and store at room temperature.*

Cut tart into wedges and serve at room temperature.

Chocolate and Mixed Nut Tart in Cookie Crust

The crust of this tart is like a shortbread cookie, and the rich filling is similar to a pecan pie—except that it features a variety of nuts and chocolate chips. Serve the tart warm so that the chocolate chips are nice and gooey. **10 to 12 servings**

Crust

1½	cups unbleached all purpose flour
¼	cup sugar
½	cup (1 stick) plus 1 tablespoon chilled salted butter, cut into ½-inch cubes
2	tablespoons (or more) chilled heavy whipping cream
1½	teaspoons vanilla extract

Filling

¾	cup whole almonds, toasted, cooled
¾	cup hazelnuts, toasted, husked, cooled
¾	cup walnuts, toasted, cooled
¾	cup light corn syrup
¼	cup (packed) golden brown sugar
¼	cup (½ stick) salted butter, melted, cooled
3	large eggs
1	teaspoon vanilla extract
½	teaspoon almond extract
1	cup semisweet chocolate chips

CRUST: Blend flour and sugar in processor. Add butter; using on/off turns, cut in until mixture resembles coarse meal. Add 2 tablespoons cream and vanilla extract. Using on/off turns, blend until moist clumps form, adding more cream by teaspoonfuls if dough is dry. Gather dough together; break into small pieces and scatter over bottom of 11-inch-diameter tart pan with removable bottom. Using fingertips, press dough evenly onto bottom and up sides of pan.

DO AHEAD: *Can be made 1 day ahead. Cover and chill. Let stand at room temperature 30 minutes before filling.*

FILLING: Preheat oven to 350°F. Combine almonds, hazelnuts, and walnuts in processor; using on/off turns, coarsely chop nuts. Whisk corn syrup, brown sugar, and melted butter in large bowl to blend. Whisk in eggs and vanilla and almond extracts. Mix in chocolate chips, then nuts. Transfer filling to prepared crust.

Bake tart until filling is firmly set in center and top is deep golden brown, about 50 minutes. Cool in pan on rack 30 minutes. Remove pan sides from tart. Serve warm or at room temperature.

Mixed Nut Tart

Walnuts, pecans, cashews, and almonds combine in this orange-scented, caramel-colored tart. If you prefer, use any combination of two or more kinds of nuts in the filling. Just be sure to use 2⅔ cups nuts in total. This tart travels well, as the filling is firm after baking. Adding vegetable shortening and apple cider vinegar helps ensure that the crust will be tender and flaky. **12 servings**

Crust

1¼	cups unbleached all purpose flour
2	teaspoons sugar
½	teaspoon salt
⅓	cup chilled non-hydrogenated solid vegetable shortening, cut into ½-inch pieces
¼	cup (½ stick) chilled unsalted butter, cut into ½-inch cubes
3	tablespoons (or more) ice water
1	teaspoon apple cider vinegar

Filling

1½	cups heavy whipping cream
⅔	cup sugar
⅓	cup (packed) golden brown sugar
⅓	cup honey
1	teaspoon finely grated orange peel
⅔	cup chopped walnuts
⅔	cup pecan halves
⅔	cup roasted unsalted cashews, coarsely chopped
⅔	cup sliced almonds

  Whipped cream
  Orange-Cranberry Compote (optional; see recipe)

CRUST: Blend flour, sugar, and salt in processor. Add shortening and butter; using on/off turns, process until mixture resembles coarse meal. Combine 3 tablespoons ice water and vinegar in small bowl; pour over flour mixture. Using on/off turns, process until moist clumps form, adding more ice water by teaspoonfuls if mixture is dry. Gather dough into ball; flatten into disk. Wrap in plastic and chill 30 minutes.

DO AHEAD: *Can be made 1 day ahead. Keep chilled. Let stand at room temperature 20 minutes to soften slightly before rolling out.*

Roll out dough disk on lightly floured surface to 13-inch round. Transfer to 11-inch-diameter tart pan with removable bottom. Press dough onto bottom and up sides of pan. Trim dough overhang and reserve. Freeze crust 30 minutes.

Preheat oven to 450°F. Bake crust until golden, about 17 minutes, pressing with back of fork if crust bubbles. Cool on rack. Reduce oven temperature to 400°F.

FILLING: Meanwhile, mix cream, both sugars, and honey in heavy large saucepan. Bring to boil over high heat. Reduce heat to medium and simmer until mixture bubbles thickly and darkens slightly, stirring occasionally, about 8 minutes. Remove from heat; stir in orange peel. Let stand 20 minutes to cool slightly. Stir in walnuts, pecans, cashews, and almonds.

Spoon filling into crust, distributing nuts evenly. Bake tart until filling is bubbling thickly and deep amber in color, about 22 minutes. Cool completely on rack. Serve with whipped cream and Orange-Cranberry Compote, if desired.

Orange-Cranberry Compote

Almond syrup, used to flavor coffee, desserts, and cocktails, is usually found in the coffee section of most supermarkets and at specialty foods stores. You can also use sirop d'amandes *(also called orgeat syrup), which is almond syrup with orange-flower water. If you prefer compote with a kick, use amaretto liqueur instead.* **Makes about 1¼ cups**

6	oranges
1	cup dried cranberries
2	tablespoons almond syrup or amaretto

Cut peel and white pith from oranges. Working over medium bowl, cut between membranes to release orange segments. Add cranberries and almond syrup to bowl. Toss to combine. Refrigerate at least 1 hour and up to 6 hours.

Chocolate-Pecan Tart

This delicious take on the classic southern dessert features an exceptionally easy crust—it's simply stirred together, pressed into a tart pan, and baked. The bourbon adds a spirited flavor, but if you prefer something nonalcoholic, substitute two teaspoons of vanilla for the bourbon in both the filling and the whipped cream. **10 servings**

Crust

1¼	cups unbleached all purpose flour
3	tablespoons (packed) golden brown sugar
½	teaspoon salt
½	cup (1 stick) unsalted butter, melted

Filling

1	cup (packed) golden brown sugar
2	large eggs
2	tablespoons bourbon
2	tablespoons (¼ stick) unsalted butter, melted
¼	teaspoon salt
1½	cups pecan halves and pieces, toasted
3	ounces bittersweet or semisweet chocolate, chopped into small chunks (about ½ cup)

Bourbon Whipped Cream

1	cup chilled heavy whipping cream
1	to 2 tablespoons bourbon
1½	tablespoons sugar

CRUST: Preheat oven to 375°F. Butter 9-inch-diameter tart pan with removable bottom. Whisk flour, brown sugar, and salt in medium bowl to blend. Add melted butter and stir with fork until moist clumps form. Break into small pieces and scatter over bottom of prepared pan. Using fingertips, press dough evenly onto bottom and up sides of pan. Bake crust until just golden brown, about 15 minutes.

FILLING: Meanwhile, beat brown sugar, eggs, bourbon, butter, and salt in large bowl until well blended. Stir in pecans and chocolate.

Pour filling into crust. Bake tart until just set, about 25 minutes. Cool completely.

DO AHEAD: *Can be made 1 day ahead. Cover tart loosely and keep at cool room temperature.*

BOURBON WHIPPED CREAM: Using electric mixer, beat cream, bourbon, and sugar in large bowl until soft peaks form.

Cut tart into wedges and serve with bourbon whipped cream.

Mexican Chocolate Tart with Cinnamon-Spiced Pecans

Cinnamon gives Mexican chocolate its unique flavor, and combines with the sugar and cayenne pepper in the sweet-spicy pecans. Mexican chocolate, available at some supermarkets, at Latin markets, and online at amazon.com, has a granular texture; when making the filling, be sure to whisk the chocolate until the sugar dissolves and the chocolate is smooth. **8 to 10 servings**

Pecans

Nonstick vegetable oil spray
1   **large egg white**
2   **tablespoons sugar**
1   **tablespoon (packed) golden brown sugar**
1   **teaspoon ground cinnamon**
¼   **teaspoon salt**
⅛   **teaspoon cayenne pepper**
1½   **cups pecan halves**

Crust

1   **cup chocolate wafer cookie crumbs (about half of one 9-ounce package cookies, finely ground in processor)**
¼   **cup sugar**
½   **teaspoon ground cinnamon**
⅛   **teaspoon salt**
5   **tablespoons unsalted butter, melted**

Filling

1   **cup heavy whipping cream**
4   **ounces bittersweet or semisweet chocolate, chopped**
1   **3.1-ounce disk Mexican chocolate (such as Ibarra), chopped**
¼   **cup (½ stick) unsalted butter, cut into 4 pieces, room temperature**
2   **teaspoons vanilla extract**
1   **teaspoon ground cinnamon**
¼   **teaspoon salt**

Lightly sweetened whipped cream

PECANS: Preheat oven to 350°F. Spray rimmed baking sheet with nonstick spray. Whisk egg white, both sugars, cinnamon, salt, and cayenne pepper in medium bowl. Stir in pecans. Spread nuts in single layer on sheet, rounded side up. Bake until just browned and dry, about 30 minutes. Cool on sheet. Separate nuts, removing excess coating.

DO AHEAD: *Can be made 2 days ahead. Store airtight at room temperature.*

CRUST: Preheat oven to 350°F. Blend cookie crumbs, sugar, cinnamon, and salt in processor. Add melted butter; process until crumbs are moistened. Press crumbs into 9-inch-diameter tart pan with removable bottom to within ⅛ inch of top. Bake until set, about 20 minutes. Cool on rack.

FILLING: Bring cream to simmer in medium saucepan. Remove from heat. Add both chocolates; whisk until melted. Add butter, 1 piece at a time, whisking until smooth between additions. Whisk in vanilla, cinnamon, and salt. Pour filling into crust. Chill until filling begins to set, 15 to 20 minutes.

Arrange nuts in concentric circles atop tart. Chill until set, about 4 hours.

DO AHEAD: *Can be made 1 day ahead. Cover loosely with foil and keep chilled.*

Serve tart with whipped cream.

Chocolate-Raspberry Tart

For an extra hit of fruit flavor, the crust is spread with a little raspberry jam midway through baking. To create a glistening raspberry topping, skip the cocoa powder and powdered sugar and brush the berries with warm raspberry jam instead. **6 servings**

Crust

1	**cup unbleached all purpose flour**
¼	**cup sugar**
3	**tablespoons natural unsweetened cocoa powder**
¼	**teaspoon salt**
6	**tablespoons (¾ stick) chilled unsalted butter, cut into ½-inch cubes**
1½	**tablespoons (or more) ice water**
1	**large egg yolk**
6	**tablespoons raspberry jam**

Filling

1	**cup heavy whipping cream**
4	**ounces bittersweet or semisweet chocolate (do not exceed 61% cacao), chopped**
2	**½-pint containers raspberries**
1	**teaspoon powdered sugar**
1	**teaspoon natural unsweetened cocoa powder**

CRUST: Combine flour, sugar, cocoa, and salt in medium bowl. Add butter; using fingertips, rub in until mixture resembles coarse meal. Add 1½ tablespoons ice water and egg yolk; mix in with fork until moist clumps form, adding more ice water by teaspoonfuls if mixture is dry. Gather dough into ball; flatten into rectangle. Wrap in plastic and chill 30 minutes.

DO AHEAD: *Can be made 1 day ahead. Let stand at room temperature 20 minutes to soften slightly before rolling out.*

Butter and flour 13¾x4-inch rectangular tart pan with 1-inch-high sides and removable bottom. Roll out dough between 2 sheets of waxed paper to 15x6-inch rectangle. Peel off 1 sheet of waxed paper. Invert dough into prepared pan; peel off second sheet of waxed paper. Press dough onto bottom and up sides of pan, trimming edges if needed. Freeze until firm, about 30 minutes.

Preheat oven to 375°F. Line crust with foil; fill with dried beans or pie weights. Bake until crust is set, about 12 minutes. Remove foil and beans. Continue to bake until crust just begins to darken around edges, piercing with toothpick if crust bubbles, about 12 minutes longer. Remove from oven; maintain oven temperature. Spread jam over bottom of crust. Bake until jam is set, about 3 minutes. Transfer tart in pan to rack; cool crust completely.

FILLING: Bring cream to boil in heavy small saucepan. Remove from heat. Add chocolate and whisk until melted and smooth. Transfer chocolate ganache to bowl and refrigerate until chilled but not firm, about 45 minutes.

Using electric mixer, beat ganache until very thick and semi-firm. Spread ganache over jam in crust.

DO AHEAD: *Can be made 8 hours ahead. Refrigerate.*

Arrange raspberries atop ganache, rounded side up. Stir powdered sugar and cocoa in bowl. Sift over tart.

Mocha Custard Tart

Cream cheese gives the custard a luxurious texture. The tart needs to chill overnight, so be sure to start this recipe a day ahead. Look for chocolate-covered coffee bean candies at some supermarkets, and at candy shops and specialty foods stores. **12 servings**

Crust

	Nonstick vegetable oil spray
1	9-ounce package chocolate wafer cookies
½	cup walnuts
5	tablespoons unsalted butter, melted

Filling

2	cups heavy whipping cream
¾	cup whole milk
⅓	cup water
⅓	cup unsweetened cocoa powder (preferably Dutch-process)
2	tablespoons chocolate liqueur (such as dark crème de cacao)
2	teaspoons instant espresso powder
2	teaspoons vanilla extract
1	8-ounce package Philadelphia-brand cream cheese, room temperature
1	cup plus 2 tablespoons sugar
4	extra-large eggs
2	extra-large egg yolks

Ganache

½	cup heavy whipping cream
1	teaspoon instant espresso powder or coffee powder
1	teaspoon light corn syrup
1	teaspoon vegetable oil
8	ounces bittersweet or semisweet chocolate (do not exceed 61% cacao), chopped
½	teaspoon vanilla extract

Chocolate-covered coffee bean candies (optional)

> ### Technique Tip: **Is It Ready?**
> To test if the ganache is ready to decorate, run the icing comb or fork in it: If the ganache doesn't hold the impression from the comb, chill the tart 10 minutes and test again. Icing combs are available at cookware stores and restaurant supply stores.

CRUST: Position rack in center of oven and preheat to 350°F. Spray 10-inch-diameter springform pan with nonstick spray. Wrap outside of pan tightly with triple layer of heavy-duty foil. Finely grind cookies and walnuts in processor. Add melted butter; process to blend. Press mixture firmly onto bottom (not sides) of prepared pan. Chill crust while making filling.

FILLING: Bring cream, milk, and ⅓ cup water to simmer in heavy small saucepan. Remove from heat. Whisk in cocoa powder, chocolate liqueur, espresso powder, and vanilla.

Using electric mixer, beat cream cheese in large bowl until smooth. Add sugar and beat until well blended. Add whole eggs 1 at a time, then egg yolks, beating well after each addition and occasionally scraping down sides of bowl. Gradually add hot cream mixture and beat until smooth. Pour mixture into prepared crust. Place springform pan in large roasting pan. Pour enough boiling water into roasting pan to come halfway up sides of springform pan.

Bake tart until custard moves just slightly in center when pan is gently shaken and tester inserted into center comes out with some custard still attached, about 1 hour 20 minutes. Remove pan from water; remove foil. Cool tart in pan on rack. Cover with foil and refrigerate overnight.

GANACHE: Bring cream, espresso powder, corn syrup, and oil to simmer in heavy small saucepan. Remove from heat. Add chocolate and vanilla; whisk until chocolate is melted and smooth. Let ganache stand until slightly cooled but still pourable, about 10 minutes.

Run small knife around pan sides to loosen tart. Remove pan sides. Place tart on platter. Pour ganache atop tart. Using thin metal spatula, spread ganache evenly over top of tart, being careful not to allow ganache to drip down sides. Let ganache set 15 minutes. Using icing comb or tines of fork, make decorative concentric circles in wave pattern in ganache. Garnish top of tart with chocolate-covered coffee bean candies, if desired. Refrigerate until ganache is softly set, about 15 minutes.

DO AHEAD: *Can be made 2 days ahead. Cover and keep chilled. Let stand at room temperature 45 minutes before serving.*

Chocolate Ganache Tart with Toasted Pecan Crust

Ganache is a French pastry term for a rich chocolate filling or icing—it's generally a simple mixture of dark chocolate and cream. Don't use chocolate that has more than 61% cacao, as the results will be too firm and bitter. You can use toasted hazelnuts or almonds in place of the pecans in the crust. **8 to 12 servings**

Crust

Nonstick vegetable oil spray

9	whole graham crackers, broken
½	cup pecans, toasted
¼	cup (packed) dark brown sugar
	Generous pinch of salt
5	tablespoons unsalted butter, melted
½	teaspoon vanilla extract

Filling

1	cup plus 2 tablespoons heavy whipping cream
2	tablespoons (packed) dark brown sugar
	Generous pinch of salt
6	ounces bittersweet or semisweet chocolate (do not exceed 61% cacao), chopped
1	tablespoon brandy
1	teaspoon vanilla extract
3	ounces high-quality white chocolate (such as Lindt or Perugina), chopped

CRUST: Preheat oven to 350°F. Spray 9-inch-diameter tart pan with removable bottom with nonstick spray. Combine graham crackers, pecans, sugar, and salt in food processor and blend until nuts and crackers are finely ground. Mix in melted butter and vanilla. Press crumbs evenly on bottom and up sides of prepared pan (crust will be thick). Bake until set and just beginning to turn golden brown, about 10 minutes. Cool.

FILLING: Bring cream, sugar, and salt to simmer in heavy medium saucepan over medium heat. Remove from heat. Add bittersweet chocolate and whisk until melted and smooth. Whisk in brandy and vanilla. Pour filling into crust.

Melt white chocolate in heavy small skillet, stirring constantly over very low heat. Transfer white chocolate to resealable plastic bag; twist bag just above point where filled. Snip tip of bag to create very small opening. Or transfer chocolate to pastry bag fitted with very small pastry tip (about ⅟₁₆-inch diameter). Starting in center of tart, pipe white chocolate in 1 continuous spiral, working outward to edge, spacing lines ½ inch apart. Using small sharp knife, draw knife tip through white chocolate lines from center to outer edge. Lift knife tip and draw second line from outer edge to center. Repeat several more times, alternating direction of lines from center to edge and edge to center, spacing evenly, to create floral pattern. Chill until set, about 2 hours.

DO AHEAD: *Can be made 3 days ahead. Tent with foil. Keep chilled.*

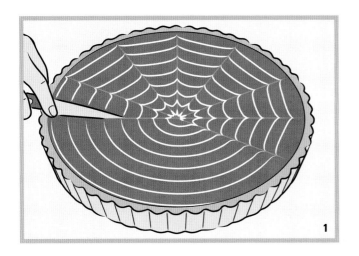

Spooky Design

Creating a spiderweb design on the tart makes this an excellent Halloween treat. Starting in the center of the tart, pipe the white chocolate in one continuous spiral, working outward to the edge, spacing lines ½ inch apart. Using a small sharp knife, draw the knife tip through the white chocolate lines from the center to the outer edge [1]. Repeat about 15 more times, spacing evenly, to create a spiderweb pattern.

Chocolate Tart with Candied Cranberries

Who says cranberries are only for making relish? Here, the tangy berries get tossed with sugar and baked until they're sweet-tart and pretty enough to top a decadent chocolate tart. **10 servings**

Crust

1²⁄₃	cups unbleached all purpose flour
2	tablespoons sugar
¼	teaspoon salt
10	tablespoons (1¼ sticks) chilled unsalted butter, cut into ½-inch pieces
2½	tablespoons (or more) ice water
1	large egg yolk
1	teaspoon vanilla extract

Filling

½	cup heavy whipping cream
8	ounces bittersweet or semisweet chocolate (do not exceed 61% cacao), chopped
3	tablespoons crème de cassis (black currant liqueur)

Candied Cranberries

	Nonstick vegetable oil spray
1½	12-ounce packages frozen cranberries (unthawed)
1	cup sugar

CRUST: Blend flour, sugar, and salt in processor. Add butter; using on/off turns, cut in until mixture resembles coarse meal. Add 2½ tablespoons ice water, egg yolk, and vanilla. Blend until moist clumps form, adding more ice water by ½ tablespoonfuls if dry. Gather dough into ball; flatten into disk. Wrap in plastic; chill at least 2 hours.

DO AHEAD: *Can be made 2 days ahead. Keep chilled. Let soften slightly at room temperature before rolling out.*

Preheat oven to 375°F. Roll out dough disk on lightly floured surface to 13- to 14-inch round. Transfer dough to 9-inch-diameter tart pan with removable bottom. Cut dough overhang to ¾ inch; fold overhang in and press, forming sides that extend ¼ inch above top of pan. Pierce crust all over with fork. Freeze 15 minutes.

Bake crust 15 minutes. If sides of crust fall, press up with back of fork. Continue to bake crust until beginning to brown, about 15 minutes longer. Cool on rack.

FILLING: Bring cream to simmer in heavy medium saucepan. Remove from heat. Add chocolate and whisk until smooth. Whisk in crème de cassis. Pour filling into crust. Chill until filling is firm, at least 2 hours and up to 1 day.

CANDIED CRANBERRIES: Preheat oven to 375°F. Spray rimmed baking sheet with nonstick spray. Toss cranberries and sugar in medium bowl to blend. Spread out mixture on baking sheet. Bake 10 minutes. Using metal spatula, stir berries gently. Bake until berries are thawed and most sugar is dissolved, about 5 minutes longer. Cool on sheet 5 minutes. Spoon berries atop filling; drizzle with syrup from sheet. Chill 1 hour.

DO AHEAD: *Can be made 1 day ahead. Keep chilled.*

Chocolate Truffle Linzer Heart

In this take on a classic Linzertorte, a hazelnut-based crust is filled with chocolate-raspberry ganache. The finishing touch? A pre-baked top crust that's decorated with whipped cream and fresh raspberries. **10 servings**

Crust

1	cup hazelnuts, toasted
2/3	cup sugar
1¼	cups sifted unbleached all purpose flour (sifted, then measured)
1¼	teaspoons ground cinnamon
½	teaspoon salt
¼	teaspoon ground cloves
¼	teaspoon ground ginger
½	cup plus 2 tablespoons (1¼ sticks) chilled unsalted butter, cut into ½-inch cubes
1	ounce Philadelphia-brand cream cheese, cut into small pieces, frozen
1	large egg, beaten to blend
½	ounce bittersweet or semisweet chocolate, finely chopped
1	egg white, beaten to blend
1/3	cup seedless raspberry jam

Filling

9	ounces bittersweet or semisweet chocolate (do not exceed 61% cacao), chopped
5	tablespoons unsalted butter, room temperature
3	tablespoons heavy whipping cream
1/3	cup plus 2 tablespoons seedless raspberry jam
1	½-pint container raspberries
	Lightly sweetened whipped cream

CRUST: Position rack in lowest third of oven. Set baking sheet on rack and preheat to 375°F. Remove bottom from 10½x9½-inch heart-shaped tart pan with 1-inch-high sides and removable bottom. Place pan bottom on parchment paper and trace heart shape.

Finely chop nuts with sugar in processor. Add flour, cinnamon, salt, cloves, and ginger. Process just to blend. Add butter and cream cheese to processor. Process until mixture resembles coarse meal. Add egg and chocolate. Using on/off turns, process until large moist clumps form.

Recipe Tip: Linzertorte

Austria is known for its delicious pastries, including the Linzertorte, which hails from the city of Linz. Some people believe that the Linzertorte—a buttery, hazelnut- or almond-based crust spread with raspberry jam and topped with a lattice crust—is the world's oldest-known cake, dating back to the 1650s.

To form top crust, transfer 1⅓ cups dough to pastry bag fitted with No. 4 (⅜-inch-diameter) plain tip. Chill remaining dough. Pipe 7 parallel diagonal lines about ¾ inch apart across heart outline on parchment. Pipe border around edge of heart inside traced line, touching ends of diagonal lines (some dough may be left over in pastry bag). Freeze 10 minutes. Brush dough with some egg white. Slide parchment with heart onto heated baking sheet and bake until crust is golden and edges are beginning to brown, about 15 minutes. Run long thin spatula between crust and parchment to loosen crust. Slide parchment with heart-shaped crust onto rack and cool completely. Maintain oven temperature.

Return removable bottom to heart-shaped pan. Press remaining dough onto bottom and ¾ inch up sides of pan, using plastic wrap if necessary to prevent dough from sticking to hands. Freeze until dough is firm, about 10 minutes. Brush lightly with egg white. Set pan on heated baking sheet and bake until crust is golden brown and sides are beginning to pull away from pan, about 23 minutes. Spread bottom crust evenly with jam. Bake 3 more minutes. Cool crust completely on rack.

FILLING: Stir chocolate, butter, and cream in heavy medium saucepan over medium-low heat until chocolate and butter are melted and mixture is smooth. Mix in 2 tablespoons jam. Cool slightly. Pour filling evenly into bottom crust; smooth top. Chill until filling is firm, about 30 minutes.

Spread remaining ⅓ cup jam over filling and outer edge of bottom crust. Carefully place cooled heart-shaped top crust atop jam. Press gently to seal. Cover with foil and chill overnight.

DO AHEAD: *Can be made 2 days ahead. Keep chilled.*

Remove torte from pan. Transfer to platter. Let stand at room temperature 45 minutes. Arrange raspberries in row in first space between crust lines. Spoon whipped cream into pastry bag fitted with small star tip. Pipe row of small rosettes in second space between crust lines. Continue decorating torte, alternating rows of raspberries and whipped cream rosettes between crust lines.

Dark Chocolate and Peppermint Whipped Cream Tart

There are two advantages to using a resealable plastic bag snipped at one corner to pipe the whipped cream: You can simply throw it away when you're done, and the bag's seam leaves behind a decorative line in the piped cream, creating a professional-looking finish. The entire tart can be assembled well in advance, but wait until just before serving to garnish it with the crushed peppermint candies, so they'll stay crunchy and their color won't bleed into the cream. **8 to 10 servings**

Crust

1¼   cups unbleached all purpose flour
⅓   cup powdered sugar
¼   teaspoon baking powder
¼   teaspoon salt
10   tablespoons (1¼ sticks) chilled unsalted butter, cut into
       ½-inch cubes
1   teaspoon vanilla extract
4½   teaspoons chilled whole milk

Filling

1¼   cups heavy whipping cream
¼   cup light corn syrup
12   ounces bittersweet or semisweet chocolate (do not exceed
       61% cacao), chopped
1   ounce unsweetened chocolate, chopped
½   cup coarsely crushed red-and-white-striped hard peppermint
       candies

Topping

3½   cups chilled heavy whipping cream
¾   cup powdered sugar
1¾   teaspoons peppermint extract
1   tablespoon coarsely crushed red-and-white-striped hard
       peppermint candies

CRUST: Blend flour, sugar, baking powder, and salt in processor. Add butter and vanilla; using on/off turns, cut in until butter forms pea-size pieces. Add milk; using on/off turns, blend in until mixture forms small moist clumps. Gather dough into ball; flatten into disk. Wrap dough in plastic; chill 1 hour.

Roll out dough disk between sheets of floured parchment to 12-inch round. Press dough onto bottom and up sides of 10-inch-diameter tart pan with removable bottom. Fold dough edges over and press to form thick sides. Using thumb, press dough around sides to extend crust ⅛ inch above edge of pan. Freeze 20 minutes.

Preheat oven to 350°F. Bake crust until brown, piercing with fork if bubbles form, about 30 minutes. Transfer to rack; cool.

FILLING: Bring cream and corn syrup to simmer in medium saucepan; remove from heat. Add both chocolates; whisk until smooth. Cool 30 minutes. Pour filling into crust. Sprinkle with peppermint candies. Chill until set, about 3 hours.

DO AHEAD: *Can be made 1 day ahead. Cover and keep chilled.*

TOPPING: Using electric mixer, beat all ingredients in large bowl to stiff peaks. Spread 2 cups whipped cream over filling, mounding slightly in center. Spoon remaining whipped cream into 1 bottom corner of large resealable plastic bag. Twist bag at top and grasp top firmly. Using scissors, cut ¾ inch off filled corner of bag to form opening; turn bag so that 1 seam faces up. Pipe 2-inch-long ovals of whipped cream side by side around edge of tart. Pipe more ovals to form second ring inside first, then pipe ovals in center. Chill at least 30 minutes and up to 3 hours. Remove tart from pan; place on platter. Sprinkle top of tart with crushed peppermint candies and serve.

Sugarplum Tart with Semisweet Chocolate Glaze

This elegant double-crusted tart evokes the kind of classic Christmas captured in Clement Clarke Moore's "A Visit from St. Nicholas." The tart is filled with caramel, walnuts, and dried fruit—which is what sugarplums are actually made of (there are no plums in them at all). The presentation of the tart with all the components is stunning, but the tart is also fantastic without the sugarplums.

10 servings

Crust

1½	**cups unbleached all purpose flour**
¼	**cup sugar**
10½	**tablespoons chilled unsalted butter, cut into ½-inch cubes**
1	**egg yolk**
1	**tablespoon heavy whipping cream, chilled**

Filling

½	**cup walnuts, coarsely chopped**
¼	**cup raisins**
¼	**cup golden raisins**
¼	**cup dried apricots, cut into ½-inch pieces**
¼	**cup dried pineapple, cut into ½-inch pieces**
3	**tablespoons brandy**

Caramel

1	**cup plus 2 tablespoons sugar**
¾	**cup water**
¾	**cup plus 2 tablespoons heavy whipping cream**
5	**tablespoons unsalted butter, cut into 5 pieces**

Semisweet Chocolate Glaze (see recipe)
Sugarplums (see recipe)

CRUST: Mix flour and sugar in large bowl. Add butter and cut in until mixture resembles coarse meal. Mix egg yolk with cream in small bowl to blend. Add to flour mixture and stir until dough comes together. Gather dough into 2 balls, 1 slightly larger than the other. Flatten into disks. Wrap separately in plastic and chill 30 minutes.

DO AHEAD: *Can be made 1 day ahead. Keep chilled. Let soften slightly at room temperature before rolling out.*

FILLING: Combine all ingredients in medium metal bowl. Let mixture soak at least 2 hours and up to 6 hours.

Roll larger dough disk out on floured surface to 12-inch round. Roll dough up on rolling pin and transfer to 9-inch-diameter tart pan with removable bottom. Trim and finish dough edges. Roll second dough disk out to 10-inch round. Transfer to baking sheet. Chill tart shell and dough round 1 hour.

CARAMEL: Cook sugar and ¾ cup water in heavy medium saucepan over medium-low heat, stirring until sugar dissolves. Increase heat and boil without stirring until syrup is deep amber color, occasionally brushing down sides of pan with wet pastry brush and swirling pan, about 10 minutes. Add cream and butter and whisk to combine (mixture will bubble vigorously). Continue cooking until candy thermometer registers 238°F. Pour caramel into medium metal bowl. Cool to room temperature, about 1 hour.

Preheat oven to 350°F. Line baking sheet with parchment paper or foil. Spread filling evenly in crust. Pour caramel over. Press dough round on top. Trim off excess. Pierce in several places with tip of small sharp knife.

Place tart on prepared sheet. Bake until crust is golden brown, about 35 minutes (some caramel may leak out). Cool on rack, about 6 hours.

(continued next page)

Sugarplum Tart with Semisweet Chocolate Glaze *(continued)*

Turn tart over onto rack. Set over rimmed baking sheet. Spoon some Semisweet Chocolate Glaze over sides of tart. Set aside ½ cup glaze. Pour remaining glaze over tart. Smooth top and sides of tart with spatula if necessary.

Line small baking sheet with waxed paper. Rewarm reserved ½ cup glaze in top of double boiler over simmering water until just lukewarm, stirring occasionally. Grasp 1 sugarplum between thumb and index finger; dip halfway into glaze. Remove from glaze and allow excess to drip back into pan. Place on prepared sheet, chocolate side up. Repeat with remaining sugarplums. Chill sugarplums until glaze is set, about 30 minutes.

Garnish top of tart with glazed sugarplums.

DO AHEAD: *Can be made 1 day ahead. Cover and chill.*

Cut into wedges. Serve at room temperature.

Semisweet Chocolate Glaze

Be sure to use the glaze after it has stood just long enough to cool but is still pourable. Try it on cakes and bar cookies, as well. **Makes about 1½ cups**

½   **cup heavy whipping cream**
¼   **cup (½ stick) unsalted butter, room temperature**
10   **ounces bittersweet or semisweet chocolate (do not exceed 61% cacao), chopped**

Bring cream and butter to simmer in heavy medium saucepan. Remove from heat. Add chocolate; whisk until melted and smooth. Let glaze stand until just cool to touch.

Sugarplums

These Christmas classics are made primarily of walnuts, dried apricots, raisins, coconut, and dates. A food processor makes mixing the ingredients quick and easy; a smidgen of brandy and a little sugar add a festive touch. You might also consider adding a pinch of holiday spices, such as cinnamon, cloves, or nutmeg. This recipe can be doubled, if desired. **Makes about twenty-five ½-inch balls**

¼   **cup walnuts**
¼   **cup dried apricots**
2   **tablespoons golden raisins**
2   **tablespoons sweetened flaked coconut**
2   **tablespoons pitted dates**
1   **tablespoon brandy**
¼   **cup sugar**

Using on/off turns, finely chop walnuts, apricots, raisins, coconut, and dates in processor (do not puree). Transfer to small bowl; mix in brandy. Form mixture into ½-inch balls by rolling teaspoonfuls between hands. Roll balls in sugar.

DO AHEAD: *Sugarplums can be made 1 day ahead. Store at room temperature in airtight container.*

More Sugarplums

Various dried fruits—raisins, apricots, and pineapple—are used in this tart, but you can substitute any dried fruit of your choice. Dried tart cherries make good alternatives to the golden raisins, and dried peaches or nectarines are good in place of the apricots. Look for the finest dried fruits at local farmers' markets and natural foods stores.

Chocolate-Cognac Truffle Tartlets

In this decadent dessert, part of the slightly boozy chocolate truffle filling is spooned into the tartlet crusts. The remainder is turned into chocolate truffles for garnish. Any leftover truffles can be kept frozen for an instant special-occasion treat. Be sure to start this recipe one day ahead. **Makes 4 tartlets (4 to 8 servings)**

Crust

1	cup unbleached all purpose flour
¼	cup plus 2 tablespoons natural unsweetened cocoa powder
	Pinch of salt
½	cup (1 stick) unsalted butter, room temperature
½	cup (packed) golden brown sugar
1½	teaspoons vanilla extract
	Nonstick vegetable oil spray

Filling and Truffles

1¼	cups heavy whipping cream
2	tablespoons (¼ stick) unsalted butter
10	ounces bittersweet or semisweet chocolate (do not exceed 61% cacao), chopped
3	tablespoons Cognac or other brandy
⅔	cup pecans, toasted, finely chopped
4	½- by 5-inch parchment paper strips
	Natural unsweetened cocoa powder

CRUST: Mix flour, cocoa powder, and salt in small bowl. Using electric mixer, beat butter, brown sugar, and vanilla in medium bowl until creamy. Add flour mixture and stir with fork until coarse meal forms. Gather dough into ball; flatten into disk. Wrap in plastic and chill 30 minutes.

Divide dough into 4 equal pieces. Press 1 dough piece evenly over bottom and up sides of 4½-inch-diameter tartlet pan with removable bottom. Repeat with remaining 3 dough pieces. Freeze 20 minutes.

DO AHEAD: *Can be made 1 day ahead. Cover and keep frozen.*

Preheat oven to 350°F. Spray four 7-inch foil squares with nonstick spray. Line crusts with foil, sprayed side down. Fill with dried beans or pie weights. Bake crusts until set, about 20 minutes. Remove foil and beans. Continue baking until crusts feel dry, about 5 minutes longer. Transfer to rack; cool completely.

FILLING AND TRUFFLES: Combine cream and butter in medium saucepan. Stir over low heat until butter melts. Add chocolate; stir until melted. Whisk in Cognac. Cool filling 15 minutes.

Spoon enough filling into crusts to fill (about ½ cup for each); reserve remaining filling. Refrigerate tartlets and reserved filling overnight.

Line small baking sheet with foil. Form reserved filling into balls, using generous rounded ½ teaspoonful for each. Place on prepared sheet. Freeze 15 minutes. Roll each truffle in chopped pecans, coating completely. Freeze until truffles are firm, about 1 hour.

Let tartlets stand at room temperature 15 minutes. Place parchment paper strips in lattice pattern atop 1 tartlet. Sift cocoa over. Remove strips. Repeat with remaining tartlets. Garnish each with 3 truffles.

Chocolate-Whiskey Soufflé Tarts

Two dessert favorites come together in this treat: A chocolate soufflé rises out of a tender tart crust. The tarts can be assembled and frozen up to one week ahead, making this the perfect dessert to keep on hand for unexpected guests. **Makes 8**

Crust

1½   cups unbleached all purpose flour
¾   cup (1½ sticks) chilled unsalted butter, cut into ½-inch cubes
¾   cup powdered sugar
½   teaspoon (scant) salt

Filling

10   ounces bittersweet or semisweet chocolate (do not exceed 61% cacao), chopped
¼   cup Irish whiskey
1½   teaspoons vanilla extract
1¼   teaspoons instant coffee crystals
    Pinch of salt
4   large eggs, room temperature, separated
½   cup sugar

    Sweetened whipped cream
    Chocolate shavings (optional)

CRUST: Preheat oven to 350°F. Blend flour, butter, sugar, and salt in processor just until dough gathers together. Shape dough into log; cut into 8 equal rounds. Using fingertips, press 1 dough round over bottom and up sides of 4½-inch-diameter tartlet pan with removable bottom. Repeat with remaining 7 dough rounds. Pierce crusts with fork; bake until pale golden, about 18 minutes. Cool in pans on rack.

FILLING: Finely chop generous ⅓ cup chopped chocolate and set aside. Stir remaining chopped chocolate in medium metal bowl set over saucepan of barely simmering water until melted and smooth. Remove bowl from over water. Whisk in whiskey, vanilla, coffee, and salt, then egg yolks. Beat room-temperature egg whites in another medium bowl until soft peaks form. Gradually add sugar, beating until stiff but not dry. Fold half of whites into chocolate mixture. Fold in reserved ⅓ cup finely chopped chocolate, then remaining egg whites. Divide mixture among crusts. Freeze at least 3 hours.

DO AHEAD: *Can be made 1 week ahead. Cover and keep frozen.*

Preheat oven to 375°F. Release pan sides from frozen tartlets. Arrange tartlets on their pan bottoms on baking sheet. Bake until filling puffs and begins to crack, about 20 minutes.

Place tartlets on plates. Spoon whipped cream alongside. Top with chocolate shavings, if desired.

♪♪♪ Caramel-Hazelnut Mini Tartlets

There's a reason these are miniature in size: They are incredibly rich. Freezing the crusts before baking reduces buckling and helps the tartlets hold their shape in the oven. Silicone mini muffin pans, which make the tartlets really easy to unmold, are available online and at cookware stores. **Makes 30**

Crust

1½	cups unbleached all purpose flour
2	tablespoons sugar
¼	teaspoon salt
½	cup (1 stick) chilled unsalted butter, cut into ½-inch cubes
5	tablespoons (or more) chilled heavy whipping cream
1	teaspoon vanilla extract
1	cup (about) hazelnuts, toasted, husked (about 5 ounces)

Filling

1⅓	cups (packed) golden brown sugar
7	tablespoons unsalted butter
6	tablespoons light corn syrup
2	tablespoons water
½	teaspoon salt
6	tablespoons heavy whipping cream
3	ounces bittersweet or semisweet chocolate (do not exceed 61% cacao), chopped

CRUST: Butter 30 metal or silicone mini muffin cups (1- to 1½-tablespoon capacity). Blend flour, sugar, and salt in processor. Add butter; using on/off turns, blend until coarse meal forms. Add 5 tablespoons cream and vanilla; using on/off turns, blend until moist clumps form, adding more cream by teaspoonfuls if dough is dry. Press 2 teaspoonfuls dough evenly onto bottom and up sides of each prepared mini muffin cup. Pierce tartlet crusts all over with fork. Freeze crusts 30 minutes.

DO AHEAD: *Can be made 1 day ahead. Cover and keep frozen.*

Preheat oven to 350°F. Bake frozen crusts until golden and baked through, about 25 minutes. Transfer to rack and cool in muffin cups 10 minutes. Carefully loosen crusts from muffin cups. Transfer crusts to rimmed baking sheet and cool completely. Place 2 to 3 hazelnuts in each crust.

FILLING: Combine brown sugar, butter, corn syrup, 2 tablespoons water, and salt in heavy large saucepan. Stir over medium heat until sugar dissolves. Bring mixture to boil, then boil 2 minutes without stirring (mixture will bubble up and thicken slightly). Remove pan from heat. Add cream (mixture will bubble vigorously); stir until smooth. Pour caramel into medium heatproof bowl; cool 10 minutes. Spoon caramel over hazelnuts in crusts, filling crusts almost to top. Refrigerate until caramel begins to firm up slightly, about 1 hour.

Stir chocolate in small bowl set over saucepan of simmering water until melted and smooth. Remove bowl from over water. Using spoon, drizzle melted chocolate over top of tartlets. Chill until chocolate is set, about 30 minutes.

DO AHEAD: *Can be made 1 day ahead. Keep refrigerated. Let stand at room temperature 1 hour before serving.*

Milk Chocolate–Pecan Tartlets

Milk chocolate is often relegated to the candy jar, but it's just right for these cute little tartlets, which have an easy press-in crust. **Makes 18**

Crust
1¼   **cups unbleached all purpose flour**
⅓   **cup pecans, toasted**
¼   **cup sugar**
     Pinch of salt
6   **tablespoons (¾ stick) chilled unsalted butter, cut into**
         ½-inch cubes
1   **large egg yolk**
1½   **teaspoons (or more) heavy whipping cream**
     Nonstick vegetable oil spray

Filling
9   **ounces imported milk chocolate (such as Lindt), chopped**
⅓   **cup plus 1 tablespoon heavy whipping cream**
3   **tablespoons finely chopped toasted pecans**

¼   **cup (about) apricot preserves**
18   **pecan halves, toasted**
     Grated milk chocolate

> ## Equipment Tip: **Tartlet Pans**
> This recipe calls for eighteen 3-inch-diameter tartlet pans, which are available at some specialty foods stores and restaurant supply stores.

CRUST: Blend flour, pecans, sugar, and salt in processor until nuts are finely chopped. Add butter; using on/off turns, process until mixture resembles coarse meal. Mix egg yolk and 1½ teaspoons cream in bowl. Add to flour mixture; process until moist clumps form, adding more cream by teaspoonfuls if dough is dry. Gather dough into ball; flatten into disk. Wrap in plastic and chill 4 hours. Let stand at room temperature 20 minutes to soften slightly.

Preheat oven to 350°F. Spray eighteen 3-inch-diameter tartlet pans with nonstick spray. Using fingertips, press 1 tablespoon dough onto bottom and up sides of each prepared pan. Arrange tartlet pans on heavy large baking sheet. Bake until crusts are golden, piercing with fork if bubbles form, about 10 minutes. Transfer pans to rack; cool completely.

FILLING: Stir milk chocolate in medium bowl set over saucepan of simmering water until melted and smooth. Remove from heat. Bring cream just to simmer in small saucepan. Pour hot cream into chocolate; stir until smooth. Stir in chopped pecans. Transfer filling to small bowl. Cover and chill until filling is consistency of thick pudding, stirring occasionally, about 2 hours.

Using small knife, loosen crusts from pans. Turn crusts out onto work surface. Spread 1 teaspoon preserves in each crust. Spoon 1 tablespoon filling over each. Garnish with pecan halves and grated chocolate. Chill until filling is firm, about 1 hour. Serve tartlets cold.

DO AHEAD: *Can be made 1 day ahead. Cover and chill.*

White Chocolate–Raspberry Crème Brûlée Tartlets

This elegant sweet is a marriage of smooth crème brûlée and a raspberry tart. These tartlets would be perfect for a special romantic dinner. If your broiler doesn't get hot enough, a small kitchen torch, available at cookware stores, can be used to caramelize the sugar. If fresh raspberries are unavailable, thawed whole frozen raspberries will work in a pinch. Start preparing the tarts at least one day before serving to allow the custard to set. **Makes 2**

Crust

¾	**cup unbleached all purpose flour**
4	**teaspoons sugar**
⅛	**teaspoon salt**
¼	**cup (½ stick) chilled unsalted butter, cut into ½-inch cubes**
1½	**teaspoons minced crystallized ginger**
1	**tablespoon (or more) ice water**
1	**tablespoon raspberry preserves, stirred to loosen**

Filling

6	**tablespoons heavy whipping cream**
1	**ounce high-quality white chocolate (such as Lindt or Perugina), chopped**
2	**large egg yolks**
¼	**teaspoon vanilla extract**
2	**teaspoons sugar**
	Fresh raspberries

CRUST: Blend flour, sugar, and salt in processor. Add butter and ginger; using on/off turns, process until mixture resembles coarse meal. Add 1 tablespoon ice water and blend until moist clumps form, adding more ice water by teaspoonfuls if dough is dry. Gather dough into ball; divide in half. Flatten each half into disk and wrap in plastic. Chill until firm, about 1 hour.

DO AHEAD: *Can be made 1 day ahead. Keep refrigerated. Let soften slightly at room temperature before rolling out.*

Roll out dough disks on lightly floured surface to 6-inch rounds. Press 1 round into 4½-inch-diameter tartlet pan with removable bottom. Trim dough overhang to ½ inch; fold in, pressing to form double-thick sides. Repeat with remaining dough round. Pierce crusts all over with fork. Freeze 30 minutes.

Preheat oven to 375°F. Bake crusts until golden, piercing with fork if crusts bubble, about 25 minutes. Transfer to rack. Immediately spoon ½ tablespoon preserves over bottom of each crust. Cool completely. Reduce oven temperature to 350°F.

FILLING: Bring cream to simmer in heavy medium saucepan. Remove from heat; add white chocolate and whisk until melted. Whisk egg yolks and vanilla in medium bowl. Slowly whisk cream mixture into yolk mixture to blend well. Divide custard between crusts. Bake tartlets until centers are just set, about 20 minutes. Cool on rack. Chill tartlets overnight.

Preheat broiler. Sprinkle each tartlet with 1 teaspoon sugar. Broil just until sugar melts and browns, covering crusts with foil to prevent burning, about 2 minutes. Refrigerate tartlets until cold, at least 1 hour and up to 3 hours. Remove pan sides from tartlets. Arrange raspberries around edge of tartlets.

Cherry-Almond Tartlets

These tartlets have a classic French "brown butter" filling. Butter is swirled over medium-low heat until it becomes golden brown, giving it a rich, nutty flavor. The filling is slightly cakey—making the tartlets durable enough to transport to a picnic or a party. (For best results, transport the tartlets in their pans.) Morello cherries can be found at Trader Joe's, at other specialty foods stores, and online. Sweetened whipped cream makes a good substitute for the crème fraîche.

Makes 8

Crust

1	cup unbleached all purpose flour
½	cup slivered almonds, toasted
¼	cup sugar
½	teaspoon salt
½	cup (1 stick) chilled unsalted butter, cut into ½-inch cubes
1	large egg yolk

Filling

½	cup (1 stick) unsalted butter
½	cup sugar
2	large eggs
3	tablespoons unbleached all purpose flour
¼	teaspoon almond extract
⅛	teaspoon salt
1	24.7-ounce jar dark Morello cherries in light syrup, well drained, syrup reserved

Sweetened Crème Fraîche

1	cup crème fraîche
2	tablespoons sugar

CRUST: Blend flour, almonds, sugar, and salt in processor until almonds are finely chopped. Add butter; using on/off turns, cut in until mixture resembles coarse meal. Add egg yolk and process until moist clumps form. Gather dough into ball; flatten into disk. Wrap in plastic and freeze 15 minutes.

Butter bottoms of eight 4-inch-diameter tartlet pans with ¾-inch-high sides and removable bottoms. Divide dough into 8 equal pieces. Press dough evenly onto bottom and up sides of each prepared tartlet pan. Place tartlets on large rimmed baking sheet. Chill while preparing filling.

DO AHEAD: *Can be made 1 day ahead. Cover and keep chilled.*

FILLING: Preheat oven to 375°F. Melt butter in heavy small saucepan over medium-low heat. Continue to cook, swirling pan occasionally, until butter turns golden brown, about 12 minutes. Whisk sugar, eggs, flour, almond extract, and salt in medium bowl to blend. Whisk in browned butter to form a smooth batter.

Divide cherries among tartlets (about 10 per tartlet). Spoon batter over cherries, dividing evenly. Bake tartlets until golden brown and set in center, about 25 minutes. Cool on rack at least 30 minutes. Remove pan sides from tartlets and cool completely.

Meanwhile, boil reserved cherry syrup in heavy small saucepan over medium-high heat until reduced to ⅓ cup, about 25 minutes.

SWEETENED CRÈME FRAÎCHE: Stir crème fraîche and sugar in small bowl to blend.

DO AHEAD: *Can be made 1 day ahead. Cover tartlets and keep at room temperature. Transfer reduced cherry syrup to small bowl and chill. Return sweetened crème fraîche to container; cover and chill.*

Transfer tartlets to plates. Spoon crème fraîche alongside. Drizzle with reduced cherry syrup and serve.

Nectarine Tartlets with Puff Pastry and Almond Filling

Frozen puff pastry makes an instant crust for the nectarines. Look for delicious all-butter frozen puff pastry (in 1-pound packages) in some markets and at specialty foods stores, or use regular puff pastry. Marzipan can be found in the baking aisle of most supermarkets. **Makes 6**

- **1 sheet frozen puff pastry (half of 16-ounce package all-butter puff pastry or half of 17.3-ounce package regular puff pastry), thawed**
- **1 large egg, beaten to blend**
- **6 ounces marzipan, very thinly sliced**
- **3 firm but ripe nectarines, halved, pitted**
- **8 teaspoons sugar, divided**
- **⅔ cup chilled heavy whipping cream**
- **Drop of almond extract**

Line heavy large baking sheet with parchment paper or silicone baking mat. Roll out puff pastry sheet on lightly floured surface to 18x11-inch rectangle with about ⅛-inch thickness. Cut pastry into six 6x5½-inch rectangles. Cut off ½-inch-wide strip from each side of 1 rectangle. Brush strips with beaten egg. Place 2 long strips, egg side down, atop long edges of 1 rectangle. Place short strips, egg side down, atop short edges, trimming to fit. Repeat with remaining rectangles. Place pastries on prepared baking sheet.

DO AHEAD: *Can be made 1 day ahead. Cover and chill.*

Preheat oven to 400°F. Divide marzipan into 6 equal portions. Press marzipan to fit and cover bottom of pastries. Thinly slice each nectarine half. Slightly fan slices in center of each pastry atop marzipan. Sprinkle each with 1 teaspoon sugar. Bake tartlets until crusts are golden brown, about 35 minutes. Transfer to rack and cool slightly.

Whisk cream, remaining 2 teaspoons sugar, and almond extract in medium bowl until thick and fluffy. Serve tartlets with whipped cream.

Technique Tip: **Added Beauty**

Try making the tartlets with a combination of yellow and white nectarines. For a pretty finishing touch, brush melted peach or apricot preserves over the nectarines when the tartlets come out of the oven.

Mango Meringue Tartlets

These tartlets are tropical throughout: Coconut adds flavor and texture to the crust, while pureed ripe mangoes enhanced with spices and lime create a velvety filling. **Makes 6**

- **2 cups unbleached all purpose flour**
- **2 cups powdered sugar, divided**
- **¾ cup (1½ sticks) unsalted butter, melted, lukewarm**
- **3 tablespoons sweetened flaked coconut**
- **3 large ripe mangoes, peeled, pitted, sliced, divided**
- **¼ teaspoon ground allspice**
- **¼ teaspoon ground cinnamon**
- **⅓ cup fresh lime juice**
- **1 ¼-ounce envelope unflavored gelatin**
- **1 14-ounce can sweetened condensed milk**
- **6 large egg whites, room temperature**
- **Pinch of coarse kosher salt**
- **6 fresh mint sprigs**

Using fork, mix flour, ½ cup powdered sugar, melted butter, and coconut in medium bowl until dough forms. Divide into 6 equal pieces. Press onto bottom and up sides of six 4½-inch-diameter tartlet pans with removable bottoms. Chill crusts 30 minutes.

DO AHEAD: *Can be made 1 day ahead. Cover and keep chilled.*

Preheat oven to 350°F. Bake crusts until golden, pressing down with spoon if bubbles form, about 25 minutes. Cool.

Puree 2 mangoes in processor. Measure 1¾ cups puree; mix in allspice and cinnamon. Transfer to bowl; cover and refrigerate.

Pour lime juice into small saucepan; sprinkle gelatin over. Let stand until gelatin softens, about 10 minutes. Stir over low heat just until gelatin dissolves, about 2 minutes. Remove from heat. Whisk in condensed milk, then spiced mango puree. Divide filling among cooled crusts. Chill at least 3 hours and up to 5 hours.

Using electric mixer, blend egg whites and coarse salt in large bowl. Gradually add remaining 1½ cups powdered sugar; beat until stiff peaks form, about 5 minutes.

Spoon meringue atop tartlets or pipe atop tartlets using pastry bag fitted with large star tip. Using kitchen torch, lightly brown meringue. (Alternatively, place tartlets in 500°F oven until meringue is golden in spots, watching carefully to prevent burning, about 3 minutes.) Garnish with remaining mango slices and mint sprigs.

♨ Apple, Goat Cheese, and Honey Tartlets

Dessert and cheese courses combine for one sophisticated dessert. If you want to serve the tartlets warm but don't want to do the assembling and baking immediately before serving, bake them up to six hours ahead and store at room temperature. Rewarm the tartlets in the oven at 350°F for five to ten minutes and drizzle with honey just before serving. Look for dark honey (such as forest honey) at natural foods stores and specialty foods stores. **Makes 8**

2	17.3-ounce packages frozen puff pastry (4 sheets), thawed
1	egg, beaten to blend
6	ounces soft fresh goat cheese
1	tablespoon fresh lemon juice
¼	teaspoon coarse kosher salt
3	medium Gala apples, peeled, quartered, cored, cut into ⅛-inch-thick slices
3	tablespoons unsalted butter, melted
¾	cup honey (preferably dark), divided
½	teaspoon (scant) ground allspice

Line 2 large rimmed baking sheets with parchment paper. Roll out each puff pastry sheet on lightly floured surface to 11-inch square. Using 5-inch-diameter cookie cutter or bowl, cut out 4 rounds from each pastry sheet, forming 16 rounds total. Divide 8 pastry rounds between prepared baking sheets; pierce pastry all over with fork. Using 3½-inch-diameter cookie cutter or bowl, cut out smaller rounds from center of remaining 8 pastry rounds (reserve 3½-inch rounds for another use), forming eight 5-inch-diameter rings. Brush outer 1-inch edges of 5-inch rounds on baking sheets with beaten egg; top each with 1 pastry ring. Freeze at least 30 minutes.

DO AHEAD: *Can be made 1 day ahead. Cover and keep frozen. Do not thaw before continuing.*

Preheat oven to 375°F. Mix cheese, lemon juice, and coarse salt in small bowl; spread mixture inside rings on frozen pastry rounds. Overlap apple slices atop cheese. Mix butter and ¼ cup honey in small bowl; brush over apples. Sprinkle with allspice.

Bake until apples are tender and pastry is golden, about 35 minutes. Place tartlets on plates. Drizzle 1 tablespoon honey over each and serve warm or at room temperature.

♨ Lemon Tartlets with Fresh Blueberries

Lemon and berries are a classic (and delicious) combination. Blueberries are great with the tangy lemon curd filling, but blackberries or sliced straw-berries would be nice, too. **Makes 8**

Crust

2½	cups unbleached all purpose flour
½	cup sugar
¾	teaspoon salt
1	cup (2 sticks) chilled unsalted butter, cut into ½-inch cubes
1	large egg

Filling

1	cup sugar
¾	cup (1½ sticks) chilled unsalted butter, cut into ½-inch cubes
½	cup fresh lemon juice
5	large eggs
2	large egg yolks
2	teaspoons finely grated lemon peel
1	cup blueberries

CRUST: Mix flour, sugar, and salt in processor. Add butter; using on/off turns, cut in until mixture resembles coarse meal. Add egg and blend until moist clumps form. Gather dough into ball. Place scant ⅓ cup dough in each of eight 4½-inch-diameter tartlet pans with removable bottoms. Using fingertips, press onto bottom and up sides of pan. Trim edges. Place on baking sheet. Chill 15 minutes.

DO AHEAD: *Can be made 1 day ahead. Cover and keep chilled.*

Preheat oven to 375°F. Bake crusts until golden brown, piercing with toothpick if crust bubbles, about 15 minutes. Transfer to rack and cool.

FILLING: Combine sugar, butter, lemon juice, eggs, egg yolks, and lemon peel in heavy medium saucepan. Whisk over medium heat until mixture thickens, about 9 minutes (do not boil). Pour lemon curd into bowl. Place plastic wrap directly onto surface of curd. Chill until cool, about 2 hours.

Spoon lemon curd into crusts, dividing equally. Chill until curd sets, at least 1 hour and up to 6 hours.

Remove tartlets from pans. Top each with some berries.

Spiced Plum and Caramelized Apple Tartlets with Calvados Cream

Dried plums—otherwise known as prunes—get dressed up with spices and Calvados, an apple brandy from France. If you can't find Calvados, Armagnac or Cognac would also be delicious. **Makes 8**

Spiced Plum Spread

½   cup (packed) pitted prunes
½   cup (packed) golden brown sugar
½   cup water
2   tablespoons (¼ stick) unsalted butter
2   tablespoons Calvados (apple brandy)
¼   teaspoon ground cinnamon
¼   teaspoon ground cardamom
⅛   teaspoon ground cloves

Apples and Pastry

¼   cup (½ stick) butter
¼   cup sugar
4   medium Granny Smith apples (about 2 pounds), peeled, quartered, cored
1   sheet frozen puff pastry (half of 16-ounce package all-butter puff pastry or half of 17.3-ounce package regular puff pastry), thawed

Calvados Cream

8   large egg yolks
⅔   cup plus 4 teaspoons sugar
⅔   cup Calvados (apple brandy)
1   cup chilled heavy whipping cream

SPICED PLUM SPREAD: Stir prunes, brown sugar, ½ cup water, and butter in heavy medium saucepan over medium-low heat until sugar dissolves. Cover and simmer until prunes are very soft, about 15 minutes. Uncover and simmer over low heat until mixture is reduced to ¾ cup, about 4 minutes. Add Calvados, cinnamon, cardamom, and cloves; mash prunes in pan into thick jam-like spread.

DO AHEAD: *Can be prepared 1 week ahead. Cover with plastic and refrigerate.*

APPLES AND PASTRY: Melt butter in heavy medium nonstick skillet over medium heat. Add sugar. Cook until sugar melts and turns deep amber, stirring occasionally, about 3 minutes. Add apples. Cook until just tender and browned, occasionally shifting and turning apples, about 12 minutes. Remove from heat. Cool in skillet.

Roll pastry out on lightly floured surface to thin 13x13-inch square. Using 4-inch-round cookie cutter, cut out 8 pastry rounds. Transfer to parchment-lined heavy large baking sheet. Using fork, pierce pastry rounds all over, leaving ⅓-inch border around edge. Chill pastry until firm, about 15 minutes.

Spread 1 slightly rounded tablespoon plum mixture evenly over center of each round, leaving ⅓-inch plain border. Slice each apple quarter into 5 thin wedges. Fan out 10 apple slices atop plum mixture on each round, forming rosette. Reserve any juices in small bowl.

DO AHEAD: *Can be made 1 day ahead. Cover tartlets and any juices separately and refrigerate.*

CALVADOS CREAM: Whisk egg yolks, ⅔ cup sugar, and Calvados in medium metal bowl. Set bowl over pan of gently boiling water. Whisk constantly until mixture thickens and instant-read thermometer registers 165°F, about 5 minutes. Cool, stirring occasionally. Whip cream until soft peaks form. Fold cooled egg mixture into whipped cream. Cover and chill.

DO AHEAD: *Can be prepared 1 day ahead. Keep chilled.*

Position rack in top third of oven and preheat to 400°F. Drizzle each tartlet with reserved juices and sprinkle with ½ teaspoon sugar. Bake until crust is deep golden brown, about 18 minutes. Serve tartlets warm or at room temperature with Calvados cream.

Warm Banana Tartlets with Peanut Crunch Ice Cream

An utterly decadent treat: peanut and banana tartlets paired with homemade peanut brittle ice cream. And because the tartlets use purchased puff pastry, they come together in no time. To take these completely over the top, serve with caramel sauce. Peel and slice the bananas just before using them to prevent browning. If you're running short on time, skip the homemade ice cream and simply stir the chopped peanut brittle into your favorite vanilla ice cream.

Makes 8

Ice Cream

1½	cups heavy whipping cream
1½	cups half and half
1¼	cups chopped lightly salted roasted peanuts
½	cup sugar
7	large egg yolks
⅔	cup chopped peanut brittle

Tartlets

⅔	cup plus 2 tablespoons sugar
6	tablespoons (¾ stick) unsalted butter, room temperature
2	large egg yolks
2	tablespoons unbleached all purpose flour
⅔	cup finely chopped lightly salted roasted peanuts
1	17.3-ounce package frozen puff pastry (2 sheets), thawed
1	egg, beaten to blend
4	bananas, peeled, thinly sliced into rounds

ICE CREAM: Bring cream and half and half to simmer in heavy medium saucepan. Add peanuts. Cover; remove from heat and let stand 30 minutes.

Strain cream mixture through sieve set over large bowl, pressing on solids to extract as much liquid as possible. Discard peanuts. Whisk in sugar and egg yolks. Return to saucepan. Stir over medium-low heat until custard thickens and leaves path on back of spoon when finger is drawn across and instant-read thermometer registers 160°F to 165°F when inserted into custard, about 4 minutes (do not boil). Strain into medium bowl. Chill uncovered until cold. Transfer custard to ice-cream maker and process according to manufacturer's instructions. Transfer ice cream to container. Mix in brittle. Cover and freeze until firm.

DO AHEAD: *Can be made 3 days ahead. Keep frozen.*

TARTLETS: Preheat oven to 350°F. Using electric mixer, beat ⅔ cup sugar and butter in medium bowl until well blended. Beat in egg yolks. Mix in flour, then nuts. Set peanut cream aside.

Unfold pastry onto work surface. Cut each pastry sheet into 4 squares; pierce all over with fork. Place 4 pastry squares on each of 2 baking sheets, spacing apart. Brush egg over pastry. Spread 2 tablespoons peanut cream over each, leaving ½-inch plain border. Arrange bananas in overlapping slices atop peanut cream. Sprinkle with remaining 2 tablespoons sugar.

Bake tartlets until crusts are golden brown, about 30 minutes. Transfer to plates. Serve warm with ice cream.

♈♈♈ Cappuccino Éclairs

A great twist on the traditional vanilla cream–filled éclair: The custard filling is flavored with coffee and the éclairs are topped with milk chocolate for a delicious mocha treat. **Makes about 12**

Filling

2	cups water
1	cup finely ground dark-roast coffee beans (such as French roast)
½	vanilla bean, split lengthwise
1	tablespoon heavy whipping cream
5	tablespoons sugar
1	tablespoon cornstarch
2	large egg yolks
¼	cup (½ stick) unsalted butter, diced

Éclair Dough

1	cup water
6	tablespoons (¾ stick) unsalted butter, diced
¾	teaspoon salt
1	cup bread flour
4	large eggs
4	ounces high-quality milk chocolate (such as Lindt or Perugina), melted
	Powdered sugar

FILLING: Brew 2 cups water and ground coffee in standard coffeemaker. Pour 1 cup brewed coffee into heavy medium saucepan. Scrape in seeds from vanilla bean; add bean, then cream. Bring mixture to boil.

Whisk sugar and cornstarch in medium bowl; whisk in egg yolks. Gradually whisk hot coffee mixture into yolk mixture. Return to same saucepan and cook until cream thickens and boils, whisking constantly, about 3 minutes. Add butter; whisk to blend. Discard vanilla bean. Transfer cream to small bowl. Press plastic wrap directly onto surface; chill until very cold, at least 3 hours and up to 2 days.

ÉCLAIR DOUGH: Position rack in center of oven and preheat to 400°F. Line large rimmed baking sheet with parchment paper. Bring 1 cup water, butter, and salt to boil in heavy medium saucepan over medium-high heat. Add flour all at once; using wooden spoon, stir vigorously until dough forms ball and thick film coats pan bottom, about 2 minutes. Remove from heat. Using handheld electric mixer, add eggs 1 at a time, beating until dough is smooth after each addition.

Spoon dough into pastry bag fitted with ½-inch plain round tip. Press dot of dough under each corner of parchment to anchor. Pipe 4-inch lines of dough onto paper, about 1½ inches apart and parallel to each other.

Bake éclair shells 15 minutes (do not open oven). Reduce temperature to 350°F; bake until crisp, about 20 minutes. Cool shells on baking sheet.

Using serrated knife and starting at 1 long side, cut each shell in half. Fill each shell bottom with 2 tablespoons filling; cover with top. Spread melted chocolate over. Chill until ready to serve, up to 2 hours.

Arrange éclairs on platter. Dust lightly with powdered sugar and serve.

Profiteroles with Caramel Sauce

This dessert combines two popular confections: custard-filled cream puffs and a rich caramel sauce. **Makes about 4 dozen**

Sauce

1⅓	cups sugar
⅓	cup water
⅔	cup heavy whipping cream
¼	cup (½ stick) butter, diced

Cream Puffs

1	cup water
½	cup (1 stick) unsalted butter, diced
1	cup unbleached all purpose flour
¼	teaspoon salt
4	large eggs

Filling

1	tablespoon water
½	teaspoon unflavored gelatin
2	cups whole milk
⅔	cup heavy whipping cream
1	vanilla bean, split lengthwise
6	large egg yolks
⅔	cup sugar
½	cup unbleached all purpose flour
	Pinch of salt

SAUCE: Stir sugar and ⅓ cup water in heavy large saucepan over medium-low heat until sugar dissolves. Increase heat to high and boil without stirring until syrup is deep amber color, occasionally brushing down sides of pan with wet pastry brush and swirling pan, 7 to 8 minutes. Remove from heat. Add cream (mixture will bubble vigorously). Add butter and whisk until smooth.

DO AHEAD: *Can be made 2 days ahead. Cover and chill. Rewarm before using.*

CREAM PUFFS: Bring 1 cup water and butter to boil in heavy medium saucepan over medium-high heat, stirring until butter dissolves. Reduce heat to low; add flour and salt all at once. Stir vigorously until dough is smooth, forms ball, and leaves film on pan bottom, about 2 minutes. Transfer dough to large bowl. Using handheld mixer, add eggs 1 at a time, blending well after each addition. Cover dough loosely with plastic wrap. Let stand until cool, about 1 hour.

Preheat oven to 425°F. Lightly butter 2 large rimmed baking sheets. Spoon dough into pastry bag fitted with ½-inch plain tip. Pipe 1-inch rounds onto prepared baking sheets, spacing 2 inches apart. Using moistened fingertips, smooth tops.

Bake puffs until golden brown and puffed, about 23 minutes. Remove puffs from oven; turn off heat. Pierce side of each puff with tip of small knife. Return puffs to hot oven; let stand 10 minutes with door ajar. Remove puffs from oven and cool completely.

DO AHEAD: *Can be made 1 day ahead. Store airtight at room temperature.*

FILLING: Place 1 tablespoon water in custard cup. Sprinkle gelatin over. Bring milk, cream, and vanilla bean to simmer in heavy large saucepan over medium heat. Whisk egg yolks, sugar, flour, and salt in large bowl to blend. Gradually whisk hot milk mixture into yolk mixture. Return to same saucepan. Whisk over medium heat until pastry cream thickens and boils, about 1 minute. Add gelatin mixture to hot pastry cream and stir until dissolved. Transfer filling to medium bowl. Press plastic wrap directly onto surface and chill until cold, about 3 hours.

DO AHEAD: *Can be made 1 day ahead. Keep chilled.*

Spoon pastry cream into pastry bag fitted with ¼-inch plain tip. Insert tip into cut on each puff and pipe in filling.

DO AHEAD: *Can be made 8 hours ahead. Arrange on rimmed baking sheet. Cover loosely with plastic wrap and refrigerate.*

Place 4 puffs on each plate. Drizzle puffs with warm caramel sauce.

Chocolate Croquembouches

French for "crunch in the mouth," a classic croquembouche is made with vanilla custard–stuffed cream puffs stacked into a dramatic cone-shaped tower and held together with crunchy caramel. Here, the presentation is scaled down for fun individual servings, and the pastry cream filling and silky drizzling glaze are both chocolate. **Makes 8**

Pastry Cream

²/₃	cup sugar
¹/₃	cup unbleached all purpose flour
2	cups whole milk
4	large egg yolks
5	ounces bittersweet or semisweet chocolate (do not exceed 61% cacao), chopped

Cream Puffs

½	cup water
¼	cup whole milk
¼	cup (½ stick) unsalted butter
2	tablespoons sugar
¼	teaspoon salt
¾	cup plus 2 tablespoons unbleached all purpose flour
2	tablespoons natural unsweetened cocoa powder
4	large eggs

Glaze

10	ounces bittersweet or semisweet chocolate, chopped

Technique Tips: **Secrets of Perfect Puffs**

The tops of the cream puffs need to be tapped down slightly to create a smooth top and to prevent any browned, hard nubs from forming during baking. Wet your fingertips when you pat down the top of the puffs to prevent the dough from sticking to your skin. Poking a hole in the puffs when they come out of the oven serves two purposes: It allows the puffs to cool quickly, which helps dry out the centers, and the small hole is just the right size for the tip of the pastry bag you'll use to fill the puffs with the chocolate pastry cream.

PASTRY CREAM: Whisk sugar and flour in heavy medium saucepan to blend. Gradually whisk in milk, then egg yolks. Cook over medium heat until cream thickens and boils, whisking constantly, about 10 minutes. Remove from heat. Add chocolate and whisk until melted and smooth. Transfer to medium bowl. Press plastic wrap directly onto surface of pastry cream; chill until cold and firm, at least 3 hours and up to 2 days.

CREAM PUFFS: Preheat oven to 375°F. Line 2 large baking sheets with parchment paper. Combine ½ cup water, milk, butter, sugar, and salt in heavy medium saucepan. Bring to boil, whisking until sugar dissolves and butter melts. Remove from heat. Add flour and cocoa all at once; whisk until smooth and blended (dough will form ball). Stir over low heat until dough leaves film on pan bottom, about 2 minutes. Transfer dough to large bowl; cool to lukewarm, about 8 minutes. Using electric mixer, beat in eggs 1 at a time.

Drop batter by teaspoonfuls onto prepared baking sheets in at least 64 scant 1-inch mounds. Using moistened fingertips, smooth any pointed tips on mounds. Bake puffs 20 minutes. Reduce heat to 350°F and continue to bake until puffs are firm and beginning to crack and dry on top, about 23 minutes longer. Transfer puffs to rack. Using small knife or chopstick, poke hole in side of each puff near bottom to allow steam to escape. Cool puffs completely.

Spoon pastry cream into pastry bag fitted with ¼-inch plain round tip. Pipe into each puff through hole in side.

GLAZE: Place chocolate in small microwave-safe dish. Microwave at low setting in 10-second intervals until beginning to melt; stir glaze until completely melted and smooth.

Dip bottom of 4 filled cream puffs into glaze. Arrange puffs, spaced about ¼ inch apart, in square on plate. Dip bottom of 3 more puffs into glaze. Arrange in triangle atop first 4 puffs, pressing slightly so glaze holds puffs in place. Dip bottom of 1 more puff into glaze; place on top. Drizzle mound of puffs with some of glaze. Repeat with remaining cream puffs, forming 8 desserts. Chill until glaze sets and holds puffs together, at least 1 hour and up to 1 day.

Mango-Filled Cream Puffs with Spiced Mango-Mojito Sauce

The mango sauce for these cream puffs is spiked with the flavors of the popular Cuban cocktail: rum, lime, and mint. For the lightest, crispiest texture, be sure to let the cream puffs dry 15 minutes in the oven after you've turned it off.
12 servings

Cream Puffs
1	**cup whole milk**
½	**cup (1 stick) unsalted butter, diced**
¼	**teaspoon salt**
1	**cup unbleached all purpose flour**
5	**large eggs**

Filling
2	**cups ⅓-inch cubes peeled pitted mango (from about 4 large)**
1	**cup chilled sour cream**
1	**cup chilled heavy whipping cream**
1	**cup powdered sugar, divided**

    Spiced Mango-Mojito Sauce (see recipe)

CREAM PUFFS: Position 1 rack in top third of oven and 1 rack in bottom third of oven and preheat to 375°F. Line 2 large rimmed baking sheets with parchment paper. Bring milk, butter, and salt to boil in heavy large saucepan over medium-high heat, stirring until butter melts. Add flour all at once. Reduce heat to medium and stir with wooden spoon until dough forms ball and some batter films bottom of pan, about 4 minutes. Transfer dough to medium bowl and cool 5 minutes. Using handheld electric mixer on medium speed, beat in eggs 1 at a time.

Drop dough by generous tablespoonfuls 3 inches apart onto prepared baking sheets, making 24 cream puffs. Smooth tops with wet fingertips.

Bake cream puffs 15 minutes. Reverse baking sheets and continue to bake until cream puffs are deep golden, about 10 minutes longer. Using small sharp knife, cut small slit in side of each cream puff. Return to oven, turn off heat, and let dry 15 minutes.

DO AHEAD: *Can be made 6 hours ahead. Let stand at room temperature.*

FILLING: Stir mango and sour cream in medium bowl to blend. Beat whipping cream and ½ cup powdered sugar in large bowl until peaks form. Fold whipped cream into mango mixture. Cover bowl and chill filling at least 30 minutes.

DO AHEAD: *Can be made 3 hours ahead. Keep chilled.*

Using serrated knife, cut cream puffs horizontally in half. Spoon filling into bottom halves; cover with tops. Sift remaining ½ cup powdered sugar over cream puffs.

Divide cream puffs among 12 plates. Spoon Spiced Mango-Mojito Sauce onto plates and serve.

Spiced Mango-Mojito Sauce

This refreshing dessert sauce would also be delicious on angel food cake with a tropical fruit compote. **Makes about 1⅔ cups**

2	**large mangoes, peeled, pitted, diced**
6	**tablespoons plain whole-milk yogurt**
4	**tablespoons (or more) sugar**
3	**tablespoons spiced rum**
1	**tablespoon fresh Key lime juice or regular lime juice**
1½	**teaspoons (packed) finely chopped fresh mint**

Puree mangoes in processor until smooth. Transfer 1½ cups puree to medium bowl (reserve remaining puree for another use). Mix yogurt, 4 tablespoons sugar, rum, lime juice, and mint into puree. Sweeten sauce to taste with more sugar, if desired.

DO AHEAD: *Can be made 1 day ahead. Cover and chill.*

Strawberry Cream Puffs with Strawberry Sauce

Chances are you already have everything you need to make these cream puffs—water, butter, salt, sugar, flour, and eggs. Together, these staples create puffs that are delicately crisp and golden on the outside, and hollow and tender on the inside. The cream puffs should be a rich golden brown when done and the centers should be slightly eggy and moist but no longer doughy. **Makes about 18**

Cream Puffs

- ¾ **cup water**
- 3 **tablespoons unsalted butter**
- ¼ **teaspoon salt**
- ¼ **teaspoon sugar**
- ¾ **cup unbleached all purpose flour**
- 3 **large eggs**

Filling

- 1 **cup chilled heavy whipping cream**
- 1 **teaspoon plus 2 tablespoons sugar**
- ¼ **teaspoon kirsch (clear cherry brandy)**
- ⅛ **teaspoon vanilla extract**
- 6 **large strawberries, hulled**

   Strawberry Sauce (see recipe)
   Powdered sugar

CREAM PUFFS: Preheat oven to 375°F. Line baking sheet with parchment paper. Combine ¾ cup water, butter, salt, and sugar in heavy medium saucepan. Bring to boil, stirring to melt butter. Add flour all at once; using wooden spoon, stir vigorously until mixture clumps together, forming ball. Stir 1 minute longer. Transfer dough to medium bowl. Using electric mixer, add eggs 1 at a time, beating until dough is smooth after each addition (dough will be slightly soft and shiny).

More Cream Puff Fillings

When it comes to cream puffs, the filling options are endless. Replace the strawberries with raspberries and add some finely grated orange peel or minced crystallized ginger to the whipped cream; or simply spoon a scoop of your favorite ice cream into the cream puffs and drizzle them with chocolate sauce to make profiteroles.

Using 1 rounded tablespoon dough for each cream puff, spoon dough onto prepared baking sheet, spacing about 2 inches apart and forming mounds about ¾ inch to 1 inch high and 1¼ inches in diameter. Using moist fingertips, gently press tops of cream puffs to flatten any peaks. Bake until golden brown, about 37 minutes. Using small sharp knife, cut small slit in side of each cream puff. Transfer baking sheet to rack; let cream puffs cool.

DO AHEAD: *Can be made 4 hours ahead. Let stand at room temperature.*

FILLING: Beat cream, 1 teaspoon sugar, kirsch, and vanilla in medium bowl until firm peaks form. Combine strawberries and remaining 2 tablespoons sugar in small bowl. Using fork, crush berries. Fold crushed strawberry mixture into cream mixture.

Using serrated knife, cut top third off each cream puff. Place cream puff bottoms, cut side up, on plates. Spoon filling into bottoms, mounding slightly. Ladle Strawberry Sauce over, allowing sauce to spill onto plates. Cover with cream puff tops. Dust with powdered sugar.

Strawberry Sauce

This classic dessert sauce, known also as a coulis, is delicious with the strawberry cream puffs. It's also good over vanilla ice cream or frozen yogurt, with crepes or waffles, or in a trifle layered with sponge cake, whipped cream, and fresh strawberries. **Makes about 2½ cups**

- 2 **1-pint containers strawberries, hulled**
- 3 **tablespoons sugar**

Puree 1 container strawberries with sugar in processor. Transfer to bowl. Quarter remaining strawberries; add to sauce.

Fried Lemon-Scented Ricotta and Mascarpone Cream Puffs

Pâte à choux, *the same dough used to make traditional cream puffs and éclairs, is deep-fried in this recipe, adding some crunch to the cream-filled pastries.* **Makes 3 dozen**

¾	cup whole milk
6	tablespoons (¾ stick) unsalted butter, diced
1	tablespoon sugar
	Pinch of salt
¾	cup unbleached all purpose flour
4	large eggs
	Vegetable oil (for frying)
1	cup whole-milk ricotta cheese
⅓	cup mascarpone cheese
¾	cup powdered sugar, divided
½	teaspoon finely grated lemon peel

Bring milk, butter, sugar, and salt to boil in heavy medium saucepan over medium heat, stirring until butter melts. Add flour all at once. Stir vigorously until dough is smooth, forms ball, and light film forms on pan bottom, about 2 minutes. Remove from heat and whisk in eggs 1 at a time.

Add enough oil to heavy large saucepan to reach depth of 2 inches. Attach deep-fry thermometer to side of pan and heat oil over medium heat to 350°F. Working in batches of 4 or 5, drop 1 tablespoon batter into oil for each cream puff. Fry until golden brown and puffed, adjusting heat to maintain temperature, about 5 minutes per batch. Using slotted spoon, transfer cream puffs to paper towels to drain.

DO AHEAD: *Can be made 6 hours ahead. Let stand at room temperature.*

Stir ricotta cheese, mascarpone cheese, ¼ cup powdered sugar, and lemon peel in medium bowl to blend for filling. Cut cream puffs in half horizontally. Spoon 1 rounded teaspoon filling into bottoms; cover with tops. Sift remaining ½ cup powdered sugar over. Arrange on platter. Refrigerate cream puffs until ready to serve, up to 3 hours.

Rhubarb-Raspberry Jalousie

These French rectangular pastries, similar to turnovers, are often filled with poached fruit or jam. This modern version saves time by using frozen puff pastry and combines fresh rhubarb with raspberry preserves. Cutting slits down the center of the jalousie not only makes the pastry look pretty, it also allows steam to escape, which maintains the filling's thick, jammy consistency. **6 servings**

2	tablespoons (¼ stick) unsalted butter
4	cups ½-inch pieces trimmed rhubarb (from about 1 pound)
1	cup raspberry preserves with seeds
¼	cup plus 2 tablespoons sugar
1	sheet frozen puff pastry (half of 17.3-ounce package), thawed
1	large egg, beaten to blend
	Vanilla ice cream

Melt butter in heavy medium saucepan over medium heat. Add rhubarb. Cover and simmer until rhubarb is tender and falling apart, about 10 minutes. Add preserves and ¼ cup sugar. Cook uncovered until mixture is very thick and reduced to 2 cups, stirring frequently, about 35 minutes. Chill filling uncovered until cold, at least 1 hour.

DO AHEAD: *Can be made 2 days ahead. Cover and keep chilled.*

Preheat oven to 400°F. Line large baking sheet with parchment paper. Roll out pastry on lightly floured surface to 16x12-inch rectangle. Cut pastry in half lengthwise, forming two 16x6-inch rectangles. Place 1 rectangle on prepared baking sheet. Spoon filling onto pastry and spread out in even layer, leaving 1-inch plain border. Brush border with egg. Top with second pastry rectangle; press edges firmly to seal. Brush edges with egg. Fold edges over, forming ½-inch border. Press border with tines of fork to seal. Brush top of pastry with glaze; sprinkle with 2 tablespoons sugar. Using sharp knife, cut 1½-inch crosswise slits down center of pastry at 2-inch intervals, exposing filling.

Bake pastry until golden brown, about 25 minutes. Cool pastry on sheet to lukewarm, about 45 minutes. Cut jalousie crosswise into 6 pieces. Serve with vanilla ice cream.

Raspberry Napoleon

A touch of honey added to the melted butter that's brushed over phyllo sheets creates crisp, golden brown pastry with a shiny, candy-like glaze. **6 servings**

¼	**cup (½ stick) unsalted butter**
3	**tablespoons honey**
4	**17x12-inch sheets or sixteen 14x9-inch sheets fresh or thawed frozen phyllo pastry**
1	**12-ounce package frozen raspberries, thawed**
¼	**cup plus 2 tablespoons sugar**
1	**cup chilled heavy whipping cream**
3	**tablespoons powdered sugar**
2	**tablespoons brandy, divided**
½	**teaspoon vanilla extract**
2	**½-pint containers raspberries or one 1-pint container strawberries, hulled, sliced**
	Additional powdered sugar

Preheat oven to 400°F. Butter large rimless baking sheet. Cover 2 racks with waxed paper. Combine butter and honey in heavy small saucepan; stir over medium-low heat until butter melts.

If using 17x12-inch phyllo, place 1 phyllo sheet on work surface (cover remaining phyllo with plastic wrap, then damp kitchen towel). Brush phyllo with honey butter. Top with second phyllo sheet. Brush with honey butter. Repeat layering with remaining 2 phyllo sheets, brushing each with honey butter. Cut stacked phyllo lengthwise into 3 strips, each approximately 17x4 inches.

If using 14x9-inch phyllo, place 1 phyllo sheet on work surface (cover remaining phyllo with plastic wrap, then damp towel). Place second phyllo sheet at end of first sheet with 1 short side overlapping first sheet by 2 inches. Brush with honey butter. Repeat layering with 6 more phyllo sheets, brushing each with honey butter. Trim phyllo stack to 17x14-inch rectangle, then cut stack lengthwise into two 17x4-inch strips (discard excess trimmings). Make second phyllo stack by repeating procedure with remaining 8 phyllo sheets and honey butter. Trim second stack to 17x14-inch rectangle, then cut second stack into one 17x4-inch strip (reserve remaining phyllo for another use).

Recipe Tip: Napoleon

This elegant French dessert features delicate layers of flaky pastry spread with whipped cream or pastry cream and jam, then topped with icing or powdered sugar. The dessert can be made with either phyllo dough or puff pastry, and it can be prepared as individual rectangles or as one large pastry and carefully sliced into servings.

Using 2 metal spatulas, transfer phyllo strips to prepared baking sheet. Bake until puffed and golden brown, about 8 minutes, watching closely to prevent burning. Carefully slide knife under phyllo to loosen from sheet. Transfer to prepared racks and cool completely.

Puree thawed raspberries in processor. Strain into bowl, pressing on solids in strainer to release as much puree as possible. Discard solids in strainer. Stir ¼ cup sugar into raspberry puree. Chill.

Beat cream in large bowl until soft peaks form. Add 3 tablespoons powdered sugar, 1 tablespoon brandy, and vanilla and beat until peaks form.

Mix fresh raspberries, remaining 2 tablespoons sugar, and remaining 1 tablespoon brandy in medium bowl. Arrange 1 phyllo strip, shiny side up, on platter. Spread half of whipped cream over. Top with half of berries. Top with second phyllo strip, pressing gently to adhere. Spread remaining cream over. Top with remaining berries. Cover with third phyllo strip, shiny side up.

DO AHEAD: *Can be made 1 hour ahead. Chill uncovered.*

Using serrated knife, cut pastry crosswise into 6 equal sections. Sift additional powdered sugar over. Serve with pureed raspberries.

Working with Phyllo

Phyllo dough is paper-thin, which creates that ultra-flaky pastry goodness in a host of desserts. But because it's so delicate, it dries out easily. Here are tips to handle it with ease.

Before removing the phyllo pastry from the box, clear off the counter to give yourself plenty of space, and have all of your other ingredients and equipment ready. Once the phyllo is unwrapped, you'll want to work with it quickly and without any interruptions.

Lay the phyllo pastry sheets on a baking sheet and cover them with plastic wrap and a slightly damp kitchen towel to keep them moist. Remove one sheet at a time and arrange it on the work surface, re-covering the stacked sheets each time. Immediately brush the phyllo sheet completely with melted butter or oil to keep it from drying out.

Strawberry Napoleons with Lemon Cream

These individual napoleons, made with phyllo dough, are light, crisp, and flaky; they're a nice foil for the rich and creamy lemon filling and the fresh strawberry sauce. **Makes 10**

Lemon Cream

2	tablespoons cold water
1	teaspoon unflavored gelatin
¾	cup frozen lemonade concentrate, thawed
6	tablespoons sugar
6	tablespoons (¾ stick) unsalted butter, cut into 6 pieces
4	large egg yolks
1	large egg
½	cup chilled heavy whipping cream

Pastries

5	17x12-inch sheets or ten 14x9-inch sheets fresh or thawed frozen phyllo pastry
6	tablespoons (or more) unsalted butter, melted
5	tablespoons sugar, divided

Strawberry Sauce

4½	cups sliced hulled strawberries, divided
6	tablespoons sugar
	Powdered sugar
10	whole strawberries

LEMON CREAM: Spoon cold water into small bowl; sprinkle gelatin over. Let stand until gelatin softens, about 10 minutes. Combine lemonade concentrate, sugar, butter, egg yolks, and egg in medium metal bowl. Set bowl over sauce-pan of simmering water (do not allow bottom of bowl to touch water). Whisk constantly until instant-read thermometer inserted into mixture registers 160°F, about 5 minutes. Remove bowl from over water; add gelatin mixture and whisk until dissolved. Strain mixture into large bowl. Set bowl over larger bowl filled with ice water. Stir until mixture is cool and begins to thicken but not set, about 10 minutes. Beat cream in medium bowl to firm peaks; fold into lemon mixture. Cover and chill at least 4 hours.

PASTRIES: Preheat oven to 350°F. If using 17x12-inch phyllo, place 1 sheet on work surface (cover remaining phyllo with plastic wrap, then damp kitchen towel). Brush phyllo with some melted butter; sprinkle 1 tablespoon sugar over. Top with second phyllo sheet. Brush with melted butter; sprinkle with sugar. Repeat with remaining phyllo, melted butter, and sugar. Cut phyllo stack into twenty 3-inch squares.

If using 14x9-inch phyllo, place 1 sheet on work surface (cover remaining phyllo with plastic wrap, then damp towel). Brush phyllo with melted butter; sprinkle ½ tablespoon sugar over. Top with second phyllo sheet. Brush with melted butter; sprinkle with ½ tablespoon sugar. Repeat with 3 more phyllo sheets, melted butter, and sugar. Cut phyllo stack into twelve 3-inch squares. Make second phyllo stack by repeating procedure with remaining 5 phyllo sheets, melted butter, and sugar. Cut second phyllo stack into eight 3-inch squares for 20 squares total.

Transfer pastry squares to rimmed baking sheets. Bake until deep golden, watching closely, about 12 minutes. Transfer to racks and cool.

DO AHEAD: *Lemon cream and pastry squares can be made 1 day ahead. Keep lemon cream chilled. Store pastry squares airtight at room temperature.*

STRAWBERRY SAUCE: Simmer 2¼ cups sliced strawberries and sugar in heavy medium saucepan until strawberries are soft, stirring occasionally, about 5 minutes. Transfer to processor and puree. Strain into small bowl. Chill until cold.

Place 10 pastry squares on work surface. Transfer lemon cream to pastry bag fitted with large star tip. Pipe lemon cream over squares, leaving ½-inch plain border on sides. Arrange remaining sliced strawberries in single layer over lemon cream. Pipe small rosette of lemon cream atop berries. Top each with pastry square and pipe rosette of lemon cream atop pastry. Sprinkle with powdered sugar. Garnish each with whole strawberry. Serve with sauce.

 # Fresh Plum Napoleon

Unlike many napoleons, this one holds together well when sliced, making it a great choice for a special dinner. The plum jam in this recipe is excellent on its own, so make a double batch—it keeps in the fridge for a good week—and slather it on toast in the morning. **8 to 10 servings**

Pastry Cream

5	tablespoons sugar
2½	teaspoons cornstarch
1	cup whole milk, divided
4	large egg yolks
½	vanilla bean, split lengthwise
6	ounces Philadelphia-brand cream cheese, cut into ½-inch cubes, room temperature

Plum Jam

½	cup sugar
¼	cup water
½	vanilla bean, split lengthwise
12	ounces small plums (about 5), halved, pitted, cut into ½-inch-thick slices (about 2 cups)
2	teaspoons finely grated orange peel

Napoleon

1	17.3-ounce package frozen puff pastry (2 sheets), thawed
1	pound small plums (about 6), halved, pitted, cut into ¼-inch-thick slices
	Powdered sugar

PASTRY CREAM: Whisk sugar and cornstarch in medium saucepan to blend. Add ¼ cup milk; whisk until cornstarch dissolves. Whisk in remaining ¾ cup milk and egg yolks. Scrape in seeds from vanilla bean; add bean. Place over medium heat and whisk until mixture is smooth and thick and comes to boil, about 2 minutes. Remove from heat. Add cream cheese and whisk until smooth. Strain pastry cream into small bowl; discard solids in strainer. Press plastic wrap directly onto surface of pastry cream and chill until cold, about 4 hours.

PLUM JAM: Combine sugar and ¼ cup water in heavy medium saucepan. Scrape in seeds from vanilla bean; add bean. Bring to simmer over medium-high heat, stirring until sugar dissolves and syrup begins to thicken, about 2 minutes. Add plums and orange peel; reduce heat to medium and simmer until mixture is very thick and reduced to ¾ cup, stirring often, about 20 minutes. Cool. Discard vanilla bean.

DO AHEAD: *Pastry cream and plum jam can be made 1 day ahead. Cover separately and chill.*

NAPOLEON: Preheat oven to 375°F. Place 1 puff pastry sheet on work surface. Brush 1 edge of sheet with cold water. Place 1 edge of second pastry sheet atop wet edge of first sheet, overlapping by 2 inches; press to adhere, forming 18x10-inch rectangle. Using rolling pin, roll out pastry to 1 large sheet, 19 to 20 inches long and 11 inches wide. Transfer pastry to ungreased 18x12x1-inch baking sheet. Pierce pastry all over with fork. Using sharp knife, trim pastry to fit baking sheet. Bake until golden, occasionally piercing pastry with fork to deflate slightly, about 25 minutes (pastry will shrink to about 15x10-inch rectangle). Cool pastry completely on sheet.

Carefully transfer pastry to cutting board. Using serrated knife, cut pastry into three 14x3-inch rectangles. Trim any puffed portions of pastry to flatten and even slightly.

DO AHEAD: *Can be made 8 hours ahead. Cover with foil; let stand at room temperature.*

Place 1 pastry rectangle on long serving platter. Stir pastry cream to loosen. Spread 1 cup pastry cream over pastry rectangle, leaving ½-inch plain border at all edges (reserve remaining pastry cream for another use). Place second pastry rectangle, flat side up, on cardboard rectangle or 18-inch-long ruler. Spread with half of jam (generous ⅓ cup) to cover. Top with sliced plums in neat lines, skin side facing out. Using cardboard rectangle or ruler as aid, slide pastry with plums atop pastry cream layer, plum side up. Spread remaining plum jam over flat side (underside) of third pastry rectangle; place jam side down atop plums on second pastry layer. Dust top of pastry with powdered sugar.

DO AHEAD: *Can be made 2 hours ahead. Let napoleon stand at room temperature (do not chill).*

Cut napoleon crosswise into 8 to 10 pieces and serve.

♔♔♔ Banana-Caramel Napoleons

In this rich napoleon, the usual pastry cream filling is replaced with a decadent blend of mascarpone cheese and homemade caramel. **8 servings**

1	cup plus 1½ tablespoons sugar
6	tablespoons water
1	teaspoon fresh lemon juice
⅔	cup heavy whipping cream
1	sheet frozen puff pastry (half of 17.3-ounce package), thawed
12	ounces chilled mascarpone cheese
3	large bananas (about), peeled, thinly sliced on diagonal
	Powdered sugar

Equipment Tip: **Bread Knife**

A bread knife—a long knife with a serrated edge—has many functions in the kitchen, besides cutting bread, of course. It's the best tool to use when cutting through delicate desserts that have multiple layers of pastry, fruit, and cream, such as napoleons (use a sawing motion for the best results).

Combine 1 cup sugar, 6 tablespoons water, and lemon juice in heavy medium saucepan. Stir over low heat until sugar dissolves. Increase heat and boil without stirring until syrup is deep amber color, occasionally brushing down sides of pan with wet pastry brush and swirling pan, about 10 minutes. Remove from heat. Carefully add cream (mixture will bubble vigorously). Place pan over low heat; stir until mixture is smooth and any caramel bits dissolve. Transfer caramel to small bowl. Cover and chill until thick, about 3 hours.

Preheat oven to 400°F. Line 2 heavy large baking sheets with parchment paper. Roll out puff pastry on lightly floured surface to 15x12-inch rectangle. Cut crosswise into three 12x5-inch strips. Transfer pastry strips to prepared baking sheets, spacing evenly. Pierce pastry all over with fork. Chill 10 minutes.

Bake pastry until golden, about 15 minutes. Transfer baking sheets to racks and cool pastry on sheets.

DO AHEAD: *Caramel and pastry can be made 1 day ahead. Keep caramel chilled. Wrap pastry in foil and store at room temperature.*

Set aside ½ cup caramel for decoration. Using electric mixer, beat mascarpone and remaining 1½ tablespoons sugar in medium bowl just until smooth. Add remaining caramel and beat until caramel cream is well blended, about 1 minute.

Using sharp knife, trim pastry layers so that they are flat and even. Place 1 pastry strip on work surface. Spread with ¼ of caramel cream. Arrange half of banana slices in single layer over caramel cream. Spread second pastry strip with ¼ of caramel cream. Place pastry, caramel cream side down, atop bananas. Spread top of second pastry strip with ¼ of caramel cream. Arrange remaining bananas in single layer over. Spread remaining pastry strip with remaining caramel cream. Place pastry, caramel cream side down, atop bananas. Using serrated knife, cut pastry crosswise into 8 equal pieces. Sift powdered sugar over.

DO AHEAD: *Can be made 2 hours ahead. Tent with foil and chill.*

Place napoleons on plates. Drizzle reserved caramel around napoleons and serve.

🥄 Rhubarb Napoleons

This modern, more casual rendition of the napoleon boasts a delicious jam-like rhubarb filling that's accented with orange. The crisp, caramel-glazed pastry is cut into triangles rather than the usual rectangles. **Makes 4**

Pastry
- **2** **tablespoons (¼ stick) unsalted butter, room temperature, divided**
- **1** **sheet frozen puff pastry (half of 17.3-ounce package), thawed**
- **2** **tablespoons sugar**

Filling
- **3** **cups ½-inch pieces trimmed fresh rhubarb (about 13 ounces)**
- **⅔** **cup sugar**
- **2** **tablespoons orange juice**
- **1** **tablespoon cornstarch**
- **2** **teaspoons finely grated orange peel**
- **1** **tablespoon red currant jelly**

    Powdered sugar
    Vanilla ice cream
    Orange peel strips (optional)
    Fresh mint sprigs (optional)

Technique Tip: Puff Pastry, Unpuffed
Sometimes you want to allow puff pastry to do its thing and puff as high as it can, as when you're making tartlets. But other times, as when making napoleons, it's best to keep the pastry layers more condensed. Sandwiching the pastry between two baking sheets while baking prevents it from rising out of control. Be sure to butter the baking sheets very well to prevent sticking.

PASTRY: Preheat oven to 400°F. Using ½ tablespoon butter, generously butter 1 rimmed baking sheet. Unfold pastry on work surface; sprinkle with sugar. Roll out pastry to 11-inch square. Trim edges to form 10-inch square. Cut square into four 5-inch squares, then cut squares diagonally in half to form 8 triangles. Transfer pastry triangles, sugar side up, to prepared baking sheet. Using remaining 1½ tablespoons butter, generously butter underside of second rimmed baking sheet. Place second sheet, buttered side down, atop pastry triangles.

Bake pastry triangles 15 minutes. Press top baking sheet down to flatten and continue to bake until pastries are golden brown, about 10 minutes longer. Remove top baking sheet. Using metal spatula, transfer pastries to rack and cool completely.

FILLING: Combine rhubarb, sugar, orange juice, cornstarch, and grated orange peel in medium saucepan; stir to blend. Let stand until juices form, about 10 minutes. Cook over medium-high heat until rhubarb is tender but still intact, stirring gently, about 7 minutes. Gently stir in red currant jelly. Cool 5 minutes.

DO AHEAD: *Pastries and filling can be made 1 day ahead. Store pastries airtight at room temperature. Cover and chill filling. Rewarm filling before using.*

Arrange 1 pastry triangle on each of 4 plates; top with rhubarb filling, then remaining 4 pastry triangles. Sprinkle with powdered sugar. Scoop ice cream alongside each napoleon. Garnish with orange peel strips and mint, if desired. Serve napoleons immediately.

Maple Mousse Napoleons with Macadamia Nut Brittle and Passion Fruit–Mango Sauce

These contemporary individual napoleons add a few delicious twists to the classic version: maple mousse in place of the traditional pastry cream, macadamia nut brittle between the layers, and a tropical fruit sauce. The mousse must chill overnight, and most of the other components for this impressive dessert can be made at least one day ahead. **Makes 6**

Brittle

- ⅔ **cup sugar**
- ½ **cup water**
- ½ **cup dry-roasted macadamia nuts**

Mousse

- 4 **tablespoons water, divided**
- 1 **teaspoon unflavored gelatin**
- ⅔ **cup chilled heavy whipping cream, divided**
- ⅓ **cup pure maple syrup**
- 2 **large egg yolks**
- 1½ **tablespoons unsalted butter, room temperature**
- ¼ **teaspoon maple extract**

Sauce

- 1½ **cups frozen passion fruit juice concentrate, thawed**
- 1 **15- to 16-ounce mango, peeled, pitted, chopped (about 1⅓ cups)**
- ½ **cup (about) water**
- 1 **vanilla bean, split lengthwise**

Pastry

- 1 **sheet frozen puff pastry (half of 17.3-ounce package), thawed**

  Powdered sugar

BRITTLE: Place sheet of foil on work surface. Stir sugar and ½ cup water in heavy small saucepan over low heat until sugar dissolves, occasionally brushing down sides of pan with wet pastry brush. Increase heat and boil until syrup is deep amber color, occasionally brushing down pan sides and swirling pan, about 8 minutes. Mix in nuts. Immediately pour out onto foil. Let stand until cold and hard. Coarsely chop brittle.

DO AHEAD: *Can be made 2 days ahead; store airtight at room temperature.*

MOUSSE: Place 1½ tablespoons water in small cup; sprinkle gelatin over. Let stand until gelatin softens, about 15 minutes. Whisk 3 tablespoons cream, maple syrup, egg yolks, and remaining 2½ tablespoons water in heavy medium saucepan. Stir over medium heat until custard thickens and forms path on back of spoon when finger is drawn across, about 5 minutes (do not boil). Remove from heat. Add gelatin mixture to hot custard. Stir until gelatin dissolves. Add butter and maple extract; stir until butter melts. Cool to room temperature. Whisk remaining cream in medium bowl until peaks form. Fold into custard. Cover; chill mousse overnight.

SAUCE: Puree juice concentrate and mango in blender. Thin, if desired, by adding up to ½ cup water, 1 tablespoon at a time. Scrape in seeds from vanilla bean; blend 2 seconds.

DO AHEAD: *Can be made 1 day ahead. Transfer to bowl; cover and chill.*

PASTRY: Preheat oven to 450°F. Line large rimmed baking sheet with parchment paper. Roll out pastry on lightly floured surface to 12x12-inch square. Let pastry rest 5 minutes, then if necessary, roll again to 12x12-inch square. Cut pastry into six 2-inch-wide strips, then cut each strip in half crosswise. Arrange strips on prepared sheet. Cover with more parchment; weigh down with another baking sheet.

Bake pastry strips 14 minutes. Remove top baking sheet and top piece of parchment. Bake strips until golden, about 5 minutes longer. Cool on sheet.

Place 6 pastry strips on work surface. Spoon mousse into pastry bag fitted with large star tip. Pipe mousse onto pastry strips in rows, covering completely. Sprinkle some nut brittle over mousse. Top with second pastry strip, pressing lightly to adhere.

DO AHEAD: *Napoleons can be made 4 hours ahead. Chill. Return to room temperature before serving.*

Sift powdered sugar over napoleons. Spoon sauce onto 6 plates. Arrange napoleons atop sauce. Sprinkle additional nut brittle around and serve.

Caramelized Banana Purses with White Chocolate Sauce

Here's a good choice for an elegant dinner party: Delicate "purses" of phyllo pastry hold a banana-hazelnut filling and are served with white chocolate sauce and a crunchy hazelnut crumble. Everything can be made ahead; just slide the purses into the oven before dinner. **Makes 10**

Crumble

 | | Nonstick vegetable oil spray
--- | --- | ---
1 | cup (packed) golden brown sugar
½ | cup (1 stick) unsalted butter, cut into 8 pieces
1½ | cups unbleached all purpose flour
1 | cup hazelnuts, coarsely chopped
 | Pinch of salt

Filling

¾	cup sugar
6	tablespoons (¾ stick) unsalted butter, cut into 6 pieces
¼	cup fresh lime juice
6	medium bananas (about 2 pounds), peeled, cut into ¾-inch-thick slices
2	tablespoons Frangelico (hazelnut liqueur) or amaretto

Purses

10	17x12-inch sheets or twenty 14x9-inch sheets fresh or thawed frozen phyllo pastry
¾	cup (1½ sticks) unsalted butter, melted

 | White Chocolate Sauce (see recipe)

CRUMBLE: Preheat oven to 300°F. Line rimmed baking sheet with foil; spray with nonstick spray. Stir brown sugar and butter in medium saucepan over low heat until butter melts. Remove from heat. Mix in flour, nuts, and salt; spread on prepared sheet. Bake until dry and golden, about 30 minutes. Cool. Peel off foil and break crumble into small pieces.

DO AHEAD: *Can be made 1 day ahead. Store airtight at room temperature.*

FILLING: Stir sugar, butter, and lime juice in large nonstick skillet over low heat until butter melts and sugar dissolves. Increase heat to high and stir until mixture begins to brown around edges, about 5 minutes. Add bananas and liqueur; stir until sauce is thick enough to coat bananas, about 2 minutes. Transfer to large bowl and cool. Mix 1 cup hazelnut crumble into banana mixture.

PURSES: If using 17x12-inch phyllo, place 1 sheet on work surface (keep remaining phyllo covered with plastic wrap, then damp towel). Brush phyllo with some melted butter. Fold phyllo in half crosswise, brush with melted butter, then fold in half again, forming square; brush with more butter.

If using 14x9-inch phyllo, place 1 sheet on work surface; brush with melted butter. Top with second sheet of phyllo; brush with butter. Fold phyllo sheets in half crosswise and brush with more butter.

Place generous ¼ cup filling in center of phyllo square. Bring all edges of phyllo square up toward center and squeeze firmly at top, forming purse. Place on baking sheet. Brush purse with butter. Repeat with remaining phyllo sheets, melted butter, and filling, forming 10 purses total.

DO AHEAD: *Can be made 6 hours ahead. Chill.*

Preheat oven to 350°F. Cover phyllo purses loosely with foil. Bake until purses begin to color, about 30 minutes. Remove foil and continue baking until phyllo is golden, about 15 minutes longer. Place 1 purse on each of 10 plates. Spoon 3 tablespoons warm White Chocolate Sauce around each. Sprinkle remaining hazelnut crumble over and serve.

White Chocolate Sauce

Some pleasures in life are simple—here's one. Because white chocolate can burn very easily, the cream is heated and then poured over the chocolate to melt it gently. With just two ingredients, you'll want to use high-quality chocolate for best results. Fine white chocolate is found in the baking aisle or candy aisle of supermarkets and at specialty foods stores. **Makes about 2 cups**

6	ounces high-quality white chocolate (such as Lindt or Perugina), chopped
1½	cups heavy whipping cream

Place chocolate in small bowl. Bring cream to boil in heavy small saucepan. Pour cream over chocolate; whisk until smooth.

DO AHEAD: *Can be made 1 day ahead. Cool, then cover and chill. Before serving, rewarm in saucepan over low heat, stirring often.*

Pear and Fig Strudels with Ginger Cream

This recipe makes two strudels that are divided into four servings each. The recipe calls for 17x12-inch phyllo sheets, but if only 14x9-inch phyllo sheets are available, make three strudels instead of two, dividing the filling among three phyllo stacks. **8 servings**

Filling

1½   **pounds fresh figs, stemmed, each cut into 6 wedges (about 5 cups)**

1½   **pounds firm but ripe pears (about 3 large), peeled, cored, cut into ½-inch pieces (about 3½ cups)**

½   **cup sugar**

½   **cup frozen cranberry-raspberry concentrate, thawed**

1½   **teaspoons finely grated lemon peel**

Strudels

6   **tablespoons plain dry breadcrumbs**

4   **tablespoons sugar, divided**

1½   **teaspoons ground cinnamon, divided**

10   **17x12-inch sheets fresh or thawed frozen phyllo pastry**

¾   **cup (1½ sticks) unsalted butter, melted**

    Ginger Cream (see recipe)

FILLING: Preheat oven to 450°F. Generously butter large rimmed baking sheet. Place figs and pear pieces in single layer on prepared baking sheet. Sprinkle with sugar. Roast until fruit pieces are tender and beginning to brown around edges, about 20 minutes. Transfer fruit and any juices from baking sheet to medium bowl. Cool. Stir in cranberry-raspberry concentrate and lemon peel. Chill until cold.

STRUDELS: Butter another large rimmed baking sheet. Mix breadcrumbs, 3 tablespoons sugar, and 1 teaspoon cinnamon in small bowl. Place clean kitchen towel on work surface. Place 1 phyllo sheet atop towel with short end toward edge of work surface (cover remaining phyllo with plastic wrap, then damp kitchen towel). Brush phyllo sheet with some melted butter; sprinkle with ⅛ of breadcrumb mixture. Top with second phyllo sheet. Brush with melted butter; sprinkle with ⅛ of breadcrumb mixture. Repeat with 2 more phyllo sheets, melted butter, and breadcrumb mixture. Top with fifth phyllo sheet; brush with melted butter (do not sprinkle with breadcrumb mixture).

Using slotted spoon, place half of fig mixture along 1 short side of phyllo stack; spread in 3-inch-wide strip, leaving 1-inch plain border on long sides. Sprinkle ½ tablespoon sugar and ¼ teaspoon cinnamon over fig mixture. Fold long sides of phyllo over filling; brush folded sides with melted butter. Starting at filled short side, roll up phyllo, enclosing filling completely. Brush all over with melted butter. Place strudel, seam side down, on prepared baking sheet. Repeat assembly process to make second strudel.

DO AHEAD: *Can be made 1 day ahead. Cover with plastic wrap and chill.*

Position rack in center of oven and preheat to 375°F. Brush strudels lightly with melted butter. Bake until golden brown, about 20 minutes. Cool 10 minutes.

DO AHEAD: *Can be made 6 hours ahead. Let stand at room temperature.*

Using serrated knife, cut each strudel on diagonal into 4 pieces; discard ends. Place 1 piece on each of 8 plates. Dollop Ginger Cream alongside. Serve warm or at room temperature.

Ginger Cream

This topping is also great served with plum, pear, or peach crisps and pies, and it makes a nice addition to tropical fruit compotes. It's even delicious with pumpkin pie for Thanksgiving. **Makes about 1½ cups**

¼   **cup water**

3   **tablespoons minced peeled fresh ginger**

1½   **tablespoons sugar**

1   **cup chilled heavy whipping cream**

Combine ¼ cup water, ginger, and sugar in heavy small saucepan. Stir over medium heat until sugar dissolves. Simmer until mixture is syrupy, about 5 minutes. Cool completely. Using electric mixer, beat cream in medium bowl until peaks form. Fold in ginger mixture.

DO AHEAD: *Can be made 4 hours ahead. Cover and chill. Rewhisk to thicken, if necessary, before serving.*

Apple Strudel with Cranberry Sauce

Sheets of phyllo pastry replace strudel dough in this great alternative to holiday pumpkin pie. Gingersnap crumbs are a clever addition: They lend a warm spice flavor to the apple filling while thickening the juices and create a tasty separation between the layers of phyllo. Use a food processor to grind crisp—not chewy—gingersnap cookies into fine crumbs, or enclose the cookies in a resealable plastic bag and use a rolling pin or meat mallet to crush them. Serve the strudel with lightly sweetened whipped cream or vanilla ice cream. **6 servings**

Sauce

2	cups fresh or frozen cranberries (about 8 ounces; unthawed)
1	cup sugar
1	cup water
3	tablespoons kirsch (clear cherry brandy)

Strudel

¼	cup raisins
1½	tablespoons kirsch (clear cherry brandy)
3	medium Granny Smith apples (about 18 ounces), peeled, cored, cut into ⅓-inch pieces
½	cup plus 9 teaspoons gingersnap cookie crumbs
½	cup plus 2 tablespoons sugar
½	cup (1 stick) unsalted butter, melted
9	17x12-inch sheets or eighteen 14x9-inch sheets fresh or thawed frozen phyllo pastry

Powdered sugar

SAUCE: Combine cranberries, sugar, 1 cup water, and kirsch in heavy medium sauce-pan. Bring to boil over medium-high heat, stirring until sugar dissolves. Reduce heat to medium and cook until most of berries burst, about 10 minutes. Cool slightly. Transfer to processor and puree.

DO AHEAD: *Can be made 1 day ahead. Cover and chill. Rewarm over low heat before serving.*

STRUDEL: Combine raisins and kirsch in small bowl. Let soak 1 hour.

Preheat oven to 375°F. Combine apples, ½ cup gingersnap crumbs, sugar, and raisin mixture in bowl. Brush large rimmed baking sheet with some of melted butter.

If using 17x12-inch phyllo, place 1 sheet on work surface with 1 long side parallel to edge of work surface (cover remaining phyllo with plastic wrap, then damp kitchen towel). Brush phyllo with melted butter; sprinkle 1 teaspoon gingersnap crumbs over. Top with second phyllo sheet. Brush with melted butter; sprinkle with 1 teaspoon gingersnap crumbs. Repeat with some melted butter, remaining phyllo sheets, and gingersnap crumbs. Spoon apple mixture in 3-inch-wide log along 1 long side of phyllo, leaving 2-inch plain border at long and short edges. Fold long side over filling, then fold in short sides and roll up jelly-roll style.

If using 14x9-inch phyllo, place 1 sheet on work surface with 1 long side parallel to edge of work surface (cover remaining phyllo with plastic wrap, then damp towel). Brush phyllo with melted butter; sprinkle with ½ teaspoon gingersnap crumbs. Top with second phyllo sheet. Brush with melted butter; sprinkle with ½ teaspoon gingersnap crumbs. Repeat with 7 more phyllo sheets, melted butter, and gingersnap crumbs. Spoon half of apple mixture in 2-inch-wide log along 1 long side of phyllo, leaving 2-inch plain border at long and short edges. Fold long side over filling [1], then fold in short sides and roll up jelly-roll style [2]. Make second strudel by repeating procedure with some melted butter, remaining 9 phyllo sheets, crumbs, and filling.

Carefully transfer strudel(s) to prepared baking sheet, seam side down. Brush top of strudel(s) with melted butter.

Bake strudel(s) 15 minutes. Brush with remaining melted butter. Bake until golden, about 30 minutes. Cool on baking sheet.

Lightly sift powdered sugar over strudel(s). Cut strudel(s) crosswise into thick slices. Transfer to plates. Spoon sauce around strudel(s) and serve.

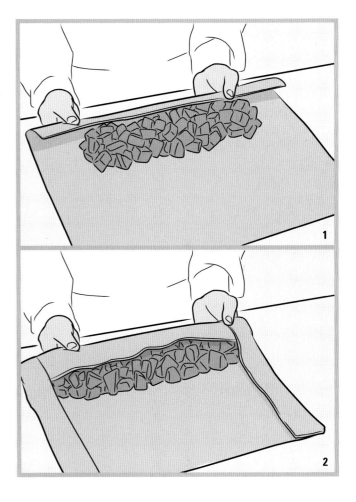

⫙⫙⫙ Dried Cherry and Walnut Strudel Bundles

These flaky phyllo bundles can be made with either dried tart cherries or dried Bing cherries, which are sweeter. Both are available at most supermarkets and at specialty foods stores. Don't brush melted butter on the tips of the phyllo bundles—the tips brown quickly on their own. **Makes 6**

1	**cup plus 2 tablespoons dried cherries**
¾	**cup boiling water**
¾	**cup walnuts, ground**
6	**tablespoons apricot preserves**
24	**14x9-inch sheets or 17x12-inch sheets fresh or thawed frozen phyllo pastry**
6	**tablespoons (¾ stick) unsalted butter, melted**
6	**6-inch-long pieces kitchen string**
	Powdered sugar

Place cherries in small bowl. Pour ¾ cup boiling water over. Let stand until cherries soften, about 30 minutes. Drain well. Pat cherries dry with paper towels. Mix cherries, nuts, and preserves in medium bowl.

Lightly oil heavy rimmed baking sheet. Stack phyllo sheets on work surface. Trim to 9-inch square if using 14x9-inch sheets, or 10-inch square if using 17x12-inch sheets (save scraps for another use). Cover phyllo stack with plastic wrap, then damp kitchen towel. Place 1 phyllo square on work surface. Brush lightly with melted butter. Arrange another phyllo square atop, with corners at slight angle. Brush lightly with melted butter. Repeat with 2 more squares, arranging corners at slight angle. Spoon ¼ cup cherry mixture in center of phyllo stack. Lift edges of phyllo and bring together around filling, forming bundle. With string, carefully tie bundle just above filling. Place on prepared sheet. Repeat with remaining phyllo and filling, forming 6 bundles total. Brush phyllo on outside of filled portion (but not tops) of each bundle with melted butter.

DO AHEAD: *Can be made 1 day ahead. Cover carefully and chill.*

Preheat oven to 325°F. Bake until phyllo is golden, about 35 minutes. Transfer baking sheet to rack and cool phyllo bundles on sheet. Carefully cut string from each bundle. Sift powdered sugar over bundles and serve.

More to Try

Try using your favorite liqueur, such as amaretto, in place of half of the boiling water. And don't hesitate to mix up the combination of nuts and fruit—hazelnuts and dried figs plumped in Port would make a tasty alternate filling.

Wondering what to do with all those phyllo trimmings? Toss them with melted butter, then cinnamon sugar; form them into mounds and bake until golden. Serve with fresh ripe peach wedges or poached pears and vanilla ice cream.

For something savory, toss trimmings with melted garlic butter and grated Parmesan cheese, then mound and bake. Serve with soup.

♥ Chocolate Chunk and Apricot Cannoli

"Leave the gun. Take the cannoli." If a dessert is good enough to be immortalized in The Godfather, *it's worth making at home. And it's easy to prepare these tube-shaped, cream-filled Italian pastries, since cannoli shells are readily available at Italian markets. Typically the ricotta and mascarpone cheese filling is studded with candied fruit, but we've used a winning combination of apricot preserves and chopped bittersweet chocolate.*

Makes 6

1	cup whole-milk ricotta cheese
¼	cup mascarpone cheese
½	cup apricot preserves
3	ounces bittersweet or semisweet chocolate, finely chopped
6	purchased cannoli shells
	Ground coffee beans
	Powdered sugar

Puree ricotta in processor. Add mascarpone and process to blend. Add preserves; process until incorporated but some small chunks remain. Add chocolate. Using on/off turns, mix until just blended (do not puree).

Transfer filling to pastry bag without tip. Pipe into shells. Sprinkle ends of cheese filling lightly with ground coffee. Arrange cannoli on platter; chill until cold.

DO AHEAD: *Can be made 6 hours ahead. Cover and keep chilled.*

Sift powdered sugar over cannoli and serve.

> ### Market Tip: **Fresh Ricotta**
> For best results, use fresh ricotta cheese. Avoid packaged brands that include preservatives, as these can be watery and have a grainy or gelatinous texture. Fresh ricotta is sometimes available at well-stocked supermarkets; otherwise, buy the ricotta at an Italian market, where the cannoli shells can also be found.

♥ Dried Cherry and Ginger Cannoli

Serve these delicious and colorful cannoli for brunch or to end an Italian feast.

Makes 25

4	cups fresh ricotta cheese (2 pounds)
2	cups powdered sugar
1	cup mascarpone cheese
1	tablespoon finely grated orange peel
½	teaspoon vanilla extract
¾	cup minced crystallized ginger
¾	cup minced dried tart cherries
4	ounces bittersweet or semisweet chocolate, finely chopped
25	purchased cannoli shells
	Chopped pistachios
	Additional powdered sugar

Working in 2 batches, blend ricotta cheese, powdered sugar, mascarpone, orange peel, and vanilla in processor until smooth. Add ginger and cherries and process until well incorporated. Using on/off turns, mix in chocolate just until blended (do not puree). Transfer filling to large bowl.

DO AHEAD: *Can be made 1 day ahead. Cover and chill. Bring to room temperature before continuing.*

Working in batches, transfer filling to pastry bag without tip. Pipe filling into cannoli shells. Sprinkle ends with pistachios. Chill at least 2 hours.

DO AHEAD: *Can be made 6 hours ahead. Cover and keep chilled.*

Sift powdered sugar over cannoli and serve.

custards & puddings

custards & puddings

stirred puddings

Double-Chocolate Pudding 334
Lime and Lemon Posset 334
Butterscotch Puddings with Whipped
    Cream and Crushed English Toffee 335
Chocolate-Espresso Puddings with
    Espresso Whipped Cream 337

pots de crème

Chocolate and Butterscotch Pots de Crème
    338
Chocolate-Orange Pots de Crème with
    Candied Orange Peel 339
Cappuccino Creams 340
Chai Pots de Crème 341
Honey-Cardamom Custards with
    Strawberry-Orange Compote 342

flans

The Perfect Flan 343
Vanilla-Lime Flans 343
Mocha Crème Caramel 344
Mango Flans 345
Sweet Potato Flans 345

crèmes brûlées

Caramel Crème Brûlée 346
Ginger Crème Brûlée 347
Cherry Crème Brûlée 347
Coffee-Brandy Crème Brûlée 349
White Pepper Crème Brûlée with Fig and
    Prune Compote 350
Pumpkin and Brown Sugar Crème Brûlée
    351

rice, tapioca & corn puddings

Vanilla Rice Pudding with Dried Cherries
    352
Rice Pudding with Cream Sherry 352
Warm Jasmine Rice Puddings with
    Passion Fruit 353
Caramelized Mango-Lime Tapioca 354
Indian Pudding 354

panna cottas

Vanilla Panna Cottas with Mixed Berry
    Compote 355
Pomegranate Panna Cottas 355
Panna Cottas with Black Mission Figs
    in Syrup 356
Piña Colada Panna Cotta 357

bread puddings

Caramel-Banana Bread Puddings 357
Dulce de Leche and Chocolate Chunk Bread
    Pudding 358
Spiced Cranberry Bread Puddings 360
Gingerbread Puddings with Candied
    Apples 361
Sticky Date and Almond Bread Pudding with
    Amaretto Zabaglione 362
Lemon-Spice Bread Pudding with Sautéed
    Peaches 363

mousse

Classic Chocolate Mousse 364
Chocolate-Cinnamon Mousse with
    Cherries 365
Spiced Coffee Mousse 365
Whiskey-Kissed White Chocolate Mousse
    with Strawberries and Lemon Shortbread
    Squares 366
Lemon Mousse with Fresh Berries 367
Chilled Lemon Mousse with Caramel
    Sauce 368
Gianduja Terrine with Hazelnut Custard
    Sauce 369–70

fools

Blackberry-Cassis Fool 371
Raspberry Fool 371

tiramisu

Berry Charlotte 372
Classic Tiramisù 373
Individual Raspberry Tiramisùs with
    Raspberry-Framboise Sauce 375

parfaits & trifles

Chocolate Cranachan 376
Mascarpone and Berry Parfaits 376
Raspberry-Nectarine Parfaits with Warm
    Peach Sabayon 377
Champagne Parfaits with Pears and
    Raspberries 377
Cranberry and Lemon-Ginger Parfaits 378
Tuaca Zabaglione with Sautéed Vanilla
    Pears 380
Tiramisù Eggnog Trifle 381
White Chocolate Trifle with Spiced Pears
    383–84
Chocolate-Cherry Trifle 385

soufflés

Chocolate Soufflés with White Chocolate
    Cream 386
Dark Chocolate Soufflés with Cardamom
    Crème Anglaise 387
Toffee Soufflés with Chocolate Sauce 388
Maple Gingerbread Soufflé 389
Lemon Soufflés with Boysenberries 390
Ricotta Soufflés with Blackberry
    Compote 390
Pear Soufflés with Chocolate Sauce 392
Salzburg Soufflé with Strawberry-Kirsch
    Sauce 393

Lemon Soufflés with Boysenberries

Double-Chocolate Pudding

This is just as quick to make as packaged pudding, but it tastes much, much better, thanks to the double dose of chocolate from both cocoa powder and bittersweet chocolate. And there are no fancy tools required—just a whisk and a saucepan. **2 servings; can be doubled**

⅓   **cup sugar**
2   **tablespoons natural unsweetened cocoa powder**
4   **teaspoons cornstarch**
     Pinch of salt
1   **cup whole milk**
½   **ounce bittersweet or semisweet chocolate, chopped**
1   **teaspoon vanilla extract**

Whisk sugar, cocoa, cornstarch, and salt in heavy medium saucepan until no lumps remain. Gradually add half of milk, whisking until mixture is smooth. Whisk in remaining milk. Cook over medium heat until pudding thickens and comes to boil, whisking constantly, about 5 minutes. Continue to boil 1 minute longer, whisking constantly.

Remove pudding from heat. Add chocolate and vanilla; whisk until chocolate melts and pudding is smooth. Divide between 2 dessert dishes. Chill puddings until cold, about 3 hours.

Lime and Lemon Posset

This dessert delivers great results with little effort. There is no need for eggs or gelatin to set the pudding; the acid in the lemon and lime juice does the trick all on its own. **Makes 6**

2¼   **cups heavy whipping cream**
¾   **cup plus 1 teaspoon sugar**
3   **tablespoons fresh lemon juice**
2   **tablespoons fresh lime juice**
1   **teaspoon finely grated lemon peel**
1   **teaspoon finely grated lime peel**

Bring cream and ¾ cup sugar to boil over medium-high heat, stirring until sugar dissolves. Boil 3 minutes, stirring constantly and adjusting heat as needed to prevent mixture from boiling over. Remove from heat. Stir in lemon juice and lime juice; cool 10 minutes. Stir pudding again and divide among six ½-cup ramekins or custard cups. Cover and chill puddings until set, at least 4 hours and up to 1 day.

Mix lemon peel, lime peel, and remaining 1 teaspoon sugar in small bowl. Sprinkle over puddings and serve.

Butterscotch Puddings with Whipped Cream and Crushed English Toffee

This is butterscotch pudding for grown-ups: It gets a splash of Scotch whisky. Whisking the hot half and half into the egg yolks gradually (instead of all at once) keeps the yolks from curdling; straining the pudding helps provide the smoothest, silkiest result. **Makes 6**

3	cups half and half, divided
2	large egg yolks
⅓	cup cornstarch
¾	cup (packed) dark brown sugar
¼	teaspoon salt
2	tablespoons (¼ stick) unsalted butter, room temperature
1	tablespoon Scotch
1	teaspoon vanilla extract
¾	cup chilled heavy whipping cream
3	tablespoons powdered sugar
1	1.4-ounce chocolate-covered English toffee bar (such as Heath), crushed with mallet or finely chopped

Technique Tip: Toffee Crush

Crushing the toffee bar with a mallet while the bar is still in its wrapper helps keep the crushed pieces contained. Or unwrap and place in a resealable plastic bag to crush.

Whisk 1 cup half and half, egg yolks, and cornstarch in large bowl until blended and cornstarch dissolves. Combine remaining 2 cups half and half, brown sugar, and salt in heavy medium saucepan. Bring just to boil, stirring until sugar dissolves. Gradually whisk hot half and half mixture into egg yolk mixture. Strain mixture back into same saucepan. Whisk over medium-low heat until mixture thickens and boils, about 10 minutes. Remove from heat; whisk in butter, Scotch, and vanilla.

Divide pudding mixture among six ¾-cup ramekins or custard cups. Cover ramekins with plastic wrap and refrigerate until cold, about 3 hours.

DO AHEAD: *Can be made 1 day ahead. Keep refrigerated.*

Whisk cream and powdered sugar in medium bowl until soft peaks form. Spoon large dollops of whipped cream atop puddings. Sprinkle with crushed toffee and serve.

Chocolate-Espresso Puddings with Espresso Whipped Cream

Chocolate-coated coffee beans would be a fun garnish for these easy-to-prepare puddings. **Makes 6**

6	tablespoons sugar, divided
2	tablespoons cornstarch
4	teaspoons instant espresso powder or instant coffee powder, divided
2	cups whole milk
1	cup bittersweet or semisweet chocolate chips
1	tablespoon unsalted butter
1½	teaspoons vanilla extract
½	cup chilled heavy whipping cream

Whisk 4 tablespoons sugar, cornstarch, and 3 teaspoons espresso powder in heavy medium saucepan until no lumps remain. Gradually whisk in milk. Whisk over medium heat until mixture thickens and boils, 3 to 4 minutes. Remove from heat. Add chocolate chips, butter, and vanilla and whisk until smooth. Divide pudding among 6 small ramekins or goblets. Cover and chill until cold, at least 2 hours and up to 1 day.

Using electric mixer, beat cream, remaining 2 tablespoons sugar, and remaining 1 teaspoon espresso powder in medium bowl until peaks form. Top each pudding with dollop of espresso whipped cream.

What's What

While many custard and pudding desserts start with the same basic elements, each has its own unique, delicious personality.

CRÈME BRÛLÉE: a chilled custard topped with a hard sugar crust made by sprinkling sugar over the top of the custard and caramelizing it with a kitchen torch or under the broiler.

FLAN (*CRÈME CARAMEL*): custard with a caramel topping. The custard is baked in a custard cup or ramekin with the caramel on the bottom, chilled, then inverted onto a plate so that the caramel coats the top and sides.

FOOL: a simple and delicious English dessert in which pureed fruit (sweetened or unsweetened) is folded together with whipped cream.

MOUSSE: a rich yet airy dessert lightened with the addition of whipped cream or beaten egg whites or both.

PANNA COTTA: a classic Italian dessert—cold, silky, eggless custard that's often embellished with fruit and sometimes flavored with liqueurs.

PARFAIT: *Parfait* ("perfect" in French) has two different culinary interpretations. The classic French parfait is a frozen custard, often layered in goblets or parfait glasses with fruit or nuts. The other, more common usage of the word refers to a layered dessert based on some sort of custard, ice cream, yogurt, or sabayon. It can be layered with anything from fruit and nuts to candy and granola.

POSSET: a simple British pudding that is thickened by the acid in the citrus fruit.

POT DE CRÈME: a rich custard, usually vanilla or chocolate, named for the small lidded pot it is traditionally served in.

Chocolate and Butterscotch Pots de Crème

Because each pudding layer needs to set overnight on its own, make sure to begin preparing this dessert two days ahead. Use clear glass ramekins to display the colored layers. **Makes 12**

Butterscotch Pudding

3½	cups heavy whipping cream
¼	teaspoon salt
½	vanilla bean, split lengthwise
6	ounces butterscotch chips
6	large egg yolks
2	tablespoons (packed) golden brown sugar
1	tablespoon water
1	tablespoon Scotch

Chocolate Pudding

6	ounces bittersweet or semisweet chocolate (do not exceed 61% cacao), chopped
½	cup plus 3 tablespoons sugar
3	tablespoons cornstarch
2	tablespoons natural unsweetened cocoa powder
	Pinch of salt
2	cups whole milk
1	cup heavy whipping cream
½	vanilla bean, split lengthwise
3	large egg yolks
1	tablespoon unsalted butter

BUTTERSCOTCH PUDDING: Preheat oven to 325°F. Combine cream and salt in heavy medium saucepan. Scrape in seeds from vanilla bean; add bean. Bring to simmer over medium-high heat, stirring occasionally. Remove from heat. Add butterscotch chips and whisk until smooth. Whisk egg yolks in medium bowl to blend. Gradually whisk cream mixture into yolks. Return mixture to same saucepan. Discard vanilla bean.

Stir brown sugar, 1 tablespoon water, and Scotch in heavy small saucepan over medium-high heat until sugar dissolves. Bring to boil; whisk brown sugar syrup into butterscotch mixture.

Divide pudding among twelve ¾-cup custard cups or ramekins. Place cups in large roasting pan. Add enough hot water to roasting pan to come halfway up sides of cups. Cover pan with foil and bake until puddings are set, about 1 hour. Remove cups from pan. Place on rimmed baking sheet and chill uncovered overnight.

CHOCOLATE PUDDING: Stir chocolate in top of double boiler over barely simmering water until melted and smooth. Cool to lukewarm.

Sift sugar, cornstarch, cocoa, and salt into heavy medium saucepan. Slowly whisk in milk and cream. Scrape in seeds from vanilla bean; add bean. Whisk in egg yolks, then melted chocolate. Place saucepan over medium heat and whisk constantly until thick and edges are bubbling, about 10 minutes. Remove chocolate pudding from heat and strain into 4-cup measuring cup. Whisk in butter. Let pudding stand at room temperature 10 minutes.

Pour warm chocolate pudding over chilled butterscotch puddings, dividing equally. Cover and refrigerate overnight.

Chocolate-Orange Pots de Crème with Candied Orange Peel

This intense chocolate pudding is the perfect finish for a romantic dinner for two—or an elegant dinner for four; the recipe doubles easily. Covering the dishes with foil before baking helps prevent a film from forming on top of the pudding as it cooks. **Makes 2**

Candied Orange Peel

1	orange
1	cup sugar, divided
¾	cup water

Pots de Crème

⅔	cup whole milk
½	cup heavy whipping cream
1	tablespoon Grand Marnier or other orange liqueur
1	teaspoon vanilla extract
1	teaspoon finely grated orange peel
4	ounces bittersweet or semisweet chocolate (do not exceed 61% cacao), chopped
4	large egg yolks
3	tablespoons sugar
	Lightly sweetened whipped cream

CANDIED ORANGE PEEL: Using vegetable peeler, remove orange part of peel from orange in long strips. Cut peel lengthwise into ⅛-inch-wide strips. Stir ¾ cup sugar and ¾ cup water in heavy small saucepan over medium-low heat until sugar dissolves. Bring to boil. Reduce heat and simmer 2 minutes. Add orange peel; simmer 15 minutes.

Place remaining ¼ cup sugar in small bowl. Using slotted spoon, remove peel from syrup and transfer to sugar. Toss to coat. Cool, tossing occasionally. Cover bowl and let stand at room temperature overnight.

DO AHEAD: *Can be made 2 days ahead. Keep covered.*

POTS DE CRÈME: Preheat oven to 350°F. Bring milk, cream, Grand Marnier, vanilla, and grated orange peel to boil in heavy medium saucepan. Remove from heat. Add chocolate and stir until melted and smooth. Whisk egg yolks and sugar in medium bowl until pale yellow, about 2 minutes. Whisk egg mixture into chocolate mixture. Strain into 2-cup measuring cup.

Divide mixture between two 8-ounce custard cups. Place cups in small baking dish. Add enough hot water to baking dish to come halfway up sides of cups. Cover dish tightly with foil. Bake until custard is set, about 40 minutes. Remove cups from water. Refrigerate uncovered until cool. Cover with plastic wrap and refrigerate until cold, about 6 hours.

DO AHEAD: *Can be made 2 days ahead. Keep refrigerated.*

Top with whipped cream, garnish with candied orange peel, and serve.

Cappuccino Creams

What could be better than a hot cappuccino topped with white chocolate cream? This cold dessert version, which features sweet espresso and white chocolate custards, comes very close. For a more playful take, bake and serve the custards in pretty coffee cups. **Makes 6**

1   2½-inch piece vanilla bean, split lengthwise
1¾   cups heavy whipping cream, divided
2   ounces high-quality white chocolate (such as Lindt or
          Perugina), finely chopped
5   tablespoons sugar
4   large egg yolks
1   large egg
¼   cup sour cream
4   teaspoons light (white) rum
      Pinch of salt
4   teaspoons instant espresso powder or instant coffee powder

Preheat oven to 350°F. Place ramekins in 13x9x2-inch metal baking pan. Scrape seeds from vanilla bean into heavy small saucepan; add bean. Mix in ½ cup cream and white chocolate. Stir over low heat just until smooth. Set aside.

Whisk remaining 1¼ cups cream, sugar, egg yolks, egg, sour cream, rum, and salt in medium bowl until smooth. Strain white chocolate mixture into egg mixture and whisk to blend. Pour ¼ cup custard mixture into each ramekin; reserve remaining custard. Add enough hot water to baking pan to come halfway up sides of ramekins. Bake until custards set, about 30 minutes. Let stand 5 minutes. Add espresso powder to remaining custard mixture; stir until dissolved. Spoon espresso custard over white chocolate custards, dividing equally.

Bake custards until set, about 30 minutes. Remove from water. Refrigerate uncovered until cold.

DO AHEAD: *Can be made 1 day ahead. Cover; keep chilled.*

Technique Tip: Ramekins
This recipe calls for wide, shallow ramekins, but the custards can also be made in 3-inch-diameter ramekins with 1¼-inch-high sides. They will need to bake a little longer, about 50 minutes instead of 35.

Chai Pots de Crème

Spiced chai tea is ubiquitous in the Indian subcontinent and in coffeehouses everywhere else. It's a blend of black tea boiled with milk and water and spiced with cinnamon, cloves, cardamom, and ginger. That combination is the inspiration for these exotic pots de crème. **Makes 6**

Custard

1	**cup heavy whipping cream**
1	**cup whole milk**
1	**tablespoon loose-leaf English Breakfast tea or jasmine tea**
1	**cinnamon stick**
8	**whole cardamom pods**
6	**whole cloves**
3	**¼-inch-thick rounds peeled fresh ginger**
4	**large egg yolks**
½	**cup (packed) golden brown sugar**
¼	**teaspoon finely grated orange peel**

Topping

1	**cup chilled heavy whipping cream**
2	**teaspoons sugar**

{ Ingredient Tip: **Jasmine Tea**
Using jasmine tea instead of English Breakfast will lend a delicate floral note to the *pots de crème*. }

CUSTARD: Combine cream, milk, tea, cinnamon, cardamom, cloves, and ginger in medium saucepan. Bring to boil. Remove from heat; cover and let steep 15 minutes to allow flavors to develop.

Preheat oven to 325°F. Place six ¾-cup custard cups or ramekins in 13x9x2-inch metal baking pan. Pour cream mixture through fine strainer into medium bowl. Discard solids in strainer.

Whisk egg yolks, sugar, and orange peel in 4-cup measuring cup to blend well. Gradually whisk in cream mixture. Pour custard mixture into custard cups, dividing equally (cups will not be full). Add enough hot water to baking pan to come halfway up sides of custard cups. Cover pan with foil. Pierce foil in several places with skewer to allow steam to escape.

Bake custards until softly set (center will move slightly when cups are shaken gently), about 30 minutes. Remove custards from water. Cool slightly on rack. Chill uncovered until cold.

DO AHEAD: *Can be made 1 day ahead. Cover; keep chilled.*

TOPPING: Beat cream and sugar in medium bowl until soft peaks form. Place dollop of whipped cream atop each pot de crème and serve.

Honey-Cardamom Custards with Strawberry-Orange Compote

Simple baked custards get a honeyed sweetness and a spicy cardamom boost. They're served straight out of the ramekins, topped with spiced sliced strawberries and orange segments. To amp up the flavor, use whole cardamom seeds, straight from the pod and freshly ground in a spice grinder or mortar and pestle. **Makes 4**

2	cups whole milk
¼	cup heavy whipping cream
1	vanilla bean, split lengthwise
2	2x1-inch orange peel strips (orange part only)
¼	teaspoon ground cardamom
⅛	teaspoon salt
⅓	cup honey
4	large egg yolks
1	large egg
	Strawberry-Orange Compote (see recipe)

Combine milk, cream, vanilla bean, orange peel strips, cardamom, and salt in heavy small saucepan. Cook milk mixture over medium heat until tiny bubbles appear around edge of saucepan. Remove from heat. Cover and let steep 20 minutes.

Preheat oven to 325°F. Remove softened vanilla bean from milk mixture. Scrape seeds from vanilla bean into milk mixture; add bean. Heat milk mixture again until tiny bubbles appear around edge of saucepan. Remove saucepan from heat, add honey, and stir until honey melts. Using fork, beat egg yolks and egg in medium bowl just until blended. Gradually mix hot milk mixture into egg mixture. Strain custard into large measuring cup with spout.

Pour custard into four 1¼-cup soufflé dishes or custard cups. Place dishes in 13x9x2-inch metal baking pan. Add enough hot water to pan to come halfway up sides of dishes. Cover pan loosely with foil. Bake custards until knife inserted into center comes out clean, about 40 minutes. Transfer dishes to rack and cool. Cover custards and refrigerate until cold.

DO AHEAD: *Can be made 1 day ahead. Keep refrigerated.*

Place custards in dishes on plates. Top each custard with Strawberry-Orange Compote and serve.

Strawberry-Orange Compote

Compotes are usually cooked—the fruit is stewed until it reaches a syrupy consistency. Here, the strawberries and orange segments are simply combined with honey and the juice from the oranges and spiced with a little cardamom. In classic French cooking, to suprême a citrus fruit is to segment it, removing the pith, peel, seeds, and membranes (see page 35 for more information on how to do this). The resulting slices are known as supremes. If you don't have the time (or perhaps the patience) for such a task, you can also cut off the peel and pith, slice the orange crosswise into rounds, and cut the rounds into pieces. **4 servings**

1	1-pint container strawberries, hulled, sliced
2	oranges, peel and white pith removed
1	tablespoon honey
¼	teaspoon ground cardamom

Place strawberries in medium bowl. Using small sharp knife, hold oranges over same bowl and cut between membranes to release segments, allowing juice and segments to fall into bowl. Squeeze orange membranes over same bowl to release any juice. Mix in honey and cardamom.

DO AHEAD: *Can be made 2 hours ahead. Cover and refrigerate.*

The Perfect Flan

This extraordinary flan starts with a few humble ingredients: eggs, cream, milk, sugar, vanilla. But with the right techniques, the results are incredible: a silky-smooth vanilla custard coated with sweet homemade caramel. Note that the flans need to chill overnight before serving. **Makes 6**

1¾   cups heavy whipping cream
1   cup whole milk
    Pinch of salt
½   vanilla bean, split lengthwise
1   cup plus 7 tablespoons sugar
⅓   cup water
3   large eggs
2   large egg yolks

Position rack in center of oven and preheat to 350°F. Combine cream, milk, and salt in heavy medium saucepan. Scrape in seeds from vanilla bean; add bean. Bring to simmer over medium heat. Remove from heat and let steep 30 minutes.

Meanwhile, combine 1 cup sugar and ⅓ cup water in another heavy medium saucepan. Stir over low heat until sugar dissolves. Increase heat to high and boil without stirring until syrup is deep amber color, occasionally brushing down sides of pan with wet pastry brush and swirling pan, about 10 minutes. Immediately pour caramel into six ¾-cup ramekins or custard cups. Using oven mitts as aid, immediately tilt each ramekin to coat sides. Place ramekins in 13x9x2-inch metal baking pan.

Whisk eggs, egg yolks, and remaining 7 tablespoons sugar in medium bowl just until blended. Gradually and gently whisk cream mixture into egg mixture without creating lots of foam. Pour custard through small sieve into prepared ramekins, dividing equally (mixture will fill ramekins). Add enough hot water to baking pan to come halfway up sides of ramekins.

Bake flans until center is gently set, about 40 minutes. Transfer flans to rack and cool. Refrigerate uncovered until cold, then cover and chill overnight.

DO AHEAD: *Can be made 2 days ahead. Keep chilled.*

Run small sharp knife around sides of 1 flan. Place plate atop ramekin. Invert flan onto plate. Shake gently to release flan. Carefully lift off ramekin, allowing caramel to run over flan. Repeat with remaining flans and serve.

Vanilla-Lime Flans

Bright lime flavors pair beautifully with vanilla in this creamy dessert. You'll want to start these one day ahead: They need to chill overnight. **Makes 8**

1⅓   cups plus ½ cup sugar
½   cup water
4   teaspoons finely grated lime peel
3   large eggs
5   large egg yolks
2   cups heavy whipping cream
1½   cups whole milk
2½   teaspoons vanilla extract
¼   teaspoon salt
    Lime slices

Preheat oven to 325°F. Place eight ⅔-cup ramekins or custard cups on work surface. Stir 1⅓ cups sugar and ½ cup water in heavy medium saucepan over low heat until sugar dissolves. Increase heat and boil without stirring until syrup is deep amber color, occasionally brushing down sides of pan with wet pastry brush and swirling pan, about 8 minutes. Immediately pour caramel into ramekins, dividing equally. Using oven mitts as aid, pick up each ramekin and tilt and rotate to coat sides with caramel. Place ramekins in large roasting pan.

Using back of spoon, mash remaining ½ cup sugar and lime peel in large bowl until sugar is moist and fragrant. Add eggs and egg yolks; whisk to blend. Bring cream and milk to boil in heavy medium saucepan. Gradually whisk cream mixture into egg mixture. Whisk in vanilla and salt. Ladle custard into caramel-lined ramekins. Add enough hot water to roasting pan to come halfway up sides of ramekins.

Bake flans until just set and beginning to color on top, about 45 minutes. Remove from water; let cool 45 minutes. Cover and refrigerate overnight.

Run small sharp knife around sides of 1 flan. Place plate atop ramekin. Invert flan onto plate, allowing caramel to run over flan. Remove ramekin. Repeat with remaining flans. Garnish with lime slices.

Mocha Crème Caramel

A nice chocolate-coffee take on traditional crème caramel: The custard is prepared with milk chocolate and instant coffee crystals, and then topped with a layer of mocha ganache. **Makes 6**

Custard

⅔	cup plus ¼ cup sugar
3	tablespoons water
1½	cups heavy whipping cream
½	cup milk
4	ounces high-quality milk chocolate (such as Lindt or Perugina), chopped
2½	teaspoons instant coffee crystals
3	large egg yolks
1	large egg

Ganache

1½	teaspoons instant coffee powder
½	teaspoon water
4	ounces high-quality milk chocolate (such as Lindt or Perugina), chopped
2	tablespoons heavy whipping cream

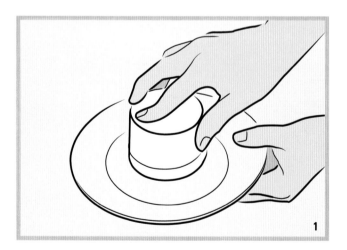

CUSTARD: Position rack in center of oven and preheat to 325°F. Place six ½-cup ramekins or custard cups in baking pan. Stir ⅔ cup sugar and 3 tablespoons water in heavy small saucepan over low heat until sugar dissolves. Increase heat to medium-high and bring mixture to boil. Boil without stirring until mixture turns deep amber color, occasionally brushing down sides of pan with wet pastry brush and swirling pan, about 9 minutes. Immediately pour caramel into ramekins, dividing equally. Carefully tilt ramekins just to coat bottom (not sides) with caramel.

Bring cream, milk, and remaining ¼ cup sugar to boil in heavy medium saucepan, whisking until sugar dissolves. Remove from heat. Add chocolate and stir until chocolate melts and mixture is smooth. Whisk in coffee crystals, egg yolks, and egg. Divide custard mixture equally among caramel-lined ramekins. Add enough hot water to baking pan to come halfway up sides of ramekins.

Bake custards until set around edges and center moves only slightly when baking pan is shaken, about 30 minutes. Remove custards from water and cool. Cover and refrigerate until very cold, about 4 hours.

DO AHEAD: *Can be made 1 day ahead. Keep refrigerated.*

GANACHE: Dissolve coffee powder in ½ teaspoon water in small bowl. Combine chocolate and cream in heavy small saucepan. Stir over low heat until chocolate melts and mixture is smooth. Remove from heat and stir in coffee mixture. Cool until just warm to touch.

Divide ganache among custards. Spread ganache with back of spoon to cover top of custards completely. Refrigerate until ganache is set, at least 1 hour.

DO AHEAD: *Can be made 2 days ahead. Cover and keep chilled.*

Run small sharp knife around sides of 1 custard to loosen. Place plate atop ramekin. Invert custard onto plate. Remove ramekin [1]. Repeat with remaining custards and ramekins.

Mango Flans

Sweet pureed mango, a bit of lime juice, and ginger give these an edge over plain old vanilla flan. Start preparing these in the morning or the night before: The flans need to chill for at least six hours after baking. **Makes 8**

1½ cups plus ⅓ cup sugar
¾ cup hot water
2 tablespoons light corn syrup
2 1-pound ripe mangoes, peeled, pitted, pureed
        (about 2¾ cups puree)
1 tablespoon plus 1 teaspoon fresh lime juice
½ teaspoon ground ginger
¾ cup plus 2 tablespoons half and half
5 large eggs

Preheat oven to 350°F. Combine 1½ cups sugar, ¾ cup hot water, and corn syrup in heavy medium saucepan. Stir over medium-low heat until sugar dissolves. Increase heat and boil without stirring until syrup is deep amber color, occasionally brushing down sides of pan with wet pastry brush and swirling pan, about 6 minutes. Immediately pour caramel syrup into eight 6-ounce custard cups, dividing equally.

Whisk mango puree, lime juice, ginger, and remaining ⅓ cup sugar in heavy medium saucepan over medium-high heat until mixture thickens and large bubbles break surface, about 5 minutes. Cool slightly, stirring occasionally. Whisk half and half and eggs in large bowl to blend. Stir in mango mixture. Strain custard.

Pour custard over caramel in custard cups, dividing equally. Place custard cups in large roasting pan. Add enough hot water to pan to come halfway up sides of custard cups. Cover pan with foil.

Bake flans until just set in center, about 35 minutes. Turn off heat. Leave flans covered in oven 30 minutes longer. Remove from roasting pan. Cool slightly. Refrigerate uncovered until cold, then cover and refrigerate at least 6 hours or overnight.

Run small sharp knife around sides of 1 flan. Place plate atop cup. Invert flan onto plate, allowing caramel to run over flan. Remove cup. Repeat with remaining flans and serve.

{ **Ingredient Tip: Mango Varieties**
The 1-pound mangoes you'll most often find in the market are known as Tommy Atkins. But you can also use the increasingly available small, sweet, golden yellow Ataulfo mangoes (sometimes referred to as Champagne mangoes). You'll need 2 pounds' worth of Ataulfo mangoes for this recipe. }

Sweet Potato Flans

Here's a southern spin on the popular Spanish custard. The flans' creamy sweetness would be nicely complemented by the Crisp Anise Cookies on page 574. **Makes 12**

1½ pounds unpeeled whole red-skinned sweet potatoes (yams)
2¾ cups sugar, divided
¾ cup water
6 large eggs
1 tablespoon vanilla extract
¾ teaspoon salt
2 cups heavy whipping cream
2 teaspoons finely grated orange peel

Cook sweet potatoes in large pot of boiling water until tender, about 35 minutes. Drain well. Cool 20 minutes. Peel potatoes. Transfer to medium bowl; mash until smooth.

Position rack in center of oven and preheat to 325°F. Stir 2 cups sugar and ¾ cup water in heavy medium saucepan over medium heat until sugar dissolves. Increase heat and boil without stirring until syrup is deep amber color, occasionally brushing down sides of pan with wet pastry brush and swirling pan, about 10 minutes. Immediately divide caramel among twelve ¾-cup custard cups or soufflé dishes, tilting cups to cover bottom (not sides) with caramel. Cool.

Whisk mashed sweet potatoes, remaining ¾ cup sugar, eggs, vanilla, and salt in large bowl to blend well. Combine cream and orange peel in heavy medium saucepan. Bring to boil. Gradually whisk cream into potato-egg mixture. Strain mixture into 2-quart measuring cup or bowl; discard solids in strainer.

Divide mixture among custard cups. Place 6 cups in each of 2 large baking pans. Add enough hot water to baking pans to come halfway up sides of cups. Bake flans until sides are set but center still moves slightly when cups are shaken, about 45 minutes. Remove cups from water and cool about 40 minutes. Cover and refrigerate at least 3 hours and up to 2 days.

Run small sharp knife around sides of 1 flan. Place plate atop cup. Invert flan onto plate, allowing caramel to run over flan. Remove custard cup. Repeat with remaining flans and serve.

Brûlée Basics

Once you've mastered custard, it's easy to transform it into restaurant-worthy crème brûlée. Here's how.

1 Sprinkle the well-chilled custards with a small amount of sugar—about 1 teaspoon. In this case, there really can be too much of a good thing. A thicker layer of sugar might not melt and caramelize (burn) evenly. Then it won't crisp completely, resulting in a slightly granular texture. White sugar is a good, classic choice. Raw sugar is even better: We find that it melts and caramelizes more easily and hardens better. Because brown sugar clumps, we recommend pressing the sugar through a sieve over each custard.

2 A small kitchen blowtorch is the easiest and the most effective way to caramelize the sugar topping. (Kitchen torches are available at cookware stores, at some hardware stores, and online for $20 to $40. See Online and Mail-Order Sources, page 632.) But if you don't have a torch (and don't want to buy one), the broiler is the next best thing. Arrange the custards on a baking sheet and place about 6 inches from the heat source. Then broil, moving sheet occasionally to ensure even browning.

3 Chill the caramelized custards until the topping hardens and any melted custard resets, about one hour and up to two hours. In other words, long enough to chill the custards, but not so long that the topping softens.

Caramel Crème Brûlée

In this twist on the classic crème brûlée, the sugar in the custard is caramelized as well as the sugar on top, which gets "brûléed," or "burnt." The custards need to chill overnight before serving, so be sure to start one day ahead. **Makes 6**

½	cup plus 6 teaspoons sugar
1	tablespoon water
2	cups heavy whipping cream
5	large egg yolks
1½	teaspoons vanilla extract
¼	teaspoon salt

Preheat oven to 300°F. Place six ½-cup ramekins or soufflé dishes in 13x9x2-inch metal baking pan. Combine ½ cup sugar and 1 tablespoon water in heavy medium saucepan. Stir over medium-low heat until sugar dissolves. Increase heat and boil without stirring until syrup is deep amber color, occasionally brushing down sides of pan with wet pastry brush and swirling pan, about 5 minutes. Slowly add cream (mixture will bubble vigorously); stir over low heat until any caramel bits dissolve and mixture is smooth. Remove from heat. Cool slightly.

Combine egg yolks, vanilla, and salt in medium metal bowl. Using electric mixer, beat until mixture is pale in color, about 3 minutes. Gradually add cream mixture and beat until blended. Divide mixture among ramekins. Add enough hot water to baking pan to come halfway up sides of ramekins.

Bake until custards are just set in center, about 45 minutes. Remove ramekins from water; cool slightly. Refrigerate uncovered until cold, then cover and refrigerate overnight.

Sprinkle each custard with 1 teaspoon of remaining sugar. Using kitchen torch, melt sugar until deep amber color. (Alternatively, use broiler. Place ramekins on rimmed baking sheet. Broil until sugar melts and is deep amber color, turning baking sheet for even browning and watching closely to avoid burning, about 3 minutes.) Refrigerate custards until topping hardens, at least 1 hour and up to 2 hours before serving.

Ginger Crème Brûlée

Fresh grated ginger gives the custards an appealing bite. Because the ginger is so flavorful, the crème brûlée needs just four ingredients and a simple garnish of fresh, ripe strawberries and mint. Be sure to make this dessert a day ahead so that the custard has plenty of time to chill. **Makes 8**

3   cups heavy whipping cream
2   tablespoons (packed) coarsely grated peeled fresh ginger
10 large egg yolks
1   cup plus 4 teaspoons sugar
    Fresh strawberries
    Fresh mint

Preheat oven to 325°F. Combine cream and ginger in heavy medium saucepan. Bring to simmer over medium heat. Remove from heat; let stand 20 minutes. Strain cream into small bowl, pressing on solids in sieve. Discard solids in sieve. Whisk egg yolks and 1 cup sugar in medium bowl to blend. Gradually whisk in warm cream mixture. Divide custard among eight ¾-cup ramekins or custard cups. Place ramekins in large roasting pan. Add enough warm water to baking pan to come halfway up sides of ramekins.

Bake custards just until set in center, about 45 minutes. Remove custards from water. Refrigerate uncovered until cold. Cover and refrigerate overnight.

Sprinkle each custard with ½ teaspoon of remaining sugar. Using kitchen torch, melt sugar until deep amber color. (Alternatively, use broiler. Place ramekins on rimmed baking sheet. Broil until sugar melts and is deep amber color, turning baking sheet for even browning and watching closely to avoid burning, about 1 minute.) Refrigerate custards until topping hardens, at least 1 hour and up to 2 hours. Garnish custards with strawberries and mint and serve.

Cherry Crème Brûlée

Beneath the crunchy sugar topping and creamy cherry-flavored custard are sweet, brandied cherries. The custards need to chill overnight. **Makes 4**

20   canned pitted sweet cherries, drained, halved
8   tablespoons sugar, divided
2   tablespoons kirsch (clear cherry brandy) or other brandy
1½   cups heavy whipping cream
½   cup milk
6   large egg yolks
1   teaspoon vanilla extract
4   tablespoons (packed) golden brown sugar

Combine cherries, 2 tablespoons sugar, and kirsch in small bowl. Let cherries soak 2 hours.

Preheat oven to 325°F. Drain cherries, reserving liquid. Divide cherries evenly among four 1-cup ramekins. Bring cream and milk to simmer in heavy medium saucepan. Whisk egg yolks and remaining 6 tablespoons sugar in medium bowl to blend. Gradually whisk in hot cream mixture. Stir in reserved cherry soaking liquid and vanilla. Divide mixture among ramekins. Place ramekins in large shallow baking dish. Add enough hot water to baking dish to come halfway up sides of ramekins.

Bake until custards are just set in center, about 35 minutes. Remove custards from water and cool. Cover and refrigerate overnight.

DO AHEAD: *Can be made 2 days ahead. Keep refrigerated.*

Press 1 tablespoon brown sugar through sieve over each custard. Using kitchen torch, melt sugar until deep amber color. (Alternatively, use broiler. Place ramekins on rimmed baking sheet. Broil until sugar melts and is deep amber color, turning baking sheet for even browning and watching closely to avoid burning, about 3 minutes.) Serve immediately.

Coffee-Brandy Crème Brûlée

If you like spiked coffee, you'll love these custards. They have all the great flavor of a classic café royale: sweetened coffee with just the right amount of brandy. You'll need to bake these a day before you plan to serve them so that the custard can chill completely. **Makes 6**

2	cups heavy whipping cream
¼	cup sugar
1½	teaspoons instant coffee crystals
4	large egg yolks
1	tablespoon brandy
1	teaspoon vanilla extract
3	tablespoons (packed) golden brown sugar

Preheat oven to 350°F. Arrange six ¾-cup ramekins or custard cups in 13x9x2-inch metal baking pan. Combine cream and sugar in heavy medium saucepan; bring almost to simmer, stirring until sugar dissolves. Remove from heat; add coffee and whisk to dissolve. Whisk egg yolks in medium bowl to blend. Gradually whisk in warm cream mixture, then brandy and vanilla. Strain custard into 4-cup measuring cup; pour into ramekins, dividing equally. Add enough hot water to pan to come halfway up sides of ramekins.

Bake custards until center moves only slightly when pan is gently shaken, about 35 minutes. Remove custards from pan. Chill uncovered until cold, then cover and chill overnight.

Arrange custards on baking sheet. Press ½ tablespoon brown sugar through sieve onto each custard, forming even layer. Using kitchen torch, melt sugar until deep amber color. (Alternatively, use broiler. Place ramekins on rimmed baking sheet. Broil until sugar melts and is deep amber color, turning baking sheet for even browning and watching closely to avoid burning, about 3 minutes.) Refrigerate custards until topping hardens, at least 1 hour and up to 2 hours before serving.

A World of Custard Cups

Stovetop custards, mousses, chilled parfaits, and panna cottas can be presented in a number of ways: wine goblets, tumblers, teacups, or mugs, for example. But baked custards are another story. For the best results (and the safest preparation), it's important to use ovenproof ramekins, soufflé dishes, or custard cups. When you're not making crème brûlée, use ramekins to serve nuts and olives, to organize your *mise en place* (all of your measured, chopped, and prepared ingredients), or to create individual chocolate fondues.

White Pepper Crème Brûlée with Fig and Prune Compote

White pepper adds a touch of heat and a delicate floral note to an elegant dessert. Raw sugar (also known as turbinado or demerara sugar) is used in this version, creating a delicious crunchy topping that is the perfect contrast to the sweet and creamy custard. **Makes 6**

Compote

2	cups apple juice
¾	cup diced dried Calimyrna figs
¾	cup diced pitted prunes
½	teaspoon (packed) finely grated orange peel

Custards

2⅓	cups heavy whipping cream
⅓	cup half and half
½	teaspoon freshly ground white pepper
1	5-inch piece vanilla bean, split lengthwise
8	large egg yolks
½	cup sugar
9	teaspoons raw sugar

COMPOTE: Combine apple juice, figs, prunes, and orange peel in heavy medium saucepan. Bring to boil, stirring occasionally. Reduce heat to medium-low and simmer gently until figs and prunes are soft, about 10 minutes. Cool compote slightly. Transfer to small bowl.

DO AHEAD: *Can be made 1 day ahead. Cover and refrigerate.*

CUSTARDS: Preheat oven to 325°F. Arrange six ¾-cup ramekins or custard cups in 13x9x2-inch metal baking pan. Combine cream, half and half, and pepper in heavy medium saucepan. Scrape in seeds from vanilla bean; add bean. Bring cream mixture to simmer over medium heat. Cover; set aside 10 minutes to steep. Discard vanilla bean. Whisk egg yolks and ½ cup sugar in medium bowl to blend. Gradually whisk in warm cream mixture.

Divide custard among ramekins. Add enough hot water to baking pan to come halfway up sides of ramekins. Bake custards until set in center, about 35 minutes. Remove custards from water; refrigerate uncovered until cold.

DO AHEAD: *Can be made 1 day ahead. Cover and keep refrigerated.*

Sprinkle 1½ teaspoons raw sugar over top of each custard. Using kitchen torch, melt sugar until deep amber color. (Alternatively, use broiler. Place ramekins on rimmed baking sheet. Broil until sugar melts and is deep amber color, turning baking sheet for even browning and watching closely to avoid burning, about 3 minutes.) Refrigerate custards uncovered until topping hardens, at least 1 hour and up to 2 hours before serving.

Serve custards with fig and prune compote.

Pumpkin and Brown Sugar Crème Brûlée

Cinnamon, cardamom, allspice, and cloves give this crème brûlée a spicy kick. Think of it as a crustless pumpkin pie with a crunchy burnt-sugar topping. Raw sugar is available at most supermarkets and at natural foods stores, but golden brown sugar works well, too. **Makes 8**

1	15-ounce can pure pumpkin
½	cup sugar
½	cup (packed) golden brown sugar
5	large egg yolks
2	teaspoons vanilla extract
1	teaspoon ground cinnamon
¼	teaspoon ground cardamom
¼	teaspoon ground allspice
¼	teaspoon ground cloves
¼	teaspoon salt
3	cups heavy whipping cream
8	tablespoons raw sugar or golden brown sugar

Preheat oven to 325°F. Whisk pumpkin, sugar, and brown sugar in large bowl. Whisk in egg yolks and vanilla, then cinnamon, cardamom, allspice, cloves, and salt. Bring cream just to boil in medium saucepan. Gradually whisk hot cream into pumpkin mixture.

Divide mixture among eight 5-inch-diameter, 1-inch-deep ramekins. Divide ramekins between 2 large roasting pans. Add enough hot water to roasting pans to come halfway up sides of ramekins.

Bake until custards are just set in center, about 35 minutes. Remove custards from water. Cool slightly. Refrigerate custards uncovered until cold.

DO AHEAD: *Can be made 2 days ahead. Cover and keep chilled.*

Sprinkle 1 tablespoon raw sugar over pumpkin custard in each ramekin. Using kitchen torch, melt sugar until deep amber color. (Alternatively, use broiler. Place ramekins on rimmed baking sheet. Press 1 tablespoon brown sugar—not raw sugar—through sieve over each custard and broil until sugar melts and is deep amber color, turning baking sheet for even browning and watching closely to avoid burning, about 3 minutes.) Refrigerate custards until topping hardens, at least 15 minutes and up to 1 hour.

The Secret of Smooth Custards

To ensure smooth custards that don't curdle or overcook, our recipes often recommend baking them in a water bath, a gentle method of baking the delicate custards. Here's the easiest and safest way to do it: First, place the soufflé dishes in a roasting pan with about 2-inch-high sides. Pull out the oven rack partway—it should still be stable and level—and place the pan on the rack. Next, fill the pan with enough hot water from a tea kettle or spouted cup to reach halfway up the sides of the soufflé dishes. Being careful not to slosh water into the custards, slide the rack back into the oven and bake the custards. Keep an eye on the water: If it starts to bubble, the custards may overcook and become tough; so throw some ice cubes into the water to cool it down a bit. Custards are done when the edges are set but the centers still tremble slightly. Bake the custards any longer and they'll be too firm when cold—not nice and creamy. Remove the pan from the oven. Slide a spatula under each dish; hold sides with tongs and lift the dish from the water.

Vanilla Rice Pudding with Dried Cherries

Dried tart cherries make a nice contrast to sweet vanilla- and cinnamon-scented rice. This pudding is equally good served warm or cold. But if you want to serve it cold, you'll have to plan ahead so that it has time to chill completely. **6 servings**

4	**cups plus 1 tablespoon whole milk**
½	**cup medium-grain white rice**
½	**cup sugar**
½	**teaspoon ground cinnamon**
¼	**teaspoon salt**
1½	**teaspoons cornstarch**
3	**large eggs**
½	**cup dried tart cherries or cranberries**
2	**teaspoons vanilla extract**
1	**teaspoon fresh lemon juice**

Combine 4 cups milk, rice, sugar, cinnamon, and salt in heavy large saucepan. Bring to boil over medium-high heat, stirring frequently. Reduce heat to medium and simmer until rice is very tender, stirring occasionally, about 25 minutes.

Whisk cornstarch and remaining 1 tablespoon milk in large bowl to blend. Add eggs; whisk to blend. Whisk in hot rice mixture. Return to same saucepan. Add cherries; stir over low heat just until mixture comes to boil. Mix in vanilla and lemon juice. Serve warm or pour pudding into buttered medium bowl. Press plastic wrap onto surface. Refrigerate until cold, at least 8 hours or overnight. Spoon pudding into bowls and serve.

Rice Pudding with Cream Sherry

Some rice puddings rely on an egg-based custard for their thick, creamy consistency. This one doesn't need it. Instead, the rice is cooked very slowly in a lot of milk (5 cups for just 1 cup of rice) and thickens gradually like a risotto. **4 servings**

5	**cups (or more) whole milk, divided**
1	**cup short-grain or medium-grain white rice**
½	**cup sugar**
2	**cinnamon sticks**
1	**vanilla bean, split lengthwise**
¼	**teaspoon salt**
½	**cup cream Sherry**
½	**cup (packed) golden brown sugar, plus additional for topping**

Combine 5 cups milk, rice, sugar, cinnamon, vanilla bean, and salt in heavy large saucepan. Bring to simmer over medium heat, stirring occasionally. Reduce heat to low and cook until rice is tender and pudding is thick, stirring frequently, about 50 minutes. Add Sherry and ½ cup brown sugar and stir until blended and sugar dissolves.

Thin with more milk by ¼ cupfuls if pudding is too thick. Discard cinnamon sticks and vanilla bean. Spoon pudding into bowls. Press additional brown sugar through sieve over puddings and serve, or cover and chill up to 1 day and top with additional brown sugar before serving.

Ingredient Tip: **The Right Sherry**
Sherry (a Spanish fortified wine) can run the gamut from very dry to super-sweet. The type called for in this recipe—cream Sherry—is on the sweet side. You'll also see it called oloroso or golden Sherry. It's darker in color and fuller in flavor than the drier varieties. Amontillado would be a fine second choice; it's somewhat sweet and rather nutty. Don't use fino or manzanilla Sherries—they're much too dry.

Warm Jasmine Rice Puddings with Passion Fruit

For a light and fluffy pudding, rinse the jasmine rice with cool water until the water runs clear. This will help prevent the grains from sticking to each other as they cook. **Makes 8**

½	cup raisins
3	tablespoons Malibu rum or other coconut-flavored rum
1½	cups nonfat milk
1¼	cups canned unsweetened coconut milk
¾	cup whole milk
1	cinnamon stick
½	teaspoon salt
½	vanilla bean, split lengthwise
1¼	cups jasmine rice
10	tablespoons sugar, divided
1	cup chilled heavy whipping cream
2½	teaspoons finely grated lime peel
6	passion fruits, halved, pulp, seeds, and juices scooped into small bowl

Market Tip: Passion Fruit

A ripe passion fruit looks like a wizened old face—impressively wrinkled. Cut the fruit in half and scoop out the intensely flavored pulp and seeds from the center.

Combine raisins and rum in small bowl. Let stand at room temperature while preparing pudding.

Combine nonfat milk, coconut milk, whole milk, cinnamon, and salt in heavy medium saucepan. Scrape in seeds from vanilla bean; add bean. Bring to simmer; remove from heat. Let steep uncovered 1 hour. Strain coconut broth into medium bowl.

Place rice in another medium bowl. Add cold water and drain. Repeat 2 more times or until water runs clear. Combine 1 cup coconut broth and rice in heavy large saucepan. Cook over medium-high heat until almost all liquid is absorbed, stirring constantly, about 3 minutes. Add remaining coconut broth; reduce heat to low. Simmer until rice is tender, stirring frequently, about 13 minutes. Remove from heat. Stir in 6 tablespoons sugar (pudding will be thick). Transfer to large bowl and cool.

Using electric mixer, beat cream in large bowl until peaks form. Fold half of whipped cream into cooled rice. Drain raisins. Fold raisins and lime peel into rice. Fold in remaining whipped cream. Divide pudding among eight ¾-cup ramekins or custard cups. Place puddings on rimmed baking sheet.

Preheat broiler. Sprinkle ½ tablespoon of remaining sugar over each pudding. Broil puddings until sugar caramelizes, watching closely to avoid burning and turning sheet for even browning, about 3 minutes. Spoon passion fruit over puddings and serve.

Caramelized Mango-Lime Tapioca

As this moist pudding is broiled, the brown sugar on top melts into a sweet, sticky syrup. Underneath that warm syrup and the lime-flavored tapioca is diced fresh mango. **8 servings**

3¾	cups whole milk
¾	cup sugar
⅓	cup quick-cooking tapioca
2	large eggs
1½	teaspoons finely grated lime peel
¼	teaspoon salt
1	teaspoon vanilla extract
1	large ripe mango, peeled, pitted, diced (about 1 cup)
⅓	cup (packed) golden brown sugar

Stir milk, sugar, tapioca, eggs, lime peel, and salt in heavy large saucepan to blend. Let stand 5 minutes. Place over medium-high heat and stir until pudding thickens and just comes to boil, about 10 minutes. Transfer pudding to large bowl; mix in vanilla. Press plastic wrap directly onto surface of pudding and cool to lukewarm.

DO AHEAD: *Can be made 1 day ahead. Cover and refrigerate. Stir to loosen before continuing.*

Preheat broiler. Divide diced mango among eight ¾-cup ramekins or custard cups. Spoon pudding atop mango, dividing equally. Smooth tops with spatula. Place puddings on rimmed baking sheet. Press 2 teaspoons brown sugar through sieve over each pudding. Let stand until sugar begins to dissolve, about 10 minutes. Broil puddings on sheet until sugar is bubbling all over, watching closely and turning sheet frequently for even browning, about 4 minutes. Serve puddings warm.

Market Tip: Mangoes

To choose the best mangoes for this pudding, simply smell them near the stem end. A strong mango-like scent equals a flavorful fruit. A ripe mango should also yield to slight pressure. For ease of preparation, you can buy a package of already chopped mango—but the fruit won't always be perfectly ripe. For help with chopping mangoes, see page 34.

Indian Pudding

If you've never tried this old-fashioned Colonial American dessert, you're really missing out. It's simple to make and great on a cold day. Its name probably derives from the fact that it is made with cornmeal, an ingredient the early settlers associated with Native Americans. **8 servings**

5½	cups whole milk
1	cup (packed) golden brown sugar
¾	cup yellow cornmeal
2	tablespoons mild-flavored (light) molasses
½	teaspoon ground ginger
½	teaspoon ground cinnamon
¼	cup (½ stick) unsalted butter
½	teaspoon vanilla extract
	Vanilla ice cream or frozen yogurt

Preheat oven to 325°F. Butter 13x9x2-inch glass baking dish. Combine milk, sugar, cornmeal, molasses, ginger, and cinnamon in heavy large saucepan. Whisk over medium-high heat until mixture thickens but is still pourable, about 15 minutes. Remove from heat. Whisk in butter and vanilla. Transfer pudding mixture to prepared baking dish.

Bake pudding until golden brown and center no longer moves when baking dish is shaken, about 1½ hours. Cool 10 minutes. Spoon pudding into bowls. Top with ice cream and serve.

Vanilla Panna Cottas with Mixed Berry Compote

Moscato is a sweet white wine made from the Muscat grape; you can find it at supermarkets and liquor stores. If unavailable, try Essensia, an orange-scented sweet dessert wine from California. **Makes 8**

¼	cup cold water
2½	teaspoons unflavored gelatin (from 2 envelopes)
3	cups heavy whipping cream
1	cup sugar, divided
1½	teaspoons vanilla extract
4	½-pint containers assorted berries (such as raspberries, blueberries, blackberries, and strawberries)
⅓	cup sweet white wine (such as Moscato)

Pour ¼ cup cold water into small custard cup. Sprinkle gelatin over. Let stand until gelatin softens, about 15 minutes. Bring 1 inch of water to simmer in small skillet. Place cup with gelatin in simmering water. Stir until gelatin dissolves. Remove cup from water.

Combine cream and ⅔ cup sugar in heavy medium saucepan. Stir over medium heat just until sugar dissolves. Remove from heat. Add vanilla and gelatin and stir to blend well. Divide mixture among eight 8- to 10-ounce wineglasses. Cover and chill until set, at least 6 hours and up to 1 day.

Combine berries and remaining ⅓ cup sugar in medium bowl. Crush berries slightly with back of spoon. Mix in wine. Let compote stand until berry juices and sugar form syrup, stirring often, at least 1 hour and up to 2 hours. Spoon compote over panna cottas.

Pomegranate Panna Cottas

After making the pomegranate syrup, don't waste the orange peel—it makes an attractive garnish. Remove it from the syrup and let it cool, then thinly slice it lengthwise. Combine it in a small bowl with 3 tablespoons of sugar and toss to coat, like candied orange peel. Then cover and chill for a few hours to use as a flavorful, crunchy finishing touch for the panna cottas. **Makes 6**

	Nonstick vegetable oil spray
3	tablespoons plus 2 cups refrigerated pomegranate juice (such as Pom)
2	teaspoons unflavored gelatin
1	cup sugar
	Peel from 1 orange, removed in strips with vegetable peeler
½	cup fresh orange juice
½	cup heavy whipping cream
1½	cups buttermilk

Spray six ¾-cup ramekins or custard cups with nonstick spray. Place 3 tablespoons pomegranate juice in small cup. Sprinkle gelatin over; let stand until gelatin softens, about 15 minutes.

Meanwhile, bring remaining 2 cups pomegranate juice, sugar, and orange peel to boil in large saucepan over high heat, stirring to dissolve sugar. Boil until syrup is reduced to 1¼ cups, about 10 minutes. Remove from heat.

Using slotted spoon, remove peel from syrup (reserve peel, if desired). Transfer ⅓ cup syrup to small bowl and reserve for sauce. Add gelatin mixture to remaining hot syrup in pan and stir until dissolved. Stir in orange juice and cream, then buttermilk. Strain into medium bowl; divide among prepared ramekins. Chill panna cottas uncovered until set, at least 4 hours and up to 1 day. Cover and chill sauce separately.

Run knife around edge of ramekins to loosen panna cottas; invert onto plates. Drizzle with sauce and serve.

Panna Cottas with Black Mission Figs in Syrup

Fig season begins toward the middle of summer and continues through early fall, and this dessert is a wonderful way to celebrate the luscious fruit. Black Mission figs (small figs with blue-black skin and crimson flesh) are called for here, but other fresh figs can be substituted. The panna cotta needs to chill overnight, so be sure to begin one day ahead. **Makes 8**

Panna Cotta

4	cups heavy whipping cream
¾	cup sugar
½	cup amaretto
1	vanilla bean, split lengthwise
3	tablespoons water
2	teaspoons unflavored gelatin

Syrup and Figs

1	cup sugar
½	cup water
½	cup Sherry wine vinegar
½	cup balsamic vinegar
2	cups fresh black Mission figs (about 1 pint), stemmed, quartered lengthwise

PANNA COTTA: Combine cream, sugar, and amaretto in heavy large saucepan. Scrape in seeds from vanilla bean; add bean. Bring mixture to boil, stirring to dissolve sugar. Remove from heat. Cover and let steep 15 minutes. Discard vanilla bean.

Meanwhile, pour 3 tablespoons water into small cup. Sprinkle gelatin over. Let stand until gelatin softens, about 15 minutes.

Return cream mixture to simmer. Add gelatin mixture and whisk until dissolved. Let cool 30 minutes, stirring occasionally. Divide cream mixture among eight 1¼-cup goblets or custard cups. Cover and refrigerate overnight.

SYRUP AND FIGS: Stir sugar and ½ cup water in heavy large saucepan over medium-low heat until sugar dissolves. Increase heat to medium-high and boil without stirring until syrup is deep amber color, occasionally brushing down pan sides with wet pastry brush and swirling pan, about 7 minutes. Add both vinegars (mixture will bubble vigorously). Continue boiling until caramel bits dissolve and mixture thickens slightly, stirring constantly, about 5 minutes. Remove from heat. Fold in figs. Cool to room temperature.

DO AHEAD: *Can be made 1 day ahead. Cover and refrigerate. Bring to room temperature and fold gently to blend before serving.*

Spoon figs and syrup over panna cottas and serve.

Piña Colada Panna Cotta

An easier-to-make dessert would be very hard to find. Piña Colada ingredients—sweet cream of coconut, crushed pineapple, cream, and rum—are blended together, then combined with gelatin. Then just put it in the fridge to chill overnight. Cream of coconut is available in the liquor section of most supermarkets. **6 servings**

1	cup sweetened cream of coconut (such as Coco Reál or Coco López)
1	cup crushed pineapple in unsweetened pineapple juice
1	cup heavy whipping cream
¼	cup dark rum
2	tablespoons water
2	teaspoons unflavored gelatin
	Ground nutmeg

Puree cream of coconut, crushed pineapple in juice, cream, and rum in blender. Transfer to bowl. Pour 2 tablespoons water into heavy small saucepan. Sprinkle gelatin over. Let stand until gelatin softens, about 15 minutes. Stir over low heat until gelatin dissolves. Add gelatin mixture to coconut mixture; stir well. Divide panna cotta among six 6- to 8-ounce wineglasses or ramekins. Cover; chill overnight. Sprinkle panna cotta with nutmeg and serve.

Caramel-Banana Bread Puddings

These fast and easy puddings become something truly special when you perk up store-bought caramel sauce with a little sea salt. **Makes 8**

1½	cups purchased caramel sauce
¼	teaspoon plus ⅛ teaspoon fine sea salt
8	5x3½-inch slices white sandwich bread (such as buttermilk bread or potato bread), very lightly toasted
3	medium bananas, peeled, thinly sliced on diagonal into 1½-inch ovals
4	large eggs
1½	cups half and half
⅓	cup whole milk
2½	tablespoons sugar, divided
1	teaspoon vanilla extract
2	tablespoons (¼ stick) unsalted butter, melted

Preheat broiler. Butter eight ¾-cup ramekins. Mix caramel sauce and ¼ teaspoon sea salt in small bowl. Spoon 1 generous tablespoon caramel into each ramekin. Place bread on rimmed baking sheet. Spread 1 generous tablespoon caramel over each bread slice. Broil until caramel is bubbling and slightly darker, watching closely to avoid burning, 1 to 2 minutes. Cool.

Cut each bread slice into 6 squares, for a total of 48 pieces. Set 1 banana slice on each bread square. Arrange 6 banana-topped bread squares standing on edge, side by side in each prepared ramekin, fitting snugly. Whisk eggs, half and half, milk, 1½ tablespoons sugar, vanilla, and remaining ⅛ teaspoon sea salt in medium bowl. Pour enough custard into each ramekin to reach top. Let stand until bread absorbs some of custard, about 30 minutes. Reserve any remaining custard.

Meanwhile, position rack in bottom third of oven and preheat to 400°F. Pour remaining custard into ramekins. Brush exposed bread pieces with melted butter. Sprinkle with remaining 1 tablespoon sugar. Set ramekins in large roasting pan. Add enough hot water to pan to come halfway up sides of ramekins.

Bake puddings until set and knife inserted into custard comes out clean, about 45 minutes. Remove from water; cool.

DO AHEAD: *Can be made 8 hours ahead. Cover and refrigerate. Bring to room temperature before serving.*

Serve bread puddings warm or at room temperature.

Dulce de Leche and Chocolate Chunk Bread Pudding

Egg bread, bittersweet chocolate, and an intense caramel sauce combine to make this the ultimate comfort dessert. It takes about half an hour for the custard to soak into the bread before it can be baked, so allow yourself enough time. **8 to 10 servings**

8   ½-inch-thick slices egg bread (about 5×4 inches), crusts trimmed, cut into ¾- to 1-inch cubes
4   tablespoons (½ stick) unsalted butter, melted, divided
1½ cups heavy whipping cream
1   cup purchased dulce de leche ice-cream topping or butterscotch-caramel sauce
4   large eggs
2   large egg yolks
2   tablespoons dark rum
1   teaspoon vanilla extract
    Pinch of salt
½   cup (about 3 ounces) bittersweet chocolate chips
2   tablespoons sugar
    Powdered sugar
    Additional purchased dulce de leche ice-cream topping or butterscotch-caramel sauce

Preheat oven to 350°F. Place bread cubes in large bowl. Drizzle with 3 tablespoons melted butter; toss. Transfer to rimmed baking sheet. Bake until bread begins to color, stirring occasionally, about 12 minutes. Cool. Brush 11×7×2-inch glass baking dish with remaining 1 tablespoon melted butter.

Stir cream and dulce de leche topping in medium saucepan over medium heat until blended and bubbling. Remove from heat. Whisk eggs and egg yolks in large bowl. Add rum, vanilla, and salt; gradually whisk in warm dulce de leche mixture. Stir in bread cubes. Let soak 30 minutes, stirring occasionally.

Mix chocolate chips into custard mixture; transfer to prepared dish. Sprinkle with 2 tablespoons sugar. Bake pudding until puffed and set in center, about 35 minutes. Cool 15 minutes. Sift powdered sugar over pudding. Serve warm, passing additional dulce de leche topping alongside.

Spiced Cranberry Bread Puddings

Treat these beautiful desserts like little upside-down cakes; turn them out of their dishes to show off the ruby red cranberries on the bottom. **Makes 6**

1   cup sugar, divided
½   cup frozen cranberry juice cocktail concentrate, thawed
½   cup orange juice
2   teaspoons finely grated orange peel
3   cups cranberries (about 12 ounces), unthawed if frozen
        Nonstick vegetable oil spray
12   slices white sandwich bread
¼   cup apricot preserves
        Ground cinnamon
        Freshly grated nutmeg
4   large eggs
1   tablespoon Grand Marnier or other orange liqueur
1   teaspoon vanilla extract
¼   teaspoon coarse kosher salt
2   cups heavy whipping cream

Bring ½ cup sugar, cranberry juice concentrate, orange juice, and orange peel to boil in heavy large saucepan, stirring until sugar dissolves. Mix in cranberries; return to simmer. Reduce heat to medium-low; simmer gently 3 minutes (cranberries should not break). Pour cranberry mixture into strainer set over bowl and drain. Return syrup to same saucepan. Boil until very thick and reduced to generous ½ cup, about 7 minutes. Fold berries into syrup. Cool to room temperature.

DO AHEAD: *Can be made 4 days ahead. Cover and chill. Bring to room temperature before using.*

Spray six 1- to 1¼-cup ramekins with nonstick spray. Measure diameter of ramekins. Line bottom of each with parchment paper round. Cut 1 round from each bread slice to fit bottom of each ramekin. Spread each bread round with 1 teaspoon preserves, then sprinkle with cinnamon and grating of nutmeg.

Spoon 1 tablespoon cranberries (with as little syrup as possible) into bottom of each ramekin. Top with 1 bread round, preserves side down. Repeat 1 time with berries and bread rounds. Reserve berry syrup.

Whisk eggs, liqueur, vanilla, coarse salt, and remaining ½ cup sugar in medium bowl until well blended. Add cream and stir until sugar dissolves. Pour custard, ¼ cup at a time, over bread in each ramekin (generous ½ cup in each). Let stand at least 15 minutes and up to 1 hour, occasionally pressing bread to submerge.

Preheat oven to 350°F. Place ramekins in 13x9x2-inch metal baking pan. Add enough lukewarm water to pan to come halfway up sides of ramekins. Bake puddings until puffed and firm to touch, about 45 minutes. Remove from water. Let cool 10 minutes. Using small sharp knife, cut around sides of puddings. Turn out onto plates; peel off parchment. Spoon some reserved syrup over. Serve warm.

Gingerbread Puddings with Candied Apples

The apples cook slowly in cider until the liquid is reduced to a thick syrup that intensifies their flavor. The time may vary depending on the size of the pot used. Happily, the gingerbread recipe makes more than you need for the puddings. Enjoy leftovers with a cup of tea for breakfast or as a mid-afternoon snack. **Makes 8**

Candied Apple Garnish

8	cups unsweetened apple cider or apple juice
1½	pounds Granny Smith apples, peeled, cored, cut into ⅓-inch cubes (about 4½ cups)
¾	cup (packed) golden brown sugar

Gingerbread

1¾	cups unbleached all purpose flour
1	tablespoon ground ginger
1	teaspoon baking soda
1	teaspoon ground cinnamon
¼	teaspoon ground cloves
¼	teaspoon salt
¼	teaspoon finely ground black pepper
½	cup (1 stick) unsalted butter, room temperature
¾	cup (packed) golden brown sugar
1	large egg
¾	cup mild-flavored (light) molasses
½	cup boiling water

Puddings

3	cups whole milk
2	4-inch-long pieces fresh ginger (about 4 ounces), peeled, thickly sliced
1	tablespoon whole black peppercorns
4	large eggs
¾	cup sugar
1	teaspoon vanilla extract
1	teaspoon ground ginger
	Pinch of salt
	Ice cream or crème fraîche

CANDIED APPLE GARNISH: Combine apple cider, apples, and sugar in large pot. Bring to boil over high heat, stirring until sugar dissolves. Reduce heat to medium and simmer until apples are soft and translucent and cider coats apples thickly, stirring occasionally, about 2 hours. Transfer to bowl and cool.

DO AHEAD: *Can be made 1 week ahead. Cover and chill. Bring to room temperature before serving.*

GINGERBREAD: Preheat oven to 350°F. Butter 9x9x2-inch metal baking pan. Whisk flour, ginger, baking soda, cinnamon, cloves, salt, and pepper in medium bowl to blend. Using electric mixer, beat butter in large bowl until fluffy. Add brown sugar and egg and beat until blended. Beat in molasses, then flour mixture. Using rubber spatula, stir in ½ cup boiling water. Transfer batter to prepared pan.

Bake gingerbread until tester inserted into center comes out clean, about 40 minutes. Transfer pan to rack and cool gingerbread completely in pan.

DO AHEAD: *Can be made 1 day ahead. Cover pan with foil; let gingerbread stand at room temperature.*

PUDDINGS: Preheat oven to 325°F. Combine milk, fresh ginger, and peppercorns in heavy medium saucepan; bring to simmer. Remove from heat. Whisk eggs, sugar, vanilla, ground ginger, and salt in medium bowl to blend. Gradually whisk hot milk mixture into egg mixture. Strain custard into medium bowl; discard solids in strainer.

Cut enough gingerbread into ½-inch cubes to measure 5⅓ cups (reserve any remaining gingerbread for another use). Divide gingerbread cubes among eight ¾-cup custard cups or ramekins. Pour custard over gingerbread in each custard cup, dividing equally. Let stand 15 minutes to allow gingerbread to absorb some custard.

Place cups in roasting pan. Add enough hot water to pan to come halfway up sides of cups. Cover pan with foil. Bake puddings until set, about 1 hour. Remove from water.

Serve puddings warm or at room temperature, topped with candied apple garnish and ice cream or crème fraîche.

Sticky Date and Almond Bread Pudding with Amaretto Zabaglione

Use freshly grated nutmeg for the best flavor in this hearty winter dessert; a Microplane grater makes the job easy. Custardy almond-flavored Amaretto Zabaglione is the perfect accompaniment to the bread pudding. Plan ahead because the bread cubes need to dry overnight. **10 to 12 servings**

8	cups 1½-inch cubes egg bread (from one 16-ounce loaf)
2¼	cups chopped pitted Medjool dates (about 12 ounces)
½	cup sliced almonds
6	large eggs
2	large egg yolks
1	cup superfine sugar or regular sugar
3½	cups half and half
1	tablespoon vanilla extract
¼	teaspoon (generous) ground nutmeg
	Powdered sugar
	Amaretto Zabaglione (see recipe)

Arrange bread cubes in single layer on rimmed baking sheet. Let stand at room temperature to dry overnight.

Butter 13x9x2-inch glass baking dish. Transfer bread cubes to prepared dish. Sprinkle dates and almonds over bread and toss to distribute evenly. Using electric mixer, beat eggs and egg yolks in large bowl until frothy. Add sugar and beat until mixture thickens and is pale yellow, about 5 minutes. Add half and half, vanilla, and nutmeg; beat until just blended.

DO AHEAD: *Bread mixture and custard can be made 2 hours ahead. Let bread mixture stand uncovered at room temperature. Chill custard; rewhisk before continuing.*

Preheat oven to 375°F. Pour custard over bread mixture; press lightly on bread with rubber spatula to submerge. Let stand 15 minutes, occasionally pressing lightly on bread to submerge.

Bake bread pudding 25 minutes. Using large spoon, press bread down, allowing custard in dish to rise to surface. Spoon custard evenly over bread mixture. Continue to bake pudding until knife inserted into center of custard comes out clean, about 20 minutes longer.

Remove bread pudding from oven and let stand 10 minutes. Spoon warm pudding onto plates. Sprinkle with powdered sugar. Serve warm with warm or chilled Amaretto Zabaglione.

Amaretto Zabaglione

Zabaglione is a delicate sauce that usually needs to be served as soon as it is made. This recipe, however, can be prepared one day ahead because whipped cream is folded in to stabilize the sauce. **Makes about 1⅔ cups**

6	large egg yolks
⅓	cup amaretto or other almond liqueur
3	tablespoons superfine sugar or regular sugar
¼	cup heavy whipping cream

Whisk egg yolks, amaretto, and sugar in medium metal bowl to blend. Set bowl over saucepan of simmering water. Whisk mixture constantly and vigorously until thickened and instant-read thermometer inserted into mixture registers 140°F for 3 minutes, about 5 minutes total. Remove mixture from over water. Add cream and whisk until incorporated. Serve warm or chilled.

DO AHEAD: *If serving chilled, zabaglione can be made 1 day ahead; cover and refrigerate. Rewhisk before serving.*

Lemon-Spice Bread Pudding with Sautéed Peaches

What better use for day-old bread could there be? The slightly dry bread soaks up the custard, both softening the bread and infusing it with the flavors of the custard. Star anise—brown, star-shaped seedpods—is available in the spice section of some supermarkets and at Asian markets and specialty foods stores. **8 servings**

6   **cups 1-inch bread cubes from day-old rustic bread with crust (about 11 ounces)**
5   **tablespoons unsalted butter, melted**
1   **vanilla bean, split lengthwise**
2   **cups whole milk**
1   **cup heavy whipping cream**
4   **cardamom pods, crushed**
2   **whole star anise**
1½   **teaspoons finely grated lemon peel**
3   **large eggs**
1¼   **cups sugar**
1   **teaspoon salt**
     Sautéed Peaches (see recipe)

Preheat oven to 350°F. Toss bread and melted butter on large rimmed baking sheet to coat. Place bread in oven and toast until golden, tossing occasionally, about 15 minutes. Cool.

Meanwhile, scrape seeds from vanilla bean into heavy medium saucepan; add bean. Add milk, cream, cardamom, star anise, and lemon peel and bring to simmer. Remove from heat, cover, and let steep 30 minutes. Strain. Discard solids.

Whisk eggs, sugar, and salt in large bowl. Gradually whisk milk mixture into egg mixture. Add bread and toss gently to combine. Cover and let stand at room temperature, stirring occasionally, at least 1 hour and up to 2 hours.

Position rack in center of oven and preheat to 350°F. Butter 11x7x2-inch glass baking dish. Transfer bread mixture to prepared dish. Bake until just set, about 55 minutes. Cool pudding at least 10 minutes. Serve warm or at room temperature with Sautéed Peaches.

Sautéed Peaches

These peaches would also taste great spooned over pancakes, waffles, or ice cream. **8 servings**

4   **peaches, halved, pitted, cut into ½-inch-thick slices**
½   **cup fresh lemon juice**
¼   **cup sugar**
¼   **cup (½ stick) unsalted butter**

Place peaches, lemon juice, and sugar in large bowl; toss to coat. Melt butter in heavy large skillet over medium-high heat. Add peaches; cook until juices thicken slightly, stirring gently, about 3 minutes.

Classic Chocolate Mousse

Undoubtedly one of the most popular French treats, mousse au chocolat *meets all the requirements of the quintessential chocolate dessert: rich, airy, creamy. Use bittersweet chocolate chips or finely chopped bars of your favorite bittersweet chocolate. (If using bars, make sure they do not exceed 61% cacao.) Have fun with the presentation—serve the mousse in wineglasses, parfait dishes, teacups, or custard cups, if you like.* **6 servings**

6	ounces bittersweet chocolate chips
⅓	cup water
¼	cup heavy whipping cream
2	large egg yolks
4	tablespoons sugar, divided
½	teaspoon vanilla extract
4	large egg whites, room temperature
	Whipped cream (optional)
	Chocolate curls (optional)

Place chocolate chips in medium bowl. Whisk ⅓ cup water, cream, egg yolks, and 2 tablespoons sugar in heavy small saucepan to blend. Place over medium-low heat and stir until mixture thickens enough to coat spoon, about 4 minutes (do not boil). Strain through sieve into bowl with chocolate. Stir until chocolate is melted and smooth. Mix in vanilla.

Using electric mixer, beat egg whites in large bowl until soft peaks form. Gradually add remaining 2 tablespoons sugar, beating until stiff but not dry. Fold egg white mixture into barely lukewarm chocolate mixture in 2 additions. Divide mousse among 6 goblets or bowls. Cover and chill until firm, about 4 hours.

DO AHEAD: *Can be made 1 day ahead. Keep chilled.*

Garnish with whipped cream and chocolate curls, if desired, and serve.

Technique Tip: **Fold with Care**

Mousse is a French term meaning "foam" or "froth"; the airy quality of mousse is achieved by the addition of whipped egg whites or whipped cream. When making a mousse, fold the whipped cream or the egg whites into the custard mixture extra carefully for the best, airiest texture.

Chocolate-Cinnamon Mousse with Cherries

Either bittersweet or semisweet chocolate will give great results, but using bittersweet provides a more intense chocolate flavor. If fresh cherries are unavailable, frozen pitted sweet dark cherries are a fine substitute. **4 servings**

Cherries
8   ounces Bing cherries, stemmed, pitted
⅓   cup black cherry preserves or other cherry preserves
⅓   cup ruby Port or cherry juice

Mousse
4   ounces bittersweet or semisweet chocolate (do not exceed 61% cacao), chopped
1¼   cups chilled heavy whipping cream, divided
⅛   teaspoon (generous) ground cinnamon

CHERRIES: Combine cherries, cherry preserves, and Port in heavy small saucepan. Bring to boil over high heat, stirring to blend. Reduce heat to medium and cook until juices thicken to syrup consistency, stirring frequently, about 10 minutes. Remove from heat. Transfer mixture to small bowl and chill until cold, about 3 hours.

DO AHEAD: *Can be made 1 day ahead. Cover and keep chilled.*

MOUSSE: Place chocolate in large bowl. Combine ¼ cup cream and cinnamon in small saucepan and bring to boil. Pour hot cream over chocolate; whisk until melted and smooth. Using electric mixer, beat remaining 1 cup cream in medium bowl until peaks form. Fold ¼ of whipped cream into lukewarm chocolate mixture. Fold remaining whipped cream into chocolate mixture in 3 additions. Divide mousse among 4 glasses or goblets. Chill until set, about 4 hours.

DO AHEAD: *Can be made 1 day ahead. Cover; keep chilled.*

Spoon cherries with syrup atop mousse and serve.

Spiced Coffee Mousse

Here's a creamy mousse spiked with rum and flavored with espresso, cloves, and nutmeg. Because this recipe uses gelatin, it's not a strictly traditional French mousse; it's similar to a rich Bavarian cream. **6 servings**

¼   cup water
2   tablespoons instant espresso powder or instant coffee powder
¼   teaspoon ground cloves
⅛   teaspoon ground nutmeg
1   teaspoon unflavored gelatin
6   large egg yolks
½   cup sugar
¼   cup dark rum
1   cup chilled heavy whipping cream
     Lightly sweetened whipped cream
     Cinnamon sticks

Mix ¼ cup water, espresso powder, cloves, and nutmeg in small cup until espresso powder dissolves. Sprinkle gelatin over. Let stand until gelatin softens, about 15 minutes.

Whisk egg yolks, sugar, and rum in large metal bowl to blend. Set bowl over saucepan of simmering water. Whisk until mixture thickens and thermometer inserted into center registers 160°F, about 10 minutes. Remove bowl from over water. Immediately add gelatin mixture to hot yolk mixture and stir until gelatin dissolves. Using electric mixer, beat yolk mixture until cool, about 5 minutes.

Using electric mixer fitted with clean dry beaters, beat heavy cream in medium bowl until peaks form. Gently fold cream into yolk mixture in 3 additions. Spoon mousse into six 6-ounce coffee mugs or small wineglasses. Chill until mousse is set, at least 4 hours.

DO AHEAD: *Can be made 1 day ahead. Cover and keep refrigerated.*

Spoon sweetened whipped cream atop mousse. Garnish with cinnamon sticks.

Whiskey-Kissed White Chocolate Mousse with Strawberries and Lemon Shortbread Squares

The strawberries get tossed with a bit of Irish whiskey for a flavorful punch. This is the perfect dessert to serve on St. Patrick's Day. **6 servings**

Mousse

10	ounces high-quality white chocolate (such as Lindt or Perugina), chopped
1	cup chilled heavy whipping cream, divided
2	tablespoons Irish whiskey
3	large egg whites, room temperature
	Pinch of salt

Strawberries

1	1-pound container strawberries, hulled, sliced
2	tablespoons Irish whiskey
1½	tablespoons (packed) golden brown sugar
½	teaspoon finely grated lemon peel
6	Lemon Shortbread Squares (see recipe)

MOUSSE: Stir chocolate and ½ cup cream in heavy small saucepan over medium-low heat just until chocolate melts and mixture is smooth. Transfer to large bowl and stir in whiskey. Cool until chocolate mixture is almost room temperature but not set.

Using electric mixer, beat egg whites and salt in medium bowl until stiff but not dry. Fold whites into chocolate mixture. Beat remaining ½ cup cream in same bowl (no need to wash bowl or beaters) until soft peaks form. Fold whipped cream into mousse. Divide mousse among 6 glass bowls (about ⅔ cup each). Chill until set, about 2 hours.

DO AHEAD: *Can be made 1 day ahead. Cover and keep refrigerated.*

STRAWBERRIES: Toss strawberries, whiskey, sugar, and lemon peel in medium bowl to blend. Let stand 10 minutes.

Spoon strawberries and accumulated juices over mousse and serve with Lemon Shortbread Squares.

Lemon Shortbread Squares

These delicious shortbread cookies, enhanced with both lemon peel and lemon juice, are rich but fresh tasting. **Makes 9**

	Nonstick vegetable oil spray
½	cup sugar
2	teaspoons finely grated lemon peel
¾	cup (1½ sticks) unsalted butter, room temperature
1	tablespoon fresh lemon juice
2	tablespoons cornstarch
½	teaspoon salt
1½	cups unbleached all purpose flour

Position rack in center of oven and preheat to 300°F. Spray 8x8x2-inch metal baking pan with nonstick spray.

Using fingertips, rub sugar and lemon peel together in large bowl to release essential oils in peel. Add butter. Using electric mixer, beat until mixture is light and fluffy. Beat in lemon juice, then cornstarch and salt. Add flour and beat just until blended. Using fingers, press dough firmly and evenly over bottom of prepared pan. Pierce dough all over with fork.

Bake shortbread until cooked through and just golden brown, about 50 minutes. Cool in pan on rack 10 minutes. Using tip of sharp knife, cut warm shortbread into 9 squares. Run knife around edge of pan to loosen shortbread. Using small offset spatula, carefully transfer shortbread squares to rack and cool completely.

DO AHEAD: *Can be made 3 days ahead. Store airtight at room temperature.*

Lemon Mousse with Fresh Berries

This mousse is a combination of delicious tart lemon curd and luscious whipped cream. It's spooned over fresh summer berries and topped with even more whipped cream. **8 servings**

1	cup plus 1 tablespoon sugar
¾	cup fresh lemon juice
6	large egg yolks
2	large eggs
1½	tablespoons finely grated lemon peel
1	12-ounce container strawberries, hulled, halved (or quartered if large), plus 8 whole strawberries for garnish
1	6-ounce container blueberries
1	6-ounce container raspberries
1	6-ounce container blackberries
2	cups chilled heavy whipping cream, divided
	Fresh mint sprigs

Combine 1 cup sugar, lemon juice, egg yolks, eggs, and lemon peel in large metal bowl. Set bowl over saucepan of simmering water. Whisk until curd thickens and thermometer inserted into center registers 160°F, 4 to 5 minutes. Chill curd until cool, whisking occasionally.

Toss halved strawberries, blueberries, raspberries, blackberries, and remaining 1 tablespoon sugar in another large bowl to blend. Let stand 10 minutes.

Using electric mixer, beat 1½ cups cream in medium bowl until medium-firm peaks form. Fold ⅓ of whipped cream into lemon curd to lighten, then fold in remaining whipped cream in 2 additions.

Divide berry mixture among 8 dessert bowls or large wineglasses. Spoon lemon mousse over berries.

DO AHEAD: *Can be made 1 day ahead. Cover and refrigerate.*

Using electric mixer, beat remaining ½ cup cream in medium bowl until stiff peaks form. Spoon whipped cream atop desserts or transfer whipped cream to pastry bag fitted with large star tip and pipe decoratively atop desserts. Garnish with whole strawberries and mint sprigs.

Ingredient Tip: Organic Peel

When a recipe calls for citrus peel, we recommend using organic fruit: Studies have shown that most of the pesticides in citrus fruit are contained in the peel.

Chilled Lemon Mousse with Caramel Sauce

The silky caramel sauce really complements the light lemon mousse. **6 servings**

¼   **cup water**
1   **teaspoon unflavored gelatin**
3   **large eggs, separated**
2   **tablespoons cornstarch**
1   **cup plus 2 tablespoons whole milk**
6   **tablespoons sugar, divided**
6   **tablespoons fresh lemon juice**
1½   **teaspoons finely grated lemon peel**
     Caramel Sauce (see recipe)

Lightly oil six ¾-cup soufflé dishes or custard cups; set aside. Pour ¼ cup water into small bowl. Sprinkle gelatin over; let stand until gelatin softens, about 15 minutes.

Meanwhile, whisk egg yolks and cornstarch in medium bowl until smooth. Combine milk and 3 tablespoons sugar in heavy medium saucepan; stir over medium heat until sugar dissolves and mixture comes to simmer. Gradually whisk hot milk mixture into yolk mixture. Return to same saucepan. Whisk constantly over medium-high heat until custard thickens and boils, about 2 minutes. Reduce heat to medium and whisk 2 minutes longer. Remove from heat; whisk in lemon juice and lemon peel. Add gelatin mixture to hot custard and stir until gelatin dissolves. Transfer custard to medium bowl; let stand 10 minutes to cool slightly.

Whisk egg whites and remaining 3 tablespoons sugar in large metal bowl to blend. Set bowl over saucepan of simmering water; whisk constantly until whites are warm, about 2 minutes. Remove from over water. Using electric mixer, beat whites until stiff but not dry; fold into warm lemon custard in 3 additions.

Divide lemon mousse among prepared dishes; level off tops with back of knife. Refrigerate uncovered overnight.

DO AHEAD: *Can be made 2 days ahead. Cover and keep refrigerated.*

Cut around mousse to loosen. Place small plate atop 1 soufflé dish and invert. Using both hands, hold plate and soufflé dish together and shake gently, allowing mousse to settle onto plate (if mousse does not release from dish, place bottom of soufflé dish in 1 inch of warm water for 20 seconds and try again). Repeat with remaining mousse. Spoon Caramel Sauce generously over top of each serving.

Caramel Sauce

Brushing down the sides of the saucepan with water helps dissolve any remaining sugar crystals (preventing them from crystallizing, which could result in a grainy sauce). There's one more reason why the sauce is practically foolproof: Corn syrup also discourages crystallization. **Makes about 1⅓ cups**

¾   **cup sugar**
½   **cup water**
¼   **cup light corn syrup**
¾   **cup heavy whipping cream**

Combine sugar, ½ cup water, and corn syrup in heavy medium saucepan. Stir over medium heat until sugar dissolves. Increase heat and boil without stirring until syrup is deep amber color, occasionally brushing down sides of pan with wet pastry brush and swirling pan, about 10 minutes. Remove from heat. Add cream (mixture will bubble vigorously). Return to low heat and stir until any caramel bits dissolve and sauce is smooth. Cool to room temperature.

DO AHEAD: *Can be made 1 day ahead. Cover and refrigerate. Rewarm over medium-low heat just until lukewarm and pourable (not hot).*

Gianduja Terrine with Hazelnut Custard Sauce

Gianduja, a ground hazelnut and chocolate confection from the Piedmont region of Italy, inspired this spectacular terrine. Rich and chocolaty, it's a cross between chocolate mousse and chocolate truffles. The filling needs to chill overnight, so plan accordingly. Use a long, thin, sharp knife, such as a carving knife, to cut thin slices. Wiping the knife with a hot damp towel after each cut will ensure that each slice is neat and clean. **12 servings**

Technique Tip: **Cooking without Scrambling**
Whisking the egg yolk mixture over simmering water until it reaches 160°F makes this dessert egg-safe. Be sure to whisk the mixture constantly and vigorously while it's over the simmering water to prevent the egg yolks from scrambling.

Filling

12	ounces high-quality milk chocolate (such as Lindt or Perugina), chopped
1	cup (2 sticks) unsalted butter, cut into 16 pieces
1/3	cup light corn syrup
1/2	cup chilled heavy whipping cream, divided
6	tablespoons Frangelico (hazelnut liqueur), divided
4	large egg yolks
2	tablespoons sugar
2	tablespoons water
1	cup very finely chopped toasted hazelnuts
1/2	cup sour cream

Glaze

9	ounces bittersweet or semisweet chocolate (do not exceed 61% cacao), chopped
1/2	cup plus 2 tablespoons (1¼ sticks) unsalted butter, cut into 10 pieces
3	tablespoons light corn syrup

Sauce

2	cups half and half
1	vanilla bean, split lengthwise
6	large egg yolks
6	tablespoons sugar
1	cup chilled heavy whipping cream
1/4	cup Frangelico (hazelnut liqueur)
3	ounces high-quality milk chocolate (such as Lindt or Perugina), chopped
12	hazelnuts, toasted, husked

FILLING: Line 5½- to 6-cup metal loaf pan with plastic wrap, overlapping sides. Melt chocolate and butter with corn syrup in heavy large saucepan over medium-low heat, stirring until smooth. Cool to lukewarm, whisking occasionally.

Whisk ¼ cup cream, 4 tablespoons Frangelico, egg yolks, sugar, and 2 tablespoons water in small metal bowl. Set bowl over saucepan of simmering water and whisk constantly until candy thermometer registers 160°F, about 3 minutes. Remove from over water. Add yolk mixture and remaining 2 tablespoons Frangelico to chocolate mixture in pan; whisk until smooth. Mix in nuts. Chill until cool, about 10 minutes. Using electric mixer, beat remaining ¼ cup cream with sour cream in large bowl to stiff peaks. Add chocolate mixture and fold together. Pour filling into prepared pan; smooth top. Cover and chill overnight.

(continued next page)

Gianduja Terrine with Hazelnut Custard Sauce

(continued)

GLAZE: Combine all ingredients in heavy medium saucepan. Stir over low heat until melted. Cool to lukewarm. Pour ½ cup glaze over filling in pan; shake pan gently to smooth top. Freeze just until glaze sets, about 20 minutes.

Line baking sheet with foil. Lift loaf from pan. Turn loaf out onto foil; peel off plastic. Whisk remaining glaze over low heat until just spreadable. Pour all but ¼ cup glaze over loaf. Working quickly, spread over top and sides with icing spatula, spreading glaze that runs onto foil up sides of loaf to cover completely. Chill 1 hour.

DO AHEAD: *Can be made 2 days ahead. Cover loaf and reserved ¼ cup glaze separately and chill.*

SAUCE: Bring half and half to simmer in heavy medium saucepan. Scrape in seeds from vanilla bean; add bean. Whisk egg yolks and sugar in medium bowl to blend. Whisk in hot half and half mixture. Return mixture to saucepan and stir over medium-low heat until custard thickens and leaves path on back of spoon when finger is drawn across, about 5 minutes (do not boil). Strain into bowl. Mix in cream and Frangelico. Cover and chill until cold.

DO AHEAD: *Can be made 2 days ahead. Keep chilled.*

Melt chocolate in top of double boiler over simmering water, stirring until smooth. Spoon all but 2 tablespoons melted chocolate into parchment cone or resealable plastic bag. Remove loaf from foil and transfer to platter. Pipe chocolate lines crosswise atop loaf, spacing ⅛ inch apart. Dip 1 hazelnut halfway into chocolate in pan; place atop center of loaf. Repeat with remaining nuts, spacing evenly and forming line down center.

DO AHEAD: *Can be made 3 days ahead. Chill.*

Using long thin knife, cut loaf into ½-inch-thick slices, wiping knife clean between cuts. Place slices on plates; surround with sauce. Whisk reserved glaze over low heat until melted. Spoon into resealable plastic bag; snip off corner of bag. Pipe Zs or other decorative design atop sauce.

Blackberry-Cassis Fool

Perhaps the easiest of all puddings to make, a fool is simply sweetened whipped cream folded into a bright fruit puree. In this case, the purple berry puree and the snow-white cream aren't completely combined: They're layered and then swirled for a lovely finish. **4 servings**

2	cups fresh or frozen blackberries, thawed, plus 4 additional berries for garnish
¼	cup sugar
2	tablespoons crème de cassis (black currant liqueur)
1	teaspoon fresh lemon juice
1¼	cups chilled heavy whipping cream

Puree 2 cups berries, sugar, crème de cassis, and lemon juice in processor. Strain into medium bowl, pressing on solids. Cover and refrigerate puree until ready to use.

DO AHEAD: *Can be made 1 day ahead. Keep refrigerated.*

Using electric mixer, beat cream in medium bowl until peaks form. Spoon ¼ cup whipped cream into each of 4 balloon-shaped wineglasses; top each with 2 tablespoons berry puree. Repeat layering 2 more times. Draw tip of small knife through layers, forming swirl pattern. Garnish each with berry. Cover and refrigerate at least 30 minutes and up to 3 hours.

Raspberry Fool

A hit of Grand Marnier and a crunchy almond topping elevate the classic, textbook fool. This is a very versatile recipe: Use your favorite frozen (or fresh, in-season) berries. Blueberries, blackberries, and strawberries all work equally well. And play around with the liqueur. Crème de cassis, limoncello, and Chambord are some good options. **12 servings**

3	12-ounce packages frozen raspberries, thawed, divided
½	cup Grand Marnier or other orange liqueur
4¼	cups chilled heavy whipping cream
1⅓	cups sugar
½	cup slivered blanched almonds, toasted

Puree half of raspberries and liqueur in processor until smooth. Strain mixture into large bowl, pressing on solids with rubber spatula. Discard solids. Gently stir remaining whole raspberries into puree. Cover and chill.

Using electric mixer, beat cream and sugar in another large bowl until peaks form. Gently fold whipped cream into raspberry mixture in 3 additions. Divide fool among 12 goblets. Cover and refrigerate at least 2 hours and up to 8 hours. Sprinkle with almonds and serve.

The Name Game

British cookbooks like to say this dessert is so easy that even a fool could make it, but the name actually comes from the French verb *fouler*, which means "to crush"—it's used in reference to the fruit, which is pureed.

# Berry Charlotte

A traditional French charlotte is made in a deep, slightly angled, smooth-sided metal container called a charlotte mold. The mold is lined with bread, cake, or ladyfingers, then filled with fruit, mousse, custard, or thick whipped cream. This charlotte is a little different: Crisp ladyfingers line a scallop-sided brioche pan, which is then filled with layers of berries and a rich mascarpone custard.

8 servings

¼	**cup sweet white wine (such as Muscat)**
2	**large egg yolks**
6	**tablespoons sugar, divided**
1	**8-ounce container mascarpone cheese**
1	**12-ounce bag frozen blackberries, thawed, drained, juices reserved**
1	**12-ounce bag frozen raspberries, thawed, drained, juices reserved**
2	**tablespoons framboise liqueur, divided**
2	**3.5-ounce packages (about) crisp ladyfingers (4-inch-long Boudoirs or Champagne biscuits)**

Whisk wine, egg yolks, and 3 tablespoons sugar in large metal bowl to blend. Set bowl over saucepan of simmering water and whisk until yolk mixture is thick and foamy and thermometer inserted into center registers 160°F, about 2 minutes. Remove bowl from over water and let custard cool. Whisk mascarpone into custard.

Meanwhile, stir reserved juices from blackberries and raspberries, 1 tablespoon sugar, and 1 tablespoon framboise in medium shallow bowl to blend. Combine drained blackberries and raspberries in another medium bowl. Add remaining 2 tablespoons sugar and remaining 1 tablespoon framboise and toss to blend for compote.

Dip ladyfingers, 1 at a time, in berry juice mixture for 1 second on each side, then use to line bottom and sides of 4½- to 5-cup nonstick metal brioche mold, inserting the ladyfingers into ridges of mold and trimming to fit as necessary. Spoon ⅓ cup berries over ladyfingers on bottom of mold. Top with ½ cup mascarpone custard, spreading evenly. Dip more ladyfingers into juice mixture and cover mascarpone mixture, trimming ladyfingers to fit as necessary. Spoon 1 cup berries over ladyfingers and spread remaining custard evenly over. Dip more ladyfingers into juice mixture and arrange over custard, covering completely. Brush ladyfingers generously with some berry juice. Cover charlotte with plastic wrap, then plate. Place heavy jar or can atop plate and refrigerate at least 2 hours and up to 1 day. Add any remaining berry juice mixture to berry compote; cover and refrigerate.

Remove weights and plastic wrap from top of charlotte. Slide thin knife between mold and charlotte all around edges. Set platter atop charlotte, then invert charlotte onto platter. Gently lift mold from charlotte and reposition any pieces of ladyfingers that may have become dislodged. Slice charlotte and serve with berry compote.

 # Classic Tiramisù

Featuring espresso- and Marsala-soaked ladyfingers layered with a mousse-like filling of Marsala-flavored mascarpone cheese, this classic Italian dessert has long been popular in the States. The egg whites can be omitted if you prefer—the mascarpone filling will still be creamy and delicious, if not quite as light and airy. **8 servings**

1	cup freshly brewed espresso
⅔	cup sweet Marsala, divided
3	tablespoons plus ¼ cup sugar, divided
3	large eggs, separated, room temperature
8	ounces mascarpone cheese, room temperature
½	cup chilled heavy whipping cream
26	crisp ladyfingers (Boudoirs, Champagne biscuits, or *savoiardi*)
½	ounce bittersweet or semisweet chocolate
1	teaspoon natural unsweetened cocoa powder, divided

Stir hot espresso, ⅓ cup Marsala, and 1 tablespoon sugar in small bowl until sugar dissolves. Chill until cold.

Meanwhile, vigorously whisk egg yolks, remaining ⅓ cup Marsala, and ¼ cup sugar in medium bowl. Set bowl over saucepan of simmering water (do not allow bottom of bowl to touch water); whisk until mixture is pale, thick, fluffy, and doubled in volume, and candy thermometer registers 160°F, about 3 minutes. Remove from heat. Whisk in mascarpone cheese until blended.

Using electric mixer, beat egg whites in large bowl until foamy. Add remaining 2 tablespoons sugar and beat just until firm peaks form. Fold egg white mixture into mascarpone mixture. Beat cream in same bowl until soft peaks form. Fold whipped cream into mascarpone mixture.

Working with 1 ladyfinger at a time, quickly dip in coffee mixture to submerge, turning to coat. Arrange ladyfingers in single layer in 9-inch square glass baking dish, trimming cookies to fit as necessary. Spread half of mascarpone mixture over ladyfingers. Using Microplane grater, grate half of chocolate over mascarpone mixture, then sift ½ teaspoon cocoa over. Repeat with remaining ladyfingers, mascarpone mixture, chocolate, and cocoa powder. Cover and chill at least 3 hours.

DO AHEAD: *Can be made 2 days ahead. Keep chilled.*

Ingredient Tip: **Ladyfingers**

Ladyfingers come in two varieties: light, crisp, oblong cookies and small, thin, spongy, oval cakes. The crisp cookies really resemble manly fingers rather than ladies' fingers, and they go by a few different names, including Champagne biscuits, Boudoirs, and *savoiardi*. You can find crisp ladyfingers in the boxed-cookie section of some supermarkets and at specialty foods stores and Italian markets. (Not all crisp ladyfingers are the same size, so it's always better to buy extra.) Soft ladyfingers are like sponge cake and are usually found in the bakery section of the supermarket (or sometimes in the produce section). They can also be found at specialty foods stores.

Individual Raspberry Tiramisùs with Raspberry-Framboise Sauce

An unexpected combination of flavors—raspberry and coffee—gives modern flair to the classic Italian dessert. Even better: The homemade ladyfinger rounds are used to make gorgeous individual servings. (Note that these ladyfingers are formed into a different shape than the traditional elongated variety.) This is a truly showstopping dessert. And there are a few extra ladyfingers for nibbling.

6 servings

Ladyfinger Rounds

½   cup unbleached all purpose flour
½   teaspoon finely ground coffee beans (preferably espresso)
3   large eggs, separated, room temperature
5   tablespoons sugar, divided
½   teaspoon vanilla extract
    Powdered sugar

Filling

3   tablespoons framboise liqueur
1   tablespoon instant espresso powder or instant coffee crystals
2   8-ounce packages Philadelphia-brand cream cheese, room temperature
⅔   cup powdered sugar
1   6-ounce container fresh raspberries or 1½ cups frozen raspberries, thawed, drained, divided

¾   cup freshly brewed strong coffee (preferably espresso), room temperature
3   tablespoons sugar
    Additional powdered sugar
    Raspberry-Framboise Sauce (see recipe)
    Fresh mint (optional)

LADYFINGER ROUNDS: Preheat oven to 350°F. Line 2 rimmed baking sheets with parchment paper. Mix flour and ground coffee in small bowl. Using electric mixer, beat egg yolks and 4 tablespoons sugar in medium bowl until very thick and slowly dissolving ribbon forms when beaters are lifted, about 4 minutes. Beat in vanilla. Mix in dry ingredients (batter will be thick). Using electric mixer fitted with clean dry beaters, beat egg whites in another medium bowl until thick and foamy. Add remaining 1 tablespoon sugar and beat until whites are stiff but not dry. Fold whites into batter in 2 additions.

Technique Tip: Shortcuts

If you don't have the patience to form little tiramisù sandwiches, just layer the ladyfingers, coffee syrup, and filling in a large dish and offer the sauce on the side. You can also use purchased ladyfingers—but we think making them yourself is half the fun.

Drop batter by rounded tablespoonfuls (8 per sheet) onto prepared sheets, spacing evenly apart. Sift powdered sugar thickly over rounds. Bake rounds until edges are golden brown, about 16 minutes. Cool on sheets on racks. Using metal spatula, lift ladyfinger rounds from parchment.

DO AHEAD: *Can be made 1 day ahead. Store in single layer in airtight container at room temperature.*

FILLING: Combine framboise and espresso powder in small bowl. Stir until espresso dissolves. Using electric mixer, beat cream cheese and powdered sugar in large bowl until light and fluffy. Beat in framboise mixture. Fold in 1 cup raspberries. Let filling stand at room temperature.

Combine brewed coffee and 3 tablespoons sugar in small bowl. Stir until sugar dissolves. Place 1 ladyfinger round, flat side up, on plate. Spoon 1 scant tablespoonful coffee syrup over. Spread ⅓ cup filling over round. Spoon 1 scant tablespoonful coffee syrup over flat side of second ladyfinger round. Place flat side down atop filling, pressing lightly to adhere. Sift additional powdered sugar over. Repeat 5 more times with remaining ladyfinger rounds, coffee syrup, filling, and powdered sugar. Spoon Raspberry-Framboise Sauce around desserts. Garnish with remaining raspberries and fresh mint and serve.

Raspberry-Framboise Sauce

Framboise liqueur can be found at liquor stores and some specialty foods stores. Buy a good-quality, imported French version. **Makes about 1¼ cups**

1   12-ounce package frozen raspberries, thawed
2   tablespoons framboise liqueur
2   tablespoons sugar

Puree raspberries, liqueur, and sugar in processor. Strain into small bowl to remove seeds.

DO AHEAD: *Can be made 2 days ahead. Cover and chill.*

Chocolate Cranachan

Cranachan is Scotland's harvest-time pudding, traditionally a blend of crowdie (an artisanal cottage cheese), cream, toasted oats, berries, whisky, and honey. For this version, the crowdie is replaced with crème fraîche, and toasted hazelnuts and grated chocolate replace the berries and honey. For flavors to reach their peak, prepare the Cranachan parfaits one day ahead and chill overnight. **Makes 6**

6   ounces coarsely grated bittersweet or semisweet chocolate
1   cup hazelnuts, toasted, husked, coarsely chopped
⅓   cup (packed) golden brown sugar
1   cup old-fashioned oats
1¾   cups chilled heavy whipping cream
⅓   cup crème fraîche or sour cream
3   tablespoons sugar
⅓   cup whisky

Preheat oven to 350°F. Mix chocolate, hazelnuts, and brown sugar in medium bowl. Spread oats on rimmed baking sheet. Bake until golden brown, stirring occasionally, about 7 minutes. Stir hot oats into chocolate mixture (hot oats will partially melt chocolate); set aside until chocolate firms, at least 2 hours.

DO AHEAD: *Can be made 1 day ahead. Cover and chill.*

Using electric mixer, beat cream, crème fraîche, and sugar in large bowl until peaks form; fold in whisky. Layer ¼ cup cream mixture and ¼ cup oat mixture in each of six 10- to 12-ounce goblets; repeat layering, ending with ¼ cup cream mixture and sprinkle of oat mixture. Cover parfaits and chill overnight.

Mascarpone and Berry Parfaits

Here's a super-fast, super-easy recipe for a luscious and beautiful dessert. Mascarpone, an Italian cream cheese, is lighter than American cream cheese. It's available at many supermarkets and at Italian markets. **Makes 4**

1   cup chopped strawberries plus 4 whole strawberries, hulled
⅔   cup plus 12 raspberries
2   tablespoons sugar
2   8-ounce containers mascarpone cheese

Blend chopped strawberries, ⅔ cup raspberries, and sugar in processor to smooth puree. Drop 1 whole strawberry into each of 4 Champagne flutes or wineglasses. Top with 2 rounded tablespoonfuls mascarpone cheese, then 2 tablespoonfuls fruit puree. Repeat layering 2 more times. Top each parfait with some of remaining cheese, then 3 raspberries. Chill at least 1 hour or cover and chill overnight.

🥄 Raspberry-Nectarine Parfaits with Warm Peach Sabayon

This is an impromptu dessert with a touch of class. It takes only a few minutes to make but must be prepared just before serving, so have your ingredients measured and ready to go. **Makes 4**

1	pound nectarines (about 4 medium), halved, pitted, thinly sliced
2½	cups raspberries, divided
½	cup sugar, divided
4	large egg yolks
⅓	cup canned peach nectar
½	cup peach liqueur
	Pinch of salt
	Sliced almonds, toasted (optional)

Toss nectarines, 2 cups raspberries, and ¼ cup sugar in medium bowl to coat evenly. Let stand until juices form, about 5 minutes.

Whisk egg yolks, nectar, liqueur, salt, and remaining ¼ cup sugar in large metal bowl to blend. Place bowl over saucepan of boiling water; whisk until sabayon is thick and thermometer inserted into center registers 160°F, about 6 minutes. Remove bowl from over water.

Divide fruit mixture among 4 large glasses or goblets. Spoon warm peach sabayon over. Garnish with remaining raspberries and sliced almonds, if desired.

Zabaglione/Sabayon

Italians call it *zabaglione*, and the French call it *sabayon*, but both words refer to the same thing: a luscious, airy soft custard. The recipe always begins with egg yolks and sugar whisked in a bowl set over a saucepan of simmering water—and then the fun begins. The next step is to whisk in wine, fortified wine, or liqueur, opening the door for all kinds of flavor options. The dessert can be served warm or chilled, on its own or as a sauce.

🥄 Champagne Parfaits with Pears and Raspberries

Sparkling wine can add a distinct effervescence—even when it's cooked. In this dessert, the Champagne is used first to poach the pears; then, that lovely poaching liquid is used again to make the custard. **Makes 4**

3	cups brut Champagne or sparkling rosé
½	teaspoon unflavored gelatin
1	cup plus 1 tablespoon sugar
2	large firm but ripe pears, peeled, quartered, cored
6	large egg yolks
2	½-pint containers raspberries
1	cup chilled heavy whipping cream
4	fresh mint sprigs
12	rose petals from unsprayed roses (optional)

Place 1 tablespoon Champagne in small cup. Sprinkle gelatin over; let stand until gelatin softens, about 15 minutes. Combine remaining Champagne and 1 cup sugar in heavy medium saucepan; stir over medium heat until sugar dissolves. Increase heat and bring to boil. Add pears; reduce heat and simmer uncovered just until pears are tender, turning pears often, about 6 minutes. Using slotted spoon, transfer pears to plate and cool. Boil poaching liquid until reduced to 1⅓ cups, about 15 minutes.

Whisk egg yolks in medium bowl to blend. Gradually whisk in hot poaching liquid. Return mixture to same saucepan. Stir over medium-low heat until custard thickens enough to leave path on back of spoon when finger is drawn across, about 4 minutes (do not boil). Remove from heat; add gelatin mixture to hot custard and stir until dissolved. Chill custard until thickened but not set, stirring occasionally, about 1 hour.

Set aside 4 raspberries for garnish. Combine remaining raspberries and remaining 1 tablespoon sugar in medium bowl; toss to coat. Let stand 10 minutes. Coarsely chop pears. Beat cream until stiff peaks form. Fold whipped cream into cooled custard.

Place ¼ cup raspberries in each of four 12- to 16-ounce goblets or balloon-shaped wineglasses. Spoon half of pears over raspberries in each goblet. Spoon ½ cup custard over. Repeat layering with remaining raspberries, pears, and custard. Cover loosely with foil; chill until custard is set, at least 6 hours and up to 1 day.

Garnish parfaits with reserved raspberries and mint sprigs, and with rose petals, if desired.

♈♈♈ Cranberry and Lemon-Ginger Parfaits

These parfaits can be prepared as early as two days ahead, making them incredibly convenient for dinner parties or holiday meals. **Makes 8**

Cranberry Custard

2	cups fresh or frozen cranberries
1	cup sugar, divided
2	tablespoons fresh lemon juice
2	teaspoons finely grated lemon peel
2	tablespoons cranberry liqueur or brandy
1½	teaspoons unflavored gelatin
1	cup whole milk
3	large egg yolks
1	cup chilled heavy whipping cream

Lemon-Ginger Custard

3	tablespoons water
¾	teaspoon unflavored gelatin
1½	cups chilled heavy whipping cream
4	ounces Philadelphia-brand cream cheese, room temperature
⅔	cup powdered sugar
2	tablespoons fresh lemon juice
1	tablespoon finely grated lemon peel
1	tablespoon minced crystallized ginger
8	crystallized ginger slices
8	fresh or frozen cranberries

CRANBERRY CUSTARD: Simmer 2 cups cranberries, ½ cup sugar, lemon juice, and lemon peel in heavy medium saucepan over medium heat until cranberries are very soft and break down, stirring frequently, about 7 minutes. Puree cranberry mixture in processor until smooth; strain into large bowl and cool.

Place cranberry liqueur in small cup. Sprinkle gelatin over and let stand until gelatin softens, about 15 minutes.

Bring milk to simmer in heavy medium saucepan. Whisk egg yolks and remaining ½ cup sugar in medium bowl to blend; gradually whisk in hot milk. Return mixture to same saucepan and stir over medium-low heat until custard thickens and leaves path on back of spoon when finger is drawn across, about 6 minutes (do not boil). Remove from heat and add gelatin mixture. Stir until gelatin dissolves.

Working with Gelatin

Gelatin is a versatile thickening agent. It is simple to use, as long as you follow two key steps. First, it must be softened by sprinkling it over a small amount of cold liquid, often water, and letting it stand at room temperature for 10 to 15 minutes. Once the gelatin is softened, it will look translucent and spongy and most of the liquid will be absorbed. Then, the mixture needs to be heated to dissolve the gelatin. This can be achieved by placing the dish with the softened gelatin into ½ inch of simmering water in a small skillet and stirring it until the granules dissolve into a clear liquid. Or add the softened gelatin to very hot liquid, such as milk or juice, then stir it until it dissolves. The gelatin is then ready to be added to other ingredients.

Stir custard into cranberry mixture. Chill until cool but not set, stirring occasionally, about 15 minutes.

Using electric mixer, beat cream in another large bowl until peaks form. Fold cream into cranberry mixture in 2 additions. Set cranberry custard aside at room temperature while preparing lemon custard.

LEMON-GINGER CUSTARD: Place 3 tablespoons water in small saucepan. Sprinkle gelatin over and let stand until gelatin softens, about 15 minutes. Stir over low heat until gelatin dissolves. Remove from heat and cover to keep warm.

Using electric mixer, beat cream in medium bowl until peaks form. Using same beaters, beat cream cheese, powdered sugar, and lemon juice in another large bowl until smooth. Mix in lemon peel and minced ginger. Stir ⅓ of cream cheese mixture into gelatin mixture. Return gelatin mixture to bowl with cream cheese mixture and beat to combine. Immediately fold in whipped cream in 2 additions.

Spoon ¼ cup cranberry custard into each of eight 10- to 12-ounce glasses. Top cranberry custard in each wineglass with ¼ cup lemon custard, then ¼ cup cranberry custard. Spoon remaining lemon custard into pastry bag fitted with large star tip. Pipe large rosette of lemon custard atop each. Garnish each parfait with 1 crystallized ginger slice and 1 cranberry. Refrigerate parfaits until set, about 4 hours.

DO AHEAD: *Can be made 2 days ahead. Cover and keep refrigerated.*

Tuaca Zabaglione with Sautéed Vanilla Pears

Zabaglione (or in French, sabayon), the airiest of all custards, is made by beating egg yolks, wine, and sugar in a bowl over simmering water. Here, that mixture is enhanced with some whipped cream, becoming a sophisticated sauce. And instead of wine, the liquor is Tuaca—a sweet citrus- and vanilla-flavored Italian liqueur. If you can't find it, Grand Marnier or any other orange liqueur would make a fine substitute. **6 servings**

Pears

2	tablespoons (¼ stick) unsalted butter
2¼	pounds firm but ripe pears (about 6 small), peeled, cored, cut into ½-inch cubes
¼	cup (packed) golden brown sugar
2	tablespoons sugar
¼	cup Pinot Grigio or other dry white wine
½	vanilla bean, split lengthwise

Zabaglione

8	large egg yolks
½	cup sugar
6	tablespoons Tuaca liqueur
2	tablespoons plus 1 cup chilled heavy whipping cream
¼	teaspoon ground cinnamon

Powdered sugar

PEARS: Melt butter in heavy large skillet over high heat. Add pears; sauté 1 minute. Add both sugars and wine and toss until sugar dissolves. Scrape in seeds from vanilla bean; add bean. Cook until pears are tender and juices in skillet form thick syrup, stirring occasionally, about 5 minutes. Remove from heat. Cool. Discard vanilla bean.

DO AHEAD: *Can be made 1 day ahead. Cover; chill.*

ZABAGLIONE: Whisk egg yolks, sugar, Tuaca, and 2 tablespoons cream in large metal bowl to blend well. Set bowl over saucepan of simmering water. Using electric mixer, beat yolk mixture constantly until zabaglione thickens and thermometer inserted into center registers 140°F for 3 minutes, about 7 minutes total. Place metal bowl in larger bowl of ice and water. Whisk occasionally until zabaglione is cool, about 3 minutes.

Using electric mixer, beat remaining 1 cup cream and cinnamon in medium bowl until peaks form. Fold whipped cream into cool zabaglione in 3 additions. Chill until cold.

DO AHEAD: *Can be made 1 day ahead. Cover and keep refrigerated.*

Divide pears among 6 dessert glasses. Spoon zabaglione over pears. Dust with powdered sugar and serve.

⫶ Tiramisù Eggnog Trifle

Brandy, rum, and nutmeg give classic tiramisù an eggnog twist; presenting it in a glass trifle dish makes it a showoff holiday dessert. As with all trifles, it's best to make this a day ahead to allow all the flavors to mingle. **16 to 18 servings**

1⅓	cups plus 2 tablespoons sugar
1¼	cups water, divided
¼	cup plus 1 teaspoon dark rum
4	tablespoons brandy, divided
12	large egg yolks
½	teaspoon ground nutmeg
4	8-ounce containers mascarpone cheese
2	cups chilled heavy whipping cream
2	teaspoons vanilla extract
6½	teaspoons instant espresso powder or instant coffee powder
7	tablespoons Kahlúa or other coffee liqueur
2	6.15-ounce boxes or four 3.5-ounce boxes crisp ladyfingers (about 60 cookies)
1	cup semisweet chocolate chips, finely ground in processor, divided

Chocolate Leaves (see recipe)

Whisk 1⅓ cups sugar, ¼ cup water, ¼ cup rum, 3 tablespoons brandy, egg yolks, and nutmeg in large metal bowl. Set bowl over saucepan of simmering water (do not allow bowl to touch water). Whisk constantly until mixture thickens and candy thermometer inserted into mixture registers 140°F for 3 minutes, about 5 minutes total. Remove bowl from over water. Whisk mascarpone, 1 container at a time, into warm custard until blended.

Using electric mixer, beat cream, vanilla, remaining 1 tablespoon brandy, and remaining 1 teaspoon rum in another large bowl until cream holds peaks. Fold in mascarpone mixture.

Bring remaining 1 cup water to simmer in small saucepan. Remove from heat. Add remaining 2 tablespoons sugar and espresso powder; stir to dissolve. Mix in Kahlúa. Submerge 1 cookie in espresso mixture, turning to coat twice; shake excess liquid back into saucepan. Place dipped cookie, sugared side facing out, around bottom side of 14-cup trifle dish, pressing against side of dish (cookie may break). Repeat with enough cookies to go around bottom sides of dish once. Dip more cookies and arrange over bottom of dish to cover.

Spoon 2 cups mascarpone mixture over cookies; spread to cover. Sprinkle ¼ cup ground chocolate over, making chocolate visible at sides of dish. Repeat with more cookies dipped into espresso mixture, mascarpone mixture, and ground chocolate in 2 more layers each. Cover with 1 more layer of dipped cookies and enough mascarpone mixture to reach top of trifle dish. Sprinkle remaining ground chocolate over, covering completely. Cover and chill overnight.

Gently press stem ends of largest Chocolate Leaves around edge of trifle. Fill center with smaller leaves.

DO AHEAD: *Can be made 8 hours ahead. Chill.*

⫶ Chocolate Leaves

Gold-dusted chocolate leaves add a magnificent look to the trifle, as well as to a host of other holiday desserts. Use them to dress up glazed brownies, cakes, or chocolate mousse. You'll find the edible gold dust at cake and candy supply stores, online at amazon.com or pastrychef.com, or from Jane's Cakes & Chocolates at 818-957-2511. **Makes about 40**

8	ounces bittersweet or semisweet chocolate, chopped
40	assorted sizes of camellia leaves or lemon leaves, wiped clean Gold dust (optional)

Line large baking sheet with foil. Melt chocolate in top of double boiler over simmering water, stirring until smooth and instant-read thermometer inserted into chocolate registers 115°F. Brush chocolate over veined side (underside) of 1 leaf, coating thickly and completely. Arrange chocolate side up on prepared baking sheet. Repeat with remaining leaves and chocolate, rewarming chocolate if necessary to maintain 115°F temperature. Chill leaves until firm, about 45 minutes. Starting at stem end, carefully pull back green leaf, releasing chocolate. Return chocolate leaves to baking sheet.

DO AHEAD: *Can be made 2 days ahead. Cover and keep chilled.*

Using small artist brush, carefully brush some leaves with gold dust, if desired.

White Chocolate Trifle with Spiced Pears

White chocolate teams with mascarpone to form a thick and creamy mousse, and pears spiced with cardamom, cinnamon, and ginger form an extra layer of luxury throughout. Using a trifle dish shows off all the layers. Soft, cake-like ladyfingers complement the fluffy mousse. **10 to 12 servings**

Spiced Pears

1	750-ml bottle dry white wine
2	cups pear juice or pear nectar
1¼	cups sugar
12	whole green cardamom pods, crushed in resealable plastic bag with mallet
4	1-inch-diameter rounds peeled fresh ginger (each about ⅛ inch thick)
2	cinnamon sticks, broken in half
5	large firm but ripe Anjou pears (3 to 3¼ pounds), peeled

Mousse

7	ounces high-quality white chocolate (such as Lindt or Perugina), chopped
⅓	cup poire Williams (clear pear brandy)
¼	cup water
½	vanilla bean, split lengthwise
1	8- to 9-ounce container mascarpone cheese
1	cup chilled heavy whipping cream

Trifle Assembly

3	3-ounce packages soft ladyfingers, separated
2	cups chilled heavy whipping cream
¼	cup minced crystallized ginger
	White chocolate curls
	Powdered sugar

SPICED PEARS: Combine white wine, pear juice, sugar, cardamom, ginger, and cinnamon in heavy large saucepan. Stir over medium-high heat until sugar dissolves. Add pears and bring to boil. Reduce heat to medium, cover, and simmer until pears are just tender when pierced with knife, about 35 minutes. Transfer liquid with pears to large bowl and chill until cold, about 3 hours.

Using slotted spoon, transfer pears to plate. Transfer poaching liquid to heavy large saucepan; boil over medium-high heat until slightly thickened and reduced to generous 1½ cups, about 15 minutes. Strain into 2-cup measuring cup; discard spices in strainer. Cool. Cover and chill pears and pear syrup until cold.

MOUSSE: Combine white chocolate, pear brandy, and ¼ cup water in top of double boiler set over simmering water. Stir until smooth (mixture will be very liquidy). Scrape in seeds from vanilla bean (reserve bean for another use). Transfer white chocolate mixture to large bowl; gradually add mascarpone, whisking until mixture is smooth. Cool mascarpone mixture until barely lukewarm.

Using electric mixer, beat cream in medium bowl until peaks form. Fold whipped cream into mascarpone mixture in 4 additions. Cover and chill white chocolate mousse until set, about 3 hours.

DO AHEAD: *Pears and mousse can be made 1 day ahead. Keep chilled.*

(continued next page)

White Chocolate Trifle with Spiced Pears *(continued)*

TRIFLE ASSEMBLY: Cut pears lengthwise in half and remove cores and stems. Cut halves lengthwise into ¼-inch-thick slices.

Arrange ladyfingers, rounded sides down, in single layer in bottom of 12-cup trifle dish (about 8 inches in diameter and 5 inches deep), covering bottom completely (using about 15 ladyfingers) [1]. Drizzle 5 tablespoons pear syrup evenly over ladyfingers. Using small offset spatula or spoon, spread ⅓ of white chocolate mousse over ladyfingers [2 and 3], making layer slightly thicker around outer edges of dish to allow mousse to be more visible (center of mousse layer will be thin). Starting at outer edges of dish, place pear slices in single layer with curved edges against sides of dish atop mousse, covering completely. Repeat layering of ladyfingers, syrup, mousse, and pears 2 more times. Cover with fourth layer of ladyfingers (some ladyfingers and pear slices may be left over). Drizzle ladyfingers evenly with 5 tablespoons syrup. Chill at least 6 hours.

DO AHEAD: *Can be made 1 day ahead. Cover and chill trifle and remaining pear syrup separately.*

Using electric mixer, beat cream in large bowl until soft peaks form. Add ¼ cup pear syrup and beat until stiff peaks form. Working in batches, transfer cream to large pastry bag fitted with large star tip. Pipe rosettes all over top of trifle, mounding slightly in center. Sprinkle with crystallized ginger. Garnish with white chocolate curls.

DO AHEAD: *Can be made 6 hours ahead. Keep chilled.*

Sift powdered sugar over trifle just before serving.

Chocolate-Cherry Trifle

This rich trifle is reminiscent of a classic Black Forest torte, with the flavors of chocolate, cherries, and kirsch. Chocolate pudding is layered with a sweet cherry filling, kirsch-scented whipped cream, and purchased pound cake. (Or use the Classic Pound Cake recipe on page 44.) **12 to 14 servings**

Pudding

⅔ cup sugar

¼ cup cornstarch

2 tablespoons natural unsweetened cocoa powder

6 large egg yolks

3 cups whole milk

8 ounces bittersweet or semisweet chocolate (do not exceed 61% cacao), chopped

Filling

2 16-ounce packages frozen pitted dark sweet cherries, thawed, juices reserved

¾ cup dried tart cherries

½ cup sugar

½ cup plus 2 tablespoons kirsch (clear cherry brandy)

1 tablespoon cornstarch

Whipped Cream

2 cups chilled heavy whipping cream

2 tablespoons sugar

2 tablespoons kirsch (clear cherry brandy)

Trifle Assembly

12 (about) ¾- to 1-inch-thick slices pound cake (cut from two 10.75-ounce pound cakes), each slice cut into 4 strips

Chocolate curls

PUDDING: Whisk sugar, cornstarch, and cocoa in heavy large saucepan to blend. Whisk in egg yolks until well blended; gradually whisk in milk. Whisk over medium-high heat until mixture thickens and comes to boil, about 5 minutes. Remove from heat. Add chocolate and stir until chocolate melts and mixture is smooth. Transfer pudding to bowl. Chill until cool, stirring occasionally, about 1 hour.

DO AHEAD: *Can be made up to 1 day ahead. When cool, press plastic wrap directly onto surface of pudding, then chill.*

FILLING: Combine sweet cherries with juices, dried cherries, sugar, and ½ cup kirsch in large saucepan; simmer over medium heat until dried cherries are slightly plumped, stirring often, about 10 minutes. Stir remaining 2 tablespoons kirsch and cornstarch in small bowl to blend. Add cornstarch mixture to cherry mixture; bring to boil. Transfer to bowl and chill until cool, stirring occasionally, about 45 minutes.

DO AHEAD: *Can be made 1 day ahead. When cool, cover with plastic and chill.*

WHIPPED CREAM: Whip cream, sugar, and kirsch in large bowl until very soft peaks form.

TRIFLE ASSEMBLY: Line bottom of 14-cup trifle bowl with single layer of cake strips. Spoon ⅓ cherry filling (about 1⅓ cups) over cake. Spoon ⅓ chocolate pudding (about 1⅓ cups) evenly over cherry filling. Carefully spread 1 cup whipped cream over pudding. Repeat layering two times, ending with all remaining whipped cream (there will be more than 1 cup). Chill until set, at least 3 hours or overnight. Garnish with chocolate curls and serve.

Chocolate Soufflés with White Chocolate Cream

There is amazing depth of flavor in these easy chocolate soufflés. The secret? A touch of brandy and a spoonful of espresso powder. A luscious white chocolate whipped cream goes on top. **Makes 4**

3 tablespoons water
1 tablespoon instant espresso powder or instant coffee powder
5 ounces bittersweet or semisweet chocolate (do not exceed 61% cacao), chopped
1 tablespoon brandy
3 large egg yolks
4 large egg whites, room temperature
2½ tablespoons sugar
   Powdered sugar
   White Chocolate Cream (see recipe)

Butter four ⅔-cup soufflé dishes; coat with sugar. Stir 3 tablespoons water and espresso powder in heavy small saucepan until espresso powder dissolves. Add chocolate and brandy. Stir over low heat until mixture is smooth. Remove from heat. Whisk in egg yolks. Cool to room temperature.

Beat egg whites in large bowl until foamy. Gradually add 2½ tablespoons sugar and beat until medium-firm peaks form. Fold chocolate mixture into whites. Divide among soufflé dishes. Place dishes on baking sheet.

DO AHEAD: *Can be made 2 hours ahead. Let stand uncovered at room temperature.*

Preheat oven to 400°F. Bake soufflés until puffed but still moist in center, about 14 minutes. Sift powdered sugar over soufflés. Serve immediately, passing White Chocolate Cream separately.

Technique Tip: **Soufflé Secrets**

As impressive as they are, soufflés are remarkably easy to make, provided you master the most important steps: beating the egg whites to firm, glossy peaks, then folding the beaten egg whites into the soufflé base. The fluffy whites are what give soufflés a lift, so you don't want to deflate them too much. To achieve this, first fold in just a quarter of the whites. This lightens the heavy base. Then gently fold in the rest of the egg whites by drawing your spatula through the whites and down into the base.

White Chocolate Cream

Whipped cream is even better when it's combined with melted white chocolate. Serve any extra cream with whole fresh strawberries. **Makes about 1 cup**

2 ounces high-quality white chocolate (such as Lindt or Perugina), chopped
½ cup chilled heavy whipping cream

Stir chocolate in top of double boiler set over simmering water until melted and smooth. Remove from over water. Let stand until cool but not set. Beat cream in medium bowl until firm peaks form. Stir half of cream into cooled chocolate; fold in remaining cream.

DO AHEAD: *Can be made 4 hours ahead. Cover; chill.*

What Makes a Soufflé?

Soufflés are created from two elements: an intensely flavored base (which can often be made ahead of time) plus beaten egg whites, which are folded into the base before baking. Some bases are thickened with a roux (flour cooked with butter), others with egg yolks and sugar. Some are made with a pastry cream, and others with an intensely sweet jam-like base. The magic begins when the beaten egg whites are folded in, and then, in the heat of the oven, the air in those tiny bubbles expands, causing the soufflés to rise dramatically.

Dark Chocolate Soufflés with Cardamom Crème Anglaise

To serve the soufflés in the classic tradition, use a small spoon to break open the soft center of the soufflé, then pour a little sauce into the indentation. Pass the remaining sauce alongside. **Makes 8**

5	ounces bittersweet or semisweet chocolate (do not exceed 61% cacao), chopped
1	tablespoon unsalted butter
¼	cup plus 3 tablespoons sugar
2	tablespoons unbleached all purpose flour
1	teaspoon natural unsweetened cocoa powder
¾	cup whole milk
¼	teaspoon vanilla extract
4	large egg yolks
5	large egg whites, room temperature
¼	teaspoon coarse kosher salt
	Cardamom Crème Anglaise (see recipe)

Place chocolate and butter in medium bowl. Whisk ¼ cup sugar, flour, and cocoa in small bowl. Bring milk and vanilla to boil in heavy small saucepan. Gradually whisk hot milk mixture into sugar mixture to blend. Return mixture to same saucepan. Cook over medium-high heat until thick paste forms, stirring constantly, about 2 minutes. Scrape mixture into bowl with chocolate and butter; stir until chocolate is melted (mixture may look curdled). Add egg yolks and whisk until mixture looks shiny and creamy.

DO AHEAD: *Soufflé base can be made 1 day ahead. Press plastic wrap directly onto surface and refrigerate. Bring to room temperature before continuing.*

Butter eight ¾-cup soufflé dishes or custard cups; dust with sugar. Using electric mixer, beat egg whites in large bowl until frothy. Gradually beat in remaining 3 tablespoons sugar, then coarse salt; beat just until soft peaks form. Fold ⅓ of whites into soufflé base until well combined. Gently fold in remaining egg whites just to blend (some white streaks may remain). Divide mixture among prepared dishes. Place dishes on rimmed baking sheet.

Preheat oven to 350°F. Bake soufflés until puffed above rim of dish, tops are flat, and edges are set, about 12 minutes. Remove from oven and serve immediately with Cardamom Crème Anglaise.

Cardamom Crème Anglaise

Crème anglaise is a classic dessert sauce that can also serve as the base for ice cream. Make a double batch and process half in an ice-cream maker for a sophisticated frozen treat. **Makes 2 cups**

2	tablespoons whole green cardamom pods, crushed
1	cup whole milk
1	cup heavy whipping cream
½	cup sugar, divided
¼	vanilla bean, split lengthwise
4	large egg yolks

Place cardamom pods with seeds in heavy medium saucepan over medium-high heat. Stir until pods brown, about 5 minutes. Add milk, cream, and ¼ cup sugar. Scrape seeds from vanilla bean into pan; add bean. Bring mixture to boil. Whisk egg yolks and remaining ¼ cup sugar in medium bowl. Gradually whisk in hot milk mixture. Return mixture to same saucepan. Stir over medium-low heat until custard thickens and leaves path on back of spoon when finger is drawn across, stirring constantly, about 2 minutes (do not boil). Refrigerate uncovered until cold, stirring occasionally. Strain into medium pitcher.

DO AHEAD: *Can be made 2 days ahead. Cover and keep refrigerated.*

Technique Tip: Skinless Custard
Custard recipes often call for pressing plastic wrap directly on top of hot custards or pastry creams. This is an important step because it prevents a rubbery skin from forming on the surface of the custard as it cools and keeps the soufflés from drying out or absorbing odors from the refrigerator.

Toffee Soufflés with Chocolate Sauce

This decadent dessert is very much like a Heath bar in soufflé form. The individual soufflés are buttery and sweet (with little crunchy pieces of chopped toffee), and they're topped with a warm homemade chocolate sauce. For a restaurant-worthy presentation, divide the chocolate sauce among six shot glasses and serve them alongside the soufflés. **Makes 6**

Sauce

½ cup heavy whipping cream
2 tablespoons (¼ stick) unsalted butter
2 tablespoons (packed) golden brown sugar
4 ounces bittersweet or semisweet chocolate (do not exceed 61% cacao), chopped

Soufflés

5 large egg yolks
⅓ cup (packed) golden brown sugar
2 tablespoons unbleached all purpose flour
½ cup milk
1 tablespoon unsalted butter
2 tablespoons Scotch whisky
3 large egg whites, room temperature
¼ cup sugar
1 cup finely chopped toffee candy (such as Heath bar or Almond Roca; about 6 ounces), divided

SAUCE: Cook cream, butter, and sugar in heavy small saucepan over medium heat, stirring until sugar dissolves. Add chocolate and stir until sauce is melted and smooth.

DO AHEAD: *Can be made 3 days ahead. Cover; chill. Before using, rewarm over low heat just until liquid.*

SOUFFLÉS: Preheat oven to 375°F. Butter and sugar six ⅔-cup soufflé dishes. Whisk egg yolks, brown sugar, and flour in medium bowl. Bring milk to simmer in heavy medium saucepan. Gradually whisk hot milk into yolk mixture. Return mixture to saucepan and whisk constantly over medium heat until mixture is very thick, about 2 minutes. Transfer mixture to large bowl. Whisk in butter and Scotch. Cool to lukewarm.

Using electric mixer fitted with clean dry beaters, beat whites in another large bowl to soft peaks. Gradually beat in ¼ cup sugar and continue beating to stiff peaks. Gently fold ¼ of whites into soufflé mixture to lighten. Fold in remaining whites. Gently fold in ¾ cup chopped toffee. Divide mixture among prepared dishes. Smooth tops.

Bake until soufflés puff and tops are golden, about 12 minutes. Transfer to plates. Sprinkle with remaining ¼ cup toffee. Serve with sauce.

Maple Gingerbread Soufflé

A great cold-weather treat that makes a delightful holiday dessert, this soufflé doesn't rise as high as many, but it more than makes up for it with its rich gingerbread flavor and luxurious texture. **6 servings**

¼	cup (½ stick) unsalted butter
¼	cup unbleached all purpose flour
1½	cups reduced-fat (2%) milk
⅔	cup (packed) dark brown sugar
⅓	cup mild-flavored (light) molasses
1	tablespoon ground ginger
1	teaspoon ground cinnamon
½	teaspoon ground nutmeg
¼	teaspoon ground cloves
1	teaspoon vanilla extract
¼	teaspoon salt
4	large egg yolks
7	large egg whites, room temperature
½	teaspoon cream of tartar
	Maple Crème Anglaise (see recipe)

Position rack in center of oven and preheat to 375°F. Butter one 6- to 8-cup soufflé dish; dust with sugar.

Melt butter in heavy medium saucepan over medium heat. Add flour; whisk until roux is smooth and bubbling, about 2 minutes. Gradually whisk in milk; bring to boil. Continue boiling mixture until smooth and thick, whisking about 1 minute. Remove from heat. Add sugar, molasses, spices, vanilla, and salt; whisk until blended. Transfer soufflé base to medium bowl. Cool until just warm, whisking occasionally, about 5 minutes. Whisk egg yolks into soufflé base.

Using electric mixer, beat egg whites and cream of tartar in large bowl until stiff but not dry. Fold ¼ of whites into soufflé base to lighten. Gradually fold soufflé base back into remaining whites. Transfer soufflé mixture to prepared dish. Bake soufflé until puffed, brown, and almost firm to touch in center, about 45 minutes. Serve immediately with Maple Crème Anglaise.

Maple Crème Anglaise

The delicate maple flavor of this silky custard sauce pairs nicely with the gingerbread soufflé, but it would also be delicious with bread pudding or flourless chocolate cake. **Makes about 1½ cups**

4	large egg yolks
¼	cup pure maple syrup
	Pinch of salt
1	cup half and half
½	teaspoon vanilla extract

Combine egg yolks, maple syrup, and salt in heavy small saucepan and whisk to blend. Gradually whisk in half and half. Stir over medium-low heat until custard thickens and leaves path on back of spoon when finger is drawn across, about 6 minutes (do not boil). Mix in vanilla. Transfer to bowl. Serve warm or at room temperature.

Technique Tip: **Plan Ahead**
Avoid last-minute prep work by making the soufflé ahead, then baking it an hour before it's time for dessert. To do ahead, just spoon the soufflé mixture into the prepared soufflé dish, cover, and chill for up to 2 hours.

🥄🥄 Lemon Soufflés with Boysenberries

Quick and easy to put together, this is a great foolproof dinner-party dessert that can be made year-round (use fresh berries when they are in season). Sifting powdered sugar over the just-baked soufflés adds an elegant touch. **Makes 6**

6	teaspoons seedless boysenberry jam
24	frozen boysenberries or blackberries
2	tablespoons finely grated lemon peel
¾	cup sugar, divided
1	tablespoon cornstarch
¾	cup whole milk
3	large eggs, separated, room temperature
2	tablespoons (¼ stick) unsalted butter
5	tablespoons fresh lemon juice
	Powdered sugar

Preheat oven to 400°F. Butter six ¾-cup ramekins; coat with sugar. Spoon 1 teaspoon jam and 4 frozen berries into bottom of each ramekin. Place on baking sheet.

Mash lemon peel and ½ cup sugar in heavy medium saucepan; whisk in cornstarch, then milk and egg yolks. Add butter. Bring to boil over medium heat, whisking constantly. Boil until thick pudding forms, whisking constantly, about 1 minute. Transfer to large bowl; mix in lemon juice. Season to taste with salt.

Using electric mixer, beat egg whites in medium bowl to soft peaks. Gradually beat in remaining ¼ cup sugar; beat until stiff but not dry. Fold whites into warm lemon pudding. Spoon mixture over berries; fill to top.

DO AHEAD: *Can be assembled up to 4 hours ahead. Chill.*

Bake until puffed, set, and golden around edges, about 14 minutes. Sift powdered sugar over soufflés and serve.

🥄🥄 Ricotta Soufflés with Blackberry Compote

Fresh ricotta cheese is quite different from most grocery store brands. It is not as watery, and has sweet creamy curds similar to cottage cheese. It gives these soufflés a texture reminiscent of cheesecake. Fresh ricotta cheese can be found at some supermarkets and at Italian markets. **Makes 6**

1	cup plus 6 tablespoons sugar, divided
1	tablespoon cornstarch
2	tablespoons plus 1 teaspoon unbleached all purpose flour
4	large egg yolks
1½	teaspoons finely grated lemon peel
1	cup whole milk
1	cup fresh ricotta cheese
2	cups frozen blackberries (about 8 ounces), thawed
¼	cup sweet vermouth
3	tablespoons fresh lemon juice
6	large egg whites, room temperature

Whisk ¾ cup sugar, cornstarch, and flour in large bowl. Add egg yolks and lemon peel; whisk to blend.

Bring milk just to simmer in small saucepan over medium-high heat. Gradually whisk hot milk into yolk mixture. Return mixture to same saucepan and bring to boil over medium heat, whisking constantly. Boil 1 minute, whisking constantly (pastry cream will be thick).

Spread pastry cream out to ⅓-inch thickness on small rimmed baking sheet. Cover completely with plastic wrap. Cool to room temperature. Transfer pastry cream to medium bowl. Whisk in ricotta. Cover and chill until cold, about 1 hour.

Bring blackberries, vermouth, lemon juice, and ¼ cup sugar to boil in small saucepan, crushing some berries and stirring to dissolve sugar. Reduce heat to medium-low; simmer until mixture thickens and measures 1 cup, about 8 minutes. Transfer blackberry compote to small bowl; cover and refrigerate.

Butter six ½-cup ramekins; coat with sugar, tapping out any excess. Using electric mixer, beat egg whites in large bowl until soft peaks form. Gradually beat in remaining 6 tablespoons sugar; continue beating until stiff but not dry. Fold egg whites into ricotta mixture. Spoon mixture into ramekins; smooth tops. Run thumb ¼ inch deep around inside edge of each ramekin.

DO AHEAD: *Can be made 4 hours ahead. Cover and chill.*

Preheat oven to 350°F. Bake soufflés until puffed and golden at edges, about 28 minutes (about 32 minutes if chilled). Serve immediately with compote.

Lemon Soufflés with Boysenberries

Pear Soufflés with Chocolate Sauce

Anjou pears are called for in this recipe because they are sweet and juicy. If unavailable, Comice or Bartlett pears would make fine substitutes. (Bosc pears are too crisp for these soufflés.) Whichever pears you use, make sure they are super-ripe. **Makes 6**

Sauce

²/₃	cup heavy whipping cream
5	ounces bittersweet or semisweet chocolate (do not exceed 61% cacao), chopped
2	tablespoons bourbon

Soufflés

2	tablespoons (¼ stick) unsalted butter, divided
5	ripe Anjou pears (about 2½ pounds), peeled, cored, cut into ½-inch cubes (6 to 7 cups)
8	tablespoons sugar, divided
2	teaspoons fresh lemon juice
3	large egg yolks, room temperature
4	large egg whites, room temperature
	Pinch of salt

SAUCE: Bring cream to simmer in small saucepan over medium heat. Remove from heat. Add chocolate and let stand until chocolate softens slightly, about 1 minute. Add bourbon and stir until chocolate is melted and sauce is smooth.

DO AHEAD: *Can be made 1 day ahead. Cover and refrigerate.*

SOUFFLÉS: Generously butter six ¾-cup ramekins or custard cups, then coat with sugar, tilting ramekins to coat bottoms and sides evenly. Gently tap out any excess sugar. Place ramekins on rimmed baking sheet.

Melt 1 tablespoon butter in large nonstick skillet over medium-high heat. Add half of pears and sauté until beginning to brown, about 8 minutes. Sprinkle with 1½ tablespoons sugar and sauté until pears are caramelized and juices are thick, 3 to 4 minutes longer. Scrape pear mixture into bowl. Repeat with remaining 1 tablespoon butter, remaining pears, and 1½ tablespoons sugar. Stir lemon juice into pear mixture. Cool to room temperature, about 45 minutes.

Using slotted spoon, transfer pear mixture to processor; add pear juices to chocolate sauce. Puree pears until smooth. Transfer pear puree (about 2 cups) to medium saucepan.

DO AHEAD: *Can be made 2 hours ahead. Cover and chill puree.*

Preheat oven to 375°F. Whisk egg yolks into pear puree in saucepan to blend. Stir pear mixture constantly over medium-low heat until steam rises and mixture is hot (do not boil). Carefully transfer pear mixture to large bowl. Using electric mixer, beat egg whites with salt in another large bowl until soft peaks form. Gradually add remaining 5 tablespoons sugar to egg whites and beat until stiff but not dry. Gently fold ⅓ of egg whites into pear mixture to lighten. Gently fold in remaining egg whites in 2 additions. Divide soufflé mixture among prepared ramekins (ramekins will be full).

Bake soufflés until puffed and golden, about 20 minutes.

Rewarm chocolate sauce over low heat. Serve soufflés immediately with warm chocolate sauce alongside.

Salzburg Soufflé with Strawberry-Kirsch Sauce

This Austrian-style soufflé (also known as Salzburger nockerl*) is baked free-form in a large pie dish—so there's no special soufflé dish or ramekin required. It's light and lemony and perfectly paired with a sweet sauce that's made from cherry brandy (kirsch) and fresh strawberries.* **4 servings**

Sauce

1	1-pint container strawberries, hulled
3	tablespoons sugar
1	tablespoon kirsch (clear cherry brandy)
¼	teaspoon vanilla extract

Soufflé

3	large eggs, separated, room temperature
⅛	teaspoon cream of tartar
¼	cup sugar
1½	tablespoons unbleached all purpose flour
1	teaspoon finely grated lemon peel
1	teaspoon vanilla extract
	Powdered sugar

SAUCE: Puree half of berries with sugar, kirsch, and vanilla in processor. Pour into medium bowl. Slice remaining berries and mix into puree. Cover and let stand 25 minutes at room temperature.

DO AHEAD: *Can be made 6 hours ahead. Refrigerate. Bring sauce to room temperature before serving.*

SOUFFLÉ: Position rack in bottom third of oven and preheat to 350°F. Butter 10-inch-diameter glass pie dish. Using electric mixer, beat egg whites and cream of tartar in large bowl until soft peaks form. Gradually beat in sugar and continue beating until stiff but not dry. Beat egg yolks in another bowl until pale yellow and slowly dissolving ribbon forms when beaters are lifted. Blend in flour, lemon peel, and vanilla. Fold in 1 heaping spoonful whites to lighten. Gently fold in remaining whites.

Spoon soufflé mixture in 4 heaping mounds into prepared dish. Bake until top is golden brown, about 14 minutes. Sift powdered sugar over soufflé. Spoon sauce onto plates. Gently separate soufflé into 4 mounds. Place 1 mound atop sauce on each plate. Serve immediately.

Technique Tip: **The Look**

For the best presentation, divide the unbaked soufflé mixture evenly into well-shaped mounds, spacing the mounds slightly apart in the pie dish. Don't worry about making it look perfect, however. *Salzburger nockerl* is meant to represent the hills outside Salzburg, so it should look somewhat rustic.

fruit desserts

fruit desserts

crisps, cobblers & crumbles

Apple-Almond Crisp 398

Apple-Cranberry Crisp with Apple Custard
Sauce 398–99

Apricot Crisp 399

Spiced Pear-Raspberry Crisp 401

Nectarine and Almond Crisp 402

Classic Peach Cobbler 404

Individual Plum Cobblers with Hazelnut
Topping 404

Peach, Plum, and Blackberry Cobbler 405

Cherry-Lime Cobbler with Vanilla–Crème
Fraîche Biscuits 407

Pear Cobbler with Dried Blueberries and
Stone-Ground Corn Biscuits 408

Blackberry Cobblers with Ginger-Cardamom
Biscuits 409

Pear and Maple Crumble 409

Individual Rhubarb and Orange Crumbles
410

clafoutis

Sweet-Cherry Clafouti 410

Pear Clafouti 411

Brandied Plum Clafoutis 411

shortcakes

Strawberry Shortcakes with
White Chocolate Mousse 412

Lemon-Blueberry Shortcakes 413

Peach Melba Shortcakes 414

Oatmeal Shortcakes with Spiced Plums 415

Pear-Cornmeal Shortcakes with
Oven-Roasted Pears 416

meringues

Floating Islands with Lemon-Scented
Custard Sauce and Raspberries 417

Spiced Plum Pavlovas 418

Coconut Pavlova with Chocolate Mousse
and Bananas 419

Pink Peppercorn Pavlovas with
Strawberries, Vanilla Cream, and
Basil Syrup 421

sautéed, baked & grilled fruit

Pears in Honey and Pine Nut Caramel with
Artisanal Cheese 422

Warm Spiced Plums with Honey Cream 422

Baked Pears with Honey and Ginger 423

Maple-Pecan Baked Apples 423

Grilled Peaches with Fresh Raspberry
Sauce 424

Grilled Bananas with Caramel-Chocolate
Sauce and Toasted Pecans 242

Grilled Pineapple with Coconut-Lime
Caramel Sauce 425

crepes & pancakes

Walnut Crepes with Raspberries and
Dried Figs 427–28

Tropical Fruit Crepes with Vanilla Bean and
Rum Butter Sauce 429

Crepes with Brown Sugar Pears and
Chocolate Sauce 430–31

Puffed Pancake with Strawberries 431

Pear and Ricotta Blintzes with
Spiced Maple Butter Sauce 432

poached & fresh fruit

Wine- and Citrus-Poached Pears with
Triple-Crème Cheese 433

Papaya Poached in Cinnamon-Lime
Syrup 433

Pink Grapefruit with Cassis 434

Nectarines, Strawberries, and Melon in
Orange-Honey Spiced Syrup 434

Vodka-Spiked Watermelon with
Crème de Cassis 435

Melon and Blueberry Coupe with
White Wine, Vanilla, and Mint 435

Oranges with Pomegranate Molasses and
Honey 436

Bittersweet Chocolate–Orange
Fondue 437

compotes

Raspberry-Apricot Compote with
Champagne and Lemon Verbena 437

Warm Rhubarb Compote with
Walnut-Coconut Crunch 439

Rhubarb and Strawberry Compote with
Fresh Mint 439

fruit with yogurt, pudding & custard

Ginger Yogurt with Berries and
Crunchy Caramel 440

Cognac-Glazed Dried Apricots with
Cinnamon-Spiced Yogurt 440

Strawberry and Blueberry Summer
Pudding 441

Raspberries with Saba Zabaglione 441

Pink Peppercorn Pavlovas with Strawberries, Vanilla Cream, and Basil Syrup

Apple-Almond Crisp

Crisps typically have a streusel or crumb topping over a baked fruit filling. In this version, a generous measure of sliced almonds gives the topping some extra crunch. **10 to 12 servings**

Topping

1½	cups unbleached all purpose flour
½	cup (packed) golden brown sugar
2	teaspoons ground cinnamon
¾	cup (1½ sticks) chilled salted butter, cut into ½-inch cubes
1	cup sliced almonds

Filling

¾	cup sugar
3	tablespoons unbleached all purpose flour
1	tablespoon finely grated lemon peel
1½	teaspoons ground cinnamon
¾	teaspoon ground nutmeg
8	small Granny Smith apples (about 4½ pounds), peeled, halved, cored, thinly sliced
1½	teaspoons vanilla extract
¾	teaspoon almond extract

TOPPING: Whisk flour, brown sugar, and cinnamon in medium bowl. Add butter and rub in with fingertips until mixture forms small, moist clumps. Mix in almonds; cover and chill until ready to use.

DO AHEAD: *Can be made up to 3 days ahead. Keep chilled.*

FILLING: Preheat oven to 350°F. Butter 13x9x2-inch glass baking dish. Whisk sugar, flour, lemon peel, cinnamon, and nutmeg in large bowl. Mix in apples, then vanilla and almond extracts.

Spoon apple filling into prepared baking dish. Sprinkle topping over. Bake until apples are tender and topping is golden and crisp, about 1 hour. Cool at least 10 minutes; serve warm.

Apple-Cranberry Crisp with Apple Custard Sauce

The natural pectin from the apples and cranberries in this crisp serves to thicken the fruit juices in the filling—no flour or cornstarch required. Cool the crisp until it is lukewarm to give the juices a chance to thicken slightly before serving. **6 servings**

Topping

1	cup unbleached all purpose flour
½	cup old-fashioned oats
½	cup (packed) golden brown sugar
½	teaspoon ground cinnamon
¼	teaspoon salt
½	cup (1 stick) chilled unsalted butter, cut into ½-inch cubes

Filling

2½	pounds large Granny Smith apples, peeled, cored, cut into ⅓-inch-thick wedges
1	cup fresh or frozen cranberries (unthawed)
⅓	cup sugar
2	tablespoons fresh lemon juice
2	teaspoons finely grated lemon peel
½	teaspoon ground cardamom
¼	teaspoon ground nutmeg
	Apple Custard Sauce (see recipe)

TOPPING: Whisk flour, oats, brown sugar, cinnamon, and salt in large bowl. Add butter and rub in with fingertips until moist clumps form.

DO AHEAD: *Can be made 1 day ahead. Cover and chill.*

FILLING: Preheat oven to 375°F. Butter 10-inch-diameter glass pie dish. Place apples in large bowl. Mix in cranberries, sugar, lemon juice, lemon peel, cardamom, and nutmeg. Transfer fruit mixture to prepared dish, mounding slightly in center.

Sprinkle topping over fruit. Bake until apples are tender, about 45 minutes. Cool on rack until lukewarm, about 20 minutes. Serve with Apple Custard Sauce.

Apple Custard Sauce

A splash of apple juice concentrate gives traditional crème anglaise a new identity. If you like, add a cinnamon stick, a whole clove, and a pinch of nutmeg when cooking the sauce to enhance its fall flavor; strain the spices before cooling the sauce. You could churn the cold sauce in an ice-cream machine to make ice cream, an equally delicious accompaniment. **Makes about 2 cups**

6	large egg yolks
1/3	cup sugar
1 1/2	cups whole milk (do not use low fat or nonfat)
3	tablespoons frozen apple juice concentrate, thawed
1/2	teaspoon vanilla extract

Whisk egg yolks and sugar in medium bowl to blend. Bring milk to simmer in medium saucepan. Gradually whisk hot milk into yolk mixture. Return mixture to saucepan. Stir over medium-low heat until custard thickens and leaves path on back of spoon when finger is drawn across, about 5 minutes (do not boil). Strain into bowl. Whisk in apple juice concentrate and vanilla. Chill until cold, about 3 hours.

DO AHEAD: *Can be made 1 day ahead. Cover and keep chilled.*

Technique Tip: Perfect Custard

When making custard sauce it is crucial to follow three simple rules: Use medium-low heat to cook the sauce gently; stir the sauce constantly so that it cooks evenly and doesn't overcook on the bottom of the pan; and never allow the sauce to simmer. Egg yolks give crème anglaise its thick, luxurious texture, but if the sauce is hotter than 180°F, the eggs in the custard will scramble. Use a thermometer to gauge the temperature, making sure it stays below 180°F.

Apricot Crisp

Apricots are highly seasonal fruits, so you'll want to make this crisp in June or July, when they are at their peak; ripe apricots have a fragrant scent and give slightly when pressed. The hazelnuts here should not be toasted or husked. The recipe calls for the topping to be mixed in a stand mixer, but a handheld electric mixer will work just as well. **8 servings**

Topping

1	cup old-fashioned oats
3/4	cup unbleached all purpose flour
1/2	cup (packed) golden brown sugar
1/2	teaspoon salt
1/2	cup (1 stick) chilled unsalted butter, cut into 1/2-inch cubes
3/4	cup chopped hazelnuts

Filling

2 1/2	pounds ripe apricots, halved, pitted, sliced (about 7 cups)
3/4	cup sugar
2	tablespoons quick-cooking tapioca

TOPPING: Using stand mixer fitted with paddle attachment, stir oats, flour, brown sugar, and salt in mixing bowl to blend. Add butter and blend until moist clumps form. Mix in hazelnuts.

DO AHEAD: *Can be made up to 2 days ahead. Place topping in airtight container and chill.*

FILLING: Preheat oven to 400°F. Butter 13-inch oval baking dish. Toss apricots, sugar, and tapioca in large bowl to blend. Let stand 15 minutes, tossing occasionally.

Transfer apricots and accumulated juices to prepared baking dish. Sprinkle topping evenly over apricots. Bake 30 minutes. Reduce heat to 350°F. Bake until topping is golden brown, juices bubble thickly, and apricots are tender when pierced with small sharp knife, about 45 minutes. Let crisp cool 20 minutes.

Spiced Pear-Raspberry Crisp

Pears and raspberries work together beautifully in this easy homespun treat. Not only do their flavors complement each other, but the creamy white pears take on a beautiful color from the raspberries. Make this crisp in the fall, when pears are juicy. Use frozen raspberries that have been picked at the height of summer, then quick-frozen to lock in their flavor and juices. **8 to 10 servings**

Topping

¾   cup unbleached all purpose flour
⅔   cup (packed) golden brown sugar
⅓   cup slivered almonds
2   teaspoons finely grated lemon peel
1   teaspoon ground cardamom
6   tablespoons (¾ stick) chilled unsalted butter, cut into
       ½-inch cubes

Filling

½   cup sugar
2   tablespoons unbleached all purpose flour
1   teaspoon ground cardamom
¼   teaspoon ground nutmeg
       Pinch of salt
2¼   pounds Bosc pears, peeled, quartered, cored, cut into
       1-inch cubes
2   cups frozen raspberries, thawed
1   tablespoon fresh lemon juice

Whipped Cream

½   cup chilled heavy whipping cream
1   teaspoon vanilla extract
1   teaspoon sugar

Crisp, Cobbler, Crumble

The familiar trio of homey fruit desserts—crisps, cobblers, and crumbles—have a lot in common: Each is a baked deep-dish dessert that pairs luscious fruit with some kind of sweet pastry topping, without a bottom crust. But subtle differences set them apart:

A **crisp** has a streusel-like topping that becomes crisp when baked. A **cobbler** traditionally has a biscuit-like topping that resembles cobblestones. A **crumble** is the British version of a crisp, sometimes with oats added to the topping.

TOPPING: Place flour, brown sugar, almonds, lemon peel, and cardamom in processor. Using on/off turns, process until nuts are finely chopped. Add butter. Using on/off turns, process until moist clumps form.

DO AHEAD: *Can be made 1 day ahead. Cover and chill.*

FILLING: Position rack in center of oven; preheat to 350°F. Butter 8x8x2-inch glass baking dish. Place dish on rimmed baking sheet. Mix sugar, flour, cardamom, nutmeg, and salt in large bowl. Add pears; toss to coat. Add berries and lemon juice; toss gently to coat. Transfer to prepared dish.

Sprinkle topping over filling. Bake until liquid thickens and topping is golden, about 55 minutes. Cool 30 minutes.

WHIPPED CREAM: Beat cream, vanilla, and sugar in large bowl until soft peaks form. Serve crisp with whipped cream.

Nectarine and Almond Crisp

This crisp can be assembled in just 20 minutes. It would be luscious topped with whipped cream, ice cream, or lightly sweetened crème fraîche. **8 servings**

Topping

¾	cup unbleached all purpose flour
¼	cup (packed) golden brown sugar
¾	teaspoon ground cardamom
½	teaspoon ground ginger
¼	teaspoon salt
2	ounces almond paste (about ⅓ cup), crumbled
6	tablespoons (¾ stick) chilled unsalted butter, cut into ½-inch cubes
1½	cups sliced almonds

Filling

2½	to 2¾ pounds nectarines, halved, pitted, each half cut into 4 wedges (about 8 cups)
½	cup apricot preserves
¼	cup (packed) golden brown sugar
1	tablespoon unbleached all purpose flour
½	teaspoon ground cardamom
½	teaspoon ground ginger

TOPPING: Blend flour, brown sugar, cardamom, ginger, and salt in processor. Add almond paste and process until fine crumbs form. Add butter; using on/off turns, process until moist clumps form. Transfer to medium bowl. Mix in almonds.

FILLING: Preheat oven to 400°F. Butter 11x7x2-inch glass baking dish or deep-dish pie dish. Toss nectarines, apricot preserves, brown sugar, flour, cardamom, and ginger in large bowl to coat.

Transfer nectarine filling to prepared dish; sprinkle topping over. Bake crisp until topping is golden, nectarines are tender, and juices are bubbling around edges, about 40 minutes. Cool at least 20 minutes before serving. Serve crisp warm or at room temperature.

Classic Peach Cobbler

The ultimate down-home summer dessert is wonderfully simple to make. The peaches don't need to be peeled and the filling is mixed right in the baking dish. The biscuit topping can be prepared in just a few minutes without any special equipment. **8 servings**

Filling
4	pounds peaches, halved, pitted, cut into wedges
¾	cup plus 2 tablespoons sugar
¼	cup unbleached all purpose flour
2	tablespoons fresh lemon juice
¼	teaspoon vanilla extract
¼	teaspoon ground cinnamon

Topping
2¼	cups unbleached all purpose flour
6	tablespoons sugar, divided
1	tablespoon baking powder
¾	teaspoon salt
¼	cup (½ stick) chilled unsalted butter, cut into ½-inch cubes
¼	cup chilled non-hydrogenated solid vegetable shortening, cut into ½-inch pieces
¾	cup plus 2 tablespoons chilled buttermilk
1	large egg, beaten to blend
1	teaspoon vanilla extract
	Vanilla ice cream

FILLING: Position rack in center of oven and preheat to 400°F. Mix all ingredients in 13x9x2-inch glass baking dish. Bake 15 minutes (juices will be hot but not bubbling).

TOPPING: Meanwhile, mix flour, 4 tablespoons sugar, baking powder, and salt in large bowl. Using fingertips, rub in butter and shortening until mixture resembles coarse meal. Whisk buttermilk, egg, and vanilla in 2-cup glass measuring cup to blend. Add to flour mixture and stir until soft dough forms.

Remove fruit from oven. Spoon dough over hot filling in 12 mounds, spacing evenly. Sprinkle with remaining 2 tablespoons sugar. Bake until juices thicken and topping is golden, about 40 minutes. Cool on rack at least 15 minutes.

Serve warm with vanilla ice cream.

Individual Plum Cobblers with Hazelnut Topping

This recipe gives everyone his or her own mini cobbler, though you could also make one large cobbler in an 8-inch-square baking dish. **Makes 8**

Filling
2	to 2¼ pounds red-skinned plums, halved, pitted, each half cut into 4 wedges
⅔	cup sugar
2	tablespoons quick-cooking tapioca
½	teaspoon ground cinnamon
2	tablespoons (¼ stick) chilled unsalted butter, cut into ½-inch cubes

Topping
¾	cup unbleached all purpose flour
2	tablespoons (packed) golden brown sugar
1	teaspoon baking powder
¼	teaspoon salt
3	tablespoons chilled unsalted butter, cut into ½-inch cubes
½	cup hazelnuts, toasted, chopped
½	cup chilled heavy whipping cream
1	tablespoon sugar
	Vanilla ice cream

FILLING: Preheat oven to 375°F. Butter eight ⅔-cup soufflé dishes or custard cups. Combine plums, sugar, tapioca, and cinnamon in large bowl; toss to blend. Let stand 15 minutes, tossing occasionally. Divide among prepared dishes (dishes will be full). Place on rimmed baking sheet. Dot fruit with butter. Bake until plums are tender and fruit bubbles thickly, about 45 minutes. Cool in dishes.

DO AHEAD: *Can be made 4 hours ahead. Let stand at room temperature.*

TOPPING: Preheat oven to 375°F. Whisk flour, brown sugar, baking powder, and salt in medium bowl. Add butter; rub in with fingertips until mixture resembles coarse meal. Mix in nuts. Gradually add cream, stirring with fork until batter holds together.

Drop large spoonful of batter atop fruit in each dish, dividing equally. Sprinkle with 1 tablespoon sugar.

Bake until biscuit topping is golden, about 25 minutes. Cool at least 15 minutes. Serve warm topped with ice cream.

Peach, Plum, and Blackberry Cobbler

Classic, homey cobblers feature biscuits baked right on top of the fruit. This one—bursting with summer fruits and topped with warm, tender biscuits and a spiced streusel—would be a great addition to a picnic or barbecue. Quick-cooking tapioca thickens the fruit juices in the cobbler to form a glossy sauce (it works well in pies and crisps, too); it's found in the baking aisle of most supermarkets. Don't use regular tapioca pearls, which are much larger and won't soften and dissolve properly. For tips on peeling peaches, see page 35.

6 servings

Filling

6	peaches, peeled, halved, pitted, sliced
2	red plums, halved, pitted, sliced
1	½-pint container fresh blackberries or 1½ cups frozen blackberries (do not thaw)
⅔	cup sugar
3	tablespoons quick-cooking tapioca

Biscuits

¾	cup unbleached all purpose flour
1	tablespoon sugar
1	teaspoon baking powder
¼	teaspoon salt
1	teaspoon finely grated lemon peel
3	tablespoons chilled unsalted butter, cut into ½-inch cubes
6	tablespoons chilled heavy whipping cream

Topping

3	tablespoons (packed) golden brown sugar
2	tablespoons unbleached all-purpose flour
½	teaspoon ground cinnamon
¼	teaspoon ground ginger
	Pinch of ground cloves
2	tablespoons (¼ stick) chilled unsalted butter, cut into ½-inch cubes
	Sweetened whipped cream

FILLING: Preheat oven to 400°F. Place peaches, plums, blackberries, sugar, and tapioca in 8x8x2-inch glass baking dish; toss to coat. Bake until fruit is tender and juices are bubbling thickly, about 50 minutes. Cool 10 minutes.

BISCUITS: Meanwhile, whisk flour, sugar, baking powder, and salt in medium bowl. Add lemon peel and butter; using fingertips, rub in until mixture resembles coarse meal. Add cream; stir until moist clumps form. Gather dough into ball. Using floured hands, pat out dough on floured surface to 6-inch square; cut into 6 equal rectangles.

TOPPING: Mix brown sugar, flour, cinnamon, ginger, and cloves in small bowl. Add butter; using fingertips, rub in until moist clumps form.

Place dough rectangles atop hot cobbler. Sprinkle topping over. Bake until biscuits are golden, about 25 minutes. Cool 30 minutes. Serve with whipped cream.

Cherry-Lime Cobbler with Vanilla–Crème Fraîche Biscuits

In this cobbler, the biscuits are baked separately and placed on the filling just before serving. You can also split the biscuits as you would shortcakes and top the biscuit halves with the filling. **6 servings**

Filling

½	cup (packed) golden brown sugar
4	teaspoons cornstarch
	Pinch of salt
½	cup water
6	cups whole pitted Bing cherries or other dark sweet cherries (from about 2¾ pounds unpitted cherries)
1	tablespoon fresh lime juice
¾	teaspoon finely grated lime peel

Biscuits

1¾	cups unbleached all purpose flour
¼	cup plus 1 tablespoon sugar
1	tablespoon baking powder
¼	teaspoon salt
1	cup crème fraîche or sour cream
1½	teaspoons vanilla paste or 2 teaspoons vanilla extract
¼	teaspoon finely grated lime peel
	Milk

FILLING: Position 1 rack in top third and 1 rack in bottom third of oven; preheat to 450°F. Whisk brown sugar, cornstarch, and salt in large ovenproof skillet. Add ½ cup water and stir over medium heat until sugar and cornstarch dissolve. Add cherries; increase heat to medium-high and bring to boil, scraping sides of skillet and stirring frequently. Reduce heat to medium-low; simmer until mixture thickens, about 2 minutes. Remove from heat. Stir in lime juice and lime peel.

BISCUITS: Whisk flour, ¼ cup sugar, baking powder, and salt in medium bowl. Whisk crème fraîche, vanilla, and lime peel in small bowl. Add crème fraîche mixture to dry ingredients; stir with fork just until dough begins to come together. Turn dough out onto floured surface and knead just until dough holds together, about 6 turns. Gather dough into round; pat out to ½-inch thickness. Using 3-inch-diameter biscuit cutter or cookie cutter dipped in flour, cut out dough rounds. Gather dough scraps together; pat out to ½-inch thickness and cut out more rounds for 6 biscuits total. Transfer rounds to rimmed baking sheet; brush tops lightly with milk, then sprinkle with remaining 1 tablespoon sugar.

Place skillet with cherries in bottom third of oven; place baking sheet with biscuits in top third of oven. Bake until cherries are bubbling and biscuits are golden, about 17 minutes.

Divide warm cherries among 6 bowls; top each with 1 biscuit and serve.

Pear Cobbler with Dried Blueberries and Stone-Ground Corn Biscuits

Dried blueberries and apple juice add understated sweetness to the filling. If you have a sweet tooth, increase the sugar by 1 or 2 tablespoons. Medium-grind stone-ground cornmeal adds an appetizing texture to the biscuits. It can be found at many supermarkets and at natural foods stores. **8 to 10 servings**

Biscuits

1	cup unbleached all purpose flour
⅔	cup medium-grind stone-ground cornmeal
¼	cup plus 3 tablespoons sugar
2	teaspoons baking powder
½	teaspoon coarse kosher salt
6	tablespoons (¾ stick) chilled unsalted butter, cut into ½-inch cubes, plus 3 tablespoons unsalted butter, melted
⅔	cup chilled heavy whipping cream

Filling

6	pounds firm but ripe Seckel, Taylor's Gold, or Bosc pears, peeled, cored, cut into ½- to ¾-inch pieces (about 12 cups)
1	cup apple juice
¼	cup fresh lemon juice
3	tablespoons cornstarch
1	teaspoon (scant) coarse kosher salt
½	teaspoon freshly grated nutmeg
2	tablespoons (¼ stick) chilled unsalted butter, diced
1½	cups dried wild blueberries
	Vanilla ice cream

BISCUITS: Whisk flour, cornmeal, ¼ cup sugar, baking powder, and coarse salt in large bowl. Add chilled butter; rub in with fingertips until mixture resembles coarse meal. Add cream; stir just until moistened. Gather dough together; form into 8-inch-long log. Cut log crosswise into eight 1-inch-thick rounds. Spread remaining 3 tablespoons sugar on plate. Dip 1 cut side of each biscuit into melted butter, then dip buttered side in sugar. Place biscuits, sugared side up, on platter; sprinkle any remaining sugar over top. Cover and chill.

FILLING: Preheat oven to 375°F. Butter 13x9x2-inch glass baking dish. Place pears, apple juice, lemon juice, cornstarch, coarse salt, and nutmeg in large bowl; toss to coat. Let stand 10 minutes, tossing occasionally.

Transfer pear filling to prepared dish. Dot with diced butter. Cover dish with foil. Bake until pears are almost tender, about 50 minutes. Remove dish from oven; stir dried blueberries into pear filling. Place biscuits atop filling. Continue to bake cobbler uncovered until filling is bubbling thickly, biscuits are pale golden, and tester inserted into biscuits comes out clean, about 35 minutes longer (biscuits may look cracked). Cool 30 minutes. Serve warm with ice cream.

Blackberry Cobblers with Ginger-Cardamom Biscuits

Cardamom lends exotic intrigue to this classic American summer dessert. This recipe can be prepared as one big cobbler, using a 13x9-inch oval baking dish or a 2-quart baking dish and arranging the biscuits over the filling. **Makes 6**

Filling
6	cups blackberries
¾	cup sugar
¼	cup unbleached all purpose flour
2	tablespoons fresh lemon juice

Biscuits
1½	cups unbleached all purpose flour
4	tablespoons sugar, divided
2	teaspoons baking powder
1	teaspoon ground cardamom
½	teaspoon salt
1	3-inch piece vanilla bean, split lengthwise
6	tablespoons (¾ stick) chilled unsalted butter, cut into ½-inch cubes
⅔	cup chilled heavy whipping cream
2	tablespoons finely grated peeled fresh ginger
	Additional heavy whipping cream

FILLING: Preheat oven to 350°F. Butter six 1¼-cup ramekins, custard cups, or baking dishes. Toss blackberries, sugar, flour, and lemon juice in large bowl to blend. Let stand while preparing biscuits, tossing occasionally.

BISCUITS: Whisk flour, 3 tablespoons sugar, baking powder, cardamom, and salt in another large bowl. Using small sharp knife, scrape seeds from vanilla bean into flour mixture (reserve bean for another use). Add butter; using fingertips, rub in until coarse meal forms. Stir ⅔ cup cream and ginger in glass measuring cup to blend. Pour cream mixture over flour mixture and stir with fork just until dough forms. Gather dough into ball; transfer to lightly floured work surface. Pat out dough to ⅓-inch-thick round. Using floured 3-inch-diameter cutter, cut out rounds for biscuits. Gather dough scraps; press out to ⅓-inch thickness and cut out additional rounds for 6 biscuits total.

Spoon filling into prepared dishes, dividing evenly. Top each with a biscuit. Brush biscuits lightly with cream; sprinkle each with ½ teaspoon sugar. Place cobblers on rimmed baking sheet and bake until filling bubbles thickly, tester inserted into center of biscuits comes out clean, and tops of biscuits are golden brown and firm all over, about 45 minutes. Cool 10 minutes and serve.

Pear and Maple Crumble

This easy crumble is sure to become a staple in your fall and winter dessert lineup: You just toss it together and it yields seemingly magical results. Sweet, floral Anjou pears are ideal for the filling, but Bartlett pears would be fine as a substitute. Typically, crumbles are served with vanilla ice cream or whipped cream, but in this case, the subtle tang of sour cream perfectly balances the sweetness of the brown sugar in the topping and the pure maple syrup in the filling. **6 to 8 servings**

Topping
1	cup unbleached all purpose flour
1	cup walnuts
⅔	cup (packed) golden brown sugar
½	cup (1 stick) chilled unsalted butter, cut into ½-inch cubes

Filling
3½	pounds firm but ripe Anjou pears, peeled, quartered, cored, cut into ½-inch cubes
⅔	cup pure maple syrup
½	cup raisins
2	tablespoons unbleached all purpose flour
2	tablespoons fresh lemon juice
1	tablespoon finely chopped crystallized ginger
	Sour cream

TOPPING: Combine flour, walnuts, brown sugar, and butter in processor. Using on/off turns, process until walnuts are coarsely chopped and small moist clumps form. Transfer topping to medium bowl. Cover and chill until firm, about 1 hour.

FILLING: Position rack in center of oven and preheat to 350°F. Place pears, maple syrup, raisins, flour, lemon juice, and ginger in large bowl; toss to coat. Let stand 15 minutes, tossing occasionally.

Transfer pear mixture to 13x9x2-inch baking dish; sprinkle topping over. Bake crumble until pears are tender, juices bubble thickly, and topping is golden and crisp, about 30 minutes. Let stand at least 10 minutes. Serve warm with sour cream.

Individual Rhubarb and Orange Crumbles

Crumbles are traditional English desserts that have a sweet, streusel-like topping over a warm, bubbling mixture of sweetened fruit. They can be prepared with almost any fruit, but this springtime rendition features rhubarb accented with orange zest and juice and includes almonds in the topping for extra crunch. **Makes 6**

Topping

²⁄₃	cup whole wheat flour
½	cup whole almonds
5	tablespoons sugar
5	tablespoons (packed) golden brown sugar
7	tablespoons chilled unsalted butter, cut into ½-inch cubes
²⁄₃	cup chopped toasted almonds

Filling

8	cups ½-inch pieces trimmed fresh rhubarb (about 2 pounds)
½	cup orange juice
6	tablespoons sugar, divided
1	tablespoon finely grated orange peel
1	tablespoon unbleached all purpose flour
	Vanilla ice cream or sweetened whipped cream

TOPPING: Combine flour, whole almonds, and both sugars in processor. Using on/off turns, blend mixture until almonds are finely ground. Add butter; using on/off turns, process until moist clumps form. Transfer to medium bowl. Mix in chopped toasted almonds.

DO AHEAD: *Can be made 1 day ahead. Cover and chill.*

FILLING: Preheat oven to 400°F. Combine rhubarb, orange juice, 5 tablespoons sugar, and orange peel in heavy large saucepan. Bring to simmer over medium heat. Cook until rhubarb is tender but still intact, stirring occasionally, about 10 minutes. Using slotted spoon, transfer rhubarb to large bowl, leaving excess juices in saucepan. Blend flour and remaining 1 tablespoon sugar in small bowl; whisk into juices in saucepan. Stir over medium-low heat until mixture boils and thickens, about 1 minute. Return rhubarb to saucepan; toss to coat. Divide warm rhubarb mixture evenly among six 1¼-cup custard cups.

Sprinkle topping over filling in each cup, dividing equally. Bake crumbles until topping is deep golden brown, about 20 minutes. Cool on rack 15 minutes. Serve warm with ice cream or sweetened whipped cream.

Sweet-Cherry Clafouti

Cherry clafouti is a classic French country fruit-filled dessert. The texture of the filling is dense, a cross between a custard and a cake. **8 servings**

1	cup sugar, divided
½	cup chilled mascarpone cheese or crème fraîche
½	cup heavy whipping cream, divided
2	tablespoons kirsch (clear cherry brandy), divided
1	pound frozen pitted sweet cherries, thawed
3	large eggs
1	vanilla bean, split lengthwise
¾	cup sour cream
½	cup whole milk
6	tablespoons unbleached all purpose flour

Using electric mixer, beat 2 tablespoons sugar, mascarpone, ¼ cup cream, and 1 tablespoon kirsch in medium bowl until peaks form. Cover and chill topping until ready to use.

Preheat oven to 375°F. Butter 10-inch-diameter glass pie dish; sprinkle with 1 tablespoon sugar to coat. Place cherries in single layer in dish. Place eggs and ¾ cup sugar in large bowl. Scrape in seeds from vanilla bean; reserve bean for another use. Whisk until blended and frothy. Whisk in sour cream, milk, remain-ing ¼ cup cream, and remaining 1 tablespoon kirsch. Sift flour over and whisk to blend. Pour batter over cherries. Sprinkle with remaining 1 tablespoon sugar.

Bake clafouti until puffed, golden brown, and set in center, about 35 minutes. Serve clafouti warm or at room temperature with mascarpone topping.

Market Tip: Rhubarb…

… is actually a vegetable, but it's usually treated like a fruit and eaten in desserts. At the market, look for thin, deep-red stalks with just a tinge of green. They'll give the most colorful, tender, and tasty results. Avoid the leaves, which are toxic.

Pear Clafouti

Cherries are traditionally used to make clafouti, *but when pears make their debut in the autumn, they are the perfect seasonal stand-in.* **8 servings**

5   tablespoons unsalted butter, melted, divided
4   Anjou pears (about 1¾ pounds), peeled, halved, cored,
        cut crosswise into thin slices
4   large eggs
1   cup whole milk
½   cup sugar
6   tablespoons unbleached all purpose flour
2   tablespoons brandy
1   teaspoon finely grated lemon peel
1   teaspoon vanilla extract
¼   teaspoon salt

Preheat oven to 325°F. Generously butter 10-inch-diameter glass pie dish. Heat 1 tablespoon melted butter in heavy large skillet over medium-high heat. Add pears and sauté until soft and beginning to brown, about 8 minutes. Cool pears in skillet.

Blend eggs, milk, sugar, flour, brandy, lemon peel, vanilla, and salt in blender until batter is smooth. Add remaining 4 tablespoons melted butter and blend to combine. Arrange pears in prepared dish. Pour batter over.

Bake clafouti until set and puffed and brown on top, about 55 minutes. Cool at least 15 minutes. Serve clafouti warm or at room temperature.

Brandied Plum Clafoutis

These warm, pudding-like individual desserts are perfect for those last-of-the-season plums. If you like, sift some powdered sugar over the clafoutis *before serving.* **Makes 6**

4   tablespoons (½ stick) salted butter, melted, divided
1½   pounds plums, pitted; 1 plum sliced thinly, the rest cut into
        ½-inch cubes
7   tablespoons plus ½ cup sugar, divided
4   tablespoons brandy, divided
¼   cup thawed frozen orange juice concentrate
½   cup (about) heavy whipping cream
3   tablespoons unbleached all purpose flour
2   large eggs

Preheat oven to 375°F. Brush six 5-inch-diameter, 1-inch-deep ramekins with 1 tablespoon melted butter; place ramekins on rimmed baking sheet. Cook cubed plums, 4 tablespoons sugar, and 2 tablespoons brandy in medium skillet over medium-high heat until juices bubble thickly, stirring often, about 5 minutes. Cover; cook until plums are just tender, stirring occasionally, 2 to 3 minutes.

Using slotted spoon, divide cubed plum mixture among prepared ramekins. Add orange juice concentrate to juices in skillet; stir to blend. Pour into 1-cup measuring cup. Add remaining 2 tablespoons brandy, then enough cream to measure ¾ cup total.

Whisk ½ cup plus 2 tablespoons sugar and flour in large bowl. Whisk in cream mixture, eggs, and remaining 3 tablespoons melted butter. Spoon batter over plum mixture in ramekins. Top with plum slices; sprinkle with remaining 1 tablespoon sugar, dividing equally.

Bake clafoutis until puffed and crusty and center is just set, about 30 minutes. Cool 15 minutes and serve warm.

Strawberry Shortcakes with White Chocolate Mousse

Two simple twists—adding white chocolate to whipped cream and bittersweet chocolate to shortcakes—spruce up the classic strawberry dessert. Macerating the strawberries (tossing them with sugar and Grand Marnier and letting them marinate) draws out their flavorful juices, so be sure to give the process plenty of time. **Makes 6**

Cakes

1½   cups unbleached all purpose flour
3   tablespoons plus 1 teaspoon sugar
2   teaspoons baking powder
½   teaspoon baking soda
¼   teaspoon salt
6   tablespoons (¾ stick) chilled unsalted butter, cut into
         ½-inch cubes
½   cup plus 1 tablespoon chilled buttermilk
3   ounces bittersweet or semisweet chocolate, chopped

Fruit and Topping

2   1-pint containers strawberries, hulled, quartered
¼   cup sugar
1   tablespoon Grand Marnier or other orange liqueur

     White Chocolate Mousse (see recipe)

CAKES: Preheat oven to 425°F. Line baking sheet with parchment paper. Blend flour, 3 tablespoons sugar, baking powder, baking soda, and salt in processor. Add butter; using on/off turns, process until mixture resembles coarse meal. Add ½ cup buttermilk; process until moist clumps form. Add chopped chocolate; using on/off turns, process just to evenly distribute.

Turn dough out onto lightly floured work surface. Dust dough lightly with flour; gently press to ½-inch thickness. Using 3¼-inch-diameter cutter, cut out rounds for shortcakes. Gather dough scraps and press to ½-inch thickness; cut out additional rounds for 6 shortcakes total. Transfer cakes to prepared baking sheet. Brush cakes with remaining 1 tablespoon buttermilk. Sprinkle with remaining 1 teaspoon sugar.

Bake cakes until golden and tester inserted into centers comes out clean, about 15 minutes. Transfer to rack and cool.

DO AHEAD: *Can be made 8 hours ahead. Let stand at room temperature.*

FRUIT AND TOPPING: Toss strawberries, sugar, and Grand Marnier in large bowl. Let stand at room temperature until juices form, tossing occasionally, about 1 hour.

Using serrated knife, cut cakes horizontally in half. Place 1 cake bottom on each of 6 plates. Spoon ⅓ cup White Chocolate Mousse over each. Spoon some of strawberry topping over, then cover each with cake top. Spoon dollops of mousse over shortcakes, then spoon more strawberry topping over each and serve.

White Chocolate Mousse

There are just two ingredients in this mousse, and two keys to creating its ethereal fluffy texture: First, the chocolate mixture has to be cool before it's folded into the whipped cream; if it's too warm, the heat will deflate the cream's foamy texture. Second, the mousse needs time to chill; the chocolate thickens the cream and locks in the airy foam. The mousse would also be delicious served with fresh berries or sandwiched between chocolate wafer cookies. **Makes about 4 cups**

8   ounces high-quality white chocolate (such as Lindt or
         Perugina), chopped
1⅔   cups chilled heavy whipping cream, divided

Stir white chocolate and ⅔ cup cream in heavy medium saucepan over low heat until chocolate is melted. Transfer chocolate mixture to large bowl. Let stand until mixture is cool and just beginning to thicken, stirring occasionally, about 30 minutes. Beat remaining 1 cup chilled cream in medium bowl until firm peaks form. Fold whipped cream into cool chocolate mixture in 2 additions. Cover and chill mousse at least 2 hours.

DO AHEAD: *Can be made 1 day ahead. Keep chilled.*

Lemon-Blueberry Shortcakes

Lemon juice and fresh blueberries make this a lovely summery dessert, but it can be prepared at any time of year with frozen blueberries. The lemon cream is ultra-simple to make. **Makes 6**

Berry Compote

7	cups wild blueberries or regular blueberries, or 16 ounces frozen wild blueberries or regular blueberries (do not thaw)
1/3	cup sugar
1	tablespoon cornstarch
1	tablespoon fresh lemon juice

Lemon Cream

1/4	cup fresh lemon juice
1/4	cup sugar
2	large egg yolks
1	cup chilled heavy whipping cream

Cakes

1/3	cup sugar
1	tablespoon finely grated lemon peel
1½	cups unbleached all purpose flour
2	teaspoons baking powder
½	teaspoon salt
6	tablespoons (¾ stick) chilled unsalted butter, cut into ½-inch cubes
1/3	cup plus 1 tablespoon chilled heavy whipping cream
2	tablespoons fresh lemon juice

BERRY COMPOTE: Cook blueberries, sugar, cornstarch, and lemon juice in heavy large saucepan over medium heat, stirring occasionally, until mixture thickens and bubbles, about 10 minutes. Continue to cook 1 minute, stirring constantly. Cool.

LEMON CREAM: Whisk lemon juice, sugar, and egg yolks in heavy small saucepan over medium-high heat until mixture is thick and creamy, about 2 minutes. Transfer lemon curd to bowl and set aside to cool completely.

DO AHEAD: *Berry compote and lemon curd can be made 2 days ahead. Cover separately and chill.*

Whip cream in large bowl until stiff peaks form. Fold half of cream into lemon curd to lighten; fold in remaining cream. Cover and chill lemon cream until ready to assemble shortcakes.

CAKES: Preheat oven to 400°F. Place sugar and lemon peel in large bowl. Press with back of spoon to release oils from peel. Reserve 2 tablespoons lemon sugar in small bowl. Add flour, baking powder, and salt to lemon sugar in large bowl; whisk to blend. Add butter and rub in with fingertips until mixture resembles coarse meal. Mix 1/3 cup cream and lemon juice in small bowl. Pour cream mixture over flour mixture and stir with fork to form dough. Gather dough into ball; press out to 1-inch thickness on lightly floured surface. Using 2½-inch-diameter cutter, cut out rounds. Gather dough scraps; press out to 1-inch thickness and cut out additional rounds to form 6 shortcakes total. Transfer cake rounds to heavy baking sheet.

Brush cake tops with remaining 1 tablespoon cream and sprinkle with reserved lemon sugar. Bake shortcakes until just golden brown, about 15 minutes. Cool slightly. Using serrated knife, cut warm or room-temperature shortcakes in half horizontally. Place bottom halves, cut side up, on each of 6 plates. Top cake halves with berry compote and lemon cream. Cover with cake tops and serve.

Peach Melba Shortcakes

Legendary French chef Auguste Escoffier created the classic peach Melba—vanilla ice cream topped with poached peaches and raspberry sauce—to honor Australian soprano Dame Nellie Melba. In this updated version, peaches and raspberries are layered between airy sponge cakes, and whipped cream replaces the ice cream. (You could also try it with nectarines and blackberries.) The tartlet pans used in this recipe can be found at cookware stores. If you don't have them, you can use mini cheesecake pans or make one large shortcake in an 8-inch-diameter tart pan and then cut the cake into wedges. **Makes 6**

Cakes

> Melted butter
½   cup (1 stick) unsalted butter, room temperature
½   cup sugar
2   large eggs
1   teaspoon vanilla extract
1¼ cups cake flour
1   teaspoon baking powder
½   teaspoon baking soda
¼   teaspoon salt
½   cup buttermilk

Sauce and Topping

1   12-ounce package frozen raspberries, thawed
¼   cup sugar
4   large peaches, peeled, halved, pitted, sliced
1   ½-pint container raspberries
6   tablespoons sugar, divided
1½ cups chilled heavy whipping cream
2   teaspoons vanilla extract
> Powdered sugar

CAKES: Preheat oven to 350°F. Brush six 4-inch-diameter tartlet pans with 1⅛-inch-high sides and removable bottoms with melted butter. Place pans on rimmed baking sheet. Using electric mixer, beat butter and sugar in large bowl until light and fluffy, about 2 minutes. Add eggs 1 at a time, beating well after each addition. Beat in vanilla. Sift flour, baking powder, baking soda, and salt over mixture in bowl. Beat until almost blended, then add buttermilk and beat just until combined. Divide batter among prepared pans (about scant ½ cup each).

Shortcake Tips

The ideal shortcakes are flaky, tender, and fluffy. Here's how to achieve that state of shortcake perfection.

FLAKY: Use very cold butter or shortening and chilled liquid, such as milk, cream, or buttermilk. Gently mix the butter or shortening with the flour just until the mixture resembles coarse meal and pea-size pieces of butter or shortening are visible—the water in the butter (plus water in the dough) releases steam during baking, which lifts the dough and makes the shortcakes flaky.

TENDER: Use a gentle hand when mixing liquid into the dough. Once it begins to clump together, pat the dough out (don't worry if it doesn't look perfectly smooth); never knead shortcake dough as you would bread dough.

FLUFFY: When cutting shortcakes with a biscuit cutter, press the cutter through the dough without twisting it; twisting seals the edges and prevents the shortcakes from rising. Alternately, use a *very sharp* knife to cut out squares or triangles.

Bake cakes until golden and tester inserted into centers comes out clean, about 25 minutes. Transfer pans to rack; cool 5 minutes. Push up bottoms of pans to release cakes. Cool cakes on rack.

DO AHEAD: *Can be made 1 day ahead. Cover and store at room temperature.*

SAUCE AND TOPPING: Puree raspberries in processor. Strain into medium bowl, pressing on solids to release sauce. Discard solids in strainer. Stir sugar into raspberry puree.

DO AHEAD: *Berry sauce can be made 1 day ahead. Cover and chill.*

Combine peaches, fresh raspberries, and 4 tablespoons sugar in medium bowl; toss to coat. Let stand until juices form, about 30 minutes. Beat cream, vanilla, and remaining 2 tablespoons sugar in medium bowl until peaks form.

Using serrated knife, cut cakes in half horizontally. Lightly sift powdered sugar over cake tops. Place 1 cake bottom on each of 6 plates. Gently toss fruit mixture. Top each cake bottom with fruit mixture, dividing equally. Spoon whipped cream atop each, then cover with cake tops. Spoon raspberry sauce around shortcakes and serve.

Oatmeal Shortcakes with Spiced Plums

A handful of oats adds texture to decadent shortcakes. The key to making the delicate, tender cakes is to handle the dough as little as possible; once the milk is added, stir gently just until the dry ingredients are moistened and come together as a dough. **Makes 6**

Cakes

2	cups unbleached all purpose flour
½	cup old-fashioned oats
½	cup (packed) golden brown sugar
1	tablespoon baking powder
½	teaspoon salt
½	cup (1 stick) chilled unsalted butter, cut into ½-inch cubes
⅔	cup whole milk
2	teaspoons sugar

Plums

1	pound firm but ripe plums (about 6), halved, pitted, each half cut into 4 wedges
⅓	cup sugar
2	teaspoons fresh lemon juice
½	teaspoon ground ginger
⅛	teaspoon ground cinnamon
2	tablespoons (¼ stick) unsalted butter
¾	cup chilled heavy whipping cream
2	tablespoons powdered sugar

CAKES: Preheat oven to 425°F. Line large baking sheet with parchment paper. Whisk flour, oats, brown sugar, baking powder, and salt in large bowl. Add butter; using fingertips, rub in until mixture resembles coarse meal. Add milk; stir just until dough forms.

Divide dough into 6 equal portions; form six 2½-inch-diameter biscuits. Place biscuits on prepared baking sheet, spacing 3 inches apart. Sprinkle with 2 teaspoons sugar. Bake biscuits until golden and tester inserted into centers comes out clean, about 20 minutes. Transfer to rack.

DO AHEAD: *Can be made 8 hours ahead. Cool completely. Store airtight at room temperature.*

PLUMS: Combine plums, sugar, lemon juice, ginger, and cinnamon in heavy medium saucepan. Cook over medium heat until plums release their juices but are still firm, stirring occasionally, about 4 minutes. Add butter; stir until melted. Cool slightly.

Using electric mixer, beat cream and powdered sugar in large bowl until peaks form. Using serrated knife, slice off top ⅓ of biscuits. Transfer biscuit bottoms to each of 6 plates. Spoon half of plum mixture over biscuits. Spoon whipped cream atop plum mixture. Spoon remaining plum mixture atop cream, dividing equally. Place biscuit tops over and serve immediately.

Pear-Cornmeal Shortcakes with Oven-Roasted Pears

Traditionally, shortcakes are filled with sweetened, uncooked fresh fruit, so the oven-roasted pears and cranberries in this recipe break some rules. If you don't have a 2¾-inch-diameter biscuit cutter, use a sharp knife to cut out six square shortcakes. **Makes 6**

Pears

4	firm but ripe Anjou or Bosc pears (about 1¾ pounds), peeled, halved, cored, each half cut into 6 wedges
½	cup apricot preserves
6	tablespoons (packed) dark brown sugar
2	tablespoons fresh lemon juice
1½	tablespoons water
½	teaspoon ground cinnamon
¾	cup fresh or frozen cranberries (do not thaw)

Cakes

1¼	cups unbleached all purpose flour
½	cup yellow cornmeal
3	tablespoons sugar
1¼	teaspoons baking powder
½	teaspoon salt
¼	teaspoon baking soda
6	tablespoons (¾ stick) chilled unsalted butter, cut into ½-inch cubes
6	tablespoons chilled buttermilk
1	large egg, beaten to blend

Whipped Cream

1¼	cups chilled heavy whipping cream
¼	cup powdered sugar

PEARS: Preheat oven to 400°F. Combine pears, preserves, sugar, lemon juice, 1½ tablespoons water, and cinnamon in 13x9x2-inch glass baking dish; toss to coat. Cover dish with foil and roast until pears are tender, stirring occasionally, about 40 minutes. Uncover. Mix in cranberries and continue baking until cranberries are tender but still hold their shape, about 15 minutes. Cool. Maintain oven temperature.

CAKES: Line baking sheet with parchment paper. Blend flour, cornmeal, sugar, baking powder, salt, and baking soda in processor. Add butter; using on/off turns, blend until butter is cut into pea-size pieces. Add buttermilk; using on/off turns, blend until moist clumps form. Pat out dough on floured surface to scant ¾-inch thickness. Using 2¾-inch-diameter cutter, cut out 4 rounds. Gather dough scraps; pat out to scant ¾-inch thickness. Cut out 2 more rounds.

Arrange rounds on prepared sheet; brush with beaten egg. Bake until golden brown and tester inserted into centers comes out clean, about 15 minutes.

WHIPPED CREAM: Beat cream and powdered sugar in medium bowl until peaks form.

Using serrated knife, cut cakes horizontally in half. Place bottoms on each of 6 plates. Top with pear mixture. Spoon whipped cream over, cover with cake tops, and serve.

More to Try

The cornmeal adds good texture to the shortcakes—they're like rich, fluffy cornbread biscuits with a bit of crunch, and would be delicious with just butter and honey. The roasted pear mixture can stand equally well on its own; try it warm with vanilla ice cream.

Floating Islands with Lemon-Scented Custard Sauce and Raspberries

In the classic French dessert, the "sea" is a lovely vanilla custard sauce and the "islands" are soft, poached meringues. Here, the meringues are baked, forming a light crust for added texture and delicate, golden wisps of color. The traditional vanilla sauce is dressed up with a little lemon and the dessert is garnished with fresh raspberries. **6 servings**

Sauce

1	cup heavy whipping cream
½	cup whole milk
6	large egg yolks
⅓	cup sugar
3	tablespoons fresh lemon juice
2	teaspoons finely grated lemon peel

Meringues

½	cup egg whites (about 4 large), room temperature Pinch of salt
⅔	cup sugar
6	paper-thin lemon slices
2	6-ounce containers fresh raspberries

SAUCE: Bring cream and milk to simmer in heavy medium saucepan. Using whisk, beat egg yolks and sugar in medium bowl until light, about 2 minutes. Gradually whisk hot cream mixture into yolks. Return mixture to saucepan and stir over medium-low heat until custard thickens and leaves path on back of spoon when finger is drawn across, about 3 minutes (do not boil). Pour custard into another medium bowl. Stir in lemon juice and lemon peel. Cool slightly, then chill uncovered until cold.

DO AHEAD: *Can be made 2 days ahead. Cover and keep chilled.*

MERINGUES: Preheat oven to 350°F. Generously butter six ¾-cup soufflé dishes, then sprinkle with sugar. Place dishes on baking sheet. Using electric mixer, beat egg whites with salt in large bowl until soft peaks form. Gradually beat in ⅔ cup sugar. Continue beating until meringue is stiff and glossy; divide among prepared soufflé dishes, mounding slightly.

Bake until meringues puff and begin to brown slightly on top and tester inserted into centers comes out clean, about 15 minutes. Cool to room temperature, at least 20 minutes.

DO AHEAD: *Can be made 3 hours ahead. Let stand at room temperature (meringues will deflate).*

Divide custard sauce among 6 shallow soup bowls. Carefully run small sharp knife around edges of meringues to loosen, if necessary. Invert meringues, then turn top side up and place atop sauce. Garnish with lemon slices and sprinkle with raspberries.

♨ Spiced Plum Pavlovas

Plums spiced with cardamom give these individual Pavlovas a nice spin. Crème fraîche is available at most supermarkets and is easy to find at specialty food stores, but if you prefer to make your own, see page 36. **Makes 6**

Plums

1½   **pounds plums, halved, pitted, cut into ¼-inch-thick slices**
½   **cup sugar**
1   **tablespoon fresh lemon juice**
½   **teaspoon ground cardamom**

Meringues

4   **large egg whites, room temperature**
¼   **teaspoon cream of tartar**
1   **cup sugar**
2   **teaspoons cornstarch**
½   **teaspoon apple cider vinegar**
½   **teaspoon vanilla extract**
¼   **teaspoon ground cardamom**

Topping

1½   **cups chilled crème fraîche**
2   **tablespoons sugar**

The Pavlova Story

Both New Zealand and Australia claim to have created this whimsical dessert, and there are definitive reports from both countries claiming their right to its birth. At least there's one thing they can agree upon: The Pavlova was created to honor the Russian ballerina Anna Pavlova. She so impressed both places when she toured in the 1920s that pastry chefs in both countries tried to create a dessert to symbolize her grace and beauty. A giant cream-filled meringue topped with fruit ultimately won the honor.

PLUMS: Combine all ingredients in large skillet; toss to coat. Cover and cook over medium-high heat until sugar dissolves, stirring occasionally, about 5 minutes. Uncover and cook until plums are tender but still hold shape, stirring occasionally, about 3 minutes longer. Cool to room temperature.

DO AHEAD: *Can be made 1 day ahead. Transfer plums to medium bowl. Cover and chill.*

MERINGUES: Preheat oven to 350°F. Line large baking sheet with parchment paper. Using electric mixer, beat egg whites in large bowl 1 minute. Add cream of tartar. Continue to beat until soft peaks form. Gradually add sugar, beating until whites are thick and resemble marshmallow creme, about 5 minutes. Beat in cornstarch, vinegar, vanilla, and cardamom. Drop meringue onto prepared sheet in 6 mounds, spacing 3 inches apart. Using back of spoon, make depression in center of each.

Place meringues in oven. Immediately reduce oven temperature to 250°F. Bake until meringues are dry outside (but centers remain soft), a pale straw color, and lift easily from parchment, about 50 minutes. Cool on sheet on rack.

DO AHEAD: *Can be made 8 hours ahead. Let stand at room temperature.*

TOPPING: Beat crème fraîche and sugar in medium bowl until peaks form. Chill up to 2 hours.

Place meringues on each of 6 plates. Spoon plum mixture into center depression of each meringue. Spoon topping and any plum juices over and serve.

Coconut Pavlova with Chocolate Mousse and Bananas

Chewy coconut meringue is topped with a rich chocolate mousse and sliced bananas in this fun twist on the classic Pavlova. Slice the bananas just before serving to prevent browning. **8 to 10 servings**

Meringue

2	cups sweetened flaked coconut, divided
6	large egg whites, room temperature
1½	teaspoons cornstarch
1	teaspoon apple cider vinegar
½	teaspoon vanilla extract
¼	teaspoon salt
1½	cups sugar
4	tablespoons boiling water

Mousse

2	large eggs, separated, room temperature
4	tablespoons sugar, divided
2	tablespoons (¼ stick) unsalted butter, cut into small pieces, room temperature
2	tablespoons water
1	tablespoon dark rum
4	ounces bittersweet or semisweet chocolate chips (about ⅔ cup)
2	bananas, peeled, cut into ¼-inch-thick rounds
¾	cup chilled heavy whipping cream

MERINGUE: Position rack in center of oven and preheat to 350°F. Spread 1½ cups coconut on large rimmed baking sheet. Toast until golden, stirring twice, about 15 minutes. Cool. Maintain oven temperature.

Line another large rimmed baking sheet with foil. Using electric mixer, beat egg whites, cornstarch, vinegar, vanilla, and salt in large bowl until foamy. Gradually add sugar and beat until stiff but not dry. Beat in boiling water, 1 tablespoon at a time. Continue beating until whites are stiff and glossy. Fold in 1 cup toasted coconut (reserve remaining ½ cup toasted coconut for garnish). Mound meringue in center of prepared baking sheet and, using back of large spoon, spread to 9-inch round with slightly raised edges. Sprinkle with remaining ½ cup untoasted coconut.

Bake meringue 10 minutes. Reduce oven temperature to 200°F. Bake until meringue is dry and crisp outside and just cooked through but not crisp inside, about 1 hour. Turn off oven. Let meringue stand in oven with door closed 1 hour. Remove from oven and cool completely on sheet.

MOUSSE: Whisk egg yolks, 2 tablespoons sugar, butter, 2 tablespoons water, and rum in medium metal bowl to blend. Set bowl over saucepan of simmering water. Whisk until mixture is thickened and thermometer inserted into center registers 160°F, about 6 minutes. Add chocolate and whisk until melted and smooth. Turn off heat; leave bowl over water.

Using electric mixer, beat egg whites in another medium bowl until soft peaks form. Gradually add remaining 2 tablespoons sugar and beat until stiff but not dry. Fold ⅓ of egg whites into chocolate mixture to lighten. Fold in remaining whites. Remove from over water and let mousse cool 20 minutes.

Place meringue on platter. Spread mousse over center of meringue; top with sliced bananas. Whisk cream in medium bowl until peaks form. Spread whipped cream over bananas and chill Pavlova at least 20 minutes and up to 3 hours. Sprinkle Pavlova with remaining toasted coconut. Cut into wedges and serve.

Pink Peppercorn Pavlovas with Strawberries, Vanilla Cream, and Basil Syrup

This airy dessert—light meringue shells that are traditionally topped with fresh fruit—was created to honor Anna Pavlova, a Russian ballerina. In this modern take on the classic recipe, crushed pink peppercorns lend a slight floral note to the meringues. **Makes 6**

Basil Syrup
⅓   cup (packed) fresh basil leaves
½   cup light corn syrup

Meringues
4   large egg whites, room temperature
1   cup sugar, divided
1½   teaspoons cornstarch
½   teaspoon white wine vinegar
1   tablespoon pink peppercorns, lightly crushed

Strawberry Coulis
1   1-pint container strawberries, hulled
2   tablespoons sugar

Vanilla Cream
¾   cup chilled heavy whipping cream
1   tablespoon sugar
½   vanilla bean, split lengthwise

1   1-pint container strawberries, hulled, sliced
    Fresh basil leaves

Technique Tip: **Make It Easy**
This recipe may look ambitious, but each simple element can be prepared in advance: The basil syrup should be made a day ahead to really bring out the flavors, and the meringue can be made a day ahead as well. The strawberry coulis and the vanilla cream can be made up to six hours before being served.

BASIL SYRUP: Blanch basil leaves in small saucepan of boiling water 30 seconds. Drain and transfer basil to bowl of ice water to cool. Drain and squeeze out excess water from basil. Puree basil with corn syrup in blender. Cover and chill at least 2 hours or overnight to allow flavors to develop. Bring basil syrup to room temperature. Strain syrup through sieve into small bowl; discard solids in strainer.

MERINGUES: Position rack in center of oven and preheat to 375°F. Firmly trace six 2½-inch circles on parchment paper, spacing apart. Invert paper onto baking sheet. Using electric mixer, beat egg whites in large bowl until soft peaks form. Gradually add ¾ cup sugar, beating until medium-firm peaks form. Mix remaining ¼ cup sugar and cornstarch in small bowl. Gradually beat sugar-cornstarch mixture into meringue; continue beating until very stiff. Beat in vinegar. Fold in peppercorns. Divide meringue equally among circles, mounding and filling circles completely. Bake meringues 10 minutes. Reduce oven temperature to 325°F and continue baking until outsides are dry, about 30 minutes. Turn oven off and keep meringues in oven with door closed for 30 minutes. Open door slightly and let meringues cool in oven until almost completely dry in center, about 30 minutes longer.

DO AHEAD: *Can be made 1 day ahead. Cool completely. Store in airtight container at room temperature.*

STRAWBERRY COULIS: Puree berries and sugar in processor until smooth.

VANILLA CREAM: Combine cream and sugar in medium bowl. Scrape in seeds from vanilla bean (reserve bean for another use). Using electric mixer, beat cream until soft peaks form.

DO AHEAD: *Coulis and vanilla cream can be made 6 hours ahead. Cover separately and chill.*

Place small dollop of vanilla cream in center of each of 6 plates. Spoon circle of strawberry coulis around vanilla cream. Top each with 1 meringue. Spoon generous amount of vanilla cream atop meringues. Top with sliced strawberries and fresh basil leaves. Drizzle basil syrup over and serve.

Pears in Honey and Pine Nut Caramel with Artisanal Cheese

This extraordinary dessert is both sweet and savory: Pear halves are cooked in a butter-honey caramel sauce, then topped with artisanal cheese and sea salt–dusted pine nuts bathed in caramel. Any variety of pears can be used in this recipe, but Bosc pears hold up especially well because of their firm texture. You can use whatever artisanal cheese you like, such as Point Reyes Original Blue, Humboldt Fog, dry Monterey Jack, sheep's-milk ricotta, tangy soft fresh goat cheese, or another local cheese. Head to your local farmers' market or a well-stocked cheese shop and get some good recommendations (and, ideally, a few tastes) from a knowledgeable cheesemonger. **6 servings**

¼ cup (½ stick) unsalted butter
3 firm but ripe Bosc pears or other pears, peeled, halved lengthwise, cored
3½ tablespoons mild honey (such as orange blossom or clover)
4 ounces artisanal cheese, sliced or crumbled, room temperature
3 tablespoons pine nuts
Pinch of fine sea salt

Cook butter in large nonstick skillet over medium-high heat until beginning to brown. Add pear halves, cut side down, to skillet. Drizzle honey over pears and swirl pan slightly to blend butter and honey. Reduce heat to medium, cover, and cook until pears are tender when pierced with paring knife, swirling skillet occasionally and adding a few tablespoons water to skillet if caramel sauce turns deep amber before pears are tender, about 12 minutes.

Transfer pears, cut side up, to serving platter. Top pears with cheese. Return skillet with caramel sauce to medium-high heat; add pine nuts and sprinkle lightly with sea salt. Cook until sauce in skillet is brown and bubbling, about 2 minutes. Spoon sauce and nuts over pears and serve.

Warm Spiced Plums with Honey Cream

A little heat and sugar is all that's needed to get the plum juices flowing in this simple dessert, and a touch of cinnamon adds nice spice. Begin making the honey cream at least six hours ahead, since it takes time to thicken. Try any extra with oatmeal, waffles, or fresh fruit. **4 servings**

1½ cups half and half
3 tablespoons low-fat (2%) buttermilk
3 tablespoons honey
2 pounds ripe plums, halved, pitted, cut into ¾-inch-thick wedges
½ cup sugar
½ teaspoon (scant) ground cinnamon

Whisk half and half, buttermilk, and honey in medium glass bowl to blend. Let stand, uncovered, in warm place until thick, at least 6 hours or overnight. Chill until ready to serve.

DO AHEAD: *Can be made 1 week ahead. Keep chilled.*

Heat large skillet over medium-high heat. Add plums and sugar; stir until sugar dissolves and forms glaze and plums are tender, about 8 minutes. Sprinkle cinnamon over plums. Spoon into bowls. Pour honey cream over.

Baked Pears with Honey and Ginger

This dessert is truly elegant, yet it couldn't be easier to make. Honey, brown sugar, lemon, and ginger coat the pears as they bake, then melt into a warm, delicious sauce. **8 servings**

	Nonstick vegetable oil spray
8	firm but ripe Bartlett pears, peeled, halved, cored
1	cup (packed) golden brown sugar
3	teaspoons ground ginger
6	tablespoons honey
3	tablespoons fresh lemon juice
2	teaspoons finely grated lemon peel
10	tablespoons (1¼ sticks) unsalted butter, divided
	Vanilla frozen yogurt or vanilla ice cream
	Fresh mint sprigs (optional)
	Lemon peel strips (optional)

Preheat oven to 375°F. Spray 2 large ovenproof skillets with nonstick spray. Arrange half of pears, cut side down, in each skillet. Sprinkle ½ cup brown sugar and 1½ teaspoons ginger over pears in each skillet. Mix honey, lemon juice, and grated lemon peel in small bowl. Drizzle over pears in each skillet, dividing equally. Dot pears with 6 tablespoons butter total.

Place skillets with pears in oven and bake until juices bubble thickly and pears are tender when pierced with small sharp knife, basting occasionally, about 15 minutes. Turn pears over. Bake 5 minutes longer. Remove pears from oven.

DO AHEAD: *Can be made 1 day ahead. Cool. Transfer pears and cooking syrup to large glass baking dish; cover and chill. Rewarm uncovered in 375°F oven 15 minutes before continuing.*

Arrange 2 pear halves on each of 8 plates. Transfer cooking syrup to 1 large skillet. Bring syrup to simmer; whisk in remaining 4 tablespoons butter. Spoon over pears. Place 1 scoop frozen yogurt or ice cream alongside. Garnish with mint and lemon peel strips, if desired.

Technique Tip: **Into the Fire**
You'll need two large ovenproof skillets for this dessert, such as cast-iron skillets or stainless steel sauté pans with metal handles that won't burn under extreme heat. Plastic handles could melt and wooden handles could burn. Remember to use oven mitts or thick potholders to remove the skillets from the oven, as the handles get extremely hot.

Maple-Pecan Baked Apples

Eating baked stuffed apples is like opening a gift: It's fun to find out what goodies are hidden inside. Spiced pecans, raisins, and coconut fill these apples, and as they bake, maple syrup, butter, and apple juice form a luscious pan sauce. The apples are great served with vanilla ice cream. **6 servings**

6	large Golden Delicious apples (about 3½ pounds)
⅔	cup plus 6 tablespoons coarsely chopped pecans
⅓	cup golden raisins
¼	cup sweetened flaked coconut
2	tablespoons pure maple syrup
1	teaspoon finely grated lemon peel
¼	teaspoon ground cinnamon
¼	teaspoon ground nutmeg
6	tablespoons peach or apricot preserves
1	cup unfiltered apple juice or apple cider
2	tablespoons (¼ stick) unsalted butter

Preheat oven to 375°F. Core apples. Peel top third of each apple. Using small sharp knife, cut ¼-inch-deep line all around each apple where peel and flesh meet. Using small sharp knife, increase opening in top of each apple to 1¼ inches wide and 1 inch deep. Cut off thin slice from bottom of each to allow apples to stand flat. Place apples in 13x9x2-inch glass baking dish.

Finely chop ⅔ cup pecans, raisins, and coconut in processor. Transfer to small bowl. Mix in maple syrup, lemon peel, cinnamon, and nutmeg. Divide filling equally among hollows in apples.

Spread 1 tablespoon preserves over top of each apple and into hollows. Press 1 tablespoon chopped pecans atop each.

Combine apple juice and butter in small saucepan. Stir over medium heat until butter melts. Pour into dish around apples. Cover dish loosely with foil. Bake apples 30 minutes. Remove foil; continue to bake until apples are tender, basting with juices every 10 minutes, about 35 minutes longer. Serve apples warm with pan juices.

Grilled Peaches with Fresh Raspberry Sauce

A melted butter–brown sugar mixture is brushed over peaches before grilling, caramelizing the fruit and lending great flavor to this simple treat. It's a wonderful way to create a summer dessert that doesn't involve the oven. The peaches are delicious with vanilla ice cream, shortbread cookies, or both.
6 servings

2¼	cups (lightly packed) raspberries
3	tablespoons water
3	tablespoons sugar
1	tablespoon fresh lemon juice
3	tablespoons unsalted butter
1½	tablespoons (packed) dark brown sugar
6	medium-size firm but ripe peaches, halved, pitted

Combine raspberries and 3 tablespoons water in processor. Puree until smooth. Strain raspberry puree through fine-mesh strainer, pressing on solids to release as much liquid as possible; discard solids in strainer. Stir sugar and lemon juice into raspberry sauce.

DO AHEAD: *Can be made 1 day ahead. Cover and chill.*

Prepare barbecue (medium heat). Melt butter with brown sugar in heavy small skillet over medium heat. Remove skillet from heat. Brush peach halves all over with melted butter mixture. Grill peaches until tender, about 8 minutes, turning occasionally. Transfer 2 peach halves to each of 6 plates. Spoon sauce alongside and serve.

Grilled Bananas with Caramel-Chocolate Sauce and Toasted Pecans

The sauce is a wonderful cross between chocolate and caramel. To ensure a silky texture, the sugar must be completely dissolved before the sauce boils.
4 servings

1	cup (packed) golden brown sugar
¼	cup water
2	tablespoons (¼ stick) unsalted butter
½	cup heavy whipping cream
1½	ounces bittersweet or semisweet chocolate (do not exceed 61% cacao), chopped
1	tablespoon Kahlúa or other coffee-flavored liqueur
½	teaspoon vanilla extract
	Nonstick vegetable oil spray
2	firm but ripe bananas, peeled, halved crosswise, then lengthwise
1	cup vanilla ice cream
	Coarsely chopped toasted pecans

Stir brown sugar and ¼ cup water in heavy medium saucepan over medium-low heat until sugar dissolves. Increase heat and boil without stirring until syrup is deep amber color, occasionally brushing down sides of pan with wet pastry brush, 3 to 4 minutes. Add butter; stir until melted. Gradually stir in cream. Boil sauce 2 minutes, stirring often. Remove from heat. Add chocolate, Kahlúa, and vanilla; stir until chocolate is melted and smooth.

DO AHEAD: *Can be made 5 days ahead. Cool completely. Cover and chill. Rewarm before using.*

Spray grill with nonstick spray. Prepare barbecue (high heat). Brush bananas with some of caramel-chocolate sauce. Grill bananas until heated through and sauce is slightly charred, occasionally brushing with more sauce, about 1 minute per side.

Divide bananas among 4 plates; top with ice cream. Drizzle sauce over, sprinkle with pecans, and serve.

Grilled Pineapple with Coconut-Lime Caramel Sauce

Cream and butter usually play a key role in caramel sauce, but here coconut milk takes their place, which gives the sauce a tropical flavor that partners perfectly with fresh lime and grilled pineapple. Serve this dessert as is, or try it with a scoop of the Rum-Ginger Ice Cream (page 125) for a Southeast Asian–style sundae. Or serve it fondue-style by cutting the grilled pineapple slices in half, then serving them with the caramel sauce and bowls of coconut and pecans to sprinkle on top. When it's cold outside, grill the pineapple slices on an indoor grill, or broil them on a baking sheet in the oven for about three minutes.

8 servings

Caramel Sauce

1	14-ounce can unsweetened coconut milk
½	cup sugar
¼	cup water
2	teaspoons (not packed) finely grated lime peel
2	teaspoons fresh lime juice

Pineapple

1	medium pineapple, peeled, cored, halved lengthwise, each half cut crosswise into 12 slices
2	teaspoons (about) canola oil
½	cup toasted pecans, very coarsely chopped
3	tablespoons shredded sweetened coconut, toasted

Technique Tip: Don't Shake the Can

The instructions on cans of coconut milk often advise shaking the can before opening it, which helps blend the heavy, thick cream with the thinner milky liquid. For this recipe, do not shake the can; you want just the heavy, thick cream that floats to the top of the can for the caramel sauce. This thick cream is also delicious in puddings and custards.

CARAMEL SAUCE: Spoon 1 cup thick coconut cream from atop coconut milk in can and set aside (reserve any remaining cream and milk from can for another use).

Stir sugar and ¼ cup water in heavy medium saucepan over medium heat until sugar dissolves, about 2 minutes. Simmer over medium heat without stirring until syrup is golden brown, occasionally brushing down sides of pan with wet pastry brush and swirling pan, about 8 minutes. Remove pan from heat and add coconut cream (mixture will bubble vigorously). Simmer over medium heat until caramel melts and sauce darkens and thickens slightly, whisking often, about 5 minutes. Remove caramel sauce from heat. Stir in lime peel and lime juice.

DO AHEAD: *Caramel sauce can be made 2 days ahead. Cover and chill. Rewarm before serving.*

PINEAPPLE: Prepare barbecue (medium-high heat). Lightly coat pineapple slices with oil. Grill until heated through and grill marks appear, rotating to form even grill marks, about 2 minutes per side.

Spoon some caramel sauce decoratively onto 8 plates. Arrange 3 pineapple slices on each plate. Spoon remaining caramel sauce over pineapple. Sprinkle with toasted pecans and coconut and serve.

Making Perfect Crepes

Light, delicate crepes are not difficult to achieve; just use some care, and don't try to rush the process.

1 Mix the batter just until blended (if the batter is overmixed, the crepes will become tough). Crepe batter must rest for a couple of hours before it is used, so plan accordingly. The resting time allows the flour in the batter to fully absorb the moisture from the milk, while any air bubbles dissipate. This makes it less likely the crepes will tear during cooking.

2 The batter thickens as it chills (this is a sign that the flour has fully absorbed the moisture). When making the crepes, the batter should be the consistency of heavy cream and coat a spoon thinly; add more milk as needed to thin the batter to the desired consistency.

3 Pour the appropriate amount of batter into the *center* of the skillet [1], then quickly tilt the skillet [2] until the batter coats the bottom evenly [3].

4 Use a thin-tipped, firm silicone spatula to loosen the crepe from the pan before turning [4]. Silicone is heat resistant and won't scratch a nonstick surface.

5 Crepes can be made ahead and refrigerated or frozen. Stack the crepes between sheets of waxed paper and store them in an airtight container in the fridge or freezer. To reheat, wrap the crepes in foil and bake at 300°F for about 20 minutes.

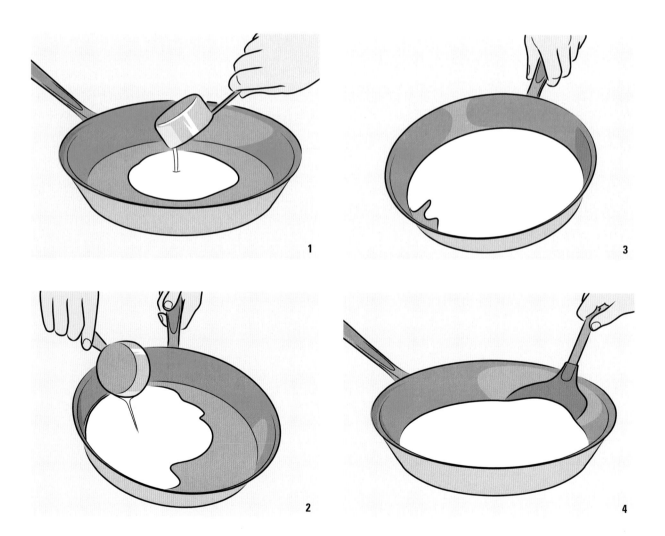

1

2

3

4

♯♯ Walnut Crepes with Raspberries and Dried Figs

In Provence, crepes are often served simply, embellished with just sugar, jam, or liqueur. Here, the addition of walnuts and orange peel to the crepe batter adds a bit of flair, and a fig and raspberry filling flavored with Muscat and vanilla bean dresses them up even more. If Muscat is unavailable, Essensia, a sweet orange Muscat wine made in California, is a great substitute. **6 servings**

Filling

½	vanilla bean, split lengthwise
1½	cups chopped dried Calimyrna figs
1	12-ounce package frozen raspberries (about 3 cups), thawed, juices reserved
1	cup Muscat
1	cup water
¼	cup (packed) dark brown sugar
2	tablespoons honey
2	teaspoons finely grated orange peel

Crepes

1	cup (or more) whole milk
1	cup unbleached all purpose flour
3	large eggs
¼	cup chopped walnuts
2	tablespoons sugar
2	tablespoons (¼ stick) unsalted butter, melted
1	teaspoon finely grated orange peel
¼	teaspoon salt
	Additional melted butter
	Additional sugar
1	8-ounce container crème fraîche or sour cream
2	tablespoons honey

FILLING: Scrape seeds from vanilla bean into heavy medium saucepan; add bean. Add figs, raspberries with juices, Muscat, 1 cup water, brown sugar, honey, and orange peel. Bring to simmer, stirring until sugar dissolves. Simmer over medium heat until figs are tender, about 30 minutes. Cool. Remove vanilla bean.

DO AHEAD: *Can be made 3 days ahead. Cover and chill.*

CREPES: Combine 1 cup milk, flour, eggs, walnuts, 2 tablespoons sugar, 2 tablespoons butter, orange peel, and salt in blender. Blend until smooth, occasionally scraping down sides of blender. Cover and chill batter in blender 2 hours. Reblend batter 5 seconds. If necessary, thin batter with additional milk, 1 tablespoon at a time, to consistency of heavy cream.

Place paper towel on plate. Heat 9-inch-diameter nonstick skillet with 7-inch-diameter bottom over medium-high heat. Brush skillet with additional melted butter. Pour scant ¼ cup crepe batter into skillet, tilting skillet quickly to coat bottom. Cook until top of crepe appears dry and bottom is golden, loosening sides of crepe with spatula, about 35 seconds. Turn crepe over; cook until brown spots appear on bottom, about 20 seconds. Turn crepe out onto prepared plate. Repeat with remaining batter. Stack crepes on plate, layering between paper towels.

(continued next page)

Walnut Crepes with Raspberries and Dried Figs

(continued)

Brush 13x9x2-inch glass baking dish with melted butter. Spoon generous 2 tablespoons filling onto center of spotted side of 1 crepe. Spread filling over crepe, leaving 1-inch plain border. Fold crepe in half, then fold in half again, forming triangle shape. Place filled crepe in prepared dish. Repeat with remaining crepes and filling, overlapping crepes slightly in dish. Brush crepes lightly with melted butter. Sprinkle lightly with additional sugar. Cover dish with foil. Stir crème fraîche and honey in small bowl to blend.

DO AHEAD: *Crepes and honey crème fraîche can be made 1 day ahead. Cover separately and chill.*

Preheat oven to 350°F. Bake crepes, covered, until heated through, about 20 minutes. Place 2 crepes on each of 6 plates. Top with dollop of honey crème fraîche and serve.

Crepe Essentials

PAN: You can buy a special crepe pan (they start at about $20), but a 9-inch-diameter nonstick skillet works just as well.

LADLE: One-ounce ladles are available at restaurant supply stores (for about $10). Or just use a ¼-cup measuring cup, filled halfway.

SPATULA: A heat-resistant spatula made of silicone (about $9) will help you coax the crepes out of the pan.

Tropical Fruit Crepes with Vanilla Bean and Rum Butter Sauce

This recipe requires a bit of last-minute assembly. Line up the components and corral a few guests to help so that everything goes smoothly. **6 servings**

Crepes

1	**cup whole milk**
½	**cup cornstarch**
¼	**cup unbleached all purpose flour**
3	**large eggs**
3	**tablespoons unsalted butter, melted**
2	**tablespoons sugar**
1	**tablespoon dark rum**
1	**teaspoon vanilla extract**
¼	**teaspoon coarse kosher salt**

Rum Butter Sauce

½	**cup sugar**
6	**tablespoons (¾ stick) unsalted butter, room temperature**
¼	**teaspoon coarse kosher salt**
3	**tablespoons dark rum**

Tropical Fruit

2	**tablespoons (¼ stick) unsalted butter**
½	**vanilla bean, split lengthwise**
1	**cup ¾-inch cubes peeled cored fresh pineapple**
¼	**cup sugar**
¼	**teaspoon coarse kosher salt**
2	**tablespoons fresh lime juice**
1	**cup ¾-inch cubes peeled seeded papaya (from about 1 large)**
1	**cup ¾-inch cubes peeled pitted mango (from about 1 large)**

CREPES: Combine all ingredients in blender. Blend until smooth. Cover and chill in blender 4 hours. Reblend for 5 seconds before using.

Line plate with paper towel or parchment paper. Heat 9-inch-diameter nonstick skillet with 7-inch-diameter bottom over medium heat. Add 2 tablespoons crepe batter to skillet; tilt and swirl skillet to spread batter evenly over bottom. Cook until center of crepe is cooked through and edges are lightly browned, about 1 minute. Run spatula around crepe and invert onto prepared plate. Repeat with remaining batter, layering crepes between paper towels or sheets of parchment paper.

DO AHEAD: *Can be made 1 day ahead. Cover and chill.*

RUM BUTTER SAUCE: Using electric mixer, beat sugar, butter, and coarse salt in medium bowl until fluffy, about 2 minutes. Gradually add rum and beat until well blended.

DO AHEAD: *Can be made 1 day ahead. Cover and chill.*

TROPICAL FRUIT: Place butter in large nonstick skillet. Scrape in seeds from vanilla bean; add bean and stir over medium-high heat until butter melts. Add pineapple, sugar, and coarse salt; stir until sugar dissolves and pineapple and pan juices are lightly browned, about 4 minutes. Stir in lime juice. Remove from heat.

DO AHEAD: *Can be made 2 hours ahead. Let stand at room temperature.*

Preheat oven to 300°F. Place crepe stack (with paper towels between crepes) on rimmed baking sheet. Cover baking sheet with foil. Warm crepes in oven until heated through, about 15 minutes. Place rum butter sauce in small saucepan; heat over medium heat until melted and smooth, stirring occasionally. Rewarm pineapple mixture over medium heat, stirring occasionally, about 3 minutes. Stir in papaya and mango. Remove vanilla bean.

Place 1 crepe on plate, browned side down; spoon 2 teaspoons rum butter sauce over, then fold crepe into quarters. Repeat with 2 more crepes on same plate. Spoon tropical fruit over. Repeat with remaining crepes, rum butter sauce, and tropical fruit, placing 3 crepes on each of 6 plates. Spoon any remaining rum butter sauce over crepes and serve.

Crepes with Brown Sugar Pears and Chocolate Sauce

For a tasty twist, serve the crepes with caramel sauce instead of chocolate sauce (such as the one on page 503) and sprinkle them with toasted pecans. Since this recipe makes extra crepes, cool and stack any leftovers, separating them with sheets of plastic wrap and storing them in the refrigerator in a resealable plastic bag. The next day, just rewarm the crepes in the microwave and serve them with jam or maple syrup for breakfast. **6 servings**

1½   **cups whole milk**
1   **cup plus 2 tablespoons unbleached all purpose flour**
3   **large eggs**
2   **teaspoons sugar**
¼   **teaspoon salt**
1   **tablespoon unsalted butter, melted, plus additional for brushing**
      Brown Sugar Pears (see recipe)
      Vanilla ice cream
      Chocolate Sauce (see recipe)

Combine milk, flour, eggs, sugar, and salt in blender. Blend until smooth, occasionally scraping down sides of blender, about 2 minutes. Add 1 tablespoon melted butter; blend 30 seconds. Cover and chill crepe batter in blender at least 1 hour and up to 4 hours. Reblend batter 5 seconds.

Heat 10-inch-diameter nonstick skillet with 8-inch-diameter bottom over medium-high heat. Brush with melted butter. Pour ¼ cup batter into skillet, tilting skillet quickly to coat bottom evenly. Cook until top of crepe appears dry and bottom is golden, loosening edges of crepe with heatproof spatula, about 45 seconds. Turn crepe over; cook until brown spots appear on bottom, about 30 seconds. Transfer to plate. Top with plastic wrap. Repeat with remaining batter, brushing skillet with more butter as needed and layering cooked crepes between sheets of plastic wrap.

DO AHEAD: *Can be made 1 day ahead. Cover with plastic; chill.*

Preheat broiler. Line baking sheet with foil; brush with melted butter. Place 1 crepe on prepared baking sheet. Place 3 slices of warm Brown Sugar Pears side by side on 1 quarter of crepe, allowing pear slices to extend slightly over edge of crepe. Fold crepe in half over pear slices. Place 3 more pear slices on crepe above first 3 slices. Fold crepe in half over pears, forming triangle shape. Repeat with 5 crepes and pear slices. Brush crepes with some of pear syrup.

Broil crepes just until heated through and golden, watching closely to avoid burning, about 1½ minutes. Transfer to plates. Arrange any remaining pear slices atop crepes. Spoon pear syrup over. Place scoop of ice cream alongside. Drizzle with warm Chocolate Sauce. Serve, passing remaining sauce separately.

Brown Sugar Pears

Brown sugar is simply white sugar with molasses. The enriched sugar lends caramel-like notes to sautéed pears. Dark brown sugar can be substituted for golden brown sugar, if desired, for a more intense flavor. **6 servings**

¼   cup (½ stick) unsalted butter
½   cup (packed) golden brown sugar
4   large firm but ripe pears (about 1½ pounds), peeled, halved, cored, each half cut lengthwise into 6 slices
4   teaspoons fresh lemon juice

Melt butter in large nonstick skillet over medium-high heat. Add brown sugar; stir 1 minute. Add pear slices and lemon juice; cook until pears begin to release juices and syrup forms in skillet, turning pear slices frequently, about 3 minutes.

DO AHEAD: *Can be made 2 hours ahead. Let stand at room temperature. Rewarm before using.*

Chocolate Sauce

This sauce is delicious and easy to make. Keep it simple for the crepes and pears, but when serving the sauce with vanilla ice cream, add your own spin. Dissolve a little espresso powder in the half and half to make a mocha chocolate sauce, or add peppermint extract. **Makes about 1¾ cups**

1   cup half and half
¼   cup (½ stick) unsalted butter
8   ounces bittersweet or semisweet chocolate (do not exceed 61% cacao), chopped

Bring half and half and butter to simmer in medium saucepan. Remove from heat. Add chocolate; whisk until melted and smooth.

DO AHEAD: *Can be made 1 day ahead. Cover and chill. Rewarm over low heat before serving.*

Puffed Pancake with Strawberries

Also known as a Dutch Baby, this is as delicious for breakfast as it is for dessert. The soufflé-like pancake puffs up impressively, so make sure your guests see it before you cut into it. **4 servings**

1   pound small strawberries, hulled, sliced (about 1⅔ cups)
2   tablespoons powdered sugar
3   tablespoons unsalted butter
¾   cup whole milk, room temperature
3   large eggs, room temperature
¾   cup unbleached all purpose flour
      Pinch of salt
      Additional powdered sugar
      Lemon wedges

Preheat oven to 450°F. Stir strawberries and powdered sugar in medium bowl. Let stand at room temperature while preparing pancake.

Melt butter in 10-inch-diameter ovenproof skillet (preferably cast-iron) over medium-high heat, swirling to coat bottom and sides of skillet. Blend milk and eggs in blender until smooth. Add flour and salt; blend batter just until incorporated. Pour batter into hot skillet.

Transfer skillet to oven and bake pancake until puffed and golden in spots, about 11 minutes.

Immediately cut pancake into quarters. Transfer 1 wedge to each of 4 plates. Spoon strawberries on top, dust with additional powdered sugar, garnish with lemon wedges, and serve.

Pear and Ricotta Blintzes with Spiced Maple Butter Sauce

A sweet, cheesy filling with caramelized pears is encased in crepes, then smothered in a buttery maple sauce for a truly satisfying dessert or a decadent breakfast or brunch. Although there are a few components to assemble, they aren't difficult to make and each can be done in advance. Firm Bosc pears are the ideal choice for this recipe, because they hold their shape well when sautéed and baked. **8 to 10 servings**

Maple Butter Sauce

1	cup pure maple syrup
1	cup (2 sticks) unsalted butter, cut into 1-inch cubes
¾	teaspoon ground cinnamon
½	teaspoon ground allspice

Crepes

2	cups whole milk
6	large eggs
1⅓	cups unbleached all purpose flour
3	tablespoons unsalted butter, melted
2	tablespoons sugar
½	teaspoon salt
	Vegetable oil

Filling

¼	cup dried currants
1½	tablespoons dark rum
1	tablespoon unsalted butter
4	firm but ripe Bosc pears, peeled, halved, cored, cut into ¼-inch cubes
½	cup sugar, divided
1	8-ounce package Philadelphia-brand cream cheese, room temperature
2	large eggs
2	teaspoons finely grated lemon peel
½	teaspoon vanilla extract
1	15-ounce container ricotta cheese

MAPLE BUTTER SAUCE: Whisk all ingredients in heavy small saucepan over low heat until butter is melted. Cool until slightly thickened, whisking occasionally.

DO AHEAD: *Can be made 3 days ahead; chill.*

CREPES: Blend milk and eggs in blender until smooth. Add flour, butter, sugar and salt; blend until smooth batter forms. Chill in blender at least 1 hour and up to 2 hours. Reblend for 5 seconds before using.

Heat 10-inch-diameter nonstick skillet with 8-inch-diameter bottom over medium-high heat; brush with oil. Pour scant 3 tablespoons batter into skillet. Rotate and shake skillet to spread batter over bottom. Cook until crepe is brown at edges and appears dry on top, about 20 seconds. Turn crepe over. Cook until brown spots form on bottom of crepe, about 12 seconds. Turn crepe out onto paper towel; cover with another paper towel. Repeat, making about 26 crepes, occasionally brushing skillet with oil.

DO AHEAD: *Can be made 1 day ahead. Cover with plastic wrap and chill.*

FILLING: Mix currants and rum in small bowl; let stand 15 minutes. Melt butter in large skillet over medium-high heat. Mix in pears and ¼ cup sugar. Cook until pears are tender and brown, stirring often, about 10 minutes; cool.

Beat cream cheese, eggs, lemon peel, vanilla, and remaining ¼ cup sugar in medium bowl. Beat in ricotta cheese, then stir in pear and currant mixtures. Cover and chill at least 1 hour and up to 1 day.

Preheat oven to 375°F. Butter 15x10x2-inch glass baking dish. Place 1 crepe, spotted side up, on work surface. Shape ¼ cup filling into 3-inch-long log in center of crepe. Fold bottom of crepe over filling. Fold in sides; roll up. Place seam side down in prepared dish. Repeat with remaining filling and crepes.

Cover dish with foil. Bake blintzes until instant-read thermometer inserted into center of filling registers 160°F to 170°F, about 45 minutes.

Whisk sauce over low heat until just warm and smooth. Place 2 blintzes on each plate. Serve blintzes with sauce.

Wine- and Citrus-Poached Pears with Triple-Crème Cheese

The after-dinner combination of fruit and cheese is transformed here, as pear halves are cooked in a red wine–citrus poaching liquid that becomes a syrup served with the sliced and fanned pears. Placing a parchment paper round atop the pears helps keep them moist and covered with liquid as they poach. France's famed triple-crème cheese is served alongside. This cheese has a soft rind and a luscious rich texture—it contains at least 75 percent butterfat. Delicious examples include Brillat-Savarin, Le Délice de Bourgogne, Explorateur, Boursault, and Saint André. **4 servings**

1½   cups dry red wine
⅓   cup sugar
¼   cup orange juice
1   3x¾-inch strip lemon peel (yellow part only)
1   whole clove
2   medium-size firm but ripe pears, peeled, halved lengthwise,
     cored (stems left intact)
1   tablespoon crème de cassis (black currant liqueur; optional)
8   ounces triple-crème cheese, cut into 4 wedges

Combine wine, sugar, orange juice, lemon peel, and clove in heavy medium saucepan. Bring to simmer over medium heat, stirring until sugar dissolves. Add pear halves to saucepan. Cut out round of parchment paper same size as saucepan. Place parchment round atop pears, pushing edges of parchment into liquid to prevent edges from curling up. Reduce heat and barely simmer until pears are tender when pierced with knife, about 12 minutes.

Using slotted spoon, transfer pears to bowl. Boil liquid in saucepan until slightly syrupy and reduced to ¾ cup, about 14 minutes. Cool syrup to room temperature; stir in crème de cassis, if desired. Pour syrup over pears. Cover and chill at least 12 hours, turning pears occasionally.

Thinly slice pear halves lengthwise almost to stem end, leaving stems attached. Spoon generous 1 tablespoon pear syrup onto each of 4 plates. Top each with 1 pear half, pressing gently to fan. Serve with cheese.

Papaya Poached in Cinnamon-Lime Syrup

Fruit simmered in cinnamon syrup is a typical after-dinner treat throughout Mexico. In this recipe, the sweetness is balanced with sour cream and lime. Poaching is gentler than boiling, so lower the heat on the syrup when the fruit is added to allow the syrup to gently simmer and the fruit to stay intact. Use a vegetable peeler to remove just the green part of the lime peel. **6 servings**

2   cups water
1   cup sugar
3   1-pound papayas, peeled, halved, seeded, cut into ½-inch-thick
     wedges
3   tablespoons fresh lime juice
6   2x½-inch strips lime peel (green part only)
1   cinnamon stick
     Sour cream, stirred to loosen
     Additional lime peel, cut into matchstick-size strips

Bring 2 cups water and sugar to boil in heavy medium saucepan over medium-high heat, stirring until sugar dissolves. Boil until syrup thickens slightly, about 6 minutes. Add papaya wedges, lime juice, lime peel, and cinnamon stick. Reduce heat to medium and simmer until papayas are just tender, about 5 minutes. Using slotted spoon, transfer papayas to bowl. Boil syrup until reduced to 1 cup, about 6 minutes. Remove cinnamon stick. Pour syrup over papayas and chill at least 2 hours.

DO AHEAD: *Can be made 1 day ahead. Cover and keep chilled.*

Spoon papayas and syrup into dessert dishes. Drizzle with sour cream and garnish with matchstick-size strips of lime peel.

Pink Grapefruit with Cassis

With just three ingredients and a little water, this light and lovely dessert is a refreshing finish to any meal, and an excellent accompaniment to Sesame-Almond Macaroons (page 557). Crème de cassis is available at many supermarkets and at most liquor stores. If it's unavailable, Chambord (black raspberry liqueur) or Cointreau (orange liqueur) can be used instead. **4 servings**

2   **large pink grapefruits (about 14 ounces each)**
2   **tablespoons sugar**
1½ **tablespoons water**
2   **tablespoons crème de cassis (black currant liqueur)**
     Fresh mint sprigs (optional)

Using small sharp knife, remove peel and white pith from grapefruits. Working over bowl to catch juice, cut between membranes to release segments. Reserve juice in bowl. Arrange grapefruit segments decoratively on plates.

Combine sugar, 1½ tablespoons water, and reserved grapefruit juice in heavy small saucepan. Stir over low heat until sugar dissolves. Remove saucepan from heat. Stir in crème de cassis. Drizzle syrup over grapefruit. Chill at least 2 hours.

DO AHEAD: *Can be made 6 hours ahead. Keep chilled.*

Garnish with mint, if desired, and serve.

Technique Tip: **Segmenting Grapefruit**
For visual appeal and best flavor, it's important to cut away the membranes and bitter white pith of the grapefruit. Segmenting a grapefruit is no different than segmenting an orange; all you need is a small sharp knife to cut away the peel and white pith, then cut between the membranes to release the segments. For more information, see page 35.

Nectarines, Strawberries, and Melon in Orange-Honey Spiced Syrup

Melon balls are playful components of this fruity dessert. For an even easier alternative, cut the melon into cubes. Whole star anise—a brown, star-shaped seedpod—adds a licorice flavor to the syrup; it is available in the spice section of some supermarkets and at Asian markets and specialty foods stores. You can make the syrup a day ahead; however, add the fruit no more than eight hours in advance to prevent it from becoming soggy. **8 servings**

2   **large oranges**
2   **cups water**
⅓   **cup honey**
4   **large whole star anise**
1   **cinnamon stick, broken in half**
1   **vanilla bean, split lengthwise**
1   **4-pound honeydew melon, halved, seeded**
3   **large nectarines (about 1 pound), halved, pitted, cut into
     ½-inch-thick slices**
1½ **1-pint containers strawberries, hulled, quartered**
     Additional orange peel strips (optional)

Using vegetable peeler, remove peel (orange part only) from oranges. Set peel aside (reserve oranges for another use).

Combine 2 cups water, honey, star anise, and cinnamon stick in medium saucepan. Scrape in seeds from vanilla bean; add bean. Bring to boil, stirring to dissolve honey. Reduce heat to medium-low. Simmer until liquid is reduced to 1½ cups, about 8 minutes. Remove from heat. Stir in reserved orange peel. Cool syrup. Strain into large bowl; discard solids in strainer.

DO AHEAD: *Can be made 1 day ahead. Cover and chill.*

Using melon baller, scoop out enough fruit from melon to equal 4 cups. Combine melon balls, nectarines, and strawberries in large bowl. Add syrup; toss to coat. Cover and chill at least 5 hours.

DO AHEAD: *Can be made 8 hours ahead. Keep chilled.*

Ladle fruit mixture into bowls. Garnish with additional orange peel strips, if desired.

Vodka-Spiked Watermelon with Crème de Cassis

Use a combination of red and yellow seedless watermelon for the most colorful presentation. Store-bought butter cookies or brownies make a great accompaniment. **8 servings**

1	8-pound watermelon, peeled, cut into 1-inch pieces (about 16 cups)
1	cup fresh lemon juice
2/3	cup sugar
1/2	cup vodka
6	tablespoons crème de cassis (black currant liqueur)
1/4	cup chopped fresh mint

Place watermelon in large bowl. Whisk lemon juice and sugar in medium bowl until sugar dissolves. Whisk in vodka and crème de cassis. Season mixture to taste with salt. Pour mixture over watermelon. Cover and chill at least 1 hour and up to 2 hours. Sprinkle with chopped mint and serve.

Fruits of the Seasons

Every fruit is most flavorful at the peak of its season, and when a fruit is more abundant it's also less expensive. Selecting locally grown seasonal fruit is even better: Since it doesn't need to travel far, it can be picked as close to ripeness as possible, allowing it to develop fuller flavor. What's at its peak each season?

SPRING: rhubarb (although technically a vegetable, it's used in many fruit desserts) and strawberries

SUMMER: apricots, blackberries, blueberries, cherries, figs, melons, nectarines, peaches, plums, and raspberries

FALL: apples, pears, persimmons, pomegranates, and quinces

WINTER: cranberries and citrus fruits, including kumquats, Meyer lemons, blood oranges, and tangerines

Melon and Blueberry Coupe with White Wine, Vanilla, and Mint

The different colors of the melons—red, orange, and pale green—dotted with purple blueberries, mint, and flecks of vanilla make a festive and refreshing finale to a summer meal. The wine syrup brings out the aromas of the melons and marries all the flavors. Serve your favorite sugar cookies alongside.
6 servings

1½	cups dry white wine, divided
½	cup sugar
1	vanilla bean, split lengthwise
2⅓	cups cantaloupe cubes (about ⅓ small melon)
2⅓	cups honeydew cubes (about ⅓ small melon)
2⅓	cups watermelon cubes (about ¼ small melon)
3	cups fresh blueberries
½	cup chopped fresh mint

Combine ½ cup wine and sugar in small saucepan. Scrape in seeds from vanilla bean; add bean. Stir over low heat until sugar dissolves and syrup is hot, about 2 minutes. Remove from heat and let steep 30 minutes. Remove vanilla bean.

Combine all fruit in large bowl. Add mint and remaining 1 cup wine to sugar syrup. Pour over fruit. Cover and chill at least 2 hours.

DO AHEAD: *Can made 6 hours ahead. Keep chilled.*

Spoon fruit and some syrup into large stemmed goblets and serve.

Presentation Tip:
Glass coupe dishes—wide, deep dessert bowls with stems—make ideal pedestals for the fruit, but any pretty, see-through bowls will lend the same effect.

Oranges with Pomegranate Molasses and Honey

This simple yet sophisticated dessert would be perfect after a Middle Eastern dinner. Thick, sweet-tart pomegranate molasses is delicious drizzled over citrus fruit (as here) or over goat cheese sprinkled with herbs, and it also adds brightness when whisked into meat marinades. Pomegranate molasses is available at many supermarkets, Middle Eastern markets, and specialty food stores. **8 to 10 servings**

8   large navel oranges (preferably Cara Cara), all peel and
           white pith cut away, oranges sliced into thin rounds
¼   cup floral honey (such as tupelo or orange blossom)
3   tablespoons pomegranate molasses
½   teaspoon ground cinnamon
¼   teaspoon fine sea salt
8   large Medjool dates, pitted, chopped

Arrange orange slices, overlapping slightly, on large rimmed platter. Whisk honey, pomegranate molasses, cinnamon, and sea salt in small bowl to blend; drizzle evenly over oranges. Sprinkle oranges evenly with chopped dates.

DO AHEAD: *Can be made 2 hours ahead. Let stand at room temperature.*

Keeping Cool with Summer Fruits

Summer fruits hit the spot for cool and easy desserts that don't require using the oven.

Macerate fruit to infuse flavor. Macerating is simply marinating fruit in sugar syrup flavored with wine, liqueur, fresh herbs, citrus, or spices. Serve the fruit with the syrup and some cookies, or layer with pound cake and whipped cream in parfait glasses.

Freeze summer fruit to enjoy in smoothies and shakes. Pit, peel, and stem fruits, then cut into large chunks. Arrange in a single layer on a baking sheet and freeze. Once frozen, store them in freezer bags or containers.

Grill fruit while the coals are still hot in the barbecue. Wipe the grill clean with a wet cloth before grilling fruit. Grill until the fruit is heated through and marks form—just a couple of minutes per side. Serve with ice cream, yogurt, mascarpone cheese, or your favorite dessert sauce.

Bittersweet Chocolate–Orange Fondue

Fondue originated in Switzerland and gained fame in America during the 1970s. Simple to make and fun to eat, this chocolate version is spiked with Grand Marnier and grated orange peel, then served with skewers and an array of fresh and dried fruit and bits of cake as dippers. So none of it gets cooked away, don't allow the fondue to simmer once the final amount of liqueur is added. **4 servings**

⅓	cup heavy whipping cream
1½	teaspoons (packed) finely grated orange peel
8	ounces bittersweet or semisweet chocolate (do not exceed 61% cacao), chopped
3	tablespoons Grand Marnier or other orange liqueur, divided
8	1-inch pieces pound cake
8	1-inch pieces angel food cake
8	strawberries, hulled
2	kiwis, peeled, each cut into 4 rounds
1	small pear, cored, cut into 1-inch pieces
1	large banana, peeled, cut into 8 rounds
1	orange, peel and white pith removed, cut into sections
8	dried Calimyrna figs
8	dried apricot halves

Bring cream and grated orange peel to simmer in heavy medium saucepan. Reduce heat to low. Add chopped chocolate and 1 tablespoon Grand Marnier; whisk until mixture is smooth. Remove fondue from heat and whisk in remaining 2 tablespoons Grand Marnier.

Transfer fondue to fondue pot. Place over candle or canned heat burner. Serve with cake pieces and fruit for dipping.

> ### Ingredient Tip: **Better Chocolate**
> Since no sugar is added to this fondue, the sweetness will be determined by the percentage of cacao in the chocolate you use. Remember: the lower the cacao percentage, the sweeter the chocolate. Bittersweet chocolate with no higher than 61% cacao will provide a perfect balance of bitter-sweet flavors.

Raspberry-Apricot Compote with Champagne and Lemon Verbena

Lemon verbena, an herb with a lovely lemon perfume flavor, can be found at some farmers' markets and at nurseries. Fresh peaches would be wonderful here in place of the apricots (you'll need to use about four). If you don't want to pop open a bottle of Champagne just for the compote, feel free to substitute cava (Spanish sparkling wine), Prosecco or Moscato d'Asti (Italian sparkling wines), or even Sauvignon Blanc. This would be delicious served with the Lemon Cream Tart (page 272). **8 servings**

¼	cup brut Champagne
2	tablespoons sugar
1	teaspoon minced fresh lemon verbena or fresh tarragon
2	½-pint containers raspberries
8	apricots, halved, pitted, cut into ½-inch pieces

Stir Champagne, sugar, and lemon verbena in medium bowl until sugar dissolves. Fold in berries and apricots.

DO AHEAD: *Can be made 1 hour ahead. Cover and chill.*

Warm Rhubarb Compote with Walnut-Coconut Crunch

Warm Rhubarb Compote with Walnut-Coconut Crunch

This super-quick dessert can be assembled in less than half an hour, but it's also a great make-ahead treat. Unsweetened flaked organic coconut is available at natural foods stores and specialty foods stores. **4 servings**

4   cups ½-inch pieces trimmed fresh rhubarb (about 1 pound)
⅔   cup plus 5 tablespoons sugar
¼   cup crème de cassis (black currant liqueur) or Chambord
        (black raspberry liqueur)
½   cup walnut pieces
½   cup ¼-inch-thick strips unsweetened flaked organic coconut
⅔   cup plain Greek-style yogurt
       Wildflower honey

Bring rhubarb, ⅔ cup sugar, and crème de cassis to boil in heavy medium saucepan, stirring until sugar dissolves. Reduce heat to low; cover and simmer until rhubarb is soft, about 10 minutes. Cool slightly.

DO AHEAD: *Can be made 1 day ahead. Cover and chill. Rewarm, if desired.*

Place walnuts and remaining 5 tablespoons sugar in medium nonstick skillet. Stir constantly over high heat until sugar melts and turns deep amber color, about 3 minutes. Remove from heat. Add coconut and stir until well combined, about 30 seconds. Press onto bottom of skillet. Cool in skillet. Break walnut-coconut crunch into shards.

DO AHEAD: *Can be made 1 day ahead. Store airtight at room temperature.*

Divide rhubarb compote among 4 large wineglasses. Spoon dollop of yogurt atop compote, drizzle with honey, and top with walnut-coconut crunch.

Rhubarb and Strawberry Compote with Fresh Mint

This versatile springtime compote is great over waffles, pancakes, vanilla ice cream, and angel food cake or pound cake. **Makes about 3 cups**

3   cups ½-inch pieces trimmed fresh rhubarb (about 13 ounces)
¾   cup sugar
¼   cup water
1   1-pint container strawberries, hulled, halved
2   tablespoons chopped fresh mint

Combine rhubarb, sugar, and ¼ cup water in heavy large saucepan. Bring to simmer over medium heat, stirring occasionally until sugar dissolves, about 3 minutes. Simmer gently until rhubarb is tender but not falling apart, stirring occasionally, about 7 minutes. Remove from heat. Stir in strawberries. Transfer to bowl and stir in mint. Chill until cold, about 1 hour.

DO AHEAD: *Can be made 4 hours ahead. Cover and keep chilled.*

Varietal Honeys

When bees forage in a single location—an orange grove or a thyme patch, for example—the honey that results assumes a special character and is known as a varietal honey. Here are a few varietal honeys worth trying. They're listed from mild to intense.

ORANGE BLOSSOM: floral and subtle

LAVENDER: perfumey and complex

THYME: aromatic and resinous

TUPELO: maple-y and buttery

BUCKWHEAT: flavors of dark caramel

CHESTNUT: earthy and intense (best paired with cheese)

Ginger Yogurt with Berries and Crunchy Caramel

This makes a wonderful brunch dish as well as a light, refreshing dessert. The berries and yogurt can be put together a few hours ahead. Fifteen minutes or so before the meal, make the caramel and pour it over the berries; it needs to harden for a few minutes before being served. **6 servings**

Berries and Yogurt
5¼ cups plain Greek-style yogurt (about 42 ounces)
¾ cup minced crystallized ginger
1 ½-pint container raspberries
1 ½-pint container blackberries
1 ½-pint container blueberries
1 1-pint container strawberries, hulled, halved
 (quartered if large)

Caramel
1 cup sugar
¼ cup water

BERRIES AND YOGURT: Mix yogurt and ginger in medium bowl. Spread mixture in large shallow serving bowl. Cover yogurt with all the berries.

DO AHEAD: *Can be made 4 hours ahead. Cover and chill.*

CARAMEL: Stir sugar and ¼ cup water in heavy medium saucepan over low heat until sugar dissolves. Increase heat and boil without stirring until syrup is deep amber color, occasionally brushing down sides of pan with wet pastry brush and swirling pan, about 7 minutes. Immediately pour hot caramel over berries, avoiding pouring down inner sides of bowl. Let stand until caramel hardens, about 5 minutes, and serve.

> Ingredient Tip: **Greek-Style Yogurt**
> For more information on Greek-style yogurt, see page 8. To make your own, see page 36.

Cognac-Glazed Dried Apricots with Cinnamon-Spiced Yogurt

This would be the perfect dessert following a Greek, Turkish, or Moroccan meal. Igniting the Cognac burns off the alcohol while preserving the lovely flavor; make sure you have long matches on hand for this step. **6 servings**

Yogurt
3 cups plain Greek-style yogurt or drained plain whole-milk yogurt
¾ teaspoon ground cinnamon

Apricots
1 tablespoon finely slivered orange peel
1 tablespoon unsalted butter
2 tablespoons sugar
1 pound dried pitted whole Mediterranean-style apricots
 (about 3 cups), halved crosswise
1 cup plus 2 tablespoons orange juice
⅓ cup Cognac or other brandy

 Unsalted natural pistachios, toasted
 Fresh mint leaves, slivered

YOGURT: Stir yogurt and cinnamon in medium bowl to blend. Cover and chill at least 1 hour.

DO AHEAD: *Can be made 1 day ahead. Keep chilled.*

APRICOTS: Cook orange peel in small saucepan of boiling water 5 minutes. Drain and reserve peel.

Melt butter in medium skillet over medium heat. Whisk in sugar. Add apricots; toss. Sauté until beginning to brown in spots, about 8 minutes. Add 1 cup orange juice and reserved orange peel. Simmer uncovered until juice is reduced to thick syrup and apricots are tender, stirring occasionally, about 8 minutes.

DO AHEAD: *Can be made 1 day ahead. Cover and chill. Bring to simmer before continuing.*

Remove apricots from heat; add Cognac. Carefully ignite with long match. Let flames subside and return skillet to heat, shaking skillet occasionally. Mix in remaining 2 tablespoons orange juice and simmer 1 minute, stirring constantly. Spoon chilled yogurt into 6 dessert dishes. Spoon warm apricots and syrup over. Sprinkle with pistachios and mint.

Strawberry and Blueberry Summer Pudding

This simple and delicious British concoction is much more than the sum of its parts: Fresh berries with buttered bread and sugar are transformed into a surprisingly light and luscious dessert. Removing the strawberry's hull, the tough bit of pulp at the stem end, is easy with a huller (stub-ended tweezers designed expressly for hulling strawberries) or a paring knife. **8 servings**

2	pounds strawberries, hulled, sliced
6	tablespoons sugar, divided
	Pinch of salt
1	pound blueberries
¼	cup (½ stick) unsalted butter, room temperature
12	slices firm-textured white bread (such as Pepperidge Farm), crusts removed
2	cups chilled heavy whipping cream
¼	cup powdered sugar
1	teaspoon vanilla extract

Combine strawberries, 2 tablespoons sugar, and salt in large bowl. Mash to coarse puree. Stir blueberries and remaining 4 tablespoons sugar in large saucepan over medium heat until sugar dissolves and berries release juices, about 7 minutes. Increase heat and boil until mixture thickens slightly, stirring often, about 5 minutes. Remove from heat; add strawberry mixture.

Line 6-cup bowl with 3 sheets of plastic wrap, leaving 6-inch overhang. Generously butter 1 side of bread slices. Line bowl with bread, buttered side up, cutting pieces to cover bowl completely. Pour berry mixture into bread-lined bowl. Top with remaining bread, buttered side down, cutting pieces to cover completely. Fold plastic wrap over bread. Place plate slightly smaller than top of bowl atop pudding. Weigh down plate with 4 pounds of canned goods or dried beans and chill at least 12 hours.

DO AHEAD: *Can be made 3 days ahead. Keep chilled.*

Beat cream, powdered sugar, and vanilla in large bowl until peaks form. Remove weights and plate from pudding. Open plastic wrap. Place large plate atop bowl and invert pudding onto plate. Remove bowl, then plastic. Spoon pudding onto 8 serving plates. Serve with whipped cream.

Raspberries with Saba Zabaglione

Zabaglione is a velvety Italian custard. This one is enhanced with saba, a thick, syrupy Italian vinegar that is made with unfermented grape juice. It's dark in color, with an intense, sweet-tart flavor. Saba is available at specialty foods stores and from online retailers. **4 servings**

4	large egg yolks
¼	cup powdered sugar
¼	cup saba vinegar
2	tablespoons water
½	cup chilled heavy whipping cream
12	ounces raspberries

Whisk egg yolks, sugar, saba, and 2 tablespoons water to blend in top of double boiler over barely simmering water (do not allow upper pot to touch water); whisk constantly until mixture thickens and instant-read thermometer inserted into mixture registers 160°F, about 4 minutes. Place top of double boiler with saba mixture over large bowl filled with ice water; continue whisking until mixture cools, about 3 minutes. Beat cream in small bowl until soft peaks form; fold into saba mixture. Cover sabayon with plastic wrap and chill until cold, at least 1 hour.

DO AHEAD: *Can be made 4 hours ahead. Keep chilled.*

Divide raspberries among 4 dessert coupes. Spoon sabayon over and serve.

frozen desserts

frozen desserts

ice cream, gelato & sorbet

Vanilla Ice Cream 446
French Quarter Chocolate Ice Cream 447
Coffee-Molasses Ice Cream with
  Molasses-Glazed Pecans 447
Brown Butter and Peanut Brittle
  Ice Cream 449
Brown Sugar Ice Cream with Cayenne-
  Spiced Walnuts 450
Orange Ice Cream 451
Lemon Verbena Ice Cream 451
Persimmon Ice Cream 452
Brandied-Prune Ice Cream 453
Lemon-Ginger Frozen Yogurt 453
Zabaglione Gelato 454
Pistachio Gelato 454
Chocolate-Cinnamon Gelato with Toffee
  Bits 456
Hazelnut Gelato Profiteroles with Warm
  Kahlúa Sauce 457
Coffee Gelato 458
Strawberry Sorbato 458
Buttermilk Sorbet with Fresh
  Strawberries 459
Sparkling Strawberry and Orange
  Sorbet 459
Plum-Raspberry Sorbet 460
Plum Sorbet with Black Currant
  Liqueur 460
Rhubarb Sorbet with Gingered Orange
  Compote 461
Watermelon-Lime Sorbet 461
Cantaloupe Sorbet with Melon Confetti
  Compote 463
Gingered Lychee Sorbet 464
Rich Chocolate Sorbet 464
Margarita Sorbet 465
Mai Tai Sorbet 465
Mint Julep Sorbet 466
White Russian Sorbet 466

granitas

Strawberry Granita with Whipped Cream 467
Honeydew Bellini Granita with Minted
  Raspberries 468
Red and Green Grape Granitas with Muscat
  and Frozen Sugared Grapes 468
Spiced Apple Cider Granita with Ginger
  Whipped Cream 470
Lime Granita with Candied Mint Leaves and
  Crème Fraîche 471
Cranberry Granita with Orange Whipped
  Cream 471

ice pops, sandwiches & cones

Watermelon-Lemonade Ice Pops 473
Apple Cider and Rosemary Ice Pops 473
Royal Blueberry Ice Pops 473
Oatmeal-Raisin Cookie Ice-Cream
  Sandwiches 474
Mini S'mores Ice-Cream Sandwiches 474
Chocolate–Peanut Butter Ice-Cream
  Sandwiches 475
Dark Chocolate–Dipped Cherry Ice-Cream
  Cones 476

sundaes

Banana Split Split 476–77
Mexican Hot Fudge Sundaes 477
Sour Cream–Brown Sugar Ice-Cream
  Sundaes with Peaches 477
Black and Tan Sundaes 478
Orange Muscat Ice-Cream Sundaes with
  Spiced Apricots 479
Strawberry Sorbet Sundaes with Prosecco
  Sabayon 480
Cherry "Pie" à la Mode Sundaes 481
Lemon and Honey Ice-Cream Sundaes 482
Caramelized Blood Orange and Almond
  Sundaes 482
Iced Maple Cream with Berries 483
Vanilla Ice Cream with Sesame Candies and
  Halvah 483
Coupe Marron with Coffee Ice Cream 483
Pear Ice Cream with Spiced Pear Compote 484
Macadamia Crunch Ice Cream with Mango
  Sauce 485

specialty frozen desserts

Frozen Plum Soufflés with Cardamom-Plum
  Sauce 486
Brandy Snaps with Lemon Curd Ice Cream
  and Blackberries 487
Boysenberry–Grand Marnier Ice-Cream
  Bonbons 488–89
Pistachio Ice Cream in Phyllo Nests with
  Rose Water–Splashed Strawberries 490
Frozen Milky Way Mousse with Chocolate
  Sauce 491
Pera Bella Helena 492

parfaits, semifreddos & bombes

Coffee-Caramel Parfaits 493
Limoncello Parfaits 494
Italian Semifreddo 494
Meyer Lemon Semifreddo with Summer
  Berries 495
Boysenberry Sorbet and Lemon Ice-Cream
  Bombe 496
Frozen Nougat Terrine with Bittersweet
  Chocolate and Raspberry-Fig Sauces
  497–98
Mint-Truffle Ice-Cream Terrine with Mint
  and Chocolate Sauces 499

ice-cream pies & cakes

Rocky Road Sundae Pie 500
Chocolate-Peppermint Crunch Ice-Cream
  Pie 501
Raspberry Brownie Ice-Cream Pie 502
Peach-Pecan Ice-Cream Pie with Caramel
  Sauce 503
Lemon Meringue Ice-Cream Pie in Toasted
  Pecan Crust 505
Coconut-Rum Pie with Pineapple 506
Peanut Brittle and Caramel Crunch
  Ice-Cream Pie 507
Pumpkin Swirl Ice-Cream Pie with
  Chocolate-Almond Bark and Toffee
  Sauce 508-09

Lemon Meringue Ice-Cream Pie in Toasted Pecan Crust

# Vanilla Ice Cream

Master the recipe for classic vanilla ice cream, and the rest will follow. This version is guaranteed to have you feeling like a pro. It has an intense vanilla flavor—and is speckled with tiny black flecks—thanks to the vanilla bean.

Makes about 1 quart

2	cups heavy whipping cream
1	cup whole milk
1	vanilla bean, split lengthwise
5	large egg yolks
²⁄₃	cup sugar

Combine cream and milk in heavy medium saucepan. Scrape in seeds from vanilla bean; add bean. Bring to simmer over medium-high heat. Remove from heat.

Whisk egg yolks and sugar in large bowl until well blended. Gradually whisk in hot cream mixture; return mixture to same saucepan. Stir constantly over low heat until custard thickens and leaves path on back of spoon when finger is drawn across, about 12 minutes (do not boil). Strain custard into medium metal bowl. Set bowl of custard over large bowl of ice water and stir until mixture is cold.

Process custard in ice-cream maker according to manufacturer's instructions. Transfer ice cream to airtight container and freeze until firm, about 4 hours.

DO AHEAD: *Can be made 3 days ahead. Keep frozen. Let soften slightly at room temperature before serving.*

Recipe Tip: **Ice-Cream Styles**

This vanilla ice cream is French style, which simply means that it's made from a cooked custard that includes egg yolks. Philadelphia style, on the other hand, is just sweetened, flavored cream (or cream and milk). Those egg yolks make the French variety both smoother and silkier, and give it a pale-cream color. Philadelphia style is quicker to prepare and lighter tasting.

Infused with Flavor

Our Vanilla Ice Cream is a classic dessert—and is the perfect base for some delicious variations. Just steep one of the following ingredients in the hot cream and milk mixture for about 20 minutes, strain, then continue with the recipe. To taste the pure flavor of the infusion, skip the vanilla bean, or cut back on the amount you add to the custard. Taste the milk mixture after about 15 minutes to see if you need to add more of the ingredient. Keep in mind that adding the eggs and freezing the mixture will mute the flavor of the infusion.

Cinnamon sticks
Whole star anise
Fresh sliced peeled ginger
Cardamom pods
Chopped fresh lemongrass
White, black, or pink peppercorns
Fresh mint leaves
Lavender (make sure it hasn't been sprayed with pesticides)
Coffee beans
Strips of orange, lemon, or lime peel

French Quarter Chocolate Ice Cream

Molasses and a little bourbon give this dessert its New Orleans accent. Chicory coffee, a favorite beverage in that southern city, would be a delicious accompaniment. **Makes about 1 quart**

½   cup mild-flavored (light) molasses
4   extra-large egg yolks
1   tablespoon (packed) dark brown sugar
     Pinch of ground ginger
     Pinch of ground cinnamon
     Pinch of salt
2   cups chilled heavy whipping cream, divided
6   ounces bittersweet or semisweet chocolate (do not exceed 61% cacao), chopped
3   tablespoons chilled unsalted butter, cut into pieces
2   tablespoons bourbon

Whisk molasses, egg yolks, sugar, ginger, cinnamon, and salt in medium bowl to blend. Bring 1 cup cream to simmer in heavy medium saucepan. Gradually whisk hot cream into molasses mixture. Return to same saucepan and stir constantly over medium heat until custard thickens and leaves path on back of spoon when finger is drawn across, about 3 minutes (do not boil). Remove from heat. Add chocolate and butter and stir until smooth. Strain custard into medium bowl. Mix in remaining 1 cup chilled cream and bourbon. Cover and refrigerate until well chilled.

Process custard in ice-cream maker according to manufacturer's instructions. Transfer ice cream to airtight container and freeze until firm, about 4 hours.

DO AHEAD: *Can be made 3 days ahead. Keep frozen.*

Ingredient Tip: Molasses
Molasses comes from the liquid that's left over after the sugar-making process is complete. It is available in three strengths—light, dark, and blackstrap. For this recipe, be sure to use light molasses; dark or blackstrap would be too pungent.

Coffee-Molasses Ice Cream with Molasses-Glazed Pecans

Sweet-savory pecans are the perfect counterpoint to coffee ice cream. Consider making a double batch of the addictive pecans for snacking. **6 servings**

Ice Cream
3   cups heavy whipping cream, divided
1   cup whole milk
6   large egg yolks
¾   cup mild-flavored (light) molasses
¼   cup sugar
2   tablespoons instant coffee crystals

Pecans
¼   cup mild-flavored (light) molasses
¼   cup sugar
     Pinch of salt
2   cups pecan halves

ICE CREAM: Bring 2 cups cream and milk to boil in heavy medium saucepan. Remove from heat. Whisk egg yolks, molasses, and sugar to blend in large bowl. Gradually whisk in hot cream mixture. Return mixture to same saucepan and stir constantly over medium-low heat until mixture thickens and leaves path on back of spoon when finger is drawn across, about 12 minutes (do not boil). Strain custard into medium bowl. Mix in coffee crystals, then remaining 1 cup cream. Cover and refrigerate coffee custard until well chilled.

Process coffee custard in ice cream maker according to manufacturer's instructions. Transfer ice cream to airtight container and freeze until firm, about 4 hours.

DO AHEAD: *Can be made 1 week ahead. Keep frozen.*

PECANS: Position rack in center of oven and preheat to 350°F. Butter large baking sheet. Line another large baking sheet with waxed paper. Combine molasses, sugar, and salt in heavy medium saucepan. Boil 1 minute. Remove from heat. Add pecans and stir to coat well. Spread pecans on buttered baking sheet. Bake until pecans are just beginning to brown, about 10 minutes. Immediately transfer pecans to waxed paper–lined baking sheet and separate with 2 forks. Cool completely.

DO AHEAD: *Can be made 1 week ahead. Store airtight at room temperature.*

Brown Butter and Peanut Brittle Ice Cream

Brown butter is simply butter that has been cooked until it has an amber color and nutty flavor. But what it does to this ice cream is nothing less than spectacular, adding rich complexity. It's perfect with the stirred-in bits of sweet, crunchy peanut brittle. **Makes about 1 quart**

6	tablespoons (¾ stick) unsalted butter
2	cups heavy whipping cream
1	cup whole milk
6	large egg yolks
⅓	cup sugar
⅓	cup (packed) dark brown sugar
¼	teaspoon salt
¾	teaspoon vanilla extract
¾	cup coarsely chopped peanut brittle

Melt butter in small skillet over medium-low heat. Cook until butter is dark amber, stirring occasionally and watching closely to avoid burning, about 6 minutes. Pour through fine strainer into small bowl.

Bring cream and milk to simmer in large saucepan. Whisk egg yolks, both sugars, and salt in large bowl until thick and well blended. Add brown butter; whisk to blend. Gradually whisk hot cream mixture into yolk mixture; return to same saucepan. Stir constantly over medium-low heat until custard thickens and leaves path on back of spoon when finger is drawn across, about 5 minutes (do not boil). Strain custard into large bowl [1]. Set bowl over larger bowl of ice water. Stir until custard is cold. Stir in vanilla.

Process custard in ice-cream maker according to manufacturer's instructions. Transfer ice cream to airtight container [2] and stir in peanut brittle [3]. Freeze until firm, about 4 hours.

DO AHEAD: *Can be made 2 days ahead. Keep frozen.*

Technique Tip: Browning Butter

How does butter brown? It's simple: Butter is made up of three basic components—water, milk solids, and milk fat. As the melted butter cooks in the skillet, the water boils off and the milk solids begin to turn brown. You'll know your brown butter is ready when it's a deep amber color and smells nutty.

Brown Sugar Ice Cream with Cayenne-Spiced Walnuts

Ice cream goes southwestern. Spicy cayenne and black pepper walnuts are stirred in at the last minute, and brown sugar gives the ice cream a subtle caramel flavor. **Makes about 1½ quarts**

1½   **cups whole milk**
1½   **cups heavy whipping cream**
1   **cup (packed) golden brown sugar**
6   **large egg yolks**
      Pinch of salt
1   **cup walnut pieces**
1   **tablespoon vegetable oil**
½   **teaspoon cayenne pepper**
½   **teaspoon freshly ground black pepper**

Preheat oven to 375°F. Bring milk and cream to simmer in heavy medium saucepan over medium heat. Whisk sugar, egg yolks, and salt in medium bowl to blend; gradually whisk in hot milk mixture. Return mixture to same saucepan. Stir constantly over medium heat until custard thickens and leaves path on back of spoon when finger is drawn across, about 4 minutes (do not boil). Strain custard into bowl; chill until cold.

Meanwhile, toss walnuts, oil, cayenne, and black pepper in medium bowl. Spread nuts on rimmed baking sheet. Toast nuts in oven until golden brown, stirring often, about 6 minutes.

Process custard in ice-cream maker according to manufacturer's instructions, adding walnuts during last 5 minutes of churning. Transfer ice cream to airtight container and freeze until firm, about 4 hours.

DO AHEAD: *Can be made 3 days ahead. Keep frozen.*

Frozen Desserts, Defined

ICE CREAM: A frozen dessert made from milk and/or cream. By law, commercial ice cream must contain at least 10% milk fat (or 8% for chocolate ice cream). In the context of home cooking, traditional ice cream is made from a sweetened custard (a mixture of milk and/or cream and egg yolks), which gives it a rich taste and a creamy texture.

GELATO: Italian ice cream that is often more intense in flavor than American-style ice cream. There are many styles of gelato, but it is usually lower in fat than ice cream.

SORBET: A frozen dessert made without milk. Most sorbets are made from water, sugar, and fruit puree (egg whites are sometimes added). Sorbets are intensely flavored and have a somewhat icy texture.

GRANITA: Granitas are like shaved ice—only better. They're not topped with a sweet syrup; instead, the ice is made from the syrup (usually a sweetened fruit puree or juice) and flaked into crystals using a fork.

PARFAIT: A layered frozen dessert, usually served in a tall parfait glass that shows off each of the layers.

SEMIFREDDO: Meaning "half cold," *semifreddo* is a classic Italian dessert that is partially frozen in a baking pan (no ice-cream maker required). Mixing whipped cream and a little alcohol into ice cream prevents the mixture from freezing solid.

Orange Ice Cream

Sometimes plain old vanilla just won't do. A scoop of orange-flavored ice cream—so simple to prepare—adds intrigue to warm cherry pie, spiced apple crumble, or dark chocolate cake. **Makes about 2⅓ cups**

4 large egg yolks
⅓ cup sugar
2 cups half and half
2 teaspoons finely grated orange peel

Whisk egg yolks and sugar in medium bowl until blended. Bring half and half and orange peel to simmer in heavy medium saucepan. Gradually whisk into yolk mixture; return to same saucepan and stir constantly over medium-low heat until custard thickens slightly and leaves path on back of spoon when finger is drawn across, about 4 minutes (do not boil). Pour custard into medium bowl. Refrigerate custard until cold.

Process custard in ice-cream maker according to manufacturer's instructions. Transfer ice cream to airtight container and freeze until firm, about 4 hours.

DO AHEAD: *Can be made 4 days ahead. Keep frozen.*

Technique Tip: Softening Ice Cream

To mix ingredients into ice cream, or to make a frozen terrine, torte, or pie, the ice cream needs to be soft enough to stir or spread. The quickest and easiest way to get rid of that hard chill is to place the carton in the microwave. Heat it in 10-second intervals on the lowest power setting; stir between intervals to get even softening. You can also put the ice cream in the refrigerator or leave it out at room temperature, checking the consistency every 10 minutes or so.

Lemon Verbena Ice Cream

Lemon verbena is a South American herb with a strong lemon flavor and haunting floral fragrance. You can find it at plant nurseries and some farmers' markets. **Makes about 2½ cups**

1 cup heavy whipping cream
1 cup whole milk
½ cup sugar, divided
¼ cup fresh lemon verbena leaves
7 large egg yolks

Bring cream, milk, ¼ cup sugar, and lemon verbena just to boil in medium saucepan, stirring until sugar dissolves. Remove from heat; cover and let steep 2 hours.

Whisk egg yolks and remaining ¼ cup sugar in medium bowl. Return cream mixture to boil. Strain hot cream mixture; gradually whisk into yolk mixture. Return custard to same saucepan. Stir over medium-low heat until custard thickens and leaves path on back of spoon when finger is drawn across, about 4 minutes (do not boil). Strain custard into medium bowl. Chill until cold.

Process custard in ice-cream maker according to manufacturer's instructions. Transfer ice cream to airtight container and freeze until firm, about 4 hours.

DO AHEAD: *Can be made 4 days ahead. Keep frozen.*

Persimmon Ice Cream

Freshly crushed black peppercorns bring out the faint spiciness of the persimmons. Serve with Vanilla Shortbread Cookies (page 542) or the Apple-Spice Cake with Brown Sugar Glaze (page 53). **Makes about 1 quart**

1½ teaspoons whole black peppercorns
1 cup water
¾ cup sugar
¼ teaspoon (scant) salt
8 large ripe Hachiya persimmons, halved, seeded
1 cup chilled heavy whipping cream

Heat heavy small skillet over medium heat. Add peppercorns and toast until fragrant and beginning to smoke, stirring often, about 3 minutes. Transfer to small bowl to cool. Coarsely crush peppercorns in mortar with pestle, or place in resealable plastic freezer bag, seal, and crush with mallet.

Transfer crushed peppercorns to small saucepan. Add 1 cup water, sugar, and salt. Bring to boil, stirring until sugar dissolves. Boil mixture until reduced to 1 cup, about 4 minutes. Refrigerate until cold.

DO AHEAD: *Black pepper syrup can be made 1 day ahead. Cover and keep refrigerated.*

Scoop persimmon flesh from skins into blender. Puree until smooth. Measure 2 cups puree for making ice cream (reserve any remaining puree for another use). Cover and chill puree until cold.

Strain black pepper syrup into large bowl. Whisk in 2 cups persimmon puree and cream. Process custard in ice-cream maker according to manufacturer's instructions. Transfer ice cream to airtight container and freeze until firm, about 4 hours.

DO AHEAD: *Can be made 1 day ahead. Keep frozen.*

Market Tip: Persimmons

Persimmons are fall-winter fruits that range in color from yellow-orange to red. There are two common varieties of persimmons, Fuyu and Hachiya; you can find both varieties at farmers' markets, supermarkets, and specialty foods stores from October to February. This recipe calls for the large, elongated persimmons known as Hachiyas, which aren't ripe until they're very soft. Fuyus, on the other hand, are ready to eat when they're still quite firm. To ripen a Hachiya persimmon, let it sit on the counter for a few days. To ripen it more quickly, place it in a brown paper bag with an apple or banana.

How to Buy an Ice-Cream Maker

Which ice-cream machine is right for you? It all depends on your budget, your lifestyle, and your passion for frozen desserts.

ICE AND ROCK SALT MACHINES: Want a workout along with your ice cream? Then this is the machine for you. Pour the custard into the metal container, place the metal container into the larger bucket-style container, then pack layers of ice and rock salt between the two containers. (The salt helps lower the temperature and keeps the brine solution nice and chilly—between 8° and 12°.) The next step? Hand-cranking the machine until the ice cream freezes. For folks looking for less exercise, this type of machine is also available with an electric motor. These machines often make a large quantity of ice cream.

MACHINES WITH A SEPARATE CANISTER: This affordable type of machine is widely available in many models and brands. To make ice cream, first place the container (which is filled with a liquid coolant) in the freezer for at least 24 hours. Once the container is completely frozen, pour in the custard, flip the switch, and let the ice-cream-making begin. This style of ice-cream maker requires freezer space for the container and some pre-planning, but it's a good choice for those who make ice cream a few times a month.

ALL-IN-ONE UNITS: For ice cream on demand, this is your machine; it's more expensive, but the extra cost means that you can go from custard to ice cream in less than an hour. These machines have built-in compressors, which eliminates the need to pre-freeze the canister. They are larger than other machines, so are not the best bet for small kitchens. But if you're an ice-cream fanatic and have the space, consider investing in an all-in-one machine.

Brandied-Prune Ice Cream

Don't be put off by the thought of prunes for dessert. Jazz them up with some brandy and you'll be amazed at what they do to vanilla ice cream. You can use a purchased premium ice cream or, for an entirely homemade treat, make our Vanilla Ice Cream (page 446). Pair this sophisticated dessert in the fall with a simple walnut cake (such as the Walnut-Orange Cake on page 79) or a slice of apple pie. And if you have Armagnac (the excellent full-flavored brandy from Gascony), use it. It's the classic French pairing for prune ice cream. **12 servings**

1	**cup pitted prunes, cut into quarters**
½	**cup plus 2 tablespoons brandy**
1	**quart vanilla ice cream, slightly softened**

Combine prunes and ½ cup brandy in heavy large saucepan. Cover and simmer over medium heat until brandy is absorbed, about 4 minutes. Cool.

Place softened ice cream in large shallow plastic freezer container. Mix in prunes and remaining 2 tablespoons brandy. Cover and freeze until firm, about 4 hours.

DO AHEAD: *Can be made 4 days ahead. Keep frozen.*

Lemon-Ginger Frozen Yogurt

The fresh, sophisticated flavors of this frozen yogurt are so irresistible that its healthful properties come as a bonus. If you like, set out a toppings bar with granola, fresh fruit, and berries. You can use agave nectar—a low-glycemic sweetener—instead of corn syrup; it's available at some supermarkets, in the aisle where other syrups are sold. **6 servings**

¾	**cup water**
¾	**cup sugar**
¼	**cup light corn syrup or agave nectar**
2	**teaspoons finely grated peeled fresh ginger**
1	**cup plain nonfat yogurt**
1	**cup buttermilk**
¼	**cup fresh lemon juice**
1	**teaspoon finely grated lemon peel**

Bring ¾ cup water, sugar, corn syrup, and ginger to boil in medium saucepan, stirring until sugar dissolves. Boil 2 minutes. Strain ginger syrup into medium bowl and chill until cool.

DO AHEAD: *Syrup can be made 1 day ahead. Keep refrigerated.*

Whisk yogurt, buttermilk, lemon juice, and lemon peel into ginger syrup. Process mixture in ice-cream maker according to manufacturer's instructions. Serve immediately or transfer to airtight container and freeze up to 3 hours.

Serving Tip: **Soft Touch**

For the best texture, serve this frozen yogurt right out of the machine or after it's been frozen for just a few hours. Overnight freezing will make it too hard. In that case, you'll need to thaw it briefly in the microwave, stopping to stir, or let it sit at room temperature for about 15 minutes.

♥♥ Zabaglione Gelato

Marsala is a Sicilian fortified wine and is traditionally used in zabaglione, the light dessert custard. In this recipe, rum is also added for an even more intense flavor. **Makes about 3½ cups**

4	large egg yolks
½	cup sugar
1	cup whole milk
1	cup heavy whipping cream
6	tablespoons imported dry Marsala
2	tablespoons dark rum
1	teaspoon vanilla extract

Whisk egg yolks and sugar in medium bowl until thick, about 2 minutes. Heat milk and cream in medium saucepan over medium heat until mixture bubbles at edges. Gradually whisk hot milk mixture into yolk mixture; return to same saucepan. Stir over medium heat until custard leaves path on back of spoon when finger is drawn across, about 6 minutes (do not boil). Strain into medium bowl. Mix Marsala, rum, and vanilla into custard. Cover and refrigerate custard until cold.

Process custard in ice-cream maker according to manufacturer's instructions. Transfer to airtight container and freeze.

DO AHEAD: *Can be made 2 days ahead. Keep frozen.*

Don't Hurry

The first rule of making frozen desserts: Don't try to rush it. When preparing ice cream or gelato, the cooked custard has to be well chilled before being churned in the ice-cream maker, and the finished product usually has to freeze for at least a few hours before serving. Ice-cream pies and cakes have to freeze for several hours or overnight. Follow the instructions in the recipe carefully: Your patience will be rewarded.

♥♥ Pistachio Gelato

Green food coloring makes this creamy gelato say "pistachio," but it can also be prepared without. For a sophisticated ice-cream-sandwich presentation, serve scoops of the gelato inside halved small sweet brioche buns. **6 servings**

¾	cup unsalted natural pistachios
¾	cup sugar, divided
2	cups whole milk
1	teaspoon almond extract
5	large egg yolks
2	drops green food coloring (optional)
	Additional chopped unsalted natural pistachios

Finely grind pistachios and ¼ cup sugar in processor. Combine pistachio mixture, milk, and almond extract in heavy medium saucepan. Bring to boil. Whisk egg yolks and remaining ½ cup sugar in large bowl to blend. Gradually whisk hot milk mixture into yolk mixture. Return mixture to same saucepan. Stir over medium-low heat until custard thickens slightly and leaves path on back of spoon when finger is drawn across, about 8 minutes (do not boil). Remove from heat. Whisk in food coloring, if using. Refrigerate custard until cold, about 3 hours.

Process custard in ice-cream maker according to manufacturer's instructions. Transfer gelato to airtight container and freeze.

DO AHEAD: *Can be made 2 days ahead. Keep frozen.*

Scoop gelato into glasses or bowls. Garnish with additional chopped pistachios.

Pistachio Gelato

Chocolate-Cinnamon Gelato with Toffee Bits

Creamy meets crunchy when luscious chocolate-cinnamon gelato is punctuated with pieces of crushed toffee candy bars. **Makes about 3 cups**

½	**cup sugar**
2	**tablespoons cornstarch**
1¼	**teaspoons ground cinnamon**
	Pinch of salt
2	**cups whole milk, divided**
5	**ounces bittersweet or semisweet chocolate (do not exceed 61% cacao), chopped**
½	**cup chilled heavy whipping cream**
⅓	**cup coarsely crushed toffee candy (such as Skor, Heath bar, or Almond Roca)**

Whisk sugar, cornstarch, cinnamon, and salt in heavy medium saucepan until blended. Gradually add ¼ cup milk, whisking until cornstarch dissolves. Whisk in remaining 1¾ cups milk. Whisk over medium-high heat until mixture thickens and comes to boil, about 6 minutes. Reduce heat to medium and cook 1 minute longer, whisking occasionally. Remove from heat; add chocolate. Let stand 1 minute, then whisk until melted and smooth.

Transfer gelato mixture to medium bowl. Mix in cream. Place bowl over large bowl filled with ice water and cool, stirring often, about 30 minutes.

Process gelato mixture in ice cream maker according to manufacturer's instructions, adding toffee during last 1 minute of churning. Transfer to airtight container and freeze.

DO AHEAD: *Can be made 2 days ahead. Keep frozen.*

The Scoop on Ice-Cream Scoops

Find an ice-cream scoop to match your personality.

THE TRADITIONALIST: Looking for perfectly round scoops that drop easily from the scoop to the bowl? Consider buying an ice-cream scoop that has antifreeze sealed right into the handle. The antifreeze begins to melt the ice cream on contact, making it easier to scoop out the frozen dessert—and making it possible to get the ice cream out of the scoop without a release mechanism. This type of scoop is available at many online retailers and at housewares stores. Zeroll, a company that's been around since the 1930s, makes many sizes of this type of scoop (zeroll.com).

THE ICE-CREAM ARTIST: At fancy restaurants, ice cream is sometimes served in egg-shape scoops called *quenelles*. With some practice, you can learn to create the shape using two spoons, or you can buy an oval-shape ice cream scoop. Matfer Bourgeat makes a nice sturdy version, available at culinarycookware.com.

THE CROWD-PLEASER: For scooping mass quantities of ice cream quickly, try an ice-cream spade. The flat, shovel-like contraption won't make pretty scoops, but it will make serving a hungry crowd quick and easy. Many manufacturers make this type of scoop. Head to your local housewares store and see which one feels most comfortable in your hand.

Hazelnut Gelato Profiteroles with Warm Kahlúa Sauce

In a sophisticated twist on traditional profiteroles—cream puffs filled with custard or vanilla ice cream—these feature hazelnut gelato and a drizzle of Kahlúa-spiked chocolate sauce. If you have any unfilled cream puffs left over, you can freeze them to enjoy later. **12 servings**

Hazelnut Gelato

1	cup hazelnuts, toasted, husked
1	quart half and half
¾	cup sugar
3	large egg yolks
1½	teaspoons vanilla extract

Sauce

1	cup half and half
¾	cup sugar
2	tablespoons (¼ stick) unsalted butter
1¼	pounds bittersweet or semisweet chocolate (do not exceed 61% cacao), chopped
¼	cup Kahlúa or other coffee liqueur
1	teaspoon vanilla extract

Cream Puffs

1	cup whole milk
½	cup (1 stick) unsalted butter, cut into ½-inch cubes
½	teaspoon salt
1¼	cups unbleached all purpose flour
5	large eggs

HAZELNUT GELATO: Finely grind hazelnuts in processor. Bring half and half to simmer in large saucepan. Whisk sugar and egg yolks in large bowl to blend. Gradually whisk hot half and half into sugar mixture; return to same saucepan. Stir over medium heat until custard thickens slightly, about 3 minutes (do not boil). Strain into large bowl. Stir in ground hazelnuts and vanilla. Refrigerate custard until cold, about 4 hours. Process custard in ice-cream maker according to manufacturer's instructions. Transfer to airtight container and freeze.

DO AHEAD: *Can be made 2 days ahead. Keep frozen.*

SAUCE: Bring half and half, sugar, and butter to simmer in heavy medium saucepan, stirring until sugar dissolves. Remove from heat; add chocolate and whisk until melted and smooth. Stir in Kahlúa and vanilla.

DO AHEAD: *Can be made 1 day ahead. Cool completely, cover, and refrigerate. Rewarm before serving.*

CREAM PUFFS: Preheat oven to 425°F. Line 2 large baking sheets with parchment paper. Bring milk, butter, and salt to boil in heavy medium saucepan. Remove from heat. Stir in flour. Cook over medium heat until mixture is smooth, pulls away from sides of pan, and forms ball, constantly stirring vigorously, about 1½ minutes. Remove from heat. Using electric mixer, mix dough at low speed until dough cools slightly but is still very warm. Beat in eggs 1 at a time at medium speed, blending well after each addition.

Drop walnut-size pieces of dough onto prepared sheets. Bake until puffed and beginning to brown, about 15 minutes. Reduce oven temperature to 375°F; continue baking until puffs are brown and very crisp, about 10 minutes. Cool on baking sheets.

Cut 36 cream puffs in half horizontally. Place scoop of gelato in bottom half of each cream puff; cover with top half.

DO AHEAD: *Can be made 1 day ahead. Cover and freeze.*

Place 3 profiteroles on each plate. Drizzle with warm sauce.

Coffee Gelato

A classic, pure and simple. Instant espresso powder gives a more intense flavor, but if you can't find it, you can use instant coffee powder. **6 servings**

5	large egg yolks
1	cup sugar
1½	cups whole milk
1	tablespoon instant espresso powder dissolved in ½ cup hot water

Whisk egg yolks and sugar in large bowl to blend. Bring milk to boil in heavy medium saucepan. Gradually whisk hot milk into egg mixture, then whisk in espresso mixture. Return mixture to same saucepan. Stir over medium heat until custard thickens and leaves path on back of spoon when finger is drawn across, about 8 minutes (do not boil). Refrigerate until cold, about 3 hours.

Process custard in ice-cream maker according to manufacturer's instructions. Transfer to airtight container and freeze.

DO AHEAD: *Can be made 2 days ahead. Keep frozen.*

Strawberry Sorbato

"Sorbato" is a cross between sorbet and gelato—it is made from a fruit puree like a sorbet, but with the addition of cream. **8 servings**

1½	pounds strawberries, hulled, sliced
1	cup sugar
	Pinch of salt
¾	cup heavy whipping cream
1½	tablespoons fresh lemon juice

Toss berries, sugar, and salt in large bowl. Let stand until juices form, about 30 minutes. Puree mixture in batches in blender. Press through fine strainer into medium bowl. Mix cream and lemon juice into puree.

Process mixture in ice-cream maker according to manufacturer's instructions. Transfer to airtight container and freeze.

DO AHEAD: *Can be made 2 days ahead. Keep frozen.*

Buttermilk Sorbet with Fresh Strawberries

Just because it's a sorbet doesn't mean it has to be sweet and fruity; this one has the refreshing tang of buttermilk and the floral sweetness of strawberries. The sorbet's texture is best when freshly made, but if you do prepare it ahead, be sure to let it soften before serving. **4 to 6 servings**

2	cups chilled buttermilk
¼	cup plus 2 tablespoons sugar
¼	cup light corn syrup
1	pound strawberries, hulled, sliced
½	teaspoon finely grated lemon peel

Stir buttermilk, ¼ cup sugar, and corn syrup in medium bowl until sugar dissolves. Process mixture in ice-cream maker according to manufacturer's instructions.

DO AHEAD: *Sorbet can be made 3 days ahead. Transfer to an airtight container and freeze. Let stand 15 minutes at room temperature to soften before serving.*

Toss strawberries, lemon peel, and remaining 2 tablespoons sugar in another medium bowl; let stand until juices form, about 10 minutes. Spoon berries into shallow bowls. Top with scoop of sorbet and serve immediately.

> ## Technique Tip: **Easy Does It**
> Not ready to try making the custard needed for homemade ice cream? Then start with a sorbet. This buttermilk version calls for just three ingredients. Mix them together until the sugar dissolves, then let your ice-cream maker do the rest. It really is that easy.

Sparkling Strawberry and Orange Sorbet

Cava, a Spanish sparkling wine, adds a mild effervescence to this refreshing dessert. For a pretty presentation, serve the sorbet in wide-mouth Champagne coupes. **8 servings**

¾	cup sugar
¼	cup water
1	12-ounce package frozen strawberries, thawed
1	cup orange juice
1	cup brut cava (Spanish sparkling wine)

Stir sugar and ¼ cup water in small saucepan over medium-low heat until sugar dissolves. Bring to boil. Transfer to large bowl. Puree strawberries in processor. Add to syrup. Mix in orange juice and cava. Refrigerate strawberry mixture until well chilled.

Process mixture in ice-cream maker according to manufacturer's instructions. Transfer sorbet to airtight container and freeze.

DO AHEAD: *Can be made 4 days ahead. Keep frozen.*

Plum-Raspberry Sorbet

Serve this light and refreshing dessert with a few crisp, buttery cookies.
Makes about 1 quart

¾   cup plus 2 tablespoons sugar
⅔   cup water
1¼   pounds plums, halved, pitted
2½   ½-pint containers raspberries
¼   to 1 teaspoon fresh lemon juice
    Pinch of salt
    Additional sliced plums
    Additional raspberries
    Fresh mint sprigs

Stir sugar and ⅔ cup water in heavy small saucepan over low heat until sugar dissolves. Increase heat to high; boil syrup 1 minute. Chill until cold, about 1 hour.

Puree plums and raspberries in processor. Strain puree through fine sieve into medium bowl; discard solids in sieve. Add syrup, lemon juice to taste, and salt and blend well.

Process in ice-cream maker according to manufacturer's instructions. Transfer sorbet to airtight container and freeze.

DO AHEAD: *Can be made 2 days ahead. Keep frozen.*

Scoop sorbet into bowls. Garnish with additional sliced plums, additional raspberries, and mint sprigs.

Plum Sorbet with Black Currant Liqueur

Sweet, black currant–flavored crème de cassis intensifies the fruitiness of this plum sorbet. It also gives the sorbet a soft, creamy texture. That's because alcohol freezes at a much colder temperature than the other ingredients, so it prevents hard ice crystals from forming. **Makes about 1 quart**

1   cup sugar
1   cup water
1½   pounds ripe purple plums, quartered, pitted
¼   cup crème de cassis (black currant liqueur) plus additional for drizzling (optional)

Stir sugar and 1 cup water in small saucepan over medium heat until sugar dissolves. Boil until syrup is reduced to generous 1 cup, about 6 minutes. Chill syrup until cold.

Puree plums in processor until smooth. Pour mixture through medium-mesh strainer set over 4-cup measuring cup, pressing on solids to extract as much pulp and liquid as possible. Discard solids in strainer. Stir chilled syrup and crème de cassis into plum puree.

Process mixture in ice-cream maker according to manufacturer's instructions. Transfer sorbet to airtight container and freeze until firm.

DO AHEAD: *Can be made 4 days ahead. Keep frozen.*

Scoop sorbet into dessert glasses or small bowls. Drizzle with additional crème de cassis, if desired.

Rhubarb Sorbet with Gingered Orange Compote

Vibrant red pomegranate juice gives this light, tangy sorbet its pretty pink color. **6 servings**

Sorbet

1½	cups sugar
1½	cups water
8	cups ½-inch pieces trimmed fresh rhubarb (about 2 pounds)
½	cup orange juice
½	cup pomegranate juice
2½	tablespoons Grand Marnier or other orange liqueur
⅛	teaspoon salt

Compote

6	large navel oranges
⅔	cup orange juice
½	cup sugar
½	cup thinly sliced peeled fresh ginger (about 2½ ounces)
1	cinnamon stick

SORBET: Bring sugar and 1½ cups water to boil in heavy medium saucepan, stirring until sugar dissolves. Cool syrup.

Stir rhubarb, orange juice, and ¾ cup syrup in large saucepan over medium heat until rhubarb falls apart and mixture thickens slightly, about 15 minutes. Puree in processor. Press through strainer into large bowl; discard solids in strainer. Mix pomegranate juice, Grand Marnier, salt, and ¾ cup syrup into puree (reserve remaining syrup for another use). Chill until cold.

Process rhubarb mixture in ice-cream maker according to manufacturer's instructions. Transfer sorbet to airtight container and freeze.

DO AHEAD: *Can be made 2 days ahead. Keep frozen.*

COMPOTE: Cut peel and white pith from oranges. Working over medium bowl and using small sharp knife, cut between membranes to release segments.

Mix orange juice, sugar, ginger, and cinnamon in small saucepan over medium heat. Simmer 3 minutes to blend flavors. Cover; cool 5 minutes. Strain syrup into medium bowl. Drain orange segments; add to syrup and cool completely.

Spoon compote into shallow bowls or wineglasses. Top with sorbet.

Watermelon-Lime Sorbet

Don't have an ice-cream maker? This sorbet can also be made in a food processor. You simply freeze the watermelon mixture, stirring occasionally, then throw it into the processor to create the lovely smooth texture. **6 servings**

½	cup dry white wine
½	cup sugar
¼	cup fresh lime juice
5	cups 1-inch cubes peeled seedless watermelon
2	tablespoons frozen orange juice concentrate, thawed
	Lime slices
	Watermelon wedges

Combine wine, sugar, and lime juice in heavy medium saucepan. Bring to simmer, stirring until sugar dissolves. Simmer gently 3 minutes. Cool completely. Puree watermelon in processor. Strain puree through sieve set over large bowl, pressing on solids with back of rubber spatula. Discard solids in sieve. Stir wine mixture and orange juice concentrate into watermelon puree.

To prepare in processor: Pour melon mixture into 8x8x2-inch glass baking dish. Freeze until semi-firm, stirring occasionally, about 2 hours. Cover; freeze until solid, at least 8 hours or overnight. Chill processor work bowl and metal blade. Transfer melon mixture to processor. Using on/off turns and scraping bottom and sides of bowl, process until very smooth.

DO AHEAD: *Can be made 1 day ahead. Transfer sorbet to airtight container and freeze.*

To prepare in ice-cream maker: Process melon mixture in ice cream maker according to manufacturer's instructions. Transfer sorbet to airtight container and freeze.

DO AHEAD: *Can be made 1 day ahead. Keep frozen.*

Freeze 6 small bowls 30 minutes. Scoop sorbet into frozen bowls. Garnish with lime slices and watermelon wedges. Serve immediately.

Cantaloupe Sorbet with Melon Confetti Compote

Essensia, a sweet California dessert wine, heightens the sweetness of cantaloupe. The "confetti" compote is a pretty mix of diced watermelon, honeydew, and cantaloupe—all tossed in a slightly spicy star anise syrup. Look for star anise (brown, star-shaped seedpods) in the spice section of some supermarkets, at specialty foods stores, and at Asian markets. **6 servings**

2	pounds cantaloupe, peeled, seeded, cut into large pieces
1¼	cups Essensia or other sweet dessert wine, divided
¾	cup sugar, divided
1	whole star anise (optional)
1	cup ¼-inch-dice peeled seeded watermelon
1	cup ¼-inch-dice peeled seeded cantaloupe
1	cup ¼-inch-dice peeled seeded honeydew melon
	Fresh mint sprigs

Puree large cantaloupe pieces in blender. Add ½ cup Essensia and ½ cup sugar; blend until sugar dissolves. Process mixture in ice-cream maker according to manufacturer's instructions. Transfer to airtight container and freeze.

DO AHEAD: *Can be made 4 days ahead. Keep frozen.*

Combine remaining ¾ cup Essensia, remaining ¼ cup sugar, and star anise, if using, in heavy small saucepan. Stir over medium heat until sugar dissolves. Simmer until reduced to ½ cup, about 4 minutes. Chill until cold.

DO AHEAD: *Can be made 1 day ahead. Keep chilled.*

Discard star anise. Add diced watermelon, cantaloupe, and honeydew to syrup and toss gently. Scoop sorbet into glasses. Spoon compote over. Garnish with mint.

Market Tip: Cantaloupe
At the market, choose heavy, fragrant cantaloupes with not much of a green tinge. Skip melons with the stems still attached; they were picked too early. If you hear sloshing when you pick up the melon, choose a different one. Keep in mind that once you bring a cantaloupe home, it will soften but will not get any sweeter.

Ingredient Tip: Essensia
Muscat, a dessert wine made from Muscat grapes, lends a delicate sweetness to frozen desserts. It goes by a few different names, including Essensia, a California brand made from Orange Muscat grapes, and Italian *moscato*. You can find Muscat wines at liquor or wine stores, or at some supermarkets.

Gingered Lychee Sorbet

Canned lychees, a Chinese fruit, and moscato *give this sorbet a delicate sweetness; grated fresh ginger adds a little kick.* **Makes about 1 quart**

¾   **cup water**
⅓   **cup sugar**
1   **tablespoon grated fresh ginger**
2   **20-ounce cans lychees in syrup**
½   **cup *moscato* or other sweet white dessert wine**

Stir ¾ cup water, sugar, and ginger in heavy small saucepan over low heat until sugar dissolves. Simmer 5 minutes. Strain. Cool ginger syrup completely.

Drain lychees, reserving ½ cup syrup from can. Puree lychees in blender or processor with ½ cup reserved canned syrup until smooth. Strain. Combine pureed lychees, ginger syrup, and wine. Process mixture in ice-cream maker according to manufacturer's instructions. Transfer sorbet to container and freeze.

DO AHEAD: *Can be made 3 days ahead. Keep frozen.*

Technique Tip: **DIY Sorbet**

No ice-cream maker? No problem. First, transfer the lychee mixture to a shallow 6-cup baking dish. Freeze until the edges are firm and the center is slushy, about three hours. Puree the mixture in a food processor until smooth, then return the mixture to the baking dish and freeze until almost firm, about an hour and a half. Puree the sorbet in the processor once more, then return to the dish and freeze until firm. Using this method, the sorbet can be made one day ahead.

Rich Chocolate Sorbet

This deluxe sorbet is delicious all by itself, but it also makes a great accompaniment to Vanilla Chiffon Cake (page 50). The egg yolks disqualify it as a sorbet in the strictest sense, but it contains neither milk nor cream and is also kosher, so it's a good choice for Passover. **Makes about 3 cups**

1   **vanilla bean, split lengthwise**
2   **cups water**
1   **cup sugar**
⅛   **teaspoon coarse kosher salt**
12 **ounces bittersweet or semisweet chocolate (do not exceed 61% cacao), chopped**
3   **large egg yolks**
2   **tablespoons brandy**

Scrape seeds from vanilla bean into heavy medium saucepan; add bean. Add 2 cups water, sugar, and coarse salt. Whisk over medium heat until sugar dissolves. Reduce heat to low. Add chocolate; whisk until completely melted and smooth. Remove from heat.

Whisk egg yolks in medium bowl to blend. Gradually whisk in hot chocolate mixture; return to same saucepan. Stir over medium heat until custard thickens slightly and leaves path on back of spoon when finger is drawn across, about 3 minutes (do not boil). Strain into medium bowl. Chill uncovered until cold, about 2 hours. Mix in brandy.

Process sorbet mixture in ice-cream maker according to manufacturer's instructions (sorbet will be very soft).

Spoon sorbet into container. Cover and freeze until firm, at least 8 hours.

DO AHEAD: *Can be made 4 days ahead. Keep frozen.*

Margarita Sorbet

This refreshing treat takes one of our favorite drinks and sends it to the deep freeze. Complete the homage by serving the sorbet in sugar-rimmed Margarita glasses garnished with lime slices. **4 servings**

2	cups water
1	cup sugar
2/3	cup fresh lime juice
6	tablespoons triple sec
6	tablespoons tequila
1	teaspoon finely grated lime peel

Stir 2 cups water and sugar in heavy medium saucepan over medium heat until sugar dissolves. Increase heat and bring to boil. Pour into medium bowl. Mix in lime juice, triple sec, tequila, and lime peel. Refrigerate until cold, about 2 hours.

Process sorbet mixture in ice-cream maker according to manufacturer's instructions. Transfer sorbet to airtight container and freeze until firm, about 2 hours.

DO AHEAD: *Can be made 2 days ahead. Keep frozen.*

Freeze 4 Margarita glasses 1 hour. Scoop sorbet into frozen glasses and serve immediately.

Granita Style

It's easy to turn the Margarita Sorbet into a granita. First, mix an additional 1 cup of water into the sorbet mixture. Freeze the mixture in a bowl until semi-firm, whisking occasionally, about three hours. Cover the bowl and freeze until solid, at least six hours. Using a fork, scrape the surface of the granita to form crystals. Scoop the granita into frozen glasses and serve immediately.

Mai Tai Sorbet

The Mai Tai, a mixture of fruit juices and rum, is a classic tropical drink. This frozen treat would be great at a backyard barbecue—paper umbrellas optional. To turn this into a granita, see Granita Style (below)—but add only half a cup of water to the sorbet mixture. **4 servings**

1/2	cup pineapple juice
1/2	cup mango–passion fruit nectar
1/2	cup guava nectar
6	tablespoons dark rum
1/4	cup sugar
4	teaspoons grenadine
1	tablespoon fresh lime juice
4	fresh pineapple wedges (optional)

Combine all ingredients except pineapple wedges in medium metal bowl and stir until sugar dissolves. Process sorbet mixture in ice-cream maker according to manufacturer's instructions. Transfer sorbet to airtight container and freeze until firm, about 2 hours.

DO AHEAD: *Can be made 2 days ahead. Keep frozen.*

Freeze 4 Martini glasses 1 hour. Scoop sorbet into frozen glasses. Garnish with pineapple wedges, if desired, and serve.

Mint Julep Sorbet

In this recipe, Kentucky's famous bourbon-based cocktail becomes a dessert. This is a natural for a Kentucky Derby party but would be a fantastic way to beat the heat all summer long. Serve in julep cups or pretty glasses. To turn this into a granita, see Granita Style (page 465)—but mix only an additional half cup of water into the sorbet mixture. **4 servings**

1½	cups water
¾	cup (loosely packed) fresh mint leaves (from about 2 small bunches)
½	cup sugar
3	tablespoons bourbon
1	tablespoon green crème de menthe
1	teaspoon minced fresh mint leaves
4	fresh mint sprigs

Combine 1½ cups water, mint leaves, and sugar in heavy large saucepan. Stir over medium heat until sugar dissolves. Increase heat and bring to boil. Pour into medium bowl. Refrigerate until cold, about 2 hours.

Strain mint syrup through sieve set over bowl, pressing on mint leaves. Discard mint leaves in sieve. Mix bourbon, crème de menthe, and minced mint into mint syrup. Process sorbet mixture in ice-cream maker according to manufacturer's instructions. Transfer sorbet to airtight container and freeze until firm, about 2 hours.

DO AHEAD: *Can be made 2 days ahead. Keep frozen.*

Freeze 4 parfait glasses 1 hour. Scoop sorbet into frozen glasses. Garnish with mint sprigs; serve immediately.

White Russian Sorbet

The coffee and cream flavors of a White Russian cocktail make a delicious frozen dessert. Scoop the sorbet into glass coffee mugs and garnish each serving with a coffee bean (plain or chocolate covered). To turn this into a granita, see Granita Style (page 465)—but mix only an additional half cup of water into the sorbet mixture and serve in frozen coffee cups. **4 servings**

1¾	cups water
½	cup sugar
3½	teaspoons instant espresso powder
1	tablespoon dark corn syrup
½	cup heavy whipping cream
¼	cup vodka
¼	cup Kahlúa or other coffee liqueur
	Coffee beans

Stir 1¾ cups water and sugar in heavy medium saucepan over medium heat until sugar dissolves. Increase heat and bring to boil. Remove from heat. Add espresso powder and stir to dissolve. Pour into medium bowl. Mix in corn syrup, then cream, vodka, and Kahlúa. Refrigerate mixture until cold, about 2 hours.

Process sorbet mixture in ice-cream maker according to manufacturer's instructions. Transfer sorbet to airtight container and freeze until firm, about 2 hours.

DO AHEAD: *Can be made 2 days ahead. Keep frozen.*

Freeze 4 coffee cups 30 minutes. Scoop sorbet into frozen cups. Garnish with coffee beans and serve immediately.

Strawberry Granita with Whipped Cream

This easy summer ice has a berry sweetness that's perfectly paired with a dollop of rich whipped cream. **6 to 8 servings**

1	**pound strawberries, hulled, sliced (about 1⅔ cups)**
¾	**cup sugar**
	Pinch of salt
1½	**cups cold water**
¼	**cup fresh lemon juice**
1	**cup chilled heavy whipping cream**

Puree strawberries, sugar, and salt in processor until smooth. Add 1½ cups cold water and lemon juice and process to blend. Strain into 8x8x2-inch metal baking pan. Cover with foil and place in freezer. Stir with fork every hour until frozen, about 4 hours.

DO AHEAD: *Can be made 2 days ahead. Keep frozen.*

Using fork, scrape granita until entire mixture is mass of crystals. Return to freezer. Beat cream until firm peaks form. Divide whipped cream among dishes. Spoon granita over and serve immediately.

Great Granitas

Granitas are easy to make—no fancy equipment needed, just a pan and a fork. Here's how to make them perfect every time.

THE PAN: A stainless steel, earthenware, plastic, or porcelain pan is fine, but avoid using aluminum (it can discolor certain granitas and leave a metallic taste). The pan should be large enough that the granita can freeze quickly, but not so large that it won't fit in your freezer.

THE PROCESS: To form perfect, fine ice crystals, begin by freezing the granita mixture for about an hour (times will vary from recipe to recipe). If it's starting to freeze around the edges, break up the frozen bits with a fork and rake them toward the center of the pan. Return the pan to the freezer and repeat this procedure every 30 minutes or so (check the recipe) until it looks like shaved ice. If it gets too hard, leave the pan out at room temperature for a few minutes, then rake the granita again.

THE PRESENTATION: Granitas are delicious on their own, but they're even better served with crisp cookies or biscotti, topped with zabaglione or whipped cream, or spooned over ice cream or sorbet.

Honeydew Bellini Granita with Minted Raspberries

Both the granita and the raspberry topping have a splash of Prosecco, Italian sparkling wine. The recipe calls for using a large baking pan so that the melon mixture will freeze quickly. But if you don't have room in your freezer, just use a smaller pan and chill it longer. **8 servings**

½   large ripe honeydew melon, seeded, peeled, cut into 1½-inch cubes (about 2½ pounds)
½   cup chilled Prosecco, divided
4½ tablespoons (about) sugar, divided
2   5.6-ounce containers raspberries
1   tablespoon minced fresh mint plus 8 fresh mint sprigs

Puree melon in processor until smooth. Strain through fine strainer into large bowl, pressing gently to extract 2½ cups juice; discard solids in strainer. Mix ¼ cup Prosecco into melon juice. Stir 3 tablespoons sugar into juice, 1 tablespoon at a time, to sweeten to taste (mixture should be sweet). Transfer mixture to 13x9x2-inch metal baking pan and freeze until slushy, about 30 minutes. Stir with fork and continue to freeze until set, about 45 minutes longer.

DO AHEAD: *Can be made 1 day ahead. Cover and keep frozen.*

Gently toss raspberries, minced mint, remaining ¼ cup Prosecco, and remaining 1½ tablespoons sugar in large bowl to coat.

Using fork, scrape granita until entire mixture is mass of crystals. Spoon granita into goblets or glasses and top with raspberry mixture. Garnish with mint sprigs.

Red and Green Grape Granitas with Muscat and Frozen Sugared Grapes

A truly gorgeous dessert: Red and green granitas are spooned over Muscat wine and topped with small clusters of frozen sugared grapes. If you prefer, you can also serve the granitas separately. **6 servings**

⅔   cup water
⅔   cup sugar
¼   cup fresh lemon juice
3   cups green seedless grapes, stemmed (about 1 pound)
3   cups red seedless grapes, stemmed (about 1 pound)
6   small grape clusters (about 3 grapes per cluster)
2   tablespoons plus ¾ cup chilled Muscat
     Additional sugar

Combine ⅔ cup water and sugar in small saucepan. Bring to boil, stirring until sugar dissolves. Boil 1 minute. Cool syrup. Stir in lemon juice.

Puree green grapes and half of lemon syrup in blender (some bits of grape peel will remain). Transfer to 13x9x2-inch metal baking pan. Puree red grapes and remaining lemon syrup in blender. Transfer to another 13x9x2-inch metal baking pan. Freeze 1 hour. Stir with fork every hour until frozen, about 4 hours.

Meanwhile, dip grape clusters into 2 tablespoons Muscat to moisten, then dip grapes into additional sugar to coat. Place grapes on small tray and freeze until frozen, about 4 hours.

DO AHEAD: *Granitas and grapes can be made 1 day ahead. Cover separately and keep frozen.*

Using fork, scrape granita until entire mixture is mass of crystals. Pour 2 tablespoons Muscat into each of 6 wide wineglasses. Divide green grape granita among glasses. Spoon red grape granita alongside green grape granita in each glass. Garnish each with sugared grape cluster and serve.

More to Try

The two granita mixtures would be equally lovely as the base for ice pops. Simply fill the molds halfway with the red grape mixture, and freeze until it's pretty firm. Then top it with the green grape mixture and continue freezing.

Red and Green Grape Granitas with Muscat and Frozen Sugared Grapes

Spiced Apple Cider Granita with Ginger Whipped Cream

Apple cider is steeped with allspice and cloves and sweetened with brown sugar before it's frozen into an icy treat. For the very best flavor, look for fresh apple cider in the fall at your local farmers' market. **6 servings**

4 cups apple cider
²⁄₃ cup (packed) golden brown sugar
20 whole allspice
10 whole cloves
   Ginger Whipped Cream (see recipe)

Stir cider, sugar, allspice, and cloves in saucepan over medium heat until sugar dissolves. Remove from heat, cover, and let steep 1 hour. Strain mixture into 8x8x2-inch metal baking pan. Freeze until edges begin to set, about 1 hour. Whisk; freeze again until mixture is slushy, about 1 hour. Whisk again to blend well. Freeze without stirring until granita is frozen solid, at least 3 hours or overnight. Using fork, scrape granita until entire mixture is mass of crystals. Cover and freeze until ready to serve.

Scoop granita into 6 chilled glasses. Top with Ginger Whipped Cream.

Ingredient Tip: Juice vs. Cider

This recipe calls for apple cider—not juice—but do you know the difference? True cider is pure, unfiltered juice with the coarse pulp and sediment included. Apple juice is filtered (so it looks clearer and tastes milder) and usually pasteurized, and it may have added water or sugar. But many commercial brands sell so-called cider that's really just apple juice made with tangier apple varieties. You can find true cider at orchards, farmstands, farmers' markets, and some supermarkets in the fall.

Ginger Whipped Cream

Crystallized ginger adds spice to whipped cream. This topping is also nice on pie—especially pumpkin or apple—but you'll want to double the recipe. **Makes about 1 cup**

½ cup chilled heavy whipping cream
1 tablespoon (packed) dark brown sugar
2 tablespoons minced crystallized ginger

Beat cream and sugar in medium bowl until peaks form. Fold in ginger.

DO AHEAD: *Can be made 8 hours ahead. Cover and refrigerate. Before serving, rewhisk to thicken, if necessary.*

Lime Granita with Candied Mint Leaves and Crème Fraîche

For an eye-catching presentation, serve this tart granita in little bowls made out of lime halves. To prepare the "bowls," cut the limes in half, snip the membranes with kitchen scissors, and scrape out the pulp with a grapefruit spoon (which has serrated edges). The candied mint leaves are a lively garnish. **6 servings**

Granita

2   cups water
1   cup sugar
½   cup fresh lime juice

Candied Mint Leaves

¼   cup sugar
12   fresh mint leaves, washed, patted dry
1   large egg white, beaten until foamy

Crème Fraîche

½   cup crème fraîche or sour cream
1½   tablespoons powdered sugar

GRANITA: Bring 2 cups water and sugar to boil in medium saucepan, stirring until sugar dissolves. Reduce heat to medium and simmer 5 minutes. Cool syrup. Stir in lime juice. Transfer lime syrup to 11x7x2-inch glass baking dish. Cover and place in freezer. Stir every 45 minutes until frozen, about 3 hours.

DO AHEAD: *Can be made 2 days ahead. Cover and keep frozen.*

CANDIED MINT LEAVES: Place sugar on small shallow plate. Brush both sides of 1 mint leaf lightly with egg white; dredge in sugar. Transfer mint leaf to rack. Repeat with remaining mint leaves. Let mint stand at room temperature until dry, about 3 hours.

DO AHEAD: *Can be made 1 day ahead. Store mint leaves in airtight container at room temperature.*

CRÈME FRAÎCHE: Mix crème fraîche and sugar to blend.

DO AHEAD: *Can be made 1 day ahead. Cover and chill.*

Using fork, scrape granita until entire mixture is mass of crystals. Spoon granita into bowls; drizzle with crème fraîche, garnish with candied mint leaves, and serve immediately.

Cranberry Granita with Orange Whipped Cream

You already know just what to do with that leftover Thanksgiving turkey—but how about the cranberry sauce? With very little effort, you can transform it into a delicious dessert. This granita is tart and nicely spiced; it's topped with a sweet orange syrup and orange-flavored whipped cream. **6 servings**

2   cups cranberry juice cocktail
½   cup plus 2 tablespoons sugar
¼   teaspoon (scant) ground cloves
1½   cups cooked cranberry sauce
½   cup orange juice
1½   teaspoons finely grated orange peel
¾   cup chilled heavy whipping cream

Bring cranberry juice, ½ cup sugar, and cloves to boil in small saucepan, stirring often. Puree cranberry sauce in processor; add juice mixture and blend. Pour mixture into 8x8x2-inch glass baking dish; freeze until firm, at least 4 hours.

Boil orange juice and remaining 2 tablespoons sugar in small saucepan until reduced to ¼ cup, stirring occasionally, about 4 minutes. Mix in orange peel. Cool orange syrup.

Whisk cream and 3 tablespoons orange syrup in medium bowl to soft peaks. Using fork, scrape granita until entire mixture is mass of crystals. Mound generous ½ cup granita to 1 side in each of 6 glasses. Mound ¼ cup whipped cream on opposite side of granita in each glass. Drizzle remaining orange syrup over whipped cream in each.

Watermelon-Lemonade Ice Pops

Watermelon-Lemonade Ice Pops

What could be more refreshing than frozen watermelon-flavored lemonade? For the best-tasting results, wait until prime watermelon season, which lasts only from mid-June through late August. For a fun twist, freeze the mixture in ice cube trays and use the cubes in a pitcher of lemonade. **Makes 8**

2	cups (packed) finely chopped seeded watermelon
¾	cup frozen lemonade concentrate (half of 12-ounce can), thawed
3	tablespoons sugar
	Pinch of salt

Combine all ingredients in processor. Puree until very smooth. Divide mixture among 8 ice pop molds (each ¼- to ⅓-cup capacity). Insert ice pop covers and sticks. Freeze until firm, at least 4 hours and up to 5 days.

Apple Cider and Rosemary Ice Pops

Ice pops aren't just for summer. These have intense autumnal flavor, thanks to the whole spices and just a bit of apple cider vinegar. **Makes 12**

4	cups apple juice
½	cup water
½	cup sugar
2	tablespoons chopped fresh rosemary
1	cinnamon stick, broken in half
2	whole cloves
4	teaspoons apple cider vinegar
¼	teaspoon vanilla extract

Combine apple juice, ½ cup water, sugar, rosemary, cinnamon, and cloves in saucepan. Bring mixture to boil, stirring until sugar dissolves. Reduce heat to medium; simmer until mixture is reduced to 3½ cups, 20 to 25 minutes. Strain into 4-cup measuring cup; cool to room temperature. Stir in vinegar and vanilla. Divide among 12 ice pop molds (each ¼- to ⅓-cup capacity). Insert ice pop covers and sticks. Freeze until firm, overnight or up to 5 days.

Royal Blueberry Ice Pops

Here's a frozen treat you don't have to feel guilty about: It's mostly berries and yogurt, plus some honey and sugar. And that vivd blue color? It's all natural. **Makes 8**

2	½-pint containers blueberries
1	8-ounce container blueberry yogurt
¼	cup water
¼	cup honey
2	tablespoons sugar

Combine all ingredients in processor and puree until smooth. Divide mixture among 8 ice pop molds (each ¼- to ⅓-cup capacity). Insert ice pop covers and sticks. Freeze until firm, at least 4 hours and up to 5 days.

Technique Tip: **No Molds?**
If you don't have any molds, just use little paper cups. Partially freeze the ice pop mixture in the paper cups before inserting a wooden stick into the center of each. Then freeze overnight. If you have trouble unmolding them, cut a slit in the paper and peel it off.

Oatmeal-Raisin Cookie Ice-Cream Sandwiches

Tender oatmeal cookies form a sweet sandwich with purchased vanilla ice cream. The cookies are so good that you might want to make a double batch and fill up the cookie jar. **Makes 12**

	Nonstick vegetable oil spray
1	cup (2 sticks) unsalted butter, room temperature
⅔	cup sugar
⅔	cup (packed) golden brown sugar
2	large eggs
1½	cups unbleached all purpose flour
4	teaspoons baking powder
½	teaspoon salt
2	cups old-fashioned oats
⅔	cup raisins
1	quart vanilla ice cream, slightly softened

Preheat oven to 350°F. Spray 2 large baking sheets with nonstick spray. Using electric mixer, beat butter and both sugars in large bowl until well blended. Beat in eggs 1 at a time. Combine flour, baking powder, and salt in medium bowl. Add to butter mixture and beat just until combined. Stir in oats and raisins.

Using generous 3 tablespoons dough per cookie, place 6 dough mounds on each baking sheet, spacing mounds 3 inches apart. Bake cookies until light golden, about 15 minutes. Cool cookies on baking sheets 5 minutes. Transfer cookies to racks; cool completely. Cool baking sheets and repeat with remaining dough, making 24 cookies total. Freeze cookies 30 minutes.

Place 1 cookie, flat side up, on work surface. Spoon ⅓ cup ice cream onto cookie. Top with another cookie, flat side down; press gently. Wrap sandwich in plastic wrap; freeze until firm. Repeat with remaining cookies and ice cream.

DO AHEAD: *Can be made 4 days ahead. Keep frozen.*

Let sandwiches stand at room temperature 5 minutes before serving.

Mini S'mores Ice-Cream Sandwiches

When marshmallow s'mores meet ice-cream sandwiches, the results are delectable. Purchased rocky road ice cream and marshmallow creme are sandwiched between graham crackers and frozen until quite firm. Then the sandwiches get a coating of melted bittersweet chocolate before going back into the freezer. **Makes 8**

1	pint rocky road ice cream
½	cup (about) marshmallow creme
8	whole graham cracker rectangles, broken in half into squares
12	ounces bittersweet or semisweet chocolate, chopped

Line small rimmed baking sheet with parchment paper. Soften ice cream just until spreadable but still firm. Spread 1 tablespoon (about) marshmallow creme over each of 8 graham cracker squares. Working quickly, spread ice cream atop remaining 8 graham cracker squares. Place marshmallow-coated crackers atop ice cream, marshmallow side down, forming sandwiches; press gently to adhere and smooth sides. Set sandwiches on prepared baking sheet and freeze until firm, at least 8 hours.

DO AHEAD: *Can be made 3 days ahead. Wrap each sandwich in plastic wrap and keep frozen.*

Stir chocolate in small metal bowl set over small saucepan of simmering water until melted and smooth and just warm (not hot) to touch. Remove bowl from over water. Working quickly, dip 1 sandwich halfway into melted chocolate. Return sandwich to same parchment-lined baking sheet. Repeat with remaining sandwiches. Immediately return to freezer and freeze until chocolate is completely set, about 30 minutes. Rewarm remaining chocolate in bowl over saucepan of simmering water, if chocolate has set. Remove sandwiches from freezer and dip second side of sandwiches in melted chocolate to coat. Return to same baking sheet and freeze until firm, at least 1 hour.

DO AHEAD: *Can be made 2 days ahead. Cover with plastic; keep frozen.*

Chocolate–Peanut Butter Ice-Cream Sandwiches

These ice-cream sandwiches are dipped halfway into melted milk chocolate. Use cookies that are about 2½ inches in diameter. If you'd like to use homemade cookies, the Classic Peanut Butter Cookies (page 538) would be the perfect choice. **Makes 6**

12   peanut butter cookies (purchased or homemade)
1   pint chocolate–peanut butter swirl ice cream or chocolate ice cream, slightly softened
6   tablespoons creamy (smooth) natural peanut butter (made only with peanuts and salt)
6   ounces high-quality milk chocolate (such as Lindt or Perugina), finely chopped

Line 2 rimmed baking sheets with waxed paper. Place 6 cookies, flat side up, on work surface. Spoon enough ice cream atop each cookie to form ½- to ¾-inch-thick layer. Spoon 1 tablespoon peanut butter atop ice cream on each cookie. Top with another cookie, flat side down, and press gently to adhere. Transfer sandwiches to 1 prepared baking sheet. Cover and freeze until firm, about 30 minutes.

Stir chocolate in small bowl set over saucepan of simmering water until melted and smooth. Dip 1 sandwich halfway into melted chocolate, allowing excess chocolate to drip back into bowl. Place sandwich on second prepared baking sheet. Repeat with remaining sandwiches. Immediately place in freezer; freeze until chocolate is firm, about 10 minutes.

DO AHEAD: *Can be made 2 weeks ahead. Wrap each sandwich in plastic wrap and keep frozen.*

D.I.Y. Ice-Cream Sandwiches

Great homemade ice cream plus delicious cookies or brownies equals the ultimate ice-cream sandwiches. To make them yourself:

CHOOSE A COOKIE RECIPE. The cookies shouldn't be too thick and hard, or too thin and fragile.

FREEZE THE COOKIES. They'll be less likely to break or to absorb any of the ice cream, which can make them soggy.

MAKE THE SANDWICH. Spread some ice cream on the flat side of one cookie and top the ice cream with another cookie. Freeze until firm.

EVEN BETTER: Dip the ice-cream sandwiches halfway into melted dark, milk, or white chocolate, then roll the dipped side in granola, toffee bits, flaked coconut, or chopped nuts.

In this book, you'll find plenty of ice-cream and cookie recipes to mix and match, but may we suggest . . .

CRANBERRY-ORANGE DROP COOKIES (page 537) with Orange Ice Cream (page 451)

CHEWY GINGER COOKIES (page 541) with Lemon Verbena Ice Cream (page 451)

DARK AND WHITE CHOCOLATE CHUNK COOKIES WITH GINGER (page 533) with Vanilla Ice Cream (page 446)

CHOCOLATE-MINT COOKIES (page 547) with French Quarter Chocolate Ice Cream (page 447)

CHERRY–CHOCOLATE CHIP OATMEAL COOKIES (page 534) with Buttermilk Sorbet (page 459)

OLD-FASHIONED BROWNIES (page 584) with Hazelnut Gelato (page 457)

CINNAMON-ALMOND COOKIES (page 546) with Chocolate-Cinnamon Gelato with Toffee Bits (page 456)

Dark Chocolate–Dipped Cherry Ice-Cream Cones

It's fun (and easy) to make dipped ice-cream cones at home. This version features a winning combination of purchased cherry ice cream and a dark chocolate coating. But feel free to mix it up: Banana, strawberry, or peanut-butter-cup ice cream would also be a great choice. **Makes 8**

3 pints premium cherry ice cream
8 sugar cones
1 11.5-ounce package bittersweet chocolate chips
¼ cup vegetable oil
2 ounces high-quality white chocolate (such as Lindt or Perugina), chopped
1½ cups coarsely chopped toasted almonds

Spoon enough ice cream into 1 cone to fill, packing gently. Dip large (¼ cup) round ice-cream scoop into bowl of hot water. Scoop large mounded ball of ice cream onto filled cone, pressing gently. Stand cone in small glass; place in freezer. Repeat with remaining cones and ice cream, placing each cone in separate glass. Freeze 2 to 8 hours.

Place bittersweet chocolate and oil in small microwave-safe bowl. Microwave on medium-high setting until chocolate is melted, stopping occasionally to stir, about 1½ minutes. Let stand just until cool, about 10 minutes. Place white chocolate in another small microwave-safe bowl; microwave on medium-high setting until chocolate is melted, stopping occasionally to stir, about 1 minute.

Place nuts on plate. Working quickly and tilting bowl of bittersweet chocolate to form deep pool, dip ice-cream end of cone into chocolate, turning to coat. Gently shake cone, allowing excess chocolate to drip back into bowl. Immediately roll bottom half of chocolate-dipped scoop in nuts. Dip fork into white chocolate; drizzle lines over top of cone. Place cone in glass; return to freezer. Repeat with remaining cones. Freeze 1 hour.

DO AHEAD: *Can be made 1 day ahead. Wrap cones in foil; keep frozen.*

Banana Split Split

An ice-cream dessert shared by two. No ice-cream maker required—this calls for purchased vanilla, strawberry, and chocolate ice creams. If you don't have a banana split dish, use a shallow bowl or small platter instead. **2 servings**

1 cup sliced hulled strawberries
2 teaspoons sugar
1 banana, peeled, halved lengthwise
1 large scoop vanilla ice cream
1 large scoop strawberry ice cream
1 large scoop chocolate or coffee ice cream
   Sticky Fudge Sauce (see recipe)
   Scotch Butterscotch Sauce (see recipe)
   Whipped cream
   Chopped nuts

Combine strawberries and sugar in small bowl; toss to coat. Place banana halves in banana split dish. Top banana halves with scoops of ice cream. Top vanilla ice cream with strawberries, strawberry ice cream with Sticky Fudge Sauce, and chocolate ice cream with Scotch Butterscotch Sauce. Top all with whipped cream and nuts. Serve with 2 spoons.

Sticky Fudge Sauce

A rich sauce that really clings to the ice cream. Any leftover sauce will keep in the fridge for up to two weeks. **Makes about 1 cup**

6 tablespoons heavy whipping cream
⅓ cup sugar
¼ cup natural unsweetened cocoa powder
¼ cup light corn syrup
2 ounces unsweetened chocolate, chopped
2 tablespoons (¼ stick) unsalted butter
1 teaspoon vanilla extract

Bring cream, sugar, cocoa, and corn syrup to simmer in heavy small saucepan over medium heat, stirring constantly. Continue simmering until sugar dissolves, stirring occasionally, about 2 minutes. Add chocolate and butter and stir until melted and smooth. Remove from heat; stir in vanilla.

DO AHEAD: *Can be made 2 weeks ahead. Cover and refrigerate. Before serving, stir over low heat until sauce is just hot.*

Scotch Butterscotch Sauce

A little bit of whisky jazzes up this sweet sauce. **Makes about 1 cup**

1	cup (packed) golden brown sugar
⅓	cup heavy whipping cream
¼	cup (½ stick) unsalted butter
2	tablespoons light corn syrup
2	tablespoons Scotch
1	teaspoon vanilla extract

Stir sugar, cream, butter, and corn syrup in heavy large saucepan over low heat until sugar dissolves. Increase heat and simmer until sauce thickens enough to coat spoon, about 4 minutes. Cool slightly. Stir in Scotch and vanilla.

DO AHEAD: *Can be made 4 days ahead. Cover and chill. Before serving, stir over low heat until sauce is just hot.*

Mexican Hot Fudge Sundaes

Brew some coffee for after dinner, then use half a cup of it to make this quick and easy hot fudge sauce. With its hints of cinnamon and vanilla, the sauce has all the great flavor of Mexican chocolate. **Makes 8**

¾	cup heavy whipping cream
½	cup freshly brewed coffee
16	ounces semisweet chocolate chips (2⅔ cups)
1	teaspoon ground cinnamon
½	teaspoon vanilla extract
	Vanilla ice cream
	Pine nuts, toasted
	Fresh mint leaves

Bring cream and coffee to simmer in medium saucepan. Remove from heat. Add chocolate chips and cinnamon. Whisk until chocolate is melted and sauce is smooth. Mix in vanilla. Scoop vanilla ice cream into bowls. Top with warm chocolate sauce, pine nuts, and mint.

Sour Cream–Brown Sugar Ice-Cream Sundaes with Peaches

The ice cream gets tangy flavor and rich texture from sour cream. Running short on time? Simply top the ice cream with slices of ripe, fresh peaches. For tips on peeling peaches, see page 35. **Makes 6**

Ice Cream

2	cups heavy whipping cream
2	cups sour cream
6	large egg yolks
1	cup plus 2 tablespoons (packed) golden brown sugar
¾	teaspoon vanilla extract

Peach Topping

2	pounds peaches, peeled, sliced
6	tablespoons sugar
½	teaspoon finely crushed cardamom seeds
	Whipped cream
	Sliced almonds, toasted

ICE CREAM: Bring cream to simmer in heavy medium saucepan over medium heat. Whisk sour cream, egg yolks, and sugar in medium bowl to blend. Gradually whisk in hot cream. Return to same saucepan. Stir over medium-low heat until custard thickens and leaves path on back of spoon when finger is drawn across, about 3 minutes (do not boil). Strain custard into large bowl. Whisk 1 minute to cool. Stir in vanilla. Refrigerate custard until cold, at least 3 hours.

DO AHEAD: *Can be made 1 day ahead. Cover and keep chilled.*

Process custard in ice-cream maker according to manufacturer's instructions. Transfer to container; cover and freeze until firm.

DO AHEAD: *Ice cream can be made 4 days ahead. Keep frozen.*

PEACH TOPPING: Combine peaches, sugar, and cardamom seeds in large bowl. Let stand until juices form, stirring occasionally, at least 20 minutes and up to 1 hour.

Scoop ice cream into sundae dishes. Spoon peaches and syrup over. Top with dollop of whipped cream. Sprinkle almonds over and serve immediately.

Black and Tan Sundaes

In this case, "black and tan" refers to chocolate sauce and caramel sauce (not the equally appealing Guinness and pale ale combination). These are simple sundaes—feel free to add sliced bananas, some crushed malted milk balls, or a cherry on top. **Makes 6**

- ¾ cup chilled heavy whipping cream
- 1 cup plus 2 tablespoons Chocolate Fudge Sauce (see recipe)
- 12 scoops vanilla ice cream
- ¾ cup Caramel Sauce (see recipe)
- ⅓ cup chopped toasted pecans

Whisk cream in large bowl until soft peaks form. Spoon 1 tablespoon warm Chocolate Fudge Sauce into each of 6 pilsner glasses. Place scoop of ice cream atop sauce in each glass. Spoon 2 tablespoons Caramel Sauce over ice cream in each glass. Top each with second scoop of ice cream, then 2 tablespoons Chocolate Fudge Sauce. Spoon whipped cream atop sundaes. Sprinkle with nuts and serve immediately.

Chocolate Fudge Sauce

The sauce would be excellent with almost any flavor of ice cream—and also makes a great gift presented in a mason jar. **Makes about 1⅓ cups**

- ½ cup (packed) golden brown sugar
- 2 tablespoons natural unsweetened cocoa powder
- ¼ cup water
- ½ cup heavy whipping cream
- 4 ounces bittersweet or semisweet chocolate (do not exceed 61% cacao), chopped
- ½ teaspoon vanilla extract
- ¼ teaspoon salt

Whisk sugar and cocoa in heavy medium saucepan to blend. Gradually whisk in ¼ cup water, then cream. Bring mixture to boil over medium heat, whisking occasionally to dissolve sugar. Remove from heat and add chocolate. Let stand 1 minute. Add vanilla and salt; whisk until chocolate is melted and sauce is smooth.

DO AHEAD: Can be made 1 week ahead. Cool, cover, and chill. Rewarm slightly before using.

Caramel Sauce

This delicious sauce has just a hint of salt to balance the sweetness. Caramel sauce isn't difficult to make once you get the hang of it; see page 31 for some tips that demystify the process. **Makes about 1¼ cups**

- ¾ cup sugar
- ¼ cup water
- ¾ cup heavy whipping cream
- 2 tablespoons (¼ stick) unsalted butter
  Pinch of salt

Using wooden spoon, stir sugar and ¼ cup water in heavy medium saucepan over medium-low heat until sugar dissolves, occasionally brushing down sides of pan with wet pastry brush. Increase heat to medium and boil without stirring until syrup is deep amber color, occasionally brushing down sides of pan and swirling pan, about 12 minutes. Remove pan from heat. Immediately add cream (mixture will bubble vigorously). Whisk to blend. Add butter and salt and whisk until sauce is smooth.

DO AHEAD: Can be made 1 week ahead. Cool, cover, and chill. Rewarm slightly before using.

Orange Muscat Ice-Cream Sundaes with Spiced Apricots

Essensia gives the ice cream and the apricot topping a sophisticated flavor. If you can't find Essensia, use another Orange Muscat. Crumbled amaretti cookies add a nice crunch to this dessert. **Makes 6**

Essensia Ice Cream

1	cup half and half
⅔	cup sugar
6	large egg yolks
2	cups heavy whipping cream
1½	cups Essensia (sweet dessert wine) or other Orange Muscat wine

Apricot Topping

2¼	cups water
¾	cup sugar
3	¼-inch-thick orange slices with peel
½	cinnamon stick
1½	pounds apricots, halved, pitted, quartered
¼	cup Essensia or other Orange Muscat wine

Amaretti cookies (Italian macaroons), crushed

{ **Ingredient Tip:** **Amaretti Cookies**
Amaretti are light, airy, crunchy Italian almond macaroons; they're available at some supermarkets and at Italian markets. }

ESSENSIA ICE CREAM: Bring half and half and sugar to simmer in heavy medium saucepan over medium heat, stirring until sugar dissolves. Whisk egg yolks in medium bowl to blend. Gradually whisk in hot half and half mixture. Return to same saucepan. Stir over medium-low heat until custard thickens and leaves path on back of spoon when finger is drawn across, about 3 minutes (do not boil). Strain custard into large bowl. Whisk in cream, then Essensia. Refrigerate custard until cold, at least 3 hours.

DO AHEAD: *Can be made 1 day ahead. Cover and keep chilled.*

Process custard in ice-cream maker according to manufacturer's instructions. Transfer to container; cover and freeze until firm.

DO AHEAD: *Ice cream can be made 4 days ahead. Keep frozen.*

APRICOT TOPPING: Combine water, sugar, orange slices, and cinnamon in heavy medium saucepan. Stir over low heat until sugar dissolves. Increase heat and simmer 10 minutes. Add apricots. Adjust heat so liquid barely simmers and cook until apricots are just tender, about 1 minute. Using slotted spoon, transfer apricots to medium bowl. Boil syrup, orange slices, and cinnamon until syrup is reduced to 1 cup, returning any juices that accumulate in apricot bowl to saucepan, about 15 minutes. Add Essensia to syrup. Pour syrup with orange slices and cinnamon over apricots. Cover and refrigerate until well chilled.

DO AHEAD: *Topping can be made 2 days ahead. Discard orange slices and cinnamon before using.*

Scoop ice cream into sundae dishes. Spoon apricots with some syrup over. Sprinkle sundaes with crushed amaretti and serve.

Strawberry Sorbet Sundaes with Prosecco Sabayon

This is no ordinary sundae: Instead of ice cream, there's cool strawberry sorbet. Instead of sauce, a strawberry compote and sabayon (light, foamy custard) made with Prosecco, the Italian sparkling wine. And on top? No cherry—but crunchy sugary almonds. **Makes 6**

Sugared Almonds

   Nonstick vegetable oil spray
1   cup sliced almonds
1   tablespoon light corn syrup
2   tablespoons sugar

Compote

4   cups sliced hulled strawberries (about 16 ounces), divided
4   tablespoons sugar, divided
3   tablespoons Prosecco or other sparkling white wine

Sabayon

½   cup chilled heavy whipping cream
4   large egg yolks
¼   cup sugar
½   cup Prosecco or other sparkling white wine

2   pints strawberry sorbet

SUGARED ALMONDS: Preheat oven to 325°F. Line rimmed baking sheet with parchment paper; spray parchment with nonstick spray. Toss almonds and corn syrup in small bowl to coat, then add sugar and toss to coat evenly (sugar coating will resemble wet sand). Spread almonds in single layer on prepared sheet. Bake until almonds are golden, stirring occasionally, about 20 minutes. Cool slightly on baking sheet, then break up any large clusters of almonds and cool completely.

DO AHEAD: *Can be made 1 day ahead. Store in airtight container at room temperature.*

COMPOTE: Combine 1 cup strawberries, 2 tablespoons sugar, and Prosecco in processor. Puree until smooth. Pour puree through strainer set over bowl, pressing on solids to extract as much liquid and pulp as possible. Discard solids in strainer. Toss remaining 3 cups strawberries and 2 tablespoons sugar in medium bowl; let stand at room temperature until juices form, tossing occasionally, about 30 minutes. Mix strawberry puree into sliced strawberries.

DO AHEAD: *Can be made 8 hours ahead. Cover and chill.*

SABAYON: Beat cream in medium bowl until peaks form; refrigerate until ready to use. Fill large bowl halfway with ice water. Whisk egg yolks and sugar to blend in medium metal bowl; add Prosecco and whisk to blend. Set bowl over saucepan of simmering water (do not allow bowl to touch water). Whisk constantly until sabayon is thick, resembles softly beaten whipping cream, and thermometer inserted into center registers 160°F, about 6 minutes. Set bowl with sabayon on ice in bowl of cold water and whisk until sabayon is cool, about 6 minutes. Fold in chilled whipped cream.

DO AHEAD: *Sabayon can be made 8 hours ahead. Cover and chill.*

Spoon ¼ cup strawberry compote into each of 6 dessert glasses or bowls. Top each with scoop of strawberry sorbet; sprinkle each with 1 tablespoon sugared almonds. Repeat layering with ¼ cup strawberry compote, scoop of sorbet, and 1 tablespoon sugared almonds. Top each sundae with large spoonful of sabayon, then 1 tablespoon sugared almonds, and serve.

Cherry "Pie" à la Mode Sundaes

Is it a deconstructed cherry pie? Or a sundae served on puff pastry? Either way, it's delicious. The cherry compote calls for two kinds of cherries: the familiar frozen, dark sweet variety as well as sour Morello cherries, sold in jars in a sweet syrup. They can be found at Italian markets and specialty foods stores.
Makes 6

Cherry Compote

1   24- to 29-ounce jar dark **Morello** cherries in light syrup, drained, syrup reserved
1   10- to 12-ounce bag frozen pitted unsweetened dark cherries, thawed, drained, juices reserved
¼   cup sugar
1   cinnamon stick
1   tablespoon cornstarch

Pastries

1   sheet frozen puff pastry (half of 17.3-ounce package), partially thawed, trimmed to 9×6-inch rectangle
1   large egg, beaten to blend
6   teaspoons raw sugar

1   pint vanilla ice cream

CHERRY COMPOTE: Combine reserved syrup from Morello cherries, reserved juices from frozen cherries, sugar, and cinnamon in heavy medium saucepan. Bring to boil over medium-high heat, stirring until sugar dissolves. Boil until syrup is reduced to 1 cup, about 20 minutes. Combine all cherries and cornstarch in large bowl; toss to coat. Add cherry mixture to syrup in saucepan and cook until compote thickens and boils, stirring frequently, about 5 minutes. Discard cinnamon stick.

DO AHEAD: *Compote can be made 2 days ahead. Cover and refrigerate. Rewarm before using.*

PASTRIES: Preheat oven to 400°F. Line large rimmed baking sheet with silicone pan liner or parchment paper. Cut puff pastry into three 6×3-inch rectangles (reserve remaining dough for another use). Cut each rectangle diagonally into 2 triangles. Transfer triangles to prepared baking sheet. Lightly brush pastry triangles with egg and sprinkle with raw sugar. Using fork, pierce entire surface of dough. Bake until pastries are golden brown, about 12 minutes.

DO AHEAD: *Can be made 2 days ahead. Cool completely. Store in resealable plastic bag at room temperature. Rewarm pastries in 350°F oven 8 to 10 minutes before continuing.*

Spoon warm cherry compote into 6 shallow bowls. Top each with 1 pastry. Spoon vanilla ice cream alongside and serve immediately.

Lemon and Honey Ice-Cream Sundaes

For a delicately flavored ice cream, use a mild honey (such as orange blossom). Candied violets, which are available at specialty foods stores and cookware shops, are a nice finishing touch. Or top the sundaes with edible flowers, which are available at farmers' markets and in the produce section of many supermarkets. **Makes 6**

Ice Cream

2	cups heavy whipping cream
2	cups half and half
6	large egg yolks
1	cup plus 2 tablespoons honey
3	tablespoons finely grated lemon peel
¾	cup fresh lemon juice
¼	teaspoon vanilla extract

Sauce

¾	cup honey
¼	cup fresh lemon juice
3	tablespoons orange marmalade, melted
¼	teaspoon (scant) ground cloves
	Lightly toasted slivered almonds
	Candied violets (optional)

ICE CREAM: Bring cream and half and half to simmer in heavy medium saucepan over medium heat. Whisk egg yolks in medium bowl to blend. Gradually whisk in hot cream mixture. Return to same saucepan and stir over medium-low heat until custard thickens and leaves path on back of spoon when finger is drawn across, about 3 minutes (do not boil). Strain custard into large bowl. Mix in honey and lemon peel. Let steep 10 minutes. Mix in lemon juice and vanilla. Refrigerate until custard is cold, at least 3 hours.

DO AHEAD: *Can be made 1 day ahead. Cover and keep chilled.*

Process custard in ice-cream maker according to manufacturer's instructions. Transfer to container; cover and freeze until firm.

DO AHEAD: *Ice cream can be made 4 days ahead. Keep frozen.*

SAUCE: Whisk honey, lemon juice, marmalade, and cloves in small bowl.

Scoop ice cream into sundae dishes. Top with sauce, then nuts. Garnish with candied violets, if desired, and serve.

Caramelized Blood Orange and Almond Sundaes

Blood oranges are small, sweet oranges with an attractive scarlet hue. Their peels are thinner and less bitter than navel orange peels, so they're good to eat. You'll see for yourself when you try the caramel orange sauce, which needs no more accompaniment than some good vanilla ice cream and a sprinkling of almonds and fleur de sel, a sea salt that provides a lovely finishing touch. Look for the salt at the supermarket or specialty foods stores. **Makes 6**

3	blood oranges, divided
⅔	cup (packed) golden brown sugar
3	tablespoons unsalted butter, diced
1	quart vanilla ice cream
½	cup sliced almonds, toasted
	Fleur de sel (optional)

Squeeze juice from 1 orange (about ¼ cup) into small bowl. Cut ends off remaining 2 oranges to expose flesh. Cut oranges lengthwise into quarters; pull out and discard white center pith. Cut orange quarters crosswise into ⅛-inch-thick slices. Place orange slices and any accumulated juices in another bowl.

Sprinkle sugar evenly over bottom of heavy 10-inch-diameter skillet; scatter butter pieces over and drizzle with 2 tablespoons orange juice. Stir over medium heat until mixture begins to melt and bubble, then swirl pan to blend. Cook until syrup is dark amber color, occasionally scraping down sides of skillet with heatproof spatula, about 6 minutes. Stir in remaining 2 tablespoons orange juice and cook until sauce is smooth and thick, about 2 minutes. Add orange slices with juices to sauce in skillet and stir to coat, about 1 minute. Cool.

DO AHEAD: *Caramelized orange sauce can be made up to 3 hours ahead. Let stand at room temperature.*

Scoop ice cream into bowls and spoon caramelized orange sauce over. Top sundaes with toasted almonds and sprinkle with fleur de sel, if desired.

Iced Maple Cream with Berries

No ice-cream maker required: Whipped cream lightens a maple custard base, turning this frozen treat into something smooth and creamy. Serve it with crisp butter cookies and whatever berries are in season. **6 servings**

¾ cup chilled heavy whipping cream, divided
3 large egg yolks
⅓ cup pure maple syrup
¼ teaspoon maple extract
2 tablespoons raspberry jam
3 cups mixed berries (such as blackberries, raspberries, and blueberries)

Whisk ¼ cup cream, egg yolks, and maple syrup in medium metal bowl. Set bowl over saucepan of simmering water (do not allow bowl to touch water). Whisk constantly until thermometer inserted into center registers 175°F, about 3 minutes. Remove bowl from over water. Using electric mixer, beat custard until cool and thick, about 3 minutes.

Whisk remaining ½ cup cream and maple extract in large bowl until soft peaks form. Fold whipped cream into custard. Cover and freeze maple cream until firm, at least 6 hours and up to 1 day.

Whisk jam in medium bowl to loosen. Add berries; toss to coat and let stand 15 minutes. Spoon berry mixture into dishes; top with maple cream.

Vanilla Ice Cream with Sesame Candy and Halvah

This ridiculously simple dessert is as delicious as any elaborate treat. If you prefer to make your own ice cream, try the classic Vanilla Ice Cream (page 446). Sesame candies, sometimes called "sesame crunch," are thin crisp bars crammed with tiny sesame seeds. Halvah is a Middle Eastern sweet made from crushed sesame seeds, honey, and (sometimes) dried fruit or pistachios. You can find them at some super-markets and at many delicatessens and Middle Eastern markets. **6 servings**

3½ ounces sesame candies
1½ pints vanilla ice cream
    Halvah, coarsely crumbled
    Honey

Place sesame candies in large resealable plastic bag; crush candies with rolling pin or mallet until broken into small pieces. Divide ice cream among 6 bowls. Top with crushed candies and crumbled halvah. Drizzle with honey and serve.

Coupe Marron with Coffee Ice Cream

This dessert is a riff on a classic French sundae (called coupe glacée*) made with vanilla ice cream,* marrons glacés *(candied chestnuts), and Chantilly cream (softly whipped cream). Here, purchased coffee ice cream is topped with the chestnuts and a coffee-brandy cream. Look for* marrons glacés *(also labeled chestnuts in vanilla syrup) at some supermarkets and at specialty foods stores.* **6 servings**

1 cup chilled heavy whipping cream
¼ cup powdered sugar
1 tablespoon instant coffee powder
2 teaspoons brandy
1 teaspoon vanilla extract
3 pints coffee ice cream, divided
1 cup chopped *marrons glacés* (chestnuts in vanilla syrup)

Using electric mixer, beat cream, sugar, coffee powder, brandy, and vanilla in large bowl until peaks form. Scoop half of ice cream into 6 large wineglasses or bowls. Top each with 1 tablespoon chestnuts. Scoop remaining ice cream over, dividing equally. Spoon whipped cream into pastry bag fitted with large star tip. Pipe border of whipped cream around ice cream. Fill center of cream with remaining chestnuts.

Pear Ice Cream with Spiced Pear Compote

This delicious fall treat would be great with a few gingersnaps. Gewürztraminer is an aromatic white wine that works beautifully with the pears and cloves.

8 servings

Ice Cream

2¼	pounds ripe Anjou or Comice pears, peeled, halved, cored, thinly sliced (about 4 cups)
1	cup pear nectar
1	tablespoon fresh lemon juice
6	large egg yolks
¾	cup sugar
2	cups heavy whipping cream, divided
1	2-inch piece vanilla bean, split lengthwise
½	cup light corn syrup

Pear Compote

2	cups Gewürztraminer
½	cup sugar
2	whole cloves
1	4½-inch piece vanilla bean, split lengthwise
2½	pounds firm but ripe Anjou or slightly underripe Comice pears (about 6 small), peeled, halved, cored, sliced crosswise into ⅓-inch-thick slices

Market Tip: Anjou and Comice Pears

This recipe calls for Anjou or Comice pears, two varieties that are excellent for cooking and eating fresh. Anjou pears, large and bell shaped (heavy on the bottom) with thick greenish yellow skins, are in season from October through June. Comice pears, which have a softer texture than Anjou, are medium yellow with areas of light green when ripe. Look for Comice pears in the market from August through March.

ICE CREAM: Combine pears, pear nectar, and lemon juice in heavy medium saucepan. Bring to boil over medium-high heat. Transfer to processor; puree until smooth. Chill until cold.

Whisk egg yolks and sugar in medium bowl to blend. Bring 1 cup cream to simmer in heavy medium saucepan. Gradually whisk hot cream into yolk mixture. Return to same saucepan. Scrape in seeds from vanilla bean; add bean. Stir over low heat until custard thickens and leaves path on back of spoon when finger is drawn across, about 7 minutes (do not boil). Pour custard through strainer into large bowl. Mix in remaining 1 cup cream. Cool custard 15 minutes.

Add corn syrup and 3 cups pear puree to custard and whisk until blended (reserve any remaining pear puree for another use). Chill custard until cold, at least 4 hours and up to 1 day.

Process custard in ice-cream maker according to manufacturer's instructions. Transfer to container; cover and freeze.

DO AHEAD: *Can be made 2 days ahead. Keep frozen.*

PEAR COMPOTE: Combine wine, sugar, and cloves in heavy large saucepan. Scrape in seeds from vanilla bean; add bean. Stir over medium heat until sugar dissolves. Bring to boil. Add pears; simmer until tender, about 5 minutes. Using slotted spoon, transfer pears to medium bowl. Boil syrup in saucepan until slightly thickened, adding any accumulated juices from bowl of pears, about 12 minutes. Pour over pears. Chill compote until cold, at least 4 hours and up to 1 day.

DO AHEAD: *Can be made 1 day ahead. Cover and keep chilled.*

Discard vanilla bean and cloves from compote. Scoop ice cream into goblets. Spoon pears and syrup over and serve.

Macadamia Crunch Ice Cream with Mango Sauce

In this tropical treat, bits of sweet-salty macadamia nut toffee are stirred into homemade vanilla ice cream. For a fun touch, serve in sundae glasses and garnish with paper umbrellas. **6 servings**

Toffee

- ⅔ cup roasted salted macadamia nuts, coarsely chopped
- ¼ teaspoon baking soda
- ⅓ cup sugar
- 2 tablespoons water
- 2 tablespoons (¼ stick) unsalted butter

Ice Cream

- 1½ cups heavy whipping cream
- 1½ cups whole milk
- ½ cup sugar
- 6 large egg yolks
- 2 teaspoons vanilla extract

Mango Sauce (see recipe)
Mango slices (optional)
Fresh mint (optional)

TOFFEE: Butter small rimmed baking sheet. Combine nuts and baking soda in small bowl. Stir sugar, 2 tablespoons water, and butter in heavy small saucepan over medium heat until sugar dissolves and butter melts, about 2 minutes. Increase heat to medium-high. Boil until candy thermometer inserted into mixture registers 290°F, tilting pan to submerge thermometer bulb and stirring constantly, about 3 min-utes. Mix in nut mixture. Imme-diately pour toffee onto prepared baking sheet, spreading with back of spoon. Cool completely. Break toffee into small pieces.

DO AHEAD: *Can be made 1 month ahead. Store in airtight container at room temperature up to 1 day or freeze up to 1 month.*

ICE CREAM: Bring cream and milk to simmer in heavy large saucepan. Whisk sugar and egg yolks to blend in medium bowl. Gradually whisk hot cream mixture into yolk mixture. Return mixture to same saucepan. Stir over medium-low heat until custard thickens slightly and leaves path on back of spoon when finger is drawn across, about 5 minutes (do not boil). Transfer to bowl; stir in vanilla. Refrigerate until cold.

Process custard in ice-cream maker according to manufacturer's instructions. Add toffee during last 5 minutes of churning. Transfer ice cream to container, cover, and freeze until firm.

DO AHEAD: *Can be made 4 days ahead. Keep frozen.*

Scoop ice cream into bowls. Top with Mango Sauce. Garnish with mango slices and mint, if desired, and serve.

Mango Sauce

This simple sauce is packed with fresh mango flavor. It would also be delicious over coconut ice cream, topped with a little shredded coconut. Because mango is a fairly fibrous fruit, it's important to strain the sauce. **Makes about 1½ cups**

- 1½ pounds ripe mangoes (about 3), peeled, pitted, chopped
- 2 tablespoons fresh orange juice
- 1 tablespoon fresh lemon juice
- 1 tablespoon sugar

Puree mangoes, orange juice, lemon juice, and sugar in processor or blender until smooth. Strain sauce into medium bowl, cover, and chill until cold.

DO AHEAD: *Can be made 2 days ahead. Keep chilled.*

Frozen Plum Soufflés with Cardamom-Plum Sauce

Aluminum foil collars help these dramatic soufflés keep their shape. Any leftover sauce would be delicious on waffles or pancakes. **Makes 4**

Soufflés

2¼	cups chopped pitted purple-fleshed plums (such as Santa Rosa; about 1 pound)
¾	cup sugar, divided
4	large egg yolks
⅓	cup light corn syrup
3	tablespoons unsalted butter
¼	teaspoon ground cardamom
1	cup chilled heavy whipping cream
1	teaspoon vanilla extract

Sauce

2¼	cups chopped pitted purple-fleshed plums (such as Santa Rosa; about 1 pound)
⅓	cup sugar
6	tablespoons water
⅛	teaspoon ground cardamom
2	plums, halved, pitted, sliced

SOUFFLÉS: Cut four 14x6-inch foil strips. Fold each in half lengthwise. Wrap 1 foil strip around each of four ¾-cup soufflé dishes, forming collars that extend from base to above rim. Fold and crimp ends to secure or secure ends with paper clips.

Combine plums and ¼ cup sugar in heavy medium saucepan. Simmer over medium heat until mixture turns bright red and is reduced to 1½ cups, stirring often, about 8 minutes. Transfer mixture to processor; puree until smooth. Cover; chill until cold.

Whisk egg yolks, corn syrup, butter, and ¼ cup sugar in medium metal bowl. Set bowl over saucepan of simmering water (do not allow bowl to touch water); whisk constantly until thermometer inserted into center registers 170°F, about 5 minutes. Remove bowl from over water. Whisk in cardamom. Using electric mixer, beat egg mixture until cool and thick, about 5 minutes.

Beat cream, vanilla, and remaining ¼ cup sugar in large bowl until stiff peaks form. Gradually fold cold plum puree into cream, then fold in egg mixture. Spoon soufflé mixture into prepared dishes, dividing equally (soufflé will extend above rim of dishes). Cover tops with plastic wrap. Freeze overnight.

DO AHEAD: *Can be made 1 week ahead. Keep frozen.*

SAUCE: Combine chopped plums and sugar in heavy medium saucepan. Simmer over medium heat until mixture turns bright red and is reduced to 1⅓ cups, stirring often, about 10 minutes. Mix in 6 tablespoons water and cardamom. Transfer to processor and puree. Transfer sauce to bowl. Cover; chill until cold, at least 3 hours and up to 1 day.

Carefully remove foil from soufflés. Drizzle some sauce over each. Top with plum slices. Serve with remaining sauce.

Brandy Snaps with Lemon Curd Ice Cream and Blackberries

A treat from across the pond: Brandy snaps are thin wafer cookies popular in Great Britain. Here they are transformed into edible cookie bowls filled with lemony ice cream and a lemon curd topping. **6 servings**

Lemon Curd

1	cup plus 2 tablespoons sugar
²⁄₃	cup fresh lemon juice
½	cup (1 stick) unsalted butter, cut into pieces
3	tablespoons finely grated lemon peel
3	large eggs
1	cup heavy whipping cream
½	cup whole milk

Cookies

3	tablespoons dark corn syrup
2	tablespoons (packed) dark brown sugar
2	tablespoons (¼ stick) unsalted butter
1	tablespoon brandy
⅓	cup unbleached all purpose flour
2	½-pint containers blackberries

LEMON CURD: Bring 1 cup sugar, lemon juice, butter, and lemon peel to boil in heavy large saucepan, stirring until sugar dissolves. Whisk eggs in large bowl to blend. Gradually whisk in hot butter mixture. Return to same saucepan and stir over low heat until curd thickens and leaves path on back of spoon when finger is drawn across, about 2 minutes (do not boil).

Divide curd equally between 2 medium bowls. Add remaining 2 tablespoons sugar, then cream and milk to 1 bowl and whisk to combine for lemon cream. Cover and chill lemon curd and lemon cream until cold, at least 2 hours and up to 1 day.

Process lemon cream in ice-cream maker according to manufacturer's instructions. Transfer to container; cover and freeze.

DO AHEAD: *Can be made 3 days ahead. Keep curd refrigerated. Keep ice cream frozen.*

COOKIES: Preheat oven to 350°F. Butter nonstick rimmed baking sheet. Combine corn syrup, sugar, butter, and brandy in heavy small saucepan. Stir over medium heat until sugar dissolves. Bring to boil. Remove from heat; whisk in flour.

Form 2 cookies by spooning 1 tablespoon batter for each onto prepared sheet, spacing 4 to 5 inches apart. Bake until cookies are lacy and golden, about 10 minutes. Cool cookies on sheet just until firm enough to lift without breaking, about 30 seconds. Working quickly and using spatula, lift 1 cookie from sheet. Drape over inverted ¾-cup custard dish. Gently flatten cookies on dish bottom; mold and crimp sides to form cup, and let stand until cool and crisp. Repeat with remaining cookie, returning baking sheet to oven briefly to soften cookie if hardened.

Repeat baking and molding of remaining batter. Cool all cookie cups. Gently remove cookie cups from dishes.

DO AHEAD: *Can be made 1 day ahead. Store in airtight container at room temperature.*

Stir lemon curd over low heat just until slightly warm. Place 1 cookie cup on each plate. Fill with scoops of ice cream. Spoon some lemon curd over. Sprinkle with berries.

Technique Tip: **Creamy Curd**

For smooth, creamy lemon curd, keep stirring. This action prevents the protein in the eggs from bonding, giving you a creamy sauce rather than a curdled one. As you stir, pay special attention to the corners where the sides and bottom of the pan meet. That's a prime location for sticking.

ᵧᵧᵧᵧ Boysenberry–Grand Marnier Ice-Cream Bonbons

These attractive ice-cream treats are decorated five different ways. You'll have some leftover ice cream—pack it into a container and freeze it to enjoy after the bonbons are gone. Begin this recipe at least a day ahead (or up to a week ahead). Once you've mastered the technique here, create all kinds of delicious bonbons of your own using other flavors of homemade or purchased ice cream.
Makes 30

Boysenberry Ice Cream

²/₃	cup sugar
12	ounces frozen boysenberries or raspberries (about 2½ cups), thawed
1⅓	cups heavy whipping cream
3	large egg yolks

Grand Marnier Ice Cream

2	oranges
2	cups heavy whipping cream, divided
1	cup half and half
¾	cup sugar
6	large egg yolks
1½	teaspoons finely grated orange peel
2	tablespoons Grand Marnier or other orange liqueur

Dipping

1¼	pounds bittersweet or semisweet chocolate (do not exceed 61% cacao), chopped
¼	cup plus 1 tablespoon non-hydrogenated solid vegetable shortening
6	ounces high-quality white chocolate (such as Lindt or Perugina), chopped
	Milk chocolate shavings
5	walnut halves
	Natural unsweetened cocoa powder

BOYSENBERRY ICE CREAM: Sprinkle sugar over berries in small bowl. Let stand 45 minutes at room temperature. Puree berries in processor. Strain through sieve into large bowl, pressing on solids with back of spoon. Bring cream to simmer in heavy medium saucepan. Whisk egg yolks in medium bowl to blend. Gradually whisk in hot cream. Return mixture to saucepan and stir over medium-low heat until custard thickens and leaves path on back of spoon when finger is drawn across, about 2 minutes. Strain custard into berry puree. Chill until cold, about 2 hours.

Place 13x9x2-inch baking dish in freezer. Transfer berry custard to ice-cream maker and process according to manufacturer's instructions. Spread ice cream in bottom of chilled dish. Freeze.

GRAND MARNIER ICE CREAM: Using vegetable peeler, remove peel (orange part only) from oranges in long wide strips. Place in heavy medium saucepan. Add 1 cup cream, half and half, and sugar. Bring to boil, stirring occasionally. Remove from heat. Cover and let steep 30 minutes.

Using slotted spoon, remove peel from cream and discard. Bring cream mixture to simmer. Whisk egg yolks in medium bowl to blend. Gradually whisk in hot cream mixture. Return mixture to saucepan and stir over medium-low heat until custard thickens and leaves path on back of spoon when finger is drawn across, about 2 minutes. Strain into large bowl. Mix in grated orange peel, then remaining 1 cup cream. Chill until cold, about 2 hours. Mix in Grand Marnier.

Transfer custard to ice-cream maker and process according to manufacturer's instructions. Spoon over boysenberry ice cream in dish; smooth top. Cover with waxed paper. Freeze until very firm, at least 6 hours or overnight.

Line 4 small baking sheets with foil. Place in freezer for 20 minutes. Remove 1 sheet. Dip 1½-inch-diameter ice-cream scoop into cup of hot water. Working quickly, scoop up layered ice cream. Round off edges with index finger. Release ice-cream ball onto frozen sheet. Repeat, forming 15 ice-cream balls. Insert 1 toothpick into center of each ball. Return sheet to freezer. Remove second sheet from freezer. Repeat process to form 15 more ice-cream balls. Return sheet to freezer. Pack remaining ice cream into container and freeze. Freeze ice-cream balls until very firm, at least 6 hours or overnight. Using metal icing spatula, loosen ice-cream balls from foil; refreeze.

DIPPING: Melt bittersweet chocolate with ¼ cup shortening in heavy medium saucepan over very low heat, stirring until smooth. Cool to lukewarm. Remove 1 sheet of ice-cream balls and 1 foil-lined frozen sheet from freezer. Fill ¼-cup measuring cup with melted chocolate. Working quickly, hold 1 ice-cream ball by toothpick over saucepan of chocolate; pour chocolate in cup over ball, turning to coat. Allow excess chocolate to drip off into saucepan. Place bonbon on foil-lined sheet. Repeat with remaining ice-cream balls. Twist and turn toothpicks to loosen; remove from bonbons. Freeze. Repeat dipping process with remaining ice-cream balls and frozen baking sheet. Freeze 30 minutes.

Melt white chocolate with remaining 1 tablespoon shortening in heavy small saucepan over very low heat, stirring constantly. Cool to lukewarm. Rewarm bittersweet chocolate to lukewarm over very low heat, stirring constantly. Remove 1 sheet of bonbons from freezer. Dip 1 bonbon halfway into white chocolate, covering 1 side and hole left from toothpick. Place on same frozen sheet. Repeat with 4 more bonbons. Dip spoon into melted bittersweet chocolate and quickly move from side to side over double-dipped bonbons, allowing chocolate to fall in zigzag lines. Dip another spoon into melted white chocolate and wave from side to side over 5 solid chocolate bonbons, allowing chocolate to fall in zigzag lines. Dip finger into melted bittersweet chocolate and dab over tops of remaining bonbons on sheet 1 at a time, covering holes left from toothpicks. Sprinkle chocolate shavings over each. Return bonbons to freezer.

Remove second sheet of bonbons from freezer. Dip half of one walnut half into bittersweet chocolate. Place atop 1 bonbon. Repeat with 4 more walnuts and bonbons. Roll remaining 10 bonbons in bowl of cocoa. Brush off excess and place on same sheet. Freeze at least 4 hours or overnight.

DO AHEAD: *Can be made 1 week ahead. Keep bonbons frozen in single layer in airtight container.*

Pistachio Ice Cream in Phyllo Nests with Rose Water–Splashed Strawberries

Here's a good choice for a springtime brunch or party. The recipe is easily doubled (or even tripled). If you can't find 17x12-inch sheets of phyllo, use about 6 smaller sheets. Butter and sugar one sheet; fold lengthwise in half, then lengthwise in half again. Cut crosswise into 4-inch-long strips. Repeat buttering and folding with enough phyllo to make a total of sixteen 4-inch-long strips, then proceed with recipe. **8 servings**

4	17x12-inch sheets fresh or thawed frozen phyllo pastry
½	cup (1 stick) unsalted butter, melted
5	tablespoons sugar (or more), divided
2	half-pint containers strawberries, hulled, sliced
1	teaspoon (or more) rose water
1	pint pistachio ice cream
½	cup chopped unsalted natural pistachios, toasted
	Organic rose petals (optional)

Ingredient Tips: Rose Water and Rose Petals

This recipe gets its lovely fragrance from two special ingredients. Rose water is essentially distilled rose petals; it's an intensely perfumed liquid—so a little goes a long way. You can find it at some supermarkets, specialty foods stores, and Middle Eastern markets or order it from adrianascaravan.com. Organic rose petals are those that haven't been sprayed with pesticides. If you don't have any in your own garden, ask your friends. Or check out the flower stand at your favorite farmers' market.

Preheat oven to 400°F. Butter 8 standard (⅓-cup) muffin cups. Place 1 phyllo sheet on work surface with long side facing you (keep remaining phyllo covered with plastic wrap and damp kitchen towel to prevent drying). Brush phyllo sheet with melted butter and sprinkle with 1 teaspoon sugar. Fold phyllo sheet in half lengthwise. Brush with more butter and sprinkle with ½ teaspoon sugar. Fold phyllo sheet in half lengthwise again, creating strip. Cut strip into 4 equal pieces. Press 1 piece of phyllo into buttered muffin pan (ends will come up higher than sides). Brush with butter. Place another piece of phyllo crosswise atop phyllo in muffin pan [1]. Brush with butter. Repeat, forming another cup. Repeat entire process with remaining phyllo sheets, forming 8 cups total. Bake until golden brown, about 12 minutes. Cool completely in pan on rack.

Toss strawberries, 1 teaspoon rose water, and remaining 3 tablespoons sugar in large bowl to coat. Let stand until juices form, tossing occasionally, about 15 minutes. Add more rose water and sugar to taste, if desired.

Place 1 phyllo nest in center of each of 8 dessert plates. Place scoop of ice cream in each nest. Spoon strawberries and juices around nests. Sprinkle with pistachios, garnish with rose petals, if desired, and serve immediately.

Frozen Milky Way Mousse with Chocolate Sauce

Some people swear by frozen Milky Way bars. This grown-up dessert takes the popular candy bar and incorporates it into a light and airy mousse that's simply frozen in a loaf pan. An intense chocolate sauce is the perfect finishing touch.

12 servings

Chocolate Sauce

1	cup heavy whipping cream
½	cup sugar
⅓	cup natural unsweetened cocoa powder
3	tablespoons unsalted butter
1	teaspoon vanilla extract
½	teaspoon instant coffee powder

Mousse

1½	cups ½-inch pieces Milky Way bars (about 8¼ ounces)
6	ounces bittersweet or semisweet chocolate (do not exceed 61% cacao), chopped
3	ounces unsweetened chocolate, chopped
¼	cup (½ stick) unsalted butter
½	cup sugar
3	tablespoons water
3	large egg whites, room temperature
¼	teaspoon cream of tartar
1¼	cups chilled heavy whipping cream
1	teaspoon vanilla extract

CHOCOLATE SAUCE: Combine cream, sugar, cocoa, and butter in heavy medium saucepan. Bring to simmer over medium-low heat, whisking constantly until butter melts and sugar and cocoa dissolve. Remove from heat and whisk in vanilla and coffee powder. Cool sauce.

DO AHEAD: *Can be made 1 week ahead. Cover and refrigerate.*

MOUSSE: Line 9x5x3-inch metal loaf pan with parchment paper. Combine Milky Way pieces, semisweet chocolate, unsweetened chocolate, and butter in large metal bowl set over saucepan of simmering water. Stir constantly until melted (mixture will look grainy). Remove bowl from over water and cool mixture slightly.

Combine sugar and 3 tablespoons water in heavy small saucepan. Stir over low heat until sugar dissolves. Increase heat to high and boil syrup until candy thermometer inserted into mixture registers 230°F, tilting pan to submerge thermometer bulb.

Meanwhile, beat egg whites and cream of tartar to soft peaks in medium bowl. Gradually pour boiling syrup into egg whites, beating until stiff peaks form and whites are cool, about 5 minutes. Using rubber spatula, fold whites into chocolate mixture in 2 additions. Beat cream and vanilla in medium bowl to soft peaks. Using rubber spatula, fold cream into chocolate mixture in 2 additions. Spoon mousse into prepared pan. Cover with plastic wrap and freeze until firm, at least 6 hours.

DO AHEAD: *Can be made 1 week ahead. Keep frozen.*

Heat sauce to lukewarm over low heat. Remove plastic wrap from top of mousse. Invert mousse onto platter. Remove pan and peel off parchment. Slice mousse crosswise into 12 slices. Cut each slice diagonally into 2 triangles. Arrange 2 mousse triangles on each plate; spoon warm chocolate sauce over and around mousse and serve.

Pera Bella Helena

This is an Italian take on the French dish poire Belle-Hélène, *poached pears with vanilla ice cream and chocolate sauce. Here, the poached pears are served with a hazelnut-orange* semifreddo *and a chocolate sauce spiked with Frangelico, the Italian hazelnut liqueur.* **4 servings**

Semifreddo

¾	cup chilled heavy whipping cream
1	pint vanilla ice cream, slightly softened
½	cup chopped husked toasted hazelnuts
3	tablespoons Frangelico (hazelnut liqueur) or other nut liqueur
1	ounce bittersweet or semisweet chocolate, finely grated
½	teaspoon finely grated orange peel

Sauce

¼	cup heavy whipping cream
¼	cup Frangelico or other nut liqueur
	Pinch of salt
6	ounces bittersweet or semisweet chocolate (do not exceed 61% cacao), chopped
¼	cup light corn syrup

Pears

6	cups water
1½	cups sugar
8	3x1-inch orange peel strips
2	teaspoons vanilla extract
4	small firm but ripe Anjou, Bartlett, or Comice pears, peeled
¼	cup chopped husked toasted hazelnuts
4	orange slices

SEMIFREDDO: Line 8x8x2-inch metal baking pan with plastic wrap. Whip cream to soft peaks in medium bowl. Mix ice cream, hazelnuts, liqueur, chocolate, and orange peel in large bowl just until blended. Gently fold in whipped cream. Transfer mixture to prepared pan; smooth top. Cover and freeze until firm, at least 4 hours.

DO AHEAD: *Can be made 4 days ahead. Keep frozen.*

SAUCE: Bring cream, liqueur, and salt to boil in heavy small saucepan. Remove from heat and add chocolate. Let stand 3 minutes. Whisk until chocolate is melted and sauce is smooth. Whisk in corn syrup.

DO AHEAD: *Can be made 3 days ahead. Cover and refrigerate.*

PEARS: Stir 6 cups water, sugar, orange peel, and vanilla in heavy medium saucepan over medium heat until sugar dissolves. Bring to boil. Reduce heat; add pears and simmer until pears are just tender, about 20 minutes. Remove pears from poaching liquid. Cool pears and poaching liquid separately. Return pears to poaching liquid and refrigerate until cold.

DO AHEAD: *Can be made 8 hours ahead. Keep chilled.*

Stir chocolate sauce over low heat until warm. Cut semifreddo into 4 squares. Place 1 square in each of 4 bowls. Using slotted spoon, remove pears from poaching liquid. Place pears atop semifreddo. Spoon chocolate sauce over pears to coat, allowing extra sauce to drizzle onto semifreddo and plate. Sprinkle with nuts. Garnish with orange slices and serve.

Coffee-Caramel Parfaits

You won't need an ice-cream machine for this rich and decadent frozen custard. It's layered with homemade caramel sauce and crunchy toasted walnuts, then topped with whipped cream. These are pretty generous portions; if you like, divide the parfait mixture among six small glasses instead of four large ones.

Makes 4

Sauce

¾	cup sugar
¼	cup water
¼	cup light corn syrup
¼	cup plus 2 tablespoons heavy whipping cream
5	tablespoons unsalted butter
⅓	cup sour cream
4	teaspoons chopped toasted walnuts

Parfaits

1	cup chilled heavy whipping cream, divided
⅓	cup sugar
6	large egg yolks
2	tablespoons instant espresso powder or instant coffee powder
2	ounces high-quality white chocolate (such as Lindt or Perugina), chopped
2	tablespoons Kahlúa or other coffee liqueur
½	cup sour cream
½	cup chopped toasted walnuts
	Whipped cream
4	walnut halves or chocolate-covered coffee beans

SAUCE: Stir sugar, ¼ cup water, and corn syrup in heavy medium saucepan over low heat until sugar dissolves. Increase heat and boil without stirring until syrup is deep golden brown, occasionally brushing down sides of pan with wet pastry brush and swirling pan, about 10 minutes. Add cream and butter (mixture will bubble vigorously); whisk until smooth. Remove from heat and whisk in sour cream.

Spoon scant 1 tablespoon sauce into each of 4 Margarita glasses or wine glasses. Sprinkle each with 1 teaspoon nuts. Place glasses in freezer.

PARFAITS: Whisk ¼ cup cream, sugar, egg yolks, and espresso powder in small metal bowl to blend. Set bowl over saucepan of simmering water (do not allow bowl to touch water). Whisk mixture constantly until thermometer inserted into center registers 160°F, about 3 minutes. Remove bowl from over water. Add white chocolate and Kahlúa and whisk until smooth. Using electric mixer, beat custard until cool and thick, about 5 minutes.

Combine remaining ¾ cup cream and sour cream in large bowl; whisk until stiff peaks form. Gradually fold yolk mixture into cream.

Pour ⅓ cup parfait mixture into each glass. Chill remaining parfait mixture. Freeze parfaits in glasses 1 hour.

If necessary, stir remaining sauce over low heat just until pourable. Spoon 2 tablespoons sauce over each parfait, tilting glasses slightly to cover parfait. Sprinkle each with 2 tablespoons chopped walnuts. Place in freezer until sauce sets, about 20 minutes. Divide remaining parfait mixture among glasses. Freeze 1 hour. Drizzle 1 tablespoon sauce over each parfait in zigzag lines. Cover and freeze overnight.

DO AHEAD: *Can be made 1 week ahead. Keep frozen.*

Let parfaits stand 10 minutes at room temperature. Spoon whipped cream into pastry bag fitted with medium star tip. Pipe 1 rosette of whipped cream atop each parfait. Garnish each parfait with walnut half and serve.

Limoncello Parfaits

A simple but sophisticated treat, these parfaits feature purchased vanilla ice cream and lemon sorbet, topped with sweet, fresh raspberries, then drizzled with limoncello, the Italian lemon liqueur. Storing limoncello in the freezer will make it icy cold; because of the high alcohol content, it won't freeze solid. Look for it at liquor stores and some supermarkets. **Makes 8**

1	pint vanilla ice cream
1	pint lemon sorbet
4	cups raspberries
16	tablespoons frozen limoncello or other lemon liqueur

Scoop ice cream into 8 parfait glasses, dividing equally. Scoop lemon sorbet atop ice cream, dividing equally. Sprinkle ½ cup raspberries into each glass. Drizzle 2 tablespoons limoncello over each and serve immediately.

Italian Semifreddo

This shortcut semifreddo (made without whipped cream) starts with purchased vanilla ice cream, which gets triple-almond flavor from toasted sliced almonds, amaretti cookies, and amaretto. It is then served with an intense amaretto-chocolate syrup. **6 servings**

Semifreddo

1	pint vanilla ice cream, slightly softened
2	tablespoons amaretto
2	ounces (about 9) amaretti cookies (Italian macaroons), coarsely chopped (about 1 cup)
⅓	cup sliced almonds, toasted

Chocolate Syrup

¼	cup water
3	ounces bittersweet or semisweet chocolate, chopped
1	tablespoon amaretto
	Additional sliced almonds, toasted

SEMIFREDDO: Line 8x4½x2½-inch loaf pan with waxed paper. Mix ice cream and amaretto in medium bowl. Stir in cookies and almonds. Transfer mixture to prepared pan; smooth top. Cover and freeze until firm, about 2 hours.

CHOCOLATE SYRUP: Bring ¼ cup water to simmer in heavy small saucepan over high heat. Remove from heat and add chocolate. Whisk until sauce is smooth. Stir in amaretto.

DO AHEAD: *Semifreddo and sauce can be made 3 days ahead. Keep semifreddo frozen. Cool, cover, and refrigerate sauce. Rewarm sauce slightly before using.*

Remove semifreddo from pan and discard waxed paper. Dip heavy large knife in hot water; cut semifreddo into 6 slices. Place 1 slice on each of 6 plates. Let stand about 5 minutes to soften slightly. Drizzle warm chocolate syrup atop semifreddo. Sprinkle with additional almonds and serve.

Meyer Lemon Semifreddo with Summer Berries

This dessert is much like a frozen mousse with a softer and denser mouthfeel than ice cream. The lemony custard is aerated with an electric mixer—not in an ice-cream maker—and then it's lightened with some freshly whipped cream and simply placed in the freezer. **8 to 10 servings**

½   **cup sliced almonds, toasted**
1¾   **cups chilled heavy whipping cream**
1¼   **cups plus 2 tablespoons sugar**
7   **large egg yolks**
½   **cup fresh Meyer lemon juice or regular lemon juice**
1   **tablespoon plus 2 teaspoons finely grated Meyer lemon peel or regular lemon peel**
¼   **teaspoon salt**
4   **cups mixed berries (such as raspberries, blackberries, blueberries, and quartered hulled strawberries)**

Line 9x5x3-inch metal loaf pan with plastic wrap, leaving generous overhang. Sprinkle almonds evenly over bottom of pan. Using electric mixer, beat cream in large bowl until soft peaks form. Refrigerate whipped cream while making custard.

Whisk 1¼ cups sugar, egg yolks, lemon juice, lemon peel, and salt in large metal bowl to blend. Set bowl over large saucepan of simmering water and whisk constantly until yolk mixture is thick and fluffy and instant-read thermometer inserted into mixture registers 170°F, about 4 minutes. Remove bowl from over water. Using electric mixer, beat mixture until cool, thick, and doubled in volume, about 6 minutes. Fold in chilled whipped cream. Transfer mixture to prepared loaf pan and smooth top. Tap loaf pan lightly on work surface to remove air pockets. Fold plastic wrap overhang over top to cover. Freeze semifreddo until firm, at least 8 hours or overnight.

DO AHEAD: *Semifreddo can be made 3 days ahead. Keep frozen.*

Gently mix all berries and remaining 2 tablespoons sugar in large bowl.

DO AHEAD: *Can be made 3 hours ahead. Cover and refrigerate.*

Unfold plastic wrap from top of semifreddo and invert dessert onto platter; remove plastic wrap. Dip heavy large knife into hot water; cut semifreddo crosswise into 1-inch-thick slices. Transfer to plates; spoon berries alongside and serve.

Boysenberry Sorbet and Lemon Ice-Cream Bombe

Ice-cream bombes date back to the Victorian era and got their name (French for—what else—"bomb") because they were often made in spherical molds. In this version, alternating scoops of berry sorbet and lemon ice cream in a ring mold give the dessert a modern, striped look. A berry sauce and fresh berries make a pretty, simple garnish. **12 servings**

Ice Cream

2¼	cups heavy whipping cream, divided
1	cup half and half
¾	cup sugar
6	egg yolks
½	cup fresh lemon juice
2	tablespoons finely grated lemon peel

Sorbet

1¼	cups sugar
½	cup water
8	cups frozen boysenberries or blackberries (about 32 ounces), thawed

Sauce

4	cups frozen boysenberries or blackberries (about 16 ounces), thawed
⅓	cup sugar
¼	cup water
4	cups fresh boysenberries, blackberries, and/or raspberries
	Fresh mint leaves
	Assorted cookies (optional)

ICE CREAM: Bring 1¼ cups cream, half and half, and sugar to simmer in heavy large saucepan, stirring occasionally. Whisk egg yolks in large bowl to blend. Gradually whisk in cream mixture. Return mixture to same saucepan. Stir over medium-low heat until mixture thickens and leaves path on back of spoon when finger is drawn across, about 4 minutes (do not boil). Strain mixture into bowl. Mix in remaining 1 cup cream, lemon juice, and lemon peel. Refrigerate until cold. Process mixture in ice-cream maker according to manufacturer's instructions. Transfer ice cream to container and freeze.

SORBET: Stir sugar and ½ cup water in heavy medium saucepan over low heat until sugar dissolves. Puree berries with sugar syrup in processor. Strain through coarse sieve into bowl, pressing firmly on seeds. Discard solids in sieve. Chill until cold. Process mixture in ice-cream maker according to manufacturer's instructions.

Carefully line 12-cup ring mold with foil, pressing as smoothly as possible to eliminate wrinkles and extending over sides. Fill prepared ring mold alternately with ⅓-cup scoops of sorbet and ⅓-cup scoops of ice cream. Freeze 1 hour. Cover bombe with plastic wrap. Press down firmly to pack. Freeze bombe overnight.

DO AHEAD: *Can be made 1 week ahead. Keep frozen.*

SAUCE: Puree thawed berries with sugar and ¼ cup water in processor. Strain through coarse sieve into bowl, pressing firmly on seeds. Discard solids in sieve. Cover sauce and chill until cold.

DO AHEAD: *Can be made 2 days ahead. Keep chilled.*

Place round platter in freezer 30 minutes. Using foil as aid, lift bombe from mold. Invert bombe onto platter; peel off foil. Mound some fresh berries in center of bombe. Arrange more berries around sides. Garnish top and sides with mint. Cut into slices and arrange on plates. Spoon sauce and berries around each. Serve with cookies, if desired.

Frozen Nougat Terrine with Bittersweet Chocolate and Raspberry-Fig Sauces

This impressive dessert was inspired by nougat, a French confection made of egg whites, honey, and nuts. The nougat mousse is frozen in a loaf pan (no ice-cream maker necessary) and needs to stay in the freezer overnight, so plan accordingly. The terrine is the ideal dessert for the busy cook: It can be made up to one week in advance. **8 servings**

5	tablespoons cold water, divided
1	teaspoon unflavored gelatin
6	ounces high-quality white chocolate (such as Lindt or Perugina), chopped
5	large eggs, separated, room temperature
6	tablespoons honey, divided
1	tablespoon Grand Marnier or other orange liqueur
¾	cup chilled heavy whipping cream
1	teaspoon vanilla extract
3	tablespoons almonds, toasted, finely chopped
3	tablespoons walnuts, toasted, finely chopped

Bittersweet Chocolate Sauce with Honey (see recipe)
Raspberry-Fig Sauce (see recipe)

Line 9x5x2¾-inch metal loaf pan with plastic wrap, leaving overhang. Pour 1 tablespoon cold water into small bowl. Sprinkle gelatin over. Let stand until gelatin softens, about 10 minutes. Stir white chocolate in top of double boiler set over simmering water until melted (do not allow bottom of pan to touch water). Remove chocolate from over water.

Whisk egg yolks, 2 tablespoons honey, Grand Marnier, and 3 tablespoons cold water in large metal bowl to blend. Set over saucepan of gently boiling water (do not allow bottom of bowl to touch water) and whisk until mixture thickens and thermometer registers 160°F, about 3 minutes. Remove bowl from over water; add gelatin mixture and whisk until dissolved.

Stir remaining 1 tablespoon cold water and 4 tablespoons honey in small saucepan over low heat until honey dissolves. Increase heat and boil until candy thermometer inserted into mixture registers 220°F, tilting pan to submerge thermometer bulb, about 2 minutes.

Using electric mixer, beat egg whites in large bowl until soft peaks form. Gradually beat hot honey syrup into whites. Continue beating until whites are cool and very stiff, about 4 minutes. Fold barely lukewarm white chocolate into yolk mixture; then fold whites into yolk mixture in 3 additions.

Beat cream and vanilla in medium bowl until medium-firm peaks form. Fold cream and nuts into mousse. Transfer mixture to prepared pan; smooth top. Cover with plastic; freeze overnight.

DO AHEAD: *Can be made 1 week ahead. Keep frozen.*

Freeze oval platter 15 minutes. Uncover terrine. Place platter on pan. Invert terrine onto platter; peel off plastic. Spoon Bittersweet Chocolate Sauce onto center of plates. Slice terrine; place atop sauce. Spoon Raspberry-Fig Sauce over center of terrine slices and serve immediately.

(continued next page)

Frozen Nougat Terrine with Bittersweet Chocolate and Raspberry-Fig Sauces

(continued)

Bittersweet Chocolate Sauce with Honey

A little bit of honey and a shot of brandy amp up the flavor of this sauce.
Makes about 1¾ cups

1   cup heavy whipping cream
2   tablespoons honey
1   tablespoon brandy
    Pinch of salt
8   ounces bittersweet or semisweet chocolate (do not exceed 61% cacao), chopped
2   teaspoons vanilla extract

Combine cream, honey, brandy, and salt in medium saucepan. Stir over high heat until mixture comes to boil. Remove from heat. Add chocolate and whisk until melted. Whisk in vanilla. Let stand until cool but still pourable, about 1 hour.

DO AHEAD: *Can be made 3 days ahead. Cover and chill. Before serving, stir over low heat until just liquid but not warm.*

Raspberry-Fig Sauce

Dried figs and frozen raspberries make this a dessert sauce for all seasons.
Makes about 2 cups

5   ounces dried Calimyrna figs, stemmed, quartered (about 1 cup)
1   cup water
3   tablespoons honey
½   vanilla bean, split lengthwise
1   12-ounce package frozen raspberries, thawed
¼   cup sugar

Combine figs, 1 cup water, honey, and vanilla bean in heavy small saucepan. Stir over low heat until honey dissolves. Increase heat to medium and simmer until figs are tender and liquid is reduced to thick syrup, stirring frequently, about 20 minutes. Add raspberries and sugar and simmer until thickened to sauce consistency, stirring occasionally, about 5 minutes. Cool.

DO AHEAD: *Can be made 1 day ahead. Cover and refrigerate. Bring to room temperature before serving.*

Mint Truffle Ice-Cream Terrine with Mint and Chocolate Sauces

The chocolate, peppermint, and cream mixture here does double duty: First, it's rolled into truffles, which become mint chocolate polka dots when pressed into the vanilla ice cream terrine. The remaining chocolate mixture is then melted into a decadent sauce that's drizzled around the terrine, along with a mint sauce, before serving. **12 servings**

Truffles and Chocolate Sauce

1½	cups heavy whipping cream
16	ounces bittersweet or semisweet chocolate (do not exceed 61% cacao), chopped
2	teaspoons pure peppermint extract
	Natural unsweetened cocoa powder
2½	pints vanilla ice cream, slightly softened

Mint Sauce

¾	cup sugar
⅓	cup water
2	cups (loosely packed) fresh mint leaves

TRUFFLES AND CHOCOLATE SAUCE: Bring cream to simmer in heavy large saucepan; remove from heat. Add chocolate; let stand 1 minute. Whisk until mixture is smooth. Whisk in peppermint extract. Freeze until firm, about 4 hours, or chill overnight.

Line baking sheet with foil. Drop scant 1 tablespoon chocolate mixture for each of 16 truffles onto prepared sheet. Dust hands with cocoa; roll chocolate mounds into rounds. Cover and freeze truffles. Cover and chill remaining chocolate mixture for sauce.

DO AHEAD: *Truffles and sauce can be made 2 days ahead. Keep truffles frozen; keep chocolate mixture chilled.*

Line 8½x4½x2½-inch metal loaf pan with plastic wrap, leaving generous overhang. Spread ⅓ of ice cream (about 1⅔ cups) over bottom of prepared pan. Press 8 truffles in random pattern (and spaced apart) into ice-cream layer. Spread ½ of remaining ice cream over. Press remaining 8 truffles in random pattern (and spaced apart) into second ice-cream layer. Spread remaining ice cream over. Cover terrine with plastic wrap overhang. Freeze at least 6 hours and up to 2 days.

MINT SAUCE: Bring sugar and ⅓ cup water to boil in small saucepan, stirring until sugar dissolves. Pour syrup into blender; cool 10 minutes. Add mint leaves to syrup and puree until smooth. Transfer sauce to bowl; cool.

DO AHEAD: *Mint sauce can be made 1 day ahead. Cover and chill. Whisk to blend before using.*

Stir remaining chocolate mixture over low heat until warm. Transfer to pitcher. Turn ice cream terrine out onto platter; peel off plastic. Cut terrine crosswise into slices; arrange on plates. Drizzle chocolate sauce and mint sauce around slices.

Rocky Road Sundae Pie

Ice-cream pies are ideal for summer entertaining: There's little or no baking required, they're easy to prepare, they can be made well in advance, and they're guaranteed crowd-pleasers. In this pie, rocky road ice cream is deconstructed into its essential elements: chocolate, marshmallow, vanilla, and nuts. It all starts with a chocolate crust, which is topped with purchased chocolate ice cream, dotted with a rich milk chocolate fudge sauce, drizzled with melted marshmallow cream, and sprinkled with toasted walnut pieces. **12 servings**

Fudge Sauce

- ⅔ **cup heavy whipping cream**
- 8 **ounces high-quality milk chocolate (such as Lindt or Perugina), chopped**
- ½ **teaspoon vanilla extract**

Marshmallow Sauce

- 4 **cups mini marshmallows (about 7½ ounces)**
- ⅓ **cup heavy whipping cream**
- 1 **teaspoon vanilla extract**

Pie

- 2 **quarts chocolate ice cream, slightly softened, divided**
  Chocolate Crumb Crust (see recipe)
- 1 **cup walnuts, toasted, coarsely chopped, divided**

FUDGE SAUCE: Bring cream just to simmer in heavy medium saucepan over medium heat. Remove from heat. Add chocolate; let stand 1 minute. Whisk until chocolate is melted and smooth. Whisk in vanilla. Let stand at room temperature until sauce cools and thickens slightly, stirring occasionally, about 20 minutes.

MARSHMALLOW SAUCE: Combine marshmallows and cream in large metal bowl. Set bowl over saucepan of barely simmering water. Stir until marshmallows melt and sauce is smooth, about 3 minutes. Remove bowl from over water; stir in vanilla. Let stand until slightly cooled but still pourable, about 10 minutes.

PIE: Spread 1 quart ice cream evenly in prepared crust. Drop half of fudge sauce by tablespoonfuls over ice cream, spacing drops apart. Sprinkle half of walnuts over sauce. Drizzle half of marshmallow sauce over walnuts. Freeze until sauces are set, about 10 minutes. Spread second quart of ice cream evenly over. Drop remaining fudge sauce by tablespoonfuls over ice cream. Drizzle remaining marshmallow sauce over, allowing some fudge sauce to show through. Sprinkle with remaining walnuts. Freeze until pie is firm, about 4 hours.

DO AHEAD: *Can be prepared 5 days ahead. Cover tightly with foil. Keep frozen.*

Let pie soften slightly at room temperature, about 10 minutes. Cut around pan sides to loosen pie. Remove pan sides. Cut pie into wedges and serve.

 ## Chocolate Crumb Crust

This two-ingredient crust couldn't be easier—or more delicious. Try it as the base for an ice-cream pie of your own invention, using your favorite flavors of ice cream and a chocolate or caramel sauce on the side.
Makes one 9-inch crust

- 1 **9-ounce package chocolate wafer cookies, crushed to crumbs**
- 6 **tablespoons (¾ stick) unsalted butter, melted**

Position rack in center of oven and preheat to 325°F. Butter 9-inch-diameter springform pan with 2¾-inch high sides. Mix crumbs and melted butter in medium bowl until crumbs are evenly moistened. Press crumb mixture firmly onto bottom and 1 inch up sides of prepared pan. Bake crust 10 minutes. Cool crust completely on rack.

Chocolate-Peppermint Crunch Ice-Cream Pie

Feel free to experiment with the ice cream in this pie. Almost any flavor of purchased ice cream—strawberry, coffee, dulce de leche—would be delicious. Note to busy cooks: The chocolate crunch topping will keep for a week in the freezer. The pie must freeze overnight, so begin preparing it a day ahead.
10 to 12 servings

Chocolate Crunch
6   ounces bittersweet or semisweet chocolate (do not exceed 61% cacao), chopped
1½   tablespoons vegetable oil
1   9-ounce package chocolate wafer cookies, crushed to crumbs

Pie
2   quarts peppermint or mint chocolate chip ice cream, slightly softened, divided
      Chocolate Crumb Crust (see recipe on page 500)
      Chocolate Truffle Sauce (see recipe)

CHOCOLATE CRUNCH: Line large baking sheet with waxed paper. Stir chocolate and oil in medium metal bowl set over saucepan of simmering water until chocolate is melted and smooth. Remove bowl from over water. Mix in cookie crumbs. Spread chocolate mixture thinly over waxed paper on sheet. Freeze until chocolate mixture is firm, about 10 minutes. Chop chocolate crunch into pea-size pieces.

DO AHEAD: *Can be made 1 week ahead. Store airtight in freezer.*

PIE: Spread half of ice cream in prepared crust. Sprinkle half of chocolate crunch over. Top with remaining ice cream. Sprinkle remaining chocolate crunch over. Freeze pie until just firm, about 1 hour. Wrap pie and freeze overnight.

DO AHEAD: *Can be made 1 week ahead. Keep frozen.*

Unwrap pie and let stand at room temperature 10 minutes. Cut around pan sides to loosen crust. Remove pan sides. Warm Chocolate Truffle Sauce. Cut pie into wedges and serve, passing sauce separately.

Chocolate Truffle Sauce

A rich, thick sauce that really clings to ice cream. Any leftover sauce will keep in the fridge for two weeks and would be great drizzled over ice cream or as a dip for banana chunks or strawberries. **Makes about 2 cups**

½   cup plus 1 tablespoon heavy whipping cream
¼   cup (½ stick) unsalted butter, diced
12   ounces bittersweet or semisweet chocolate (do not exceed 61% cacao), chopped
1   teaspoon vanilla extract

Bring cream and butter to simmer in heavy medium saucepan. Remove from heat. Add chocolate and vanilla and whisk until chocolate is melted and sauce is smooth.

DO AHEAD: *Can be made 2 weeks ahead. Cool, cover, and chill. Before using, rewarm over medium-low heat, stirring frequently.*

Raspberry Brownie Ice-Cream Pie

The rich, fudgy brownies are perfect in this dessert because they keep their soft texture even when frozen. And they're delicious in combination with the purchased raspberry sherbet and vanilla ice cream. Be sure to make the brownies (and try not to eat them all) a day before you make the pie.

10 to 12 servings

Brownies

½   **cup (1 stick) unsalted butter, diced**
2   **tablespoons freshly brewed strong coffee**
8   **ounces bittersweet or semisweet chocolate, chopped**
2   **large eggs**
¾   **cup sugar**
1   **teaspoon vanilla extract**
¼   **cup unbleached all purpose flour**
    Large pinch of salt

Pie

1   **quart raspberry sherbet or sorbet, slightly softened**
    Chocolate Crumb Crust (see recipe on page 500)
    Chocolate Truffle Sauce (see recipe on page 501)
1   **quart vanilla ice cream, slightly softened**

Technique Tip: **Even Easier**

For a fast variation, try a brownie sundae: Just make and cool the brownies and cut them into squares. Then top with either vanilla ice cream or raspberry sorbet (or small scoops of both). Finish with a drizzle of Chocolate Truffle Sauce (page 501).

BROWNIES: Position rack in center of oven and preheat to 375°F. Line 8x8x2-inch metal baking pan with foil, leaving overhang. Butter foil. Stir ½ cup butter and coffee in heavy medium saucepan over medium heat until butter melts and mixture comes to simmer. Remove from heat. Add chocolate and stir until melted and smooth. Cool 5 minutes.

Using electric mixer, beat eggs, sugar, and vanilla in large bowl until thick, about 2 minutes. Stir in chocolate mixture, then flour and salt. Transfer batter to prepared pan.

Bake brownies until cracked around edges, about 25 minutes. Cool. Cover and chill overnight. Cut brownies into ⅓-inch pieces.

PIE: Spread raspberry sherbet in prepared crust. Sprinkle half of brownie pieces over. Stir 1 cup Chocolate Truffle Sauce in heavy medium saucepan over low heat until just warm. Drizzle ½ cup warm sauce over brownies. Spread vanilla ice cream over. Sprinkle remaining brownie pieces over, then drizzle ½ cup warm sauce over. Freeze pie until just firm, about 1 hour. Wrap and freeze pie overnight.

DO AHEAD: *Can be made 2 days ahead. Keep frozen. Cover and refrigerate remaining sauce.*

Let pie stand at room temperature 10 minutes. Cut around pan sides to loosen pie. Remove pan sides. Stir remaining chocolate sauce in medium saucepan over low heat until just warm. Cut pie into wedges and serve, passing warm sauce separately.

Peach-Pecan Ice-Cream Pie with Caramel Sauce

This pie features a winning southern influence, with purchased peach ice cream and a pecan-caramel combination that's reminiscent of Louisiana pecan pralines. **12 servings**

Crust

2½   cups finely ground or crushed pecan shortbread cookies (such as pecan Sandies; about 11 ounces)
¼   cup (½ stick) unsalted butter, melted

Caramel Sauce

2   cups sugar
½   cup water
1¼   cups heavy whipping cream
¾   teaspoon vanilla extract

Pie

2   quarts peach ice cream, slightly softened, divided
1   cup pecans, toasted, coarsely chopped
1   cup (about) pecan halves, toasted

CRUST: Preheat oven to 325°F. Butter 9-inch-diameter springform pan with 2¾-inch-high sides. Mix cookie crumbs and melted butter in medium bowl until crumbs are evenly moistened. Press crumb mixture firmly onto bottom and 1 inch up sides of prepared pan. Bake until crust is set and pale golden, about 15 minutes. Cool completely.

CARAMEL SAUCE: Combine sugar and ½ cup water in heavy medium saucepan. Stir over medium-low heat until sugar dissolves. Increase heat to medium-high and boil without stirring until syrup is deep amber color, occasionally brushing down sides of pan with wet pastry brush and swirling pan, about 8 minutes. Remove from heat. Gradually add cream (mixture will bubble vigorously). Stir over low heat until any caramel bits dissolve and sauce is smooth, about 1 minute. Stir in vanilla. Let stand until caramel sauce is cool but still pourable, about 1 hour.

PIE: Drizzle ¼ cup cooled caramel sauce over bottom of crust. Freeze until caramel sets, about 10 minutes. Spread 1 quart ice cream over caramel in crust. Sprinkle chopped pecans over. Drizzle ½ cup caramel sauce over ice cream. Freeze until caramel sets, about 10 minutes. Spread remaining 1 quart ice cream over. Freeze until top of pie is firm, about 1 hour. Arrange pecan halves in 3 concentric circles on top of pie. Drizzle ¼ cup caramel sauce over. Freeze pie until frozen, at least 4 hours.

DO AHEAD: *Can be made 5 days ahead. Cover tightly with foil; keep frozen. Cover and chill remaining caramel sauce.*

Rewarm remaining caramel sauce over low heat, stirring often. Let pie stand at room temperature 10 minutes. Cut around pan sides to loosen pie. Remove pan sides. Serve pie with warm caramel sauce.

Lemon Meringue Ice-Cream Pie in Toasted Pecan Crust

It doesn't get much better than a sweet-tart lemon meringue pie. That is, unless you add a crunchy pecan crust and two layers of creamy vanilla ice cream. Incredible. You can also make this beautiful pie in a tart pan, if you prefer. Just be sure to place the tart pan on a baking sheet before putting it in the oven; this will catch any butter that might seep from the crust. **8 servings**

Lemon Curd

2	large eggs
2	large egg yolks
6	tablespoons (¾ stick) unsalted butter
1	cup sugar
6	tablespoons fresh lemon juice
2	teaspoons finely grated lemon peel
	Pinch of salt

Crust

1½	cups finely chopped pecans
¼	cup sugar
¼	cup (½ stick) unsalted butter, melted
3	cups vanilla ice cream, slightly softened, divided

Meringue

4	large egg whites, room temperature
	Pinch of cream of tartar
6	tablespoons sugar

LEMON CURD: Whisk eggs and egg yolks in medium bowl to blend. Melt butter in medium metal bowl set over large saucepan of simmering water. Whisk in sugar, lemon juice, lemon peel, and salt; gradually whisk in egg mixture. Whisk until curd is thick and thermometer inserted into center registers 178°F to 180°F, about 8 minutes. Transfer to small bowl. Press plastic wrap directly onto surface of curd; chill 4 hours.

DO AHEAD: *Can be made 2 days ahead. Keep chilled.*

CRUST: Preheat oven to 400°F. Mix pecans, sugar, and melted butter in medium bowl until evenly moistened. Press pecan mixture onto bottom and up sides of 9-inch-diameter glass pie dish (mixture will be crumbly). Bake until crust is lightly toasted, about 12 minutes (crust will slip down sides of dish). Use back of spoon to press crust back into place. Cool crust on rack. Freeze crust 30 minutes.

Spoon 1½ cups ice cream into crust; spread to even layer. Spread lemon curd over ice cream; freeze until firm, about 2 hours. Spoon remaining 1½ cups ice cream over lemon curd; spread to even layer. Cover and freeze pie until firm, about 2 hours.

MERINGUE: Using electric mixer, beat egg whites in medium bowl until frothy. Beat in cream of tartar. Gradually add sugar, beating until stiff but not dry. Spoon meringue over pie, spreading to seal at edges and swirling decoratively. Freeze pie 1 hour.

DO AHEAD: *Can be made 1 day ahead. Keep frozen.*

Using kitchen torch, toast meringue until golden in spots or place pie in a preheated 500°F oven until meringue is golden in spots, watching closely to avoid burning, about 3 minutes. Cut pie into wedges; serve immediately.

Coconut-Rum Pie with Pineapple

Sweetened cream of coconut, which is available in the liquor or mixers section of most supermarkets, gives this icebox pie an intense coconut flavor. The filling is simply frozen in a mixing bowl for a few hours before being spooned into the crust, so the recipe doesn't require an ice-cream maker. **8 servings**

Crust

1   cup (packed) sweetened flaked coconut, toasted
1   cup graham cracker crumbs
3   tablespoons unsalted butter, melted
1   large egg white

Filling

1   15-ounce can sweetened cream of coconut (such as Coco Reál or Coco López), divided
6   large egg yolks
2   tablespoons fresh lemon juice
2   cups chilled heavy whipping cream
½   teaspoon coconut extract
3   tablespoons dark rum
1   cup plus 1 tablespoon sweetened flaked coconut, toasted
1   pineapple, peeled, quartered lengthwise, cored, thinly sliced crosswise
¼   cup apricot preserves, stirred to loosen

CRUST: Preheat oven to 350°F. Blend toasted coconut, graham cracker crumbs, melted butter, and egg white in processor until sticky crumbs form. Press crumbs onto bottom and up sides of 9-inch-diameter metal pie pan. Freeze 10 minutes.

Bake crust until golden brown, about 10 minutes. Cool crust to room temperature, then freeze.

FILLING: Whisk 1 cup cream of coconut, egg yolks, and lemon juice in large metal bowl to blend. Set bowl over saucepan of simmering water; whisk constantly until thermometer inserted into center registers 160°F, about 3 minutes. Remove bowl from over water. Using electric mixer, beat mixture until cool and thick, about 5 minutes.

Combine cream, coconut extract, and remaining cream of coconut in another large bowl. Beat until soft peaks form. Add rum and beat until stiff peaks form. Fold whipped cream mixture and 1 cup toasted coconut into egg mixture. Freeze until filling is softly set, stirring occasionally, about 3 hours.

Spoon filling into frozen crust, mounding slightly in center. Cover and freeze pie overnight.

DO AHEAD: *Can be made 1 week ahead. Keep frozen.*

Cut around pan sides to loosen crust. Arrange enough pineapple slices atop pie in overlapping circles to cover. Brush pineapple with preserves. Sprinkle with remaining 1 tablespoon toasted coconut.

More to Try

Sliced papaya or mango—or a combination of pineapple, mango, and papaya—would also be great on top of this pie.

♦♦♦ Peanut Brittle and Caramel Crunch Ice-Cream Pie

Nothing beats the enticing combination of sweet and salty flavors. Here, salted peanuts add a savory hint to the pie crust, and the homemade caramel sauce includes a generous sprinkling of sea salt. A freshly opened and stirred jar of natural peanut butter (made with just peanuts and salt) is soft enough to drizzle over the ice cream when assembling the pie. **8 to 10 servings**

Caramel Sauce

¾	cup heavy whipping cream
½	vanilla bean, split lengthwise
2	tablespoons (¼ stick) unsalted butter
¼	teaspoon fine sea salt
¾	cup sugar
⅓	cup water
¼	cup light corn syrup

Crust

9	whole graham crackers
¼	cup (packed) dark brown sugar
5	tablespoons unsalted butter, melted, hot
1½	teaspoons vanilla extract
½	cup salted roasted cocktail peanuts

Pie

3	pints premium vanilla ice cream, slightly softened, divided
5	tablespoons creamy (smooth) natural peanut butter (made only with peanuts and salt), divided
1	cup coarsely chopped purchased peanut brittle, divided

CARAMEL SAUCE: Place cream in small saucepan. Scrape in seeds from vanilla bean; add bean. Bring cream to simmer. Add butter and sea salt; stir until butter melts and salt dissolves. Set vanilla cream aside.

Stir sugar, ⅓ cup water, and corn syrup in heavy medium saucepan over medium heat until sugar dissolves. Increase heat and boil without stirring until syrup is deep amber color, occasionally brushing down sides of pan with wet pastry brush and swirling pan, about 12 minutes. Remove from heat. Whisk in vanilla cream (mixture will bubble vigorously). Set sauce aside.

CRUST: Preheat oven to 375°F. Line 9-inch-diameter glass pie dish with foil. Finely grind graham crackers and brown sugar in processor. Add melted butter and vanilla; blend until moist crumbs form. Add nuts; blend just until finely chopped. Using plastic wrap as aid, press crumbs firmly onto bottom and up sides of prepared dish. Freeze 15 minutes. Bake crust until brown, about 15 minutes, then place in freezer for 1 hour. Using foil as aid, lift crust from dish; carefully peel off foil. Return frozen crust to same dish.

PIE: Drizzle ½ cup caramel sauce over bottom of crust. Freeze 30 minutes. Spoon 1½ pints ice cream evenly over caramel sauce; smooth top. Drizzle 3 tablespoons peanut butter over, then 2 tablespoons sauce. Sprinkle with ½ cup brittle. Freeze 1 hour. Spoon remaining 1½ pints ice cream evenly over; smooth top. Drizzle remaining 2 tablespoons peanut butter over, then 2 tablespoons sauce. Sprinkle remaining ½ cup brittle around edge of pie. Freeze 4 hours.

DO AHEAD: *Pie can be made 3 days ahead. Tent with foil and keep frozen. Cover and chill remaining sauce.*

Rewarm sauce; discard vanilla bean. Cut pie into wedges and serve, passing sauce separately.

⚞⚞⚞ Pumpkin Swirl Ice-Cream Pie with Chocolate-Almond Bark and Toffee Sauce

Here's a fun alternative for Thanksgiving dessert: a frozen pumpkin pie. The filling has the expected pure pumpkin and spices, but they're swirled into purchased vanilla ice cream. And the best part? You can make most of the elements up to two days ahead. Then all that's left to do is add the whipped cream topping, decorate the top with pieces of chocolate bark, and warm up the toffee sauce.

8 servings

Crust

12	whole graham crackers
¼	cup sugar
7	tablespoons unsalted butter, melted

Filling

1	cup canned pure pumpkin
¾	cup (packed) golden brown sugar
¼	cup heavy whipping cream
1	teaspoon vanilla extract
½	teaspoon ground ginger
½	teaspoon ground cinnamon
½	teaspoon freshly grated nutmeg
¼	teaspoon ground allspice
¼	teaspoon salt
2	quarts premium vanilla ice cream, divided

Bark

	Nonstick vegetable oil spray
6	ounces bittersweet or semisweet chocolate, chopped
½	cup slivered almonds, toasted, coarsely chopped

Sauce

1	cup (packed) golden brown sugar
¼	cup dark corn syrup
3	tablespoons water
3	tablespoons unsalted butter
½	cup chilled heavy whipping cream
1	teaspoon vanilla extract
⅛	teaspoon salt

Whipped Cream

1½	cups chilled heavy whipping cream
2	tablespoons sugar

CRUST: Preheat oven to 350°F. Finely grind graham crackers in processor. Mix in sugar. Add melted butter; process to blend. Press crumb mixture onto bottom and up sides of 10-inch-diameter glass pie dish. Bake crust until light brown around edges, about 12 minutes. Cool completely.

FILLING: Whisk pumpkin, sugar, cream, vanilla, ginger, cinnamon, nutmeg, allspice, and salt in medium bowl. Slightly soften ice cream in microwave on low setting in 10-second intervals. Measure 1 cup ice cream; cover and freeze (reserve for another use). Place remaining ice cream in large bowl. Working quickly, add pumpkin mixture and fold just until swirled into ice cream (do not blend completely). If ice cream begins to melt, place in freezer until almost firm again. Spoon ice cream filling into cooled crust, cover with plastic wrap, and freeze until firm, at least 6 hours.

DO AHEAD: *Can be made 2 days ahead. Keep frozen.*

BARK: Line large rimmed baking sheet with parchment paper; spray parchment with nonstick spray. Stir chocolate in medium metal bowl set over saucepan of simmering water until melted and smooth. Pour onto prepared sheet. Using offset spatula, spread chocolate in even layer into 12x9-inch rectangle. Sprinkle chocolate with nuts. Place in freezer until hard, at least 30 minutes. Invert onto work surface. Peel off parchment. Chop coarsely. Place bark in airtight container and freeze.

DO AHEAD: *Bark can be made 2 days ahead. Keep frozen.*

SAUCE: Bring brown sugar, corn syrup, 3 tablespoons water, and butter to boil in heavy medium saucepan over medium-high heat, stirring until butter melts and sugar dissolves. Reduce heat to medium and boil until mixture is dark brown, stirring occasionally, about 5 minutes. Carefully stir in cream, vanilla, and salt (mixture will bubble vigorously). Boil 1 minute longer. Cool slightly, whisking occasionally.

DO AHEAD: *Sauce can be made 2 days ahead. Cool, cover, and chill. Rewarm before serving.*

WHIPPED CREAM: Using electric mixer, beat cream and sugar in medium bowl until peaks form.

Spoon whipped cream decoratively over pie. Sprinkle chocolate-almond bark over. Cut pie into wedges and serve, passing warm sauce separately.

The Perfect Slice

You've created a beautiful frozen torte, terrine, or pie—don't let all your hard work go to waste by serving messy portions. To cut the cleanest slice, dip a chef's knife into hot water, wipe it dry, and then cut a piece of the pie. Continue dipping and wiping the knife between each slice.

❦ Heavenly Haystack Ice-Cream Pie

An eye-catching dessert that's super-easy to make—it's prepared with purchased ice cream and just a few other ingredients. The crispy "haystacks" are a mixture of white chocolate and toasted coconut, nestled in the middle of the ice-cream pie. The "heavenly" part will be evident after the first bite.
10 to 12 servings

6	ounces high-quality white chocolate (such as Lindt or Perugina), chopped
4	teaspoons vegetable oil
2	cups shredded sweetened coconut, toasted, divided
2	quarts chocolate ice cream, slightly softened, divided
	Chocolate Crumb Crust (see recipe on page 500)

Stir white chocolate and oil in medium metal bowl set over saucepan of simmering water until chocolate is melted and smooth. Mix in 1 cup coconut. Remove bowl from over water. Cool 10 minutes.

Spread half of chocolate ice cream evenly in prepared crust. Drop all of white chocolate mixture by teaspoonfuls over ice cream. Freeze until haystacks are firm, about 10 minutes. Spread remaining ice cream over. Sprinkle remaining 1 cup coconut evenly over. Freeze pie until just firm, about 1 hour. Wrap pie and freeze overnight.

DO AHEAD: *Can be made 2 days ahead. Keep frozen.*

Let pie stand at room temperature 10 minutes. Cut around pan sides to loosen pie. Remove pan sides. Cut pie into wedges and serve.

Frozen Italian Zabaglione Tart with Marsala-Lemon Sauce

You won't need an ice-cream maker here; the zabaglione filling is simply frozen in a mixing bowl before being spooned into a crunchy crust made from amaretti cookies. Marsala, a sweet fortified wine from Italy, is the base for a pretty and delicious sauce. **8 servings**

Crust

1	**5.5-ounce package amaretti cookies (Italian macaroons)**
5	**tablespoons unsalted butter, melted, hot**

Filling

1½	**cups Marsala, divided**
½	**cup dried currants**
¾	**cup sugar**
10	**large egg yolks**
2	**tablespoons dark corn syrup**
2	**teaspoons vanilla extract**
¼	**teaspoon ground nutmeg**
1⅓	**cups chilled heavy whipping cream**

Sauce

2	**cups Marsala**
½	**cup sugar**
2	**teaspoons finely grated lemon peel**
⅛	**teaspoon ground nutmeg**
5	**strawberries, hulled, halved**

CRUST: Preheat oven to 350°F. Finely grind amaretti cookies in processor. With processor running, gradually add hot melted butter and blend until crumbs begin to stick together. Press crust mixture onto bottom and up sides of 9-inch-diameter tart pan with removable bottom. Bake crust until pale golden, about 6 minutes. Cool. Gently press up bottom of pan just to loosen crust from sides, then lower crust back into place (do not remove from pan). Place crust in pan in freezer.

FILLING: Combine ½ cup Marsala and currants in small bowl; let steep 1 hour.

Whisk remaining 1 cup Marsala, sugar, and egg yolks in large metal bowl to blend. Set bowl over saucepan of rapidly simmering water (do not allow bowl to touch water). Whisk until thermometer inserted into center registers 170°F, about 4 minutes. Remove bowl from over water. Whisk in corn syrup, vanilla, and nutmeg. Refrigerate zabaglione uncovered until cool, whisking occasionally, about 20 minutes.

Beat cream in another large bowl until stiff peaks form. Add zabaglione and beat just until smooth. Drain currants (reserve Marsala for another use). Fold currants into zabaglione. Freeze until slightly firm but not frozen, about 1 hour.

Spoon zabaglione cream into crust, mounding in center. Freeze tart until almost firm, about 2 hours. Cover and freeze until firm, at least 6 hours and up to 1 day.

SAUCE: Stir Marsala and sugar in heavy medium saucepan over medium heat until sugar dissolves. Increase heat and boil until sauce is reduced to generous ⅔ cup, about 17 minutes. Add lemon peel and nutmeg and boil 1 minute. Cool sauce slightly.

DO AHEAD: *Can be made 8 hours ahead. Let stand at room temperature. Rewarm over low heat before serving.*

Push up pan bottom to release tart from pan. Transfer tart to platter. Arrange strawberries around top edge of tart. Cut into wedges. Serve, passing warm sauce separately.

Frozen Grand Marnier Torte with Dark Chocolate Crust and Spiced Cranberries

Frozen desserts are great for entertaining—they can be made well in advance and safely stashed away in the freezer, freeing up valuable refrigerator space. This easy torte has it all: chocolate cookie crust, rich creamy orange filling, and a glistening tumble of cranberries on top. The crust and filling need to freeze overnight, and the finished torte with topping needs to chill for at least another six hours, so plan ahead. **12 servings**

Crust

1	9-ounce package chocolate wafer cookies
½	cup semisweet chocolate chips
3	tablespoons sugar
7	tablespoons unsalted butter, melted

Filling

8	large egg yolks
1	cup sugar
¼	cup water
½	teaspoon ground nutmeg
⅛	teaspoon ground allspice
2	cups chilled heavy whipping cream
½	cup chilled sour cream
5	tablespoons Grand Marnier or other orange liqueur
3	tablespoons frozen orange juice concentrate, thawed
1	tablespoon finely grated orange peel

Topping

½	cup ruby Port
1	tablespoon cornstarch
1	cup sugar
¼	cup honey
1	teaspoon ground nutmeg
1	teaspoon ground allspice
½	teaspoon ground cinnamon
5	cups fresh or partially thawed frozen cranberries, divided

White chocolate curls (optional)

CRUST: Finely grind cookies, chocolate chips, and sugar in processor. Add melted butter; blend until wet crumbs form. Set aside ½ cup crumb mixture. Press remaining crumb mixture onto bottom and 2 inches up sides of 9-inch-diameter springform pan with 2¾-inch-high sides.

FILLING: Whisk egg yolks, sugar, and ¼ cup water in medium metal bowl. Set over saucepan of simmering water and whisk vigorously until candy thermometer registers 175°F, about 8 minutes. Remove bowl from over water. Add nutmeg and allspice. Using electric mixer, beat until thick and cool, about 5 minutes.

Using electric mixer, beat cream, sour cream, Grand Marnier, orange juice concentrate, and orange peel in large bowl until peaks form. Add egg yolk mixture and fold together. Pour ⅔ of filling into crust. Sprinkle with reserved ½ cup crumb mixture. Gently spoon remaining filling over. Cover torte and freeze overnight.

DO AHEAD: *Can be made 3 days ahead. Keep frozen.*

TOPPING: Whisk Port and cornstarch in large skillet to blend. Add sugar, honey, nutmeg, allspice, and cinnamon. Bring mixture to boil over high heat, stirring often. Add 3 cups cranberries; cook until mixture boils and cranberries begin to pop but still hold shape, about 5 minutes. Mix in remaining 2 cups cranberries. Chill topping at least 6 hours or overnight.

Release pan sides from torte. Transfer torte to platter. Spoon topping over filling. Garnish torte with white chocolate curls, if desired.

Frozen Orange Mousse Torte with Boysenberry Sauce

The frozen mousse filling has an intense orange flavor, thanks to orange juice, orange peel, and Grand Marnier. In the simple, pressed-in crust, pistachios provide an appealing crunch. You'll need to start this recipe one day ahead, since the mousse needs to freeze overnight. **12 to 14 servings**

Crust

1½	cups unsalted natural pistachios
¼	cup (packed) golden brown sugar
2	tablespoons unbleached all purpose flour
½	teaspoon finely grated orange peel
3	tablespoons unsalted butter, melted

Mousse

1	cup sugar
½	cup fresh orange juice
6	large egg yolks
¼	cup Grand Marnier or other orange liqueur
2	cups chilled heavy whipping cream
1	tablespoon finely grated orange peel
	Lightly sweetened whipped cream (optional)
1	orange, thinly sliced into rounds, then cut into small triangles (optional)
	Whole pistachios (optional)
	Boysenberry Sauce (see recipe)

CRUST: Preheat oven to 350°F. Blend pistachios, sugar, flour, and orange peel in processor until nuts are coarsely chopped. Add melted butter and blend until moist crumbs form. Press nut mixture onto bottom (not sides) of 9-inch-diameter springform pan with 2¾-inch-high sides. Bake crust until golden, about 8 minutes. Freeze while preparing mousse.

MOUSSE: Whisk sugar, orange juice, and egg yolks in medium metal bowl to blend. Set bowl over saucepan of simmering water (do not allow bowl to touch water). Whisk until thermometer inserted into center registers 170°F, about 4 minutes. Remove bowl from over water. Using electric mixer, beat yolk mixture until cool and thick, about 6 minutes. Beat in liqueur.

Beat cream and orange peel in large bowl until stiff peaks form. Gradually fold in yolk mixture. Pour mousse into crust. Cover and freeze overnight.

DO AHEAD: *Can be made 3 days ahead. Keep frozen.*

Cut around pan sides to loosen torte. Remove pan sides. Transfer torte to platter. If desired, spoon lightly sweetened whipped cream into pastry bag fitted with medium star tip. Pipe rosettes of cream around top edge of torte; place orange triangles between rosettes. Garnish with whole pistachios. Cut torte into wedges. Serve with Boysenberry Sauce.

Boysenberry Sauce

Use any leftover sauce as a waffle topping, along with some sweetened whipped cream. **Makes about 2 cups**

1   vanilla bean, split lengthwise
2   12-ounce packages frozen boysenberries or blackberries
⅔   cup sugar
½   cup water
¼   cup fresh orange juice
½   teaspoon finely grated orange peel

Scrape seeds from vanilla bean into heavy medium saucepan; add bean. Add berries, sugar, and ½ cup water. Cook over medium-high heat until berries thaw, sugar dissolves, and mixture boils, stirring often, about 10 minutes. Transfer berry mixture with vanilla bean to processor and puree. Strain puree through sieve set over bowl, pressing on solids; discard solids. Mix orange juice and peel into puree. Cover and chill until cold.

DO AHEAD: *Can be made 2 days ahead. Keep chilled.*

Nutella Ice-Cream Torte

In this crowd-pleasing dessert, purchased ice cream (or frozen yogurt) is layered with Nutella, a creamy chocolate-hazelnut spread. Because of Nutella's soft texture, even though it freezes firmly on the ice cream, it is still easy to cut through. Nutella is available at the supermarket and specialty foods stores. Look for it in the section where peanut butter is sold. **12 servings**

1   13-ounce jar Nutella (chocolate-hazelnut spread), divided
2   pints nut or chocolate chip ice cream or frozen yogurt, slightly softened
2   pints strawberry ice cream or frozen yogurt, slightly softened
2   pints vanilla ice cream or frozen yogurt, slightly softened
    Coarsely chopped toasted hazelnuts (optional)

Spoon 3 tablespoons Nutella into small pastry bag fitted with small plain tip; or spoon into resealable plastic bag and snip off one corner of bag. Set aside to use for topping.

Wrap outside of 9-inch-diameter springform pan with 2¾-inch-high sides with foil. Spread nut ice cream evenly in prepared pan. Drop half of remaining Nutella by teaspoonfuls over ice cream, spacing drops evenly apart (do not spread). Freeze until firm, about 30 minutes. Spread strawberry ice cream evenly over. Drop remaining Nutella by teaspoonfuls over ice cream, spacing drops evenly apart (do not spread). Freeze again until firm, about 30 minutes. Spread vanilla ice cream evenly over. Using spatula, smooth top. Using pastry bag, pipe Nutella decoratively over top. Freeze torte just until Nutella is firm, about 30 minutes. Wrap torte in plastic wrap and freeze at least 6 hours or overnight.

DO AHEAD: *Can be made 1 week ahead. Keep frozen.*

Let torte stand briefly at room temperature to soften slightly. Remove foil and plastic from pan. Cut around sides of pan to loosen torte; remove pan sides. Press hazelnuts into sides of torte, if desired, and serve.

Ingredient Tip: Nutella
Nutella was created in Italy in the 1940s. Because of rationing during World War II, chocolate was in short supply, so Nutella creator Pietro Ferrero blended hazelnuts into a chocolate mixture as a way to make the chocolate go further.

Lime Ice-Cream Torte Topped with Berry Sorbets

Here's a playful yet sophisticated treat: purchased ice cream and sorbet with a hint of cardamom. A sugar cookie and hazelnut crust encloses the cardamom-scented lime ice cream. On top is a dazzling array of scoops of sorbet in brilliant pink, red, and purple hues. **12 servings**

Crust

1	5.25-ounce package sugar cookies
⅓	cup (packed) dark brown sugar
⅛	teaspoon salt
7	tablespoons unsalted butter, melted, hot
1½	teaspoons vanilla extract
1¼	cups hazelnuts, toasted, hot

Filling

⅔	cup fresh lime juice
⅔	cup sugar
3	tablespoons finely grated lime peel
¼	teaspoon finely crushed cardamom seeds
2	quarts premium vanilla ice cream, slightly softened
3	pints assorted berry sorbets (such as strawberry, raspberry, and blackberry)

Sauce and Berries

⅓	cup water
¼	cup sugar
1	12-ounce package frozen unsweetened blackberries (do not thaw)
4	cups mixed fresh berries (such as blackberries, raspberries, and blueberries; about 20 ounces)

{ **Technique Tip: Crushing Seeds**
To crush the whole cardamom seeds, you can use a mortar and pestle, or place the seeds in a resealable plastic bag and tap them with a rolling pin. }

CRUST: Preheat oven to 375°F. Finely grind cookies, sugar, and salt in processor. Add hot butter and vanilla; blend until moist crumbs form. Add hot nuts; blend just until finely chopped. Press crust mixture onto bottom and up sides of 9-inch-diameter springform pan with 2¾-inch-high sides to within ¼ inch of top edge. Freeze crust 15 minutes. Bake until golden, about 15 minutes. Freeze 30 minutes.

FILLING: Stir lime juice, sugar, and lime peel in large bowl until sugar dissolves and syrup forms. Pour ⅓ cup lime syrup into small bowl; mix in cardamom. Cover; chill until ready to serve. Mix ice cream into remaining lime syrup in large bowl. Spoon all but 2½ cups ice cream into crust; smooth top. Freeze torte and remaining ice cream separately until firm, about 2 hours.

Top torte with large scoops of ice cream, spacing apart and dipping ice cream scoop into hot water between scoops for easy release. Top with large scoops of sorbets, spacing apart. Using measuring spoons of various sizes dipped into hot water, scoop remaining sorbets; place among larger scoops on torte. Freeze 3 hours.

SAUCE AND BERRIES: Stir ⅓ cup water and sugar in medium saucepan over medium heat until sugar dissolves. Add frozen berries. Increase heat; boil until berries are soft and liquid is slightly reduced, about 8 minutes. Puree mixture in processor. Strain through sieve set over bowl, pressing on solids. Discard solids in sieve. Cover; chill sauce until cold.

DO AHEAD: *Can be made 1 day ahead. Cover torte; keep frozen. Keep lime syrup and berry sauce chilled.*

Cut around pan sides to loosen crust. Remove pan sides. Tuck some fresh berries into spaces between ice cream and sorbet scoops. Mix remaining berries into berry sauce. Cut torte into wedges. Drizzle reserved lime syrup over wedges. Spoon berry mixture alongside.

Mocha Crunch Ice-Cream Cake

This showstopping treat features layers of purchased chocolate and coffee ice cream and a homemade chocolate-coffee sauce. It can be made up to three days ahead, so it's a great dessert for a party. **10 to 12 servings**

Sauce

1½	cups water
½	cup sugar
2½	tablespoons instant espresso powder
12	ounces bittersweet or semisweet chocolate (do not exceed 61% cacao), chopped
6	tablespoons (¾ stick) unsalted butter

Crust

	Nonstick vegetable oil spray
2	cups shortbread cookie crumbs (about 10 ounces)
¼	cup (½ stick) unsalted butter, melted
¼	teaspoon coconut extract

Pie

2	pints chocolate ice cream
1	cup shortbread cookie crumbs (about 5 ounces)
2	pints coffee ice cream
¾	cup chopped Almond Roca or Heath bars (about 5 ounces; or 14 Almond Roca or 12 miniature Heath bars)

SAUCE: Cook 1½ cups water, sugar, and espresso powder in heavy medium saucepan over low heat, stirring until sugar dissolves. Add chocolate and butter. Stir until chocolate and butter are melted and sauce is smooth. Cool completely.

DO AHEAD: *Can be made 3 days ahead. Cover and refrigerate. Bring to room temperature before using.*

CRUST: Spray 9-inch-diameter springform pan with nonstick spray. Blend cookie crumbs, melted butter, and coconut extract in processor until moist crumbs form. Press firmly into bottom of prepared pan. Freeze until firm.

PIE: Soften chocolate ice cream in refrigerator until spreadable but not melted. Spread on crust in pan and smooth top. Freeze until firm.

Spoon ½ cup chocolate-coffee sauce over ice cream and sprinkle with cookie crumbs. Freeze until firm.

Soften coffee ice cream in refrigerator until spreadable but not melted. Spread in pan and smooth top. Freeze until firm. Spread ½ cup sauce over coffee ice cream. Sprinkle with chopped Almond Roca and freeze until firm.

DO AHEAD: *Can be made 3 days ahead. Cover tightly; keep frozen.*

Soften cake slightly in refrigerator if necessary. Rewarm remaining sauce over low heat until lukewarm, stirring frequently. Run sharp knife around pan sides to loosen cake. Release pan sides from cake. Cut cake into wedges. Serve, passing warm mocha sauce separately.

Peppermint Ice Cream Candyland Cake

This whimsical cake is a fun holiday dessert that kids and adults will love. While it's perfect for Christmas, the type of ice cream and candies used can be changed to suit any celebration. The candy brittle—delicious on its own—can also be used to decorate any other type of cake. (When not frozen, the brittle will look best if it's used the same day it's made.) The brittle hardens quickly, so make swift work of applying the candies and be careful not to burn yourself on the hot sugar syrup. **12 servings**

Cake

1½	cups unbleached all purpose flour
1½	cups sugar
¾	teaspoon baking soda
¼	teaspoon salt
¾	cup (1½ sticks) unsalted butter
6	tablespoons bittersweet or semisweet chocolate chips
¾	cup water
½	cup natural unsweetened cocoa powder
1½	teaspoons vanilla extract
1	large egg, room temperature
3½	quarts (about) peppermint stick ice cream, slightly softened

Brittle

1½	cups sugar
½	cup water
1½	tablespoons light corn syrup
1	to 2 cups assorted candies (such as sliced gummy candies, spice drops, Swedish mints, butter mints, rock candy pieces, and candy cane pieces)

Sauce

½	cup water
8	ounces bittersweet or semisweet chocolate chips

CAKE: Preheat oven to 350°F. Butter 15x10x1-inch baking sheet; line with parchment. Butter parchment. Whisk flour, sugar, baking soda, and salt in large bowl. Melt butter in medium saucepan. Remove from heat. Add chocolate chips; stir until melted. Whisk in ¾ cup water, cocoa, and vanilla until blended. Whisk in egg. Add to flour mixture; whisk to blend. Pour batter onto prepared baking sheet.

Technique Tip: DIY Peppermint Ice Cream
Purchased peppermint ice cream will vary in color from pale pink to bright pink, so if you don't find one you like, you can quickly create your own by mixing 3½ quarts of softened premium vanilla ice cream with 2 cups of coarsely crushed red-and-white-striped hard peppermint candies and 2½ teaspoons of peppermint extract.

Bake cake until tester inserted into center comes out with some moist crumbs attached, about 22 minutes. Cool cake on baking sheet on rack 15 minutes. Run knife around pan sides to loosen cake. Turn cake out onto sheet of foil; cool. Cut cake crosswise into 3 equal strips. Freeze cake strips 1 hour.

Place 1 cake strip on platter. Working quickly, spoon 3½ cups peppermint ice cream in dollops over cake; spread evenly to edges. Top with second cake strip. Spoon 3½ cups ice cream in dollops over cake; spread evenly to edges. Top with third cake strip; freeze 1 hour. Spread enough remaining ice cream over top and sides of cake to cover generously (about 6 cups). Freeze until firm, about 3 hours.

BRITTLE: Place 20-inch-long sheet of foil on work surface. Mark off 16x12-inch rectangle. Stir sugar, ½ cup water, and corn syrup in heavy small saucepan over medium-low heat until sugar dissolves, brushing down sides of pan with wet pastry brush. Increase heat and boil without stirring until candy thermometer registers 300°F, tilting saucepan slightly to submerge bulb, about 15 minutes.

Being very careful (syrup is extremely hot), pour boiling syrup in wide zigzag lines across foil. Using offset metal spatula and working quickly, spread syrup evenly to 16x12-inch rectangle. Immediately sprinkle generously with candies, pressing larger pieces into syrup to adhere (do not touch hot syrup). If syrup hardens before all candies have been applied, slide foil with brittle onto large rimless baking sheet and place baking sheet directly over burner set on high heat to soften syrup, about 10 seconds, rotating sheet. Remove from heat and immediately apply remaining candies. Cool completely.

Starting at one end of brittle, break off pieces in irregular shapes, peeling foil as you go. Press brittle upright, candy side out, onto top and sides of cake and freeze.

DO AHEAD: *Can be made 2 days ahead. Cover and keep frozen.*

SAUCE: Bring ½ cup water to simmer in small saucepan. Remove from heat. Add chocolate chips; whisk until smooth.

DO AHEAD: *Can be made 2 days ahead. Cover and chill.*

Slice cake. Serve with sauce.

Meringue Hearts with Mint Ice Cream and Fudge Sauce

This dessert is a study in contrasts: crispy, delicate meringue cookies, smooth and creamy purchased ice cream, and a puddle of rich fudge sauce. **Makes 6**

Sauce

6	tablespoons (¾ stick) unsalted butter
¼	cup dark corn syrup
5	ounces bittersweet or semisweet chocolate (do not exceed 61% cacao), chopped
¼	cup powdered sugar, sifted
2	tablespoons heavy whipping cream

Meringues

4	large egg whites, room temperature
1	cup sugar

Ice Cream

2	pints vanilla ice cream, softened slightly
½	cup finely crushed red-and-white-striped hard peppermint candies
⅛	teaspoon peppermint extract
	Powdered sugar
	Additional red-and-white-striped hard peppermint candies, coarsely crushed

Technique Tip: Shape-Shifting
The heart-shaped meringues make for a romantic dessert, but feel free to use any large cookie cutter with a simple shape to form the cookies. Or, simply spoon the meringue batter onto the foil-lined sheet and spread evenly into a 3¾-inch round.

SAUCE: Melt butter with corn syrup in heavy small saucepan over medium-low heat, stirring occasionally. Add chocolate, sugar, and cream. Whisk until chocolate melts and sugar dissolves.

DO AHEAD: *Can be made 1 week ahead. Cover; chill.*

MERINGUES: Preheat oven to 225°F. Line 2 baking sheets with foil; butter foil. Place 3¾-inch heart-shaped cookie cutter on foil-lined sheet. Using electric mixer, beat egg whites in large bowl to soft peaks. Gradually add 1 cup sugar; continue beating until stiff and shiny. Spoon ¼ cup meringue inside cookie cutter on prepared sheet. Using back of spoon, spread meringue evenly. Lift up cookie cutter; place on another section of foil-lined sheet. Repeat with remaining meringue, forming 6 hearts on each sheet.

Bake meringues until crisp and dry, about 1 hour. Cool meringues on sheets 10 minutes. Peel meringues off foil.

DO AHEAD: *Can be made 1 day ahead. Cool completely. Store in airtight container at room temperature.*

ICE CREAM: Mix ice cream, finely crushed peppermint candies, and peppermint extract in medium bowl. Cover and freeze until semi-firm, about 2 hours.

Place meringues flat side up on baking sheet and freeze 15 minutes. Spoon ½ cup ice cream atop 1 meringue. Top with another meringue, flat side up. Press gently to flatten, forming sandwich. Run spatula around sides of ice cream to even sides. Freeze. Repeat with remaining meringues and ice cream. Cover and freeze at least 1 hour and up to 6 hours.

Stir sauce over medium-low heat just until warm. Sift powdered sugar over tops of meringues, coating completely. Place on plates. Spoon sauce around. Sprinkle coarsely crushed peppermint candies over sauce.

Frozen Raspberry Zabaglione on Meringues with Chocolate Sauce

Zabaglione, an Italian custard, is blended with raspberries and frozen in a container (not processed in an ice-cream maker) for this recipe. Creating an indentation in each meringue before baking makes room for a scoop of the fruity zabaglione. For a party-perfect presentation, garnish the dessert with fresh raspberries, orange segments, and a sprinkling of toasted sliced almonds.

Makes 8

Raspberry Puree

2	12-ounce bags frozen raspberries, thawed, with juices
2	tablespoons light corn syrup

Zabaglione

8	large egg yolks
¾	cup sugar
6	tablespoons Grand Marnier or other orange liqueur
5	tablespoons frozen orange juice concentrate, thawed

Sauce

6	ounces bittersweet or semisweet chocolate, chopped
1	tablespoon light corn syrup
1	tablespoon water

Meringues

3	large egg whites, room temperature
¼	teaspoon cream of tartar
¾	cup sugar
1	cup sliced almonds, lightly toasted, divided

RASPBERRY PUREE: Puree raspberries with juices in blender. Strain puree into bowl, pressing firmly on fruit to release all pulp and juices. Mix corn syrup into puree. Cover and chill while preparing zabaglione.

ZABAGLIONE: Combine egg yolks, sugar, Grand Marnier, and orange juice concentrate in large bowl. Using electric mixer, beat 1 minute. Set bowl over large saucepan of simmering water and beat at high speed until very thick and thermometer registers 160°F, about 12 minutes.

Place bowl over larger bowl filled with ice water and cool zabaglione, whisking occasionally, about 15 minutes. Fold in ¾ cup raspberry puree. Transfer to covered container and freeze.

DO AHEAD: *Can be made 2 days ahead. Keep frozen.*

SAUCE: Stir chocolate, corn syrup, 1 tablespoon water, and ½ cup plus 3 tablespoons raspberry puree in heavy medium saucepan over low heat until chocolate melts and sauce is smooth. Cover and chill.

DO AHEAD: *Can be made 2 days ahead. Keep chilled.*

MERINGUES: Preheat oven to 200°F. Line large baking sheet with foil; grease foil lightly. Using electric mixer, beat egg whites and cream of tartar in large bowl until soft peaks form. Gradually add sugar, beating until meringue is stiff and shiny. Fold in half of almonds.

Drop meringue in 8 mounds onto prepared baking sheet. Using back of spoon, make indentation in each mound. Sprinkle meringues with remaining almonds. Bake 1 hour. Turn off oven; leave oven door closed and let meringues dry in oven overnight.

Place meringues on platter or baking sheet and fill each with large scoop of frozen zabaglione. Wrap meringues tightly and freeze at least 8 hours and up to 1 day.

Rewarm chocolate sauce over low heat. Place each filled meringue on plate. Spoon warm chocolate sauce over and serve immediately.

Working with Meringue

Meringues are made by beating egg whites to soft peaks, then adding sugar and beating until firm, glossy peaks form. Soft meringue is used as a topping for pies (such as lemon meringue pie) and other desserts, like baked Alaskas, and to add airy lightness to mousses and soufflés. Hard meringues are baked for a long time at a low temperature so they become dry while remaining white. Here are tips to make perfect meringues every time.

1. Use egg whites that are at room temperature; they will reach a greater volume.

2. When separating the eggs, make sure none of the yolk gets into the whites.

3. Your bowl and whisk or beater must also be completely clean. Any trace of yolks or fat on your equipment will make it very difficult to stiffen the egg whites.

4. Add cream of tartar or lemon juice to the egg whites before they're beaten to help stabilize the foam.

5. Use an electric mixer or a large balloon whisk and a metal or glass bowl.

6. Beat the egg whites to soft peaks, and then gradually add the sugar. Adding the sugar too early will slow down the stiffening process; adding the sugar after the whites have reached stiff peaks could cause the meringue to become too dry.

Once the meringue is formed, use it immediately, since it will weep and lose volume quickly. Store hard meringues in an airtight container to maintain their dry, crisp texture.

Frozen White Chocolate and Hazelnut Dacquoise

A dacquoise is one of the greatest French cakes, combining wonderful textures and flavors into one luxurious dessert. Here, crunchy hazelnut meringue layers are sandwiched with a fudgy dark chocolate ganache and a light and creamy white chocolate mousse. This one is rectangular, but you can also make it round. Start preparing this layered treat at least one day before you plan to serve it, as it needs to freeze overnight. **10 servings**

Meringue
1¼	cups hazelnuts, toasted, husked, divided
¾	cup sugar, divided
6	large egg whites, room temperature
⅛	teaspoon cream of tartar

Ganaches
2	cups heavy whipping cream, divided
4	tablespoons light corn syrup, divided
24	ounces bittersweet or semisweet chocolate (do not exceed 61% cacao), finely chopped
	White Chocolate Mousse (see recipe)
8	ounces high-quality white chocolate (such as Lindt or Perugina), chopped
24	hazelnuts, toasted, husked

MERINGUE: Preheat oven to 300°F. Line large baking sheet with parchment paper. Draw three 9x5-inch rectangles on parchment. Turn paper over. Finely grind 1 cup nuts with ¼ cup sugar in processor. Coarsely chop remaining ¼ cup nuts; set aside for garnish.

Beat egg whites and cream of tartar in large bowl until foamy. Gradually add remaining ½ cup sugar, beating until stiff and glossy. Fold ground hazelnut mixture into whites in 2 additions. Divide meringue among traced rectangles on parchment, spreading to edges. Bake meringues until crisp and light golden, about 1 hour 30 minutes. Turn oven off; cool meringues in oven 1 hour. Remove from oven.

(continued next page)

Frozen White Chocolate and Hazelnut Dacquoise

(continued)

GANACHES: Bring 1½ cups cream and 3 tablespoons corn syrup to simmer in medium saucepan. Remove from heat. Add bittersweet chocolate; stir until smooth. Chill until slightly thickened but still spreadable, about 1 hour.

Line 9x5x2½-inch metal loaf pan with plastic wrap, leaving 3-inch overhang on all sides. Run thin knife under meringues to loosen from parchment. Gently transfer meringues to work surface. Using serrated knife and gentle sawing motion, trim each to 8x4-inch rectangle.

Spread ⅓ cup chocolate ganache over each of 2 meringues. Place on baking sheet. Freeze until ganache is set, about 10 minutes. Place third meringue, smooth side down, in prepared loaf pan. Spread half of White Chocolate Mousse over. Sprinkle with reserved ¼ cup chopped hazelnuts. Top with 1 meringue, ganache side down. Spread remaining mousse over. Top with remaining meringue, ganache side down. Fold plastic overhang over cake; freeze overnight. Chill remaining bittersweet chocolate ganache.

Bring remaining ½ cup cream and remaining 1 tablespoon corn syrup to simmer in small saucepan. Remove from heat. Add white chocolate; stir until smooth. Chill just until thick enough to spread, about 30 minutes.

Invert cake onto small baking sheet; remove plastic. Working quickly, spread white chocolate ganache thinly over top and sides of cake. Place 24 hazelnuts around top edge of cake. Freeze cake until frosting is firm, about 30 minutes.

DO AHEAD: *Can be made 1 week ahead. Cover cake tightly and keep frozen.*

Keep bittersweet chocolate ganache chilled. Before serving, rewarm ganache over low heat, stirring just until liquid.

Serve cake, passing remaining bittersweet ganache as sauce.

 ## White Chocolate Mousse

Frangelico is used in this mousse to pair well with the hazelnut dacquoise, but other liqueurs can also be used. For instance, if you're making meringues with almonds or pistachios, use amaretto in the mousse. Be sure the chocolate mixture is completely cool before folding in the whipped cream, or the cream will melt and the mousse won't have an airy texture. Don't worry if the mousse is soft at first; it sets up nicely as it chills. **Makes about 2½ cups**

2	**large eggs**
⅓	**cup sugar**
3	**tablespoons Frangelico (hazelnut liqueur)**
6	**ounces high-quality white chocolate (such as Lindt or Perugina), chopped**
1	**cup chilled heavy whipping cream**

Whisk eggs, sugar, and Frangelico in large metal bowl to blend. Set bowl over saucepan of simmering water (do not allow bowl to touch water); whisk constantly until mixture thickens and candy thermometer inserted into mixture registers 140°F for 3 minutes, about 7 minutes total. Remove bowl from over water. Add white chocolate; whisk until smooth. Cool completely, whisking occasionally. Beat cream in medium bowl to medium-firm peaks. Fold whipped cream into white chocolate mixture in 3 additions (mixture will be soft). Chill until spreadable, about 3 hours.

Strawberry and Chocolate Baked Alaskas

Baked Alaskas are like an edible magic trick: Sponge cake and a layer of ice cream are covered with meringue, then browned in a hot oven—without melting the ice cream. These individual baked Alaskas pair chocolate cake with purchased strawberry ice cream and a meringue topping. Even better: They can be assembled up to two days ahead. **Makes 6**

6	ounces bittersweet or semisweet chocolate (do not exceed 61% cacao), chopped
6	tablespoons (¾ stick) unsalted butter
¾	ounce unsweetened chocolate, chopped
1½	cups sugar, divided
2	large eggs
⅓	cup unbleached all purpose flour
2	tablespoons natural unsweetened cocoa powder
½	teaspoon baking powder
⅛	teaspoon salt
1	pint strawberry ice cream, slightly softened
3	large egg whites

Quick Browning

If you have a kitchen torch, you can use it to brown the meringue on these baked Alaskas, instead of baking them in a hot oven.

Recipe Tip: How Does It Work?

Why doesn't the ice cream melt when you bake this dessert? For one thing, all of the elements (the cake, the ice cream, and the meringue) start out very cold. For another, the baking time is brief—5 minutes or less. Plus, the meringue topping insulates the ice cream, protecting it from the oven's heat.

Preheat oven to 350°F. Butter 9x9x2-inch metal baking pan; line bottom with parchment paper. Stir bittersweet chocolate, butter, and unsweetened chocolate in heavy small saucepan over low heat until chocolates melt and mixture is smooth. Cool 10 minutes. Whisk ¾ cup sugar and eggs in large bowl until well blended, about 1 minute. Whisk in chocolate mixture. Sift flour, cocoa, baking powder, and salt over; stir to blend. Transfer batter to prepared pan. Bake cake until top looks dry and tester inserted into center comes out with some thick sticky batter attached, about 17 minutes. Cool cake in pan to room temperature.

Cut around cake in pan. Place cutting board over pan and invert, tapping out cake. Peel off parchment. Using 3-inch round cutter, cut out 6 cake rounds (reserve remaining cake for another use). Line small baking sheet with parchment paper. Arrange cake rounds on prepared sheet. Using 2¼- to 2½-inch-diameter ice cream scoop, place scoop of strawberry ice cream in center of each round, leaving about ¼-inch plain border. Freeze until ice cream is solid, about 2 hours.

Combine remaining ¾ cup sugar and egg whites in large metal bowl. Set bowl over saucepan of gently simmering water and whisk until mixture is very warm, about 2 minutes. Remove bowl from over water. Using electric mixer, beat meringue at high speed until very thick and billowy, about 2 minutes. Place baking sheet with cake rounds on work surface. Mound 2 heaping tablespoons meringue atop ice cream on 1 cake round. Spread meringue evenly over to cover, sealing meringue to plain cake border and swirling decoratively. Repeat with remaining desserts. Freeze uncovered on baking sheet until meringue is solid, at least 4 hours and up to 2 days.

Preheat oven to 500°F. Transfer desserts still on baking sheet from freezer directly to oven. Bake until meringue is deep brown in spots, turning sheet as needed for even cooking, about 3 minutes. Transfer to plates.

♀♀♀♀ Pumpkin Baked Alaska

In this fall-themed version of the classic dessert, tender pecan cake is topped with a frozen spiced pumpkin custard (no ice-cream maker required), then covered in meringue and browned in the oven. **10 to 12 servings**

Cake

3	large eggs, separated, room temperature
7	tablespoons sugar, divided
1	cup finely ground pecans
1	tablespoon unbleached all purpose flour
⅛	teaspoon cream of tartar
	Pinch of salt

Filling

	Nonstick vegetable oil spray
6	large egg yolks
½	cup sugar
½	cup (packed) dark brown sugar
1	cup milk
1	cup mini marshmallows
1	15-ounce can pure pumpkin
1½	teaspoons ground cinnamon
1	teaspoon ground ginger
1	teaspoon ground nutmeg
½	teaspoon ground allspice
¼	teaspoon ground cloves
⅛	teaspoon salt
1	cup chilled heavy whipping cream
4	large egg whites, room temperature
¼	teaspoon cream of tartar
⅔	cup superfine sugar
	Pinch of salt

Meringue

4	large egg whites, room temperature
¼	teaspoon cream of tartar
¼	teaspoon salt
½	teaspoon vanilla extract
½	cup superfine sugar

Assembly

½	pound English toffee or toffee candy bars, coarsely crushed
¼	cup chopped pecans

CAKE: Position rack in center of oven and preheat to 350°F. Butter 9-inch-diameter cake pan with 2-inch-high sides. Line bottom with waxed paper; butter paper thoroughly.

Using electric mixer, beat egg yolks in medium bowl until thick and pale yellow. Gradually add 6 tablespoons sugar, beating until mixture is thick and ribbon forms. Mix nuts and flour in small bowl; fold into egg yolk mixture (mixture will be thick). Using electric mixer fitted with clean dry beaters, beat egg whites in large bowl until foamy. Add cream of tartar and salt; continue beating until soft peaks form. Gradually add remaining 1 tablespoon sugar; continue beating until whites are stiff but not dry. Mix ⅓ of egg white mixture into yolk mixture, then fold in remaining whites. Transfer batter to prepared pan, spreading evenly. Bake just until cake springs back when touched with fingers and is lightly browned, about 22 minutes. Cool in pan on cake rack 30 minutes (cake will shrink). Remove cake from pan. Cool completely. Wrap in plastic and freeze until ready to assemble, at least

FILLING: Spray 8¾-inch-diameter metal bowl (about 3¼ inches deep) with nonstick spray. Line with plastic wrap, allowing to extend a few inches over sides.

Using electric mixer, beat egg yolks until creamy. Add both sugars; continue beating until thick and creamy.

Combine milk and marshmallows in medium bowl. Set over saucepan of simmering water, stirring occasionally until marshmallows are melted, about 3 minutes. Add egg yolk mixture; cook until mixture thickens and ribbons dissolve slowly, whisking frequently, about 20 minutes. Add pumpkin, spices, and salt; whisk to blend. Cool completely.

Using electric mixer, beat cream in large bowl to soft peaks. Using clean dry beaters, beat egg whites in another large bowl until foamy. Add cream of tartar; beat until soft peaks form. Gradually add superfine sugar; continue beating until stiff but not dry. Beat in salt. Fold cream into pumpkin mixture. Add meringue; fold gently but thoroughly. Transfer the mixture to plastic-lined bowl. Cover well and freeze at least 24 hours.

MERINGUE: Just before assembling and serving, beat egg whites in large bowl until foamy. Add cream of tartar and salt; continue beating until soft peaks form. Add vanilla. Gradually beat in superfine sugar about 1 tablespoon at a time, beating well after each addition, until sugar is completely dissolved and meringue is stiff and glossy. Set aside.

ASSEMBLY: Combine toffee with pecans. Sprinkle toffee-pecan mixture over frozen pumpkin cream to within ¼ inch of sides. Unwrap cake; invert onto toffee-pecan mixture and peel off waxed paper. Place tart pan bottom atop cake. Invert ice cream and cake onto tart pan bottom. Remove bowl and peel off plastic. Place cake on baking sheet. Immediately cover filling and cake completely with meringue (make sure all surfaces are well sealed). Freeze at least 4 hours.

DO AHEAD: *Can be made 1 day ahead. Keep frozen.*

Preheat oven to 500°F. Bake until meringue is golden brown, watching closely to avoid overbrowning, about 3 minutes. Transfer to platter and serve.

Coffee-Almond Baked Alaska with Coffee-Caramel Sauce

Instead of the traditional layer of sponge cake, this baked Alaska gets two delicious layers of buttery, amaretti-espresso crust. And instead of one ice cream, it has two: purchased toasted almond and coffee, which are molded and frozen into a "bombe" using a 10-cup bowl. **10 to 12 servings**

Sauce

1	cup (packed) golden brown sugar
½	cup heavy whipping cream
¼	cup (½ stick) unsalted butter
3	tablespoons brandy, divided
2	tablespoons dark corn syrup
1½	teaspoons instant espresso powder or instant coffee powder

Crust and Ice Cream Layers

2	cups coarsely broken amaretti cookies (Italian macaroons; about 4 ounces)
1	cup sliced almonds, toasted
2	teaspoons instant espresso powder or instant coffee powder
3	tablespoons unsalted butter, melted
3	pints toasted almond ice cream
2	pints coffee ice cream

Meringue

6	large egg whites, room temperature
½	teaspoon vanilla extract
1	cup sugar

SAUCE: Combine sugar, cream, butter, 2 tablespoons brandy, corn syrup, and espresso powder in medium saucepan. Whisk over medium heat until sugar dissolves. Increase heat to medium-high and boil until sauce is thickened and reduced to 1 cup, whisking often, about 8 minutes. Remove from heat; cool 15 minutes. Whisk in remaining 1 tablespoon brandy. Transfer to microwave-safe bowl.

CRUST AND ICE CREAM LAYERS: Grind amaretti, almonds, and espresso powder in processor. Add melted butter and 1 tablespoon sauce. Blend just until crumbs cling together.

Line 10-inch-diameter, 3½-inch-deep bowl (10-cup capacity) with plastic wrap, leaving generous overhang. Slightly soften almond ice cream in microwave on defrost setting in 10-second intervals. Spoon into bowl. Spread ice cream in even layer over bottom and up sides of bowl, leaving hollow center. Freeze 15 minutes. Sprinkle ⅔ cup crust mixture over ice cream and press gently. Slightly soften coffee ice cream in microwave on defrost setting in 10-second intervals. Spoon into hollow center of almond ice cream; smooth top. Press remaining crust mixture over ice cream. Cover with plastic. Freeze at least 3 hours.

DO AHEAD: *Can be made 2 days ahead. Keep frozen. Cover and chill remaining sauce.*

MERINGUE: Using electric mixer, beat egg whites and vanilla in large bowl until soft peaks form. Gradually add sugar, beating until meringue is stiff, about 5 minutes.

Uncover bombe. Place 11-inch-diameter tart pan bottom on crust. Turn bombe over. Remove bowl; peel off plastic wrap. Spread meringue thickly over ice cream, swirling decoratively and sealing meringue to tart pan bottom. Freeze bombe uncovered at least 4 hours.

DO AHEAD: *Can be made 2 days ahead. Keep frozen.*

Preheat oven to 500°F for 20 minutes. Rewarm sauce in microwave; transfer to pitcher. Place large rack on baking sheet. Place bombe on rack. Bake until meringue is pale golden but dark brown in spots, about 4 minutes; transfer to platter. Let stand 5 minutes.

Dipping heavy large knife into very hot water before each slice, cut baked Alaska into wedges. Serve with sauce.

Recipe Tip: **That Name**

Food historians can agree that baked Alaska was created in the 19th century, but that's where the consensus ends. Some believe the dessert, which was encased in pastry instead of meringue, was first served by Thomas Jefferson in 1802 or created by a Chinese chef visiting Paris around the middle of the 19th century. Others credit scientist Benjamin Thompson, who studied the insulating powers of egg whites. Another school of thought says that the dessert was named at Delmonico's restaurant in New York in the 1870s and was an homage to the District of Alaska.

Strawberry Milk Shakes

These rich, creamy shakes have twice the strawberry flavor: from the ice cream, and from a fresh-strawberry syrup, which is blended in and then also drizzled on top. **Makes 4**

2 pints strawberry ice cream, slightly softened, divided
1 cup Strawberry Syrup (see recipe)
1 cup whole milk
   Additional Strawberry Syrup
4 whole strawberries with stems (optional)

Freeze four 12-ounce glasses 1 hour.

Place 1 pint ice cream, 1 cup Strawberry Syrup, and milk in blender; puree until smooth. Add second pint of ice cream and puree until almost smooth. Divide shake among frozen glasses. Drizzle each with additional Strawberry Syrup, garnish with strawberry, if desired, and serve with spoons and straws.

Strawberry Syrup

You'll have plenty of syrup left over after making the milk shakes. Use it to create your own homemade strawberry soda (just add sparkling water and a squeeze of lime), drizzle over vanilla ice cream or Greek yogurt, or add (just a splash) to a glass of Champagne. **Makes 2½ cups**

1   pound strawberries, hulled, sliced
½   cup water
½   cup sugar
⅓   cup light corn syrup
     Pinch of salt
2   tablespoons fresh lemon juice

Bring strawberries, ½ cup water, sugar, corn syrup, and salt to boil in large saucepan over medium-high heat, stirring until sugar dissolves. Boil uncovered 10 minutes, stirring occasionally and adjusting heat to prevent mixture from boiling over. Mix in lemon juice. Strain mixture into large bowl, pressing on solids in strainer to extract as much juice as possible; discard solids in strainer. Cover and chill syrup.

DO AHEAD: *Can be made 1 week ahead. Keep chilled.*

Ginger-Mango Floats

Forget root beer: These ginger beer floats are a fresh and tropical take on the classic soda fountain treat, enhanced with mango sorbet and spicy crystallized ginger. Ginger beer is a nonalcoholic carbonated drink that's made from ginger, fruit juices, and spices. You can find it alongside the sodas at the supermarket or specialty foods store. **Makes 8**

1 pint vanilla ice cream
4 tablespoons finely diced crystallized ginger, divided
1 pint mango sorbet
4 12-ounce bottles all-natural ginger beer (such as Reed's), chilled

Place scoop of ice cream in each of 8 medium-size glasses. Sprinkle scant 1 teaspoon crystallized ginger over ice cream in each glass. Top each with scoop of sorbet, then second scoop ice cream. Pour ginger beer into glasses. Sprinkle remaining crystallized ginger over floats and serve immediately.

cookies

cookies

Classic Chocolate Chip Cookies

The iconic American cookie, at its most gooey and delicious. The dough can be made one day ahead. Just scoop and bake the next day for a batch of freshly baked warm chocolate chip cookies. **Makes about 3 dozen**

    Nonstick vegetable oil spray (optional)
2½   **cups unbleached all purpose flour**
1   **teaspoon baking soda**
1   **teaspoon salt**
1   **cup (2 sticks) unsalted butter, room temperature**
1   **cup (packed) golden brown sugar**
¾   **cup sugar**
2   **large eggs**
2   **teaspoons vanilla extract**
2   **cups semisweet or bittersweet chocolate chips**
1   **cup pecans, toasted, chopped (optional)**

Butter 2 large baking sheets or spray with nonstick spray. Whisk flour, baking soda, and salt in medium bowl. Using electric mixer, beat butter in large bowl until smooth. Add both sugars; beat to blend. Add eggs and vanilla; beat to blend. Add flour mixture and beat at low speed just to blend. Stir in chocolate chips and nuts, if using. Cover and chill dough at least 2 hours.

DO AHEAD: *Can be made 1 day ahead. Keep chilled.*

Preheat oven to 375°F. Drop dough by 2 level tablespoonfuls onto prepared sheets, mounding one atop the other, spacing 2 inches apart. Bake until edges are browned and tops are golden brown, 11 to 12 minutes. Transfer cookies to racks and cool completely. Repeat with remaining dough.

Chocolate Toffee Cookies

This is a chocolate cookie with crunchy almonds and rich, buttery English toffee bits. Almond Roca candy, Heath bars, or any English toffee candy will do here. Serve the cookies with English toffee ice cream for dessert. **Makes about 3 dozen**

½   **cup (1 stick) unsalted butter, room temperature**
1   **cup plus 2 tablespoons sugar**
1   **large egg**
1   **tablespoon dark rum**
1   **teaspoon vanilla extract**
1   **cup unbleached all purpose flour**
½   **cup natural unsweetened cocoa powder**
½   **teaspoon baking soda**
¼   **teaspoon salt**
1½   **cups crushed chocolate-covered English toffee (such as Heath bars; about 7 ounces)**
½   **cup chopped almonds**

Position rack in center of oven and preheat to 350°F. Using electric mixer, beat butter and sugar in large bowl until fluffy. Add egg, rum, and vanilla and beat until well blended. Sift flour, cocoa powder, baking soda, and salt into small bowl. Add flour mixture to butter mixture and stir until well blended. Mix in toffee and chopped almonds.

Drop batter by heaping tablespoonfuls onto heavy large ungreased baking sheet, spacing 2 inches apart. Bake until cookies puff slightly and crack on top but are still soft to touch, about 11 minutes. Let cookies cool on baking sheet 1 minute. Transfer cookies to rack and cool completely (cookies will become crisp). Repeat shaping and baking with remaining batter.

DO AHEAD: *Cookies can be made 2 days ahead. Store in airtight container at room temperature.*

White Chocolate–Granola Cookies

Packed with dried fruit, oatmeal, granola, and white chocolate, these cookies lift the classic oatmeal recipe to a whole new level. Be sure to use high-quality white chocolate, such as Lindt, Perugina, or Callebaut, for the best flavor.

Makes about 4 dozen

½	cup chopped dried apricots
½	cup chopped dried pineapple
1	cup hot water
2	cups unbleached all purpose flour
¾	teaspoon baking soda
¾	teaspoon ground cinnamon
1	cup (2 sticks) unsalted butter, room temperature
2¼	cups (packed) golden brown sugar
⅔	cup sugar
2	large eggs
1½	teaspoons vanilla extract
2¼	cups old-fashioned oats
2	cups coarsely chopped high-quality white chocolate (such as Lindt or Perugina)
1	cup granola, crumbled

Place apricots and pineapple in medium bowl. Add 1 cup hot water and let soak until fruit is soft, about 15 minutes. Drain.

Whisk flour, baking soda, and cinnamon in medium bowl to blend. Using electric mixer, beat butter and both sugars in large bowl until fluffy. Beat in eggs and vanilla. Add flour mixture; mix on low speed just until blended. Using wooden spoon, stir in apricot-pineapple mixture, oats, chocolate, and granola.

Using 2 heaping tablespoons dough for each cookie, drop batter onto 3 heavy large rimmed baking sheets, spacing 1 inch apart. Chill 30 minutes.

DO AHEAD: *Can be made 1 day ahead. Cover and keep chilled.*

Preheat oven to 325°F. Bake cookies until golden, about 15 minutes. Transfer cookies to rack and cool completely.

DO AHEAD: *Cookies can be made 2 days ahead. Store in airtight containers at room temperature.*

Cookie Basics: Getting Started

It's tempting to dive right in and start baking when you know there will soon be cookies coming out of the oven, but take a minute to do the proper prep work—it will pay off in the end.

• Be sure that you have all the ingredients for the recipe.

• Assemble and measure all ingredients before beginning.

• Make sure that your ingredients are at the proper temperature. If a recipe calls for chilled butter, use it directly from the refrigerator. If room-temperature butter is required, allow it to stand until it is slightly soft when gently pressed with a fingertip.

• If the recipe calls for toasted nuts, allow them to cool completely before adding them to the dough or batter; if still warm, they could melt the cookie mixture.

Dark and White Chocolate Chunk Cookies with Ginger

The addition of crystallized ginger gives these chocolate chip cookies a surprising kick. Crystallized ginger can be found in the spice section or the Asian foods section of most supermarkets. **Makes about 2 dozen**

2⅔   **cups bittersweet or semisweet chocolate chips, divided**
¼   **cup (½ stick) unsalted butter**
2   **large eggs**
½   **cup (packed) golden brown sugar**
2   **teaspoons vanilla extract**
¾   **cup self-rising flour**
½   **cup chopped crystallized ginger**
3½   **ounces high-quality white chocolate (such as Lindt or Perugina), very coarsely chopped**

Preheat oven to 350°F. Line 2 heavy large rimmed baking sheets with parchment paper. Stir 2 cups chocolate chips with butter in heavy small saucepan over low heat until melted and smooth; cool 10 minutes. Beat eggs and brown sugar in large bowl until well blended. Beat in melted chocolate mixture and vanilla, then flour. Stir in ginger and remaining ⅔ cup chocolate chips; let stand 10 minutes.

Drop cookie dough by rounded tablespoonfuls onto prepared baking sheets, spacing cookies 1½ to 2 inches apart. Press white chocolate pieces into tops of cookies, dividing equally. Bake until cookies look puffed and slightly dry on top, about 13 minutes. Cool cookies on baking sheets.

DO AHEAD: *Cookies can be made 2 days ahead. Store in airtight container at room temperature.*

Cookie Basics: The Proper Tools

Most cookies can be made without fancy equipment or even electrical appliances. (Drop cookies, for example, can often be mixed with a large wooden spoon in a deep bowl. And you can use your fingers to combine flour, butter, and sugar into a mixture resembling coarse meal for shortbread and other cookies.) But there's no denying that electric mixers and food processors can dramatically simplify the cookie-making process. Here are other essential tools you'll turn to again and again:

• A large chef's knife, for chopping nuts and chocolate

• A rolling pin and a smooth, large work surface, for rolling out cookie dough

• Good-quality, heavy cookie sheets, to ensure that cookies bake and brown evenly. Thin cookie sheets tend to burn the bottom of cookies. Owning at least three cookie sheets allows you to have two batches of cookies in the oven while you're getting another batch ready to go in.

• Two baking racks, for cooling up to two dozen cookies at a time

• A pastry brush, for brushing cookies with glaze and for removing excess flour from rolled cookies

• An offset spatula, for spreading jam, chocolate, or other fillings, and for transferring cutout cookies from the work surface to the baking sheet

• A ruler, for measuring the thickness of rolled dough, for measuring the diameter of cookie cutters and pans, and for cutting rectangles and strips

• Parchment paper or silicone baking mats, for lining cookie sheets. Silicone baking mats, such as the ones made by Silpat, are available at cookware stores. These are thin liners that are made to fit cookie sheets and baking pans and provide an excellent nonstick baking surface that doesn't need to be greased. They also add a thin layer of insulation to safeguard against burned cookies. The mats may seem expensive at first, but they can be used over and over again.

• An accurate—and loud—kitchen timer, to prevent ruining a good batch of cookies. Because cookies are small, they overbake and burn easily. Consider getting a timer that clips on to your clothing, so you'll never miss the signal.

Oatmeal Cookies

These raisin-studded beauties make a great snack—or even a breakfast treat. If you like extra crunch, add 1 cup of chopped walnuts or pecans to the batter along with the raisins. **Makes about 2 dozen**

1	cup unbleached all purpose flour
½	teaspoon baking powder
½	teaspoon baking soda
¼	teaspoon salt
1	cup (packed) golden brown sugar
½	cup (1 stick) unsalted butter, room temperature
1	large egg
1	teaspoon vanilla extract
1⅔	cups old-fashioned oats
1	cup raisins

Position 1 rack in top third and 1 rack in bottom third of oven and preheat to 350°F. Line 2 heavy large rimmed baking sheets with silicone baking mats or parchment paper. Whisk flour, baking powder, baking soda, and salt in medium bowl to blend. Using electric mixer, beat brown sugar and butter in large bowl until very well blended. Beat in egg and vanilla. Mix in flour mixture, then stir in oats and raisins.

Using trigger cookie scoop and about 2 tablespoons dough per cookie, arrange mounds of dough on prepared baking sheets, spacing 2 inches apart. Bake cookies until golden brown, reversing baking sheets halfway through baking, about 14 minutes total. Transfer cookies to rack and cool completely.

DO AHEAD: *Cookies can be made 1 day ahead. Store in airtight container at room temperature.*

Equipment Tip: **The Scoop**

A trigger cookie scoop makes simple work of dropping cookie dough balls onto the baking sheet—a much easier task than scraping the dough off of spoons or out of measuring cups. The scoop looks like a small ice-cream scoop and comes in several sizes. Look for them at kitchen supply stores or order online (see Online and Mail-Order Sources, page 632).

Cherry–Chocolate Chip Oatmeal Cookies

Not the usual oatmeal-raisin cookie. Dried tart cherries replace the raisins, and chocolate chips, almonds, and almond extract add new twists to the classic. Enjoy them as an afternoon snack or with cherry or fudge marble ice cream for dessert. **Makes about 2 dozen**

1	cup unbleached all purpose flour
½	teaspoon baking soda
¼	teaspoon salt
10	tablespoons (1¼ sticks) unsalted butter, room temperature
½	cup sugar
½	cup (packed) dark brown sugar
1	large egg
1	teaspoon vanilla extract
½	teaspoon almond extract
1	cup old-fashioned oats
1½	cups semisweet chocolate chips
1	cup dried tart cherries
½	cup slivered almonds, toasted

Position 1 rack in center and 1 rack in top third of oven and preheat to 325°F. Line 2 heavy large rimmed baking sheets with parchment paper. Sift flour, baking soda, and salt into medium bowl. Using electric mixer, beat butter and both sugars in large bowl until well blended. Mix in egg and both extracts. Beat in flour mixture. Stir in oats, then chocolate chips, cherries, and almonds.

Drop dough by rounded tablespoonfuls onto prepared baking sheets, spacing 2 inches apart. Bake cookies 12 minutes. Reverse baking sheets and continue to bake cookies until golden, about 6 minutes longer. Cool cookies on baking sheets (cookies will firm as they cool).

DO AHEAD: *Cookies can be made 1 week ahead. Store in airtight container at room temperature.*

Spice Cookies with Raisins and Walnuts

These cake-like cookies combine spices, plump raisins, and walnuts. They are an excellent addition to a lunch box or a great pick-me-up on a hike. **Makes about 6 dozen**

1⅓ cups unbleached all purpose flour
2 teaspoons baking powder
1 teaspoon ground cinnamon
¾ teaspoon ground allspice
½ teaspoon ground cloves
½ teaspoon salt
½ cup (1 stick) unsalted butter, room temperature
½ cup (packed) golden brown sugar
½ cup sugar
¼ cup whole milk
1 large egg
1 teaspoon vanilla extract
1 cup chopped raisins
1 cup chopped walnuts

Whisk flour, baking powder, cinnamon, allspice, cloves, and salt in medium bowl to blend. Using electric mixer, beat butter and both sugars in large bowl until creamy. Beat in milk, egg, and vanilla. Add flour mixture and beat until blended. Stir in raisins and walnuts. Cover dough and chill until cold, about 2 hours (dough will be sticky).

Preheat oven to 375°F. Drop dough by rounded teaspoonfuls onto heavy large rimmed baking sheets, spacing evenly. Bake until cookies are pale golden, about 12 minutes. Cool cookies on baking sheet 5 minutes. Transfer cookies to racks and cool completely.

DO AHEAD: *Cookies can be made 2 days ahead. Store in airtight containers at room temperature.*

Pine Nut Cookies

These Italian favorites are rolled in a decidedly American ingredient: crushed cornflakes. **Makes about 2 dozen**

2½ cups unbleached all purpose flour
2 teaspoons baking powder
11 tablespoons (1 stick plus 3 tablespoons) unsalted butter, room temperature
1 cup sugar
3 large eggs
1 cup pine nuts, toasted
4 cups cornflakes, crushed
Powdered sugar (optional)

Preheat oven to 350°F. Line 2 heavy large rimmed baking sheets with parchment paper. Whisk flour and baking powder in medium bowl to blend. Using electric mixer, beat butter and sugar in large bowl until blended. Add eggs 1 at a time, beating well after each addition. Add flour mixture and beat until blended. Stir in pine nuts.

Place crushed cornflakes in shallow baking dish. Using 1 heaping tablespoon dough for each cookie, form into balls (dough will be soft and sticky). Roll each ball in cornflakes, pressing gently to adhere. Transfer balls to baking sheets, spacing 1 inch apart. Bake cookies until deep golden, about 23 minutes. Transfer to rack and cool completely. Dust cookies with powdered sugar, if desired.

DO AHEAD: *Cookies can be made 2 days ahead. Store in airtight containers at room temperature.*

Chocolate-Dipped Lace Cookies

The small amount of flour in the batter is just enough to hold the dough together but still allow the cookies to spread out as they bake, forming thin, lacy designs.

Makes about 20

1	cup (packed) golden brown sugar
⅔	cup old-fashioned oats
½	cup unbleached all purpose flour
½	cup sliced almonds
2	teaspoons finely grated orange peel
½	teaspoon baking powder
¼	teaspoon salt
½	cup (1 stick) unsalted butter, melted
¼	cup whole milk
4	ounces bittersweet or semisweet chocolate, chopped

Position rack in top third of oven and preheat to 350°F. Line heavy rimless baking sheet with silicone baking mat or foil. Stir sugar, oats, flour, almonds, orange peel, baking powder, and salt in medium bowl to blend. Add melted butter and milk and stir well. Let batter stand 10 minutes.

Drop batter by level tablespoonfuls onto prepared cookie sheet, spacing 4 inches apart (cookies will spread considerably). Bake until cookies are bubbly, lacy, and golden brown, about 12 minutes. Carefully slide baking mat or foil from cookie sheet onto work surface. Let cookies cool completely. Using spatula, carefully transfer cookies to paper towels to absorb any excess butter. Repeat with remaining batter, wiping baking mat or lining cooled cookie sheet with clean foil for each batch.

Line 2 clean baking sheets with waxed paper or parchment paper. Stir chocolate in small metal bowl set over small saucepan of gently simmering water until melted and smooth. Partially dip 1 cookie into melted chocolate, coating ¼ of cookie. Transfer to prepared baking sheet. Repeat with remaining cookies and melted chocolate. Chill until chocolate is set. Carefully remove cookies from waxed paper.

DO AHEAD: *Can be made 1 week ahead. Store in airtight container in cool place.*

Lacy Sandwich Cookies

This recipe can also be used to make small lacy chocolate sandwich cookies. Use a rounded teaspoonful of dough to make the cookies smaller, and bake them for only about 10 minutes. Once they have cooled, spread a small amount of the melted chocolate over the bottom side of one cookie, then top with a second cookie, bottom side down. Repeat with the remaining cookies and chocolate for a total of about two dozen sandwich cookies.

Equipment Tip: **Clean Chopping**

For easy chocolate chopping that's also easy to clean up, use a wide, heavy chef's knife or Chinese cleaver and chop the chocolate on a thin, flexible plastic cutting board; the board makes it easy to transport the chopped chocolate to the double boiler, and it's lightweight, so a snap to rinse off. Flexible cutting boards can be found at bedbathandbeyond.com, amazon.com, and some kitchen supply and cookware stores.

Cranberry-Orange Drop Cookies

Use a razor-sharp Microplane (available at Bed, Bath, and Beyond and kitchenware stores) to grate the orange peel. It makes the job so easy and creates a delicate grated peel. **Makes about 4 dozen**

2	cups (packed) dried sweetened cranberries
1/3	cup orange juice
2	cups unbleached all purpose flour
1	teaspoon ground cinnamon
1	teaspoon baking powder
3/4	teaspoon ground ginger
1/4	teaspoon baking soda
1/4	teaspoon salt
1	cup (2 sticks) unsalted butter, room temperature
1	cup (packed) golden brown sugar
1	large egg
1	tablespoon minced peeled fresh ginger
2	teaspoons vanilla extract
1½	teaspoons finely grated orange peel
3/4	cup chopped walnuts
3/4	cup chopped unsalted natural pistachios
1/2	cup coarsely chopped fresh or frozen cranberries (do not thaw)

Combine dried cranberries and orange juice in small bowl. Let stand until cranberries soften slightly, stirring occasionally, about 30 minutes.

Position rack in center of oven and preheat to 350°F. Butter 3 heavy large rimmed baking sheets. Whisk flour, cinnamon, baking powder, ground ginger, baking soda, and salt in medium bowl until just blended.

Using electric mixer, beat butter and brown sugar in large bowl until smooth. Add egg, minced ginger, vanilla, and orange peel; beat until well blended, about 2 minutes. Beat in flour mixture. Stir in walnuts, pistachios, fresh or frozen cranberries, and dried cranberries with juices.

Drop cookie dough by rounded tablespoonfuls onto prepared baking sheets, spacing about 1½ inches apart. Bake cookies, 1 baking sheet at a time, until golden and almost firm to touch in center, about 18 minutes. Cool cookies on baking sheets 5 minutes. Transfer cookies to rack and cool completely.

DO AHEAD: *Can be made 2 days ahead. Store in airtight containers at room temperature.*

Technique Tip: Chopping Cranberries

It's easier to cut whole fresh cranberries when they are firm. If using frozen cranberries, chop them while they are still frozen and don't allow them to thaw before adding them to the dough or they will be too mushy to chop.

Cookie Basics: The Big Freeze

There is a way to enjoy fresh-baked cookies any time: Make the dough or cookies ahead of time and freeze them.

FREEZING DOUGH: This works well for low-moisture batters or doughs, such as for drop cookies, slice-and-bake cookies, and cutout cookies. (Any cookie batter that spreads prior to baking won't work.) To freeze cookies that are shaped into mounds or balls before baking, shape the dough and freeze the mounds or balls on waxed paper–lined baking sheets until firm. Transfer the mounds to a resealable bag and return to the freezer. When you're ready to bake, let them thaw briefly on a baking sheet while the oven preheats. Then bake according to the recipe instructions. To freeze slice-and-bake cookie dough, simply wrap the log of dough in foil or plastic wrap and store it in a freezer bag. To bake the cookies, thaw the dough slightly and then slice into rounds. Bake according to the recipe directions.

FREEZING BAKED COOKIES: Cookies such as chocolate chip and oatmeal cookies fare best when wrapped individually and tightly in plastic wrap or aluminum foil, then frozen in a cookie tin, food storage container, or resealable plastic bag. Bring them to room temperature, or warm them in a 300°F oven for 5 to 10 minutes. Bar cookies, such as brownies, are best frozen uncut in the pan they were baked in; shortbread and other crisp cookies can be frozen in resealable bags or food storage containers. These are best when just brought to room temperature.

Classic Peanut Butter Cookies

These delicious treats can be transformed into thumbprint cookies that mimic the popular PB&J combo. Instead of flattening the dough balls, use your finger-tip to make a deep indentation in the center of each, then fill each indentation with 1 level teaspoon of your favorite jam. Bring the kids into the kitchen for this baking project—they'll love the job of making the indentations in the dough. **Makes about 2½ dozen**

2   cups unbleached all purpose flour
½   teaspoon baking soda
½   teaspoon salt
½   cup (1 stick) unsalted butter, room temperature
¾   cup sugar
½   cup (packed) golden brown sugar
2   large eggs
1   cup old-fashioned (natural) salted crunchy peanut butter
        (preferably organic)

Preheat oven to 350°F. Line 2 heavy large rimmed baking sheets with parchment paper or silicone baking mats. Whisk flour, baking soda, and salt in small bowl to blend. Using electric mixer, beat butter and both sugars in large bowl until fluffy. Beat in eggs. Add peanut butter and mix just until combined (do not overmix). Stir in flour mixture.

Form dough into golf-ball-size balls and arrange on baking sheets, spacing 1 inch apart. Using fork, flatten and make crosshatch pattern in each dough ball. Bake cookies until golden brown on bottom, about 20 minutes. Transfer to rack and cool.

DO AHEAD: *Cookies can be made 2 days ahead. Store in airtight container at room temperature.*

Lime Snowball Cookies

This delicious cookie offers deep lime flavor, thanks to lime juice, lime peel, and lime oil, an intense essence derived from lime peels. Lime oil can be found at specialty foods stores and online at chefshop.com. **Makes about 2½ dozen**

1½   cups unbleached all purpose flour
½   cup cornstarch
1   cup (2 sticks) unsalted butter, room temperature
½   cup powdered sugar
2   tablespoons fresh lime juice
1   teaspoon (packed) finely grated lime peel
½   teaspoon lime oil
        Additional powdered sugar

Whisk flour and cornstarch in medium bowl to blend. Using electric mixer, beat butter and powdered sugar in large bowl until light and fluffy. Mix in lime juice, lime peel, and lime oil. Beat in flour mixture until smooth. Chill dough until just firm, about 45 minutes.

Preheat oven to 350°F. Line 2 heavy large rimmed baking sheets with parchment paper. Using scant 1 tablespoon for each, form dough into balls and place on prepared baking sheets, spacing 1 inch apart. Bake cookies until pale golden on top and browned on bottom, about 23 minutes. Transfer baking sheets to racks; immediately sift generous amount of additional powdered sugar over cookies. Cool cookies completely on baking sheets.

DO AHEAD: *Can be made ahead. Store in airtight container at room temperature up to 5 days, or freeze up to 2 weeks. Dust with more powdered sugar before serving.*

Almond Thumbprints

Use your favorite fruit preserves in these delicious, crumbly almond cookies. For a pretty presentation, choose a variety of different-colored preserves, such as blueberry, raspberry, and peach. **Makes about 3 dozen**

1	cup blanched whole almonds, toasted
½	cup sugar
2	cups unbleached all purpose flour
½	cup powdered sugar
½	teaspoon baking powder
¼	teaspoon salt
1	cup (2 sticks) unsalted butter, room temperature
1	large egg yolk
1	teaspoon vanilla extract
½	teaspoon almond extract
½	cup (about) fruit preserves

Combine almonds and sugar in processor and blend until almonds are finely chopped.

Mix flour, powdered sugar, baking powder, and salt in medium bowl. Using electric mixer, beat butter, egg yolk, and almond mixture in large bowl until blended. Beat in vanilla and almond extracts. Mix flour mixture into butter mixture in 3 additions. Cover dough and chill until firm, about 1 hour.

Preheat oven to 350°F. Using hands, roll 1 generous tablespoonful of dough for each cookie into 1¼-inch-diameter ball. Place cookies on 2 heavy large ungreased baking sheets, spacing 2 inches apart. Make depression in center of each cookie with fingertip or handle of wooden spoon. Bake cookies 10 minutes.

Press back of teaspoon into cookies to re-form depressions. Fill each depression with ½ teaspoon preserves. Continue baking cookies until light golden brown around edges and on bottom, about 8 minutes longer. Cool on baking sheets 2 minutes. Using metal spatula, transfer cookies to rack and cool completely.

DO AHEAD: *Can be made 3 days ahead. Store between sheets of waxed paper in airtight container at room temperature.*

Deep Dark Chocolate Cookies

Made without butter or flour, these dense, chewy cookies will satisfy even the most intense chocolate craving. **Makes about 2 dozen**

	Nonstick vegetable oil spray
1½	cups bittersweet chocolate chips (about 9 ounces), divided
3	large egg whites, room temperature
2½	cups powdered sugar, divided
½	cup natural unsweetened cocoa powder
1	tablespoon cornstarch
¼	teaspoon salt

Preheat oven to 400°F. Spray 2 heavy large rimmed baking sheets with nonstick spray. Melt 1 cup chocolate chips in glass bowl in microwave, stirring twice, about 2 minutes. Cool slightly.

Using electric mixer, beat egg whites in large bowl until soft peaks form. Gradually beat in 1 cup powdered sugar. Continue beating until mixture resembles soft marshmallow creme. Whisk 1 cup powdered sugar, cocoa powder, cornstarch, and salt in medium bowl to blend. On low speed, beat dry ingredients into meringue. Stir in lukewarm chocolate and remaining ½ cup chocolate chips (dough will become very stiff).

Place remaining ½ cup powdered sugar in small bowl. Roll 1 rounded tablespoon dough into ball; roll in powdered sugar, coating thickly. Place on prepared sheet. Repeat with remaining dough, spacing 2 inches apart. Bake cookies until puffed and tops crack, about 10 minutes. Cool on sheets on rack 10 minutes. Transfer cookies to rack and cool completely.

Technique Tip: **The Cracked Look**
Roll the cookies thickly in powdered sugar before baking. When the cookies begin to expand in the oven, cracks will form, dramatically showing the dark chocolate cookie underneath. This style of cookie is often called an Earthquake Cookie.

Mexican Chocolate-Cherry Rounds

Rich chocolate cookies take on Mexican flair when spiced with cinnamon, cloves, and cayenne pepper. Whole blanched almonds, shelled pistachios, and walnut halves can be used to decorate the cookies instead of the candied cherries. This recipe makes a generous amount, but the cookies store well—up to a week in an airtight cookie jar or a month in the freezer. **Makes about 5 dozen**

6	ounces unsweetened chocolate, chopped
2	cups plus 2 tablespoons unbleached all purpose flour
1	tablespoon ground cinnamon
2	teaspoons baking powder
1	teaspoon salt
¼	teaspoon cayenne pepper
¼	teaspoon ground cloves
1¾	cups sugar
½	cup (1 stick) unsalted butter, room temperature
3	large eggs
1	teaspoon vanilla extract
⅔	cup powdered sugar
60	(about) candied cherry halves

Stir chocolate in top of double boiler over simmering water until melted and smooth. Cool slightly.

Combine flour, cinnamon, baking powder, salt, cayenne pepper, and cloves in medium bowl. Using electric mixer, beat sugar and butter in large bowl until light. Beat in eggs 1 at a time, then vanilla and melted chocolate. Gradually add flour mixture and beat just until blended. Chill dough until firm, about 2 hours.

Preheat oven to 350°F. Lightly butter 2 heavy large rimmed baking sheets. Place powdered sugar in shallow bowl. Form dough into 1-inch balls. Roll each ball in powdered sugar to coat; shake off excess sugar. Arrange cookies on prepared baking sheets, spacing 1½ inches apart. Press 1 cherry half into center of each cookie. Bake until cookies puff and crack but are still soft, about 10 minutes. Transfer cookies to rack and cool completely.

DO AHEAD: *Can be made ahead. Store in airtight containers at room temperature up to 1 week, or freeze up to 1 month.*

Pistachio and Cranberry Mexican Wedding Cakes

Classic Mexican wedding cakes are actually cookies—nut-studded, crumbly confections coated in powdered sugar. They get a delicious and colorful twist here with the addition of dried cranberries and chopped pistachios. The dough doesn't use eggs, baking powder, or baking soda for leavening, so the cookies are similar in texture to shortbread cookies. They also don't incorporate much sugar, but instead get most of their sweetness after baking: The cookies are rolled in powdered sugar twice—first when they are still warm and again after they are cooled, giving them a nice generous coating of snowy sugar. **Makes about 6½ dozen**

2	cups (4 sticks) unsalted butter, room temperature
1	cup powdered sugar
2	tablespoons vanilla extract
1	teaspoon salt
1	cup unsalted natural pistachios (about 4 ounces), chopped
1	cup dried cranberries
3⅓	cups sifted cake flour (sifted, then measured)
1⅔	cups sifted unbleached all purpose flour (sifted, then measured)
	Additional powdered sugar

Preheat oven to 350°F. Butter 3 heavy large rimmed baking sheets. Using electric mixer, beat butter and powdered sugar in large bowl until light and fluffy. Beat in vanilla and salt, then pistachios and cranberries. Using spatula, stir in both flours (do not overmix dough).

Shape dough by generous tablespoonfuls into football-shape ovals. Place on prepared sheets, spacing 1 inch apart. Bake cookies, 1 sheet at a time, until bottoms just begin to color, about 16 minutes. Cool cookies on sheets 10 minutes before coating.

Pour generous amount of additional powdered sugar into medium bowl. Working with 5 or 6 warm cookies at a time, add cookies to bowl of sugar; gently turn to coat thickly. Transfer cookies to sheet of waxed paper. Let cool. Return cookies to bowl of sugar and gently turn to coat again; cool completely.

DO AHEAD: *Cookies can be made 4 days ahead. Store in airtight containers at room temperature.*

Pfeffernüsse

These spicy cookies get their name from the German word for "peppernuts," or black pepper. They are popular holiday treats in many European countries. **Makes about 2½ dozen**

2¼	cups unbleached all purpose flour
½	teaspoon crushed aniseed
½	teaspoon freshly grated nutmeg
½	teaspoon ground cinnamon
½	teaspoon salt
¼	teaspoon baking soda
¼	teaspoon ground allspice
¼	teaspoon (scant) ground cloves
¼	teaspoon freshly ground black pepper
½	cup (1 stick) unsalted butter, room temperature
¾	cup (packed) dark brown sugar
¼	cup mild-flavored (light) molasses
1	large egg
2	cups (about) powdered sugar

Preheat oven to 350°F. Line 2 heavy large rimmed baking sheets with parchment paper or silicone baking mats. Whisk flour, aniseed, nutmeg, cinnamon, salt, baking soda, allspice, cloves, and pepper in medium bowl to blend. Using electric mixer, beat butter, brown sugar, and molasses in large bowl until light and fluffy. Beat in egg, then stir in flour mixture.

DO AHEAD: *Can be made 3 days ahead. Cover with plastic and chill.*

Using 1 tablespoon for each cookie, roll dough into balls. Place balls on prepared baking sheets, spacing about 2 inches apart. Bake until golden brown on bottom and just firm to touch, about 14 minutes. Transfer baking sheets to racks and cool cookies on sheets 5 minutes.

Place powdered sugar in brown paper bag. While still warm, drop 3 cookies into bag; close bag and shake gently to coat cookies with sugar. Transfer sugar-coated cookies to racks. Repeat with remaining cookies. Serve warm or at room temperature.

DO AHEAD: *Can be made ahead. Store in airtight container at room temperature up to 2 days, or freeze up to 1 week.*

Chewy Ginger Cookies

These soft, chewy cookies have a double dose of ginger: Ground ginger lays the flavor foundation, while crystallized ginger makes the cookies a little punchier and chewier. **Makes about 2 dozen**

2⅓	cups unbleached all purpose flour
2	teaspoons baking soda
2	teaspoons ground ginger
1½	teaspoons ground cinnamon
¾	teaspoon salt
¼	teaspoon ground cloves
¾	cup (packed) dark brown sugar
6	tablespoons non-hydrogenated solid vegetable shortening, room temperature
6	tablespoons (¾ stick) unsalted butter, room temperature
¼	cup sugar
¼	cup mild-flavored (light) molasses
1	large egg
½	cup chopped crystallized ginger
	Additional sugar

Whisk flour, baking soda, ground ginger, cinnamon, salt, and cloves in medium bowl to blend. Using electric mixer, beat brown sugar, shortening, butter, and sugar in large bowl until fluffy. Add molasses and egg and beat until blended. Add flour mixture and mix just until blended. Mix in crystallized ginger. Cover and chill 1 hour.

Preheat oven to 350°F. Line 2 heavy large rimmed baking sheets with parchment paper or silicone baking mats. Spoon additional sugar in thick layer onto small plate. Using 2 tablespoons of dough for each cookie, form dough into balls using hands, then roll in sugar to coat completely. Place balls on prepared baking sheets, spacing 2 inches apart.

Bake cookies until cracked on top but still soft to touch, about 14 minutes. Cool on baking sheets 1 minute. Carefully transfer cookies to racks and cool completely.

DO AHEAD: *Cookies can be made 5 days ahead. Store in airtight container at room temperature.*

Ingredient Tip: Shortening
Solid vegetable shortening used to be loaded with trans fats because of all of the hydrogenated oils. Fortunately, companies have begun to make non-hydrogenated solid vegetable shortening, a much healthier alternative.

Vanilla Shortbread Cookies

European butter adds extra flavor to the already incredible crumbly richness of this classic shortbread. For more information on European butter, see page 4. Swapping the baking sheets between the higher and lower racks halfway through baking allows the cookies to brown evenly. **Makes about 3 dozen**

2	cups unbleached all purpose flour
¾	cup powdered sugar
¼	cup cornstarch
¼	teaspoon salt
1	cup (2 sticks) unsalted European-style butter, room temperature
¼	cup sugar
1	teaspoon vanilla extract

Sift flour, powdered sugar, cornstarch, and salt into medium bowl. Using electric mixer, beat butter in large bowl until fluffy. Gradually beat in sugar and vanilla. Stir in flour mixture in 3 additions, mixing until just blended each time. Gather dough into ball; divide in half. Roll each half into 6-inch-long log; wrap each log in plastic wrap and chill at least 2 hours.

DO AHEAD: *Can be made 1 day ahead. Keep chilled.*

Position 1 rack in top third and 1 rack in center of oven and preheat to 325°F. Cut each log crosswise into ⅓-inch-thick slices. Arrange slices on 2 heavy large rimmed baking sheets, spacing ½ inch apart (cookies will spread very little). Bake cookies 9 minutes. Switch baking sheets on racks and bake just until cookies turn golden brown at edges, about 9 minutes longer. Cool cookies on sheets 1 minute. Using thin metal spatula, transfer cookies to racks and cool.

DO AHEAD: *Cookies can be made 3 days ahead. Store in airtight container at room temperature.*

Almond Shortbread

This tender shortbread is made the traditional way: as one large cookie that's cut into wedges after baking. It's important to cut the shortbread into wedges while it's still warm; cooled shortbread is crisp and will break into pieces. **Makes 8**

6	tablespoons (¾ stick) chilled unsalted butter, cut into 8 pieces
¼	cup (packed) golden brown sugar
¾	teaspoon vanilla extract
	Pinch of salt
¾	cup unbleached all purpose flour
1	tablespoon cornstarch
¼	cup sliced almonds

Preheat oven to 375°F. Place 9-inch-diameter metal pie pan in freezer to chill. Combine butter, brown sugar, vanilla, and salt in processor. Blend until smooth, about 20 seconds. Add flour and cornstarch. Using on/off turns, process until dough clumps together. Press dough evenly onto bottom of chilled pie pan. Sprinkle almonds over and press lightly into dough to adhere. Freeze until chilled, about 5 minutes.

Bake shortbread until edges are golden brown, about 22 minutes. Cut warm shortbread (still in pan) into 8 wedges. Transfer pan to rack and cool shortbread completely in pan.

DO AHEAD: *Cookies can be made 1 day ahead. Store in airtight container at room temperature.*

Brown Butter–Pecan Shortbread

Brown butter (often called beurre noisette, *or hazelnut butter, for its color) is unsalted butter that has been cooked for a few minutes over medium heat, just until the milk solids at the bottom of the pan turn golden brown. It lends a wonderfully complex, nutty flavor to this tender shortbread cookie.* **Makes 32**

1	cup (2 sticks) unsalted butter, room temperature, divided
1	cup pecans, toasted
2	cups sifted unbleached all purpose flour (sifted, then measured)
¼	teaspoon coarse kosher salt
½	cup sugar
1	teaspoon vanilla extract

Melt ½ cup butter in small skillet over medium heat. Cook until deep amber, stirring often, about 6 minutes (do not burn). Pour through fine strainer into small bowl. Chill just until firm, about 1 hour. Meanwhile, grind pecans in processor until coarse meal forms.

Preheat oven to 300°F. Whisk flour and coarse salt in medium bowl to blend. Using electric mixer, beat brown butter, remaining ½ cup butter, and sugar in large bowl until creamy. Beat in vanilla, then pecans. Gradually beat in flour mixture just to blend.

Transfer dough to sheet of parchment paper. Form dough into rectangle. Place second sheet of parchment paper over dough. Press or roll dough into 12x8-inch rectangle. Remove top sheet of parchment. Transfer dough on parchment to heavy baking sheet. Using fork, pierce dough all over, spacing 1 inch apart.

Bake shortbread until golden brown and firm to touch, about 55 minutes. Cut warm shortbread (still on baking sheet) lengthwise into 8 strips. Cut each strip crosswise into quarters. Cool 10 minutes on baking sheet on rack. Transfer cookies to rack and cool completely.

DO AHEAD: *Cookies can be made 3 days ahead. Store in airtight container at room temperature.*

Italian Hazelnut–Espresso Shortbread

Favorite Italian flavors—espresso and hazelnuts—come together in these appealing treats. The cookies are drizzled with a coffee-flavored dark chocolate topping, but they would be equally delicious without embellishment. **Makes 4 dozen**

2	cups unbleached all purpose flour
1	cup (packed) golden brown sugar
3	tablespoons cornstarch
1	tablespoon plus 1 teaspoon instant espresso powder
¾	teaspoon salt
1	cup (2 sticks) chilled unsalted butter, cut into ½-inch cubes
1	teaspoon vanilla extract
⅔	cup hazelnuts, toasted, husked, coarsely chopped
2	tablespoons hot water
2	ounces bittersweet or semisweet chocolate, chopped

Preheat oven to 350°F. Blend flour, brown sugar, cornstarch, 1 tablespoon espresso powder, and salt in processor. Add butter and vanilla. Using on/off turns, process until mixture resembles coarse meal. Add nuts; blend until finely chopped. Transfer dough to floured work surface. Knead briefly just until dough comes together. Divide dough in half.

Press each half into 9-inch-diameter tart pan with removable bottom. Bake until deep golden brown, about 25 minutes. Transfer shortbread to rack and cool 2 minutes. Carefully remove pan sides. Cut each warm shortbread round into 24 wedges. Transfer shortbread to rack and cool completely.

Mix 2 tablespoons hot water and remaining 1 teaspoon espresso powder in small saucepan. Add chocolate. Stir over medium-low heat until chocolate is melted and smooth. Remove from heat. Cool slightly. Drizzle chocolate mixture over cookies. Let stand until chocolate sets.

DO AHEAD: *Can be made ahead. Store in airtight containers at room temperature up to 1 week, or freeze up to 1 month.*

Pistachio Shortbread Cookies

The dough for this delicious and easy-to-make cookie comes together quickly in a food processor. The dough logs need to chill for at least four hours before they are firm enough to slice, so be sure to begin several hours ahead. **Makes about 5 dozen**

1½	cups unbleached all purpose flour
½	cup plus 2 tablespoons powdered sugar
½	teaspoon salt
¾	cup (1½ sticks) chilled unsalted butter, cut into ½-inch cubes
½	cup unsalted natural pistachios, lightly toasted, chopped
1	large egg yolk
¾	teaspoon vanilla extract

Mix flour, powdered sugar, and salt in processor. Add butter, pistachios, egg yolk, and vanilla. Using on/off turns, mix until moist ball forms. Transfer dough to work surface and divide in half. Form each half into 8x1¼-inch log (if dough is too soft, chill until firm, about 30 minutes). Wrap logs in plastic and chill until firm, about 4 hours.

DO AHEAD: *Can be made 3 days ahead. Keep chilled.*

Preheat oven to 325°F. Slice logs into ¼-inch-thick rounds, rolling each log on work surface after every few slices to retain round shape. Place rounds on heavy ungreased rimmed baking sheets, spacing 1 inch apart. Bake shortbread until barely golden, about 18 minutes. Cool shortbread completely on baking sheets.

DO AHEAD: *Cookies can be made 4 days ahead. Store in airtight containers at room temperature.*

Mexican Chocolate and Pepita Shortbread Stars

Green hulled pumpkin seeds are also known as pepitas. *They are popular in Central American, Mexican, and southwestern cuisines. They stand up well to cooking and give a crunchy texture and subtle, nutty flavor to all sorts of dishes, including these lovely shortbread stars. You can find pumpkin seeds at many supermarkets and at natural foods stores and Latin markets.* **Makes about 1½ dozen**

¾	cup shelled unsalted pumpkin seeds (*pepitas*), toasted
4	ounces bittersweet or semisweet chocolate, chopped
1	cup (2 sticks) unsalted butter, room temperature
½	cup plus 2 tablespoons sugar
¾	teaspoon ground cinnamon
¼	teaspoon salt
2¼	cups unbleached all purpose flour
1	large egg white, lightly whisked to loosen

Preheat oven to 325°F. Grind pumpkin seeds in coffee grinder or processor until coarsely ground. Stir chocolate in top of double boiler set over simmering water until melted and smooth. Transfer to large bowl and cool slightly.

Add butter, ½ cup sugar, cinnamon, and salt to melted chocolate. Using electric mixer, beat until well blended. Add flour and ground pumpkin seeds and stir until just blended.

Roll out dough on floured surface to ½-inch thickness. Using 3-inch star-shape cookie cutter dipped into flour, cut out cookies. Transfer cookies to heavy ungreased rimmed baking sheets, spacing 1 inch apart. Reroll dough scraps; cut out additional cookies and place on baking sheets. Brush cookies with egg white; sprinkle with remaining 2 tablespoons sugar.

Bake cookies until just firm to touch, about 18 minutes. Cool 5 minutes on baking sheets. Transfer to rack and cool completely.

DO AHEAD: *Cookies can be made 2 days ahead. Store in airtight container at room temperature.*

Equipment Tip: Impromptu Pastry Bag

Small resealable plastic bags are convenient alternatives to using pastry bags for decorating cookies. Fill one corner of the bag with icing or melted chocolate, then twist the bag and snip off just the tip of the corner for piping fine-line decorations.

Mocha Shortbread

Cocoa powder and instant espresso powder flavor this version of Scottish shortbread. To set the chocolate piping more quickly, place the cookies in the freezer in a single layer for 15 to 20 minutes until the chocolate is firm.
Makes 2 dozen

1¼   cups unbleached all purpose flour
¼   cup cornstarch
¼   cup unsweetened cocoa powder (preferably Dutch-process)
¾   teaspoon instant espresso powder or instant coffee powder
¼   teaspoon salt
1   cup (2 sticks) unsalted butter, room temperature
1   cup powdered sugar
3   ounces high-quality white chocolate (such as Lindt or Perugina), chopped
3   ounces bittersweet or semisweet chocolate, chopped

Position 1 rack in top third and 1 rack in bottom third of oven and preheat to 325°F. Line 2 heavy large rimmed baking sheets with parchment paper. Sift flour, cornstarch, cocoa powder, espresso powder, and salt into medium bowl. Using electric mixer, beat butter in large bowl until fluffy. Beat in powdered sugar. Add flour mixture and beat until well blended.

Gather dough into ball; divide into 3 equal pieces. Place 1 dough piece close to each end of 1 prepared sheet. Place third piece in center of second prepared sheet. Using moistened fingertips, press each dough piece to 7-inch-diameter round. Using small sharp knife, mark each round at equal intervals to form 8 wedges after baking. Press fork tines around edge of each to make notched design.

Bake shortbread 12 minutes. Reverse baking sheets. Bake until shortbread looks dry and feels firm to touch, about 12 minutes longer. Cool on sheets 5 minutes. Cut warm shortbread into wedges along marked lines. Cool completely on sheets on racks. Transfer wedges to work surface.

Place white chocolate in metal bowl set over saucepan of barely simmering water. Stir until chocolate is melted and smooth. Remove bowl from over water. Place bittersweet chocolate in another bowl set over same simmering water. Stir until melted and smooth.

Fit 2 pastry bags with ⅛-inch plain tips; spoon white chocolate into 1 and bittersweet chocolate into other. Or spoon chocolate into 2 small plastic bags (cut off 1 tip from each bag). Pipe chocolates decoratively over cookies. Let stand at room temperature until chocolate sets, about 1 hour.

DO AHEAD: *Can be made 2 days ahead. Store in airtight container in single layers between sheets of waxed paper at room temperature.*

White Chocolate and Peppermint Cookie Brittle

This dough is baked into one giant shortbread-style cookie, which is then topped with coarsely crushed peppermint candies and drizzled with melted white chocolate. Once the chocolate is set, the cookie gets broken into irregular pieces that look spectacular when arranged upright at angles in a basket or bowl.
Makes about 24 pieces

1½   cups unbleached all purpose flour
½   teaspoon baking soda
¼   teaspoon salt
¾   cup (1½ sticks) unsalted butter, melted, cooled slightly
½   cup sugar
⅓   cup (packed) golden brown sugar
1   teaspoon vanilla extract
10   ounces high-quality white chocolate (such as Lindt or Perugina), chopped into ⅓-inch pieces, divided
¾   cup coarsely crushed red-and-white-striped hard peppermint candies (about 6 ounces), divided

Preheat oven to 350°F. Line heavy rimmed baking sheet with parchment paper. Whisk flour, baking soda, and salt in medium bowl to blend. Whisk melted butter, both sugars, and vanilla in large bowl until smooth. Stir in flour mixture until just blended. Stir in 1 cup chopped white chocolate and ½ cup crushed peppermint candy.

Transfer dough to prepared baking sheet. Press dough into 14x8-inch rectangle, about ⅜ inch thick. Bake cookie until top is firm and dark golden, about 30 minutes. Cool on sheet 10 minutes. Transfer to rack and cool completely.

Stir remaining white chocolate in top of double boiler over barely simmering water until melted and smooth. Using small spoon, drizzle about half of melted chocolate in thin lines over cooled cookie. Sprinkle remaining crushed peppermint candies over chocolate. Drizzle remaining white chocolate over top. Let stand until white chocolate sets, about 1 hour. Break cookie into irregular 2- to 3-inch pieces.

DO AHEAD: *Cookie brittle can be made 2 days ahead. Store in airtight container at room temperature.*

{ **Ingredient Tip: Peppermint Candy**
Round red-and-white-striped hard peppermint candies are called for in this recipe, but candy canes would be a great substitute. Place the candies in a resealable plastic freezer bag, then crush them gently with a mallet or rolling pin. }

♟ Cinnamon-Almond Cookies

The nice thing about these simple, irresistible cookies is that you can have them anytime you've got a craving—the recipe makes a lot of dough, so you can freeze any extra that you don't use. For impromptu entertaining, slice the still-frozen dough into rounds and pop them in the oven for a quick dessert. Serve with a cup of hot chai tea. **Makes about 12 dozen**

3	cups unbleached all purpose flour
1	teaspoon ground cinnamon
½	teaspoon baking powder
½	teaspoon baking soda
1	cup (2 sticks) unsalted butter, room temperature
¾	cup sugar
¾	cup (packed) golden brown sugar
1	large egg
1	large egg yolk
1	teaspoon vanilla extract
½	teaspoon salt
1¾	cups sliced or blanched slivered almonds

Sift flour, cinnamon, baking powder, and baking soda into medium bowl. Beat butter in large bowl until fluffy. Beat in both sugars. Add egg and egg yolk; beat to blend. Beat in vanilla and salt. Add flour mixture and beat until dough comes together in moist clumps. Add almonds and knead gently in bowl with hands until blended.

Divide dough into 4 equal portions. Roll each into 10-inch-long log, about 1¼ to 1½ inches in diameter. Wrap dough in 2 layers of plastic and place in freezer until frozen, at least 4 hours.

DO AHEAD: *Can be made 1 month ahead. Keep frozen.*

Preheat oven to 350°F. Working with 1 log at a time, remove plastic and cut dough crosswise into ¼-inch-thick rounds. Place rounds on heavy ungreased rimmed baking sheet, spacing 1 inch apart. Bake until light golden brown, about 12 minutes. Transfer cookies to rack and cool completely.

DO AHEAD: *Cookies can be made 4 days ahead. Store in airtight containers at room temperature.*

♟ Chocolate-Espresso Cookies

These crisp, full-flavored wafers are a classic icebox-style cookie—meaning that they achieve their thinness by being formed into a log, chilled, and sliced before baking. Enjoy the cookies as a light, sophisticated finish to a dinner party. **Makes about 4 dozen**

1	cup unbleached all purpose flour
½	cup unsweetened Dutch-process cocoa powder
½	teaspoon salt
¼	teaspoon baking soda
3	tablespoons unsalted butter, room temperature
3	tablespoons non-hydrogenated stick margarine, room temperature
½	cup plus 2 tablespoons sugar
½	cup (packed) golden brown sugar
1½	tablespoons instant espresso powder or instant coffee powder
1	teaspoon vanilla extract
1	large egg white

Sift flour, cocoa powder, salt, and baking soda into small bowl. Using electric mixer, beat butter and margarine in large bowl until creamy. Add both sugars, espresso powder, and vanilla and beat until blended. Mix in egg white. Add flour mixture and beat just until incorporated. Using hands, knead dough briefly in bowl until smooth.

Form dough into 14-inch-long, 2-inch-diameter log. Wrap log in waxed paper and chill until cold, at least 1 hour.

DO AHEAD: *Can be made 3 days ahead. Keep chilled.*

Position 1 rack in top third and 1 rack in bottom third of oven and preheat to 350°F. Slice cookie log crosswise into ¼-inch-thick rounds. Place cookies on heavy large rimmed baking sheets. Bake cookies until cracked and almost firm to touch in center, reversing sheets from top to bottom oven racks after 7minutes, about 14 minutes total. Transfer cookies to racks and cool completely.

DO AHEAD: *Cookies can be made 2 weeks ahead. Store in airtight containers at room temperature.*

Chocolate-Mint Cookies

There's a reason that Thin Mints are the best sellers of all Girl Scout cookies: The combination of a crisp chocolate-mint cookie topped with chocolate icing is irresistible. Now you can make your own any time of the year with this simple recipe. Note that the dough needs to chill for a couple of hours before you roll it out, so plan ahead. Dutch-process cocoa has been treated with an alkali to neutralize its natural acidity. It has a milder, more delicate flavor and a darker, richer color than regular cocoa. **Makes about 3½ dozen**

1½	cups unbleached all purpose flour
¾	cup unsweetened cocoa powder (preferably Dutch-process)
¼	teaspoon salt
¾	cup (1½ sticks) unsalted butter, room temperature
¾	teaspoon peppermint extract
½	teaspoon vanilla extract
1	cup sugar
1	large egg
6	ounces bittersweet or semisweet chocolate, chopped

Whisk flour, cocoa, and salt in medium bowl to blend. Using electric mixer, beat butter in large bowl until smooth. Beat in peppermint and vanilla extracts. Beat in sugar in 3 additions. Add egg and beat until blended. Add flour mixture and beat just until blended (dough will be sticky).

Divide dough between 2 sheets of plastic wrap. Using plastic as aid, form dough on each into 2-inch-diameter log. Wrap with plastic and refrigerate dough until well chilled, at least 2 hours.

DO AHEAD: *Can be made 1 day ahead. Keep chilled.*

Position 1 rack in center and 1 rack in top third of oven; preheat to 350°F. Line 2 heavy large rimmed baking sheets with parchment paper. Unwrap dough; roll briefly on work surface to form smooth round logs. Cut logs crosswise into ¼-inch-thick rounds. Place rounds on prepared baking sheets, spacing 1 inch apart. Bake cookies until tops and edges are dry to touch, about 15 minutes. Transfer baking sheets with cookies to racks; cool completely.

Stir chocolate in top of double boiler set over simmering water until melted and smooth. Remove from over water. Cool melted chocolate until slightly thickened but still pourable, about 10 minutes. Dip fork into melted chocolate, then wave fork back and forth over cookies, drizzling melted chocolate thickly in zigzag pattern. Chill cookies on baking sheets until chocolate is set, about 10 minutes.

DO AHEAD: *Can be made 1 week ahead. Chill in airtight container between sheets of parchment paper or waxed paper.*

Caramel Cookies

This unusual cookie starts with a deep amber-colored homemade caramel. Brown sugar and flour are then added to form the dough. Once the dough is prepared, it needs to chill overnight before it's sliced and baked, so be sure to begin making these crisp cookies a day ahead. **Makes about 4 dozen**

¾	cup sugar
⅓	cup water
½	vanilla bean, split lengthwise
2	tablespoons heavy whipping cream
¾	cup (1½ sticks) unsalted butter, cut into ½-inch cubes
2	tablespoons (packed) golden brown sugar
¼	teaspoon salt
2	cups unbleached all purpose flour, sifted (measured, then sifted)

Combine sugar and ⅓ cup water in heavy medium saucepan. Scrape in seeds from vanilla bean; add bean. Stir over medium heat until sugar dissolves. Increase heat and boil without stirring until syrup is deep amber color, occasionally brushing down sides of pan with wet pastry brush and swirling pan, about 8 minutes. Remove from heat. Discard vanilla bean. Pour in cream (mixture will bubble vigorously); add butter and whisk until smooth. Cool 5 minutes. Stir in brown sugar and salt. Add flour and stir until well blended and dough forms. Turn dough out onto floured work surface; divide dough in half. Form each dough half into 9-inch-long log; wrap in plastic and chill overnight.

Preheat oven to 350°F. Line 2 heavy large rimmed baking sheets with parchment paper. Cut dough logs crosswise into ¼-inch-thick slices. Place slices on prepared baking sheets, spacing 1 inch apart. Bake cookies until firm to touch and slightly darker in color, about 13 minutes. Transfer cookies to racks to cool.

DO AHEAD: *Cookies can be made 3 days ahead. Store in airtight containers at room temperature.*

Spiced Snowflakes

This is a wonderful cookie to bake with children—it's basically a spiced sugar cookie with a pretty dusting of powdered sugar. You can have the kids cut out their own snowflake stencils, then let the powdered sugar fly. Lace doilies also work well as stencils. Of course, the holiday design options are endless: cutout hearts for Valentine's Day, pumpkins for Halloween . . . just use your imagination. The dough log needs to chill overnight, so plan accordingly. **Makes about 2 dozen**

1½	**cups sifted unbleached all purpose flour (sifted, then measured)**
1½	**teaspoons baking powder**
1¼	**teaspoons ground cinnamon**
1	**teaspoon ground ginger**
½	**teaspoon ground nutmeg**
¼	**teaspoon ground cloves**
¼	**teaspoon salt**
½	**cup (1 stick) unsalted butter, room temperature**
¾	**cup sugar**
1	**large egg**
2	**teaspoons vanilla extract**
	Powdered sugar

Sift flour, baking powder, cinnamon, ginger, nutmeg, cloves, and salt into medium bowl. Using electric mixer, beat butter in large bowl until light. Gradually beat in sugar. Beat in egg and vanilla. Gradually beat in flour mixture. If dough is too soft to mold, chill until firm.

Spoon dough onto large sheet of plastic wrap. Roll into 7-inch-long, 2¼-inch-diameter log. Wrap tightly and chill overnight.

Preheat oven to 350°F. Butter 2 heavy large rimmed baking sheets. Unwrap dough and cut into ¼-inch-thick slices. Place on baking sheets, spacing slices 1 inch apart. Bake until light golden brown, about 12 minutes. Transfer cookies to rack and cool.

DO AHEAD: *Cookies can be made 1 week ahead. Store in airtight container at room temperature.*

Place doilies or snowflake stencils atop cookies. Sift powdered sugar over. Carefully remove doilies or stencils and serve.

Decorating Cookies: After Baking

• Cool cookies completely before decorating. This is especially important if topping with frosting, chocolate, or royal icing (the decorative icing that hardens when it dries), so that the topping doesn't melt or drip. If using white icing or frosting, or melted white chocolate, you can add a few drops of vegetable food coloring, if you like—or even divide the topping among a few bowls and create several different colors.

• Frosting can be spread on cookies with an offset spatula or piped through a pastry bag (see page 38 for tips on piping). Do a few practice rounds on a plate; then just scoop the frosting back into the bag and move on to the cookies.

• Icing and melted chocolate can be drizzled over cookies (using a fork makes it easy) or piped from a pastry bag. Or simply dip the cookies into the icing or chocolate.

• To design with icing, first pipe a thin line of icing around the border of the cookie or in the pattern of your choice; give the icing a few minutes to set, then fill in the design with additional icing. The border will help the icing stay in place.

• Before the frosting, icing, or chocolate becomes firm, press in any decorations you like, including any that might otherwise melt during baking, such as crushed candy canes and chocolate chips. You don't need to ice the whole cookie to apply decorations; use icing as the glue to hold each decoration in place.

• After the topping sets, create decorations using an icing pen—a food-safe pen, available at some supermarkets and at kitchen supply stores, that works like a marker. (Kids love them because they're so easy to use.) Or sprinkle the cookie with sparkly edible glitter for a special effect.

Sweet Almond "Biscotti"

Almond paste adds extra flavor and texture to these delicious cookies. The word biscotti *takes quotation marks here because this cookie doesn't have to be baked twice. However, if you prefer a crisper cookie, you can continue with the second baking.* **Makes about 2½ dozen**

1	**cup unbleached all purpose flour**
1	**teaspoon baking powder**
¼	**teaspoon salt**
½	**cup sugar**
¼	**cup (½ stick) unsalted butter, room temperature**
6	**ounces almond paste, crumbled**
1	**large egg**
⅔	**cup sliced almonds**

Preheat oven to 325°F. Line heavy large rimmed baking sheet with parchment paper. Whisk flour, baking powder, and salt in medium bowl to blend. Using electric mixer, beat sugar and butter in large bowl just to blend. Add almond paste and mix until very well blended. Mix in egg. Stir in flour mixture and almonds. Mix just until combined, occasionally scraping down sides of bowl.

Form dough into two 8-inch-long, 2-inch-wide logs and place on prepared baking sheet, spacing 3 inches apart. Bake until golden brown and tender but set in center, about 40 minutes. Cool on baking sheet. Transfer to cutting board and cut crosswise into ½-inch-thick slices.

DO AHEAD: *Soft biscotti can be made 2 days ahead. Store in airtight containers at room temperature.*

For crisp biscotti, arrange slices, cut side down, on same baking sheet. Continue baking at 325°F until just golden, about 20 minutes. Cool completely (biscotti will crisp as they cool).

DO AHEAD: *Cookies can be made 1 week ahead. Store in airtight containers at room temperature.*

Cookie Basics: Preparing and Rolling Dough

As with pie crust dough, making and rolling out cookie dough requires some care. So follow the recipe instructions carefully and precisely.

• If a recipe says to "beat butter and sugar until light and fluffy," continue beating until the mixture is noticeably paler in color and the texture is light and airy. This step is essential, as it incorporates air into the batter, resulting in a finer product.

• If a recipe calls for chilling the dough, do so. Chilled dough is easier to shape, roll, and mold.

• If the dough is too cold and firm, and cracks when you attempt to roll it out, allow it to stand for a minute or two at room temperature to soften slightly. If it's too soft and sticky, return it to the refrigerator to chill briefly.

• Be sure that the work surface is generously floured.

• Lift and turn the dough as you roll it out so that it does not stick to the work surface; add more flour as necessary.

• Use a ruler to make sure that the cookie dough is rolled to the right thickness; rolling dough too thinly or unevenly can result in burned cookies.

• Dip the cookie cutter into flour before cutting shapes from the dough; this will keep the dough from sticking to the cutter.

• Use a small metal spatula to transfer cutout cookies to the cookie sheet.

Almond, Lemon, and Anise Biscotti with Chocolate

A quick dip in melted chocolate adds a touch of decadence to these crispy cookies. **Makes about 3½ dozen**

1½	**cups sugar**
½	**cup (1 stick) unsalted butter, room temperature**
1	**tablespoon finely grated lemon peel**
2	**large eggs**
3	**cups unbleached all purpose flour, divided**
2	**teaspoons aniseed**
1	**teaspoon baking soda**
½	**teaspoon salt**
1½	**cups slivered almonds**
8	**ounces (about) bittersweet or semisweet chocolate or high-quality white chocolate (such as Lindt or Perugina), chopped**
	Natural unsweetened cocoa powder or powdered sugar

Position rack in center of oven and preheat to 350°F. Line heavy large rimmed baking sheet with parchment paper. Using stand mixer fitted with paddle attachment, beat sugar, butter, and lemon peel in large bowl until blended; mix in eggs. Mix in 1 cup flour, aniseed, baking soda, and salt. Mix in remaining 2 cups flour and almonds.

Transfer dough to lightly floured work surface and gather together. Shape into three 7½-inch-long, 3-inch-wide loaves. Transfer to prepared baking sheet, spacing evenly (at least 3 inches apart). Bake until golden and firm to touch, about 40 minutes. Cool until warm.

Reduce oven temperature to 300°F. Using long metal spatula, carefully transfer loaves to work surface. Using large serrated knife, cut loaves crosswise (not on diagonal) into ½-inch-thick slices. Arrange slices, cut side down, on baking sheet. Bake until golden, about 20 minutes (biscotti will crisp as they cool). Cool completely.

Stir chocolate in heavy medium skillet over very low heat just until melted. Remove skillet with melted chocolate from heat. Dip 1 cut side of biscotti into chocolate; drag biscotti gently on edge of skillet to remove excess chocolate. Arrange biscotti, chocolate side up, on baking sheet. Repeat with remaining biscotti. Chill until chocolate is set. Brush cocoa powder over bittersweet chocolate-dipped biscotti or brush powdered sugar over white chocolate-dipped biscotti.

DO AHEAD: *Can be made ahead. Store in airtight containers at room temperature up to 4 days, or freeze airtight up to 1 month.*

🥢 Lemon-Walnut Biscotti

Because this recipe makes so many biscotti, store some of the cookies in an airtight container and freeze for up to a month. (Wrap them tightly in foil and enclose in a resealable plastic freezer bag. When you're ready to enjoy them, let them come to room temperature. If you prefer them warm, pop them in a 350°F oven for 5 minutes.) These biscotti are very tender, so work carefully with a serrated knife when slicing the logs for their second baking. **Makes about 5 dozen**

3	**cups unbleached all purpose flour**
1	**teaspoon salt**
1	**teaspoon baking powder**
¼	**teaspoon baking soda**
10	**tablespoons (1¼ sticks) unsalted butter, room temperature**
1⅓	**cups sugar**
1½	**tablespoons finely grated lemon peel**
2	**large eggs**
3	**tablespoons fresh lemon juice**
3	**cups chopped walnuts**
1	**large egg, beaten to blend**
	Raw sugar

Whisk flour, salt, baking powder, and baking soda in medium bowl. Using electric mixer, beat butter, sugar, and lemon peel in large bowl until blended. Add eggs 1 at a time, beating just to blend after each addition. Beat in lemon juice, then flour mixture. Stir in walnuts.

Divide dough into 3 equal pieces. Place each piece on sheet of plastic wrap. Using plastic wrap as aid, form dough into 8-inch-long logs; press each slightly, flattening to 2½-inch-wide logs. Enclose in plastic wrap and chill until firm, at least 3 hours.

DO AHEAD: *Can be made 2 days ahead. Keep chilled.*

Position rack in top third of oven and preheat to 325°F. Line heavy large rimmed baking sheet with parchment paper. Unwrap logs and set atop plastic. Brush tops of logs with egg. Sprinkle with raw sugar. Lift logs from plastic and transfer to prepared baking sheet, spacing evenly. Bake until golden brown and just firm to touch, about 50 minutes. Carefully transfer to rack and cool completely. Reduce oven temperature to 300°F.

Line 2 heavy rimmed baking sheets with parchment paper. Using long serrated knife, carefully cut logs crosswise into ⅓-inch-thick slices. Arrange biscotti, cut side down, on prepared baking sheets. Bake cookies until golden brown around edges, about 20 minutes. Cool completely (biscotti will crisp as they cool).

DO AHEAD: *Can be made 3 days ahead. Store in airtight containers at room temperature.*

Hazelnut-Cinnamon Biscotti

Biscotti *means "twice-baked" in Italian; this extra-crisp cookie is delicious dunked into coffee or into a sweet dessert wine.* **Makes about 2½ dozen**

  Nonstick vegetable oil spray
3 cups unbleached all purpose flour
1 tablespoon baking powder
½ teaspoon salt
¼ teaspoon ground cinnamon
1 cup hazelnuts, toasted, husked
¾ cup sugar
½ cup (1 stick) unsalted butter, room temperature
1 tablespoon finely grated orange peel
1 teaspoon vanilla extract
3 large eggs

Preheat oven to 350°F. Spray heavy large rimmed baking sheet with nonstick spray. Mix flour, baking powder, salt, and cinnamon in medium bowl. Coarsely chop hazelnuts in processor. Transfer to small bowl. Combine sugar and butter in processor; blend until fluffy. Add orange peel and vanilla and blend well. Add eggs 1 at a time, blending just until incorporated after each addition. Add flour mixture; using on/off turns, mix until just blended. Add chopped hazelnuts; using on/off turns, mix until just blended.

Turn dough out onto floured work surface. Divide dough in half. Roll each half into 9-inch-long, 2-inch-wide log. Space logs 3 inches apart on prepared baking sheet. Flatten each to 12-inch-long, 2½-inch-wide log. Bake until very light golden and firm to touch, about 25 minutes. Cool on baking sheet 5 minutes. Maintain oven temperature.

Using metal spatula, carefully transfer logs to work surface. Using serrated knife, cut logs diagonally into ¾-inch-wide slices. Place slices, cut side down, on large baking sheet. Bake 15 minutes. Turn biscotti over; bake until light golden and firm, about 15 minutes longer. Transfer biscotti to racks and cool.

DO AHEAD: *Cookies can be made 3 days ahead. Store in airtight container at room temperature.*

Pistachio, Raspberry, and White Chocolate Biscotti

This recipe calls for one end of the biscotti to be dipped into melted chocolate, but don't let that limit your decorating fun. For variety, dip half the biscotti in melted white chocolate and the other half in dark chocolate. Or, if desired, add a few drops of food coloring to the melted white chocolate and drizzle over the biscotti in contrasting colors. Or simply drizzle the melted chocolate over the undipped biscotti. **Makes about 3 dozen**

3	cups unbleached all purpose flour
2	teaspoons baking powder
½	teaspoon salt
1	cup sugar
3	large eggs
2	tablespoons canola oil
2½	teaspoons almond extract
¾	cup raw unsalted natural pistachios
1	cup dried raspberries or chopped dried strawberries (about 5 ounces)
½	cup chopped high-quality white chocolate (such as Lindt or Perugina)
8	ounces high-quality white chocolate (such as Lindt or Perugina) and/or 8 ounces bittersweet or semisweet chocolate, chopped

Preheat oven to 350°F. Line heavy large rimmed baking sheet with parchment paper. Whisk flour, baking powder, and salt in medium bowl to blend. Using electric mixer, beat sugar, eggs, oil, and almond extract in large bowl until well blended. Add flour mixture and beat until smooth. Stir in pistachios, dried berries, and ½ cup chopped white chocolate. Drop dough by heaping tablespoonfuls in two 12-inch-long strips on prepared baking sheet, spacing strips 3 inches apart. Using wet fingertips, shape each strip into 3-inch-wide log, pressing evenly (logs may look slightly lumpy).

Bake logs until lightly browned and almost firm to touch, about 30 minutes. Cool logs on baking sheet 30 minutes. Reduce oven temperature to 325°F.

Carefully transfer logs to cutting board. Line same baking sheet with parchment paper. Cut each log crosswise into generous ½-inch-thick slices. Stand biscotti upright, spacing about ¼ inch apart, in 3 rows on prepared baking sheet. Bake until pale golden (biscotti may be soft but will firm as they cool), about 20 minutes. Cool completely on baking sheet.

Line another large baking sheet with parchment paper. Place 8 ounces chopped white chocolate in medium glass bowl. Place 8 ounces chopped bittersweet chocolate in another medium glass bowl, if desired. Microwave separately on low power in 10-second intervals, stirring in between intervals, just until chocolate is soft to touch, about 40 seconds total (do not overheat or chocolate will burn or seize). Stir chocolate until smooth.

Dip 1 end or 1 side of each biscotti in chocolate; place on prepared baking sheet. Chill until chocolate is set, about 30 minutes.

DO AHEAD: *Can be made ahead. Arrange in single layer in airtight containers and chill up to 5 days, or freeze up to 2 weeks. Bring to room temperature before serving.*

Chocolate-Orange Biscotti

Orange liqueur and finely grated orange peel combine to bring a bright citrus note to chocolaty, nutty, crisp cookies. Because the dough is slightly sticky, dust your hands with flour while forming the logs. These are delicious served with orange sorbet. **Makes about 3 dozen**

2	cups plus 2 tablespoons unbleached all purpose flour
1½	teaspoons baking powder
¼	teaspoon salt
¾	cup sugar
½	cup (1 stick) unsalted butter, room temperature
2	large eggs
2	tablespoons Grand Marnier or other orange liqueur
1	tablespoon finely grated orange peel
1	cup pecans, lightly toasted, coarsely chopped
6	ounces bittersweet or semisweet chocolate, chopped

Line heavy large rimmed baking sheet with parchment paper. Whisk flour, baking powder, and salt in medium bowl to blend. Using electric mixer, beat sugar and butter in large bowl to blend. Beat in eggs 1 at a time, then Grand Marnier and orange peel. Add flour mixture and beat until blended. Stir in pecans and chocolate. Gather dough together; divide in half. Wrap in plastic and freeze 20 minutes to firm.

Position rack in center of oven; preheat to 350°F. Using floured hands, form each dough piece into 14-inch-long, 2½-inch-wide log. Transfer logs to prepared baking sheet, spacing 2 inches apart. Bake until light golden, about 30 minutes. Transfer parchment with logs to rack. Cool 20 minutes. Reduce oven temperature to 300°F.

Place 1 log on cutting board. Using serrated knife, cut log on diagonal into ½-inch-thick slices. Stand slices upright on baking sheet. Repeat with remaining log.

Bake biscotti until dry to touch and pale golden, about 30 minutes. Cool completely on rack.

DO AHEAD: *Cookies can be made 1 week ahead. Store in airtight container at room temperature.*

Vanilla Meringues

These meringues are sweet, crispy treats. For variety, fold in chocolate chips, or substitute almond extract for the vanilla and sprinkle the meringues with sliced almonds before baking. If adding the extra goodies, drop the meringue from a spoon instead of piping it onto the baking sheet. Using superfine sugar (which dissolves easily) is the key to making meringues that are smooth, not grainy.
Makes about 2½ dozen

2	large egg whites, room temperature
1/16	teaspoon cream of tartar
7	tablespoons superfine sugar, divided
	Pinch of salt
¼	teaspoon vanilla extract

Position rack in center of oven and preheat to 200°F. Line large rimmed baking sheet with parchment paper. Using electric mixer, beat egg whites and cream of tartar in medium bowl until firm peaks form when beaters are lifted. Add superfine sugar 1 tablespoon at a time, beating 10 to 15 seconds after each addition. Beat in salt, then vanilla. Continue to beat until sugar is completely dissolved, 15 to 30 seconds longer.

Drop meringue by level tablespoonfuls 1 inch apart onto prepared sheet. Or spoon meringue into large pastry bag fitted with ½-inch plain tip. For each cookie, pipe meringue onto prepared sheet in 1½-inch-diameter round, then lift bag, forming peak in center (meringue will look like candy kiss).

Bake meringues until dry and firm to touch but still white, about 3 hours. Cool completely on sheet, about 30 minutes. Lift meringues off parchment.

DO AHEAD: *Meringues can be made 2 weeks ahead. Store in airtight container at room temperature.*

Hazelnut Meringue Drops

These airy, crunchy meringue nuggets gain distinctive flavor from hazelnuts (yet are surprisingly low in fat and calories). If you don't own a piping bag and star tip, simply spoon the meringue mixture onto prepared baking sheets, forming 1-inch rounds. **Makes about 6 dozen**

	Nonstick vegetable oil spray
½	cup hazelnuts, toasted, husked
4	large egg whites, room temperature
⅛	teaspoon cream of tartar
½	cup sugar, divided
½	teaspoon vanilla extract
2	tablespoons cornstarch

Position 1 rack in center and 1 rack in top third of oven and preheat to 300°F. Spray 2 heavy large rimmed baking sheets with nonstick spray. Finely grind hazelnuts in processor. Using electric mixer, beat egg whites in large bowl until foamy. Add cream of tartar and beat until soft peaks form. Gradually add ¼ cup sugar and beat until stiff and glossy but not dry. Beat in vanilla. Sift cornstarch and remaining ¼ cup sugar into small bowl. Sift half of cornstarch mixture over meringue mixture. Using rubber spatula, carefully fold into meringue. Sift remaining half of cornstarch mixture over and fold into meringue. Gently fold in nuts.

Working in batches, spoon meringue into large pastry bag fitted with large star tip. Pipe meringue onto prepared baking sheets, forming 1-inch rounds and spacing ½ inch apart. Bake until meringues are light golden brown and set, about 35 minutes. Let meringues cool 5 minutes on baking sheets. Carefully transfer meringues to rack and cool completely.

DO AHEAD: *Meringues can be made 2 days ahead. Store in airtight containers at room temperature.*

Chocolate-Dipped Coconut Macaroons

Toasting some of the coconut before adding it to the cookie dough gives these macaroons a rich, nutty flavor. **Makes about 1½ dozen**

5	cups sweetened flaked coconut, divided
½	cup sweetened condensed milk
½	vanilla bean, split lengthwise
2	large egg whites
¼	teaspoon salt
1	tablespoon sugar
8	ounces (about) bittersweet or semisweet chocolate, melted

Position rack in center of oven and preheat to 350°F. Sprinkle 2 cups coconut evenly over large rimmed baking sheet. Toast in oven until golden, stirring occasionally and watching closely to avoid overbrowning, about 12 minutes. Cool slightly. Maintain oven temperature.

Line 2 heavy large rimmed baking sheets with parchment paper or silicone baking mats. Pour sweetened condensed milk into large bowl. Scrape seeds from vanilla bean into milk (reserve bean for another use). Stir in toasted coconut and remaining 3 cups untoasted coconut. Using electric mixer, beat egg whites and salt in another clean large bowl until frothy. Add sugar and beat until soft peaks form. Carefully fold whites into coconut mixture.

Using about 3 tablespoons coconut mixture per cookie, form into 2-inch-diameter mounds on prepared baking sheets, spacing about 2 inches apart. Bake until macaroons are golden brown on bottom, about 14 minutes. Transfer macaroons to rack; cool completely.

Line large baking sheet with waxed paper. Melt chocolate in heavy small saucepan over low heat, stirring constantly. Dip bottoms of macaroons into melted chocolate and transfer to prepared baking sheet, chocolate side down. Freeze until chocolate sets, about 5 minutes. Pull macaroons from waxed paper.

DO AHEAD: *Can be made ahead. Store in waxed paper–lined airtight containers in refrigerator up to 2 days, or freeze up to 2 weeks.*

Sesame-Almond Macaroons

These soft, chewy almond macaroons have the added bonus of toasty sesame flavor. They go particularly well with tea. Be sure not to overbake the cookies, as they will become too crisp. **Makes about 3 dozen**

½	cup plus 1 tablespoon raw sesame seeds (about 3 ounces)
1	7-ounce package almond paste, broken into small pieces
½	cup sugar
2	large egg whites

Preheat oven to 325°F. Sprinkle sesame seeds on large baking sheet. Place in oven; toast until light golden, stirring occasionally, about 20 minutes. Cool.

Line 2 heavy large rimmed baking sheets with foil. Butter and flour foil. Using electric mixer, beat almond paste and sugar until only very small pieces of almond paste remain. Add egg whites and mix on high speed until mixture is smooth, about 5 minutes. Mix in toasted sesame seeds. Drop by rounded teaspoonfuls onto prepared baking sheets, spacing 2 inches apart.

Bake cookies until puffed and pale golden and edges begin to brown, about 14 minutes. Transfer foil with cookies to rack and cool completely. Carefully peel cookies from foil.

DO AHEAD: *Macaroons can be made 2 days ahead. Store in airtight containers at room temperature.*

Linzer Macaroon Sandwiches

In this variation of the classic jam-filled Austrian nut cookie, the nut shortbread is replaced by a slightly chewy almond macaroon. The cookies keep well at room temperature and can also be frozen. They may soften slightly while stored, but they'll still be wonderful. **Makes about 2 dozen**

1²/₃   **cups blanched slivered almonds**
1¹/₃   **cups sugar**
2   **large egg whites**
1   **teaspoon almond extract**
¹/₃   **cup sliced almonds**
¹/₂   **cup raspberry preserves**
2   **tablespoons water**
   Powdered sugar

Position rack in center of oven and preheat to 375°F. Line 2 heavy large rimmed baking sheets with parchment paper. Finely grind slivered almonds and sugar in processor. Add egg whites and almond extract; process until well blended (dough will be sticky).

Using slightly rounded teaspoonful for each cookie, roll dough between damp palms of hands into balls. Place on prepared baking sheets, spacing 1 inch apart. Flatten each ball slightly to 1¼-inch-diameter round. Gently press a few sliced almonds into each cookie.

Bake cookies, 1 baking sheet at a time, until light golden, about 18 minutes. Slide parchment with cookies onto racks and cool completely.

Stir preserves and 2 tablespoons water in heavy small saucepan over medium-high heat until mixture boils. Reduce heat and simmer until mixture thickens slightly, about 4 minutes. Cool slightly.

Spoon ½ teaspoon raspberry preserves onto bottom side of 1 cookie. Top with second cookie, bottom side down. Press to adhere. Repeat with remaining cookies and preserves.

DO AHEAD: *Can be made ahead. Store airtight at room temperature up to 1 week, or freeze up to 1 month. Cookies may soften slightly.*

Sift powdered sugar over cookies.

Pecan Lace Sandwich Cookies with Orange Buttercream

It is especially important to use parchment paper when baking these Florentine-style lace cookies—they are a cross between a cookie and candy, so they tend to be sticky and would otherwise be difficult to remove from the baking sheet. Lining baking sheets with parchment paper creates a nonstick surface, protects the cookie bottoms from burning, and ensures easy cleanup. **Makes about 1½ dozen**

Cookies
¹/₄   **cup (½ stick) unsalted butter, room temperature**
¹/₃   **cup sugar**
2   **tablespoons light corn syrup**
¹/₃   **cup unbleached all purpose flour**
1   **cup coarsely ground pecans**
1   **teaspoon vanilla extract**

Filling
1   **cup powdered sugar**
¹/₄   **cup (½ stick) unsalted butter, room temperature**
1   **tablespoon orange juice**
³/₄   **teaspoon finely grated orange peel**

COOKIES: Position rack in center of oven and preheat to 350°F. Line 2 heavy large rimmed baking sheets with parchment paper. Stir butter, sugar, and corn syrup in heavy medium saucepan over low heat until melted and smooth. Bring to boil over medium-high heat, stirring constantly. Remove from heat. Stir in flour. Add pecans and vanilla; stir to combine.

Drop dough by teaspoonfuls onto prepared baking sheets, spacing 2 inches apart. Bake cookies, 1 sheet at a time, until bubbling and lightly browned, about 11 minutes. Cool on sheets 10 minutes. Carefully transfer to rack; cool completely.

FILLING: Whisk all ingredients in medium bowl until smooth. Spread 1 teaspoon filling onto bottom of 1 cookie. Top with second cookie, bottom side down, pressing lightly to adhere. Repeat with remaining cookies and filling.

DO AHEAD: *Can be made 2 days ahead. Store between sheets of waxed paper in airtight container at room temperature.*

Pecan Lace Sandwich Cookies with Orange Buttercream

Vanilla Crescents with Pistachio Filling

Tender crescent-shaped pastry encloses a filling that resembles marzipan in texture, but has a delicate pistachio flavor. The filling, pastry, and aromatic vanilla sugar can all be made ahead, but the cookies are best eaten the same day they're baked. **Makes 2 dozen**

Vanilla Sugar

¾   **cup sugar**

1   **2-inch piece vanilla bean, split lengthwise, chopped**

Filling

1   **cup unsalted natural pistachios**

1   **large egg white**

1   **drop of vanilla extract**

1   **drop of almond extract**

Dough

1¼   **cups sifted unbleached all purpose flour (sifted, then measured)**

⅛   **teaspoon salt**

½   **cup (1 stick) chilled unsalted butter, cut into ½-inch cubes**

⅓   **cup sour cream**

1   **large egg yolk**

1   **egg yolk, beaten to blend with 1 teaspoon water (for glaze)**

VANILLA SUGAR: Mix sugar and vanilla bean in processor 2 minutes, stopping every 30 seconds to scrape down sides of bowl. Spoon into jar and seal tightly. Let stand at room temperature at least 1 day.

DO AHEAD: *Can be made 3 days ahead. Store at room temperature.*

FILLING: Sift vanilla sugar through fine strainer set over small bowl. Combine pistachios, 2 tablespoons vanilla sugar, egg white, vanilla extract, and almond extract in processor. Using on/off turns, blend until chunky paste forms, occasionally scraping down sides of bowl. Transfer filling to bowl.

DO AHEAD: *Can be made 1 day ahead. Cover and chill.*

DOUGH: Place flour and salt in processor. Add butter; using on/off turns, cut in until mixture resembles coarse meal. Add sour cream and egg yolk; using on/off turns, blend until small moist clumps form. Turn dough out onto plastic wrap; flatten into disk. Wrap and chill at least 2 hours.

DO AHEAD: *Can be made 1 day ahead. Keep chilled.*

Position rack in center of oven and preheat to 375°F. Line 2 heavy large rimmed baking sheets with parchment paper. Lightly butter parchment. Divide dough disk in half. Wrap and chill 1 half. Shape remaining dough half into round. Sprinkle 1 tablespoon vanilla sugar on work surface. Place dough round atop sugar. Sprinkle 1 tablespoon vanilla sugar over. Roll dough out to 12-inch round, about ⅛ inch thick, sprinkling top and bottom of dough round with 2 tablespoons more vanilla sugar while rolling. Using fluted pastry cutter, cut dough round into 12 wedges. Shape half of pistachio filling by slightly rounded teaspoonfuls into 12 ovals. Set 1 oval at base of each wedge. Roll wedges up from base to point to form cylinder. Arrange cylinders on prepared baking sheet. Form into horseshoes (crescents will form while baking). Repeat with remaining dough half, vanilla sugar, and filling. Bake 15 minutes. Meanwhile, whisk 1 tablespoon vanilla sugar into glaze.

Brush glaze lightly over hot crescents. Continue baking until light golden, about 5 minutes. Slide parchment with crescents onto rack and cool 5 minutes. Remove crescents from parchment and cool completely on rack.

DO AHEAD: *Crescents can be made 1 day ahead. Store in airtight container at room temperature.*

Hazelnut-Apricot Windows

These shortbread-like cookies are inspired by the Austrian Linzertorte, which also features a jam filling inside a buttery crust flavored with nuts and lemon peel. Dividing the dough into four equal parts and working with only one portion at a time ensures that the dough remains properly chilled for easy rolling. The cookies work just as well with raspberry, cherry, or plum preserves. **Makes about 4 dozen**

1	**cup hazelnuts, toasted, husked**
1	**tablespoon plus ⅔ cup sugar**
14	**tablespoons (1¾ sticks) unsalted butter, room temperature**
1	**large egg**
1	**large egg yolk**
1	**teaspoon finely grated lemon peel**
½	**teaspoon lemon extract**
½	**teaspoon salt**
¼	**teaspoon ground cinnamon**
2⅔	**cups unbleached all purpose flour**
	Apricot preserves
	Powdered sugar

Combine hazelnuts and 1 tablespoon sugar in processor; grind nuts finely. Using electric mixer, beat remaining ⅔ cup sugar and butter in large bowl until fluffy. Beat in hazelnut mixture, then egg, egg yolk, lemon peel, lemon extract, salt, and cinnamon. Beat in flour. Gather dough into ball. Divide into 4 equal pieces. Flatten each into disk and wrap in plastic. Chill at least 1 hour.

DO AHEAD: *Can be made 2 days ahead. Keep chilled.*

Position 1 rack in top third and 1 rack in bottom third of oven and preheat to 325°F. Line 2 heavy large rimmed baking sheets with parchment paper. Roll out 1 dough disk between sheets of parchment paper to scant ¼-inch thickness, sprinkling dough with flour to prevent sticking and occasionally peeling off top parchment to remove wrinkles. Peel off top sheet of parchment. Using 2-inch-diameter fluted pastry cutter, cut out cookies. Transfer to prepared baking sheets, spacing ½ inch apart. Gather dough scraps and reroll, cutting out more cookies and placing on baking sheets. Using 1-inch-diameter fluted pastry cutter, cut out centers from half of cookies, making rings. Gather centers as scraps. Bake cookies 5 minutes. Reverse baking sheets and bake cookies until light golden, about 6 minutes longer. Cool cookies on baking sheets 2 minutes. Transfer to racks and cool completely. Repeat with remaining dough.

Arrange whole cookie rounds on work surface. Drop generous ½ teaspoon preserves in center of each. Arrange cookie rings on work surface. Sift powdered sugar over. Place 1 cookie ring atop each whole cookie round, forming sandwich with preserves in cutout center.

DO AHEAD: *Can be made 3 days ahead. Store in airtight containers between sheets of waxed paper in refrigerator.*

Lemon–Poppy Seed Sandwich Cookies

These are wonderful sugar cookies with the crunch of poppy seeds and a lemony cream cheese filling. Assemble the sandwiches shortly before serving to keep them crisp. If you like, skip the filling and serve the tasty cookies on their own. If you can't find a fluted pastry cutter, use a plain round cutter; the only thing that will be missing is the scalloped edge. **Makes about 2 dozen**

Cookies

2¾	cups unbleached all purpose flour
½	teaspoon salt
½	teaspoon baking powder
1	cup (2 sticks) unsalted butter, room temperature
1¼	cups sugar
1	large egg
2	tablespoons poppy seeds
2	teaspoons finely grated lemon peel
1	teaspoon vanilla extract
½	teaspoon lemon extract

Filling

8	ounces Philadelphia-brand cream cheese, room temperature
⅓	cup plus 1 tablespoon sugar
½	teaspoon lemon extract
¼	teaspoon vanilla extract

Technique Tip: A Few Good Turns

When rolling out dough on a lightly floured work surface, lift and rotate the dough frequently to keep it from sticking, and dust the surface lightly with additional flour as needed.

COOKIES: Whisk flour, salt, and baking powder in medium bowl to blend. Using electric mixer, beat butter in large bowl until light. Gradually beat in sugar. Beat in egg, then poppy seeds, lemon peel, and both extracts. Mix in flour mixture in 3 additions. Gather dough into ball. Divide dough in half; flatten each half into disk. Wrap each in plastic and chill 2 hours.

Position rack in center of oven and preheat to 325°F. Butter 2 heavy large rimmed baking sheets. Roll out 1 dough disk on floured surface to ⅛-inch thickness. Using 2½-inch-diameter fluted pastry cutter, cut out cookies. Arrange cookies 1 inch apart on prepared baking sheets. Gather dough scraps; reroll and cut out more cookies. Chill cookies on baking sheets 15 minutes.

Bake cookies, 1 baking sheet at a time, until edges just begin to color, about 18 minutes. Cool cookies on baking sheets 3 minutes. Transfer cookies to racks and cool completely. Repeat rolling, cutting, and baking with remaining dough.

DO AHEAD: *Can be made ahead. Store in airtight container at room temperature up to 2 weeks, or freeze up to 1 month.*

FILLING: Beat all ingredients in large bowl until light and fluffy. Spread 2 teaspoons filling over bottom side of 1 cookie. Press second cookie, bottom side down, onto filling. Repeat with remaining cookies and filling.

DO AHEAD: *Can be made 2 hours ahead. Cover and chill.*

Lemon Ladyfinger Sandwiches

Ladyfingers are little sponge cakes. You will need a pastry bag and a No. 6 star tip for this recipe, as the ladyfingers are shaped by piping the batter onto foil in short, thin lines that resemble fingers. The dainty sandwich cookies are assembled just before serving, but the tart lemon curd filling can be made two days ahead. These would be an excellent addition to an afternoon tea. **Makes 18**

Lemon Curd

¼	cup fresh lemon juice
2	teaspoons cornstarch
6	tablespoons sugar
3	tablespoons unsalted butter
3	large egg yolks, room temperature
1	large egg, room temperature
2	teaspoons finely grated lemon peel

Ladyfingers

3	large egg yolks, room temperature
2½	teaspoons fresh lemon juice
½	teaspoon vanilla extract
½	teaspoon finely grated lemon peel
3	large egg whites
2	pinches of salt
½	cup superfine sugar
⅔	cup sifted unbleached all purpose flour (sifted, then measured)
½	cup powdered sugar

LEMON CURD: Whisk lemon juice and cornstarch in small bowl until cornstarch dissolves. Combine sugar, butter, egg yolks, egg, and lemon peel in heavy small skillet. Whisk in dissolved cornstarch mixture. Whisk constantly over medium-low heat until mixture is thickened and smooth, about 5 minutes. Transfer lemon curd to bowl. Press plastic wrap directly onto surface of curd to prevent skin from forming. Chill until cold.

DO AHEAD: *Can be made 2 days ahead. Keep chilled.*

LADYFINGERS: Position rack in center of oven and preheat to 325°F. Dab butter in each corner of 2 heavy large rimmed baking sheets. Line baking sheets with foil, leaving 1-inch overhang at short ends. Butter and flour foil, shaking off excess.

Whisk egg yolks, lemon juice, vanilla, and lemon peel in small bowl. Using electric mixer, beat egg whites and salt in large bowl until soft peaks form. Gradually add superfine sugar and beat until stiff and shiny. Gently fold in yolk mixture. Sift in flour in 4 additions, folding gently after each addition. Spoon batter into pastry bag fitted with No. 6 star tip. Pipe eighteen 4-inch-long ladyfingers onto each baking sheet. Sift powdered sugar over ladyfingers. Let stand 2 minutes. Using fingertip, press down points at ends of ladyfingers. Bake until lightly colored and crisp, 17 to 18 minutes. Transfer foil with ladyfingers to rack and let cool 15 minutes. Gently peel ladyfingers off foil and cool completely on rack. Fill within several hours, or layer with paper towels in airtight container and store overnight.

Spread 2 teaspoons lemon curd on flat surface of 1 ladyfinger. Press flat surface of another ladyfinger onto lemon curd to form sandwich. Set on platter. Repeat with remaining ladyfingers and lemon curd. Serve immediately.

Chocolate–Chocolate Chip Cookies with Mocha Cream Filling

These ultra-rich and chocolaty sandwich cookies have creamy, coffee-spiked centers. **Makes 20**

Filling

½   cup semisweet chocolate chips (about 3 ounces)
½   cup heavy whipping cream
1   tablespoon instant coffee crystals
¾   cup powdered sugar
6   tablespoons (¾ stick) unsalted butter, room temperature
1   teaspoon vanilla extract

Cookies

1   cup unbleached all purpose flour
3   tablespoons natural unsweetened cocoa powder
1   teaspoon baking soda
½   teaspoon salt
½   cup (1 stick) unsalted butter, room temperature
⅔   cup (packed) golden brown sugar
¼   cup sugar
1   large egg
2   teaspoons water
1   teaspoon vanilla extract
1   teaspoon instant coffee crystals
2   cups semisweet chocolate chips (about 12 ounces)
1   cup pecans, coarsely chopped

Equipment Tip: Sliding Help

When cookies are baked on parchment paper or a silicone baking mat, such as Silpat, transferring them to a cooling rack becomes a simple task. There's no need to transfer the cookies one by one; just slide the sheet of parchment (or the baking mat), cookies and all, off the baking sheet and onto the rack. Once cooled, the cookies will be firm enough to peel off of the parchment paper or the baking mat for picture-perfect results.

FILLING: Stir chocolate chips, cream, and coffee crystals in heavy small saucepan over medium heat until chocolate melts and coffee dissolves. Cool to room temperature, about 20 minutes. Using electric mixer, beat powdered sugar, butter, and vanilla in medium bowl until blended. Beat in chocolate mixture. Chill until beginning to firm, about 8 minutes.

DO AHEAD: *Can be made 2 days ahead. Cover and keep chilled. Before using, let stand at room temperature until just soft enough to spread, about 2 hours.*

COOKIES: Position rack in center of oven and preheat to 325°F. Line 2 heavy large rimmed baking sheets with parchment paper. Sift flour, cocoa, baking soda, and salt into medium bowl. Using electric mixer, beat butter and both sugars in large bowl until well blended. Add egg, 2 teaspoons water, vanilla, and coffee crystals and blend well. Beat in flour mixture. Stir in chocolate chips and chopped pecans.

Drop dough by tablespoonfuls onto prepared sheets, spacing 2 inches apart. Bake cookies, 1 baking sheet at a time, until tops are just firm to touch and no longer shiny, about 13 minutes. Cool cookies on baking sheets 10 minutes. Transfer cookies to racks and cool completely.

Place half of cookies, bottom side up, on work surface. Spread each with 1 tablespoon filling, leaving ¼-inch plain border. Top each with second cookie, bottom side down, pressing to adhere. Cover and chill at least 2 hours.

DO AHEAD: *Can be made 2 days ahead. Keep chilled.*

Arrange cookies on platter and serve cold.

Milk Chocolate–Peanut Butter Sandwich Cookies

These treats are pure decadence. Be sure to use creamy peanut butter—not old-fashioned or freshly ground—for the best consistency in the cookie batter and the filling. **Makes about 2½ dozen**

Cookies

1¾	cups unbleached all purpose flour
1	teaspoon baking powder
½	teaspoon baking soda
½	teaspoon coarse kosher salt
½	cup plus ⅓ cup powdered sugar
½	cup plus 1 tablespoon (packed) dark brown sugar
6	tablespoons (¾ stick) unsalted butter, room temperature
½	cup creamy peanut butter
½	cup vegetable oil
1½	teaspoons vanilla extract
1	large egg
1⅓	cups milk chocolate chips (about 8 ounces)

Filling

3	ounces high-quality milk chocolate (such as Lindt or Perugina), chopped
¼	cup creamy peanut butter
2	tablespoons powdered sugar
¼	teaspoon coarse kosher salt
6	tablespoons heavy whipping cream

COOKIES: Position rack in center of oven and preheat to 350°F. Whisk flour, baking powder, baking soda, and coarse salt in medium bowl to blend. Using electric mixer, beat powdered sugar, brown sugar, and butter in large bowl to blend. Add peanut butter and beat until creamy. Gradually beat in oil and vanilla, then egg. Add flour mixture and beat just until blended. Stir in milk chocolate chips.

Drop cookie dough by level tablespoonfuls onto ungreased heavy rimmed baking sheets, spacing about 1½ inches apart. Bake cookies, 1 baking sheet at a time, until puffed and golden brown, about 12 minutes. Cool slightly, then transfer cookies to rack to cool completely.

FILLING: Place chopped chocolate, peanut butter, powdered sugar, and coarse salt in medium bowl. Bring whipping cream to boil in heavy small saucepan. Pour hot cream over chocolate mixture; stir until mixture is melted and smooth. Chill until filling is thick and spreadable, about 1 hour.

Spread about 1 rounded teaspoonful filling onto bottom side of 1 cookie. Top with second cookie, bottom side down, forming sandwich. Repeat with remaining filling and cookies.

DO AHEAD: *Cookies can be made 1 day ahead. Store in airtight container at room temperature.*

♥♥ Cream Cheese Strudel Cookies

Strudel is an Austrian pastry in which the filling is wrapped in a multilayered dough. This recipe uses cream cheese to create a flaky, tender dough that is similar to that of a strudel; the dough is then spread with preserves, topped with coconut and cherries, rolled up jelly-roll style, and sliced into individual strudel cookies and baked. If you're not a fan of coconut, substitute an equal amount of chopped nuts. **Makes about 2 dozen**

1	cup unbleached all purpose flour
4	ounces chilled Philadelphia-brand cream cheese, cut into ½-inch cubes
½	cup (1 stick) chilled unsalted butter, cut into ½-inch cubes
½	cup apricot preserves, divided
1	cup sweetened flaked coconut, divided
1	cup dried tart or Bing cherries, divided

Combine flour, cream cheese, and butter in processor; blend until moist clumps form. Gather dough into ball; flatten into square. Wrap in plastic; freeze until cold enough to roll, about 15 minutes.

DO AHEAD: *Can be made 1 day ahead. Keep chilled.*

Preheat oven to 375°F. Butter heavy large rimmed baking sheet. Cut dough crosswise in half. Roll out each half on floured surface to 12x8-inch rectangle. Spread each with ¼ cup preserves. Top each with ½ cup coconut and ½ cup cherries. Starting at 1 long side, roll dough up jelly-roll style; pinch long seam together to seal. Cut each roll crosswise into 12 pieces. Arrange pieces, cut side up, on prepared sheet. Flatten each to ½-inch thickness.

Bake cookies until golden brown, about 25 minutes. Transfer to rack and cool completely.

DO AHEAD: *Cookies can be made 1 day ahead. Store in airtight container at room temperature.*

♥♥ Cottage Cheese Rugelach with Walnuts

Rugelach are classic cookies from the Jewish culinary repertoire. The surprise ingredient in this version is cottage cheese (most rugelach is made with cream cheese). The cottage cheese makes for extra-tender, rich cookies. **Makes 32**

⅔	cup small-curd cottage cheese
⅔	cup plus 3 tablespoons non-hydrogenated stick margarine, room temperature
1⅓	cups unbleached all purpose flour
½	cup (packed) golden brown sugar
½	cup chopped walnuts
½	teaspoon ground cinnamon
½	teaspoon vanilla extract
1	egg, beaten to blend with 2 tablespoons milk

Mix cottage cheese and ⅔ cup margarine in medium bowl. Stir in flour. Knead in bowl until dough is smooth, about 1 minute. Divide dough in half. Flatten each half into disk. Wrap each in plastic and freeze until firm enough to roll out, about 10 minutes.

Meanwhile, combine remaining 3 tablespoons margarine, brown sugar, walnuts, cinnamon, and vanilla in processor. Blend until almost smooth paste forms.

Preheat oven to 350°F. Line heavy large rimmed baking sheet with parchment paper. Roll out 1 dough disk on lightly floured surface to 10-inch-diameter round. Spread half of brown sugar mixture evenly over. Cut round into 16 wedges. Starting at wide ends, roll up wedges to point to form cylinders. Bend ends in, forming crescents. Transfer to prepared baking sheet. Repeat with remaining dough disk and brown sugar mixture.

Brush egg mixture over crescents. Bake until light brown and baked through, about 25 minutes. Cool 5 minutes on baking sheet. Transfer cookies to racks and cool completely.

DO AHEAD: *Cookies can be made 2 days ahead. Store in airtight containers at room temperature.*

Chocolate–Candy Cane Cookies

These festive chocolate sandwich cookies are first filled with peppermint buttercream, then the edges are rolled in crushed candy canes for a festive look. The cookies freeze well for up to two weeks. **Makes about 1½ dozen**

Cookies

1¾ cups unbleached all purpose flour
½ cup unsweetened cocoa powder (preferably Dutch-process)
¼ teaspoon salt
1 cup sugar
¾ cup (1½ sticks) unsalted butter, room temperature
1 large egg

Filling

1 cup plus 2 tablespoons powdered sugar
¾ cup (1½ sticks) unsalted butter, room temperature
¾ teaspoon peppermint extract
2 drops (or more) red food coloring

½ cup crushed red-and-white-striped candy canes or hard peppermint candies (about 4 ounces)

Technique Tip: **A Touch of Glass**
Flattening the cookies with the bottom of a drinking glass before baking them makes the edges of the dough crack slightly, forming a pretty, scalloped look.

COOKIES: Whisk flour, cocoa, and salt in medium bowl to blend. Using electric mixer, beat sugar and butter in large bowl until well blended. Beat in egg. Add flour mixture and beat until blended. Chill dough 1 hour.

Position rack in center of oven and preheat to 350°F. Line 2 heavy large rimmed baking sheets with parchment paper. Scoop out dough by level tablespoonfuls, then roll into smooth balls. Place balls on prepared baking sheets, spacing about 2 inches apart. Using bottom of glass or hands, flatten each ball to 2-inch-diameter round (edges will crack). Bake 1 sheet at a time until cookies no longer look wet and small indentation appears when tops of cookies are touched lightly with fingers, about 11 minutes (do not overbake or cookies will become too crisp). Cool on baking sheet 5 minutes. Transfer cookies to racks and cool completely.

FILLING: Using electric mixer, beat powdered sugar and butter in medium bowl until well blended. Add peppermint extract and 2 drops food coloring. Beat until light pink and well blended, adding more food coloring by dropfuls if darker pink color is desired.

Spread 2 generous teaspoons filling evenly over bottom side of 1 cookie, spreading to edges. Top with another cookie, bottom side down, pressing gently to adhere. Repeat with remaining cookies and filling.

Place crushed candy canes on plate. Roll edges of cookie sandwiches in crushed candies (candies will adhere to filling).

DO AHEAD: *Can be made ahead. Store in single layer in airtight container at room temperature up to 3 days, or freeze up to 2 weeks.*

Glazed Raisin-Nut Spice Cookies

These diamond-shaped cookies, called papassinos *in Italy, are especially good with a cup of coffee. Spoon the glaze over the cookies while they are hot; when the glaze melts slightly from the heat, it will be easier to spread. The flavor of these cookies gets even better after a few days.* **Makes about 2½ dozen**

Nonstick vegetable oil spray
1 cup powdered sugar
8 teaspoons (about) whole milk, divided
1 cup whole almonds, toasted, cooled
½ cup walnut pieces, toasted, cooled
1¾ cups all purpose flour
¾ cup (1½ sticks) unsalted butter, cut into ½-inch cubes, room temperature
⅔ cup sugar
1 teaspoon finely grated lemon peel
1 teaspoon finely grated orange peel
1 teaspoon aniseed
¾ teaspoon salt
½ teaspoon ground cinnamon
¼ teaspoon ground cloves
¼ teaspoon baking soda
2 large egg yolks
1 cup golden raisins

Position rack in center of oven and preheat to 350°F. Spray 2 heavy large rimmed baking sheets with nonstick spray.

Place powdered sugar in small bowl. Mix in enough milk by teaspoonfuls (about 5) to form thick, smooth glaze. Cover glaze; set aside. Combine almonds and walnuts in processor. Using on/off turns, blend until most nuts are reduced to ¼-inch pieces (some will be very finely ground).

Combine flour, butter, sugar, lemon peel, orange peel, aniseed, salt, cinnamon, cloves, and baking soda in large bowl. Using electric mixer, beat at low speed until fine meal forms. Add egg yolks and beat until clumps form. Add ground nuts and raisins. Beat until dough holds together, adding milk by teaspoonfuls (about 3) if dough is dry. Knead dough briefly in bowl to compact. Divide dough into 3 equal pieces.

Roll out 1 dough piece on lightly floured surface to ¼- to ⅓-inch-thick rectangle. Cut lengthwise into 2-inch-wide strips. Cut each strip on diagonal into 1½- to 2-inch diamonds. Transfer diamonds to prepared baking sheet. Gather dough scraps and reserve. Repeat with remaining dough. Reroll scraps, cutting out more cookies, until all dough is used.

Bake cookies, 1 sheet at a time, until golden, about 17 minutes. Spoon generous ½ teaspoon glaze over each hot cookie and spread with back of spoon to coat. Let cookies stand on baking sheets until completely cool and glaze is set.

DO AHEAD: *Can be made 1 week ahead. Store in airtight container between sheets of waxed paper at room temperature.*

Classic Christmas Cutout Cookies

If you prefer thick cookies, roll the dough out to ⅜-inch thickness and bake the cookies a little longer. The number of cookies produced here depends on the thickness of the dough and the size of the cookie cutters. **Makes about 3 dozen**

2⅔	cups unbleached all purpose flour
1	teaspoon baking powder
½	teaspoon salt
1	cup (2 sticks) unsalted butter, room temperature
¾	cup sugar
3	large egg yolks
2	teaspoons vanilla extract
	Assorted colored sugar crystals or sprinkles

Whisk flour, baking powder, and salt in medium bowl to blend. Using electric mixer, beat butter and sugar in large bowl until light and fluffy. Mix in egg yolks and vanilla. Stir in flour mixture. Divide dough into 4 equal portions; flatten into disks. Wrap each disk in plastic and chill until firm, about 2 hours.

DO AHEAD: *Can be made 2 days ahead. Keep chilled. Let soften slightly at room temperature, if necessary, before rolling out.*

Preheat oven to 350°F. Line heavy large rimmed baking sheets with parchment paper or silicone baking mats. Roll out 1 dough disk on lightly floured surface to ¼-inch thickness, frequently lifting and rotating dough to prevent sticking. Cut out cookies with desired cookie cutters and transfer to prepared baking sheets. Gather dough scraps; reroll and cut out additional cookies.

Sprinkle cookies decoratively with assorted colored sugars or sprinkles. Bake until just golden brown at edges, about 12 minutes. Transfer cookies to racks and cool completely. Repeat with remaining dough disks and colored sugars.

More to Try: The Frosted Look

These cookies are also beautiful topped with an icing made with meringue powder, a fine white powder used in place of fresh egg whites. It's available in the baking aisle of many supermarkets.

Bake cookies without colored sugars and cool completely. Store cooled cookies in airtight container at room temperature until ready to decorate.

Whisk ¼ cup meringue powder and ½ cup room-temperature water in large bowl to blend. Let stand until powder dissolves, about 5 minutes. Using electric mixer, beat meringue mixture until medium peaks form. Gradually add 4 cups powdered sugar, beating until thick, glossy, firm peaks form. Mix in about 3 tablespoons water, 1 tablespoon at a time, until icing is just thin enough to drizzle thickly.

Dip surface of undecorated cooled baked cookies into icing to coat lightly. Shake off excess icing back into bowl. Using offset metal spatula, gently wipe off any excess icing, if necessary. Sprinkle colored sugars decoratively over icing. Let stand until icing sets, about 2 hours.

DO AHEAD: *Can be made 1 week ahead. Store cookies in single layers between sheets of waxed paper in airtight containers at room temperature.*

Stained Glass Lemon Cookies

Ground hard candies melt in the center cutouts of these cookies while they bake, achieving a gorgeous stained glass effect. If you don't have small cookie cutters (about 1 inch in diameter) to cut the "windows" from the centers, use the wide end of a small pastry bag tip instead. These cookies would make a striking gift displayed in a glass canister tied with a brightly colored ribbon.

Makes about 2½ dozen

1	cup (2 sticks) unsalted butter, room temperature
¾	cup sugar
1	large egg yolk
2	teaspoons finely grated lemon peel
1	teaspoon vanilla extract
2¼	cups unbleached all purpose flour
½	teaspoon salt
6	ounces (about) red and/or green hard candies
	Additional sugar

Using electric mixer, beat butter and sugar in large bowl until well blended. Beat in egg yolk, lemon peel, and vanilla. Add flour and salt and beat until mixture begins to clump together. Divide dough into 3 equal pieces. Flatten each piece into disk; wrap each in plastic and chill at least 4 hours or overnight.

DO AHEAD: *Can be made 2 days ahead. Keep chilled. Soften dough slightly at room temperature before rolling out.*

Roll out each dough disk between 2 sheets of parchment paper to ¼-inch thickness. Transfer rolled-out dough disks (still on parchment) to baking sheets and chill 30 minutes.

Finely grind red and/or green hard candies separately in processor. Transfer each color of candy to separate small bowl; cover candies and set aside. Position 1 rack in center and 1 rack in top third of oven and preheat to 375°F. Line 2 heavy large rimmed baking sheets with parchment paper. Working with 1 rolled-out dough disk at a time, peel off top layer of parchment paper; use 2¼- to 2¾-inch-diameter cookie cutter or biscuit cutter to cut out cookies [1]. Using small (about 1-inch-diameter) cookie cutter, make cutouts in center of each cookie [2].

Transfer cookies to prepared baking sheets. Spoon ground hard candies into cookie cutouts [3], filling cutouts completely to same thickness as cookies.

(continued next page)

Stained Glass Lemon Cookies *(continued)*

Sprinkle cookies lightly with additional sugar. Return cookies and dough scraps to refrigerator; chill 15 minutes. Repeat with remaining dough disks, ground hard candies, and additional sugar. Reroll dough scraps and cut out additional cookies. Place on baking sheets; fill with hard candies and sprinkle with additional sugar. Chill filled cookies on baking sheets 15 minutes.

Bake cookies until firm and light golden and ground candies look translucent, 8 to 12 minutes. Cool cookies completely on baking sheets.

DO AHEAD: *Can be made ahead. Store in airtight container at room temperature up to 1 week, or freeze up to 1 month.*

Cookie Ornaments

To create hanging decorations, use a straw to make a hole near the top of the cookie—leave at least half an inch of dough around the hole so that the cookie doesn't break when it's hung.

Maple Stars

Crisp, buttery, maple-flavored cookies are transformed by a sprinkling of bright white sparkling sugar crystals, which can be found at some supermarkets, cake and candy supply stores, and online at lacuisineus.com.
Makes about 6 dozen

Cookies
2¾ **cups unbleached all purpose flour**
2 **teaspoons baking powder**
¼ **teaspoon salt**
1 **cup (2 sticks) unsalted butter, room temperature**
1 **cup sugar**
½ **cup (packed) golden brown sugar**
1 **large egg**
2 **teaspoons maple extract**

Icing
2¼ **cups powdered sugar**
3 **tablespoons whole milk**
   Bright white sparkling sugar crystals or other white sprinkles

COOKIES: Whisk flour, baking powder, and salt in medium bowl to blend. Using electric mixer, beat butter and both sugars in large bowl until light and fluffy. Beat in egg and maple extract. Beat in flour mixture until just blended. Divide dough in half. Flatten each half into disk; wrap disks separately in plastic and chill until firm enough to roll out, about 1 hour.

DO AHEAD: *Can be made 1 day ahead.*

Preheat oven to 375°F. Line heavy large rimmed baking sheets with parchment paper. Roll out 1 dough disk on lightly floured work surface to 11-inch-diameter round, about ⅓ inch thick. Using 2-inch star-shaped cookie cutter dipped into flour, cut out cookies from dough. Place cookies on prepared baking sheets, spacing 1 inch apart. Reroll dough scraps on lightly floured surface and cut out additional cookies. Repeat with remaining dough disk.

Bake cookies until lightly browned, about 12 minutes. Cool cookies on baking sheets 5 minutes, then transfer to racks and cool completely.

ICING: Stir powdered sugar and milk in medium bowl until smooth (icing will be thick). Using small offset spatula or butter knife, spread icing over top of 1 cookie, then sprinkle top with sugar crystals. Repeat with remaining cookies, icing, and sugar crystals. Let cookies stand at room temperature until icing is dry and firm, at least 1 hour.

DO AHEAD: *Can be made ahead. Store in single layer in airtight containers at room temperature up to 5 days, or freeze up to 2 weeks.*

New England Molasses Gingerbread Cookies

A ginger cookie without the "snap," this is a soft cake-like version with all the flavor of the classic. Because the dough is soft, be sure to keep it very cold before rolling it out. Once you've cut out the cookies, chill them in the refrigerator until they are firm. This will help them to hold their shape as they bake. **Makes about 4 dozen**

Dough

6	cups (about) unbleached all purpose flour, divided
1	tablespoon ground cinnamon
2	teaspoons ground ginger
1½	teaspoons ground cloves
¾	teaspoon salt
11	tablespoons (1 stick plus 3 tablespoons) unsalted butter, room temperature
⅔	cup non-hydrogenated solid vegetable shortening
1	cup sugar
1	cup mild-flavored (light) molasses
1½	teaspoons finely grated lemon peel
1	large egg
¼	cup chilled buttermilk
2	teaspoons water
1	teaspoon baking soda

Icing

3	cups powdered sugar
1½	tablespoons fresh lemon juice
1½	teaspoons light corn syrup
	Water
	Food coloring (optional)
	Decorations (such as colored sugar crystals)

DOUGH: Combine 5¼ cups flour, cinnamon, ginger, cloves, and salt in medium bowl; whisk to blend well. Using electric mixer, beat butter and shortening in large bowl to blend. Add sugar, molasses, and lemon peel and beat until smooth. Beat in egg and buttermilk. Stir 2 teaspoons water and baking soda in small cup to blend; beat into butter mixture. Beat in flour mixture in 2 additions. Stir in more flour, ¼ cup at a time, until slightly firm dough forms. Divide dough into 3 equal parts. Shape each into disk. Wrap each disk in plastic and chill until firm enough to roll out, at least 2 hours.

DO AHEAD: *Can be made 2 days ahead. Keep chilled. Soften only slightly at room temperature before rolling out.*

Working with 1 disk at a time, roll out dough between sheets of parchment paper or waxed paper to 16x12-inch rectangle, occasionally lifting paper to smooth out wrinkles. Using 4- to 5-inch gingerbread cookie cutters, cut out gingerbread people. Pull away excess dough around cutouts; flatten, wrap, and chill excess dough. Slide rimless baking sheet or inverted baking sheet under waxed paper with cutouts and chill until firm. Repeat with remaining dough disks, chilling cutouts on waxed paper on baking sheets. Roll out excess dough and make more cookies, using all of dough.

DO AHEAD: *Can be made 1 day ahead. Cover and keep chilled.*

Position rack in center of oven and preheat to 350°F. Using thin metal spatula, lift chilled cookies off waxed paper and transfer to baking sheet, spacing 1 inch apart. Bake until darker at edges and just firm to touch in center, about 12 minutes. Cool on sheet 5 minutes. Transfer cookies to rack and cool completely. Bake remaining cookies, 1 sheet at a time.

ICING: Sift powdered sugar into medium bowl. Mix in lemon juice and corn syrup. Mix in enough water by teaspoonfuls to form smooth icing soft enough to pipe but firm enough to hold shape. Divide into 3 or 4 portions and tint with food coloring, if desired.

Spoon icing into pastry bag (or bags if using more than 1 color) fitted with small (1/16- to 1/8-inch) plain tip. Arrange cookies on work surface. Pipe icing onto cookies in desired patterns. Apply decorations as desired. Let cookies stand until icing is dry.

DO AHEAD: *Can be made 3 days ahead. Store cookies in airtight containers between sheets of waxed paper at room temperature.*

⚓ Joe Frogger Spice Cookies

Joe Froggers, New England favorites that reportedly go back to the 18th century, are said to be named for an Uncle Joe who lived by a frog pond in Marblehead, Massachusetts. The chewy molasses cookies—flavored with spices, raisins, and rum—are a Sunday night supper tradition. The dough needs to chill overnight, so be sure to start a day ahead. **Makes about 2½ dozen**

½	cup chopped raisins
¼	cup dark rum
4	cups unbleached all purpose flour
1½	teaspoons salt
1	teaspoon baking soda
1½	teaspoons ground ginger
½	teaspoon ground cloves
½	teaspoon ground nutmeg
¼	teaspoon ground allspice
1	cup (2 sticks) unsalted butter, room temperature
1	cup sugar
1	cup mild-flavored (light) molasses
	Additional sugar

Place raisins in small bowl. Add rum and let soak at least 1 hour.

Combine flour, salt, baking soda, and spices in large bowl. Using electric mixer, beat butter and sugar in another large bowl to blend. Beat in molasses. Beat in flour mixture. Stir in raisin-rum mixture. Cover bowl with plastic wrap and chill dough overnight.

Preheat oven to 375°F. Divide dough in half. Roll out 1 dough piece on lightly floured surface to ¼-inch thickness. Using 3-inch-diameter cookie cutter, cut dough into rounds. Transfer rounds to nonstick baking sheets. Sprinkle cookies with additional sugar. Bake until puffed, about 8 minutes. Cool on baking sheets on racks 5 minutes. Transfer cookies to racks and cool completely (cookies will firm as they cool). Repeat with second dough piece.

DO AHEAD: *Can be made 3 days ahead. Store airtight at room temperature.*

⚓ Crisp Anise Cookies

Aniseed, also referred to as anise, has a fresh licorice flavor. Toasting the spice in a dry skillet intensifies the flavor. Enjoy these cookies with custards and flans. **Makes about 2 dozen**

1½	cups unbleached all purpose flour
¾	teaspoon baking powder
¼	teaspoon salt
½	cup (1 stick) unsalted butter, room temperature
⅓	cup plus 2 tablespoons sugar
1	large egg yolk
2	tablespoons brandy
½	teaspoon aniseed, toasted

Preheat oven to 325°F. Sift flour, baking powder, and salt into small bowl. Beat butter and ⅓ cup sugar in large bowl until light. Beat in egg yolk, brandy, and aniseed. Add flour mixture and beat just until smooth dough forms.

Spread remaining 2 tablespoons sugar on small plate. Roll out dough on lightly floured surface to ¼-inch thickness. Using 2-inch-diameter cookie cutter, cut out rounds from dough. Gather scraps; reroll on lightly floured surface and cut out more dough rounds.

Place dough rounds, 1 at a time, on sugar on plate, then transfer, sugar side up, to 2 heavy large ungreased baking sheets. Bake cookies until bottom and edges are golden, about 20 minutes. Transfer cookies to rack and cool completely.

DO AHEAD: *Can be made 3 days ahead. Store airtight at room temperature.*

Decorating Cookies: Before Baking

• One of the easiest ways to dress up a cookie is to press decorations gently into the dough before the cookies are baked. Use decorations that won't melt, such as M&M's, nonpareils, nuts, or currants or chopped dried fruit.

• Sprinkle unbaked cookies with sparkling colored sugars and sprinkles. First, lightly brush the cookie with beaten egg white; you can paint the whole cookie or create a design—the sugar or sprinkles will adhere only to the design formed by the egg white.

Puff Pastry Pinwheel Cookies with Jam

Supermarket staples—puff pastry and fruit jams—are transformed into delicate treats that require very little effort to make. Use any flavor of jam you like. These cookies freeze well, so they make excellent holiday gifts—the recipients can just take a few out of the freezer and let them come to room temperature whenever they have a cookie craving. **Makes 40**

1	**17.3-ounce package frozen puff pastry (2 sheets), thawed**
1	**egg, beaten to blend**
½	**cup (about) sugar**
½	**cup (about) assorted jams or fruit preserves (such as raspberry, apricot, and plum)**
	Powdered sugar (optional)

Preheat oven to 400°F. Lightly butter 2 heavy large rimmed baking sheets. Roll out 1 puff pastry sheet on lightly floured surface to 16x13-inch rectangle. Trim edges neatly, forming 15x12-inch rectangle. Cut rectangle into twenty 3-inch squares. Using small sharp knife, make 1-inch-long diagonal cut in all 4 corners of 1 square, cutting toward center (do not cut through center). To form pinwheels, fold every other point of puff pastry toward center of square [1, 2], pressing to adhere. Repeat with remaining puff pastry squares.

Brush pinwheels lightly with egg. Sprinkle each with ½ teaspoon sugar. Place scant ½ teaspoon jam in center of each. Transfer to prepared baking sheet. Bake until pinwheels are golden and puffed, about 13 minutes. Using metal spatula, transfer cookies to rack and cool completely. Repeat with remaining puff pastry sheet, glaze, sugar, and jam.

DO AHEAD: *Can be made ahead. Place cookies between waxed paper sheets in airtight containers and store at room temperature up to 3 days or freeze up to 2 weeks.*

Sprinkle cookies with powdered sugar, if desired.

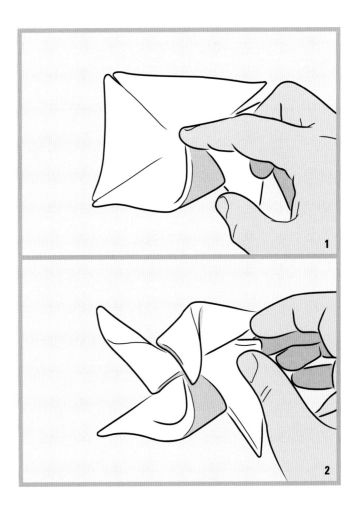

♕♕ Madeleines

It was a madeleine—a small, shell-shaped cake-cookie—that launched a surge of memories for the narrator of Marcel Proust's Swann's Way. Perhaps this simple recipe will help you create memories of your own. Madeleines must be baked in a special pan: a metal or silicone mold with scallop-shaped indentations. The pans are sold at cookware stores and online. **Makes about 1½ dozen**

2	large eggs
⅔	cup sugar
1	teaspoon vanilla extract
½	teaspoon finely grated lemon peel
	Pinch of salt
1	cup unbleached all purpose flour
10	tablespoons (1¼ sticks) unsalted butter, melted, cooled slightly
	Powdered sugar

Preheat oven to 375°F. Generously butter and flour pan for large madeleines (about 3 x 1¾ inches). Using electric mixer, beat eggs and sugar in large bowl just to blend. Beat in vanilla, lemon peel, and salt. Add flour; beat just until blended. Gradually add cooled melted butter in steady stream, beating just until blended.

Spoon 1 tablespoon batter into each indentation in pan. Bake until puffed and golden brown, about 16 minutes. Cool in pan 5 minutes. Gently remove madeleines from pan. Repeat process, buttering and flouring pan before each batch.

DO AHEAD: *Can be made 1 day ahead. Store airtight at room temperature.*

Dust cookies with powdered sugar.

♕♕♕ Langues-de-Chat

The French name translates as "cats' tongues," which refers to the long thin shape of these crisp, light cookies. They are traditionally served with sorbet or ice cream. For a fancy presentation, dip one end of each cookie into melted white, milk, or dark chocolate and chill on waxed paper until the chocolate is set. **Makes about 2½ dozen**

¼	cup (½ stick) unsalted butter, room temperature
¼	cup sugar
½	teaspoon finely grated lemon peel
½	teaspoon vanilla extract
¼	cup egg whites (about 2 large)
6	tablespoons unbleached all purpose flour
	Pinch of salt

Preheat oven to 350°F. Butter 2 heavy large rimmed baking sheets. Using electric mixer, beat butter and sugar in medium bowl until well blended. Beat in lemon peel and vanilla. Add egg whites and beat 30 seconds. Add flour and salt; beat just until blended.

Spoon batter into pastry bag fitted with ⅓-inch plain round tip. Pipe batter onto prepared baking sheets in 2½-inch-long strips, spacing 2 inches apart. Bake until edges are golden, about 10 minutes. Carefully transfer cookies to racks and cool completely (cookies will crisp as they cool).

DO AHEAD: *Can be made 2 days ahead. Store airtight at room temperature.*

Orange and Rosemary Butter Blossoms

A bit of fresh rosemary adds an herbal, slightly savory flavor to these pretty cookies. Gold sparkling sugar is available at some supermarkets and at specialty foods stores. A cookie press with assorted disks can be found at cookware stores and at williams-sonoma.com and amazon.com. **Makes about 7 dozen**

1	cup sugar
2	teaspoons finely grated orange peel
1	cup (2 sticks) unsalted butter, room temperature
½	teaspoon minced fresh rosemary
1	large egg
½	teaspoon (scant) salt
2⅓	cups unbleached all purpose flour
	Freshly ground black pepper (optional)
	Raw sugar or gold sparkling sugar (optional)

Preheat oven to 375°F. Using electric mixer, beat sugar and orange peel in large bowl until sugar becomes pale orange. Add butter and rosemary and beat until light and fluffy. Beat in egg and salt. Add flour and stir until well blended.

Pack dough into barrel of cookie press fitted with 5-point star/flower disk. Press cookies out onto heavy ungreased rimmed baking sheets, spacing about 1 inch apart. Sprinkle centers very lightly with freshly ground pepper and raw or sparkling sugar, if desired.

Bake cookies until just golden brown at edges, about 12 minutes. Using metal spatula, immediately transfer cookies to rack and cool completely. Repeat with any remaining dough, pepper, and raw or sparkling sugar.

DO AHEAD: *Can be made ahead. Store in airtight containers at room temperature up to 3 days, or freeze up to 1 week.*

Cookie Basics: Keeping Cookies Fresh

Cookies are generally best the same day they're baked, but most will also keep well for about three days when stored in an airtight container, such as a cookie tin or plastic storage container. (Cookie jars are often not airtight, so crisp cookies can become soft and soft cookies can dry out.) It's usually not a good idea to store cookies in the refrigerator, as they can become stale quickly and also pick up flavors from other foods. A few exceptions are noted in the recipes here—just be sure to wrap the cookies tightly with foil or plastic wrap.

Beignet Twists

♨♨♨ Beignet Twists

Orange peel and brandy flavor these fried cookies from New Orleans. Enjoy the cookies as a snack, as dessert with brandy-spiked orange slices, or for breakfast with café au lait. A deep-fry thermometer is essential for determining when the oil is hot enough for frying. **Makes about 4 dozen**

6	tablespoons sugar
2	large egg yolks
2	tablespoons brandy
2	tablespoons heavy whipping cream
1½	teaspoons finely grated orange peel
1	teaspoon vanilla extract
1	teaspoon baking soda
¼	teaspoon salt
1	tablespoon vegetable oil plus additional for frying
1½	cups unbleached all purpose flour
	Powdered sugar

Combine sugar, egg yolks, brandy, whipping cream, orange peel, vanilla, baking soda, and salt in medium bowl; add 1 tablespoon oil and whisk to blend. Add flour ½ cup at a time, mixing until very thick dough forms; scrape out onto lightly floured surface. Knead until no longer sticky, about 3 minutes. Roll out dough to 12x10-inch rectangle. Cut lengthwise into 3 strips, then cut each strip crosswise into ¾-inch-wide strips. Twist each strip of dough several times and place on large baking sheet; chill twists to set dough, about 30 minutes.

Pour enough oil into large saucepan to reach depth of 1 inch. Attach deep-fry thermometer to side of saucepan and heat oil to 350°F. Working in batches, drop twists into oil. Fry until golden, turning occasionally, about 2 minutes. Using slotted spoon, transfer beignets to paper towels and drain. Sift powdered sugar over. Serve warm or at room temperature.

DO AHEAD: *Beignets can be made 2 days ahead. Store in airtight containers at room temperature.*

♨♨♨ Cinnamon Fritters

These deep-fried cookies—called sfingi, sfinci, *or* zeppole *in Italy—hail from a time when many Italian homes didn't have stoves for baking. The cream-puff dough contains no sugar; rolling the freshly fried cookies in cinnamon sugar is what makes them sweet.* **Makes about 6 dozen**

2	cups sugar
2	teaspoons ground cinnamon
¾	cup water
6	tablespoons (¾ stick) unsalted butter
½	teaspoon salt
¾	cup unbleached all purpose flour, sifted (measured, then sifted)
3	large eggs
4	cups vegetable oil (for deep frying)

Mix sugar and cinnamon in shallow bowl. Set aside. Combine ¾ cup water, butter, and salt in heavy medium saucepan. Stir over medium heat until butter melts. Increase heat and bring to boil. Add flour all at once and stir with wooden spoon to blend. Stir over medium heat until dough forms a ball in center of saucepan, about 1 minute. Transfer dough to bowl. Using electric mixer, beat dough 15 seconds. Add eggs 1 at a time, beating until blended after each addition.

Attach deep-fry thermometer to side of heavy large deep saucepan. Add oil to saucepan and heat to 370°F. Working in batches, carefully drop mounded ½ teaspoonfuls of dough into hot oil and cook until golden brown, adjusting heat as necessary to maintain temperature and turning fritters occasionally, about 3 minutes per batch. Using slotted spoon, transfer fritters to paper towels and drain 10 seconds. Immediately roll fritters in cinnamon sugar. Serve fritters hot, or cool up to 3 hours and serve at room temperature.

bar cookies & brownies

bar cookies & brownies

Coconut Checkerboard Brownies

Old-Fashioned Brownies

Sometimes all you want is a good, simple, classic chocolate brownie. Look no further. **Makes 2 dozen**

	Nonstick vegetable oil spray
5	ounces unsweetened chocolate, chopped
½	cup (1 stick) unsalted butter, cut into 8 pieces
2	cups sugar
2	teaspoons vanilla extract
4	large eggs
¼	teaspoon salt
1	cup unbleached all purpose flour

Preheat oven to 350°F. Line 13x9x2-inch metal baking pan with aluminum foil, leaving 2-inch overhang on both long sides. Spray foil with nonstick spray. Stir chocolate and butter in heavy large saucepan over low heat until melted and smooth. Cool 15 minutes.

Whisk sugar and vanilla into chocolate mixture. Whisk in eggs and salt, then stir in flour. Spread batter in prepared pan.

Bake brownies until tester inserted into center comes out with moist crumbs attached, about 20 minutes. Cool in pan.

DO AHEAD: *Brownies can be made 1 day ahead. Cover and let stand at room temperature.*

Using foil as aid, lift brownies from pan and cut into bars.

Fudge Brownies with Walnuts

A classic brownie with a bit of crunch. Don't care for walnuts? Try chopped toasted pecans instead. **Makes about 2 dozen**

Brownies

	Nonstick vegetable oil spray
5	ounces bittersweet or semisweet chocolate (do not exceed 61% cacao), chopped
¾	cup (1½ sticks) unsalted butter, cut into 12 pieces
2	ounces unsweetened chocolate, chopped
2	cups sugar
4	large eggs
2	teaspoons vanilla extract
¼	teaspoon salt
1	cup unbleached all purpose flour
1	cup chopped walnuts
1	cup bittersweet or semisweet chocolate chips

Glaze

½	cup heavy whipping cream
3	ounces bittersweet or semisweet chocolate (do not exceed 61% cacao), chopped

BROWNIES: Preheat oven to 350°F. Spray 9x9x2-inch metal baking pan with nonstick spray. Stir bittersweet chocolate, butter, and unsweetened chocolate in medium saucepan over low heat until melted and smooth. Remove from heat.

Whisk sugar, eggs, vanilla, and salt in large bowl until fluffy. Stir in melted chocolate mixture. Mix in flour, then nuts and chocolate chips; spread in prepared pan. Bake until tester inserted into center comes out with moist crumbs attached, about 35 minutes.

GLAZE: Meanwhile, bring cream to boil in small saucepan. Remove from heat. Whisk in bittersweet chocolate. Pour glaze over brownies in pan. Chill uncovered 1 hour. Cut into squares. Serve cold or at room temperature.

Chocolate–Chocolate Chip Brownies with Pecans and Raisins

This quick and easy dessert would be great made with almost any kind of nut. Three others to try: walnuts, almonds, and peanuts. **Makes 16**

²⁄₃   **cup unbleached all purpose flour**
1   **teaspoon baking powder**
¼   **teaspoon salt**
3   **ounces unsweetened chocolate, chopped**
2   **large eggs**
1   **teaspoon vanilla extract**
1   **cup sugar**
½   **cup (1 stick) unsalted butter, room temperature**
½   **cup chopped pecans**
⅓   **cup raisins**
⅓   **cup bittersweet or semisweet chocolate chips**

Preheat oven to 350°F. Butter 9x9x2-inch metal baking pan. Whisk flour, baking powder, and salt in small bowl. Stir chocolate in medium metal bowl set over saucepan of simmering water until melted and smooth. Cool slightly.

Whisk eggs and vanilla into chocolate. Using electric mixer, beat sugar and butter in large bowl until blended. Beat in chocolate mixture. Mix in flour mixture. Stir in pecans, raisins, and chocolate chips. Transfer batter to prepared pan.

Bake until tester inserted into center comes out with moist crumbs attached, about 25 minutes. Cool. Cut into squares.

DO AHEAD: *Can be made 1 day ahead. Store airtight at room temperature.*

Chocolate–Espresso Brownies with Chocolate Glaze

A little instant espresso powder really heightens the chocolate flavor in these extra-thick brownies. If you can't find espresso powder, you can use instant coffee powder. **Makes 16**

¾   **cup (1½ sticks) unsalted butter, cut into 12 pieces**
5   **ounces unsweetened chocolate, chopped**
1   **tablespoon instant espresso powder or instant coffee powder**
2   **cups sugar**
1   **teaspoon vanilla extract**
4   **large eggs**
¾   **cup unbleached all purpose flour**
½   **cup heavy whipping cream**
6   **ounces bittersweet or semisweet chocolate (do not exceed 61% cacao), chopped**

Position rack in center of oven and preheat to 325°F. Line 8x8x2-inch metal baking pan with aluminum foil, leaving 2-inch overhang. Butter foil. Stir butter, unsweetened chocolate, and espresso powder in heavy medium saucepan over low heat until melted and smooth. Pour chocolate mixture into large bowl and cool 10 minutes.

Using electric mixer, beat sugar and vanilla into chocolate mixture. Add eggs 1 at a time, beating well after each addition. Add flour; beat at low speed just until blended. Pour batter into prepared pan.

Bake until just firm to touch and tester inserted into center comes out with some thick wet batter still attached, about 45 minutes. Cool brownies in pan on rack 10 minutes. Using metal spatula, press down brownie edges to level top. Cool completely.

Bring cream to simmer in heavy medium saucepan. Reduce heat to low. Add bittersweet chocolate; whisk until smooth. Pour glaze over brownies in pan. Chill until firm, about 3 hours.

Using foil as aid, lift brownies from pan. Fold down foil sides. Cut into squares; remove from foil. Serve cold or at room temperature.

DO AHEAD: *Can be made 2 days ahead. Keep refrigerated.*

Fudgy Hazelnut Brownies with Marbled Chocolate Glaze

This recipe, which makes nearly 75 brownies, is perfect for a big buffet dinner. The marbled topping is easy to create—keep it in mind for topping some of your other favorite bar cookies. **Makes about 6 dozen**

Brownies

2½	cups semisweet chocolate chips
1	cup (2 sticks) unsalted butter, cut into 16 pieces
1	cup sugar
4	large eggs
¼	teaspoon salt
2	teaspoons vanilla extract
¾	cup unbleached all purpose flour
1	cup coarsely chopped hazelnuts, toasted

Topping

12	ounces bittersweet or semisweet chocolate, chopped
3	ounces high-quality white chocolate (such as Lindt or Perugina), chopped

BROWNIES: Preheat oven to 350°F. Butter and flour 15x10x1-inch baking sheet. Stir chocolate chips and butter in heavy medium saucepan over medium-low heat until melted and smooth. Remove from heat. Combine sugar, eggs, and salt in heavy large saucepan. Whisk constantly over low heat just until sugar dissolves, about 5 minutes (do not boil). Remove from heat. Whisk in chocolate mixture and vanilla. Whisk in flour and nuts. Spread batter in prepared pan.

Bake until tester inserted into center comes out with some moist crumbs attached, about 30 minutes. Cool brownies completely in pan on rack.

TOPPING: Stir semisweet chocolate in medium metal bowl set over saucepan of barely simmering water until melted and smooth. Spread over brownies.

Stir white chocolate in another medium metal bowl set over saucepan of barely simmering water until melted and smooth. Spoon into resealable plastic bag. Cut small tip off 1 corner of bag. Pipe lines of white chocolate crosswise atop brownies, spacing lines 1 inch apart. Draw toothpick lengthwise across lines, alternating direction from left to right and right to left, to create marbled pattern. Chill just until firm enough to cut, about 30 minutes. Cut brownies into small squares.

DO AHEAD: *Can be made 3 days ahead. Refrigerate in single layer in airtight containers. Bring to room temperature before serving.*

♯♯ Fudgy Toffee Brownies

A quick chocolate ganache–toffee topping turns these brownies into something unforgettable. Purchase the toffee bits or make them yourself without making a mess by putting a toffee candy bar, such as a Heath bar, inside a resealable plastic bag and gently crushing it with a rolling pin or mallet. **Makes 16**

Brownies

1	cup semisweet chocolate chips
¾	cup (1½ sticks) unsalted butter, cut into 12 pieces
4	ounces unsweetened chocolate, chopped
1¾	cups sugar
4	large eggs
¾	cup unbleached all purpose flour
1	cup toffee bits or chopped toffee bars (such as Skor or Heath)

Topping

⅔	cup heavy whipping cream
1	cup semisweet chocolate chips
1	ounce unsweetened chocolate, chopped
¾	cup whole almonds, toasted, coarsely chopped
¼	cup toffee bits or chopped toffee bars (such as Skor or Heath)

BROWNIES: Preheat oven to 350°F. Line 9x9x2-inch metal baking pan with aluminum foil, leaving overhang on 2 sides. Butter foil. Combine chocolate chips, butter, and unsweetened chocolate in heavy large saucepan. Stir over low heat until melted and smooth. Remove from heat. Whisk in sugar, then eggs. Whisk in flour, then toffee bits. Pour batter into prepared pan.

Bake brownies until tester inserted into center comes out with moist crumbs attached, about 45 minutes. Cool 15 minutes. Using metal spatula, press down brownie edges to level top.

TOPPING: Bring cream to simmer in heavy small saucepan. Add chocolate chips and unsweetened chocolate; whisk topping until smooth. Pour topping over brownies in pan. Sprinkle with almonds and toffee bits. Chill brownies until cold, at least 2 hours and up to 1 day.

Using foil as aid, lift brownies from pan. Fold down foil sides. Cut into 16 squares and serve cold.

♯♯ Mint Chocolate Brownies

Mint chocolate chips and mint liqueur add fresh flavor to these rich chocolate brownies. If you prefer, you can use ¼ teaspoon peppermint extract in place of the crème de menthe. **Makes about 2 dozen**

Brownies

1¼	cups mint chocolate chips
1½	ounces unsweetened chocolate, finely chopped
½	cup (1 stick) unsalted butter, cut into 8 pieces
½	cup sifted unbleached all purpose flour (sifted, then measured)
	Pinch of salt
1½	teaspoons heavy whipping cream
1½	teaspoons instant espresso powder or instant coffee powder
½	teaspoon white (clear) crème de menthe
3	extra-large eggs, room temperature
¾	cup plus 2 tablespoons sugar

Glaze

6	tablespoons mint chocolate chips
½	ounce unsweetened chocolate, finely chopped
5	tablespoons unsalted butter, cut into 5 pieces

BROWNIES: Position rack in bottom third of oven and preheat to 350°F. Butter sides of 9x9x2-inch metal baking pan. Fold 18x12-inch piece of aluminum foil in half crosswise. Line pan with foil, leaving overhang on 2 sides. Butter foil. Stir mint chocolate chips, unsweetened chocolate, and butter in heavy medium saucepan over very low heat until melted and smooth. Cool.

Sift flour and salt into small bowl. Mix cream, espresso powder, and crème de menthe in small cup. Using electric mixer, beat eggs and sugar in large bowl until frothy. Fold in cream mixture, then melted chocolate. Fold in dry ingredients. Spread batter evenly in prepared pan.

Bake until tester inserted in center comes out with some moist crumbs attached, about 25 minutes (surface may crack). Using metal spatula, press down brownie edges to level top. Cool 30 minutes on rack.

GLAZE: Stir mint chocolate chips, unsweetened chocolate, and butter in heavy small saucepan over low heat until melted and smooth. Let cool until thick enough to spread. Spread glaze over brownies. Let brownies stand 4 hours at room temperature.

Using foil as aid, lift brownies from pan. Fold down foil sides. Cut into squares.

DO AHEAD: *Can be made 1 day ahead. Store airtight at room temperature.*

Coconut Checkerboard Brownies

This dessert has a chocolate brownie on the bottom and alternating squares of chocolate and coconut brownie on the top. It looks impressive but doesn't require any special equipment or a sophisticated technique. Canned sweetened cream of coconut is available in the liquor or mixers section of most supermarkets. **Makes 16**

Coconut Batter

1	**7-ounce package sweetened flaked coconut**
¼	**cup powdered sugar**
¼	**cup canned sweetened cream of coconut (such as Coco Reál or Coco López)**
2	**ounces Philadelphia-brand cream cheese, cut into 1-inch cubes, room temperature**
1	**extra-large egg**
⅛	**teaspoon almond extract**
⅛	**teaspoon fresh lemon juice**
	Pinch of salt

Chocolate Batter

6	**tablespoons (¾ stick) unsalted butter, cut into 6 pieces**
3½	**ounces unsweetened chocolate, chopped**
2	**extra-large eggs**
¼	**teaspoon vanilla extract**
1½	**cups (packed) golden brown sugar**
¾	**cup sifted unbleached all purpose flour (sifted, then measured)**
¼	**teaspoon baking powder**
⅛	**teaspoon salt**

COCONUT BATTER: Measure ⅓ cup flaked coconut; cover and set aside. Place remaining coconut and sugar in processor; finely chop. Add cream of coconut and cream cheese to processor and blend well. Add egg, almond extract, lemon juice, and salt and blend well, stopping occasionally to scrape down sides of bowl. Transfer to bowl. Cover and refrigerate until very firm, about 3 hours.

CHOCOLATE BATTER: Butter 9x9x2-inch metal baking pan. Melt butter with chocolate in heavy small saucepan over low heat, stirring until smooth. Pour into medium bowl. Cool to lukewarm. Whisk in eggs and vanilla. Whisk sugar, flour, baking powder, and salt in small bowl; sift over chocolate mixture. Mix until blended and smooth. Spread 1¼ cups chocolate batter in prepared pan (cover and refrigerate remaining batter). Cover pan tightly with aluminum foil. Refrigerate batter until very firm, about 3 hours.

Position rack in center of oven and preheat to 325°F. Alternate 1 tablespoon remaining chocolate batter and 1 tablespoon coconut batter over chocolate layer, filling pan completely. Sprinkle reserved ⅓ cup flaked coconut over coconut mounds; press gently to adhere. Cover pan tightly with foil.

Bake 45 minutes. Remove foil and bake until tester inserted in center of 1 chocolate mound comes out almost clean, about 40 minutes. Cool brownies completely in pan on rack.

DO AHEAD: *Can be made 1 day ahead. Cover brownies tightly and store at room temperature.*

Cut into squares.

Chocolate Brownies with Orange–Cream Cheese Frosting

Baking in a disposable pan creates brownies with soft edges. If you prefer brownies with chewy edges, use a 13x9x2-inch metal baking pan instead and bake for 30 minutes. Finish these brownies with toasted pistachios, toasted flaked coconut, or untoasted coconut—or go all out and top with all three.

Makes 1½ dozen

Brownies

Nonstick vegetable oil spray
- ⅔ cup unbleached all purpose flour
- ½ teaspoon baking powder
- ½ teaspoon salt
- 4 ounces bittersweet or semisweet chocolate, chopped
- 2 ounces unsweetened chocolate, chopped
- 10 tablespoons (1¼ sticks) unsalted butter, cut into 10 pieces
- 1¼ cups sugar
- 2 teaspoons vanilla extract
- 3 large eggs

Frosting

- 1 8-ounce package Philadelphia-brand cream cheese, room temperature
- ⅔ cup powdered sugar
- 2 tablespoons (¼ stick) unsalted butter, room temperature
- 1½ teaspoons finely grated orange peel

- ½ cup toasted unsalted natural pistachios, toasted sweetened flaked coconut, or untoasted sweetened flaked coconut

BROWNIES: Position rack in center of oven; preheat to 325°F. Spray 13x9x2-inch disposable aluminum baking pan with nonstick spray. Press 18x12-inch sheet aluminum foil over bottom and up long sides of pan, leaving overhang on both long sides. Spray foil with nonstick spray. Whisk flour, baking powder, and salt in small bowl. Stir both chocolates and butter in medium saucepan over medium-low heat until melted and smooth; remove from heat. Whisk sugar and vanilla, then eggs, into chocolate mixture. Whisk until glossy and smooth, about 1 minute. Add dry ingredients and whisk just to blend. Pour batter into prepared pan.

Bake until tester inserted into center comes out with some moist crumbs attached, about 24 minutes. Cool completely in pan on rack.

FROSTING: Using electric mixer, beat cream cheese, powdered sugar, butter, and orange peel in medium bowl until smooth. Spread cream cheese frosting over brownies. Sprinkle nuts or coconut over.

DO AHEAD: *Can be made 1 day ahead. Cover and chill.*

Using foil as aid, lift brownies from pan. Cut into squares; serve cold or at room temperature.

🥄 Chocolate Brownies with Peanut Butter Frosting

Who can resist the combination of chocolate and peanut butter? You can finish the brownies with a sprinkling of chopped salted peanuts, if you like.
Makes 2 dozen

Brownies

Nonstick vegetable oil spray
5   ounces unsweetened chocolate, coarsely chopped
4   ounces bittersweet or semisweet chocolate, coarsely chopped
½   cup (1 stick) unsalted butter, cut into 8 pieces
1½ cups sugar
4   large eggs
1   teaspoon vanilla extract
½   cup unbleached all purpose flour
¼   teaspoon salt

Frosting

1   cup creamy peanut butter (do not use old-fashioned style or freshly ground)
3   tablespoons unsalted butter, room temperature
⅔   cup powdered sugar
1   teaspoon vanilla extract

BROWNIES: Preheat oven to 350°F. Line 13x9x2-inch metal baking pan with aluminum foil, leaving 2-inch overhang on both long sides. Spray foil with nonstick spray. Combine unsweetened chocolate, bittersweet chocolate, and butter in heavy small saucepan. Stir over low heat until melted and smooth. Cool to barely lukewarm. Using electric mixer, beat sugar, eggs, and vanilla in large bowl at high speed until mixture is thick and pale yellow, about 5 minutes. Reduce mixer speed to low; beat in flour and salt, then melted chocolate mixture. Transfer mixture to prepared baking pan.

Bake brownies until tester inserted into center comes out with moist crumbs attached, about 20 minutes. Transfer pan to rack; cool 15 minutes. Using metal spatula, press down brownie edges to level top. Cool completely in pan.

FROSTING: Place peanut butter and butter in medium bowl. Using electric mixer, beat until smooth. Add sugar and vanilla and beat until well blended and smooth. Spread frosting evenly over brownies in pan. Refrigerate at least 1 hour. Using foil as aid, lift brownies from pan. Cut into squares.

DO AHEAD: *Can be made 1 day ahead. Cover and keep refrigerated. Let stand at room temperature 30 minutes before serving.*

🥄 Raspberry Brownies

Berries and chocolate are natural partners. In this variation on that theme, chocolate brownies are sprinkled with fresh raspberries just before baking, then drizzled with a chocolate glaze that contains just a hint of raspberry brandy.
Makes 1½ dozen

Brownies

Nonstick vegetable oil spray
1   cup (2 sticks) unsalted butter, room temperature
1¼ cups sugar
½   cup (packed) golden brown sugar
4   large eggs
½   cup natural unsweetened cocoa powder
1   tablespoon framboise (clear raspberry brandy) or brandy
1   teaspoon vanilla extract
¼   teaspoon salt
1¼ cups unbleached all purpose flour
1   ½-pint container raspberries

Glaze

4   ounces bittersweet or semisweet chocolate, chopped
2   tablespoons framboise (clear raspberry brandy) or brandy
2   teaspoons hot water
    Powdered sugar

BROWNIES: Preheat oven to 325°F. Spray 13x9x2-inch metal baking pan with nonstick spray. Beat butter and both sugars in large bowl until fluffy. Add eggs 1 at a time, beating to blend after each addition. Stir in cocoa, framboise, vanilla, and salt. Add flour; stir just to blend. Pour batter into prepared pan. Sprinkle raspberries evenly over batter. Bake until tester inserted into center comes out clean, about 30 minutes. Cool completely in pan on rack.

GLAZE: Stir chocolate, framboise, and 2 teaspoons hot water in medium metal bowl set over saucepan of barely simmering water until melted and smooth. Cool slightly.

Cut brownies into 18 bars. Sift powdered sugar lightly over brownies. Dip fork into glaze and drizzle glaze decoratively over brownies. Let stand until glaze sets, about 30 minutes.

DO AHEAD: *Can be made 8 hours ahead. Cover; store at room temperature.*

Transfer brownies to plate and serve.

White Chocolate Suzette Brownies

This white chocolate brownie was inspired by crepes suzette, a classic French dessert that consists of crepes warmed in a buttery orange sauce, then soaked in orange liqueur and flambéed. This slightly less dramatic (but equally delicious) version features brownies flavored with orange liqueur, dried apricots, lemon and orange peel, and ginger. The finishing touch? An orange-flavored glaze. **Makes about 2 dozen**

Brownies

½	cup finely chopped dried apricots
2	tablespoons Grand Marnier or other orange liqueur
1	tablespoon frozen orange juice concentrate, thawed
1	tablespoon finely grated orange peel
1	teaspoon fresh lemon juice
1	teaspoon finely grated lemon peel
½	teaspoon vanilla extract
2	tablespoons (¼ stick) unsalted butter, cut into 2 pieces
2	ounces Philadelphia-brand cream cheese, cut into 2 pieces
4	ounces high-quality white chocolate (such as Lindt or Perugina), finely chopped
1	cup sifted unbleached all purpose flour (sifted, then measured)
½	teaspoon salt
½	teaspoon ground ginger
2	extra-large eggs, room temperature
⅔	cup sugar
4	ounces high-quality white chocolate (such as Lindt or Perugina), very coarsely chopped

Glaze

⅔	cup powdered sugar
2¼	teaspoons Grand Marnier or other orange liqueur
2¼	teaspoons frozen orange juice concentrate, thawed

BROWNIES: Position rack in center of oven and preheat to 350°F. Butter sides of 9x9x2-inch metal baking pan. Fold 18x12-inch piece of aluminum foil in half crosswise. Line pan with foil, leaving overhang on 2 sides. Butter foil. Dust pan and foil with flour; tap out excess.

Mix apricots, Grand Marnier, orange juice concentrate, orange peel, lemon juice, lemon peel, and vanilla in medium bowl. Melt butter and cream cheese in heavy small saucepan over low heat, stirring constantly. Remove from heat. Add finely chopped white chocolate and let stand 5 minutes. Stir gently to combine. Cool.

Sift flour, salt, and ginger into small bowl. Whisk eggs and sugar in large bowl until thickened, about 1 minute. Whisk in cream cheese mixture. Fold in apricot mixture and coarsely chopped white chocolate. Fold in dry ingredients. Spread batter in prepared pan. Bake until tester inserted into center comes out clean, about 25 minutes. Transfer pan to rack and cool.

GLAZE: Mix all ingredients in small bowl. Spread glaze evenly over brownies. Let stand until glaze sets, about 20 minutes. Using foil as aid, lift brownies from pan. Fold down foil sides. Cut into squares.

DO AHEAD: Can be made 1 day ahead. Store airtight at room temperature.

Presentation Tip: **Top It Off**

For another pretty presentation, drizzle the glaze over the brownies and sprinkle with chopped dried apricots or chopped crystallized ginger (or both).

Double-Lemon Bars

Healthy doses of lemon juice and lemon peel give these bars their extra-tangy flavor. To get the most juice out of the lemons (or any other citrus), firmly roll room-temperature fruit along the countertop with your palm before squeezing.

Makes 32

Crust

	Nonstick canola oil spray
1½	cups unbleached all purpose flour
½	cup powdered sugar
⅛	teaspoon salt
¾	cup (1½ sticks) chilled unsalted butter, cut into ½-inch cubes
1	teaspoon vanilla extract

Filling

2½	cups sugar
6	large eggs, room temperature
1	cup strained fresh lemon juice
3	tablespoons unbleached all purpose flour
2½	tablespoons finely grated lemon peel
	Powdered sugar

CRUST: Position rack in center of oven and preheat to 350°F. Line 9x9x2-inch metal baking pan with aluminum foil, leaving 1-inch overhang on 2 sides of pan. Spray with nonstick spray. Blend flour, sugar, and salt in processor. Add butter and cut in, using on/off turns, until mixture resembles coarse meal. Add vanilla and process until dough begins to come together. Press dough evenly onto bottom of prepared pan. Bake crust until golden brown, about 26 minutes.

FILLING: Whisk sugar and eggs in large bowl to blend. Whisk in lemon juice, then flour. Strain into another bowl. Mix in lemon peel.

Reduce oven temperature to 325°F. Pour filling over hot crust. Bake until sides are set and filling no longer moves in center when pan is shaken, about 35 minutes. Cool on rack. Cover and chill at least 4 hours or overnight.

Using foil as aid, lift dessert from pan. Fold down foil sides. Cut into 16 squares. Cut each square diagonally in half, forming triangle. Sift powdered sugar over.

DO AHEAD: *Can be made 1 day ahead. Refrigerate in airtight containers.*

Raising the Bar

Transform the humble bar cookie into a dramatic dessert.

INFINITE SUNDAES: Top warm bar cookies with scoops of ice cream, chocolate or caramel sauce, dollops of whipped cream, and sprinklings of chopped salted peanuts.

BROWNIE BITES: Slice a pan of chocolate brownies into ½-inch cubes. Using a toothpick, dip each brownie bite into melted dark or white chocolate. While the chocolate is still wet, dip into chopped nuts, sprinkles, or crushed cookie crumbs. Place the brownie bites on a rimmed baking sheet lined with aluminum foil and chill until the chocolate sets.

THE LAYERED LOOK: Make a parfait by layering chopped brownies or bar cookies with lightly sweetened whipped cream and fresh berries. Use a medium-size clear bowl or arrange in small clear glasses to make individual servings.

CHOP SHOP: Dice cookies and sprinkle them over ice cream.

BAKED ALASKAS: Top bar cookies with scoops of ice cream and freeze until firm (up to 2 days ahead). Place the cookie-ice cream combos on a foil-lined baking sheet. Make a simple meringue (see the baked Alaska recipes on pages 521–24) and swirl it over the combos, leaving about ¼ inch of space between the bottom of the meringue and the baking sheet. Bake in a 500°F oven until the meringue browns in spots (no more than 5 minutes), or use a kitchen torch to brown the meringues.

🥄 Lemon-Coconut Bars

The buttery coconut crust tempers the tang of the lemony filling in these delicious bars. For a tropical twist, substitute fresh lime juice and lime peel for the lemon in the filling. **Makes 16**

Crust

1	cup unbleached all purpose flour
¼	cup sugar
¼	teaspoon salt
¾	cup sweetened flaked coconut, toasted, cooled
6	tablespoons (¾ stick) chilled unsalted butter, cut into ½-inch cubes

Filling

¾	cup sugar
2	large eggs
¼	cup fresh lemon juice
1	tablespoon finely grated lemon peel
1	teaspoon unbleached all purpose flour
½	teaspoon baking powder
	Pinch of salt
¼	cup powdered sugar

CRUST: Preheat oven to 350°F. Line 8x8x2-inch metal baking pan with aluminum foil, leaving overhang on 2 sides of pan. Butter foil. Blend flour, sugar, and salt in processor. Add coconut and butter; process until mixture resembles fine meal and begins to clump together. Gather dough into ball. Press dough evenly over bottom of prepared pan. Bake crust until golden at edges, about 25 minutes.

FILLING: Meanwhile, combine sugar, eggs, lemon juice, lemon peel, flour, baking powder, and salt in processor. Blend filling until smooth.

Remove crust from oven. Pour filling evenly over hot crust. Return to oven and bake until filling begins to brown at edges and is just set and springy to touch in center, about 30 minutes. Transfer pan to rack; cool lemon bars completely.

Using foil as aid, transfer lemon bars to work surface. Fold down foil sides. Cut into bars. Sift powdered sugar over.

DO AHEAD: *Can be made 5 days ahead. Refrigerate lemon bars in single layer in airtight containers.*

🥄 White Chocolate and Lime Cheesecake Bars

Here's a no-bake bar cookie that's just perfect for a summer barbecue. Chocolate curls are an easy way to dress up your desserts and impress guests—just soften a chocolate bar briefly on low power in the microwave, then run a vegetable peeler along one long side. **Makes 9**

7	ounces high-quality white chocolate (such as Lindt or Perugina), chopped
27	chocolate sandwich cookies (about 11 ounces)
½	cup chilled heavy whipping cream
1	8-ounce package Philadelphia-brand cream cheese, room temperature
3	tablespoons sugar
3	tablespoons fresh lime juice
1	tablespoon finely grated lime peel
	Lime slices or lime twists
	White chocolate curls (optional)

Line 8x8x2-inch metal baking pan with aluminum foil, leaving overhang on all sides. Stir chopped white chocolate in medium metal bowl set over saucepan of barely simmering water until melted and smooth. Remove bowl from over water. Finely grind cookies in processor. Add 2 tablespoons melted white chocolate and blend until mixture clumps together. Firmly press mixture onto bottom of prepared pan. Chill while making filling.

Beat cream in medium bowl until peaks form. Beat cream cheese, sugar, lime juice, and lime peel in large bowl until smooth. Beat in remaining melted white chocolate. Fold in whipped cream in 2 additions; spread over prepared crust. Chill until filling is slightly firm, at least 2 hours. Using foil as aid, lift cheesecake from pan. Fold down foil sides. Cut into bars. Garnish with lime slices or twists and white chocolate curls, if desired.

Apricot-Walnut Bars

Crisp shortbread crust topped with a moist apricot cake makes a delicious dessert, but these bars would also be terrific as a breakfast or brunch treat.
Makes 1½ dozen

Shortbread Layer

	Nonstick vegetable oil spray
1	cup unbleached all purpose flour
¼	cup sugar
	Pinch of salt
½	cup (1 stick) chilled unsalted butter, cut into ½-inch cubes

Apricot Layer

⅔	cup (packed) dried apricot halves, coarsely chopped
⅓	cup unbleached all purpose flour
½	teaspoon baking powder
¼	teaspoon salt
2	large eggs
1	cup (packed) golden brown sugar
½	teaspoon vanilla extract
½	cup chopped toasted walnuts

Powdered sugar

SHORTBREAD LAYER: Preheat oven to 350°F. Spray 8x8x2-inch glass baking dish with nonstick spray. Blend flour, sugar, and salt in processor. Add butter; using on/off turns, process until coarse meal forms. Press crumbs firmly onto bottom of prepared dish. Bake until center is golden, about 25 minutes. Maintain oven temperature.

APRICOT LAYER: Meanwhile, place apricots in small saucepan; add enough water to cover. Boil until soft, about 4 minutes; drain. Set aside and cool.

Sift flour, baking powder, and salt into small bowl. Using electric mixer, beat eggs in large bowl. Add brown sugar and vanilla; beat until blended. Stir in flour mixture, then nuts and apricots. Spread over shortbread.

Bake until puffed and dark brown and tester inserted into topping comes out with small moist crumbs attached, about 35 minutes. Cool in dish.

Cut into bars. Transfer to waxed paper. Sift powdered sugar over bars.

A Cut Above

Bar cookies don't have to be sliced into traditional squares and rectangles. Try these shapes instead.

CIRCLES: Use a round cookie cutter to give your cookies some flattering curves. For clean edges, push straight down with the cookie cutter and wipe it clean after each cut.

MODERN RECTANGLES: Think thin. Use a ruler to divide the pan of cookies lengthwise into even strips. Make short, crosswise cuts to form bars. You can cut the bars all the same length, or mix things up and make some longer and some shorter.

DIAMONDS OR TRIANGLES: Look sharp with these pointy shapes. For diamonds, use a ruler to make diagonal cuts across the pan, then make diagonal cuts in the opposite direction. These cuts will form triangles along the edges of the pan. Serve the triangles with the diamonds or cut all the cookies into triangles by slicing the diamonds in half.

Triple-Cherry Streusel Bars

Dried sweet cherries, tart cherry preserves, and cherry brandy give these bars their triple hit of fruit flavor. If you don't have kirsch (clear cherry brandy) on hand, you can use regular brandy or amaretto (almond-flavored liqueur) instead.

Makes 2 dozen

Filling

1	cup dried Bing (sweet) cherries
1	cup tart red cherry preserves
1	tablespoon kirsch (clear cherry brandy)

Dough and Streusel

	Nonstick vegetable oil spray
2	cups unbleached all purpose flour
⅔	cup sugar
½	teaspoon ground cinnamon
¼	teaspoon salt
¾	cup (1½ sticks) chilled unsalted butter, cut into ½-inch cubes
1¾	teaspoons vanilla extract
¼	teaspoon almond extract
3	tablespoons whole milk
1	cup (packed) sweetened flaked coconut
¾	cup sliced almonds

FILLING: Combine all ingredients in processor; blend to chunky puree.

DO AHEAD: *Filling can be made 1 day ahead. Transfer filling to bowl; cover and refrigerate.*

DOUGH AND STREUSEL: Preheat oven to 375°F. Line 13x9x2-inch metal baking pan with heavy-duty aluminum foil, leaving overhang on both long sides. Spray foil with nonstick spray. Blend flour, sugar, cinnamon, and salt in processor. Add butter, vanilla, and almond extract. Blend, using on/off turns, until mixture resembles coarse meal. Add milk and blend, using on/off turns, until mixture comes together in small clumps. Transfer 1 cup (packed) mixture to medium bowl and reserve for streusel.

Blend remaining mixture in processor until large moist clumps form. Gather dough together in large ball. Press dough over bottom of prepared pan; pierce all over with fork. Bake dough until golden, about 22 minutes; cool crust 15 minutes. Maintain oven temperature.

Add coconut and almonds to reserved 1 cup dough. Mix with fork, breaking streusel topping into small clumps.

Spread cherry filling over baked crust. Sprinkle streusel topping over. Bake until cherry filling is bubbling and streusel topping is golden brown, about 30 minutes. Cool in pan on rack. Using foil as aid, lift cookie from pan. Fold down foil sides. Cut into bars.

DO AHEAD: *Can be made 2 days ahead. Refrigerate in airtight container.*

Classic Date Bars

The oat mixture does double duty in this recipe: Half of the mixture is pressed into the pan to form a buttery crust; the remainder is sprinkled over the filling, streusel-style. **Makes 16**

1½	**cups water**
1½	**cups chopped pitted dates**
1	**teaspoon vanilla extract**
1½	**cups unbleached all purpose flour**
1	**cup (packed) dark brown sugar**
1	**cup old-fashioned oats**
1½	**teaspoons ground cinnamon**
½	**teaspoon baking soda**
½	**teaspoon salt**
¾	**cup (1½ sticks) unsalted butter, diced, room temperature**

Preheat oven to 350°F. Butter 8x8x2-inch metal baking pan. Bring 1½ cups water to simmer in medium saucepan. Add dates; simmer until very soft and thick, stirring occasionally, about 10 minutes. Cool to room temperature. Stir in vanilla.

Combine flour, sugar, oats, cinnamon, baking soda, and salt in large bowl; stir to blend. Add butter. Using fingertips, rub in until moist clumps form. Press half of oat mixture evenly over bottom of prepared pan. Spread date mixture over. Sprinkle with remaining oat mixture; press gently to adhere.

Bake until brown at edges and golden brown and set in center, about 40 minutes. Cool completely in pan on rack. Cut into bars and serve.

Fig and Rum Squares

A little rum in the spiced fig filling adds an adult edge to these tender bar cookies. **Makes 1½ dozen**

2	**cups unbleached all purpose flour**
1	**cup (2 sticks) chilled unsalted butter, cut into ½-inch cubes**
1	**cup (packed) golden brown sugar, divided**
¼	**teaspoon salt**
1	**tablespoon ice water**
1	**9-ounce package dried black Mission figs, stemmed**
6	**tablespoons orange juice**
2	**tablespoons dark rum**
1	**tablespoon finely grated orange peel**
1	**teaspoon ground cinnamon**
¾	**cup sliced almonds**

Preheat oven to 350°F. Blend flour, butter, ½ cup sugar, and salt in processor until coarse meal forms. Add 1 tablespoon ice water; blend until moist dough forms. Measure 1 cup dough; reserve for topping. Press remaining dough into 11½x7½-inch metal baking pan (do not clean processor).

Blend remaining ½ cup sugar, figs, orange juice, rum, orange peel, and cinnamon in processor to coarse paste. Spread filling over crust. Mix almonds into reserved 1 cup dough. Drop topping by small clumps onto filling. Bake until golden, about 35 minutes. Cool completely in pan. Cut into bars.

DO AHEAD: *Can be made 8 hours ahead. Cover; store at room temperature.*

Pumpkin Cheesecake Crumble Squares

Four layers of deliciousness: a crispy nutty crust, a creamy pumpkin filling, a tangy sour cream topping, and a sprinkling of streusel. These squares would be a natural addition to a Thanksgiving dessert lineup—but they're irresistible any time of the year. **Makes 16**

Crust and Streusel

1	cup unbleached all purpose flour
¾	cup (packed) golden brown sugar
½	teaspoon salt
½	cup (1 stick) chilled unsalted butter, cut into ½-inch cubes
1	cup pecan halves
¾	cup old-fashioned oats

Filling

1	8-ounce package Philadelphia-brand cream cheese, room temperature
¾	cup canned pure pumpkin
½	cup sugar
1	large egg
1½	teaspoons ground cinnamon
1	teaspoon ground ginger

Topping

1	cup sour cream
2	tablespoons sugar
¼	teaspoon vanilla extract

CRUST AND STREUSEL: Preheat oven to 350°F. Generously butter 9x9x2-inch metal baking pan. Line rimmed baking sheet with parchment paper. Using on/off turns, blend flour, sugar, salt, and butter in processor until coarse meal forms. Add pecans; using on/off turns, process until nuts are chopped. Add oats; using on/off turns, process until mixture is moistened but not clumping. Press 3½ cups crumbs onto bottom of prepared square pan. Transfer remaining crumbs to prepared baking sheet (do not clean processor). Bake crumbs on sheet until golden, stirring once, about 12 minutes. Cool crumbs. Bake crust in pan until golden, about 30 minutes. Remove from oven while preparing filling. Maintain oven temperature.

FILLING: Blend all ingredients in same processor until smooth. Spread filling over warm crust; bake until set, dry in center, and beginning to rise at edges, about 20 minutes. Maintain oven temperature.

TOPPING: Whisk all ingredients in small bowl. Spread topping evenly over hot filling. Bake until topping sets and is bubbling at edges, about 5 minutes. Cool completely in pan on rack. Sprinkle crumbs over topping; gently press into topping. Cover; chill until cold, about 2 hours.

DO AHEAD: *Can be made 2 days ahead. Keep chilled.*

Cut into squares.

Banana-Oatmeal Bars with Chocolate Chunks

The dynamic duo of banana and oats makes these cookies perfect for breakfast or an afternoon snack. **Makes about 2 dozen**

2	cups unbleached all purpose flour
1	cup quick-cooking oats
1	tablespoon baking powder
¾	teaspoon salt
1	cup (2 sticks) unsalted butter, room temperature
1¼	cups sugar
1¼	cups (packed) golden brown sugar
2	large eggs
⅔	cup mashed ripe bananas (about 2 large)
2	teaspoons vanilla extract
4	2.6-ounce bars semisweet chocolate (such as Hershey's Special Dark), cut into ¾-inch pieces
1	cup pecans, toasted, chopped

Preheat oven to 350°F. Butter and flour 15x10x1-inch baking sheet. Blend flour, oats, baking powder, and salt in medium bowl. Beat butter in large bowl until fluffy. Add both sugars and beat until well blended. Add eggs 1 at a time, beating well after each addition. Beat in bananas, then vanilla. Stir in flour mixture, then chocolate and pecans.

Spread batter in prepared pan. Bake until tester inserted into center comes out clean and top is golden, about 45 minutes. Cool in pan on rack. Cut into bars.

Ingredient Tip: Bananas
Don't waste that one lonely overly ripe banana that hasn't been eaten—peel it, place it in a resealable plastic freezer bag, and stick it in the freezer. Once you've collected a few bananas, use them in these delicious bar cookies or in banana bread. Thaw, then mash them in a bowl, and they are ready to use.

Coconut Macaroon Bars

These bar cookies have all the moist, chewy appeal of traditional macaroons.
Makes 2 dozen

Crust
	Nonstick vegetable oil spray
1¼	cups unbleached all purpose flour
⅓	cup sugar
½	teaspoon salt
10	tablespoons (1¼ sticks) chilled unsalted butter, cut into ½-inch cubes
1	large egg yolk
1	tablespoon heavy whipping cream

Filling
1	cup sugar
3	large eggs
¼	cup (½ stick) unsalted butter, melted, cooled
2	tablespoons unbleached all purpose flour
2	teaspoons vanilla extract
¼	teaspoon salt
1	7-ounce package sweetened flaked coconut

CRUST: Preheat oven to 350°F. Spray 13x9x2-inch metal baking pan with nonstick spray. Blend flour, sugar, and salt in processor. Add butter and process, using on/off turns, until mixture resembles coarse meal. Add egg yolk and cream; blend until dough comes together in clumps. Press dough evenly over bottom of prepared pan. Bake crust until pale golden, about 15 minutes. Transfer to rack. Maintain oven temperature.

FILLING: Beat sugar, eggs, melted butter, flour, vanilla, and salt in medium bowl to blend. Beat in coconut. Pour filling over crust.

Bake dessert until golden brown on top and set in center, about 25 minutes. Cool in pan. Cut around pan sides to loosen. Cut into bars.

DO AHEAD: Can be made 2 days ahead. Store in airtight container and chill.

More to Try: Add Chocolate
For a delicious variation, spread a thin layer of melted semisweet chocolate over the crust before pouring on the coconut topping. After the bars are baked, drizzle them with more melted chocolate.

Double-Nut Maple Bars

This sweet and sticky bar cookie gets its deep caramel flavor from brown sugar and maple syrup. **Makes 16**

Crust

1¼	cups unbleached all purpose flour
⅓	cup sugar
	Pinch of salt
6	tablespoons (¾ stick) chilled unsalted butter, cut into ½-inch cubes
1	large egg yolk
1	tablespoon whole milk

Filling

⅓	cup pure maple syrup
⅓	cup (packed) golden brown sugar
¼	cup heavy whipping cream
2	tablespoons (¼ stick) unsalted butter
¾	cup pecans, toasted, coarsely chopped
¾	cup walnuts, toasted, coarsely chopped
½	teaspoon vanilla extract

CRUST: Preheat oven to 350°F. Butter 8x8x2-inch metal baking pan. Blend flour, sugar, and salt in processor. Add butter; using on/off turns, process until mixture resembles coarse meal. Combine egg yolk and milk in small bowl. Drizzle egg mixture into processor; using on/off turns, process just until dough clumps together but is still dry. Transfer dough crumbs to prepared pan. Press crumbs onto bottom and halfway up sides of pan. Bake until crust is set and pale golden, about 25 minutes. Cool crust in pan on rack. Maintain oven temperature.

FILLING: Combine maple syrup, sugar, cream, and butter in heavy medium saucepan. Boil 2 minutes. Remove from heat, Stir in all nuts and vanilla.

Pour filling over crust, spreading nuts evenly. Bake until filling is bubbling all over, about 8 minutes. Transfer to rack and cool completely. Cut into bars and serve at room temperature.

DO AHEAD: *Can be made 1 day ahead. Store between sheets of waxed paper in airtight container at room temperature.*

Brown Sugar Bars with Milk Chocolate and Pecans

A bit of orange liqueur and some candied orange peel add a bright citrus note to these bars. **Makes 16**

1	cup unbleached all purpose flour
1	teaspoon baking powder
¼	teaspoon salt
¾	cup (packed) golden brown sugar
6	tablespoons (¾ stick) unsalted butter, melted
1	large egg
3	tablespoons Grand Marnier or other orange liqueur, divided
½	teaspoon vanilla extract
6	ounces high-quality milk chocolate (such as Lindt or Perugina), cut into ½-inch pieces
⅓	cup chopped pecans
¼	cup chopped candied orange peel

Preheat oven to 350°F. Butter 8x8x2-inch metal baking pan. Whisk flour, baking powder, and salt in small bowl. Whisk sugar, butter, egg, 2 tablespoons liqueur, and vanilla in large bowl to blend. Add dry ingredients; stir to blend. Stir in chocolate, pecans, and orange peel. Transfer batter to prepared pan.

Bake until golden and tester inserted into center comes out clean, about 25 minutes. Transfer pan to rack. Brush top with remaining 1 tablespoon liqueur. Cool completely in pan. Cut into squares.

DO AHEAD: *Can be made 2 days ahead. Wrap in plastic; store cookies at room temperature.*

Technique Tip: **Soften Up**

Brown sugar is a mixture of white sugar and molasses, the molasses giving it a soft, moist texture. To keep brown sugar from drying out, be sure to store it in an airtight container at room temperature. If it does harden, there are easy ways to revive it. Add a piece of apple or a damp paper towel to the airtight container; keep it closed for a few days. You can also transfer the sugar to a microwave-safe dish, cover with damp paper towels, and microwave on high for 30 to 60 seconds, or simply let stand overnight.

Chocolate-Caramel Slice

A "slice," a delicious dessert popular in Australia, has a shortbread base that is topped with a layer of caramel and a chocolate glaze. Balancing all that sweetness is a sprinkling of sea salt. **Makes 20 to 24**

Crust

1	cup unbleached all purpose flour
¼	cup (packed) golden brown sugar
2	teaspoons cornstarch
¼	teaspoon salt
½	cup (1 stick) chilled unsalted butter, cut into ½-inch cubes
1	tablespoon ice water
1	large egg yolk

Caramel Topping

1	14-ounce can sweetened condensed milk
½	cup (packed) golden brown sugar
6	tablespoons (¾ stick) unsalted butter, diced
2	tablespoons golden syrup (such as Lyle's Golden Syrup) or dark corn syrup
1	teaspoon vanilla extract

Chocolate Glaze

6	ounces bittersweet or semisweet chocolate (do not exceed 61% cacao), chopped
3	tablespoons heavy whipping cream
	Flaked sea salt (such as Maldon)

(continued next page)

> ### Ingredient Tip: **Sweet and Salty**
> This recipe uses two ingredients from the U.K.—Lyle's Golden Syrup (a popular British sweetener with a mild butterscotch flavor) and Maldon salt (salt crystals made from evaporated seawater). Both products are available at some supermarkets and specialty foods stores and online from amazon.com.

Chocolate-Caramel Slice

(continued)

CRUST: Preheat oven to 350°F. Butter 12x8¼x1-inch fluted tart pan with removable bottom. Blend flour, sugar, cornstarch, and salt in processor. Add butter. Using on/off turns, blend until coarse meal forms. Add 1 tablespoon ice water and egg yolk. Blend until moist clumps form. Press dough onto bottom (not sides) of pan; pierce all over with fork [1]. Bake until golden, piercing if crust is bubbling, about 22 minutes. Cool completely.

CARAMEL TOPPING: Whisk milk, sugar, butter, syrup, and vanilla in heavy medium saucepan over medium heat until sugar dissolves, butter melts, and mixture comes to boil. Attach clip-on candy thermometer to side of pan. Boil gently until caramel is pale golden and thick and thermometer registers 225°F, whisking constantly, about 8 minutes. Pour caramel evenly over crust [2], then spread almost to edge of crust [3]; cool 15 minutes to set.

CHOCOLATE GLAZE: Meanwhile, melt chocolate with cream in microwave in 15-second intervals, stirring occasionally until smooth (do not overheat or chocolate will separate). Spread chocolate over warm caramel; sprinkle with sea salt. Refrigerate until chocolate is set, at least 1 hour.

DO AHEAD: *Can be made 3 days ahead. Cover and keep refrigerated.*

Cut dessert lengthwise into 4 strips. Cut each strip crosswise into 5 or 6 slices. Transfer to platter and serve.

Pecan Squares

This combination of a crispy, buttery crust and chewy pecan topping is reminiscent of a pecan pie—but much simpler to make. **Makes about 20**

2	cups unbleached all purpose flour
½	cup powdered sugar
1	cup (2 sticks) chilled unsalted butter, cut into ½-inch cubes
2	cups pecan pieces
¾	cup (packed) golden brown sugar
¾	cup honey
6	tablespoons heavy whipping cream

Preheat oven to 350°F. Butter 13x9x2-inch metal baking pan. Blend flour and powdered sugar in processor. Add butter and cut in, using on/off turns, until moist clumps form. Press dough onto bottom of prepared pan. Bake until golden, about 20 minutes. Maintain oven temperature.

Stir pecans, brown sugar, honey, and cream in heavy small saucepan over medium heat until sugar dissolves. Cook until mixture is bubbling around edges, about 2 minutes.

Pour pecan mixture over crust. Bake until filling is bubbling all over and is light caramel color, about 20 minutes. Cool completely.

DO AHEAD: *Can be made 1 day ahead. Cover baking pan tightly and let stand at room temperature.*

Cut into squares and serve.

Dried Fruit and Nut Bars

Looking for a healthful snack that actually tastes like something you'd want to eat anyway? These granola-type bars are packed with flavor and with good ingredients: whole grain cereal, walnuts, peanut butter, and three kinds of dried fruit. **Makes about 1½ dozen**

	Nonstick vegetable oil spray
3	cups puffed whole grain cereal (such as from Kashi)
½	cup walnuts, chopped
¼	cup chopped pitted dates
¼	cup chopped dried tart cherries
¼	cup raisins
⅓	cup creamy peanut butter (do not use old-fashioned style or freshly ground)
¼	cup honey
¼	cup light corn syrup

Preheat oven to 350°F. Spray 9x9x2-inch metal baking pan with nonstick spray. Mix cereal, walnuts, dates, cherries, and raisins in medium bowl. Combine peanut butter, honey, and corn syrup in heavy small saucepan. Bring to boil, whisking constantly. Continue whisking until mixture is bubbling vigorously and thickens slightly, about 1 minute. Pour peanut butter mixture over cereal mixture in bowl; stir to blend. Transfer mixture to prepared pan; press to compact.

Bake until just golden around edges, about 10 minutes. Cool completely. Cut into bars.

DO AHEAD: *Can be made 3 days ahead. Store in single layer between sheets of foil in airtight container at room temperature.*

All Dressed Up

The quickest and easiest way to decorate your bar cookies is to melt some milk chocolate or bittersweet chocolate and spread it over the baked cookies, then choose your topping:

S'MORES: Sprinkle mini marshmallows over the melted chocolate. Broil just until the marshmallows brown in spots. This will happen quickly, so be sure to keep a close eye on the pan.

A NEW KIND OF CANDY BAR: For a kids' party treat, top the melted chocolate with chopped up candy. Coarsely chopped toffee bars (such as Heath or Skor), Butterfinger candy bars, or peanut butter cups would all be delicious.

SNOWSTORM: Sprinkle sweetened coconut (toasted or untoasted) over the melted chocolate.

FRUITS AND NUTS: Top with your favorite combination. We like dried cranberries and chopped almonds or dried chopped apricots and pistachios.

ZIG AND ZAG: Melt some white chocolate and use a fork or spoon to drizzle it in a zigzag pattern over the dark chocolate.

CHILL OUT: Top the melted chocolate with fresh mint leaves or crushed peppermint candies (a nice choice for a holiday treat).

candy

candy

Espresso-Chocolate Fudge

This fudge has the silky texture of a no-beat fudge (and is almost as easy to make) and the rich taste of an old-fashioned, hand-beaten fudge. The secret is its mix of creamy ingredients—marshmallow creme, sweetened condensed milk, and whipping cream. Espresso intensifies the flavor of bittersweet chocolate. **Makes 30 pieces**

6	ounces bittersweet or semisweet chocolate (do not exceed 61% cacao), chopped
¼	cup marshmallow creme
1	ounce unsweetened chocolate, chopped
1	teaspoon vanilla extract
½	cup water
2	tablespoons instant espresso powder or instant coffee powder
1½	cups sugar
¾	cup canned sweetened condensed milk
⅓	cup heavy whipping cream
¼	cup (½ stick) unsalted butter
2	ounces high-quality white chocolate (such as Lindt or Perugina)
30	espresso beans
30	paper candy cups

Line 8x8x2-inch glass baking dish with aluminum foil, leaving overhang. Combine bittersweet chocolate, marshmallow creme, unsweetened chocolate, and vanilla in medium bowl. Mix ½ cup water and espresso powder in heavy large saucepan until espresso powder dissolves. Add sugar, milk, cream, and butter and stir over medium heat until sugar dissolves, occasionally brushing down sides of pan with wet pastry brush. Attach clip-on candy thermometer to side of pan. Increase heat to high and bring mixture to boil. Reduce heat to medium-high and stir constantly but slowly with wooden spoon until candy thermometer registers 234°F, about 12 minutes.

Immediately pour mixture over ingredients in bowl (do not scrape pan). Stir vigorously with wooden spoon until all chocolate melts and fudge thickens slightly, about 3 minutes (mixture will still be glossy). Transfer fudge mixture to prepared baking dish. Smooth top of fudge with rubber spatula. Refrigerate fudge uncovered until firm enough to cut, about 2 hours.

Technique Tip: Don't Scrape

When a candy recipe involves boiling, the instructions often specify "do not scrape pan" when the boiled mixture is poured into another container. This is important, as you don't want to scrape in any sugar crystals that might be clinging to the sides of the pan. The crystals could ruin the texture of the candy.

Using foil as aid, lift fudge from pan. Trim edges of fudge. Cut into 30 pieces. Melt white chocolate in top of double boiler over simmering water. Using fork, drizzle white chocolate decoratively over fudge. Press 1 espresso bean onto top of each piece of fudge. Place fudge in paper candy cups. Refrigerate fudge until white chocolate sets, about 20 minutes.

DO AHEAD: Can be made 1 week ahead. Refrigerate in airtight container. Bring to room temperature before serving.

Milk Chocolate–Peanut Butter Fudge

You don't need a big slab of marble and an audience of tourists to make great fudge. All it takes is a loaf pan, a metal bowl, a heavy saucepan, and most importantly, a candy thermometer. **Makes 24 pieces**

Milk Chocolate Fudge

3	ounces high-quality milk chocolate (such as Lindt or Perugina), chopped
½	ounce unsweetened chocolate, chopped
½	teaspoon vanilla extract
¾	cup sugar
⅓	cup canned sweetened condensed milk
⅓	cup water
¼	cup heavy whipping cream
2	tablespoons (¼ stick) unsalted butter, cut into pieces

Peanut Butter Fudge

⅓	cup super-chunky peanut butter (do not use old-fashioned style or freshly ground)
¾	cup sugar
⅓	cup canned sweetened condensed milk
⅓	cup water
¼	cup heavy whipping cream
1	ounce high-quality milk chocolate (such as Lindt or Perugina), chopped, melted
2	tablespoons very coarsely chopped roasted unsalted peanuts
24	paper candy cups

MILK CHOCOLATE FUDGE: Line 9x5x3-inch loaf pan with aluminum foil, leaving overhang. Place both chocolates and vanilla in medium metal bowl. Combine sugar, milk, ⅓ cup water, cream, and butter in heavy 2-quart saucepan. Stir over medium-low heat until sugar dissolves. Brush down sides of pan with wet pastry brush. Attach clip-on candy thermometer to side of pan. Increase heat to high and bring to rolling boil. Reduce heat to medium-high and stir constantly but slowly with wooden spoon until candy thermometer registers 230°F, about 10 minutes.

Immediately pour mixture over ingredients in bowl (do not scrape pan). Stir vigorously with wooden spoon until chocolate melts and fudge thickens slightly, about 1 minute (mixture will still be glossy). Transfer fudge mixture to prepared pan. Smooth top of fudge with rubber spatula. Cover with plastic wrap. Using hand, press gently into even layer. Remove plastic. Refrigerate mixture uncovered while preparing peanut butter fudge.

PEANUT BUTTER FUDGE: Place peanut butter in medium metal bowl. Stir sugar, milk, ⅓ cup water, and cream in heavy 2-quart saucepan over medium-low heat until sugar dissolves. Brush down sides of pan with wet pastry brush. Attach clip-on candy thermometer to side of pan. Increase heat to high and bring to rolling boil. Reduce heat to medium-high and stir constantly until candy thermometer registers 230°F, about 8 minutes.

Pour mixture over peanut butter in bowl (do not scrape pan). Stir vigorously with wooden spoon until fudge thickens slightly, about 3 minutes (mixture will begin to lose gloss).

Spoon peanut butter fudge over chocolate fudge in pan. Smooth top with rubber spatula. Cover with plastic wrap. Using hand, press gently into even layer. Remove plastic. Drizzle melted milk chocolate over fudge. Sprinkle nuts over. Refrigerate until firm enough to cut, about 2 hours.

Using foil as aid, lift fudge from pan. Fold down foil sides. Trim ends of fudge. Cut into 24 pieces. Transfer fudge to paper candy cups.

DO AHEAD: *Can be made 1 week ahead. Refrigerate in airtight container. Bring to room temperature before serving.*

Caramel-Pecan Fudge

Even people who don't love chocolate can find something to love here. This fudge is also known as penuche or brown sugar fudge. Its flavor is reminiscent of the very best pecan praline, but the texture is not grainy at all—it's smooth and creamy. **Makes 24 pieces**

1¼   cups sugar
1   cup (lightly packed) golden brown sugar
1   cup heavy whipping cream
⅔   cup canned sweetened condensed milk
¼   cup (½ stick) unsalted butter, cut into pieces
⅓   cup water
2   tablespoons light corn syrup
¾   cup very coarsely chopped toasted pecans
24   pecan halves, toasted
24   paper candy cups

Line 9x5x3-inch loaf pan with aluminum foil, leaving overhang. Mix both sugars in heavy 3-quart saucepan, breaking up any lumps with fingertips. Add cream, milk, butter, ⅓ cup water, and corn syrup. Stir over medium-low heat until sugar dissolves. Brush down sides of pan with wet pastry brush. Attach clip-on candy thermometer to side of pan. Increase heat to high and bring to rolling boil. Reduce heat to medium-high and cook until candy thermometer registers 232°F, stirring frequently, about 15 minutes. Pour onto rimmed baking sheet (do not scrape pan). Cool 10 minutes.

Using rubber spatula, scrape mixture into medium metal bowl. Using hand-held electric mixer, beat fudge at high speed until thick and creamy, about 5 minutes. Beat with wooden spoon until fudge begins to lose its gloss and thickens even more, about 2 minutes. (To test for proper consistency, mound fudge mixture on spoon; turn upside down. If mixture falls off spoon, beat fudge again and repeat test.) Mix in chopped nuts. Transfer fudge to prepared loaf pan. Using rubber spatula, spread into smooth, even layer. Arrange pecan halves lengthwise in 3 rows atop fudge, spacing evenly. Press to adhere. Refrigerate uncovered until firm enough to cut, about 2 hours.

Using foil as aid, lift fudge from pan. Fold down foil sides. Trim ends of fudge. Cut between pecan halves into 24 pieces. Transfer fudge to paper candy cups.

DO AHEAD: *Can be made 1 week ahead. Refrigerate in airtight container. Bring to room temperature before serving.*

Melting Chocolate

Tempering is a technique that involves melting and cooling chocolate to specific temperatures in order to create good cocoa crystal structure. This produces chocolate that is glossy with a crisp, clean snap. Because the process can be time-consuming and difficult to master without a machine, our recipes use a simplified alternative technique: The chocolate is melted to specific temperatures, then chilled to set the chocolate quickly (this helps prevent bloom—streaks of cocoa butter that affect the appearance of the chocolate). The finished chocolates should be stored in the refrigerator, but for the best texture, allow them to stand at room temperature for about 15 minutes before serving.

When melting chocolate for dipping truffles and other candy centers, moisture is the enemy. Be careful not to let any steam or water come in contact with the chocolate or it will seize, or become lumpy, making it unsuitable for dipping. For the same reason, never cover chocolate when melting.

Leftover melted chocolate that remains in the pan after dipping truffles or other centers can be used several ways:

1. Add nuts and drop by spoonfuls onto foil-lined sheets and chill to form nut clusters.

2. Dip whole fresh strawberries into the chocolate; place on a foil-lined baking sheet and chill until firm.

3. Add enough cream to thin the chocolate to a pourable consistency. Use as a fondue for fresh fruits, cubes of angel food cake, and cookies.

4. Spoon chocolate into small disks on a foil-lined sheet and chill until set. Store disks in resealable plastic bags in the freezer for future use. You can also add them to milk and heat them to make rich hot chocolate.

Pine Nut and Orange Fudge

This sophisticated fudge is subtly flavored with finely grated orange peel and studded with tiny, delicate pine nuts instead of the usual walnuts or almonds. **Makes 24 pieces**

2¼	cups sugar
¾	cup heavy whipping cream
⅔	cup canned sweetened condensed milk
½	cup sour cream
⅓	cup water
2	tablespoons (¼ stick) unsalted butter, cut into pieces, room temperature
2	tablespoons light corn syrup
1	tablespoon finely grated orange peel
¾	cup pine nuts, toasted
24	paper candy cups

Line 9x5x3-inch loaf pan with aluminum foil, leaving overhang. Combine sugar, cream, milk, sour cream, ⅓ cup water, butter, corn syrup, and orange peel in heavy 3-quart saucepan. Stir over medium-low heat until sugar dissolves, about 15 minutes. Brush down sides of pan with wet pastry brush. Attach clip-on candy thermometer to side of pan. Increase heat to high and bring to boil. Reduce heat to medium-high and cook until candy thermometer registers 234°F, stirring frequently, about 12 minutes. Pour mixture onto rimmed baking sheet (do not scrape pan). Cool 15 minutes.

Using rubber spatula, scrape mixture into medium metal bowl. Using electric mixer, beat fudge until thick and creamy and no longer glossy, about 5 minutes. (To test for proper consistency, mound fudge mixture on spoon; turn upside down. If mixture falls off spoon, beat fudge again and repeat test.) Mix in pine nuts and immediately transfer fudge to prepared pan. Cover with plastic wrap and press to flatten fudge into even layer. Refrigerate until firm enough to cut, about 1 hour.

Using foil as aid, lift fudge from pan. Fold down foil sides. Trim ends of fudge. Cut into 24 pieces. Transfer fudge to paper candy cups.

DO AHEAD: *Can be made 1 week ahead. Refrigerate in airtight container. Bring to room temperature before serving.*

Ingredient Tip: **Pine Nuts**

Pine nuts—which do, in fact, come from pine cones—are very high in fat, so they can go rancid rather quickly. For this reason, they should be stored in an airtight container in the refrigerator or freezer.

Tools of the Trade

When making candy, which can be more demanding than preparing other kinds of desserts, it's important to have the appropriate equipment.

CANDY THERMOMETERS: If a recipe calls for a candy thermometer, it's essential to use one for the most accurate results. Don't be tempted to merely follow the cooking time provided in a recipe. Candymaking is very precise; being even a few degrees off can make a big difference in the texture of your candy.

Select a candy thermometer with a bulb attached to a metal backing that's set low enough to measure the heat of the candy mixture, but that won't touch the bottom of the pan. The ideal thermometer has easy-to-read numbers in 2-degree increments and a clip that will easily attach to the side of the pan. This allows you the freedom to constantly stir the candy mixtures without having to hold a thermometer in place.

Always check the thermometer's accuracy before you get started. Place the thermometer in a saucepan of boiling water for a few minutes. It should read 212°F. If it registers above or below, add or subtract the same number from the temperature in the recipe.

When reading a thermometer, do it at eye level for accuracy.

SAUCEPANS: Use high-quality, heavy-duty pans with evenly thick bottoms and sides. Thin, flimsy pans won't work, as the candy mixtures will cook unevenly and may even burn at the sides of the pan. If a recipe calls for a specific size saucepan, use it, as candy mixtures can rise considerably as they boil.

WOODEN SPOONS: A long-handled, sturdy wooden spoon is best for candymaking; it won't conduct heat and the temperature of the candy mixture will be more accurate. Wood also allows you to stir comfortably, because it never gets hot.

PASTRY BRUSHES: You'll use these to brush down the sides of the pan when dissolving sugar in the candy mixture, as well as for a host of other dessert-making uses.

Caramel–Dark Chocolate Truffles with Fleur de Sel

Salted caramels meet truffles in these indulgent treats. They get their slight saltiness from fleur de sel, a fine French sea salt that's becoming more widely available. If you can find Maldon sea salt—an English salt that comes in larger flakes—sprinkle the chocolate-coated truffles with it at the end for a very attractive finished look. Look for both fleur de sel and Maldon sea salt in well-stocked supermarkets and specialty foods stores, or order online from amazon.com. Start this recipe at least a day ahead as the truffles need to chill overnight. **Makes about 32**

20 ounces bittersweet or semisweet chocolate (do not exceed 61% cacao), finely chopped, divided
⅓ cup sugar
2 tablespoons water
⅔ cup heavy whipping cream
¼ teaspoon fleur de sel plus additional for sprinkling
½ cup natural unsweetened cocoa powder

Stir 8 ounces chocolate in metal bowl set over saucepan of barely simmering water (do not allow bowl to touch water) until chocolate is melted and smooth. Remove bowl from over water.

Combine sugar and 2 tablespoons water in heavy small saucepan. Stir over medium heat until sugar dissolves, occasionally brushing down sides of pan with wet pastry brush. Increase heat; boil until syrup is deep amber color, occasionally brushing down pan sides and swirling pan, about 4 minutes. Add cream (mixture will bubble vigorously). Stir over very low heat until caramel is smooth. Mix caramel and ¼ teaspoon fleur de sel into melted chocolate. Chill until truffle filling is firm, at least 3 hours.

Place cocoa in bowl. Using 1 tablespoon truffle filling for each truffle, roll into balls, then roll in cocoa. Arrange on baking sheet. Cover; chill overnight.

Line rimmed baking sheet with aluminum foil. Stir remaining 12 ounces chocolate in medium metal bowl set over saucepan of barely simmering water (do not allow bowl to touch water) until chocolate is melted and smooth and thermometer inserted into chocolate registers 115°F. Remove bowl from over water. Working quickly, submerge 1 truffle in melted chocolate. Using dinner fork, lift out truffle and tap fork against side of bowl, allowing excess chocolate to drip back into bowl. Using small knife, push truffle off fork and onto prepared sheet. Repeat with remaining truffles. Sprinkle truffles lightly with additional fleur de sel. Refrigerate until coating sets, at least 1 hour.

DO AHEAD: *Can be made 1 week ahead. Refrigerate in airtight container. Bring to room temperature before serving.*

That's a Wrap

The candies in this chapter are even more impressive when they're cleverly packaged and presented. Discount and import stores are a terrific source for unusual and decorative containers, including tins, boxes, and baskets. For candies that can be stacked (bark and brittle, for example), a box or container with 5-inch-high sides is fine. But for the more delicate candies (such as truffles, or anything inside a paper cup), keep them in a single layer in a box no more than 2 inches deep.

• **Create a tiered tower of decorative holiday tins in graduated sizes.** Wrap the whole tower in colored cellophane and tie it with a French silk ribbon. Decorate the ribbon with anything you like: A Christmas ornament, a sprig of pine or eucalyptus, silk flowers. This is a great way to deliver several different types of candies—truffles, toffees, caramels—each in its own tin. Holiday tins are often sold in nesting sets at stores.

• **Package the candies using an item of kitchen equipment that itself makes a great gift.** Use a fluted tart pan, baking dish, or decorative platter, for example. Stroll through a housewares store and let your imagination go. If possible, link the type of candy to the gift in some way—presenting the Layered Peppermint Crunch Bark (page 621) on a large baking sheet, or enclosing the Asian-influenced New-Wave Rocky Road (page 622) with crystallized ginger inside a Chinese bamboo steamer.

• **Think beyond traditional candy boxes—way beyond.** Use ceramic containers, papier-mâché or fabric-covered boxes, wicker baskets, star-shaped metal mesh containers (often available in silver or gold at import stores during the holidays), Shaker birch boxes. Line them with waxed paper, or put the candies inside a clear cellophane bag inside the container.

Recipe Tip: Truffles

Chocolate truffles are a decadent treat—rich mixtures of melted chocolate and cream and/or butter, plus other ingredients that may include fruit, nuts, spices, or liqueurs. The chocolate mixture is chilled and rolled into balls, then usually coated with cocoa powder or melted chocolate. Present them in paper candy cups, available at baking or candymaking supply stores (or see Online and Mail-Order Sources on page 632).

Fig and Walnut Truffles

Cognac gives a heady flavor to these easy-to-make truffles. When rolling the truffles in your hands to shape, be sure to work quickly so that the ganache doesn't melt. **Makes 36**

¾	cup heavy whipping cream
6	tablespoons (¾ stick) unsalted butter
3	tablespoons light corn syrup
12	ounces bittersweet or semisweet chocolate (do not exceed 61% cacao), chopped
1	tablespoon Cognac or other brandy
⅔	cup chopped dried Calimyrna figs
⅔	cup chopped toasted walnuts
	Natural unsweetened cocoa powder

Line 8x8x2-inch metal baking pan with aluminum foil, leaving overhang. Heat cream, butter, and corn syrup in heavy medium saucepan over medium heat until just boiling, stirring occasionally. Remove saucepan from heat. Add chocolate and stir until chocolate melts and mixture is smooth. Mix in Cognac, then figs and walnuts. Pour into prepared pan; refrigerate just until firm enough to handle, about 1 hour.

Using foil as aid, lift chocolate block from pan; place on work surface. Flatten foil at edges.

Cut chocolate mixture into 36 squares. Roll each square by hand to form ball. Dust lightly with cocoa. Cover and chill until firm, at least 4 hours.

DO AHEAD: *Can be made 4 days ahead. Refrigerate in airtight container. Bring to room temperature before serving.*

Dark Chocolate Truffles with Honey and Lime

Lime flavors the bittersweet chocolate three ways: It's infused into the cream that melts the chocolate, it's stirred into the melted honey that sweetens the ganache, and it's combined with the cocoa powder that coats the truffles. Make the cocoa-lime truffle coating a day ahead; it needs to dry overnight. **Makes about 55**

1½	teaspoons finely grated lime peel, divided
⅔	cup sugar
1	cup natural unsweetened cocoa powder
15	ounces bittersweet or semisweet chocolate (do not exceed 61% cacao), finely chopped
1	cup heavy whipping cream
¼	cup fresh lime juice
¼	cup honey
6	tablespoons (¾ stick) unsalted butter, room temperature

Place 1 teaspoon lime peel on work surface. Chop very finely; transfer to medium bowl. Add sugar and rub together with fingertips until mixture is slightly moist. Mix in cocoa. Spread on rimmed baking sheet. Let dry uncovered at room temperature 1 day.

Place chocolate in medium bowl. Finely chop remaining ½ teaspoon lime peel; transfer to medium saucepan. Add cream to pan and bring just to boil over medium heat. Cover and set aside 10 minutes. Uncover cream mixture, return to boil, and pour over chocolate. Let stand 30 seconds. Stir until chocolate is smooth.

Meanwhile, combine lime juice and honey in small saucepan. Stir over low heat until honey melts and mixture is warm. Gradually stir warm honey mixture into chocolate mixture. Add butter 2 tablespoons at a time, stirring until ganache is smooth. Cover; chill until firm, at least 4 hours or overnight.

Line 2 rimmed baking sheets with aluminum foil. Drop cold ganache by heaping teaspoonfuls onto prepared sheets. Refrigerate 30 minutes. Working quickly, roll ganache between palms into balls and return to baking sheets, briefly freezing ganache on sheets if becoming too soft to shape. Chill truffles until firm, about 45 minutes.

Roll truffles in cocoa mixture to coat; shake off excess.

DO AHEAD: *Can be made 2 weeks ahead. Refrigerate in airtight container.*

Chocolate-Orange Truffles with Almonds

These truffles are flavored with Grand Marnier and covered in a crunchy almond coating—not the usual cocoa powder or melted chocolate. If you don't have orange liqueur, try a berry variety like Chambord or crème de cassis. **Makes 25**

¾	**cup heavy whipping cream**
12	**ounces bittersweet or semisweet chocolate (do not exceed 61% cacao), finely chopped**
2	**tablespoons Grand Marnier or other orange liqueur**
1½	**teaspoons finely grated orange peel**
1¼	**cups almonds, toasted, finely chopped**

Line 8x8x2-inch metal baking pan with aluminum foil, leaving overhang. Bring cream to boil in heavy medium saucepan. Remove from heat. Add chocolate and whisk until melted and smooth. Whisk in Grand Marnier and orange peel. Pour into prepared pan; freeze just until firm, about 30 minutes.

Using foil as aid, lift chocolate block from pan; place on work surface. Fold down foil sides. Cut chocolate mixture into 25 squares. Place nuts in small bowl. Press 1 chocolate square into nuts, coating completely. Roll truffle between palms into ball. Place on small baking sheet. Repeat with remaining chocolate and nuts. Cover; refrigerate until very firm, about 2 hours. Serve cold.

Truffle Techniques

You might not guess it by looking at them, but truffles are among the easiest candies to make once you learn the right techniques. When rolling the chocolate base, it's important to handle it as little as possible (so it doesn't start to melt). We recommend scooping out the well-chilled ganache with a mini ice-cream scoop with a release. If you don't have the right-size scoop, form spheres of chocolate with a teaspoon-size measuring spoon, then use your hands to smooth out the spheres (work quickly so that the chocolate doesn't melt). There are two primary techniques for coating truffles in chocolate:

For a hand-coated chocolate with a thin coating, start by scooping a little bit of melted chocolate into your palm. Next, roll a chilled truffle in your palm until it's evenly coated, then drop it onto a waxed paper–lined baking sheet or roll it in a bowl of chopped nuts. It's a bit messy (your kids will love it), but it's also easy and effective.

For a dipped chocolate with a thicker chocolate shell, submerge a truffle in melted chocolate. Using a fork, remove the dipped truffle and tap the fork on the side of the pan to allow the excess chocolate to drip back into the pan [1]. Next, run a small knife under the base of the truffle, gently pushing it onto a foil-lined sheet [2].

1

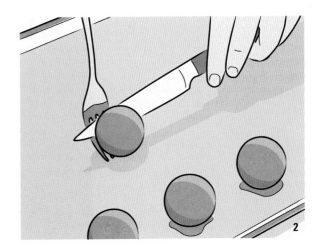

2

Chocolate Truffle Croquembouche

A traditional croquembouche *(customarily served at French weddings) is a stunning tower of custard-filled cream puffs glued together with caramelized sugar. This twist on a classic* croquembouche *is made with chocolate truffles instead of cream puffs, and is decorated with candied violet petals and fresh flowers. You'll find candied violet petals at some supermarkets, at cake decorating stores and specialty foods stores, and online at cheftools.com. Styrofoam cones are available at most floral and party supply stores.*

Makes 76 truffles

Truffles

1	cup plus 2 tablespoons heavy whipping cream
¾	cup (1½ sticks) unsalted butter, cut into 12 pieces
2¼	pounds bittersweet or semisweet chocolate (do not exceed 61% cacao), chopped
¾	cup sour cream
6	tablespoons Grand Marnier or other orange liqueur
1½	tablespoons finely grated orange peel
1½	cups powdered sugar
1½	cups natural unsweetened cocoa powder

Dipping

1¾	pounds high-quality white chocolate (such as Lindt or Perugina), chopped
1½	pounds bittersweet or semisweet chocolate, chopped
38	candied violet petals (optional)

Assembly

1	12-inch-tall Styrofoam cone
	Rose leaves and miniature white roses or other small flowers

Technique Tip: Dipping Truffles

Before dipping the truffles in the melted chocolate, brush off any excess powdered sugar or cocoa powder to prevent it from affecting the sheen of the chocolate. Keep the melted chocolate at 115°F—at this temperature, the chocolate is the perfect consistency for dipping. Use high-quality chocolates and make enough room in the freezer to fit all the truffles.

TRUFFLES: Bring cream and butter to simmer in heavy large saucepan. Reduce heat to medium; stir until butter melts. Add chocolate; whisk until melted and smooth. Remove from heat. Whisk in sour cream, liqueur, and orange peel. Pour into 13x9x2-inch baking dish. Chill mixture until firm enough to hold shape, about 1 hour.

Line 4 large baking sheets with foil; sift sugar over 2 sheets and cocoa over 2 sheets. Using ¾-ounce ice-cream scoop (1½ tablespoons), scoop truffle mixture, mounding slightly, and release onto sugar-dusted sheet. Repeat to form total of 28 large truffles on sugar-dusted sheets and 28 on cocoa-dusted sheets. Using ¼-ounce ice-cream scoop (1½ teaspoons), scoop truffle mixture and release onto sugar-dusted sheet. Repeat to form total of 10 small truffles on sugar-dusted sheets and 10 on cocoa-dusted sheets. Freeze truffles 10 minutes.

Roll each truffle on sugar-dusted sheets in sugar; roll between palms of hands into smooth round and place on clean baking sheet. Roll each truffle on cocoa-dusted sheets in cocoa; roll between palms of hands into smooth round and place on same baking sheet as sugar-dusted truffles. Freeze 1 hour.

DIPPING: Line 2 baking sheets with foil. Melt white chocolate in top of double boiler over simmering water, stirring until candy thermometer registers 115°F. Remove from over water. Submerge 1 large sugar-dusted truffle in white chocolate, tilting pan if necessary. Using long fork, lift truffle from chocolate. Tap fork gently against side of pan (if necessary) to remove excess chocolate. Using knife as aid, slide truffle off fork and onto clean prepared baking sheet. Wipe fork clean. Repeat process with all remaining sugar-dusted truffles. Freeze truffles 15 minutes.

Reheat remaining white chocolate to 115°F over simmering water. Repeat dipping process to give truffles a double coating of white chocolate.

Melt bittersweet chocolate in top of clean double boiler over simmering water, stirring until candy thermometer registers 115°F. Dip spoon into bittersweet chocolate and wave quickly over white chocolate-coated truffles, creating zigzag lines. Chill truffles.

Pretty Enough to Eat

Whether it's white roses tucked between these chocolate truffles or ruby red petals strewn across a single layer cake, using flowers as decoration is a simple way to make desserts look beautiful and elegant (and hide occasional flaws). Since not all fresh flowers are safe to eat, be sure what you buy is edible and chemical-free (and grown without pesticides). Which blooms are edible? Roses, gardenias, carnations, nasturtiums, pansies, violets, marigolds, Johnny-jump-ups, snapdragons, and blossoms from citrus and herbs like rosemary. You may have some of these flowers in your own garden, but supermarkets, farmers' markets, and florists are other good sources. When using fresh flowers, apply them just before serving, or use small flower holders to keep them fresh.

Line 2 more baking sheets with foil. Using same dipping process, dip cocoa-dusted truffles into bittersweet chocolate, dipping each truffle only once. Immediately top each with candied violet petal, if desired. Chill truffles 1 hour.

DO AHEAD: *Can be made 3 weeks ahead. Cover truffles and remaining melted bittersweet chocolate separately and chill.*

ASSEMBLY: Remelt remaining bittersweet chocolate. Brush melted bittersweet chocolate in 2-inch-wide strip down length of Styrofoam cone. Wrap waxed paper around cone, covering completely and pressing against chocolate to adhere [1]. Place cone on platter. Holding toothpick at sharp angle, press ⅔ of toothpick into cone near base. Press 1 large truffle onto toothpick [2]. Repeat with more toothpicks and remaining large truffles, alternating dark and white truffles and attaching in spiral design toward top of cone. Begin attaching small truffles 4 inches from top of cone and continue to cover completely.

DO AHEAD: *Can be made 1 day ahead. Cover and chill.*

Press rose leaves between truffles on cone, covering any spaces [3]. Press toothpicks into roses and attach to leaves between truffles.

DO AHEAD: *Can be made 3 hours ahead. Chill.*

Layered Peppermint Crunch Bark

This bark features white chocolate, bittersweet chocolate, and peppermint candies—perfect for the holidays. To crush the candies, place them in a resealable plastic bag and tap them firmly with a rolling pin. **Makes 36 pieces**

17   ounces high-quality white chocolate (such as Lindt or Perugina), chopped
30   red-and-white-striped hard peppermint candies, coarsely crushed (about 6 ounces), divided
7   ounces bittersweet or semisweet chocolate (do not exceed 61% cacao), chopped
6   tablespoons heavy whipping cream
¾   teaspoon peppermint extract

Turn large baking sheet bottom side up. Cover tightly with aluminum foil. Mark 12x9-inch rectangle on foil. Stir white chocolate in medium metal bowl set over saucepan of barely simmering water until chocolate is melted and smooth and candy thermometer registers 110°F (chocolate will feel warm). Remove bowl from over water. Pour ⅔ cup melted white chocolate onto rectangle on foil. Using icing spatula, spread chocolate to fill rectangle. Sprinkle with ¼ cup crushed candies. Chill until set, about 15 minutes.

Stir bittersweet chocolate, cream, and peppermint extract in heavy medium saucepan over medium-low heat until just melted and smooth. Cool to barely lukewarm, about 5 minutes. Pour bittersweet chocolate mixture in long lines over white chocolate rectangle. Using offset spatula, spread bittersweet chocolate in even layer. Refrigerate until very cold and firm, about 25 minutes.

Rewarm remaining white chocolate in bowl set over barely simmering water to 110°F. Working quickly, pour white chocolate over firm bittersweet chocolate layer [1]; spread to cover [2]. Immediately sprinkle with remaining crushed candies [3]. Chill just until firm, about 20 minutes.

Lift foil with bark onto work surface; trim edges. Cut bark crosswise into 2-inch-wide strips. Using metal spatula, slide bark off foil and onto work surface. Cut each strip crosswise into 3 sections and each section diagonally into 2 triangles.

DO AHEAD: *Can be made 2 weeks ahead. Refrigerate in airtight container. Let stand 15 minutes at room temperature before serving.*

{ ## Technique Tip: **Spreading the Chocolate**
To keep the white chocolate layer from remelting when you add the bittersweet chocolate, pour out the bittersweet chocolate mixture in three thick lines down the length of the baking sheet. This speeds up the spreading so that there isn't time for the white chocolate to melt. }

Dried Fruit and Nut Chocolate Bark

Here's an incredibly versatile bark recipe: Just use whatever dried fruits and nuts you happen to have on hand. For a sweeter version, substitute semisweet chocolate chips for the bittersweet. **Makes about 1 pound**

1   11½-ounce bag bittersweet chocolate chips (about 2 cups)
⅔   cup mixed nuts (such as walnuts, pistachios, pecans, and almonds), toasted
⅔   cup mixed dried fruit (such as raisins, cranberries, cherries, quartered figs, and quartered apricots)
6   quarter-size rounds crystallized ginger, thinly sliced
⅛   teaspoon fleur de sel or coarse kosher salt (optional)

Line small baking sheet with aluminum foil. Melt chocolate chips in medium bowl over saucepan of simmering water, stirring until melted and smooth. Pour melted chocolate onto foil, spreading with offset spatula to scant ¼-inch thickness. Scatter nuts and dried fruit over chocolate. Sprinkle with ginger. Sprinkle with fleur de sel, if desired. Chill until chocolate is firm, about 30 minutes. Peel off foil. Cut chocolate into irregular pieces. Serve bark slightly chilled.

DO AHEAD: *Can be made 1 week ahead. Refrigerate in airtight container.*

New-Wave Rocky Road

Traditional rocky road candy (chocolate, nuts, and marshmallows) is amped up with orange peel, spicy crystallized ginger, and tart dried cherries. If you like, use your own Homemade Marshmallows (page 626). **Makes 40 pieces**

26   ounces bittersweet or semisweet chocolate, coarsely chopped
2   teaspoons finely grated orange peel
¾   cup walnut halves
¾   cup chopped dried tart cherries or dried cranberries
3   tablespoons finely chopped crystallized ginger
22   large marshmallows
40   paper or foil candy cups

Line 11x7x2-inch metal baking pan with aluminum foil, leaving overhang. Stir chocolate in medium metal bowl set over saucepan of simmering water (do not allow bowl to touch water) until melted and smooth and candy thermometer registers 115°F. Remove bowl from over water. Mix in orange peel, then walnuts, cherries, and ginger. Fold in marshmallows. Pour into prepared pan, spreading evenly. Chill until chocolate is just firm enough to cut, about 1 hour.

Using foil as aid, lift candy from pan. Fold down foil sides. Cut candy crosswise into 8 strips, then cut each strip lengthwise into 5 pieces. Transfer rocky road squares to paper or foil candy cups.

DO AHEAD: *Can be made 2 weeks ahead. Keep rocky road squares refrigerated in airtight container. Let stand at room temperature at least 30 minutes and up to 1 hour before serving.*

♨ Chocolate Panforte Candies

Traditional panforte *is a confection from Siena, Italy, that combines cocoa, spices, nuts, honey, and citrus with just enough flour to hold it all together. Here, those same flavors (minus the flour) become the topping for rich chocolate patties.* **Makes 14**

½   **cup quartered dried black Mission figs**
¼   **cup orange juice**
2   **tablespoons honey**
½   **teaspoon ground nutmeg**
¼   **teaspoon ground cloves**
1¼   **teaspoons finely grated orange peel, divided**
½   **teaspoon ground cinnamon**
⅔   **cup (scant) hazelnuts, toasted**
1   **cup bittersweet or semisweet chocolate chips**
14   **standard (⅓-cup) paper muffin baking cup liners**

Cook figs, orange juice, honey, nutmeg, cloves, and 1 teaspoon orange peel in heavy small saucepan over medium-high heat until liquid forms thick syrup that coats figs, stirring occasionally, about 6 minutes. Remove from heat. Mix in cinnamon, remaining ¼ teaspoon orange peel, and nuts.

Melt chocolate in microwave-safe bowl on medium setting until melted and warm, stopping once to stir, about 1½ minutes. Arrange paper cups on rimmed baking sheet. Spoon 1 mounded teaspoon chocolate into each paper cup. Tap baking sheet on work surface to spread chocolate over bottoms of cups. Top center of each with about 1 mounded teaspoon fig mixture. Refrigerate until firm, about 1 hour. Peel off paper.

DO AHEAD: *Can be made 3 days ahead. Refrigerate in airtight container. Let stand at room temperature at least 15 minutes before serving.*

 Mixed Nut Spiced Toffee

Traditional English toffee gets a hit of allspice and a blend of nuts. Instead of taking the time to melt chocolate and dip the toffee into it, this recipe efficiently utilizes the residual heat from the candy to melt bittersweet chocolate into a sweet and easy topping. **Makes about 2 pounds**

1¼   **cups (2½ sticks) unsalted butter**
1   **cup sugar**
½   **cup (packed) golden brown sugar**
⅓   **cup water**
1   **tablespoon mild-flavored (light) molasses**
½   **teaspoon salt**
¼   **teaspoon ground allspice**
2   **cups coarsely chopped toasted mixed nuts (such as cashews, almonds, and pistachios), divided**
5   **ounces bittersweet or semisweet chocolate, coarsely chopped**

Butter small rimmed baking sheet. Melt butter in heavy medium saucepan over low heat. Add both sugars, ⅓ cup water, molasses, salt, and allspice; stir until sugar dissolves. Attach clip-on candy thermometer to side of pan. Increase heat to medium; boil until thermometer registers 290°F, stirring constantly but slowly and scraping bottom of pan with wooden spatula, about 20 minutes. Remove pan from heat. Mix in 1½ cups nuts. Immediately pour candy onto prepared sheet. Spread toffee to ¼-inch thickness. Immediately sprinkle chocolate over toffee. Let stand 1 minute. Using back of spoon, spread chocolate over toffee. Sprinkle with remaining ½ cup nuts. Chill 1 hour. Break toffee into pieces.

DO AHEAD: *Can be made 2 weeks ahead. Refrigerate in airtight container. Let stand at room temperature at least 30 minutes and up to 1 hour before serving.*

Storage Tip: Why Airtight?
Even if you're presenting the toffee as a gift, it's important to keep the candy in an airtight container or bag. Otherwise, the toffee will draw moisture from the air—and extra moisture makes candy turn unappealingly soft. The toffee should be kept refrigerated until 30 minutes to 1 hour before serving.

♦♦♦ Macadamia Brittle with Fleur de Sel

Brittle is essentially caramelized sugar that is stirred together with nuts and baking soda (which aerates the candy) and then spread out on a large sheet of aluminum foil. In this brittle, the decadent sweetness is balanced by a sprinkling of sea salt. Cut the brittle into large pieces to enjoy on its own, or chop it into smaller pieces to sprinkle over ice cream. **Makes about ¾ pound**

1	cup unsalted macadamia nuts, toasted, chopped, cooled
1	tablespoon chilled butter, diced
1	teaspoon baking soda
½	teaspoon fleur de sel or other coarse sea salt
1	cup sugar
½	cup water
2	tablespoons light corn syrup

Place large sheet of aluminum foil on work surface; butter foil. Combine nuts, butter, baking soda, and fleur de sel in medium bowl.

Stir sugar, ½ cup water, and corn syrup in medium saucepan over medium heat until sugar dissolves. Boil without stirring until syrup is deep amber color, occasionally brushing down sides of pan with wet pastry brush and swirling pan, about 10 minutes. Remove caramel from heat. Immediately stir in nut mixture (caramel will bubble vigorously). Pour caramel onto prepared foil; spread thinly. Cool brittle until hard; cut into pieces.

DO AHEAD: *Can be made 1 week ahead. Store brittle in airtight container at room temperature.*

♦♦ Pecan Pralines

A southern delicacy dating back to the mid-1700s, pralines (pronounced prah-leens) are an addictive mix of pecans, brown sugar, butter, and milk. Unlike other candies, their texture is meant to be somewhat grainy and sugary. For less molasses and more caramel flavor, use golden brown sugar in place of the dark brown. **Makes about 24**

1½	cups sugar
¾	cup (packed) dark brown sugar
½	cup plus 2 tablespoons (or more) canned evaporated milk
¼	cup (½ stick) unsalted butter
1	teaspoon vanilla extract
1½	cups pecan halves, toasted

Line 2 baking sheets with waxed paper. Butter paper. Stir both sugars and ½ cup plus 2 tablespoons evaporated milk in heavy medium saucepan over medium heat until sugar dissolves. Attach clip-on candy thermometer to side of pan. Continue cooking over medium heat until thermometer registers 240°F, stirring constantly but slowly, about 5 minutes. Add butter and vanilla; stir until thermometer registers 240°F, about 2 minutes. Remove from heat. Add nuts and stir until mixture is creamy, about 1 minute.

Working quickly, drop mixture by rounded tablespoonfuls onto prepared sheets (if candy mixture begins to set in saucepan, add 2 tablespoons evaporated milk and stir over medium heat until softened). Let candies stand until firm, about 30 minutes. Peel candies off waxed paper.

DO AHEAD: *Can be made 2 weeks ahead. Store pralines in airtight container at room temperature.*

More to Try

Pralines are so great on their own that it might not occur to you to eat them any other way. But if you happen to have some left over, coarsely chop them and sprinkle over vanilla ice cream or a pan of chocolate-glazed brownies.

Coffee-Spice Caramels

Before the cream becomes caramel, it's steeped in a fragrant mix of coffee, cloves, cinnamon, and nutmeg. The caramels are great on their own—but they're even better with a chocolate coating. **Makes about 42**

2	cups (about) heavy whipping cream, divided
⅓	cup (packed) freshly ground (medium-grind) coffee
20	whole cloves
1	cinnamon stick, cut into small pieces
¼	teaspoon freshly grated nutmeg
1½	cups sugar
¼	cup light corn syrup
2	tablespoons (¼ stick) unsalted butter
1	pound bittersweet or semisweet chocolate, chopped
3	ounces high-quality milk chocolate (such as Lindt or Perugina), chopped
42	(about) paper candy cups

Line 8x8x2-inch metal baking pan with aluminum foil, leaving overhang. Generously butter foil. Bring 1¼ cups cream, coffee, cloves, cinnamon, and nutmeg to boil in heavy 2½-quart saucepan. Remove pan from heat. Cover and let steep 30 minutes.

Return mixture to boil, stirring constantly. Strain through fine sieve into measuring cup, pressing with back of spoon to extract all liquid. Add enough additional cream to measure 1½ cups. Return mixture to same saucepan. Add sugar, corn syrup, and butter. Stir over medium-low heat until sugar dissolves. Attach clip-on candy thermometer to side of pan. Increase heat to medium and bring to boil, brushing down sides of pan with wet pastry brush. Boil over medium heat until candy thermometer registers 242°F, stirring occasionally, about 20 minutes. Pour into prepared baking pan (do not scrape saucepan). Cool caramel mixture until firm enough to cut, about 2 hours.

Line baking sheet with waxed paper. Using foil as aid, lift caramel from pan. Fold down foil sides. Using buttered heavy large knife, cut caramel into 1x1¼-inch rectangles. Transfer to prepared sheet, reshaping caramel into rectangles if necessary. Refrigerate until firm, about 30 minutes.

Line 2 baking sheets with waxed paper. Melt bittersweet chocolate in top of double boiler over barely simmering water, stirring occasionally, until candy thermometer registers 115°F. Remove from over water. Working quickly, submerge 1 caramel in chocolate. Using dinner fork, lift out caramel. Tap bottom of fork on sides of pan, allowing excess chocolate to drip back into pan. Using small knife, push caramel off fork and onto prepared sheet. Repeat with remaining caramels, setting double boiler over hot water occasionally to rewarm chocolate as needed. Refrigerate candies until chocolate is firm, about 30 minutes.

Stir milk chocolate in top of double boiler over barely simmering water until melted and smooth. Immediately transfer to parchment cone or small resealable plastic bag; cut off tip. Pipe chocolate in diagonal spiral pattern on surface of each caramel. Refrigerate until firm. Transfer to paper candy cups.

DO AHEAD: *Can be made 4 days ahead. Refrigerate in airtight container. Let caramels come to room temperature before serving.*

Homemade Marshmallows

Originally, marshmallows were thickened with the extract from the root of the marshmallow plant. Gelatin replaces the extract in modern recipes. These are sweet, creamy, almost delicate—a world away from stiff supermarket marshmallows. Float them in a cup of hot chocolate, use them as the centerpiece for s'mores, or stir them into homemade rocky road (like the one on page 622). You can also make them in crazy colors and shapes. Just add a few drops of food coloring along with the vanilla, and cut the marshmallows with lightly oiled cookie cutters. This recipe calls for potato starch (sometimes called potato starch flour), a thickener made from the starch of potatoes but with no discernible flavor. It can be found at most supermarkets, often in the kosher section. **Makes about 24**

Nonstick vegetable oil spray
1 **cup cold water, divided**
3 **¼-ounce envelopes unflavored gelatin**
2 **cups sugar**
⅔ **cup light corn syrup**
¼ **teaspoon salt**
2 **teaspoons vanilla extract**
½ **cup potato starch**
½ **cup powdered sugar**

Technique Tip: Checking for Doneness
The recipe tells you to beat the hot syrup into the gelatin until the mixture is "very thick and stiff." Another clue that the mixture is ready is the temperature: It should be lukewarm.

Line 13x9x2-inch metal baking pan with aluminum foil. Coat foil lightly with nonstick spray.

Pour ½ cup cold water into bowl of heavy-duty mixer fitted with whisk attachment. Sprinkle gelatin over water. Let stand until gelatin softens and absorbs water, at least 15 minutes.

Combine sugar, corn syrup, salt, and remaining ½ cup cold water in heavy medium saucepan. Stir over medium-low heat until sugar dissolves, brushing down sides of pan with wet pastry brush. Attach clip-on candy thermometer to side of pan. Increase heat and bring syrup to boil. Boil without stirring until thermometer registers 240°F, about 8 minutes.

With mixer running at low speed, slowly pour hot syrup into gelatin mixture in thin stream down side of bowl (avoid pouring syrup onto whisk, as it may splash). Gradually increase speed to high and beat until mixture is very thick and stiff, about 15 minutes. Add vanilla and beat to blend, about 30 seconds longer.

Scrape marshmallow mixture into prepared pan. Smooth top with wet spatula. Let stand uncovered at room temperature until firm, about 4 hours.

Stir potato starch and powdered sugar in small bowl to blend. Sift generous dusting of starch-sugar mixture onto work surface, forming rectangle slightly larger than 13x9 inches. Turn marshmallow slab out onto starch-sugar mixture; peel off foil. Sift more starch-sugar mixture over marshmallow slab. Coat large sharp knife with nonstick spray. Cut marshmallows into squares. Toss each in remaining starch-sugar mixture to coat. Transfer marshmallows to rack, shaking off excess mixture.

DO AHEAD: *Can be made 2 weeks ahead. Store marshmallows in airtight container at room temperature.*

Cranberry and Tart Apple Gelées

Gelées are jellied candies flavored with fruit (in this case, cranberries and Granny Smith apples). Together, the deep red and bright green candies make a gorgeous homemade gift for Christmas. In France these popular sugar-coated gems are known as pâte de fruits, or fruit pastes. Because pan sizes vary widely, you may get as many as 128 gelées from this recipe. **Makes about 100**

Cranberry Gelées

1	12-ounce bag fresh or frozen cranberries
2½	cups sugar
2	cups coarsely chopped cored unpeeled Granny Smith apples
1	cup fresh orange juice
2	tablespoons (¼ stick) unsalted butter
1	tablespoon finely grated orange peel
12	whole cloves
2	3-ounce packages liquid pectin
¼	teaspoon ground cloves

Tart Apple Gelées

5	cups coarsely chopped cored unpeeled Granny Smith apples
2½	cups sugar
1	cup fresh apple juice
3	tablespoons fresh lemon juice
2	tablespoons (¼ stick) unsalted butter
1½	teaspoons finely grated lemon peel
2	3-ounce packages liquid pectin
	Green and yellow food coloring
1	cup coarse white sparkling sugar or regular sugar

Ingredient Tips: For Gelées

You'll need a few special ingredients to make the *gelées*; luckily, most (if not all) can be found at a well-stocked supermarket. Look for liquid pectin (typically an apple-based thickener) in the produce department or baking aisle. Fresh apple juice can be found, chilled, in the produce section or at a farmers' market. Food coloring is available in the baking aisle—as is coarse white sparkling sugar. If you don't find the sugar there, go to a specialty foods store or order it online from kingarthurflour.com.

CRANBERRY GELÉES: Wipe 8x8x2-inch glass baking dish with damp cloth. Line dish with plastic wrap, pressing to adhere. Place small plate in freezer.

Mix cranberries, sugar, apples, orange juice, butter, orange peel, and whole cloves in heavy large saucepan; bring to boil. Reduce heat to medium and simmer uncovered until fruit is very tender, stirring often, about 15 minutes. Cool slightly. Working in batches, puree mixture in blender until smooth.

Transfer puree to heavy medium saucepan. Stir in pectin and ground cloves. Bring to boil, reduce heat to medium, and simmer uncovered until puree is very thick (like applesauce), stirring frequently, about 50 minutes. (Gelée is done when ½ teaspoon puree placed on plate in freezer gels after 1 minute.)

Transfer puree to prepared dish; smooth top. Let stand 2 hours at room temperature. Cover; chill gelée until firm, about 3 hours longer.

TART APPLE GELÉES: Wipe 8x8x2-inch glass baking dish with damp cloth. Line dish with plastic wrap, pressing to adhere. Place small plate in freezer.

Combine apples, sugar, apple juice, lemon juice, butter, and lemon peel in heavy large saucepan; bring to boil. Reduce heat to medium and simmer uncovered until fruit is very tender, stirring often, about 15 minutes. Cool slightly. Working in batches, puree mixture in blender until smooth.

Transfer puree to heavy medium saucepan. Stir in pectin. Bring to boil, reduce heat to medium, and simmer uncovered until puree is very thick (like applesauce), stirring frequently, about 50 minutes. (Gelée is done when ½ teaspoon puree placed on plate in freezer gels after 1 minute.) Stir in enough food coloring to obtain appealing green color (about 20 drops of green and 5 drops of yellow).

Transfer puree to prepared dish; smooth top. Let stand 2 hours at room temperature. Cover; chill gelée until firm, about 3 hours longer.

Invert both gelées onto work surface. Peel off plastic. Cut into 1-inch squares. Roll squares in sparkling sugar to coat.

DO AHEAD: *Can be made 1 week ahead. Store gelées in airtight container at room temperature.*

Chocolate-Dipped Brown Sugar–Maple Creams

These creamy maple and brown sugar candies covered in rich milk chocolate are perfect with coffee after a holiday meal. **Makes about 30**

1½   cups (packed) golden brown sugar
1   cup heavy whipping cream
2   tablespoons pure maple syrup
2   teaspoons unsalted butter
    Powdered sugar
12   ounces high-quality milk chocolate (such as Lindt or Perugina), chopped
    Semisweet or milk chocolate shavings or chocolate sprinkles
30   (about) paper candy cups

Generously butter small metal bowl. Stir brown sugar, cream, and maple syrup in heavy 2-quart saucepan over medium heat until sugar dissolves, about 5 minutes. Attach clip-on candy thermometer to side of pan. Increase heat to medium-high and stir until candy thermometer registers 234°F, about 10 minutes. Pour into prepared bowl (do not scrape pan). Add 2 teaspoons butter to bowl (do not stir). Set bowl over larger bowl filled with ice water. Let stand 5 minutes. Fold firm outside edges of mixture into center; do not stir. Let sugar mixture cool to lukewarm.

Transfer sugar mixture to processor. Blend until creamy and no longer glossy, 3 to 5 minutes. Transfer to medium bowl. Freeze mixture just until firm enough to shape, about 1 hour.

Line 2 baking sheets with waxed paper. Roll 2 teaspoons sugar mixture into ball, dusting hands with powdered sugar if necessary. Place on 1 prepared sheet. Repeat with remaining mixture, freezing briefly if too soft to form. Freeze until firm, about 1 hour.

Stir milk chocolate in top of double boiler over barely simmering water until melted and smooth and candy thermometer registers 115°F. Remove from over water. Working quickly, submerge 1 candy in chocolate, tilting pan if necessary. Using dinner fork, lift out candy. Tap bottom of fork on sides of pan, allowing excess chocolate to drip back into pan. Using small sharp knife, push candy off fork onto second prepared sheet. Sprinkle with chocolate shavings. Repeat with remaining candies, setting double boiler over hot water occasionally to rewarm chocolate to 115°F as needed. Refrigerate until chocolate is set. Transfer candies to paper candy cups. Serve chilled.

DO AHEAD: *Can be made 3 days ahead. Keep chilled in airtight container.*

Fresh Raspberry Creams

The chocolate-coated, raspberry-flavored fondant (a soft candy mixture that can be rolled or sculpted) hides a sweet surprise: one fresh, ripe raspberry. Framboise is a potent, clear brandy distilled from fermented raspberries. Look for it at premium liquor stores and some specialty foods stores. **Makes 18**

1   cup sugar
¾   cup heavy whipping cream
1   tablespoon light corn syrup
1   teaspoon unsalted butter
1   tablespoon framboise (clear raspberry brandy)
36   raspberries, divided
    Powdered sugar
12   ounces bittersweet or semisweet chocolate, chopped
18   paper candy cups

Generously butter small metal bowl. Stir sugar, cream, and corn syrup in heavy 2-quart saucepan over medium heat until sugar dissolves. Attach clip-on candy thermometer to side of pan. Increase heat to medium-high and stir until candy thermometer registers 234°F, about 10 minutes. Pour mixture into prepared bowl (do not scrape pan). Add 1 teaspoon butter to bowl (do not stir). Set bowl over larger bowl filled with ice water. Let stand 5 minutes. Fold firm outside edges of mixture into center (do not stir). Cool to lukewarm.

Transfer mixture to processor. Add framboise and blend until mixture is creamy and no longer glossy, 3 to 5 minutes. Freeze until firm enough to shape, about 30 minutes.

Line 2 baking sheets with waxed paper. Spoon cream mixture by teaspoonfuls onto 1 prepared sheet, forming 18 mounds. Set 1 raspberry atop each. Cover each with another teaspoon of cream mixture. Using fingers, seal raspberries completely with cream mixture. Freeze until almost firm, about 20 minutes.

Using hands dusted with powdered sugar to prevent sticking, gently roll each mound into ball. Return candies to same sheet. Freeze until firm, about 4 hours.

Melt chocolate in top of double boiler over barely simmering water, stirring frequently, until candy thermometer registers 115°F. Remove from over water. Working quickly, submerge 1 cream ball in chocolate, tilting pan if necessary. Using dinner fork, lift out ball. Tap bottom of fork on sides of pan, allowing excess chocolate to drip back into pan. Using small sharp knife, push ball off fork and onto second prepared sheet. Top with 1 raspberry. Repeat with remaining cream balls, setting double boiler over hot water occasionally to rewarm chocolate to 115°F as needed. Refrigerate until chocolate is set, about 1 hour. Transfer candies to paper candy cups.

DO AHEAD: *Can be made 2 days ahead. Refrigerate in airtight container. Let stand 20 minutes at room temperature before serving.*

Peanut Butter Dreams

Inspired by the popular peanut butter cup, these are given extra appeal with a glistening coating of ground peanut praline. The peanut butter centers are incredibly easy to make: Just stir, freeze, and roll into balls. **Makes about 18**

¾	cup powdered sugar plus additional for dusting hands
⅓	cup super-chunky peanut butter (do not use old-fashioned style or freshly ground)
2	ounces Philadelphia-brand cream cheese, room temperature
2	ounces high-quality white chocolate (such as Lindt or Perugina), melted, cooled
2	tablespoons (¼ stick) unsalted butter, room temperature
12	ounces high-quality milk chocolate (such as Lindt or Perugina), chopped
	Peanut Praline (see recipe)
18	(about) paper candy cups

Blend ¾ cup powdered sugar, peanut butter, cream cheese, melted white chocolate, and butter in medium bowl. Freeze until firm enough to shape, about 20 minutes.

Line 2 baking sheets with waxed paper. Using hands dusted with powdered sugar, roll 1 tablespoon peanut butter mixture into ball. Place on 1 prepared sheet. Repeat with remaining mixture. Freeze until very firm, about 3 hours.

Stir milk chocolate in top of double boiler over barely simmering water until melted and smooth. Remove from over water. Working quickly, submerge 1 peanut butter ball in chocolate, tilting pan if necessary. Using dinner fork, lift out candy. Tap bottom of fork on sides of pan, allowing excess chocolate to drip back into pan. Using small knife, push candy off fork and onto second prepared sheet. Repeat with remaining balls, setting double boiler over hot water occasionally to rewarm chocolate to 115°F as needed. Refrigerate candies until chocolate is set, about 1 hour. (Reserve remaining chocolate in pan.)

Line another baking sheet with waxed paper. Rewarm remaining chocolate over barely simmering water. Remove from over water. Place praline in large shallow dish. Dip half of 1 candy into chocolate. Roll around in palm to cover candy with a light coating of chocolate. Set in praline and roll gently, covering completely. Transfer to prepared sheet. Repeat with remaining candies. Refrigerate until firm. Transfer candies to paper candy cups.

DO AHEAD: *Can be made 1 week ahead. Refrigerate in airtight container. Let stand 20 minutes at room temperature before serving.*

Peanut Praline

Don't confuse this praline with the brown sugar confections that abound in the South. This is a brittle candy made from caramelized sugar and nuts, and it can be eaten on its own or finely ground and used as an ingredient in other candies. Hazelnuts or almonds are usually the nuts of choice; this recipe (to pair with the Peanut Butter Dreams) calls for peanuts instead. **Makes about 2 cups**

1	cup sugar
¼	cup water
1	cup roasted salted peanuts

Butter baking sheet. Cook sugar and ¼ cup water in heavy small saucepan over low heat, stirring until sugar dissolves. Increase heat to medium and boil without stirring until syrup is deep golden brown. Mix in peanuts. Immediately pour mixture onto prepared sheet. Cool completely. Break into 2-inch pieces. Using on/off turns, grind finely in processor.

DO AHEAD: *Can be made 2 months ahead. Cover and refrigerate in airtight container.*

Smooth and Delicious

One of the first steps in candymaking is to thoroughly dissolve the sugar in the candy mixture before it boils. Take your time with this step. Undissolved sugar crystals can ultimately turn toffee, brittle, caramel, and other candies into a grainy mess. A simple test ensures that the sugar has dissolved: Rub a drop of the warm mixture between your fingertips—it should feel smooth, with no trace of granules. If it feels sandy, return it to the heat and continue warming and stirring until the mixture is smooth. Occasionally brushing down the sides of the pan with a pastry brush dipped in water will also help prevent sugar crystals from forming.

Mixed Berry Chocolate-Toffee Bites

Little "puddles" of melted chocolate are topped with fresh berries and tiny pieces of toffee. You can make these sweet bites ahead, keep them refrigerated, and then serve them with coffee after dinner. **Makes about 20**

6   ounces bittersweet or semisweet chocolate or high-quality milk chocolate (such as Lindt or Perugina), chopped
2   cups mixed berries (such as blackberries, raspberries, and blueberries)
2   1.4-ounce English toffee candy bars (such as Skor or Heath), cut into ¼-inch pieces

Line large baking sheet with aluminum foil. Stir chocolate in small metal bowl set over saucepan of simmering water until melted, smooth, and warm to touch. Remove bowl from over water. Spoon melted chocolate by teaspoonfuls onto foil, spacing about 1½ inches apart (do not spread). Top with berries and toffee, making sure toppings touch melted chocolate. Chill until chocolate sets, about 15 minutes. Remove from foil.

DO AHEAD: *Can be made 8 hours ahead. Refrigerate in airtight container. Let stand at room temperature 15 minutes before serving.*

Gianduja Gold Cups

Reminiscent of Baci, the well-known dome-shaped Italian chocolates, these cups also have a rich gianduja (chocolate-hazelnut) filling; make sure to use high-quality milk chocolate for the best flavor and texture. The chocolates start with a candy shell that's made by brushing melted chocolate inside foil candy cups. Once the shells have firmed up in the fridge, they're filled with the gianduja mixture and covered with a thin layer of melted bittersweet chocolate. If you can't find foil candy cups, use paper, but double them up to make a sturdier form. **Makes 32**

4   ounces high-quality milk chocolate (such as Lindt or Perugina), chopped
1   cup chocolate-hazelnut spread (such as Nutella)
6   tablespoons coarsely chopped toasted hazelnuts
18 ounces bittersweet or semisweet chocolate, chopped
32 1-inch-diameter gold foil candy cups
32 whole hazelnuts, toasted, husked

Stir milk chocolate in medium metal bowl set over saucepan of barely simmering water (do not allow bowl to touch water) until melted and smooth. Remove bowl from over water. Whisk in chocolate-hazelnut spread and chopped nuts.

Stir bittersweet chocolate in another medium metal bowl set over saucepan of barely simmering water (do not allow bowl to touch water) until melted and smooth and candy thermometer registers 110°F (chocolate will feel warm). Remove bowl from over water. Using 1-inch-wide pastry brush, coat insides of candy cups with just enough chocolate to cover. Rewarm chocolate as needed to maintain temperature. Place cups on baking sheet. Chill until chocolate is firm, about 15 minutes.

Spoon enough hazelnut mixture into center of each chocolate cup to fill to within ⅛ inch of top (about 1 heaping teaspoonful in each cup). Refrigerate until filling sets, about 15 minutes.

Rewarm remaining melted bittersweet chocolate in bowl set over barely simmering water to 110°F. Spoon enough chocolate over filling to cover and to fill cups completely. Immediately top each with 1 hazelnut. Refrigerate cups until firm, about 20 minutes.

DO AHEAD: *Can be made 2 weeks ahead. Refrigerate in single layer in airtight container. Let stand 20 minutes at room temperature before serving.*

online & mail-order sources

Love the sound of the Oranges with Pomegranate Molasses and Honey (page 436) but you can't get your hands on a bottle of pomegranate molasses? All ready to make The Ultimate Valentine Cake (page 156)—except for the heart-shaped cake ring? Here are a variety of online and mail-order retail sources that can supply all your dessert-making needs.

bakeware & baking supplies

Broadway Panhandler: This New York–based shop is a good source for a wide assortment of baking supplies, including essentials (heat-resistant spatulas), as well as items you didn't know you needed (like *kugelhopf* pans). Shop by brand or by specific need, such as Bundt pans or cookie cutters. 866-266-5927 / broadwaypanhandler.com

Chefs: Professional-quality gear, from oven mitts to angel food cake pans. The bakeware section of the Web site is organized by category (baking and pastry tools, cake and Bundt pans), which makes shopping very easy. 800-338-3232 / chefscatalog.com

Cooking.com: This site offers multiple listings for virtually every piece of baking equipment you might need. Most items also include a customer rating, so you can see what other folks think of the products before you decide to make any purchases. 800-663-8810 / cooking.com

Cooking Enthusiast: This store initially specialized in knives but has since broadened its offerings to include baking equipment (pie plates, springform pans, candy thermometers, etc.). 800-792-6650 / cookingenthusiast.com

Kitchen Universe: Heavy-duty baking sheets, Silpat baking mats, KitchenAid stand mixers, and more—much more. Find exactly what you need by browsing specific bakeware subcategories, or search by brand or price range. 877-517-1966 / kitchenu.com

decorating supplies

Ateco: This shop, which specializes in decorating tools (pastry bags, decorating tubes, etc.), also offers a wide selection of molds and forms, rolling pins, and pastry brushes. 800-645-7170 / atecousa.net

Beryl's Cake Decorating & Pastry Supplies: Cupcake fans will love Beryl's. The store offers nearly 175 different cupcake papers and several cupcake stands to show off your handiwork. Beryl's is also a great source for pastry bag tips (such as basketweave and petal) and sugary decorations (such as chocolate "pebbles" and the little multicolored balls called dragées) in every shape, size, and color. 800-488-2749 / beryls.com

Cincinnati Cake & Candy Supplies: This store's incredible assortment of baking supplies includes nearly 500 different cookie cutters and more than 100 varieties of sprinkles. 800-304-4536 / cincicakeandcandy.com

Fancy Flours: If you need to decorate a dessert, this is the place for you. Choose from more than 700 different cookie cutters, 50 oils and extracts, and 500 sugar-based decorations, as well as chocolate transfers and culinary stencils. 406-587-0118 / fancyflours.com

Jane's Cakes & Chocolates: This Montrose, California, shop is a good source for cake pans, decorating tips, candymaking equipment, and edible gold dust. 818-957-2511 (no Web site; only in-store or mail-order purchases)

Wilton: The place to go for cake decorating supplies, Wilton offers an assortment of pastry bags and decorating tips, as well as cake pans of every kind. 800-794-5866 / wilton.com

gadgets

Microplane: Once you use one of Microplane's graters, you won't be able to use anything else. These sturdy, super-sharp tools make quick work of citrus zest, whole nutmeg, and even carrots (for Carrot Cake with Buttermilk Glaze and Cinnamon–Cream Cheese Frosting on page 67, for example). 866-968-6665, ext. 1 / us.microplane.com

Oxo: The gadget experts. Products include sturdy silicone spatulas, great mixing bowls, and our favorite cherry pitter (it works on olives, too). 800-545-4411 / oxo.com

Zeroll: Ice-cream enthusiasts will want to check out the array of scoops from Zeroll. The sturdy aluminum alloy scoops have a heat-conductive fluid sealed in the handle, which makes dishing up frozen desserts a breeze. 800-872-5000, ext. 17 / zeroll.com

ingredients

BAKING STAPLES AND MORE

ChefShop.com: Browse this site's baking ingredients category to find candied fruits, dried fruits, extracts, nuts, and chocolates. 800-596-0885 / chefshop.com

Dean & Deluca: This New York–based specialty store is known for its first-rate ingredients. The store carries a nice assortment of honeys and is a good place to buy culinary lavender—among many other delectable things. 800-221-7714 / deandeluca.com

igourmet.com: Shop for baking staples like extracts, baking chocolate, and vanilla beans. 877-446-8763 / igourmet.com

CHOCOLATE

Chocosphere: One-stop shopping for all things chocolate (baking chocolate, chocolate sprinkles, cocoa powder). This store carries products from nearly 50 chocolate makers from around the globe, including *Bon Appétit* test kitchen favorites Valrhona and Callebaut.
877-992-4626 / chocosphere.com

Lindt: A Swiss chocolate that's great for baking. Lindt makes an especially good white chocolate. Buy products from Lindt's online store or type in your zip code to find a nearby store that carries Lindt chocolate.
877-695-4638 / lindtusa.com

Scharffen Berger: Some supermarkets carry this high-quality chocolate brand, but for cooks who can't find Scharffen Berger in their market, the company's Web site offers online ordering for all of its products, including basics like baking chocolate and cocoa powder.
866-972-6879 / scharffenberger.com

FLOUR

King Arthur Flour: This Vermont-based company is obsessed with baking. It's known for high-quality flours, but King Arthur is also a great source for cookie cutters, baking pans, and baking advice.
800-827-6836 / kingarthurflour.com

FRUITS AND NUTS

American Almond Products Company, Inc: An excellent source for almond paste. If you use a lot of marzipan or whole or sliced nuts, the company also sells those, but only in large quantities (5 pounds or more for nuts, 8 pounds or more for marzipan).
800-825-6663 / americanalmond.com

Bella Viva Orchards: This Central Valley, California-based company sells a variety of dried fruits, from prunes to Pluots. They even have diced dried fruit that's all ready to mix into your favorite recipe.
800-552-8218 / bellaviva.com

Friske Orchards: This orchard in northern Michigan is a good source for hard-to-come-by frozen sour cherries (called "tart cherries" on the site).
888-968-3554 / apples-cherries.com

Melissa's: Shop at Melissa's for dried fruits and nuts, as well as a huge selection of hard-to-find fresh fruits.
800-588-0151 / melissas.com

HONEY

Savannah Bee Company: This Georgia-based company sells honeycomb and eight kinds of fantastic artisanal honeys, from the common orange blossom variety to the ethereal tupelo honey. (And for cooks who can't get enough of the wildflower and tupelo varieties, the company offers those in 5-pound bottles.)
912-234-0688 / savannahbee.com

SPICES

Adriana's Caravan: Adriana's carries a staggering array of spices and extracts, as well as exotic ingredients that can be tough to find, like pomegranate molasses.
800-316-0820 / adrianascaravan.com

Penzeys Spices: Penzeys carries hundreds of different spices, both whole and ground, so you're sure to find what you're looking for.
800-741-7787 / penzeys.com

The Spice House: A specific baking spices category helps narrow down the spice options quickly. The store also carries other kinds of flavorful ingredients, such as orange-flower water.
847-328-3711 / thespicehouse.com

one-stop shopping

Amazon.com: Potato starch, stand mixer, cake decorating supplies, a bicycle to ride to the market—whatever you need, it's on Amazon.
amazon.com

Davidlebovitz.com: David Lebovitz, a frequent *Bon Appétit* contributor, honed his pastry skills at the legendary Chez Panisse. Today, he lives and writes—and bakes—in Paris. His Web site includes lots of helpful tips, as well as a link to his own amazon.com store, where you'll find a collection of products (ice-cream machines, ingredients, gadgets) that Lebovitz really likes.
davidlebovitz.com

Fante's Kitchen Wares Shop: A comprehensive resource for everything from aprons to zesters.
800-443-2683 / fantes.com

Kitchen Krafts: This shop focuses on hard-to-find tools and ingredients. Cherry pitter? Check. Cake turntable? Of course.
800-776-0575 / kitchenkrafts.com

Surfas: A Culver City, California–based restaurant supply store that's open to the public, Surfas is a great source for ingredients (like high-quality chocolate chips) and equipment (such as heart-shaped baking pans).
877-641-2661 / culinarydistrict.com

Sur La Table: Sur La Table's online Professional Baking Shop has product collections organized by dessert type, so you can choose gear specifically for cakes (or cookies or pastry). The store is also a good resource for decorating supplies, including sparkling sugars and edible gold and silver leaf.
800-243-0852 / surlatable.com

Williams-Sonoma: A good resource for everything from pans, fluted pastry cutters, and gadgets to baking staples like vanilla extract.
877-812-6235 / williams-sonoma.com

metric conversions & equivalents

metric conversion formulas

To Convert	Multiply
Ounces to grams	Ounces by 28.35
Pounds to kilograms	Pounds by .454
Teaspoons to milliliters	Teaspoons by 4.93
Tablespoons to milliliters	Tablespoons by 14.79
Fluid ounces to milliliters	Fluid ounces by 29.57
Cups to milliliters	Cups by 236.59
Cups to liters	Cups by .236
Pints to liters	Pints by .473
Quarts to liters	Quarts by .946
Gallons to liters	Gallons by 3.785
Inches to centimeters	Inches by 2.54

approximate metric equivalents

Volume

¼ teaspoon	1 milliliter
½ teaspoon	2.5 milliliters
¾ teaspoon	4 milliliters
1 teaspoon	5 milliliters
1¼ teaspoons	6 milliliters
1½ teaspoons	7.5 milliliters
1¾ teaspoons	8.5 milliliters
2 teaspoons	10 milliliters
1 tablespoon (½ fluid ounce)	15 milliliters
2 tablespoons (1 fluid ounce)	30 milliliters
¼ cup	60 milliliters
⅓ cup	80 milliliters
½ cup (4 fluid ounces)	120 milliliters
⅔ cup	160 milliliters
¾ cup	180 milliliters
1 cup (8 fluid ounces)	240 milliliters
1¼ cups	300 milliliters
1½ cups (12 fluid ounces)	360 milliliters
1⅔ cups	400 milliliters
2 cups (1 pint)	460 milliliters
3 cups	700 milliliters
4 cups (1 quart)	.95 liter
1 quart plus ¼ cup	1 liter
4 quarts (1 gallon)	3.8 liters

Information compiled from a variety of sources, including *Recipes into Type* by Joan Whitman and Dolores Simon (Newton, MA: Biscuit Books, 2000); *The New Food Lover's Companion* by Sharon Tyler Herbst (Hauppauge, NY: Barron's, 1995); and *Rosemary Brown's Big Kitchen Instruction Book* (Kansas City, MO: Andrews McMeel, 1998).

approximate metric equivalents

Weight

¼ ounce	7 grams
½ ounce	14 grams
¾ ounce	21 grams
1 ounce	28 grams
1¼ ounces	35 grams
1½ ounces	42.5 grams
1⅔ ounces	45 grams
2 ounces	57 grams
3 ounces	85 grams
4 ounces (¼ pound)	113 grams
5 ounces	142 grams
6 ounces	170 grams
7 ounces	198 grams
8 ounces (½ pound)	227 grams
16 ounces (1 pound)	454 grams
35.25 ounces (2.2 pounds)	1 kilogram

Length

⅛ inch	3 millimeters
¼ inch	6 millimeters
½ inch	1¼ centimeters
1 inch	2½ centimeters
2 inches	5 centimeters
2½ inches	6 centimeters
4 inches	10 centimeters
5 inches	13 centimeters
6 inches	15¼ centimeters
12 inches (1 foot)	30 centimeters

oven temperatures

Description	°F	°C	British Gas Mark
Very cool	200°	95°	0
Very cool	225°	110°	¼
Very cool	250°	120°	½
Cool	275°	135°	1
Cool	300°	150°	2
Warm	325°	165°	3
Moderate	350°	175°	4
Moderately hot	375°	190°	5
Fairly hot	400°	200°	6
Hot	425°	220°	7
Very hot	450°	230°	8
Very hot	475°	245°	9

To convert Fahrenheit to Celsius, subtract 32 from Fahrenheit, multiply the result by 5, then divide by 9.

Common Ingredients & Their Approximate Equivalents

1 cup uncooked white rice = 185 grams

1 cup all-purpose flour = 140 grams

1 stick butter (4 ounces • ½ cup • 8 tablespoons) = 110 grams

1 cup butter (8 ounces • 2 sticks • 16 tablespoons) = 220 grams

1 cup brown sugar, firmly packed = 225 grams

1 cup granulated sugar = 200 grams

contributors

recipes

Engin Akin

Katherine Anastasia

Pam Anderson

Nancy Baggett

Mary Corpening Barber

Karen Barker

Melanie Barnard

Barrington Brewery, Great Barrington,
    Massachusetts

Bridget Batson, Hawthorne Lane,
    San Francisco, California

Anna Bruni Benson

Mary Bergin

Sondra Bernstein

Lula Bertran

Lena Cederham Birnbaum

Carole Bloom

Susan S. Bradley

Frank Brigtsen

Buttersweet Bakery, Atlanta, Georgia

Lynn Buzza, Soul Kitchen, Chicago, Illinois

Cafe Paradiso, Cork, Ireland

Canyon Southwest Cafe,
    Fort Lauderdale, Florida

Andrew Carmellini

Kathleen Carroll

Cascadia, Seattle, Washington

Mary Cech

Lauren Chattman

Melissa Clark

Sally Clarke

Eugene I. Cleary

Jayne Cohen

Cat Cora

Lane Crowther

Leila Cuttino

Christine Dahl

Sanford D'Amato

Jane Spector Davis

Robin Davis

Janet Hazen de Jesus

Karen DeMasco

Lori Zimring De Mori

Kirsten Dixon, Riversong Lodge,
    Yentna River, Alaska

Brooke Dojny

Crescent Dragonwagon

Alain Ducasse, Mix, THEhotel at Mandalay Bay,
    Las Vegas, Nevada

Jill Dupleix

Philippe Duret, Auberge du Moulin Hideux,
    Belgium

Elizabeth Ellis

Extraordinary Desserts, San Diego, California

Elizabeth Falkner

Tarla Fallgatter

Susan Feniger

Claudia Fleming

Janet Fletcher

Hiroshi Fukui, L'Uraku, Honolulu, Hawaii

Gale Gand, Tru, Chicago, Illinois

Tasha Garcia and Julie Taras, Little Giant,
    New York, New York

Michelle Gayer-Nicholson, Trotter's To Go,
    Chicago, Illinois

Jason Gibbons, Zelo, Minneapolis, Minnesota

Todd Goddard

Debbie Gold

Rozanne Gold

Marcy Goldman-Posluns

Bill Granger

Dorie Greenspan

Lauren Groveman

Nancy Grubin

David Guas

Ken Haedrich

Gabrielle Hamilton

Tariq Hanna, Sucré, New Orleans, Louisiana

Angela Hartnett

Susan Haskell

Julie Hasson

Pierre Hermé

Ginny Leith Holland

Jill Silverman Hough

Jesse and Matthew Hufft

Il Giardino di Luca, Dei Dogi Hotel, Venice, Italy

Jamie's Restaurant, Pensacola, Florida

Kimball Jones, Wente Vineyards Restaurant,
    Livermore, California

Terry and Peter Kagan

Karen Kaplan

Jeanne Thiel Kelley

Kristine Kidd

Elinor Klivans

Abigail Langlas, Alan Wong's,
    Honolulu, Hawaii

Sue Lawrence

David Lebovitz

Shari Ledwidge

Rita Leinwand

Dave Lieberman

Charles P. Loan

LocoPops, Durham, North Carolina

Lori Longbotham

Emily Luchetti

Lucia Luhan

Deborah Madison

Nick Malgieri

Andrew Mandolene

Pamela Mazzola

Janet Taylor McCracken

Lori McKean

Michael McLaughlin

Alice Medrich

Ree Millan

Mary Sue Milliken

Jinx and Jefferson Morgan

Selma Brown Morrow

Eleanor Moscatel

Dawn Murray

Rebecca Naccarato

Debby Maugans Nakos

Norma at the Wharf House, St. James,
    Jamaica, West Indies

Nottoway Plantation, White Castle,
    Louisiana

Nancy Oakes

Jill O'Connor

Beatrice Ojakangas

Old Manor Estate and Hotel, Gingerland,
    Charlestown, Nevis, West Indies

Pichet Ong, Spice Market,
    New York, New York

Alex Palermo

Rochelle Palermo

Sal Passalacqua, Dimaio Cucina,
Berkeley Heights, New Jersey

Sylvia Pease

Pesce Blue, Portsmouth, New Hampshire

Christine Piccin

Anna Pump

Jamie Purviance

Susan Quick

Susan Richardson

Mary Risely

Tori Ritchie

Rick Rodgers

Douglas Rodriguez

Betty Rosbottom

Rosie's Bakery, Cambridge, Massachusetts

Michael Rosloff

Jocelyne Roux

Amelia Saltsman

Sally Sampson

Patricia Cohen Samuels

Sanders 1907, Grand Forks, North Dakota

Cathy Sandrich

Roberto Santibañez

Savory Faire, Montesano, Washington

Richard Sax

Michele Scicolone

Sarah Patterson Scott

Scratch, Durham, North Carolina

Alex Seidel, Fruition Restaurant,
Denver, Colorado

Anita Sharp

Marie Simmons

Maria Helm Sinskey

B. Smith

Michael Smith

Allen Susser

Sweet Lady Jane, Los Angeles, California

The Sweet Pea Bakery & Catering,
Phoenix, Arizona

Maureen Tatlow

Sandy Soto Teich

Sarah Tenaglia

Mary Jo Thoresen

Town Hall, San Francisco, California

Trattoria da Fagiolino, Cutigliano, Italy

Trois Pommes Patisserie, Brooklyn, New York

Harriett Tupler

Julia M. Usher

Vanilla Bake Shop, Santa Monica, California

Cyndi Verger

Waldorf A'Story, Story, Wyoming

Charlotte Walker

Ila Walrath

Sara Corpening Whiteford

Anne Willan, La Varenne at The Greenbrier,
White Sulphur Springs, West Virginia

Pat Willard

Kristen Williams

Dede Wilson

Molly Wizenberg

Alan Wong

Woodstock Inn, North Woodstock,
New Hampshire

Diane Rossen Worthington

Clifford A. Wright

Sherry Yard

for bon appétit

Amy Albert

Zoë Alexander

Lena Cederham Birnbaum

Frederika Brookfield

Susan Champlin

Nina Elder

Bailey Franklin

Gaylen Ducker Grody

Kirsten Hageleit

Camille Hahn

Julie Jamerson

Jeanne Thiel Kelley

Kristine Kidd

Katy Laundrie

Katie Levine

Marcia Hartmann Lewis

Mike Lorrig

Marcy MacDonald

Janet Taylor McCracken

Selma Brown Morrow

David Nemetz

Rachel Ng

Rochelle Palermo

Amy C. Quick

Christine Schuchart

Shayna Sobol

Amy Steinberg

Annie Taylor

Sarah Tenaglia

Victoria von Biel

for andrews mcmeel publishing

Hugh Andrews

Tammie Barker

Jennifer Barry

Leslie Barry

Jennifer Baum

John Carroll

Valerie Cimino

Carol Coe

Jean Conlon

Erika Kuster

Kristen Hall

Chris Langley

Jean Lucas

Lynne McAdoo

John McMeel

Kirsty Melville

Arthur Mount

Con Poulos

Deri Reed

Chris Schillig

David Shaw

Layla Smith

Susie Theodorou

Eliza Whipple

Amy Worley

index of whisk ratings

one whisk recipes

⫿ two whisk recipes

pies, tarts & pastries

♉♉♉ three whisk recipes

⅋⅋⅋⅋ four whisk recipes

index

A

C

Notes

Notes